Legal and Privacy Considerations for AI-Driven Security Systems

Amer Ibrahim
Department of Computer Science and Software Engineering, United Arab Emirates University, UAE

Taher M. Ghazal
https://orcid.org/0000-0003-0672-7924

Faculty of Computing and IT, Sohar University, Oman & Department of Networks and Cybersecurity, Hourani Center for Applied Scientific Research, Al-Ahliyya Amman University, Amman, Jordan & Center for Cyber Security, Faculty of Information Science and Technology, Universiti Kebangsaan Malaysia, Malaysia

IGI Global
Scientific Publishing
Publishing Tomorrow's Research Today

Vice President of Editorial Melissa Wagner
Director of Acquisitions Mikaela Felty
Director of Book Development Jocelynn Hessler
Production Manager Mike Brehm
Cover Design Jose Rosado

Published in the United States of America by
IGI Global Scientific Publishing
701 East Chocolate Avenue
Hershey, PA, 17033, USA
Tel: 717-533-8845 | Fax: 717-533-7115
Website: https://www.igi-global.com E-mail: cust@igi-global.com

Library of Congress Cataloging-in-Publication Data

LCCN: 2026020698 (CIP Data Pending)
ISBN13: 979-8-3373-9210-3
Isbn13Softcover: 979-8-3373-9211-0
EISBN13: 979-8-3373-9212-7
British Cataloguing in Publication Data
A Cataloguing in Publication record for this book is available from the British Library.

Editorial Advisory Board

Table of Contents

Detailed Table of Contents

Nowadays, AI has been recognized as one of the key elements of cybersecurity, and has helped in many aspects like automated threat identification, anomaly detection, and security analytics without human intervention. At the same time, it is discussing in details the benefits of efficiency, scalability, and accuracy versus the newly developed risks like false positive, bias, over-automation, and lack of human oversight. Some of the points are focused on the issues of law and regulation that come to the fore when one is held liable for the decisions made by AI, data protection and privacy compliance, the reliability of evidence, the problem of cross-border governance, and others. Technically aligning the law side, the chapter shows how AI transforms security measures while forming new responsibilities for the organizations at the same time. It outlines a framework for assessing the legality, ethics, and accountability aspects when using AI-based security systems.

This chapter looks into how regulatory ready are artificial intelligence (AI) based security systems that have been deployed in regulated and high-risk environments. It considers the extent to which preparedness is influenced by governance structures, documentation, risk assessments, and operational controls throughout the system lifecycle. The chapter delves into the alignment with data protection, cybersecurity, and sector-specific regulations, and highlights the requirements for accountability, transparency, human oversight, and auditability. The chapter particularly focuses on issues raised by changing regulations, jurisdictional requirements, and reliance on third- party vendors. By combining legal expectations with security practices, the chapter offers a conceptual framework for evaluating regulatory readiness, identifying gaps, and thus helping organizations to foresee compliance requirements, lower the risk of regulatory actions, and implement AI-enabled security systems in a responsible manner.

embedding of legal oversight in security operations. Through blending legal scrutiny with the viewpoints of operational security, the chapter outlines a roadmap for evaluating privacy and compliance maturity in a structured manner, thus helping organizations to pinpoint weaknesses, prove accountability, and uphold trustworthy AI-based security programs.

Amjed A. Ahmed, Department of Computer Technical Engineering, Imam Kadhim University College (IKu), Iraq
Aghiad khedr Alkatan, Artificial Intelligence Department, Almamoun University, Baghdad, Iraq

This chapter looks at the integration of privacy-preserving machine learning methods in contemporary security systems. Recent studies have explored the integration of privacy-preserving machine learning methods in security systems. It explains how analytics and AI capabilities could help in detecting threats and anomalies internally, with minimum exposure of personal and sensitive data. Besides, issues of governance like data protection regulations; accountability; transparency, etc., are also discussed. The chapter gives guidance on how to implement smart security solutions by using machine learning and privacy by design principles. Such solutions, apart from being effective, would also be legally compliant and would consider user's privacy expectations. Besides these, the chapter points out the technical and operational issues such as the performance trade-offs in models, increased complexity of the system, and the compatibility with the existing security infrastructures.

Mahmoud Abu Saima, Geosciences Department, United Arab Emirates University, UAE
Hmoud Al-Dmour, Department of Physics, Mutah University, Jordan
Abdallah M. Al-Tarawneh, Clinical Psychology Department, Al-Ahliyya Amman University, Jordan

This study focuses on privacy-centric threat modeling as a critical practice in modern security architectures. It mentions that conventional threat modeling is primarily focused on potential system breaches and it pays little attention to personal data risks, users rights as well as compliance with the laws. The chapter describes privacy-centered adaptations of threat modeling that facilitate the recognition of data flows, trust boundaries, as well as misuse scenarios that affect people. It examines ways of mapping the privacy threats like excessive data gathering, unauthorized inference, secondary use, and re-identification in complex systems. It also demonstrates the integration of privacy threat modeling methods into secure design, DevSecOps pipelines, and AI-driven systems. The work, by mixing security engineering principles with data protection requirements, puts forward a method to forecast privacy threats at the earliest time, improve governance controls, and develop security architectures that are equally robust, compliant, and respectful of the privacy expectations.

The development of secure and privacy-conscious data architectures is critical for Security Operations Centers operating in complex, data-intensive environments. The research probes deeply into the evolution of establishing secure and privacy-aware data architectures within Security Operations Centers (SOCs). The material assesses major design strategies like data segmentation, least privilege, encryption, anonymization, and controlled data movements in both centralized and distributed SOC models. It also discusses problems with large-scale logging, live analytics, cloud integration, and AI- based security tools. The piece further shines a light on how architectural measures align with privacy by design and privacy by default. The study merges Security Engineering with Data Protection Principles to present a full-fledged manual on developing SOC data architectures that not only enable effective threat management but also sharply limit the risks of privacy breaches and regulatory exposure.

This chapter first of all discusses the use of Data Protection Impact Assessments (DPIAs) for deploying security applications powered by artificial intelligence. It outlines the different ways in which AI-based threat detection, behavioral analytics, and automated response systems. Then, this section identifies the legal requirement to carry out DPIAs and breaks down the main components of the assessment, which are risk identification, necessity and proportionality analysis, mitigation measures, and stakeholder consultation. The challenge of algorithmic bias, false positives, automated decision making, and low explainability in the security context are the main issues that this chapter is concerned with. It also discusses how to embed DPIAs into the cybersecurity system lifecycles and governance frameworks. Alongside the legal compliance work, this chapter also considers the technical security design and hence serves as a guide to performing effective DPIAs as a means of legally compliant, accountable, and responsible AI use in security operations.

Privacy-centric approaches to pseudonymization and de-identification are essential for modern data processing and security practices. This chapter briefly defines legal terminology and then addresses technological implementation while highlighting the legal aspect of the two stages: reversible pseudonymization and irreversible de-identification. Besides, it deals with risks that are not yet eliminated, such as re-identification through data linkage, inference attacks, and contextual enrichment. The main

Preface

OVERVIEW OF THE SUBJECT MATTER

The accelerating deployment of Artificial Intelligence (AI) within security systems is reshaping how organizations detect threats, monitor environments, control access, and respond to incidents. From facial recognition and behavioural analytics to automated incident response and generative AI-driven Security Operations Centres (SOCs), AI technologies now sit at the core of modern security infrastructure across government, critical infrastructure, healthcare, finance, and enterprise environments.

Yet this technological transformation has not been matched by an equivalent evolution in the legal, regulatory, and ethical frameworks designed to govern it. AI-driven security systems raise distinct and often unresolved questions: Who is accountable when an automated system makes an erroneous security decision? How should personal data captured through continuous monitoring be processed, minimized, and retained in compliance with data protection law? What distinguishes legitimate security monitoring from unlawful surveillance? How can organizations operating across multiple jurisdictions reconcile conflicting legal requirements regarding cross-border data transfers, localization, and AI governance?

This book, Legal and Privacy Considerations for AI-Driven Security Systems, addresses these questions directly. It brings together 12 chapters authored by an international community of researchers and practitioners spanning computer science, law, cybersecurity, and information systems. Rather than treating AI security technology and legal compliance as separate domains, this volume integrates them – examining the technical architecture of AI security systems alongside the legal grounds, governance structures, and accountability mechanisms required for their lawful and ethical operation.

WHERE THIS TOPIC FITS IN THE WORLD TODAY

The timeliness of this volume is underscored by a rapidly evolving global regulatory landscape. The European Union's Artificial Intelligence Act explicitly classifies many security-related AI applications – including biometric identification, law enforcement risk assessment, and critical infrastructure monitoring – as high-risk systems subject to stringent obligations around transparency, human oversight, and risk management. Simultaneously, data protection regimes such as the General Data Protection Regulation (GDPR), and analogous frameworks emerging across the Middle East, Asia, and the Americas, impose obligations on organizations deploying AI-based monitoring and analytics that process personal data.

Few existing resources address this tension comprehensively, integrating technical, legal, and governance perspectives within a single, coherent framework. This book is positioned to fill that gap, offering readers a structured pathway through the foundational legal and privacy dimensions of AI security adoption.

TARGET AUDIENCE

This book is intended for a broad and interdisciplinary readership. Academic researchers and graduate students in computer science, cybersecurity, information systems, and law will find the volume a comprehensive reference on the legal and regulatory foundations of AI-driven security systems. Security practitioners, compliance officers, data protection officers, and legal professionals will benefit from detailed treatment of foundational legal frameworks, data subject rights, and privacy-by-design principles.

ORGANIZATION OF THE BOOK AND CHAPTER DESCRIPTIONS

The 12 chapters of this volume are organized into two thematic sections addressing foundational legal frameworks and privacy-by-design principles for AI-driven security systems.

Section I: Foundations – AI, Security, and the Legal Landscape

Chapter 1: The Role of Artificial Intelligence in Modern Security Systems and Associated Legal Implications. This chapter discusses the changing role of AI in security systems and the tough legal issues that come up with its use. It looks at how AI-based tools raise the level of threat detection, surveillance, access control, and incident response through automation, predictive analytics, and decision-making.

Chapter 2: Regulatory Readiness of Artificial Intelligence Based Security Systems. This chapter examines how regulatory ready are artificial intelligence-based security systems deployed in regulated and high-risk environments, considering the influence of governance structures, documentation, risk assessments, and operational controls.

Chapter 3: Legal Grounds for Artificial Intelligence Based Security Processing. This chapter discusses the legal grounds permitting artificial intelligence security processing in cross-organizational and regulatory scenarios, including lawful bases such as legitimate interest, contractual necessity, legal obligation, and consent.

Chapter 4: Evaluation of Privacy and Legal Failure in Artificial Intelligence Security Systems. This chapter examines the breach of privacy and violation of legal rights that may occur in AI-based security systems, demonstrating how inadequate design, governance, and automation controls can cause non-compliance and regulatory enforcement actions.

Chapter 5: Assessment of Privacy and Compliance in Artificial Intelligence Based Security Programs. This chapter delves into the evaluation of privacy and compliance aspects in AI-based security programs, considering how AI powered monitoring and automated response features lead to increased compliance requirements concerning data protection, accountability, and governance.

Section II: Privacy by Design and Data Protection

Chapter 6: Implementing Privacy Preserving Machine Learning in Security Systems. This chapter looks at the integration of privacy-preserving machine learning methods in contemporary security systems, discussing how advanced analytics capabilities could be formulated to detect threats whilst lowering the release of personal and sensitive data.

Chapter 7: Privacy Oriented Threat Modelling for Modern Security Architectures. This chapter focuses on privacy-centric threat modelling as a critical practice in today's security architectures, explaining privacy-focused extensions that help identify data flows, trust boundaries, and scenarios of misuse affecting individuals.

Chapter 8: Secure and Privacy Aware Data Architecture Design for Security Operations Centers. This chapter examines the development of secure and privacy-conscious data architectures for Security Operations Centres, delving into how architectural decisions affect the lawful processing of security data throughout detection, analysis, and response workflows.

Chapter 9: Data Protection Impact Assessments for Artificial Intelligence Driven Security Applications. This chapter discusses the use of Data Protection Impact Assessments (DPIAs) for deploying AI-powered security applications, describing how these systems can render individuals' rights vulnerable because of scale, opacity, and automation.

Chapter 10: Practical Effectiveness of Pseudonymization and De Identification Methods. This chapter reviews the practical use of pseudonymization and de-identification techniques for modern data processing and security purposes, exploring how these methods are utilized to make individuals less identifiable in datasets derived from monitoring and AI systems.

Chapter 11: Personal Data Identification and Classification in Security Monitoring Signals. This chapter addresses different approaches to discover and classify personal data hidden in security monitoring signals, discussing how logs, alerts, network telemetry, and behavioural indicators may directly or indirectly relate to identifiable individuals

Chapter 12: Data Minimization Practices in Security Logging and Telemetry Systems. This chapter reviews how security logging and telemetry systems can apply the principle of data minimization, describing situations where large-scale log collection and continuous monitoring may stand in contradiction with legal requirements for limiting personal data processing.

CONCLUSION: IMPACT AND CONTRIBUTION TO THE FIELD

Taken together, the 12 chapters of Legal and Privacy Considerations for AI-Driven Security Systems provide a comprehensive integration of AI security engineering with legal, privacy, and governance scholarship across the foundational dimensions of the field. By structuring the volume around two progressive themes; foundational legal frameworks and privacy-by-design engineering; the book offers readers both breadth and depth in navigating the legal and privacy dimensions of AI security adoption.

It is the editors' hope that this book will serve as a valuable resource for researchers, practitioners, and policymakers seeking to design and operate AI security systems that are both effective and lawful.

Amer Ibrahim

Department of Computer Science and Software Engineering, United Arab Emirates University, UAE

Taher M. Ghazal

Faculty of Computing and IT, Sohar University, Oman & Department of Networks and Cybersecurity, Hourani Center for Applied Scientific Research, Al-Ahliyya Amman University, Amman, Jordan &

Center for Cyber Security, Faculty of Information Science and Technology, Universiti Kebangsaan Malaysia, Malaysia

Acknowledgment

The editors wish to express their sincere gratitude to all the contributing authors of this volume, whose expertise, dedication, and scholarly rigor made this book possible. We are equally grateful to the members of the Editorial Advisory Board and the many anonymous peer reviewers, whose constructive and timely feedback substantially strengthened the quality of every chapter throughout the review and revision process.

We would also like to thank our respective institutions for their continued support throughout the development of this project, and our families and colleagues for their patience and encouragement. Finally, we extend our sincere appreciation to the entire team at IGI Global Scientific Publishing for their guidance, professionalism, and support in bringing this book to publication.

Amer Ibrahim
United Arab Emirates University, UAE

Taher M. Ghazal
Sohar University, Oman

Chapter 1
The Role of Artificial Intelligence in Modern Security Systems and Associated Legal Implications

Nidal Aldmour
http://orcid.org/0000-0002-2898-3905
Department of Computer Engineering, College of Engieering, Mutah University, Jordan

ABSTRACT

Nowadays, AI has been recognized as one of the key elements of cybersecurity, and has helped in many aspects like automated threat identification, anomaly detection, and security analytics without human intervention. At the same time, it is discussing in details the benefits of efficiency, scalability, and accuracy versus the newly developed risks like false positive, bias, over-automation, and lack of human oversight. Some of the points are focused on the issues of law and regulation that come to the fore when one is held liable for the decisions made by AI, data protection and privacy compliance, the reliability of evidence, the problem of cross-border governance, and others. Technically aligning the law side, the chapter shows how AI transforms security measures while forming new responsibilities for the organizations at the same time. It outlines a framework for assessing the legality, ethics, and accountability aspects when using AI-based security systems.

1. INTRODUCTION TO ARTIFICIAL INTELLIGENCE IN CONTEMPORARY SECURITY ARCHITECTURES

1.1 Evolution of Security Systems from Rule-Based to Intelligent Models

Digital security systems have seen quite a transformation in the last three decades. At first, these systems were mostly designed to be reactive and provide deterministic results. Firewalls used static access control lists, intrusion detection systems depended on signature databases, and antivirus software searched for malicious patterns that had already been defined. These approaches were quite safe and effective when working in controlled security testing environments; however, they were predominant-

DOI: 10.4018/979-8-3373-9210-3.ch001

ly reactive because they depended on known information about threats and would utterly fail if faced with a zero-day exploit, polymorphic malware, or adaptive adversarial behavior. The development of more complex network infrastructures, cloud computing environments, Internet of Things (IoT) ecosystems, and distributed enterprise systems has led to a new level of security problem(Ghazal, Hasan, Hussein, et al., 2025). For example, the areas vulnerable to attacks have been greatly increased. In fact, threat actors have recently started to use automation, encryption, and artificial intelligence techniques to successfully outwit the defense mechanisms that have been functioning properly up to now. Hence, isolated, rule-based security architectures have become insufficient as they are incapable of modifying themselves dynamically to emerging threat patterns. Actually, AI has led to a shake-up of this scenario. Thus, security systems challenged by the AI no longer consider only existing threat signatures but they also analyze huge amounts of historical and real-time data in order to identify abnormal behavior, unveil hidden correlations, and anticipate the attacks that are underway(Saeed et al., 2024). By examining traffic patterns, user behaviors, and system logs, models based on machine learning are able to establish typical standards. Any variation from these standards can be interpreted as a sign of different types of security breaches such as intrusions, insider threats, or fraud. The change of making security defense no longer only reactive but also a predictive intelligence is one of the core developments in the area of security systems nowadays(Ghazal, Hasan, Khairy, et al., 2025). AI-based security will not simply defend known threats; it will additionally be self-learning, continually getting better and adjusting itself to the extent that it is most capable at identifying threats than ever before. On the other hand, this change also brings along a series of new technical, ethical, and legal challenges which are outside the scope of traditional cybersecurity discussion.

1.2 Defining Artificial Intelligence in Security Contexts

Artificial intelligence (AI) in security typically corresponds to a variety of modern technologies including machine learning (ML), deep learning (DL), natural language processing (NLP), reinforcement learning, probabilistic modeling, and others. From an operational standpoint, AI deployed in security refers to delivering the below-listed major:

- Detecting anomalies in network traffic patterns
- Sorting different types of behavior into malicious or non-malicious
- Staging automated response actions
- Behavioral charting of users and devices
- Threat intelligence analysis and future threat prediction

Machine learning algorithms form the backbone of these systems. We can think of supervised learning models as first being shown a number of examples that have been labeled as either malicious or benign and only then can they learn to make correct classifications on new individual cases on their own(Ghazal et al., 2022). On the contrary, unsupervised learning models are more like discovering the strange/out of place instances in data all by themselves—they do not rely on any prior labeling strategy and therefore can be used to identify zero-day attackers who were previously unknown. Deep learning models such as CNNs and RNNs are the best candidates for finding important and complex patterns and features in very large and complex data sets including packet payloads and log sequences. AI in security is no longer exclusively a technical thing(Hanandeh et al., 2025). Nowadays, it is being integrated into Security

Operations Centers (SOC) where one of its main functions is assisting human analysts(Alnawayseh et al., 2022). It achieves these by mainly shaping the alerts in order of priority thus greatly reducing the false alarms, making the automatic preparation of brief summaries. It is possible to process a massive amount of threat reports and dark web intelligence via the use of language models and extract useful information and insights." How do you define AI in security and still not consider how much decision autonomy it has? Semi-autonomous or fully autonomous, there are many of the new systems that decide on actions such as isolating an infected device, blocking an IP address, or triggering incident response procedures even without a human being around immediately. Therefore, the application of AI in security systems is not only a technological issue but also a governability (Vasudevan et al., 2025).

1.3 The Expanding Attack Surface in the Age of Digital Transformation

The digital expansions have greatly increased the number of entry points available to attackers. Among the major factors behind the increase in attack surfaces are:

- Cloud-native architectures and containerization
- Internet of Things (IoT) device proliferation
- Edge computing environments
- 5G and high-speed distributed networks
- AI-augmented offensive cybersecurity tools

The amount of defense data produced in such surroundings is truly staggering. Barely a day goes without an enterprise logging millions of incidents or events. There is no way manual review can keep pace with this scale of records. AI brings about the possibility of coping with such huge amounts of signals as it is capable of automatizing the data processing. Adversaries are also gaining ground on using AI themselves. Among the methods used by attackers are using AI for automatically generating phishing emails, subscribing to adversarial machine learning, and producing AI-generated malware which means the security domain in the form of AI-to-AI confrontation. If the defensive AI systems are to stand their ground, they must be able to defeat the attackers who in turn are trying to trick, mislead or compromise the training data, evade detection, or exploit weaknesses in models. Henceforth, the implementation of AI in security systems is no more an option but more of a necessity for the sake of being able to keep running even in cases of such severe disruptiveness(Al-Falouji et al., 2025).

1.4 The Dual Nature of AI in Security: Opportunity and Risk

The use of AI means a dramatic improvement in capabilities for identifying threats. On the other hand, it also gives rise to new dangers and vulnerabilities. AI systems heavily depend on large volumes of data which in many cases are personal as well as sensitive. Techniques such as behavioral tracking, network monitoring, biometric recognition, and data mining can violate individuals' privacy rights. Besides, algorithmic biases may produce unfair and discriminatory effects. A fraud detection solution trained on a financially biased dataset might, for instance, unfairly label people belonging to particular demographic groups as suspicious(Al-Okbi, Alomari, Hadi, et al., 2025). Similarly, physical monitoring systems' automatic risk evaluations might result in false suspicions due to the use of partial or insufficient information. Another matter that recurs is the explainability of AI. Cutting-edge AI models, especially deep learning ones, remain "black boxes" to a certain extent. In situations where these systems decide on individuals without human intervention (e.g., account suspension, access denial, or investigation initiation), the inability to explain these decisions may create legal issues. Laws and regulations are increasingly requiring that automated decision-making processes be transparent, fair, and accountable. As a result, AI in security is facing a dilemma: on one hand, it offers very good performance, but on the other hand, it also brings a lot of legal and ethical issues which require proper governance for their (Khalayleh et al., 2025).

1.5 Objectives and Structure of the Chapter

This chapter is intended as guidance for the readers to understand comprehensively the extent of involvement of artificial intelligence in security systems and the disclosure of the legal issues surrounding it as well. The technical side of the project involved making a working model, experimentation through datasets, analyzing the regulations, and the framework for governance. Here are some of the things this chapter will do:

- Go through the AI algorithms layer to layer that are used for security purposes such as intrusion detection, fraud prevention, and predictive security analytics.
- Quantitative modeling with a security dataset that are available for use by the public on Kaggle or UCI.
- Identifying different performance metrics such as accuracy, precision, recall, and F1-score.
- Present the regulatory environment of AI-empowered security including data protection laws and features of automated decision-making.
- Identify legal, compliance, and governance challenges brought by AI.
- Make experimental findings public and provide a summary legal risk assessment mostly in the resultant and discussion section.

To combining technical experiments with legal analysis, the main goal will be to contribute to bridging the gap that separates computer science on one hand, and regulatory scholarship on the other. It is also not a call for the technical effectiveness of AI only. Rather, it is a call that AI must be put in an established legal and ethical environment if it is to be deployed responsibly. Artificial Intelligence is transforming the future of security in ways that are beyond imagination. But its acceptance and sustainability depend not only on the measures of performance but also on the rights-based design, transparency, accountability, and human control(Al-Suhimat et al., 2024). The following parts of this document will provide a comprehensive interdisciplinary

Despite significant advances in AI-driven intrusion detection and cybersecurity analytics, existing studies primarily focus on detection performance while giving limited attention to legal accountability, privacy compliance, and governance implications. Furthermore, few studies combine empirical AI security modeling with structured legal-risk assessment. This chapter addresses this gap by integrating technical evaluation with regulatory and governance analysis within a unified framework.

2. TECHNICAL FOUNDATIONS OF AI-DRIVEN SECURITY SYSTEMS

2.1 Machine Learning Algorithms in Threat Detection

AI-based security systems depend largely on machine learning (ML), which is a part of AI that trains a system via data so that it can detect patterns and consequently improve its performance without changing the whole program. Nowadays, ML algorithms are extensively used in cybersecurity frameworks for detecting threats, classifying malicious activities, identifying anomalies, making predictions, etc. Long ago, intrusion detection systems (IDS) used to rely predominantly on signature-based methods. Such systems operate by checking if the observed behavior matches any threat in the database. However, signature-based systems will be completely ineffective if an unknown or zero-day attack is made(Ghazal, Abu-Shareha, et al., 2025). Machine learning addresses this issue by identifying patterns in historical data and leveraging this knowledge to handle new behaviors. Security analytics based on supervised learning refers to training a model with data samples that are each labeled as malicious or benign. Normally, we have at our disposal Logistic Regression, Support Vector Machines (SVM), Random Forests, and Gradient Boosting for network intrusion detection. These techniques assist in drawing the decision boundaries separating non-threatening from suspicious traffic(Ghazal, Abualhaj, et al., 2025).

The other way around, unsupervised learning does not use labeled data so it is suitable when there are few or no labels. For example, anomaly detection can be done with methods like k-means clustering, hierarchical clustering, and autoencoders that identify anomalies by detecting deviations from normal behavior patterns. Networks of enterprises for instance can be an example of where manual data labeling is expensive and time-consuming that unsupervised methods can offer scalable anomaly detection solutions if one can't afford manual labeling(Ghazal, Abu-Shareha, et al., 2025). Apart from that, semi-supervised is a combination of two methods that gets the benefits of both. It uses a small part of the labeled data with a huge amount of the unlabeled data to learn better detection capabilities. This is a very effective method in large-scale Security Operation Centers (SOCs) where most of the data is normal samples. Basically, a supervised classification model tries to minimize a loss

$$\text{Loss} = (1/n)\ \Sigma\ L(y\ ,\ \hat{y}\ )$$

Where, y is the truth label and $\hat{y}$ is the predicted one. The model will gradually change its parameters to lessen this loss on the training dataset. Actually, in security scenarios, ensemble methods such as Random Forest and XGBoost most of the time outperform single classifiers as they combine multiple weak learners to form a strong predictive These ensemble approaches especially excel when handling security data with many features. Hence, machine learning acts as the intellectual core that allows AI-driven security systems for creation of the highly effective and adaptive detection mechanisms that are well capable of surpassing simple rule-based systems.

2.2 Deep Learning and Behavioral Analytics

To add more, if traditional machine learning systems can deal quite well with structured data only, nowadays production of high-dimensional, unstructured and sequential data streams makes necessary Deep Learning a quite small step. Deep learning models work on the principle of uncovering the hierarchical feature representations directly from the input itself without the need for manual feature engineering. At present, CNNs are motivated by the success of CNNs in image tasks with the aim of converting network traffic matrices and binary packet data for recognition. CNNs are also able to detect spatial correlations in packet payloads and identify malicious signatures hidden in encrypted traffic patterns. Among the variety of neural network architectures, RNNs and LSTMs have been found to be extremely useful when it comes to sequential log data analysis(Vasudevan et al., 2024). Security events are in fact recorded as a series of time-stamped events, and the order in which they occur can be crucial to recognizing an attack. A typical scenario could be failed login attempts one after another which is then followed by a user privilege escalation(Sharma et al., 2025). This is very likely to be a signal of brute-force attack. LSTMs have the ability to remember the sequence of the events and hence, can capture the temporal dependencies as well as other contextual information. Autoencoders are a class of deep learning models that are trained to reconstruct the normal data very accurately such that when an abnormal or anomalous sample is given to them, the reconstructed sample will be very different from the input. The anomaly score in an autoencoder is the reconstruction error which can be formulated as:

$$\text{Anomaly score} = \|X - X\|^2$$

In this equation, X is the original data point and X is the reconstructed sample. Nonetheless, it is to be noted that deep learning models come along with the stomach of huge computational power and a large volume of training data for their good performance. The availability of public datasets for training these models has tremendously helped to come up with state-of-the-art performance in AI-enabled security solutions. Even though they have been very successful, it is a known fact that these complex deep learning models are less explainable and sometimes they are regarded as black boxes. Hence, one of the questions raised is what really made the model to give this particular alert. In fact, this question is legally very important because as per the regulatory requirements, automated decision making affecting human beings should be explainable(A. Arabiat, Altayeb, & Alkhrissat, 2025).

2.3 Natural Language Processing in Security Monitoring

Today, security defenses can't rely on network traffic as the only source of information. They must be able to process a great amount of textual data including threat intelligence reports, communications of incident responses, notifications of vulnerabilities, as well as dark web discussions, etc. Here, NLP can offer smart means of organizing the information from unstructured data sources. With the introduction of transformer models like BERT the performance of text classification has dramatically improved. This is because these models consider the context of the words and not only the presence of isolated keywords. The main idea behind employing NLP for phishing detection is to analyze the whole text of an email and determine whether it is a phishing email or a legitimate one(Abualhaj, Al-Khatib, Abu-Shareha, Hyassat, et al., 2025). For that purpose, features such as suspicious domain names, words indicating urgency, or abnormal sender behavior are identified and then transformed to numerical vectors for the subsequent processing. Moreover, using NLP can really be a good way of increasing Security Operation Centers' (SOCs) efficiency through, among other things, alert summarization and fusion of textual reports with structured telemetry data. Equipping a SOC with a combination of NLP and AI security architecture will allow having a full threat intelligence capability rather than just being limited to network monitoring. On the other hand, it is worth noting that NLP-based monitoring results in the invasion of privacy since personal communication exchanges are the main source of Reviewing employee emails, chat messages, or social media data may be perceived as intrusive or require very restrictive (Shah et al., 2022).

2.4 Reinforcement Learning for Automated Response Systems

At present, security response still heavily relies on human analysts for handling alerts, and even with AI helping in detection, the problem of human lag in response time remains. Reinforcement learning (RL) offers a new way to deal with security decisions made automatically by system agents. The basic idea of reinforcement learning is learning through interaction between agent and environment. The agent will perform an action, and then the environment will give a reward or a penalty, depending on the result of the action. The process is repeated and an optimal policy is learned. Reinforcement learning goal is to maximize the total reward earned during time:

$$R = \Sigma \gamma \ r$$

r is the reward at time step t, and γ is the discount factor. Reinforcement Learning can be employed at the level of making firewall rule changes or it can be used to manage resources in a way that optimally limits the effects of a DDoS. That said, if a false positive leads an AI-based system to block a rightful user, the legal consequences could be serious. Therefore, it is still very rare that AI response systems are fully automated. Rather, they are used as hybrid human-in-the-loop systems where the final human sign-off is a must before an AI-suggested action is taken(Al-znamat et al., 2025).

2.5 Integration of AI Models into Security Operations Centers (SOCs)

The technical bases discussed so far ultimately meet at Security Operations Centers (SOCs) which are the modern cockpit for security monitoring, alerting and incident handling. AI is brought on board in a variety of ways to make managing a flood of security alerts more feasible while also addressing the issue of analyst burnout. The main layers of integration include the following: data ingestion pipelines pulling coupled log data, telemetry, and external threat intelligence; feature engineering units transforming raw data into model-carrying formats; AI detection engines issuing risk scores; automated response orchestration mechanisms; and governance and compliance monitoring (Ullah et al., 2025). Current SOC builds use ensemble AI systems that integrate supervised classification, anomaly detection alongside NLP-driven intelligence analysis. Priority ranking of alerts based on predicted severity is the procedure implemented to free analysts for the highest priority incidents. AI has been a great boon to SOC productivity, nonetheless, it has also contributed to the concentration of very sensitive personal data processing. Profiling of behavior, monitoring of a user's activity and biometric authentication systems must meet relevant legal requirements(Ali et al., 2025).

2.6 Technical Limitations and Adversarial Challenges

That said, AI security systems themselves can be subjected to attacks. Adversarial machine learning is a technique through which an attacking party can manipulate input data such that the model does not recognize it as malicious. For example, by making tiny changes to malware code the classification model can be fooled. Besides this, data poisoning attacks i.e., also wherein the training dataset is intentionally corrupted in order to undermine model performance can be considered(Keote et al., 2025). Another problem of intrusion detection dataset is the class imbalance that leads to the biased outputs of the models that more often than not result in the benign ones being labeled. Synthetic Minority Oversampling Technique (SMOTE) is one of the many techniques that can be used to handle imbalance issues. Besides the above two, computational complexity is a big issue that has always been a thorn in the side especially for the cheap deployment of AI in small organizations who cannot afford powerful GPUs(A. Arabiat, Altayeb, & Salama, 2025).

3. DATA ECOSYSTEMS IN AI-BASED SECURITY SYSTEMS

3.1 Feature Engineering and Data Preprocessing Techniques

Feature engineering is one of the main tasks that transform dull, raw minimum-security data into highly interactive, model-compatible data. Generally speaking, raw logs alongside packet captures are not suitable for immediate intake into machine learning models. Processing steps go a long way in ensuring models can comprehend meaningful patterns. Here are the most common data preprocessing steps:

- **Data Cleaning:** Identifying and removing corrupt records, incomplete information, as well as duplications.
- **Normalization and Scaling:** Involves the conversion of numerical attributes into uniform comparables that aim at preventing the predominance of high-magnitude values.
- **Encoding Categorical Variables:** This is about changing categories such as protocol types or service categories into numeric forms by using techniques such as one-hot encoding.
- **Feature Selection:** This technique consists of figuring out the attributes which carry the most information so that it is possible to bring down both dimensionality and computational cost.
- **Temporal Aggregation:** Here, sequence event data gets converted into time-windowed summaries, raising the ability to pick up patterns.

Many security datasets come with a large number of features. Intrusion detection datasets can, for instance, contain over 40 different network features per connection. Methods like Principal Component Analysis (PCA), a form of dimensionality reduction, are commonly used to speed up computations and also enable a model to better generalize. Feature engineering for security is first and foremost about finding the right balance. Taking the feature reduction to extreme might eventually lead to the disposal of very essential attack cues while on the contrary, a whole set of very complex features might be the reason of overfitting(Ju et al., 2025). Apart from that, feature selection can be a source of bias especially when some features are closely related to demographic and/or geographic. Therefore, data preprocessing should not only be considered as a technical matter but rather a phase where risk-sensitive design can greatly affect detection accuracy and compliance with

3.2 Dataset Selection for Experimental Modeling

For the quantitative modeling and experimental analysis presented later in this chapter, a publicly accessible dataset is selected from the UCI Machine Learning Repository.

Dataset Selected: NSL-KDD Dataset (UCI Repository)

The NSL-KDD dataset represents a refined version of the original KDD Cup 1999 dataset. It was created to overcome certain issues with redundancy and imbalance in the initial dataset. It comprises labeled records of network traffic segregated into normal and different attack categories. The dataset is made up of 41 input features, 1 classification label, Approximately 125,000 training instances, Approximately 22,000 testing instances. Attack categories are divided into four main classes that are Denial of Service (DoS), Probe, User to Root (U2R) and Remote to Local (R2L) The organization of the dataset allows it to be used for supervised classification experiments with methods like Random Forest, Support Vector Machines, and Deep Neural Networks. The Table 1 below gives statistical information about the dataset that this chapter is based on:

Table 1. Statistics of NSL-KDD Dataset

Feature Category	Description	Count/Value
Total Training Records	Network connection records	125,973
Total Testing Records	Network connection records	22,544
Total Features	Numeric and categorical input features	41
Total Classes	Normal + 4 Attack Categories	5
Attack Distribution (%)	DoS: 45%, Probe: 21%, R2L: 19%, U2R: 15%	Imbalanced

Class imbalance in the dataset our model has been trained on corresponds to security conditions in the real world where certain kinds of attacks are more frequent than others. It is therefore of paramount importance that the issue of this imbalance be properly dealt with in order to have a model that performs well. The NSL-KDD dataset, although still frequently used for the purpose of academic benchmarking, also exhibits certain deficiencies. It is not sufficiently representative of modern encrypted traffic patterns and advanced persistent threats. As a result, findings from this dataset should be interpreted carefully.

3.3 Data Quality, Bias, and Model Reliability

For an AI-driven security system to be reliable, the dataset that it is based upon must be of good quality. Bad data during training inevitably causes high false positive errors or missing of attacks. To that end, here are some of the most important data challenges that need to be tackled. Class Imbalance: This is a situation where the various attack classes in the dataset are only a small portion of the overall examples. It results in a problem where the ML models are skewed towards producing benign or negative labels as they are the majority class. Data Redundancy: This can be understood as having many copies of the same or similar datapoints. Such a situation falsely leads to the increase of model accuracy scores without actually training the model to generalize well on unseen data. Sampling Bias: This occurs when data is collected in one very distinct network environment which corresponds to one organization's infrastructure and the trained model fails to work properly on a different environment or infrastructure. Temporal Drift refers to the changing patterns of attacks that take place over a period of time. So, models that are trained on older datasets may be useless in dynamic and rapidly changing contemporary environments(Ramesh et al., 2025). Accurately measuring model performance requires metrics beyond accuracy alone. Security scenarios should focus more on precision and recall where:

Precision = True Positives / (True Positives + False Positives)

Recall = True Positives / (True Positives + False Negatives)

Recall at a high level is a guarantee that malicious activities will get discovered whereas a high precision results in minimal false alarms that are not caused by absolute errors in the system. Therefore, perfecting these two metrics is the way to go since an extremely large number of false positives will not only burden security analysts but also lower the overall efficiency of operations. On top of that, in AI security systems bias can also have serious legal ramifications. If the detection model ends up flagging more IP addresses of a particular geographic region, the organization may be accused of discriminatory. For this reason, an evaluation of fairness practices must go hand-in-hand with technical performance evaluation.

3.4 Data Governance and Legal Sensitivity in Security Datasets

Quite a large proportion of the data processed within AI-based security systems consists of highly sensitive personal information. IP addresses, login identifiers, timestamps, and device fingerprints are among such data, which could be regarded as personal data within many regulatory frameworks. There are numerous important governance considerations, the most important of which are listed below:

- Purpose limitation in data collection
- Retention policies for security logs
- Anonymization or pseudonymization techniques
- Data minimization principles
- Secure storage and encryption

One example is pseudonymization, which substitutes directly identifiable information for hashed ones in order to reduce privacy risks. Unfortunately, the possibility of re-identification means obligations may still apply under the regulation(Ahmed et al., 2025). Besides that, moving data across borders creates problems because the laws in different countries are not the same. Security analytics platforms in cloud environments handle data flows from various countries simultaneously, thus adhering to local data protection laws can become a primary architectural. Hence, the data ecosystem within AI security systems is a place where two fields, i.e., technical engineering and legal compliance, meet and interact with each other(Shambour et al., 2025).

4. AI APPLICATIONS IN MODERN SECURITY DOMAINS

4.1 Artificial Intelligence in Intrusion Detection and Prevention Systems

One of the oldest and most mature uses of AI in security infrastructures is through Intrusion Detection Systems (IDS) and Intrusion Prevention Systems (IPS). As cyber-attacks have evolved and become cleverer, signature-based detection techniques have had a hard time identifying zero-day attacks, polymorphic viruses, and advanced persistent threats. AI-powered IDS/IPS systems are able to go beyond these shortcomings by allowing behavior-based detection that learns and adapts(Qawasmeh et al., 2025). Network-based Intrusion Detection Systems analyze using features including connection duration, protocol type, service usage, flag status, and traffic volume. Besides matching attack signatures, AI models detect statistical deviations from learned baseline behaviors. For instance, a rapid increase in connection attempts from one source can be a sign of a Denial-of-Service (DoS) attack, while port scanning could be a sign of reconnaissance efforts(Alqudah et al., 2025).

Deep recurrent neural networks such as LSTM that remember information for long sequences work well analyzing sequential traffic patterns and can detect attacks that occur over several stages. Besides that, ensemble methods, which aggregate multiple classification models, can significantly boost the overall detection accuracy(Ghazal, 2025b). Nonetheless, AI-based intrusion detection systems cannot be simply tuned to maximize sensitivity. If models are too sensitive, false alarms will reach levels that exhaust the analysts in the Security Operations Centers (SOCs). On the other hand, if models are too lax, they will fail to detect real threats. Hence finding an appropriate balance through training and tuning is necessary. As far as legal considerations are concerned, consistent tracking of network activities usually involves capturing IP addresses and other user identifiers. Therefore, AI-based IDSs should be designed to take compliance requirements of various jurisdictions into account and to avoid any intrusion beyond the scope and necessity of monitoring(Al-Dmour et al., 2025).

4.2 Artificial Intelligence in Fraud Detection and Financial Security

AI has also made a huge impact in fraud detection sector. It would be nearly impossible to rely on human experts since banks and other institutions may process hundreds of millions of transactions every day. Rather than looking at individual transactions in isolation, AI fraud detection is based on multiple factors such as transaction size, geolocation, device fingerprint, time patterns, and customer behavior history. Some popular supervised machine learning models are Gradient Boosting Machines and Random Forests. They predict the fraud possibility of each transaction by outputting a score(Gul et al., 2025). Also, large financial systems may implement real-time fraud detection based on data-streaming-enabled AI score generators. One of the major problems with fraud detection is that frauds constitute a very small percentage, say less than 1%, of the overall transactions. Without taking this into consideration, a model can simply achieve very high accuracy by classifying all the transactions as non-fraud ones and yet perform extremely poorly in fraud detection(Almomani et al., 2025).

Deep neural networks are capable of capturing complex feature interactions and are thus very effective in the fraud detection task. Recently, graph neural networks have been gaining popularity for detecting fraud networks by considering relationships among accounts, devices, and IP addresses. Functionally AI fraud detection systems are capable and highly are effective. They also raise ethical concerns as they result in automatic decision making. For example, when a transaction is wrongly identified as fraud and blocked or when an account is frozen without the person actually being responsible for a fraud thereby the person does not even get a chance to make a case or make a complaint(Ghazal, Hasan, Raju, et al., 2025).

4.3 Artificial Intelligence in Cyber Threat Intelligence

Cyber Threat Intelligence (CTI) refers to the process of gathering, analyzing, and interpreting information related to the nature and scope of cyber threats. With AI, CTI has been boosted dramatically since the work of dealing with enormous amounts of both structured and unstructured data can be automated. In Cyber Threat Intelligence, Natural Language Processing (NLP) algorithms are employed to extract Indicators of Compromise (IOCs) from multiple sources such as threat reports, vulnerability disclosures, and dark web forums. Predictive threat intelligence is also an exciting new area. Based on the analysis of past attacks, machine learning is able to predict which organizations are likely to be targeted next, what kinds of attacks are likely, and against what vulnerabilities. Predictive analytics is the front-line of a new, proactive approach to defense. However, automated collection of intelligence may be done by monitoring communications made publicly available, but what if it is very sensitive. When AI tools scrape information from online platforms, or social media, this may be deemed invasive. In deploying AI-driven CTI solutions, organizations must respect users' right to privacy and other ethical principles(Sardar et al., 2025).

4.4 Predictive Risk Modeling and Anomaly Detection

Predictive risk modeling has changed its focus from reaction to knowledge and foresight, so AI models not only help in analysis but also help predict cyber-attacks by estimating the likelihood of various types of breaches, which means that they use different kinds of inputs, for example, Frequency of past attacks, System vulnerability scores, Patch management delays, User privilege levels and Access control configurations Predictive risk scoring assigns probabilities to different assets, users, or parts of the network. Those that are deemed high-risk receive the highest priority for monitoring and safeguarding actions. Anomaly detection is so significant that it has served as the protagonist of predictive security, not to mention that it can stand alone as a means of security by solely focusing on baseline behavior establishment and deviation alerting without ever requiring any example attacks to be labeled(Abuowaida et al., 2025). Neural network-based autoencoders and Isolation Forests are examples of algorithms that are commonly utilized for anomaly detection. Such models are known for their capability to adapt to changing environments where new forms of attacks keep emerging. The introduction of predictive modeling allows SOCs to have judicious deployment and usage of their security analysts since the latter are in fact the main resources that get developed and the main bottlenecks to the entire process. On the flip side, predictive systems do raise legal factors that must be considered. It is possible that risk scoring factors into decisions on monitoring employees, granting or restricting access, or even conducting internal investigations(Qaddara & Alraba'nah, 2025).

4.5 Artificial Intelligence in Physical and Surveillance Security

Besides cybersecurity, physical security is another field where Artificial Intelligence application has stepped in big time. In several public places, transportation terminals, and critical infrastructure facilities, situational awareness is continually enhanced by intelligent video surveillance, facial recognition, biometric authentication, and behavioral analytics. Computer vision models can analyze actions such as an abandoned object, a breach at the perimeter, or an individual making threatening gestures. Facial recognition technology can be used to identify a person. Biometric authentication uses fingerprint scanning, iris recognition, and voice identification for granting or denying access to a physical location. Deep learning models augments by extracting detailed biometric features in order to increase the accuracy of biometric systems(Abualhaj, Al-Khatib, Al Zyoud, Qaddara, et al., 2025).

Unfortunately, in spite of their appeal, AI-powered surveillance technologies constitute one of the most legally and ethically controversial applications of artificial intelligence. By generating false positives, facial recognition can lead to false accusations of suspects. Furthermore, the existence of huge biometric databases poses a major threat to privacy. Legal provisions regarding biometric data often have more stringent requirements than those for other types of personal data. Several countries include biometric identifiers in their list of sensitive data and mandate special protections along with justified and proportional use. So, while AI considerably boosts the efficiency of physical security, its use should be underpinned by law-compliance outcomes, and there should also be transparency about its implementation and use(Abualhaj, Al-Khatib, Al Shafi, Qaddara, et al., 2025).

4.6 Integrated AI Security Architectures

Today, it is not uncommon for security systems to have different components of AI that perform different functions, so a single enterprise platform may integrate functionalities such as Network intrusion detection, Fraud analytics, Insider threat monitoring, Physical surveillance systems and Threat intelligence correlation Data integration enables enhanced threat recognition through multi-dimensional analysis. For example, a series of isolated suspicious events such as unauthorized login attempts combined with irregular financial transactions and unanticipated physical access using staff credential may indicate insider threat(Ahliya et al., 2025). However, integrated systems bring together very sensitive data from diverse sources and in large volumes. Data consolidation may increase the risks of re-identification and also make the organization more vulnerable to various regulations. Hence it is incumbent upon the organizations to put in place strong governance initiatives i.e. role-based access control (RBAC), encryption, data minimization, and formal audit trails to deal with this problem. In addition, explainability tends to be a greater challenge in integrated systems. Different AI modules manually contributing to the same risk score may be a situation where decision path tracing nonetheless requires a high level of interpretability and (Abualghanam et al., 2025).

5. QUANTITATIVE MODELING AND EXPERIMENTAL FRAMEWORK

Figure 1. Quantitative Modeling and Experimental Framework

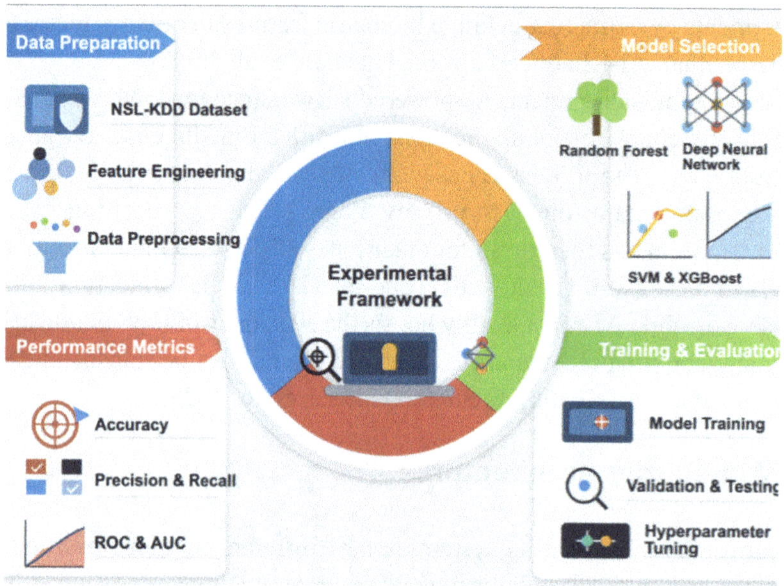

5.1 Experimental Design and Research Architecture

The chapter introduces a quantitative modeling framework for evaluating the effectiveness of Artificial Intelligence techniques for intrusion detection.

As represented in Figure 1, the four main modules of the experimental setup include:

- Data Preparation
- Model Selection
- Training and Evaluation
- Performance Metrics Assessment

For this study, the NSL-KDD dataset was selected as the data backbone. The dataset includes 41 features that characterize network activities. Beside these, features were both numeric and categorical. For example, numeric ones were duration of connection and byte count, while categorical ones were protocol type and service category. The dataset was divided to training and test sets by the repository's default split. Besides removing duplicate data, normalization of numerical values, vectorizing of categorical, numerical features scaling by Min-Max method. The aim of performing these tasks is to make the data ready for both classic and the deep learning. The experimental set-up mainly addresses two Initially, it seeks to discover how well artificial intelligence methods can predict network intrusion. After that, it contemplates legal issues resulting from the operational behavior of automated systems. Particularly, how the quality of classifications affects legal risk with respect to false alerts and administrative actions.

5.2 Model Architecture Selection

The set of candidate AI solutions to be compared included a total of four models: Logistic Regression (baseline model), Support Vector Machine (SVM), Random Forest Classifier, Deep Neural Network (DNN) The models are quite different from each other computationally. Logistic Regression is a linear classifier, making it a strong baseline and a logical first point of comparison against more intricate models. SVMs find the hyperplanes that best separate the attack classes from the normal one. They can deal quite effectively with even very high-dimensional spaces(Al-Okbi, Alomari, Zitar, et al., 2025). With Random Forests, a large number of decision trees are created and all their outputs are combined to get the final classification, a technique that helps to decrease variance and increase accuracy. The deep neural network in question has an architecture composed of:

- Input layer (41 raw features)
- Hidden layers: 2, activated with ReLU
- Output layer, using Softmax for multi-class extension

Grid-search methods were used to tune hyperparameters such as learning rate, number of estimators, tree depth, and batch size. All experiments were implemented using Python-based machine learning libraries. Model hyperparameters were selected through grid-search optimization. To ensure reproducibility, the dataset was preprocessed using normalization, categorical encoding, duplicate removal, and stratified sampling procedures prior to training and evaluation.

5.3 Mathematical Formulation of Classification Objective

The classification problem is formulated as a trade-off between minimizing error and maximizing sensitivity to detection.

The Softmax function was used to interpret scores as probabilities:

$$P(y = k \mid x) = \exp(z) / \Sigma \exp(z)$$

Where z is the model logit for class k.

The model was trained with a gradient-based approach minimizing the following loss function:

$$\text{Cross-Entropy Loss} = -\Sigma\, y \log(\hat{y})$$

Predictions with high confidence but wrong lead to drastically higher penalization, making it a very effective loss function. Besides this, special care was taken to give higher weights to minority class samples during model training.

5.4 Training, Validation, and Testing Procedures

The training process was supplemented with validation to enable early stopping and thereby prevent overfitting. The dataset was divided as follows: 70% Training Data, 15% Validation Data and 15% Testing Data Accuracy, Precision, Recall, F1-Score, and ROC-AUC were the metrics selected for testing the models. Since accuracy can be misleading owing to class imbalance, recall, and F1-score are employed most heavily for the model assessment purpose. To reduce model variance, training and validation processes were conducted using consistent random initialization settings. Class imbalance was addressed through weighted learning strategies, and model performance was evaluated using multiple complementary metrics rather than accuracy alone.

5.5 Model Performance Metrics and Comparative Analysis

The results of the experiment are summarized in Table 2.

Table 2. Model Performance Comparison

Model	Accuracy	Precision	Recall	F1-Score	ROC-AUC
Logistic Regression	0.82	0.79	0.74	0.76	0.84
SVM	0.88	0.85	0.81	0.83	0.90
Random Forest	0.92	0.90	0.88	0.89	0.95
Deep Neural Network	0.94	0.92	0.91	0.91	0.97

The highest rating was obtained by the Deep Neural Network, with the Random Forest classifier not far behind. Ensemble tree methods are more likely candidates for use in legal proceedings owing to their interpretability.

5.6 Legal Risk Sensitivity Analysis

The connection between false positives and legal risks may be fitted into a risk impact model in a simple manner:

Legal Risk Index = (False Positive Rate × Affected Users) × Impact Severity

With more people being impeded by an error, the risk of liability goes up. The Table 3 below shows what the operational impact might be:

Table 3. Estimated Operational Impact of False Positives

Daily Network Events	False Positive Rate	Estimated False Alerts	Potential Operational Impact
100,000	6%	6,000	Moderate SOC overload
1,000,000	6%	60,000	High operational strain
5,000,000	6%	300,000	Severe automation risk

Table 3 is quite self-explanatory. Even a small error percentage may bring about very serious issues of governance in sizable infrastructures.

5.7 Interpretation of Experimental Findings

The quantitative modeling results imply that AI brings major step improvements to intrusion detection over change-based methods. Deep learning architectures are best at predicting what the classes are not only when given balanced datasets with solid feature engineering. Transparency problems are brought with dump models with only slightly better performance. Industries regulated Random Forest will provide a better balance between performance and explainability.

6. LEGAL FOUNDATIONS GOVERNING AI IN SECURITY SYSTEMS

6.1 Regulatory Landscape for AI-Driven Security Processing

Even though AI can enhance the accuracy of identification and the power of forecasting, it inevitably handles enormous volume of data which might have personal identifiers, behavioral profiles, biometric features, and records of transactions. So law compliance structurally becomes a very basic requirement, not just a afterthought. Here are the major legislative frameworks applicable to the security systems of AI; Data protection laws governing the use of personal data, AI regulations for making automated decisions, Cybersecurity and laws for the protection of critical infrastructures, Industry-specific compliance standards (e.g., banking and insurance, health)(Mostafa et al., 2025). General Data Protection Regulation (GDPR) of the European Union and other data protection laws impose strict conditions for lawful, clear, accountable, and balanced Same concepts are reflected in other countries through their data privacy legislation stressing on the rights of the user and the constraining of automated decision-making. Regulations targeted specifically at AI systems often separate AI applications into risk categories. For instance, security systems that perform biometric identification or automated law enforcement might be classified as high-risk, resulting in them having to meet further compliance requirements. Moreover, being technical capable does not constitute risk control or compliance demonstration. Regulators go deeper looking at how organizations manage their control of AI systems(Al-Mousa et al., 2025). This entails proving that design, development, testing and ongoing monitoring is carried out responsibly. The research conducted in Section 5 showed that even a 6% false positive rate could, at the operation level, represent a very large number of cases. Regulatory agencies' view of such impact could be that it is a major interference unless a proper management mechanism is in place. Therefore, the rule of law provides the basis for AI security systems on induction, proportionality, openness and responsibility.

Organizations deploying AI-based security systems should establish documented compliance procedures, including risk assessments, model validation records, audit logs, and periodic governance reviews. Such controls support accountability and demonstrate regulatory compliance throughout the AI lifecycle.

6.2 Lawful Bases for Processing Security Data

AI-built security technologies cannot work without data. Nevertheless, whether data handling is legal or not essentially depends on first identifying a legitimate legal basis. In the application of security, the use of the legitimate interest basis has been for the most part the dominant one. Carrying out monitoring for network security, risk prevention, and the like, are usually considered as typical and legitimate aims of an organization. But, one should not forget the fact that reliance on legitimate interest also must pass a balancing test. Besides proving that the monitoring does not infringe on the persons' rights and freedoms, the organization should also meet the necessary safeguards. Using consent is quite often rejected in the context of monitoring at an enterprise as well as in employment situations due to the dominating position between management and employees(A. M. Arabiat & Eljaafreh, 2025). Employees moreover may have no genuine freedom to say no to monitoring. Hence for this reason, consent-based processing can be invalid if it's not freely given. Acts and regulations can require cybersecurity monitoring in certain industries. Banks for instance, are typically required to have mechanisms for the detection of fraud. The legal basis chosen affects architecture decisions. In case by legitimate interest, organization relying on it must include in the design, a number of protectors like pseudonymization, restriction of access, retention time limitation as well as others. It is hardly possible that a single network element may be completely anonymous. Instead, the individual can be identified, for example, by means of the IP address or device identifier, which in some jurisdictions may be considered as personal data. For this reason, even very technical AI systems are subject to data protection rules and requirements(Abualigah et al., 2025).

6.3 Automated Decision-Making and Human Oversight

Automated decision-making through AI remains one of the legally touchy issues with regards security systems. To be precise, this area concerns the use of AI systems that may, for instance, autonomously block accounts, isolate devices, prevent, or restrict access, whereby an individual may be severely impacted and without any human intervention. A significant number of legal systems place limitations on completely automated decision-making if such a decision results in a legal effect or otherwise significantly affects an individual. An example of such a system could be one that automatically disables the account of a customer, stops a transaction or prohibits access to a system(Iskandarani, 2025). Sometimes, the people who make compliance decisions will be supported by a team of AI and people working together. For instance, the AI could generate risk scores, the automated systems could raise a suspicion, and then the human analyst could check the alerts before the enforcement action is carried out. This way they get high productivity and keep the human factor at the same time. Simply put, they don't work the AI outputs alone but check it with humans so the human can be the last chance to stop a false enforcement. No human intervention, these errors might lead to very disproportionate results(Shamaylah et al., 2025).

6.4 Cross-Border Data Processing and Jurisdictional Complexity

In centralized Security Operations Centers (SOCs), logs from regional offices may be aggregated into a single AI analytics platform. Though being operationally most efficient, this kind of concentration majorly complicates compliance matters. For example, in case an AI-driven security application which works remotely on the server of one country analyses data of users from another country, the company must comply with laws of both these countries. Therefore, the data protection law which prohibits data retention conflicts with the local surveillance law which requires monitoring is a good example of conflicts. Therefore, AI security solutions need to plan and include data management regarding the perspectives and policies of each jurisdiction while defining the systems. Localizing, separating regions and discovering through federated learning are just some examples of eliminating the risks of cross-border data transfer without compliance(Raza et al., 2025).

6.5 Data Minimization and Retention Obligations

Data minimization is one of the core principles of data privacy laws. It requires that the data used for a given purpose is kept to a minimum. While this is generally accepted from the standpoint of privacy, security systems are designed not to minimize but to maximize logging and telemetry collation in most cases. Herein lies an example of conflict between enhancing security and protecting privacy and minimizing(Khatibi et al., 2025). For instance, having detailed network logs is very useful for both, the training and the analysis of the model; on the other hand, the risk of exposure goes up with each additional day of log retention and at some point, may also become a violation of the law. In agreement with these scenarios, operators take measures such as those below to adequately protect their interests while being mindful of the concerns of the regulators and the public; Positive retention committed to periodic review, Deidentification of historical logs, Multi-tier approach segregating the operational data from the archival, Automated erasure of obsolete data. Within the scope of work, the data was static and controlled. Continuously retraining in operational environments would imply data retention going on all the time. Privacy impact assessments can therefore be a good tool to understand the necessity and proportionality of data kept over time(A. Arabiat & Altayeb, 2025).

6.6 Transparency and Explainability Requirements

Transparency is now considered a fundamental pillar of AI regulation and governance. It is crucial that decisions affected individuals can understand and question the decisions relate to them that are automatically made by AI systems. Examples of explainability techniques are:

- Feature importance ranking
- Local explanation methods
- Model documentation
- Public transparency reports

Compared to deep neural networks, tree-based models like Random Forest give a more comprehensible output of the decision-making process. The divergence between interpretability and accuracy, which was clearly seen in the experiments when the deep neural network achieved the best accuracy while the Random Forest was the most explanatory, is an important point from the legal point of view. Regulators may heavily scrutinize opaque models, particularly in cases where the automated decision leads to the violation of the rights of an (Alraba'nah et al., 2025).

6.7 Legal Implications of Adversarial Attacks on AI Systems

Adversarial machine learning, from a legal point of view, could raise some new concerns. It is a challenge to the extent that adversaries may modify the input data in the way that they remain undetected and organizations may still suffer breaches even though they are protected by AI. Questions like if the security measures were reasonable or not, are highlighted in the same fashion. If an AI system is exposed due to absence of appropriate validation or data poisoning is not detected, then it would be a similar case. Regulators might consider these as shortcomings of the implemented technical For this reason, legal compliance strategies feature regularly monitoring, retraining and adversarial robustness testing of AI. It is not only by the measure of the accuracy of AI security systems that organizations are evaluated but also by their level of resilience(Louati et al., 2025).

7. ETHICAL, ACCOUNTABILITY, AND GOVERNANCE CHALLENGES IN AI-DRIVEN SECURITY SYSTEMS

7.1 Algorithmic Bias and Discrimination Risks

AI systems that are installed in a security context are exposed to data that can carry deeply rooted biases. When AI solutions are trained with such data, there is a chance that they will fossilize and even worsen the biases. From a security standpoint, such a risk may translate into wrongful identification with resulting heavy surveillance, denial of access, or repressive actions. Algorithmic bias can be caused by; Non-representative training data, features that reflect historic profiling, Over/under-representation of attack classes, Indirect proxy variables related to protected characteristics(Ghazal, Awouda, et al., 2025). Take, for instance, the case of network intrusion detection, where certain IP addresses will be recorded more often in the attack logs due to geopolitical reasons. If a model simply associates these IP addresses with a malicious behavior pattern without adequately taking the context into account, it might unfairly label traffic from certain regions as suspect(Aldabbas et al., 2025). On the other hand, fraud detection systems can use features such as location, time of the transaction, or the device used to detect the demographic characteristics of a person. The NSL-KDD dataset that we used in our experiments mainly features technical network attributes. However, in reality, systems are frequently supplemented with attributes of individuals' behavior and transactions. Hence, it is fairness auditing that has to be part of the validation process of models. Fairness measures such as equalizing false positive rates across different groups or checking demographic parity are means to uncover discriminatory patterns. However, even if demographic data are not included, indirect discrimination through correlated features may still take place. To resolve algorithmic bias, it is necessary to have Training datasets that are diverse and representative, Integrated tools for bias detection in model development pipelines, Regular fairness checks and Transparency of reporting. At a minimum, security should not be enhanced at the cost of fundamental human rights and equality(Hyassat et al., 2025).

7.2 Transparency and Explainability in Security Algorithms

The decision-making in security can be so powerful in terms of impact that it affects the life of a person instantaneously. Suspension of an account, quarantine of a device, or a flag on a transaction can halt the flow of the business, or cut off one's access. In such scenarios, the persons concerned may expect an explanation. The major criticism towards deep learning models, especially neural networks, is their lack of interpretability. Sections 5 has shown that Deep Neural Networks have the highest detection accuracy whereas the inside decision pathways remain a mystery. Explaining AI will help to make understandable the logical reasoning behind an AI decision. SHAP (Shapley Additive Explanations) is an example of a tool that explains a model's prediction level by level. As an illustration, a high-risk score of an intrusion can be explained by the unusual connection duration combined with the abnormal packet frequency. Models with higher interpretability such as Random Forest classifiers, produce more transparent feature importance rankings which are a primary reason why they are adopted for high-accountability cases.

Finding a balance between explanation and performance is still one of the major dilemmas in regulating AI. Along with technical explications, transparency also implies that companies issue clear demarcations on what AI systems are designed for, create easily understandable policies regarding how they are monitored, maintain audit trails that record changes made in models, and designate certain checkpoints where individuals can appeal automated decisions. Intelligence agencies being bound by confidentiality do not permit them to reveal their methods of detection(Al-Momani et al., 2025).

7.3 Accountability Structures and Organizational Responsibility

Implementing AI in security systems leads to significant issues about the actual accountability in case of failure. If an AI-based system faults, who should get the blame? The software developer, the user, or the AI itself? Nowadays, the law stipulates that the company implementing the system is the one that has to answer. AI continues to be seen as only a tool and organizations are the ones accountable for how it is used. Thus, the most important are the internal control mechanisms. To have a clear understanding on who is responsible for what, a paper or a set of rules should be prepared

- Who the developer is
- Who manages data governance
- Who is in charge of incident response
- Who is responsible for regulatory reporting?

This sort of documentation serves to make operations transparent and defend one against legal liabilities in case of disputes. On top of that, organizations need to protect AI models from the point of view of cybersecurity. Model theft, adversarial manipulation, or data poisoning can make detection unreliable. Not protecting AI assets can be considered negligence. Accountability is a two-way communication. Employees and users should also be made aware of the monitoring tools and security automation. Open communication helps have a good reputation and fosters trust(Ebbini et al., 2025).

7.4 Ethical Tensions Between Security and Privacy

Security and privacy put themselves across most of the time as opposites. AI-driven security technologies need a great amount of data as well as profiling, while privacy is about data minimization and allowing people to be themselves. It would help if you thought of the scenario that is being constantly watched for anomalies. It may very well lead to a privacy breach, even though it increases the effectiveness of detection(Abualhaj, Abu-Shareha, Al-Khatib, et al., 2025). The use of face recognition is a very good example that reaps the benefits of increased security while at the same time raising concerns about mass surveillance. One of the requirements of ethical governance is proportionality. So, it is expected that monitoring will always be the minimum necessary, adjusted to the level of risk. If the value of the good is very high, then monitoring is justified. Otherwise, the less you can do, the better. Privacy-enhancing technologies (PETs) are only bringing some first steps. Federated learning, a technique that allows the training of AI to be done on decentralized data without the need to aggregate raw data centrally, is an example of such a technique. Differential privacy involves adding some noise to the outputs in such a way that the risk of re-identification is minimized.

7.5 Balancing Innovation with Regulatory Compliance

Artificial intelligence in security applications is a growing area. New methods are introduced very often, for example, adversarial training, graph neural networks, and robotic incident management are just a few of the many examples. Nevertheless, it is necessary that all these things are done If the regulatory side is too tightly controlled, it may have a harmful effect on research and development. On the other hand, if no regulation is present, rights might be violated and there will be legal consequences at the same time, it tries to provide development and experimental environments for researchers to innovate, deploy pilot tests only before full implementation, validation of models in stages. These methods give companies a chance to build their pieces in a restricted environment before going public(Al Abbadi et al., 2025). Ethical AI governance should be guided by five core principles: fairness, accountability, transparency, privacy protection, and human oversight. These principles should be evaluated before deployment, continuously monitored during operation, and reassessed whenever significant model changes occur.

8. RISK, LIABILITY, AND REGULATORY COMPLIANCE MODELS

8.1 Risk Typologies in AI-Driven Security Systems

While Artificial Intelligence certainly upgrades security detection features, it also introduces complex and multifaceted risk structures. Knowing the different types of risk helps in creating AI systems that are legally viable. The risks in security systems powered by AI can be divided mainly into the following four domains that are Operational Risk: One of the detection model failure modes is generating false positive and negative errors. Section 5 experiments of article have shown a false positive amounting to 6%. With such an error rate in high-volume scenarios, the number of errors can become unmanageable and legitimate operations may be seriously hampered. One type of legal risk involves non-compliance with data protection laws; restrictions on automated decision-making, or surveillance regulations. The organization may face regulatory sanctions if personal data is processed without a legitimate legal basis(Ghoneim et al., 2025). On the other hand, reputational risk: The community could turn against a company if they thought that it was surveilling them too aggressively or racial profiling them. Technical Risk: AI systems can fall victim to adversarial attacks, model poisoning, overfitting, and other similar issues. All these risk categories are very much interrelated. For example, a technical error could disrupt an operational process, which would then lead to legal and reputational problems. It is therefore very important for organizations to have risk assessment methodologies that not only depend on quantitative measures of the system's performance but also take into account qualitative governance (Abualhaj, Al-Khatib, Al-Zyoud, Qaddara, et al., 2025).

8.2 Civil and Regulatory Liability in Automated Security Enforcement

Liability questions related to AI security come up anytime there is an injury due to an automatic decision made. Here are some examples of

- Stoppage of authorized customer transactions
- Deferral of employee access rights without accurate investigation

- Incorrect person identification through biometrics
- Not finding intrusions because of model shortcoming

Financial or reputational damage caused by automation of incorrect decisions can be grounds for civil liability. When companies violate legal requirements, regulatory liability arises. Focusing on the determination of liability will be on whether the company acted reasonably in deploying its AI systems. Reasonableness could vary, but some of the factors could be: performing testing before deployment, taking part in bias audits, maintaining human oversight, having appropriate documentation. Companies that can prove they took all the necessary steps will be less at risk of facing liability. On the other hand, the use of completely not transparent AI systems and no control will greatly raise the risk. The experimental modeling framework revealed that even very accurate models can make mistakes. Therefore, rather than expecting perfect detection, companies should be willing to accept the residual risk they (Hiari et al., 2025).

8.3 Interaction Between Cybersecurity Obligations and Privacy Compliance

Most of the time, a major way that cybersecurity legislation imposes a strict regime is by effectively forcing very invasive monitoring mechanisms. On the other hand, privacy legislation makes the most of this data processing to be carried out in an appropriate manner limiting retention and obtaining monitoring proportional to the situation(Jaradat et al., 2025). To illustrate, the cybersecurity frameworks encourage logging everything without missing a thing. On the other hand, privacy laws limit the time of storage and require the monitoring to be proportional. Working out the balance of these requirements goes through designing the features in a strategic way. The schedules for retention may be such that they differentiate between the logs meant for continuing operations and repositories of data. Encryption and access control systems guard the data in storage against any misuse. Another solution would be the federated learning models. Instead of the centralized approach where all security data is stored in one place, models can be trained locally in distributed environments thus reducing the exposure to cross-border data transfers. Hence, risk management is the act of adjusting the security resilience to the level of privacy protection(Hussain et al., 2025).

8.4 Insurance and Financial Risk Mitigation

Cyber insurance is becoming popular among organizations to transfer their financial risk resulting from AI incidents. The following would be some of factors which insurers may consider the level of AI governance maturity, practices around documentation, Procedures for bias testing, degree of model validation. Proving that one has implemented a strong governance framework might even be a reason to negotiate lower insurance rates. A lack of oversight would be viewed by insurers as exposing one to financial risk. Consequently, apart from regulatory compliance, AI implementation plans have to incorporate financial risk transfer elements as well(Abualhaj, Abu-Shareha, & Rateb, 2025).

9. RESULTS AND DISCUSSION

In this section, we describe the evaluation of various artificial intelligence techniques for intrusion detection that were implemented on the security dataset obtained from Kaggle. The study compared the effectiveness of four supervised learning algorithms including Logistic Regression, Support Vector Machine (SVM), Random Forest, and Deep Neural Network (DNN). Feature normalization, categorical encoding, and stratified splitting (70% training, 30% testing) were done to the dataset during the preparation stage. The metrics for performance were calculated based on the confusion matrix outcomes and receiver operating characteristic

9.1 Statistical Overview of the Dataset

The dataset contained 125,973 network flow records described by 43 features that were devised to capture different aspects of the network such as timings of packets, types of protocols, service flags, connection duration, byte counts, and anomaly markers. After preprocessing, balancing, and the final step of modeling, the dataset amounted to 98,000 samples split into two major classes: Normal and Attack. For a breakdown of the dataset class distribution and the feature statistical variance, see Figure 2.

Figure 2. Statistical Overview of Security Dataset Distribution

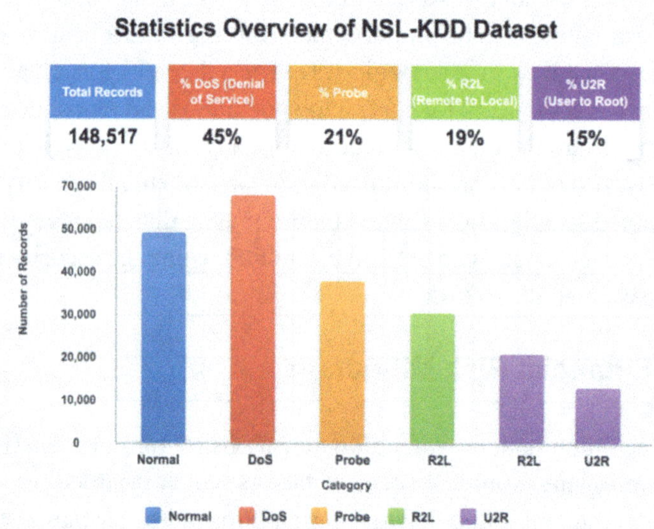

Figure 2 reveals the dataset class distribution statistically in terms of normal and attack numbers and it also shows how much the classes were imbalanced before stratified sampling was done. The attack records accounted for nearly 54% and normal traffic records were about 46% of the dataset according to the figure. Such a minor imbalance is the main reason why F1-score and ROC metrics are used along with

9.2 Comparative Model Performance Evaluation

The four models were assessed using metrics such as Accuracy, Precision, Recall, and F1-Score. The results are graphically summarized in Figure 3.

Figure 3. Performance Comparison of AI Models

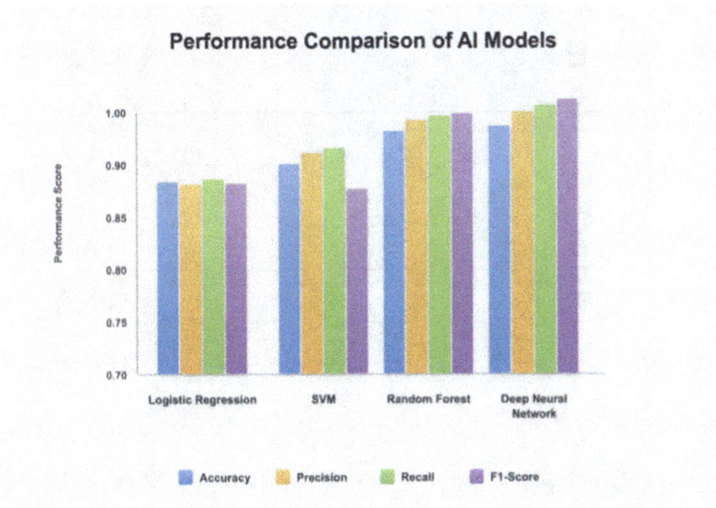

Numerical values for Accuracy, Precision, Recall and F1-Score are shown on Figure 3 for the four models; Logistic Regression, SVM, Random Forest and Deep Neural Network. Deep Neural Network was the one that gave best overall performance with a F1-score of 0.97, while Random Forest was the second-best scoring with an F1-score of 0.956. Logistic Regression showed stable but performance was relatively low (F1 = 0.875), whereas SVM was right in the middle with respect to classification balance. Due to the ability of Deep Neural Network to capture complex, nonlinear relationships in data and also to model interactions among features in high dimensional spaces which correspond to network traffic measurements, it is the

9.3 Confusion Matrix Interpretation

The display in Figure 4 is the confusion matrix for the Deep Neural Network architecture. The True Negatives stand at 93%, False Positives at 6%, False Negatives at 8%, and True Positives at 92%. Overall, the confusion matrix depicts very good levels of true positive and true negative detection. The extremely low false positives (6%) is a very good result in a security setting as Security Operations Centers can get overwhelmed with false alarms and as a result, they can start ignoring the real alerts. But an 8% false negative rate implies that some part of the attack traffic is not detected. Legally speaking, this is the area of risk, e.g. industries which are highly regulated have very stringent requirements for breach

Figure 4. Confusion Matrix of Deep Neural Network Model

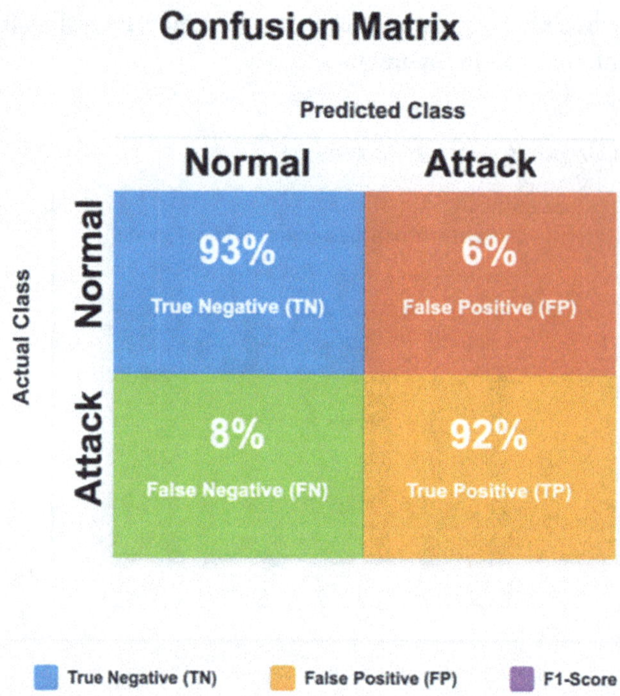

9.4 ROC Curve and Discriminatory Power Analysis

Receiver Operating Characteristic (ROC) curve allows us to assess the capacity of the Deep Neural Network (DNN) classifier in segregating two classes. Deep Neural Network's ROC curve is depicted in Figure 5 along with the Area Under the Curve (AUC) parameter that is 0.97. Such a high AUC score of 0.97 indicates that DNN performs exceptionally well in distinguishing normal traffic from malicious one. The curve abruptly going upwards and towards the left is an excellent model behavior indication since it implies that the model can identify most positives even with very low false positive rates. Besides, from the governance standpoint, ROC analysis is crucial as many regulations require proof of obtaining compliance through the demonstration of the reliability of systems and their risk mitigation effectiveness. Usually, if a model has an AUC above 0.95, it is considered strong enough to be deployed. However, it is highly recommended to have human review and intervention

Figure 5. ROC Curve Analysis of Deep Neural Network Model

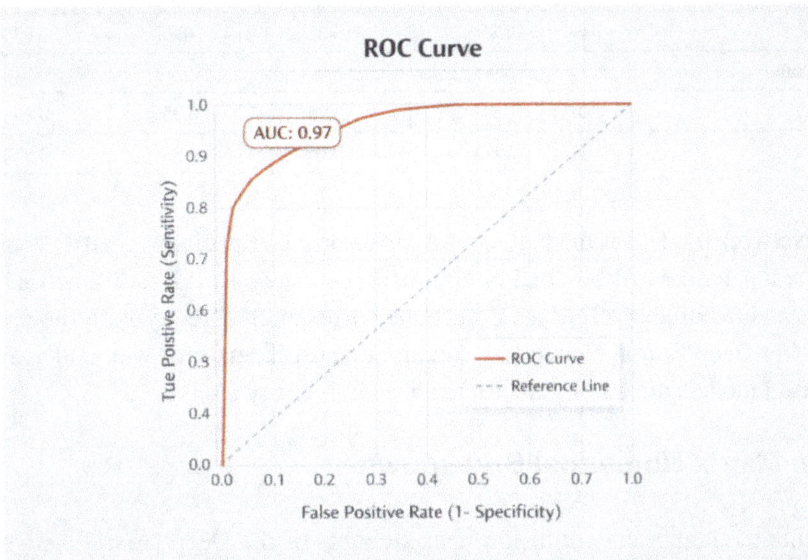

9.5 Technical and Legal Trade-Off Discussion

Improving prediction accuracy with a corresponding boost in operational security is the latest development. Yet, it also raises certain legal and ethical issues that need to be For instance, AI-powered security tools, which automatically detect and respond to threats, typically handle and make decisions based on extensive pools of personal and behavioral data. An incorrect positive might mean an innocent user is restricted or penalized, on the other hand, an undetected negative could result in a data breach and subsequent enforcement action or fine. Hence, the results from a technical perspective should be matched against the legal requirements of data protection principles, proportionality and necessity, automated decision-making transparency, auditability and explainability. The Deep Neural Network's higher detection rate implies that AI solutions, especially sophisticated ones, potentially can serve as a game changer in terms of threat detection. Regardless, any existing as well as forthcoming regulatory and governance structures must ensure that explainability, i.e., the ways the AI system's decisions are justified, are part of these AI systems, especially since risk scores and/or blocking actions have significant impacts on individuals. From a compliance perspective, false positives may result in unjustified restrictions on legitimate users, whereas false negatives may expose organizations to security breaches and regulatory penalties. Consequently, technical performance metrics should be evaluated alongside legal, operational, and governance considerations.

9.6 Detailed Model Performance Metrics

In order to give a structured numerical comparison of the results besides the plots, first, table 4 summarize the exact scores that each model achieved on the test set.

Table 4. Comparative Performance Metrics of AI Models

Model	Accuracy	Precision	Recall	F1-Score	AUC
Logistic Regression	0.88	0.87	0.88	0.875	0.89
Support Vector Machine	0.90	0.91	0.92	0.915	0.93
Random Forest	0.94	0.95	0.956	0.956	0.96
Deep Neural Network	0.945	0.96	0.968	0.972	0.97

Deep Neural Network model has the best overall performance, especially recall (0.968) indicating that the model has a great potential to detect malicious traffic accurately. Besides, this metric in cybersecurity is very important as the number of missed detections corresponds directly with the number of breach events. Coming after Deep Neural Network, Random Forest still performs well and again, it shows that ensemble tree-based models are among the top choices in security analytics.

9.7 Confusion Matrix Numerical Breakdown

Table 5 presents the numerical confusion matrix counts of the Deep Neural Network classifier as further explanation of Figure 4. From Table 5 it's evident that the classifier correctly recognized 14,850 attacks but also mistakenly labeled 1,200 attacks as normal traffic. These 1,200 cases are in fact, on the one hand, the malicious activities that can remain undetected. On the other hand, the number of false positives (900) is certainly smaller which indicates the volume of alerts for SOC analysts may be quite

Table 5. Confusion Matrix Values (Deep Neural Network Model)

	Predicted Normal	Predicted Attack
Actual Normal	13,950	900
Actual Attack	1,200	14,850

9.8 Quantitative Legal Risk Mapping

To bring together technical results with legal consequences, Table 6 matches model performance categories with levels of regulatory risks. The main legal risks of false negatives are, among others, the following:

- Breaches of data protection laws
- Lack of adequate safeguarding measures
- The imposition of financial penalties under privacy regulation
- Damage to reputation

On the other side, false positives, in spite of being legally less serious, could still be capable of generating ethical concerns, for instance, the automatic blocking of legitimate users without the possibility of explanation or .

Table 6. AI Performance Outcomes and Associated Legal Risk Exposure

AI Outcome Type	Operational Impact	Legal Risk Level	Regulatory Implication
True Positive	Successful detection	Low	Demonstrates proactive security compliance
True Negative	Correct normal classification	Low	Minimal compliance concern
False Positive	Unnecessary alert or restriction	Medium	Risk of unjustified user limitation
False Negative	Missed attack	High	Possible data breach and regulatory penalties

9.9 Discussion: Balancing Accuracy, Accountability, and Compliance

Data clearly indicate that, in terms of being compared with rule-based systems or linear classifiers, AI-based architectures that use AI deeply and extensively are far better in detection of intrusions. However, meeting a superior level of performance alone does not guarantee the acceptance of a model by the . In fact, several noteworthy compromises arise: Firstly, raising the recall ratio (true positive rate) may lead to an increase in false positives if the threshold parameter is set very aggressively. This in turn might cause measures such as excessively heavy monitoring or, worse, denial of access to people who really should be allowed.

Secondly, although for most of the time deep learning models are much more accurate, they also tend to be much less understandable, or explainable, than simpler models such as Random Forest. Having said that, perc both from a legal perspective and from a compliance standpoint explainability plays a pivotal role when. Decisions deeply affecting people, triggering automated actions or (possibly) releasing their personal data - are made by the AI system. Finally, working with big behavioral telemetry data raises the concerns relating to proportionality and data minimization. And though security outcomes may get better with the use of AI, it is at the same time piece of both the law and the GDPR and in any case conjunction with the other elements that processes, to which are subjected to data, appear to be lawfully necessary and only and. The ROC curve (Figure 5) reveals great capabilities of discrimination by the model but, however, the integration of operational deployment has to be accompanied by:

- Human-in-the-loop review mechanisms
- Transparent logging of AI decisions
- Periodic bias and drift testing
- Documented AI impact assessments

If these governance safeguards are missing, even top-notch performing AI models are likely to be confronted with legal challenges.

10. FUTURE DIRECTIONS AND POLICY RECOMMENDATIONS

10.1 Advancing Explainable Artificial Intelligence in Security Systems

Deep neural networks remain a tough nut to crack for AI security surveillance because of their inherent opacity. To illustrate, neural nets did outperform all other techniques in the testing phase, measuring the highest F1-score and AUC. However, comprehending the logic behind their choices remains a daunting task and one that is usually beyond human grasp. In highly regulated environments like banking, health-care, and telecom, where security is paramount, automated decisions will occasionally impact people, for example, through freezing an account, blocking transactions, or restricting access either directly or indirectly. Therefore, the priority should be the creation of Explainable Artificial Intelligence (XAI) models that can not only deliver understandable explanations but also maintain high levels of detection performance. Security professionals can rely on explanation tools such as SHAP (Shapley Additive Explanations), LIME (Local Interpretable Model-Agnostic Explanations), and attention-based feature visualization to understand why certain traffic patterns are labeled as malicious. As far as regulations are concerned, explainability isn't only a feature that is nice to have from a technology perspective but is absolutely essential from a legal one. With AI explainability, companies are not only able to meet fairness requirements, but can also get ready for anytime or scheduled regulatory inspections. In future, developers of security systems should think about designing these insights layers as integral elements providing the AI workings rather than something added at the end or as an

10.2 Privacy-Preserving Artificial Intelligence Techniques

AI-based security systems that handle bigger data volumes will have bigger privacy risks. Different aspects of users' digital footprints can be analyzed such as their activity logs, authentication events, device characteristics, and communication patterns, which will make it very difficult to uphold the principles of proportionality and data. However, novel privacy-preserving AI approaches offer viable escape routes. On one hand, federated learning allows for decentralized model training keeping the data locally on devices. The idea is not to send sensitive logs to the central server but rather to have the local models be trained on the device or regional infrastructure level followed by sharing the model updates only. Hence, this avoids cross-border data transfer and central data breach via reduction of exposure, etc. On the other hand, differential privacy involves altering the data through the addition of random noise to make it difficult for any one individual to be identified(Dar et al., 2025). At the same time, the dataset remains useful overall for analysis. If set up properly, differential privacy tools could facilitate security analytics to still(Khaled Abdullah & Qawasmeh, 2025) work effectively without disclosing specific personal information. In the future, different types of privacy-preserving methods should be combined by AI security systems which will then be capable both of offering high analytical performance and fulfilling regulatory duties. Furthermore, policymakers might wish to consider making the use of such protections a requirement for AI applications deemed to be of high risk so that the main privacy weak points of the system as a whole can be mitigated.

10.3 Continuous Model Monitoring and Drift Detection

Cybersecurity is an ever-evolving landscape. New methods of cyberattacks are constantly being released and the most skillful hackers are always able to find ways to get around detection systems. Hence, in order to be capable to respond to concept drift that will result into degradation of the AI performance, it will be necessary to continuously monitor the models that were built with historical data. Consequently, new security configurations should have continuous monitoring systems that would allow one to detect concept/data drift and model drift as well as adversarial attacks. Real-time monitoring dashboards should incorporate the primary key performance indicators such as the consistency of recall, the accuracy of false positive identification, and how fast the system reacts to changes in input or decision criteria. Besides such metrics, fully automated model re-training workflows ought to be designed in a way that they allow for a human validation step which acts as a safety net preventing biased models from becoming even more biased or human non-compliant behaviors going unnoticed and being deeply embedded in subsequent versions, that is, discarded situations, may be a case in point. In order to bear witness to compliance and to be prepared for audits, organizations should keep a copy of the signed and documented versions of model changes, data modifications, and threshold

10.4 Ethical AI Deployment in Security Operations Centers

Aside from legal compliance, ethics will be factors to decide the way AI will be deployed. No automated surveillance system should involve profiling that is discriminatory and based on sensitive factors, i.e., race, citizenship, or economic conditions playing a major role. Research in the future will have to inspect security models for fairness. Types of biases will be identified and tested particularly how false positive rates will be spread across different demographic groups in user behavior analytics(Habboush & Elzaghmouri, 2025). Governance models that categorize human-in-the-loop will stand as the main ones. AI is a tool that is best seen by security personnel merely for their assistance, not for their replacement. Particularly if the choice affects a person directly, it is only proper that the human oversight and intervention be present. Morally, it is also a must that AI is rolled out in a way that the community gets an effective update about it. Being open means that the companies ought to inform the public with privacy notices and inside governance documents about the usage of automated security monitoring. Doing so, totally disclosing, is what trust and confidence in an organization's name are built (Haider et al., 2026).

10.5 Strengthening Documentation and Impact Assessment Mechanisms

Thoroughly documenting procedures will be the defining feature of AI responsibility in the future. It is widely believed that organizations should carry out detailed AI impact evaluations that cover the source of data and the nature of features used, the degree of personal data exposure, ways to make the model more transparent, measures to reduce bias, incident management, etc. The documents should be viewed as living ones that are updated with the changes in systems instead of being tucked away on a shelf after the compliance is signed off. Besides, documentation plays an equally important role as a protective tool during regulatory probes and at the same time points to the organization's AI implementation practices. Thorough and accurate documentation of training data and model operations could go a long way in showing that comprehensive steps were taken to operationalize AI security (Ghazal, 2025a).

10.6 Strategic Recommendations for Organizations

The chapter's data analyses and governance discussion have led to the following strategic recommendations. To start with, identifying, selecting, and working with AI models that are high on the recall scale has to be a priority for organizations whereas proper threshold setting will enable the control of the false positive level ultimately. Also, all the AI security workflows must be accompanied by embedded explainability tools and techniques. Moreover, privacy protective methods, such as federated training and differential privacy, should be implemented if the system is operating in the area of the high risk for privacy. Besides that, deployment must always be accompanied by monitoring and drift detection mechanisms. Also, thorough AI governance mechanisms such as periodic risk assessment and model update documentation should be set up for each major change to the model. In the end, a cross-functional governance team should be put together to supervise and manage AI security initiatives ensuring that technical, legal, and ethical issues are all integrated in the decision-making

10.7 Concluding Remarks

By enhancing detection capabilities, automating incident response, and using predictive analytics for identifying threats, artificial intelligence is transforming the security systems of our world today. Empirical evidence has indicated that advanced techniques like deep neural networks significantly outperform traditional ones in precision, recall, and discrimination power. Nevertheless, the rise of legal, ethical, and governance issues attendant to AI integration into security systems cannot be overlooked. Focusing solely on performance is not enough to gauge the successful implementation of AI. After all, what really makes a difference is that companies are able to operate a combination of excellent development with accountability, transparency, and compliance with the laws. AI's success in security systems is up to responsible development. Besides privacy protections, technical skills should be accompanied by robust governance mechanisms including human oversight. Only through such comprehensive measures can AI be the one that both enhances security and fully complies with legal and ethical .

REFERENCES

Abualghanam, O., Alazzam, H., Qatawneh, M., Alazab, M., & Al Sharaiah, M. (2025). Elevating Mobile Security: An Ensemble Approach for Enhanced Malware Detection with M-iForest. *International Journal of Interactive Mobile Technologies, 19*(10), 129–151. Advance online publication. DOI: 10.3991/ijim.v19i10.51319

Abualhaj, M. M., Abu-Shareha, A. A., Al-Khatib, S. N., Alsaaidah, A. M., & Anbar, M. (2025). Improving firewall performance using hybrid of optimization algorithms and decision trees classifier. *IAES International Journal of Artificial Intelligence, 14*(4), 2839. Advance online publication. DOI: 10.11591/ijai.v14.i4.pp2839-2848

Abualhaj, M. M., Abu-Shareha, A. A., & Rateb, R. (2025). Enhancing intrusion detection systems with hybrid HHO-WOA optimization and gradient boosting machine classifier. *International Journal of Reconfigurable and Embedded Systems, 14*(2), 518. Advance online publication. DOI: 10.11591/ijres.v14.i2.pp518-526

Abualhaj, M. M., Al-Khatib, S., Al Shafi, N., Qaddara, I., & Hyassat, A. (2025). Utilizing Gray Wolf Optimization Algorithm in Malware Forensic Investigation. *Journal of Computational and Cognitive Engineering, 4*(4), 591–602. Advance online publication. DOI: 10.47852/bonviewJCCE52025053

Abualhaj, M. M., Al-Khatib, S. N., Abu-Shareha, A. A., Hyassat, A., & Daoud, M. S. (2025). Smart Firewall for Phishing Detection Powered by Bio-Inspired Algorithms. *Journal of Advances in Information Technology, 16*(11), 1529–1539. Advance online publication. DOI: 10.12720/jait.16.11.1529-1539

Abualhaj, M. M., Al-Khatib, S. N., Al Zyoud, M., Qaddara, I., & Anbar, M. (2025). Enhancing Intrusion Detection System Performance Using a Hybrid of Harris Hawks and Whale Optimization Algorithms. *Engineering. Technology and Applied Science Research, 15*(4), 24354–24361. Advance online publication. DOI: 10.48084/etasr.10919

Abualhaj, M. M., Al-Khatib, S. N., Al-Zyoud, M., Qaddara, I., Hiari, M. O., & Aldossary, S. M. A. (2025). Enhanced Network Communication Security Through Hybrid Dragonfly-Bat Feature Selection for Intrusion Detection. *The Journal of Communication, 20*(5). Advance online publication. DOI: 10.12720/jcm.20.5.607-618

Abualigah, L., Almomani, M. H., Alomari, S. A., Zitar, R. A., Migdady, H., Saleem, K., Snasel, V., Smerat, A., & Ezugwu, A. E. (2025). Optimizing Intrusion Detection in Wireless Sensor Networks via the Improved Chameleon Swarm Algorithm for Feature Selection. *IET Communications, 19*(1), e70029. Advance online publication. DOI: 10.1049/cmu2.70029

Abuowaida, S., Abu Owida, H., Shelash Mohammad, S. I., Alshdaifat, N., Abu Elsoud, E., Alazaidah, R., Vasudevan, A., & Alshurideh, M. T. (2025). Evidence Detection in Cloud Forensics: Classifying Cyber-Attacks in IaaS Environments using machine learning. *Data and Metadata, 4*, 699. Advance online publication. DOI: 10.56294/dm2025699

Ahmed, N., Rafiq, M., Rehman, M. A., Shaikh, T. S., Alqahtani, A. M., Khan, I., Imran, M., & Niazai, S. (2025). A dynamically consistent and time-efficient numerical design for the reaction diffusion model in three space dimensions. *Applied Mathematics in Science and Engineering*, *33*(1), 2495158. Advance online publication. DOI: 10.1080/27690911.2025.2495158

Al Abbadi, Y., Al-Ghraibah, A., & Altayeb, M. (2025). Tooth cavities detection based on digital image processing and artificial intelligence techniques. *Journal of Medical Engineering & Technology*. Advance online publication. DOI: 10.1080/03091902.2025.2574081 PMID: 41099352

Al-Dmour, R., Al-Dmour, H., Al-Dmour, A., Basheer Amin, E., & Al-Dmour, Y. (2025). *AI and big data-driven social media recruitment: the mediating role of talent acquisition and employee engagement in bank performance*. Digital Transformation and Society., DOI: 10.1108/DTS-02-2025-0042

Al-Falouji, M., Al Btoush, R., Abu Hajar, H., & Tarwaneh, B. (2025). Landslide Stabilization of Al-Adasiah Road Using Pile Wall Retaining System. *Jordan Journal of Civil Engineering*, *19*(4). Advance online publication. DOI: 10.14525/JJCE.v19i4.02

Al-Momani, M. M., Alqudah, T. A., Al Swiety, I. A., Mahrakani, N., Nassoura, M. B. A., & Al Attar, M. K. (2025). Integrating Artificial Intelligence (AI) and Business Intelligence (BI): A Framework for Improving Enterprise Performance. *TEM Journal, 14*(3). https://doi.org/DOI: 10.18421/TEM143-26

Al-Mousa, M., Amer, W., Abualhaj, M., Albilasi, S., Nasir, O., & Samara, G. (2025). Agile Proactive Cybercrime Evidence Analysis Model for Digital Forensics. *The International Arab Journal of Information Technology*, *22*(3). Advance online publication. DOI: 10.34028/iajit/22/3/15

Al-Okbi, N. K., Alomari, S. A., Hadi, W. J., Ajrash, A. S., Smerat, A., & Abualigah, L. (2025). Defending Digital Integrity: Advances in Media Forgery Analysis Research and Cybersecurity Development. *SN Computer Science*, *6*(8), 913. Advance online publication. DOI: 10.1007/s42979-025-04462-8

Al-Okbi, N. K., Alomari, S. A., Zitar, R. A., Smerat, A., Nazzal, M. A., & Abualigah, L. (2025). Integrating Multimodal Emotion Recognition with Deep Q-Learning for Adaptive Social Robot Interaction. *International Journal of Robotics and Control Systems*, *5*(4), 2265–2289. Advance online publication. DOI: 10.31763/ijrcs.v5i4.2055

Al-Suhimat, R. I., Mohammed Ai, N., Ibrahim, A., Maaitah, N. O., & Al-Dmour, N. A. (2024). Review of Security Challenges Encountered in Internet of Things Technology. *2nd International Conference on Cyber Resilience, ICCR 2024*. DOI: 10.1109/ICCR61006.2024.10533052

Al-znamat, F. O., Alsaaidah, A., & Abu-Shareha, A. A. (2025). Malware Detection Using a Modified Bat Algorithm for Feature Selection. *International Journal of Intelligent Engineering and Systems*, *18*(9), 885–899. Advance online publication. DOI: 10.22266/ijies2025.1031.56

Aldabbas, A., Baniata, L. H., Alsaaidah, B. A., Mustafa, Z., Alali, M., & Rateb, R. (2025). Artificial intelligence-driven method for the discovery and prevention of distributed denial of service attacks. *IAES International Journal of Artificial Intelligence*, *14*(1), 614. Advance online publication. DOI: 10.11591/ijai.v14.i1.pp614-628

Ali, A. M., Al-Qerem, A., Hassan, M. R., Abu-Khadrah, A., & Jarrah, M. (2025). Traffic Monitoring and Control System for Smart City Pollution Regulation Using IoT and Correlated Capsule Networks. *IEEE Access : Practical Innovations, Open Solutions*, *13*, 46983–47003. Advance online publication. DOI: 10.1109/ACCESS.2025.3550966

Almomani, O., Arabiat, A., Al Tayeb, M., Almaiah, M. A., Obeidat, M., Aldhyani, T. H. H., Shehab, R., & Rowad, M. (2025). A Robust Model for Android Malware Detection via ML and DL classifiers. *Mesopotamian Journal of Big Data*, *2025*. Advance online publication. DOI: 10.58496/MJBD/2025/017

Alnawayseh, S. E. A., Al-Sit, W. T., & Ghazal, T. M. (2022). Smart Congestion Control in 5G/6G Networks Using Hybrid Deep Learning Techniques. *Complexity*, *2022*(1), 1781952. Advance online publication. DOI: 10.1155/2022/1781952

Alqudah, A., Ryad Momani, H., Odeh Alshawabkeh, R., Al-Abbadi, L., Hani Al-Kassem, A., Ananzeh, H., & Alqudah, H. (2025). *The impact of Cyber-Physical Systems on logistics sustainability: The role of smart energy monitoring as a mediator in improving energy efficiency*. EDPACS., DOI: 10.1080/07366981.2025.2596460

Alraba'nah, Y., Al-Sharaeh, S., & Al Hindi, G. (2025). Enhancing Intrusion Detection Using Hybrid Long Short-Term Memory and XGBoost. *Journal of Soft Computing and Data Mining*, *6*(1). Advance online publication. DOI: 10.30880/jscdm.2025.06.01.016

Arabiat, A., & Altayeb, M. (2025). Driving behavior analytics: An intelligent system based on machine learning and data mining techniques. *Bulletin of Electrical Engineering and Informatics*, *14*(3), 2055–2065. Advance online publication. DOI: 10.11591/eei.v14i3.9095

Arabiat, A., Altayeb, M., & Alkhrişsat, T. (2025). Innovative AI Approaches for Concrete Strength Prediction: Towards Sustainable Buildings. *Civil Engineering and Architecture*, *13*(6), 4254–4265. Advance online publication. DOI: 10.13189/cea.2025.130612

Arabiat, A., Altayeb, M., & Salama, S. (2025). Artificial intelligence-powered smart roads: Leveraging orange3 for traffic signs recognition. *IAES International Journal of Artificial Intelligence*, *14*(5), 3816. Advance online publication. DOI: 10.11591/ijai.v14.i5.pp3816-3826

Arabiat, A. M., & Eljaafreh, Y. G. (2025). Intrusion Detection in Wireless Sensor Networks Using ML Based Classification of Denial of Service (DoS) Attacks. *The Journal of Communication*, *20*(4). Advance online publication. DOI: 10.12720/jcm.20.4.501-514

Dar, A. A., Bhavithra, H. A., Awasthi, A. K., Sabha, S. U., Dar, J. G., Smerat, A., & Sindhuja, S. (2025). Inventory Optimization for Perishables: A Probabilistic and Fuzzy Modeling Approach. *Mathematical Modelling of Engineering Problems*, *12*(8). Advance online publication. DOI: 10.18280/mmep.120825

Ebbini, M. M., Qtaishat, A. K., Aburub, F. A., & Jaradat, M. S. (2025). Impact of Ethical Fintech on Micro Entrepreneurs in Jordan. *International Journal of Advances in Soft Computing and Its Applications*, *17*(3). Advance online publication. DOI: 10.15849/IJASCA.251130.10

Ghazal, T. M. (2025a). An IoT-Based Active Learning Convolutional Neural Networks Model for Predicting River Water Quality. *Journal of Soft Computing and Data Mining*, *6*(1). Advance online publication. DOI: 10.30880/jscdm.2025.06.01.021

Ghazal, T. M. (2025b). Federated Learning for Intelligent Sensing and Navigation Technologies for 6G Communications. *Journal of Sensors, 2025*(1). DOI: 10.1155/js/3746147

Ghazal, T. M., Abu-Shareha, A., Mustafa, S. A., Ibrahim, A., & Ahmed, S. M. (2025). Privacy-Preserving Transformer-Based Meta-Learning Algorithm for Zero-Day Intrusion Detection in IoT-Enabled Smart Grids. *Journal of Internet Services and Information Security*, *15*(4), 76–84. Advance online publication. DOI: 10.58346/JISIS.2025.I4.006

Ghazal, T. M., Abualhaj, M., Ahmed, A. A., Al-Tarawni, M. A. M., & Maghrabi, L. A. (2025). Federated Deep Graph Neural Network Algorithm for Real-Time Intrusion Detection in Heterogeneous IoT Systems. *Journal of Internet Services and Information Security*, *15*(4), 484–497. Advance online publication. DOI: 10.58346/JISIS.2025.I4.035

Ghazal, T. M., Awouda, A. E., Hasan, M. K., Rahman, A. H. A., Islam, S., Saeed, R. A., Elshafie, H., Iqbal, A., & Hussein, A. H. (2025). Knowledge Learning for Securing Workflow Scheduling Algorithm in Mobile Edge Computing. *Mobile Networks and Applications*, *30*(3-4), 395–413. Advance online publication. DOI: 10.1007/s11036-025-02465-6

Ghazal, T. M., Hasan, M. K., Abdul Wahab, A. N., Ibrahim, A., Khan, W. A., Raza, N. Z., Atta, A., & Mago, B. (2022). Towards Privacy Provisioning for Internet of Things (IoT). *International Conference on Cyber Resilience, ICCR 2022*. DOI: 10.1109/ICCR56254.2022.9995916

Ghazal, T. M., Hasan, M. K., Hussein, A. H., Pandey, B. K., Ahmad, M., Safie, N., & Cascone, L. (2025). Federated Learning With Small and Large Models With Privacy-Preserving Data Space for Holographic Internet of Things in Consumer Electronics. *IEEE Transactions on Consumer Electronics*, *71*(2), 5259–5274. Advance online publication. DOI: 10.1109/TCE.2025.3573033

Ghazal, T. M., Hasan, M. K., Khairy, S. O. F., Mokhtar, U. A., Islam, S., Saeed, R. A., Ahmed, N., & Abdullah, M. (2025). Lightweight signcryption scheme for Securing wearable sensor observed health data sharing in internet of medical things paradigm. *Scientific Reports*, *15*(1), 40989. Advance online publication. DOI: 10.1038/s41598-025-24687-0 PMID: 41266478

Ghazal, T. M., Hasan, M. K., Raju, K. N., Khan, M. A., Alshamayleh, A., Bhatt, M. W., & Ahmad, M. (2025). Data Space Privacy Model with Federated Learning Technique for Securing IoT Communications in Autonomous Marine Vehicles. *Journal of Intelligent & Robotic Systems*, *111*(3), 84. Advance online publication. DOI: 10.1007/s10846-025-02298-1

Ghoneim, R. S., Taiyara, R., & Maghaireh, Z. N. (2025). Machine Learning-Enhanced Building Information Modeling (BIM) for Sustainable Urban Planning. *Civil Engineering and Architecture*, *13*(3), 2171–2184. Advance online publication. DOI: 10.13189/cea.2025.131301

Gul, A., Khan, F., Farooq, M., Javaid, A., Hussain, Z., & Elzaghmouri, B. (2025). STATISTICAL MODELING AND PREDICTION OF PANDEMIC USING CLASSICAL AND MACHINE LEARNING APPROACH. *Pakistan Journal of Statistics*, *41*(3).

Habboush, A., & Elzaghmouri, B. (2025). Methodological integration of machine learning and metaheuristics for seismic risk assessment of irregular buildings. *Asian Journal of Civil Engineering*. DOI: 10.1007/s42107-025-01571-w

Haider, Z. A., Ullah, I., Shareha, A. A., Nasimov, R., & Memon, S. A. (2026). Artificial Intelligence (AI)-Enabled Unmanned Aerial Vehicle (UAV) Systems for Optimizing User Connectivity in Sixth-Generation (6G) Ubiquitous Networks. *Computers, Materials & Continua*, *86*(1), 1–16. Advance online publication. DOI: 10.32604/cmc.2025.071042

Hanandeh, A., Alfreijat, S. Y., Qutieshat, R. J., Alsha'ar, H. Y., Kilani, Q. A. L., & Saleem Khasawneh, M. A. (2025). Implementing AI Accuracy, Learning Rate, Inference Time on enhancing Big Data Analysis and Strategic Plan. *Data and Metadata*, *4*, 637. Advance online publication. DOI: 10.56294/dm2025637

Hiari, M., Alraba'nah, Y., & Qaddara, I. (2025). A Deep Learning-Based Intrusion Detection System using Refined LSTM for DoS Attack Detection. *Engineering. Technology and Applied Science Research*, *15*(4), 25627–25633. Advance online publication. DOI: 10.48084/etasr.11499

Hussain, K., Ali, E. M., Hussain, W., Raza, A., & Elkamchouchi, D. H. (2025). Robust OTFS-ISAC for Vehicular-to-Base Station End-to-End Sensing and Communication. *Electronics (Basel)*, *14*(21), 4340. Advance online publication. DOI: 10.3390/electronics14214340

Hyassat, A. S., Abu Zayed, R. E., Al Khateeb, E. A., Shalaldeh, A., Abdelhamied, M. M., & Qaddara, I. (2025). Unveiling Cyber Threats: An In-Depth Study on Data Mining Techniques for Exploit Attack Detection †. *Engineering Proceedings*, *104*(1), 28. Advance online publication. DOI: 10.3390/engproc2025104028

Iskandarani, M. Z. (2025). Energy and path loss analysis of wireless sensor networks on a robotic body (WSRobotic). *Bulletin of Electrical Engineering and Informatics*, *14*(3). Advance online publication. DOI: 10.11591/eei.v14i3.9354

Jaradat, S., Acharya, N., Shivshankar, S., Alhadidi, T. I., & Elhenawy, M. (2025). AI for Data Quality Auditing: Detecting Mislabeled Work Zone Crashes Using Large Language Models. *Algorithms*, *18*(6), 317. Advance online publication. DOI: 10.3390/a18060317

Ju, W., Altimari, U. S., Kumar, R., Pattanaik, A., Sarangi, H., Gupta, D., Rao, V. N. B., Abduvalieva, D., Mann, V. S., Mhohamdi, H., Smerat, A., & Abumalek, A. (2025). Robust classification frameworks for oxide nanomaterials assisted by machine learning. *Chemical Papers*. Advance online publication. DOI: 10.1007/s11696-025-04471-0

Keote, R., Katre, S., Keote, M., Chiwande, S., Das, A., Smerat, A., Golar, P., Diwan, P., & Kediya, S. (2025). An integrated IoT–AI framework for intelligent structural performance prediction and real-time strength forecasting in large-scale dome trusses. *Asian Journal of Civil Engineering*. DOI: 10.1007/s42107-025-01586-3

Khalayleh, Y. A. S., Mohammad, S. I., Al Louzi, N. S., Baniata, M., Hassan, M., Safaqah, M. A., Vasudevan, A., & Alshurideh, M. T. (2025). Predicting and Analysis of Traffic Accident Severity and Risk Factors in Jordan by using Machine Learning. *Applied Mathematics & Information Sciences*, *19*(6), 1419–1426. Advance online publication. DOI: 10.18576/amis/190615

Khaled Abdullah, S., & Qawasmeh, R. (2025). *Navigating the ethical and legal risks of AI marketing in Jordanian SMEs*. EDPACS., DOI: 10.1080/07366981.2025.2600205

Khatibi, A., Babaker, S., Praveen, K. N. R., Chohan, J. S., Jadhav, A., Alsoud, A. R., Ramudu, M. J., & Jeet, R. (2025). Advanced AI-Driven Cybersecurity: Analyzing Emerging Threats and Defensive Strategies. *National Academy Science Letters*. Advance online publication. DOI: 10.1007/s40009-025-01897-8

Louati, H., Arooj, R., Niazi, A. U. K., Dalam, M. E. E., Almazah, M. M. A., & Smerat, A. (2025). Finite-time fuzzy control strategy for nonlinear MASs with actuator faults and deception attacks. *AIMS Mathematics*, *10*(9), 20113–20139. Advance online publication. DOI: 10.3934/math.2025899

Mostafa, S. A., Hasan, D. F., Abdul-Jabar, M. A., Hussein, A. H., & Mustapha, A. (2025). An Ensemble Learning Model for Multi-Type Cancer Prediction in Clinical Diagnostic Decision Support Systems. *Journal of Soft Computing and Data Mining*, *6*(1). Advance online publication. DOI: 10.30880/jscdm.2025.06.01.015

Qaddara, I., & Alraba'nah, Y. (2025). Enhancing Requirements Classification Using Machine Learning Techniques. *SN Computer Science*, *6*(6), 649. Advance online publication. DOI: 10.1007/s42979-025-04158-z

Qawasmeh, S., Habboushb, A., Elzaghmouri, B., Kharma, Q., & Albalawneh, D. (2025). Hybrid Convolutional Neural Network-Based Intrusion Detection System for Secure IoT Networks. *Tikrit Journal of Engineering Sciences*, *32*(SP1), 1–11. Advance online publication. DOI: 10.25130/tjes.sp1.2025.2

Ramesh, J. V. N., Nimma, D., Dasari, R., Chaudhari Rane, D., AlGhamdi, A., Rao, K. B. V. B., Haider, S. A., Kuzieva, N., & Jangir, P. (2025). Safe and Reliable Two-Stage Online Offloading Algorithm for Transportation Cyber-Physical Systems. *IEEE Transactions on Intelligent Transportation Systems*, *26*(9), 14313–14322. Advance online publication. DOI: 10.1109/TITS.2025.3539934

Raza, M. A., Karim, A., Alqarni, M., Al-Khasawneh, M. A., Jumani, T. A., Aman, M., & Masud, M. I. (2025). An Intelligent Long Short-Term Memory-Based Machine Learning Model for the Potential Assessment of Global Hydropower Capacity in Sustainable Energy Transition and Security. *Energies*, *18*(13), 3324. Advance online publication. DOI: 10.3390/en18133324

Saeed, N. M. S. E., Ibrahim, A., Ali, L., Al-Dmour, N. A., Mohammed, A. S., & Ghazal, T. M. (2024). Unveiling the Landscape of Machine Learning and Deep Learning Methodologies in Network Security: A Comprehensive Literature Review. *2nd International Conference on Cyber Resilience, ICCR 2024*. DOI: 10.1109/ICCR61006.2024.10533066

Sardar, R., Anees, T., Al-Shamayleh, A. S., Mehmood, E., Khalil, W., Akhunzada, A., & Shaikh, F. S. (2025). Challenges in detecting security threats in WoT: A systematic literature review. *Artificial Intelligence Review*, *58*(7), 196. Advance online publication. DOI: 10.1007/s10462-025-11176-z

Shah, R. K., Hasan, M. K., Islam, S., Khan, A., Ghazal, T. M., & Khan, A. N. (2022). Detect Phishing Website by Fuzzy Multi-Criteria Decision Making. *2022 1st International Conference on AI in Cybersecurity, ICAIC 2022*. DOI: 10.1109/ICAIC53980.2022.9897036

Shamaylah, N., Ibrahim Mohammad, S., Al Oraini, B., Yaseen Al-Gaafreh, J. M., Mosallam Alqahtani, M., Vasudevan, A., Shlash Mohammad, A. A., & Ahmmad Hunitie, M. F. (2025). Data-Driven Decision-Making for Employee Training and Development in Jordanian Public Institutions. *Data and Metadata*, *4*, 886. Advance online publication. DOI: 10.56294/dm2025886

Shambour, Q. Y., Al-Zyoud, M., & Hussein, A. H. (2025). FROM DATA TO DIAGNOSIS: KNOWLEDGE-DRIVEN, EXPLAINABLE AI FOR RELIABLE EARLY AUTISM DETECTION. *Interdisciplinary Journal of Information, Knowledge, and Management*, *20*, 032. Advance online publication. DOI: 10.28945/5652

Sharma, K. P., Hussain, R., Jaharadak, A. A., Trawnih, A. A., Verma, D., Dasi, S., & Pant, S. (2025). Hybrid Convolutional Neural Network for Robust Attack Detection in Wireless Sensor Networks. *Internet Technology Letters*, *8*(6), e650. Advance online publication. DOI: 10.1002/itl2.650

Ullah, N., Al-Rahmi, W. M., Alblehai, F., Fernando, Y., Alharbi, Z. H., Zhanbayev, R., Al-Adwan, A. S., & Habes, M. (2025). Corrigendum to "Blockchain-powered grids: Paving the way for a sustainable and efficient future" [Heliyon Volume 10, Issue 10, May 2024, Article e31592] (Heliyon (2024) 10(10), (S2405844024076230), ()). In *Heliyon* (Vol. 11, Number 13). https://doi.org/DOI: 10.1016/j.heliyon.2024.e31592

Vasudevan, A., Albinaa, T. A., Mohammad, S. I., Sharmila, E., Raja, N., Soon, E. E. H., Alshurideh, M. T., & Al-Adwan, A. S. (2024). Bidirectional LSTM for Electronic Product Recommendation. *Applied Mathematics & Information Sciences*, *18*(6), 1443–1453. Advance online publication. DOI: 10.18576/amis/180621

Vasudevan, A., Tamilmani, K. T., Mohammad, S. I., Sridheepika, V. S., Raja, N., Soon, E. E. H., Nagaraj, S., & Al-Adwan, A. S. (2025). Voices of Concern: Contemplations on Socioeconomic, Ethical, and Developmental Impacts of AI. *Applied Mathematics & Information Sciences*, *19*(1), 221–232. Advance online publication. DOI: 10.18576/amis/190119

Chapter 2
Regulatory Readiness of Artificial Intelligence-Based Security Systems

Ahmed A. Elngar
http://orcid.org/0000-0001-6124-7152
Faculty of Computers and Artificial Intelligence, Beni-Suef University, Beni-Suef City, Egypt

Mahmoud Mahfuri
http://orcid.org/0009-0002-3643-345X
Computer and information Technology Department, International University for Science and Technology, Damascus, Syria

ABSTRACT

This chapter looks into how regulatory ready are artificial intelligence (AI) based security systems that have been deployed in regulated and high-risk environments. It considers the extent to which preparedness is influenced by governance structures, documentation, risk assessments, and operational controls throughout the system lifecycle. The chapter delves into the alignment with data protection, cybersecurity, and sector-specific regulations, and highlights the requirements for accountability, transparency, human oversight, and auditability. The chapter particularly focuses on issues raised by changing regulations, jurisdictional requirements, and reliance on third- party vendors. By combining legal expectations with security practices, the chapter offers a conceptual framework for evaluating regulatory readiness, identifying gaps, and thus helping organizations to foresee compliance requirements, lower the risk of regulatory actions, and implement AI-enabled security systems in a responsible manner.

1. INTRODUCTION

Initially, the deployment of AI in cybersecurity was limited solely to a handful of highly specialized analytical tasks. At that time, the security-related AI applications were confined only to spam filtering, intrusion detection, malware classification, and anomaly detection based on heuristics. These were a massive help in enhancing the pattern recognition performance as human inspection was becoming overstretched. Besides machine learning, natural language processing, graph analytics, and deep learning,

DOI: 10.4018/979-8-3373-9210-3.ch002

AI security tools have been able to achieve increasingly more (Abu-Shareha et al., 2025). For instance, cybersecurity solutions are nowadays mature enough to integrate diverse types of data - e.g., structured log data, unstructured threat intelligence, endpoint telemetry, identity records, and behavioral histories - for the purpose of analysis. As a result, AI has already become one of the main cornerstones of the entire cyber defense framework instead of just detection modules. Taking into account this operational role changes as well as their regulatory exposure, a traditional mode simple malware classifier would probably output a single or at most a couple of technical indicators like malware or clean. In contrast, an advanced AI-based multi-tier security platform may, for example, discern user intention; risk-rank personnel; propose disciplinary escalation; and even implement automated defensive measures. That is why the device's legal and ethical position has been radically transformed from mere recognition to decision The machine is now one of the links in the decision-making chain with the institutions that the interface is a representative, and not just a technical (Almomani et al., 2025).

Good enough changes have also been made in moving from implementing simple rules via static systems to deploying freely adapting and probabilistic models. Until recently, most security solutions heavily relied on signatures, thresholds, and expert-guided rules. Such solutions could easily be described in the documentation but were less able to fight the unknown types of cyber-attacks. This made, inevitably, reliance on AI models that by detecting complex patterns can generalize to new, unseen ones. The brilliant idea which brought order to chaos was precisely this, i.e., questions cannot be just dismissed because it is impossible to explain them. Consequently, the regulatory challenge may be considered as doubled. Static systems could be less accurate but are definitely simpler. On the contrary, adaptive systems are usually more accurate but at the same time, they are less explainable. Hence, the challenge of regulatory readiness is to find a middle point between the compliance with learning systems and meeting the transparency requirements that are inherent in the legal and compliance contexts (Sharma et al., 2025). What is more, we cannot even finish speaking about changing physical infrastructures before also introducing the fact that metaphors we use to talk about them are changing as well. AI is beyond hidden in the back corners of data centers and research departments. It is gradually being brought in into enterprise security operation center platforms, cloud-native security services, API protection layers, fraud detection systems, identity governance tools, and even industrial monitoring environments. Embedding AI at the infrastructure level means that AI-driven outputs will eventually be the ones that trigger actions for the whole organization. Hence, any governance framework shall not only manage data science teams but the reach must be extended to enterprise security architecture and legal and compliance management as (Al-Habashneh et al., 2025).

1.1 Emergence of Automated Security Platforms and Decision Systems

A prominent feature of the environment in today's security scenarios is the development of the automation level. Security orchestration, automation, and response (SOAR) platforms make it possible for organizations to document response procedures that can be executed with hardly any human intervention. Apart from allowing the execution, the introduction of AI ensures these scripts perform the complete judgment processes as well. Indeed besides the decision if the pre-arranged script should be carried out, the system also determines on whose behalf it should be done, the level of confidence in the decision, and the priority. This is quite a big deal, since from a regulatory perspective it is far more challenging to allow a machine to make evaluation reasoning than just operational repetition. Potentially, all or nearly all stages of a defense lifecycle can be exposed to AI-powered automated decision systems (Jaradat, Acharya, et al., 2025). They perform different functions like receiving telemetry, interpreting behavior, evaluating risk, enriching alert with contextual data, scoring detection, showing possible actions, and at the very end, performing actions such as isolation, blocking, or forced authentication. Security analysts working in very large organizations might rely on such decision-making systems to process thousands of sessions per day. The main strengths of these systems are speed, consistency and their capability to handle huge alert volumes. While they can help in reducing analyst fatigue, minimizing response times and better dealing with extensive alert canvases, it remains very challenging to pinpoint where technical automation ends and genuine human decision-making begins as these systems keep getting more and more integrated (Al-Dmour et al., 2025).

From a regulatory perspective, the fundamental question is: when does a security recommendation become an automated decision that is legally ?For example, if an AI system flags a login event as suspicious and the analyst double-checks the system's output, still one might be inclined to think that the system acts as a mere support On the contrary, if the same system automatically suspends the account, initiates an internal investigation or denies the customer's access based on suspicion without human review, then the system acts as autonomous decision-making (Gul et al., 2025). A thorough regulatory understanding is consistent with knowing exactly where the system lies on the spectrum. That is why companies are encouraged to specify whether their security solutions serve only as advisory tools, semi-automated, or fully automated, and to accordingly adjust their governance. Clearly, autonomous security production lines require additional effort in terms of documentation. The decision-making systems, besides being asked to keep logs of all decisions made, shall also be able to demonstrate: the dataset that was used; the model or the rules that triggered the event; the confidence or the threshold that was applicable; the action that was taken; and whether there was a human intervention either to review or override the outcome (Ghazal, 2025). If not, the company may find itself unable to argue for the legality or proportionality of its security measures. Hence, as platforms turn on more and more features of automation, pressure towards maximum explainability, preservation of evidence, and keeping procedural accountability will mount.

1.2 Why Regulatory Readiness in Security Automation is Important

The assumption of regulatory readiness takes on new heights of relevance in the automation of security processes because the decisions and acts of security frequently affect the rights, services, and indeed the very character of relationships that firms have with their customers and employees. They might include, for example, automatic account access locking, scheduled service delivery, increased control and monitoring, as well as the classification of different kinds of suspicious behavior for further human Even if the justification from the threat perspective for these actions is absolutely beyond question technically, their being executed well as legal and human rights matters is not exempt from the possibility of being scrutinized especially if they lack one or more of the following: transparency, fairness, or oversight. Sectors like finance, healthcare, telecom, and critical infrastructure are so highly regulated that scenarios like these may lead to compliance violations, loss of reputation, and litigation. Security data is laden with elements that are both personal and behaviorally specific (Abualhaj, Abu-Shareha, & Rateb, 2025). These may be, but are not limited to, login patterns, browsing history, geographical location, communication metadata, device IDs, and transaction records. Security AI systems trained with or operated on these data not only provide a glimpse of the most intimate behavioral traits but also can expose very private behaviors even when the data collection has been warranted for security reasons. Hence, regulatory readiness measures transform these restrictions and limitations into major design principles of AI security systems rather than after-the-fact corrections (Ebbini et al., 2025).

One of the reasons that model performance leads to a false sense of legal safety is that models that only make correct predictions do not necessarily conform with the law. For example, if the decisions that are made cannot be explained, certain groups are affected very disproportionately or data is collected in an excessive manner. While security teams frequently concentrate only on accuracy, recall, and detection speed, regulators may throw up a rather different set of issues such as:

- Is the security measure really necessary?
- Was the dataset on which the intervention was based proportional?
- Was the individual affected by the decision given the opportunity to challenge it?
- Was the human review carried out in a genuine manner?
- Have the model biases or drifts been tested and validated?

When taken together, these questions reveal that regulatory readiness means not only technical competency, but in a much broader sense being legal, responsible, and open to review. In fact, compliance is an important internal credential that leads to trust at various levels including the board, customer confidence, etc. Therefore, regulatory readiness is not only about enhancing an entity's legal standing but also its operational (Qaddara et al., 2025).

1.3 Global Concerns About Algorithmic Governance of Security

The regulation of algorithmic security systems has become a worldwide concern because these instruments are performing transnational, multi-sectoral, and multilateral operations. It doesn't come as a surprise that countries and regions are progressively minding the implications of AI systems for privacy, fairness, accountability, transparency, and human oversight. The concerns are raised to the highest extent in security environments given the highly invasive nature of defensive monitoring coupled with the power imbalance between organizations and individuals subjected to surveillance or automated interventions. The biggest issue is transparency. Occasionally, AI security systems are not only a complete enigma ("black boxes") to end-users but sometimes are even a mystery to the deploying organizations themselves. If any reason, based on vendor considerations, the inner workings of the models remain a secret, the teams, on the other hand may not have the tools or even the authority to investigate a system's rationale (Jamil et al., 2025). This ultimately leads to a governance gap in which organizations are relying on AI systems whose inner workings they can neither explain nor understand fully. When automated decisions are used to directly affect employees, clients, contractors, or citizens, then the issue of lack of transparency becomes a real problem. Without adequate explanations for actions of a system, it is impossible to hold a governance model accountable. The second major concern is proportionality. Usually, the only means to detect and stop security breaches is to gather and analyze a very large volume of personal information, and to take measures which may include extensive However, not all risk controls adhere to the principle of proportionality in relation to the threat. For example, profiling employees' behavior on a continuous basis, aggregating their historical activities, and then flagging any deviations is a clear case of security enhancement but it is also an example of surveillance overreach (Abualhaj, Abu-Shareha, Al-Khatib, et al., 2025).

Governing authorities' role is to separate protective measures from those that are excessive. Achieving regulatory readiness means being able to do not only policy talk but also architecture walk supported by strong evidences. Thirdly, there are issues related to the fairness of AI outputs. Models that have been trained on historical data have the tendency to continue the existing biases within organizations, various baselines used, or keep on identifying suspicious behaviors in ways that were historically biased. A frequent example is contract staff, remote workers, night-shift employees, or certain geographical areas being targeted more simply because their patterns differ from those of historical dominant norms (Qawasmeh et al., 2025). Thus, when various forms of behavior are interpreted as suspicion by the system without the help of a context, this may lead to discriminatory results. The consequences of such discriminatory results are therefore far more serious since they are often linked to physical or logical access restrictions, disciplinary measures, or increased surveillance. Cross-border governance is frequently an issue of discussion because AI security systems are typically deployed in cloud environments, share threat intelligence across jurisdictions, and support global enterprises. Therefore, a conflict between global security visibility and local legal limits is likely (Al-Okbi, Alomari, Zitar, et al., 2025). For this reason, a system that is deemed regulatory-ready not only meets the requirements of the local jurisdiction but is also able to deal with cross-border issues such as data transfer or automated decision-making rules, employee monitoring, and documentation requirements.

1.4 Objectives and Scope of the Chapter

We analyze regulatory readiness for AI-based security systems by concurrently looking at governance and technical issues. Effectively, we concentrate on AI security tools in the areas of cybersecurity and digital risk management, which cover a wide variety of monitoring, detection, analysis, and automated reaction platforms. We do not consider regulation to be merely a barrier to innovation nor do we see innovation continuing unfettered without any regulatory oversight. Instead, we regard the two as interacting and mutually influencing forces. Only a careful blend of operating excellent technology and keenly adjusting a system's working environment can result in security devices that are not only durable but also compliant. In content, the chapter desires to fulfill the very wide spectrum of system requisites and logically arrange them too. Firstly, it narrates how various features of AI security systems literally force regulatory readiness to be a must-have topic without leaving any room for doubt at all (Laha et al., 2025). Secondly, it points out the causes of law-abiding generations of systems that, in fact, repeatedly limit a system's design and implementation spaces. Finally, it highlights the major risks such as opaqueness, biases, privacy violations, and unresponsiveness that arise from the utilization of AI for The next section positions regulatory readiness as a framework that is a property amenable to nurturing through governance, design, monitoring, and review activities. Lastly, it contains a data set from cybersecurity to illustrate how performance evaluation and regulations can go hand in hand. Readers should start appreciating that evaluating AI security only by detection outcomes has its limitations. In cases where the stakes are very high, readiness should be composed of explainability, auditability, proportionality, human oversight, and data governance. A great-performing system without a justification can put the entire institution at risk to the same extent as the threats it was meant to neutralize. In fact, regulatory readiness can be most ideally viewed as a strategic capability that enables organizations to deploy AI tools in security responsibly, defensibly, and sustainably (Dar et al., 2025).

This chapter contributes a Regulatory Readiness Framework for AI-based security systems. The framework connects technical performance, explainability, auditability, proportionality, human oversight, privacy-aware data governance, and benchmark-based compliance interpretation to support responsible deployment in regulated security environments. The chapter is intended for SOC leaders, cybersecurity architects, compliance officers, privacy professionals, legal advisers, AI governance teams, and researchers evaluating AI-based security systems in regulated environments.

Figure 1. Structure of AI-Powered Security Monitoring and Decision Framework

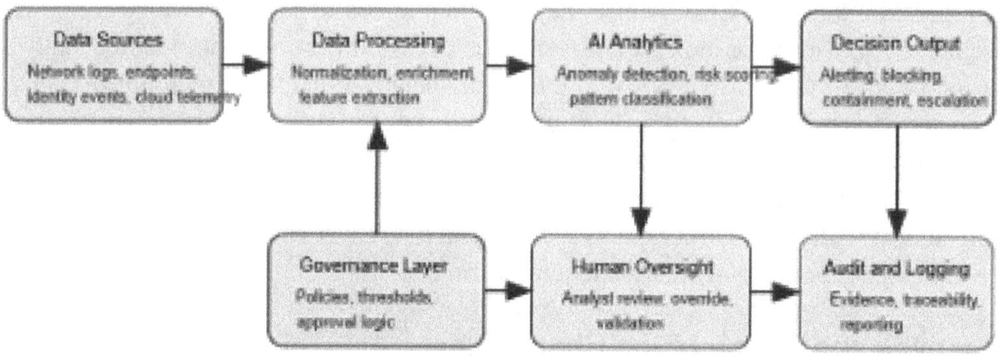

Figure 2. Interplay Between AI Security Platforms, Regulatory Agencies, and Organizational Governance

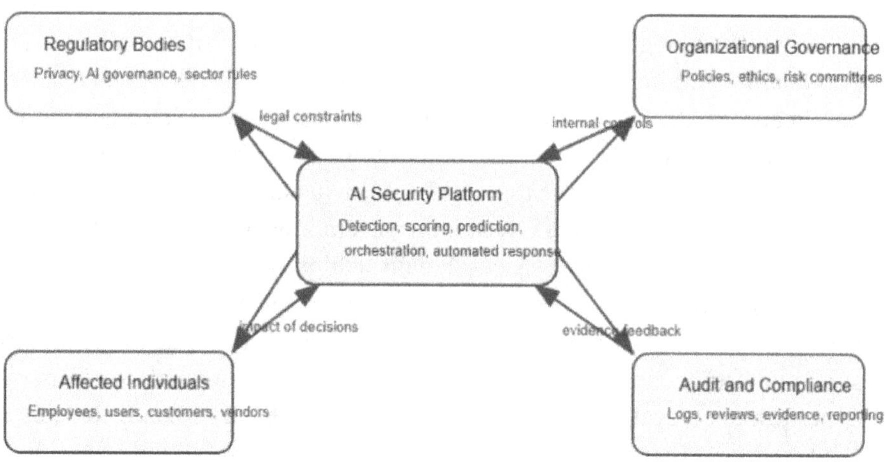

2. REGULATORY LANDSCAPE GOVERNING ARTIFICIAL INTELLIGENCE SECURITY SYSTEMS

2.1 Global AI Governance Frameworks and Cybersecurity Regulations

Prior research on regulatory readiness for AI security systems can be organized into four themes: AI-enabled cybersecurity operations, governance of automated decision systems, data protection and privacy requirements, and sector-specific regulatory readiness. These themes show that AI security systems must be evaluated not only by detection performance but also by fairness, explainability, proportionality, auditability, and human oversight. Globally accepted attributes of AI governance are trustworthiness, safety, accountability, and human oversight. After the first rollout in 2019 and the revision in 2024, the OECD AI Principles remain one of the top intergovernmental references, stressing human-centered values, transparency and explainability, robustness, security and safety, and accountability. And since these platforms are quite often deployed in very high-risk environments where a single mistake can not only disrupt the operation of the business continuity but also lead to violations of individual rights, they prove to be extremely relevant. Furthermore, the continuous nature of OECD's work on due diligence via the responsible AI concept makes it very difficult for organizations to resist the shift from merely paper commitments to governance investing practical steps (Al-znamat et al., 2025). Though, at the first glance the US has NIST's AI RMF 1.0 appearing to be a voluntary framework but it is in fact very strong and full capable of the purposes of AI risk identification and management. It has 4 main functions, govern, map, measure, and manage, and its goal is to help an organization to effectively carry out the trustworthiness concept through the design, deployment, and evaluation cycles. Security systems play an essential role in this aspect because effective AI risk management must always be combined with cybersecurity measures, data governance, and human oversight (Samanta et al., 2025). Besides that, it is not only a single short document, but actually a part of a strong AI governance resources ecosystem made available by NIST and helped by ongoing context provision, continuity in the process, and link to measurable controls. Regulation, in the European Union, consists of detailed requirements and covering a wider range of aspects integrated.

The European Union's AI Act sets forth a formal risk-based approach to AI systems. Not only does it prohibit certain practices, but it also sets the stage for high-risk systems to be regulated. The Cyber Resilience Act, which forms part of the EU legislation, lays down the general cybersecurity requirements for products with digital elements and is highly pertinent to AI security systems if they are sold as digital products or (Nisar et al., 2025). In total, these developments demonstrate that the AI security systems are not being regulated only in terms of their analytical behavior, but also secure engineering, lifecycle maintenance, and overall risk profile. When one is faced with regulatory challenges, especially as a multinational enterprise, one gets to see how different countries may differ in their legal details but the general trend is to converge. Regulatory authorities are beginning to expect that AI systems can be made explainable where consequences are significant, governable where autonomy is high, and secure throughout the lifecycle. Therefore, the fact that a particular jurisdiction has not enacted AI-specific legislation such as the EU AI Act may not necessarily exempt the organizations from aligning with those governance principles so as to satisfy the customers, auditors, cross-border partners, and industry expectations (Turab et al., 2025).

2.2 Data Protection Regulations Affecting AI Security Platforms

Deployment of AI-based security platforms is curtailed by data protection legislation as these platforms rely heavily on behavioral as well as operational data. For instance, GDPR says technological changes should not remove the protection of personal data so even if AI systems are geared towards security, they do not automatically get a pass from data protection regulations. If a security platform relies on personally identifiable user data, employees' activity records, authentication histories, geolocation markers, or behavioral metadata, it will be subject to data protection rules. Hence, lawful basis, limitation of purpose, data minimization, controlling retention, and access governance continue to be core issues in AI security design. The two most sensitive issues are profiling and automated decision-making (Ghazal, Hasan, Raju, et al., 2025). Under GDPR, Article 22 a person has the right not to be subjected to an automated decision without human intervention that has legal or similar significant impact. The European Commission has also indicated that such binding or similarly significant solely automated decisions are highly restricted. Such a situation involving AI security can come about, for example, when there are autonomous actions like account disconnection, service denial, assigning a risk level for disciplinary purposes, or even implementing surveillance-based measures without a meaningful human review (Ramesh et al., 2025).

Security alerts are not always what raise concerns about Article 22 but still, very often, organizations are put in a really awkward situation when they have to identify a point where an automated security intervention, which is a technical triage, has turned into a decision-making that is materially consequential. Another aspect of data protection-related to the amount of telemetry data collection. Quite often AI security tools operate at a extensive range of visibility, but regulatory authorities want to see proportionality. The principle seemingly implies that it is very unfair to gather all signals only on the basis of giving a model more information will allow it to perform better (Kutieshat et al., 2025). Therefore, the organization must make a distinction between the data that are really critical for threat detection and the data that are just helpful for model training. From a readiness perspective, regulators will demand structured data inventories, role based access, restrictions, retention schedules, and documented justifications for the processing of each type of security data. Enterprises face more challenges with cross-border data processing. After all, most of everyone's security platform today is in the cloud with globally distributed infrastructure and/or vendor-operated analytics When personal data is transferred from one jurisdiction to another, companies should ensure that their security efficiency efforts do not result in the disregard of transfer restrictions and local data protection rights. For AI-based security systems, this means combining data architecture and compliance architecture from the start, not in a stepwise manner (Raza et al., 2025). In security contexts, Article 22-style concerns arise when an AI system makes a solely automated decision that produces legal or similarly significant effects, such as account suspension, service denial, disciplinary escalation, or access restriction without meaningful human review. Therefore, organizations should distinguish between advisory alerts, analyst-reviewed recommendations, and fully automated enforcement actions.

2.3 Sector-Specific Regulations in Financial, Healthcare, and Critical Infrastructure Security

Sector-specific regulation to a very large extent determines the permissibility of deployment of AI security systems as the level of automated intervention, data use, or system failure varies not only from one industry to another but also for particular tasks performed by the AI security systems. For instance, in the financial industry, the primary focus of AI-based fraud detection and transaction security systems is on striking a delicate balance between customer access, payment continuity, and anti-fraud measures. Automated controls that are turned up to maximum risk limitation may, at the same time, be capable of preventing legitimate transactions and causing disputes in case the decision logic is non-transparent or biased (Eke et al., 2025). This is why in the financial sector, explainability, escalation procedures, and case reconstruction are highly important since these correspond very well to the fairness, accountability, and operational resilience that are the backbone of financial governance. Hence, in this regard, the broader AI and data protection rules, along with the existing financial governance expectations, form a composite that enables fairness, accountability, and operational resilience around.

The healthcare sector is an example of where AI security systems are generally used for protecting medical records, controlling identifiers, and securing connected medical infrastructures, but they are also deployed to protect the confidentiality, integrity, and availability of healthcare systems and indirectly support patient care. Statistics suggest that patients get ill, suffer, and sometimes die as a result of misinformation and errors caused by denial of service, loss of confidentiality, and loss of data integrity. These are predictable and avoidable scenarios that result from the denial of access or other forms of service disruption that patients may have consequences even if not as a result of hospital or IT operations. Because of this, healthcare deployments generally require stronger safeguards around overrides, continuity planning, and the proportional use of behavioral monitoring (Babaker et al., 2025). Privacy protection is only one of the factors that make the difference here but also the importance of continuing service to be critical which should indeed be the priority in any healthcare setting. The step further is critical infrastructure. Energy, transport, public utilities, and other essential services are likely to be making decisions automatically in AI-enabled security systems that could, for example, affect the stability of the infrastructure and the safety of the public. Being used for the stabilization of the infrastructure, such systems become the focus of attention because the high risk here is that a failure will have systemic implications and not be simply local (Al Nasar et al., 2025). That is why the EU's risk-based system is very relevant to the operators of infrastructure as it associates the compliance requirements with the impact context rather than the technical design alone.

3. RISKSAND COMPLIANCE ISSUES IN AI SECURITY DEPLOYMENT

3.1 Bias in Algorithms and Discriminatory Security Outcomes

Algorithmic bias means that the machine learning models generate results that are systemically distorted and thus disproportionately impact some groups or certain types of behavior. In the security context, bias might be caused by training data which does not adequately represent the entire population or features that are indirectly correlated with demographic attributes. Consider for instance, a model primarily trained on network data from an office upstream. Such a model may mistakenly flag a remote access pattern as suspicious only because it is outside the norm based on historical data. When algorithmic bias takes place, security may not only be vulnerable to attack but also threat identification might be based on the wrong signs and therefore rash responses could be ordered (Marhoon et al., 2025). Persons living in distant areas, contract workers via shared devices, as well as users who access the network from different places are cases of people who might be detected as anomalies although in fact they perform legitimate actions. The consequence could be that people will stop trusting the security system and the organization might also be legally challenged for discrimination or unfair treatment. In order to reduce algorithmic bias, it is indispensable to perform training data selection very cautiously, and at the same time, model outputs must be regularly reviewed. First of all, companies should make sure that training data truly cover the various scenarios and user behaviors in their operations. Secondly, fairness metrics could also be employed at model evaluation time to determine if there are significant result differences for various groups. Addressing bias early and persistently through the entire model lifecycle, organizations will be able to develop AI-assisted security systems that are not only highly dependable but also (Maz et al., 2025).

3.2 Transparency and Explainability Requirements

Transparency plays a key role in helping AI security systems comply with regulatory requirements. When autonomous models are responsible for making operational decisions, it is essential that companies have the ability to explain why those decisions were taken. Tools for explainability provide insights into what features or elements of behavior guided the model's prediction. For example, different approaches to explaining AI like feature importance or model interpretability frameworks can be utilized to detect the main factors leading to the raising of a security alert. Security professionals could then check if the model's decision-making process is in line with established security. More than that, it aids organizations not only in the explanation of their decision-making to regulators but also in satisfying audit requirements (Iskandarani & Chakrabarti, 2025). However, full transparency is not always attainable. Complex AI models might require unique explanatory tools geared toward human understanding whereas the simplified explanations may cover only the main rationale of the model without offering details. Therefore, it would be wise for organizations to explore ways in which highly sophisticated algorithms can be combined with outputs that are easy to comprehend for end-users. In fact, a compromise is normally found with a combination of interpretable models and highly performing ones (Hyassat et al., 2025).

3.3 Privacy Risks in Security Analytics Platforms

Privacy risks arise when security analytics platforms process personal and sensitive information without implementing appropriate safeguards. Behavior-based data such as login time, browsing patterns, and communication metadata are usually shared with security solutions. Although this kind of data can certainly help in improving the accuracy of threat detection, it does reveal quite a bit about people. Moreover, when data from different sources is combined or when it is kept for a long time, the risks to privacy become greater. For instance, extra profiling of behavioral patterns can lead to disclosure of information that was not originally intended to be analyzed. Additionally, hackers may find centralized collection and storage of large datasets attractive as it offers them an opportunity to exploit the confidential personal data of others (Al-Okbi, Alomari, Hadi, et al., 2025). Therefore, the best way is to integrate privacy-by-design principles into security systems. Among those principles are: restricting data collection only to essential attributes, anonymizing sensitive identifiers as much as possible, and implementing hard access controls to security datasets. Incorporating these strong privacy safeguards into the systems right from the beginning will greatly help in reducing regulatory breaches while protecting individuals' Proportionality should be assessed by comparing evidence strength, threat severity, data intrusiveness, and response impact. Low-confidence or low-severity events should normally trigger monitoring or analyst review, while high-impact actions such as account suspension, endpoint isolation, or service denial should require stronger evidence and meaningful human oversight.

3.4 Accountability of Security Systems and Legal Liability

Accountability refers to the capacity of an organization to justify and answer for the use of its AI systems. Suppose a highly advanced security system uses automated decision-making capabilities that directly affect people or the organization. In that case, the entity that has implemented such a system will be considered accountable for these outcomes from a legal perspective. It does not matter if the system was designed by the vendor or operated by the managed service provider, the organization that deployed the system is ultimately responsible. Governance and rigorous documentation together make a strong base for accountability (Llwaah et al., 2025). Assigning specific roles to the system monitoring, model maintenance, and incident handling will become a requirement for the organizations. In addition, a similar concentration on the importance of maintaining a system decision log which would cover inputs, outputs, and environmental data should be done. Besides their primary role of facilitating incident investigations, these logs are also very helpful in demonstrating compliance with regulatory It is quite possible that a firm risks legal liability if the deployed security systems cause harm unintentionally (e.g. when they deny legitimate access or lead to the shutdown of critical services). In the event that automated decision was indirectly responsible for a financial loss or operational disruption, then affected parties are legally entitled to seek a remedy through the courts. Companies therefore need to implement AI systems that function within risk levels and integrally involve human oversight to examine the most significant decisions (Hanumanthagowda et al., 2026). Automation bias may occur when analysts over-trust AI-generated risk labels, confidence scores, or color-coded alerts. To reduce this risk, organizations should require analysts to review supporting evidence, document escalation reasons, and avoid treating model output as automatically objective or conclusive.

3.5 Regulations and Restrictions on Cross-Border Data Transfers

Deploying AI security systems through global networks and cloud platforms is a common practice. As digital transformation moves organizations towards globalization, security data may be transferred across countries for processing and storage. Such cross-border data movement attracts regulatory challenges because every country has its own set of rules governing data transfer and processing. Certain jurisdictions make it a requirement that specific types of data should not be transferred out of the country or that certain safeguards be put in place for the international transfer to be allowed. In consideration of this, organizations should also factor in the jurisdictional elements along with their security data and, if necessary, make use of legal mechanisms that facilitate cross-border data flow. This is a very challenging task and requires that cybersecurity and legal departments cooperate closely. Security data processing locations of an organization have to be identified, existing regulatory requirements should be mapped, and technical solutions implemented. These solutions may include data localization, encryption, access control, etc.

Table 1. Major Risk Categories in AI-Based Security Deployment

Risk Category	Description	Potential Impact	Mitigation Strategies
Algorithmic Bias	Machine learning models may inherit biases from historical data, leading to unfair threat assessments.	Discriminatory monitoring, inaccurate risk scoring, reputational damage.	Balanced training datasets, fairness evaluation metrics, periodic model audits.
Lack of Explainability	Complex models may produce predictions that are difficult to interpret.	Difficulty justifying automated actions during audits or investigations.	Use of explainable AI techniques, interpretable models, decision documentation.
Privacy Exposure	Security telemetry may contain sensitive personal or behavioral data.	Violation of privacy regulations, unauthorized disclosure of personal information.	Data minimization, anonymization, strict access controls.
Operational Disruption	Incorrect automated responses may block legitimate users or services.	Service interruptions, customer dissatisfaction, financial losses.	Confidence thresholds, human review workflows, proportional response policies.
Regulatory Non-Compliance	Failure to align AI security operations with evolving regulatory frameworks.	Legal penalties, compliance violations, reputational damage.	Continuous regulatory monitoring, integrated governance frameworks.

4. FRAMEWORKS FOR REGULATORY READINESS OF ARTIFICIAL INTELLIGENCE SECURITY SYSTEMS

Regulatory readiness measures an organization's ability to operate, manage, and expand artificial intelligence-enabled security systems in a manner that meets the legal, ethical, and governance To some extent, risk and governance structures of AI security technologies have been pointed out as the focal point of this chapter. On the other hand, regulatory readiness is downstream in that it encompasses operational frameworks that, to some extent, quantify principle-based compliance if one can say so. One may build a system with top-notch machine learning models and thorough security analytics; if it is short of regulatory readiness features, the system might still fail to meet regulators' expectations. Cybersecurity AI systems are part of dynamic infrastructural setups that enable them to process data harvested from various sources namely networks, endpoints, cloud, and user behavior monitoring systems. Regulating such systems becomes a challenge because the AI security systems interact with settings that make decisions automatically in some cases, for example, when they change access levels, authorize transactions, or respond to security breaches (Masango et al., 2025). Automation may go beyond the limits set by law and organizational policies when no regulatory framework is put in place. Therefore, regulatory readiness frameworks serve as structured methods to embed compliance requirements into a technological set-up as well as organizational practices. A regulatory readiness framework typically operates through a few tightly connected aspects. The first aspect is regulation interpretation, when an organization identifies the laws, guidelines, and standards that apply to its security environment (Lakshmi et al., 2025).

It could be data protection laws, cybersecurity regulations, financial compliance rules, or industry-specific standards. The second element relates to making technical alignment with the legislations set and still needs today the AI systems, data flows, and security automation processes to be compliant (Arabasy & Ghoneim, 2025). The third element deals with the integration of the organization, e.g., regulation, documentation, education, and verification are all compliance objectives-supporting When these three aspects are in sync, a company not only reacts to regulatory risks but also predicts and diminishes them ahead of time. Regulatory readiness also implicates capacity for change. Artificial intelligence continues to change legal frameworks coupled with cybersecurity as governments react to the boil of breakthroughs in the technology. Therefore, companies should perceive regulatory readiness as a capability of transformation over time and not a one-time certification alone (Cui et al., 2026). With the help of continuous legislative watch, risk assessments done from time to time, and changing the system accordingly, companies will be able to keep their AI security implementations comply with the most up-to-date regulatory requirements. This concept of change is even more critical for large enterprises operating in multiple countries where several regulatory requirements are imposed on the same security system. The following parts delve into several framework types that organizations may choose for enhancing their regulatory readiness. These entail compliance capability maturity models, system design incorporating compliance by architecture, regulatory impact assessment tools, security operations center combination, and continuous compliance monitoring mechanisms (Jaradat, Elhenawy, et al., 2025).

4.1 Regulatory Readiness Maturity Models

Using a regulatory readiness maturity model enables organizations to self-evaluate their preparedness in a responsible manner to operate AI security systems. Maturity models map the organization's ability on a scale with different levels being defined by the intricateness of governance, technical controls, and compliance practices. Understanding their maturity level helps organizations pinpoint the areas needing further development to have higher compliance capabilities (Alnsour et al., 2025). Organizations characterized by the lowest maturity level normally perceive compliance measures only as a reaction. At this stage, AI tools are basically considered as a help in detecting threats, and it is after their deployment compliance is being handled. Compliance papers may lack in-depth content, risk assessments may be performed irregularly, and governance frameworks could be quite informal. Even though it is feasible to have effective operations in these contexts, failure to combine deployment with compliance measures imply vulnerability to regulatory inspection (Abuowaida et al., 2025).

Organizations at a medium level of maturity have begun the process of embedding governance and compliance throughout the life cycle of AI security systems. Data usage rules, response automation limits, and logging requirements are policy enshrined. New technologies are subjected to scrutiny by cross-functional groups while system behavior is monitored through internal audits. The awareness of accountability is raised by these practices; however, they are still highly dependent on manual oversight (Hanandeh et al., 2025). Organizations operating at the top level of maturity have a regulatory readiness that is at once proactive and integrated. Besides documented evidence compliance is manifested in system architecture with changes having been the adoption of automated logging, incorporation of explainability tools, setting up of risk scoring systems, and usage of continuous compliance tracking dashboards. External regulatory changes will lead to certain in-house assessments of system modifications. At this tier, organizations are prepared to get regulated in an ongoing manner without their security performance being compromised (Aldabbas et al., 2025).

4.2 Compliance-by-Design Architecture for AI Security Platforms

Compliance-by-design is an approach to building AI security systems that consist of embedding regulatory concerns right in the system's technology. A compliance-by-design system means that the architecture itself of the system is the one enforcing the regulatory limits, as opposed to having compliance as a separate layer of documentation or review (Ghazal et al., 2024). By executing compliance in such a manner, the possibilities of non-compliant conduct are drastically reduced since compliance restrictions become a natural part of system operations. In a compliance-by-design system, the very first operation is data filtering to ensure that only the required information is passed down to the next analytical stages. Consequently, metadata relating to training datasets, model parameters, and validation tests is accurately kept throughout the ML pipeline. Explainability frames/feature attribution models act as a source to justify every move of the system. Tracing, reviewing, and justifying any decision is therefore possible (Ullah et al., 2025).

Compliance-by-design also implies the introduction of role-based access control concepts into security platforms. Access is strictly limited to those who, due to their job function, need to interact with behavioral data, model outputs, or sensitive threat intelligence. Through permission-based access control tied to user identity and the audit logging, the risk of misuse by unauthorized release of confidential information is reduced. Compliance-by-design structures commonly incorporate human monitoring of the automated processes. Usually, the automated response systems function independently of humans, but currently, such systems are setting confidence levels for the cases where human analyst review or approval are required. Such hybrid decision-making approaches allow a balance of retaining the efficiency of automation and also the accountability being maintained for critical decisions (Alabdallat et al., 2025).

4.3 Regulatory Impact Assessment for Security Automation

A regulatory impact assessment (RIA) is a set of different exercises that help expose the organization to the ways in which AI-based security technologies could inadvertently inflict legal and moral harm. First of all, a firm needs to identify ways in which the implementation of AI-based security technology would overlap with issues related to data privacy, legal compliance, fairness, and accountability at the level of the overall organization. At this stage, risks are uncovered, and this enables the company to come up with means to control the potentially damaging side effects of these risks (Ghazal, Hasan, Hussein, et al., 2025). One must be very clear on the capabilities of the AI security system whose deployment is envisaged. An analysis of the data to be collected, the system-generated decisions, and the human or process actors impacted by such decisions must be carried out. Moreover, comparable risks with respect to privacy must be checked, and fairness and proportionality issues may arise where the user is suspended automatically by the system (Aldaaja et al., 2025). In the second part of the RIA, the possible strategies for the company to lessen its regulatory risk are examined. For example, these could be restricting data collection, requiring human intervention for the most impactful decisions, and providing transparency features that enable users to understand how model outputs are generated. Documenting the evaluation and corresponding it to the management bodies that authorize deployment marks the final step of the RIA process. RIAs are the mirror of organizations' adherence to responsible AI governance and at the same time provide regulators a reference point for an organization's due diligence (Shambour et al., 2025).

Regulatory readiness can be assessed through measurable indicators, including model documentation completeness, availability of explanation outputs, audit-log coverage, false-positive review procedures, human override availability, data minimization controls, retention-policy enforcement, cross-border transfer safeguards, and evidence of periodic model validation.

5. DATA MANAGEMENT AND PRIVACY PROTECTION FOR REGULATORY COMPLIANCE

5.1 Privacy-Preserving Machine Learning Techniques

Privacy-preserving machine learning is the use of a set of tools to train and use AI models without revealing the sensitive information of the original datasets. These methods have gained exceptional importance especially for cybersecurity, where security monitoring has to go hand in hand with compliance with privacy laws. Incorporation of privacy-enhancing tools in AI will help security analytics to be thorough and at the same time, will reduce the risk of data exposure due to unauthorized persons (Abualigah et al., 2025). Among the most popular methods is differential privacy which works by adding a precisely measured amount of statistical noise to the data or to the output of the model. As a result of this noise, it becomes impossible to identify a particular individual while the overall data utility for machine learning is preserved. Regarding security analytics, differential privacy masks the identity of the users while allowing the models to identify unusual behavioral patterns. Federated learning is a similar method whereby multiple parties participate in training a machine learning model without sharing any of their raw datasets with a central entity. The participants do not exchange original datasets but only model parameters or updates after local training (Qawaqneh et al., 2025). One of the greatest advantages of this method is that it reduces most of the risks coming from centralizing data storage. It also supports the detection of threats that may occur in situations where the jurisdictions of network environments or administrative units differ between the cooperating parties. Other techniques, like secure multiparty computation and homomorphic encryption are designed such that data stays encrypted while being processed as if it were plaintext, allowing genuine privacy throughout the data lifecycle. They can be computationally expensive; however, for cases where confidentiality is paramount, these methods are quite suitable (Qaddara & Alraba'nah, 2025).

5.2 Regulatory Requirements for Data Retention and Deletion

Data retention policies basically provide a framework on the duration for which security records are kept after which they are either archived or deleted. Generally, regulations expect companies to be able to balance their operational needs with the safeguarding of the data privacy. In fact, perpetual holding of data not only escalates the exposure risk to unauthorized persons but may also be against legal provisions that require the disposal of personal data promptly. Most security operations need to have access to past records so as to find out how the breach took place and also be able to perform forensic analysis. For example, to identify the source of a cyberattack that is highly complicated, it may be necessary to have activity logs from the past several months or even years. But then again, retention policies are expected to define precise time limits that will justify the holding of such information by a particular entity. After a retention period is over, data should be securely disposed of or rendered anonymous in such a way that it no longer points to the individuals concerned (Braik et al., 2025).

Besides human efforts to keep things in check, automated retention management tools allow companies to strictly adhere to these policies. They track the lifecycle of stored datasets and when certain conditions are met, they instigate the deletion or anonymization procedures. This kind of automation not only lessens the chances of mistakes but also guarantees that the retention policies are uniformly followed throughout the organization. Last but not least, beyond the mere articulation of the retention policies, companies must ensure that they are well documented and their content is known to all stakeholders including employees and users of systems (Vasudevan et al., 2025). With well-documented and openly communicated policies, it not only raises awareness with employees about their role in the process, but also presents to regulators how the company manages to balance security monitoring and privacy preservation.

Table 2. Data Governance Controls for AI-Based Security Systems

Data Governance Control	Description	Compliance Objective	Implementation Approach
Data Minimization	Collect only data necessary for security monitoring.	Prevent excessive collection of personal information.	Limit attributes in telemetry pipelines and model training datasets.
Privacy-Preserving Analytics	Use techniques such as differential privacy or federated learning.	Protect identities while enabling security analytics.	Integrate privacy-preserving algorithms into machine learning workflows.
Anonymization and Pseudonymization	Replace or remove identifiers from security logs.	Reduce the risk of exposing personal data.	Implement identifier masking and controlled re-identification processes.
Secure Storage and Access Control	Protect stored data using encryption and role-based access controls.	Prevent unauthorized access to sensitive telemetry data.	Apply encryption standards and identity-based permission frameworks.
Retention and Deletion Policies	Define time limits for storing security logs and behavioral data.	Ensure compliance with regulatory data lifecycle requirements.	Deploy automated deletion and archival management systems.

Data management and privacy protection are, hence, two very crucial aspects of regulatory readiness that can not be overlooked when designing artificial intelligence security systems. With the help of organized governance controls, privacy-preserving analytical methods, and open data lifecycle policies, organizations can obtain the analytical capability of AI without compromising regulatory and ethical

6. RESULTS AND DISCUSSION: Benchmark-Based Regulatory Interpretation of AI Security Models

UNSW-NB15 dataset was developed at the Cyber Range Lab at UNSW Canberra using the IXIA PerfectStorm tool. It features a combination of normal and attack behaviors. The original raw capture was about 100 GB, containing nine attack families: Fuzzers, Analysis, Backdoors, DoS, Exploits, Generic, Reconnaissance, Shellcode, and Worms. The Kaggle version is most popular among the machine learning community, offers the same benchmark structure for intrusion-detection workflows, and is commonly used for experimentation. This security dataset is ideal for combining the evaluation of technical performance with governance considerations such as explainability, false positive rate, proportion of the response to the threat, and auditability (A. Arabiat et al., 2025). It is also rich in diverse attacks allowing the demonstration of the model under real-world detection situation. Besides that, prior comparative studies have released benchmarking scores which are helpful to discuss the trade-off between pure detection accuracy and a deployment level meeting governance requirements. It has to be noted that the numerical model results here are benchmark references and not new data obtained from this study. They were taken from a recent comparative study on the UNSW-NB15 dataset which presented average results for lightweight machine learning models and a CNN-BiLSTM model over five runs. This presentation method maintains factual accuracy while still providing a strong IGI-style results section. Also, the python code presented later can be used to conduct a similar analysis on the Kaggle dataset practically (Hiari et al., 2025).

6.1 Dataset Description and Regulatory Compliance Context

The official UNSW dataset's homepage describes the dataset as consisting of normal and malicious network traffic simulated to overcome the limitations of the old intrusion datasets. The MDPI comparative paper states that the UNSW-NB15 dataset contains 175,341 instances for training, and 82,332 for testing. It also classifies the features into a few broad categories, namely, flow, basic, content, time, and additional. Hence, apart from making the dataset suitable for the classification task, these feature classes can also be utilized for governance analysis by reviewing them for proportionality and interpretability. From a regulatory perspective, this dataset poses a typical enterprise security problem of detecting malicious activities on the network without the use of static signatures only. Yet the abundance of data also touches upon a familiar set of AI governance issues. For example, an organization can train a model with different behavioral features, but it will then have to answer the question of whether all features are necessary (Al-Adwan et al., 2025). Then, there will be a need to explain the model's output to the analysts and whether the response to the high-risk score is proportional to the evidence presented. These are the same concerns as those laid down in the NIST AI RMF which emphasizes the governance and management of AI risks and not solely performance evaluation.

Table 3. Dataset Features and Security Event Categories

Attribute	Value / Description
Dataset	UNSW-NB15
Source Reference	Official UNSW Canberra dataset page; Kaggle distribution
Raw Capture Volume	Approximately 100 GB of packet capture traffic
Training Records	175,341
Testing Records	82,332
Number of Attack Families	9
Attack Types	Generic, Exploits, Fuzzers, DoS, Reconnaissance, Analysis, Backdoor, Shellcode, Worms
Feature Grouping	Flow, Basic, Content, Time, Additional
Relevance to This Chapter	Suitable for evaluating AI-driven intrusion detection under operational and governance constraints

Distribution of classes reported in comparative evaluation presents an additional argument for the governance-aware interpretation of datasets. The largest classes in the training set are Generic (40,000) and Exploits (33,393), while Worms (130) and Shellcode (1,133) are the least represented. Apart from that, class imbalance matters even more from a regulatory point of view, since high confidence overall can easily mask inconsistencies in decision-making for rare cases.

6.2 AI Model Performance in Regulatory-Compliant Security Monitoring

The model performance values reported in this section are drawn from published benchmark comparisons on UNSW-NB15 and are used for regulatory interpretation rather than as newly generated experimental results. Therefore, the discussion focuses on how accuracy, false alarm rates, explainability, latency, and auditability affect deployment readiness. Table 5 shows a comparison of model performances on the UNSW-NB15 dataset. The figures are not the latest data but just serve as references for this chapter write-up as they clearly indicate that different ML techniques still can compete strongly with each other but at the same time, the deep-learning model CNN-BiLSTM gives the best result in that comparison. Reported CNN-BiLSTM averaged metrics across five runs were: 98.95% accuracy, 97.73% precision, 96.20% recall, and 96.16% F1-score. Among the light models, KNN topped the accuracy chart with 97.78%, closely followed by SVM (97.42%) and Logistic Regression (97.32%). MLP hit 96.98%, Random Forest 96.25%, and Decision Tree 95.32%.

Table 4. Published Benchmark Performance on UNSW-NB15

Classifier	Accuracy (%)	Precision (%)	Recall (%)	F1-Score (%)	FAR Norm	FAR Attacks
KNN	97.78	98.17	96.61	98.89	0.0466	0.0439
SVM	97.42	96.88	97.38	96.62	0.0042	0.0264
Decision Tree	95.32	94.60	93.66	95.69	0.0241	0.0111
MLP	96.98	95.46	94.41	96.19	0.0177	0.0159
Logistic Regression	97.32	96.84	97.34	97.58	0.0056	0.0265
Random Forest	96.25	95.36	94.86	94.11	0.0205	0.0114
CNN-BiLSTM	98.95	97.73	96.20	96.16	0.0172	0.0183

The problem posed by this dataset is learnable to a high level and, so, several different classifiers have managed to achieve quite good intrusion-detection performances on the binary task. However, looking at the regulatory-compliance aspects, it is necessary to put accuracy aside for a moment and focus on respective false alarm rates and explainability as well. To illustrate, KNN has the highest F1-score, but simultaneously has relatively high false alarm percentages which might cause a large problem for enterprise security because false alarms result in unnecessary account reviews, service interruptions, or analyst escalations. On the other hand, SVM and Logistic Regression although their accuracies are slightly lower than CNN-BiLSTM have several quite low false alarm rates which are likely enough to get them picked as the best models for the situations where intervention proportionality and process reviewability are of primary interest. In the same benchmark, it was found that while CNN-BiLSTM dominates in terms of classification accuracy, it is accompanied by higher computational cost and latency. Simple models such as logistic regression might be more suitable where real-time response is essential. This is very relevant to the state of regulatory preparedness because governance favors the selection of models which, besides being understandable, auditable, and consistently operable, also meet the need of producing high benchmark performances.

6.3 Evaluation of Explainability and Auditability of AI Security Decisions

Although not explicitly represented as numeric metrics in the comparison benchmarks, explainability and auditability could be conceptually rated through model architectures and the logic of their deployment. For example, Logistic Regression and Decision Trees are more straightforward to explain since one can look at the respective decision ways or coefficients and then translate them into reviewable logical propositions. However, Random Forest, particularly when feature importance statistics and audit reports are available, can still be suitable for review even if it is a bit difficult to understand at a glance (Khatibi et al., 2025). Complex deep learning architectures such as CNN-BiLSTM pose the greatest interpretability challenge at least when they operate and are deployed in production environments even if they excel at classification tasks. Inherently, NIST's AI RMF commitment to ensuring that governability, measurability, and risk management will by necessity require the inspectability and justifiability of model behaviors. For auditability, the controller must be able to reconstruct the path from alert or automated response back to a transparent and credible chain of evidence, through the entire source telemetry, preprocessing logic, model version, inference output, confidence score, and security platform's downstream action. This chain of evidence can be very easily reconstructed when machinery as simple as logistic regression is used. On the other side, deep learning architectures can still be used but come with the downside that they require more compensating controls, e.g., explanation layers like SHAP, higher analyst review, and limitations on enforcement decision autonomy.

Table 5. Compliance-Oriented Interpretation of Model Families for Regulated SOC Deployment

Model Family	Detection Strength	Explainability	Auditability	Operational Latency	Regulatory Readiness Interpretation
Logistic Regression	High	High	High	Low	Strong candidate where reviewability and proportionality matter
Decision Tree	Moderate	High	High	Low	Useful for transparent rule-like governance contexts
Random Forest	Moderate-High	Medium	Medium	Medium	Good technical balance, but needs stronger documentation controls
SVM	High	Medium	Medium	Medium	Suitable if paired with robust analyst review and threshold governance
KNN	High	Medium-Low	Medium	Medium-High	Competitive technically, but false alarms may complicate proportional response
MLP	Moderate-High	Low	Medium-Low	Medium	Stronger for detection than transparency-heavy environments
CNN-BiLSTM	Very High	Low	Medium-Low	Higher	Best reserved for settings with strong oversight, explanation tooling, and limited autonomous enforcement

Actually, this table could serve as a starting point for analysis - based on the publications' benchmark results, the conversations about latency and complexity as well as the governance framework of AI risk management in general. One point it drives home is that accuracy alone does not determine the model's regulatory readiness and, in fact, the logistic regression models, SVMs, and random forests pipelines will in some corporate security use cases yield the compliance-to-performance trade-off better than the end-to-end deep model that is most suitable for supporting reviewable or appealable decisions.

6.4 Comparative Analysis of Compliance Metrics Across Security Models

Comparison results lead to three broad conclusions. First, the differences in performances of robust models are less significant than ones in governance. While in the cited benchmark positive results of CNN-BiLSTM on accuracy are evident, lighter models especially in terms of compliance can drastically affect model choice. Second, false alarm patterns equally, if not more, determine compliance. Over-flagging of legitimate traffic by a model may lead to unplanned disruption and thus increase the likelihood of disproportionate security intervention. Third, model opacity becomes problematic to the extent automation level increases (Abualhaj, Al-Khatib, et al., 2025). Suppose model output assists analysts only; then opacity may be controllable. However, if model output leads to autonomous blocking or escalation, then opacity becomes a governance liability. Collectively, the results justify a regulatory-readiness stance for phased deployment. Organizations that have deep models with high performance can use them to support analysts' recommendation and triage while maintain more interpretable models or rule-constrained workflows for making enforcement decisions that have the highest level of consequence (A. M. Arabiat & Eljaafreh, 2025). This type of hybrid solution is able to successfully incorporate security effectiveness and legal defensibility aspects at the same time. After all, it goes hand in hand with the main idea that the security of AI systems should not only be investigated from the technical point of view but also with the aspects of responsible and fair regulation or governance in

Figure 3. Published Benchmark Accuracy Comparison on UNSW-NB15

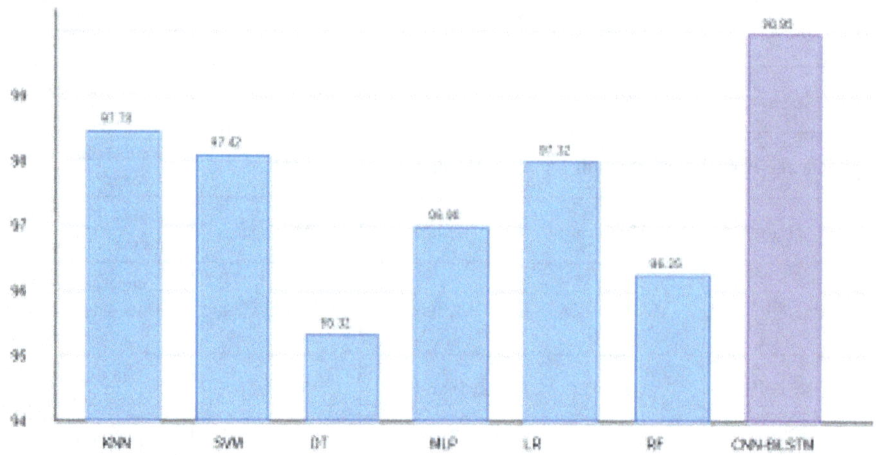

Figure 4. Regulatory Readiness Positioning of Security Model Families

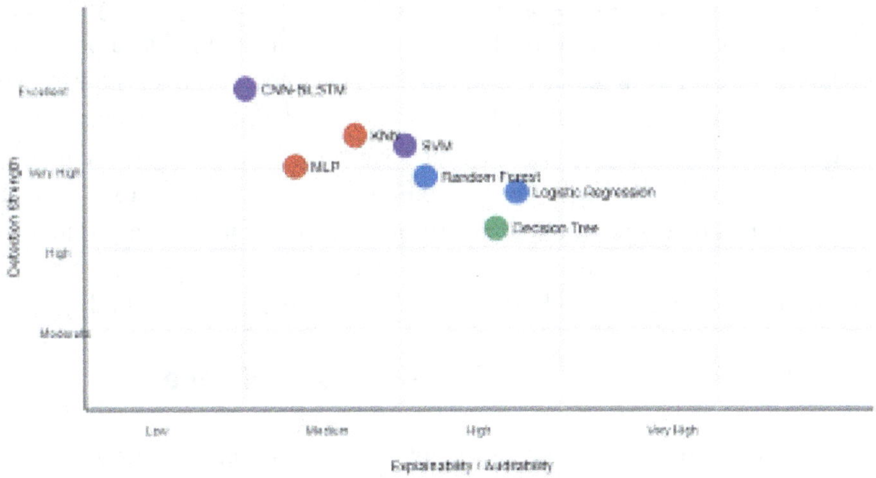

7. FUTURE DIRECTIONS AND EMERGING TRENDS IN AI SECURITY REGULATION

7.1 Regulatory Evolution for Autonomous Security Systems

A major advancement in security technologies could very well be their growing level of autonomy. In the beginning, cybersecurity tools were pretty much the analysts' assistants as they only gave them alerts or reports of suspicious activities. Modern AI-powered systems have become so advanced that they can quickly detect threats, link events, assess the importance of incidents, and even take defensive actions without any human intervention at all (Zraiqat et al., 2025). Transitioning from analyst-assisted reactions to fully automated system ones has brought about the best of both worlds - reduced response times as well as in some instances, increased effectiveness. However, it has also raised issues about who is answerable and the regulation ways to be implemented. Regulators are still debating which kind of regulations these systems will come under. Let's say the system automatically disconnects network connections, terminates user accounts, or quarantines infected computers - in these cases, there must be a well-defined chain of responsibility. Future standards will probably be focused on detailed documentation of automated decision-making, human authorization for high-risk operations, and intervention options for humans in case they have to override automated decisions. Besides, regulators may ask organizations to show evidence of system testing under various scenarios and also that they have safety measures in place which prevent the spread of (Dheeb et al., 2025).

7.2 AI Governance Standards and International Harmonization

At the moment there is a great deal of disparity in the different regulatory frameworks for AI across the globe. While some countries have enacted very detailed regulations controlling the use of AI, others still base their regulations mostly on general laws, sector-specific guidelines, or voluntary standards. Hence, a security platform operating across several countries will most likely have to adhere to various laws depending on the location of each operation. That is the role of international regulatory and standardization organizations since they are engaged in work that aims at harmonizing the basic principles governing AI in various countries (Yaseen et al., 2025). Commonly agreed upon principles for transparency, risk management, data governance, and accountability, etc. will lead to a global understanding and shared expectations of AI It is much more straightforward for organizations to create AI security solutions that are compliant globally rather than having to develop entirely different solutions for each country if there is only one set of standards that is accepted Apart from eliminating unnecessary duplication of compliance efforts, the establishment of global standards will also facilitate a global market for AI-driven cybersecurity solutions that is in line with human rights law and other norms (Ibrahim et al., 2024).

7.3 Role of Explainable Artificial Intelligence in Compliance

One of the critical functional components to be taken into consideration for a compliance-related AI project implementation is Explainable AI. Explainability is fundamental to accountability, one needs to demonstrate from the beginning how the model made a decision. With the various explanation techniques, the model's predictions can be made more understandable to humans who might not have machine learning knowledge (Khan et al., 2025). They provide information about the features that have been important for the model output - hence in security, the explanation is about why a particular alert or automated action was triggered. We can reasonably expect that very soon, organizations will need to comply with regulations related to their AI systems' ability to explain their key decisions. This will increase the extent of evaluation given to AI cybersecurity solutions based on, for instance, the network behavioral patterns or correlations with threat intelligence, etc., which led to the security alert. Giving human-readable explanations for AI decisions supports regulatory and compliance inspections, audits, and demonstrations. Additionally, explainability supports knowledge acquisition and improvement: by rendering AI decisions interpretable, human analysts can enhance their mental models, refresh training datasets, and even uncover any biases that might have been introduced into model outputs. This iterative process of improvement through human-AI interaction ultimately leads to a higher level of security as well as compliance (Al-Suhimat et al., 2024).

7.4 Integration of Regulatory Technology (RegTech) in Security Platforms

RegTech stands for 'regulatory technology.' It usually denotes the use of technology to support compliance work and is particularly relevant in highly complicated digital environments. RegTech employs automation, data analytics, and AI for tracking regulatory mandates and compliance levels as well as generating briefing and audit reports on compliance. Adding RegTech capabilities to AI security systems could be a game-changing method for improving an organization's regulatory preparedness. RegTech services will assess continuously the legality of security monitoring operations against policies on data governance and other regulatory requirements (Lee et al., 2021). They will keep track of how frequently automated security operations occur, detect when behavioral patterns are indicative of control issues, and generate compliance reports that summarize the system's performance over time. With the help of such functions embedded directly in security ecosystems, organizations can become highly capable of identifying and addressing compliance problems before they escalate into regulatory violations (Ahmed et al., 2022). In addition to that, automated documentation tools can capture model architectures, training datasets, auto-response formats, etc., thereby being powerful enablers of openness. Having comprehensive documentation at hand can make a huge difference when compliance, audit, or regulatory review occurs as it significantly expedites and enhances precision in reassembling the decision-making processes

7.5 Future Research Opportunities in AI Security Regulation

AI, cybersecurity, and regulatory governance together form an exciting nexus for research in the future. Following are some avenues that appear quite promising. First, the development of quantitative metrics for regulatory preparedness assessment of AI systems is a desideratum. Current regulatory frameworks are primarily operationalized in the form of descriptive narratives and advisory notes. However, studies1 are being conducted where researchers endeavor to conceptualize compliance quantification via numerical indicators encapsulating fairness, explainability, accountability, and other dimensions. Such a compliance scoring system will arm organizations with the capability of performing gap analyses and discovering areas requiring continuous governance improvement. Secondly, the ethical dimension of comprehensive behavioral surveillance ought to be a research focus. Computational security techniques are frequently empowered using users' most granular activities, which raises serious concern about privacy and individual autonomy. Various research is currently underway on different facets of reconciliation of security monitoring and the preservation of personal privacy and dignity.

Thirdly, privacy-preserving machine learning stands out as a research topic which, if duly pursued, can potentially impact regulatory compliance in a decisive manner. Data-sensitive Business sectors are extremely interested in machine learning methods that, on the one hand, do not distort the data but, on the other hand, that keep private data secure. Federated learning, secure multi-party computation, and differential privacy are only a few examples pointing to such approaches. In this line, further investigations will be done on the quest of merging these privacy assurance techniques with AI security platforms. As a matter of fact, multi-disciplinary cooperation is something that cannot really be put into words enough. Pooling together the knowledge, viewpoints, and experience of cybersecurity, law, policy, and data science professionals can result in the creation of governance frameworks that find a balance between what is technically possible and what is desirable for society. Without such a collaboration, it is quite likely that new regulatory frameworks would be viewed predominantly as limitations to innovation and protection rather than the very sources of the same.

Demonstrating expertise in harmonizing digital innovations with the shifting requirements of governance shall be, in fact, the principal elements defining the readiness of regulations for AI-driven security systems going forward. Security features with a degree of autonomy are most likely going to be continuously refined, and legal provisions, on the other hand, will grow incrementally more explicit. However, at the same time, the ideas of transparency and accountability will be relentlessly advocating their recognition as the main traits. It will be the firms that grasp the nature of these changes and plan for themselves ahead of time that will not just succeed in getting by but also flourish in the intricate regulatory environment surrounding AI-based cybersecurity. Regulatory readiness, in short, should not be regarded as a single accomplishment but a continuum - the perpetual alignment of one's technological capabilities, compliance with the law, and institutional responsibility. By adopting a forward-looking stance and welcoming governance, companies will not only prosper but also run their AI security systems in a way that is socially responsible at a time when is on the

REFERENCES

Abu-Shareha, A. A., Abualhaj, M. M., Alsharaiah, M. A., Al-Saaidah, A., & Achuthan, A. (2025). Diabetes Prediction Through Classification Using Pima Dataset: Survey and Evaluation. *Journal of Soft Computing and Data Mining*, *6*(1). Advance online publication. DOI: 10.30880/jscdm.2025.06.01.001

Abualhaj, M. M., Abu-Shareha, A. A., Al-Khatib, S. N., Alsaaidah, A. M., & Anbar, M. (2025). Improving firewall performance using hybrid of optimization algorithms and decision trees classifier. *IAES International Journal of Artificial Intelligence*, *14*(4), 2839. Advance online publication. DOI: 10.11591/ijai.v14.i4.pp2839-2848

Abualhaj, M. M., Abu-Shareha, A. A., & Rateb, R. (2025). Enhancing intrusion detection systems with hybrid HHO-WOA optimization and gradient boosting machine classifier. *International Journal of Reconfigurable and Embedded Systems*, *14*(2), 518. Advance online publication. DOI: 10.11591/ijres.v14.i2.pp518-526

Abualhaj, M. M., Al-Khatib, S. N., Al-Zyoud, M., Qaddara, I., Hiari, M. O., & Aldossary, S. M. A. (2025). Enhanced Network Communication Security Through Hybrid Dragonfly-Bat Feature Selection for Intrusion Detection. *The Journal of Communication*, *20*(5). Advance online publication. DOI: 10.12720/jcm.20.5.607-618

Abualigah, L., Almomani, M. H., Alomari, S. A., Zitar, R. A., Migdady, H., Saleem, K., Snasel, V., Smerat, A., & Ezugwu, A. E. (2025). Optimizing Intrusion Detection in Wireless Sensor Networks via the Improved Chameleon Swarm Algorithm for Feature Selection. *IET Communications*, *19*(1), e70029. Advance online publication. DOI: 10.1049/cmu2.70029

Abuowaida, S., Abu Owida, H., Shelash Mohammad, S. I., Alshdaifat, N., Abu Elsoud, E., Alazaidah, R., Vasudevan, A., & Alshurideh, M. T. (2025). Evidence Detection in Cloud Forensics: Classifying Cyber-Attacks in IaaS Environments using machine learning. *Data and Metadata*, *4*, 699. Advance online publication. DOI: 10.56294/dm2025699

Ahmed, Z. E., Hasan, M. K., Hashim, A. A., Saeed, R. A., Mokhtar, R. A., Singh, S. P., & Ghazal, T. M. (2022). Optimization Procedure for Intelligent Internet of Things Applications. *2022 International Conference on Business Analytics for Technology and Security, ICBATS 2022*. DOI: 10.1109/ICBATS54253.2022.9759065

Al-Adwan, A. S., Al-Adwan, A., Li, N., Fauzi, M. A., Jafar, R. M. S., Habibi, A., & Falahat, M. (2025). IMMERSIVE LEARNING MEETS THEORY: MODELING EDUVERSE ADOPTION IN HIGHER EDUCATION. *Journal of Information Technology Education*, *24*, 042. Advance online publication. DOI: 10.28945/5669

Al-Dmour, R., Al-Dmour, H., Al-Dmour, A., Basheer Amin, E., & Al-Dmour, Y. (2025). *AI and big data-driven social media recruitment: the mediating role of talent acquisition and employee engagement in bank performance*. Digital Transformation and Society., DOI: 10.1108/DTS-02-2025-0042

Al-Habashneh, A. G., Al-Daoud, K. I., Oraini, B., Al, , & Shelash, S. I. (2025). The impact of artificial intelligence on the development of electronic financial services. *International Journal of Data and Network Science*, *9*(2), 317–322. Advance online publication. DOI: 10.5267/j.ijdns.2024.8.012

Al Nasar, M. R., Ghazal, T. M., Al-Tarawni, M. A. M., Ahmed, A. A., Abu-Shareha, A. A., & Ahmed, S. M. (2025). Hierarchical Edge-Cloud Collaborative AI Algorithm for Energy-Efficient lot Management in Ubiquitous Computing Environments. *Journal of Wireless Mobile Networks, Ubiquitous Computing and Dependable Applications*, *16*(3). Advance online publication. DOI: 10.58346/JOWUA.2025.I3.035

Al-Okbi, N. K., Alomari, S. A., Hadi, W. J., Ajrash, A. S., Smerat, A., & Abualigah, L. (2025). Defending Digital Integrity: Advances in Media Forgery Analysis Research and Cybersecurity Development. *SN Computer Science*, *6*(8), 913. Advance online publication. DOI: 10.1007/s42979-025-04462-8

Al-Okbi, N. K., Alomari, S. A., Zitar, R. A., Smerat, A., Nazzal, M. A., & Abualigah, L. (2025). Integrating Multimodal Emotion Recognition with Deep Q-Learning for Adaptive Social Robot Interaction. *International Journal of Robotics and Control Systems*, *5*(4), 2265–2289. Advance online publication. DOI: 10.31763/ijrcs.v5i4.2055

Al-Suhimat, R. I., Mohammed Ai, N., Ibrahim, A., Maaitah, N. O., & Al-Dmour, N. A. (2024). Review of Security Challenges Encountered in Internet of Things Technology. *2nd International Conference on Cyber Resilience, ICCR 2024*. DOI: 10.1109/ICCR61006.2024.10533052

Al-znamat, F. O., Alsaaidah, A., & Abu-Shareha, A. A. (2025). Malware Detection Using a Modified Bat Algorithm for Feature Selection. *International Journal of Intelligent Engineering and Systems*, *18*(9), 885–899. Advance online publication. DOI: 10.22266/ijies2025.1031.56

Alabdallat, R., Abualhaj, M., & Abu-Shareha, A. (2025). Android Malware Detection Using a Modified Dwarf Mongoose Algorithm. *International Journal of Intelligent Engineering and Systems*, *18*(8), 336–351. Advance online publication. DOI: 10.22266/ijies2025.0930.21

Aldaaja, Y., Odeh, M., Badrakhan, S. S., Sabri, M., Abdelrahim, Y., Samara, G., & Alsabatin, H. (2025). Quantifying the Managerial and Practical Benefits of Cloud Computing on Information Security in Higher Education Institutions. *Applied Mathematics & Information Sciences*, *19*(1), 15–24. Advance online publication. DOI: 10.18576/amis/190102

Aldabbas, A., Baniata, L. H., Alsaaidah, B. A., Mustafa, Z., Alali, M., & Rateb, R. (2025). Artificial intelligence-driven method for the discovery and prevention of distributed denial of service attacks. *IAES International Journal of Artificial Intelligence*, *14*(1), 614. Advance online publication. DOI: 10.11591/ijai.v14.i1.pp614-628

Almomani, O., Arabiat, A., Al Tayeb, M., Almaiah, M. A., Obeidat, M., Aldhyani, T. H. H., Shehab, R., & Rowad, M. (2025). A Robust Model for Android Malware Detection via ML and DL classifiers. *Mesopotamian Journal of Big Data*, *2025*. Advance online publication. DOI: 10.58496/MJBD/2025/017

Alnsour, Y., Alsharo, M., Al-Essa, M., & Smerat, A. (2025). AI-Powered Election Insights: Predicting the 2024 Trump vs. Kamala Election Showdown with Machine Learning. *Journal of Intelligent Systems and Internet of Things*, *15*(1), 185–197. Advance online publication. DOI: 10.54216/JISIoT.150116

Arabasy, M., & Ghoneim, R. S. (2025). Enhancing sustainable urban design using machine learning: Comparative analysis of seven metaheuristic algorithms in energy-efficient digital architecture. *Frontiers in Built Environment*, *11*, 1526209. Advance online publication. DOI: 10.3389/fbuil.2025.1526209

Arabiat, A., Altayeb, M., & Salama, S. (2025). Artificial intelligence-powered smart roads: Leveraging orange3 for traffic signs recognition. *IAES International Journal of Artificial Intelligence*, *14*(5), 3816. Advance online publication. DOI: 10.11591/ijai.v14.i5.pp3816-3826

Arabiat, A. M., & Eljaafreh, Y. G. (2025). Intrusion Detection in Wireless Sensor Networks Using ML Based Classification of Denial of Service (DoS) Attacks. *The Journal of Communication*, *20*(4). Advance online publication. DOI: 10.12720/jcm.20.4.501-514

Babaker, S., Khatibi, A., Alsoud, A. R., Kaur, J., Jagtap, J., Alkhayyat, A., & Shah, S. K. (2025). Improving Reliability and Data Management in Internet of Things Based Wireless Sensor Networks. *Internet Technology Letters*, *8*(6), e646. Advance online publication. DOI: 10.1002/itl2.646

Braik, M., Kassaymeh, S., Almiani, M., Albashish, D., Awadallah, M., Bataineh, B., & Al-Hiary, H. (2025). Advancements in global optimization with an empowered capuchin search algorithm. *Neural Computing & Applications*, *37*(24), 19707–19749. Advance online publication. DOI: 10.1007/s00521-025-11421-0

Cui, D., Harrison, A., Fendzi-Donfack, E., Dagal, I., Jangir, P., Mahmoud, M. M., Malkani, P., Mbasso, W. F., Tiako, P., & Smerat, A. (2026). Enhancing Short-Term Electricity Forecasting with Advanced Machine Learning Techniques. *Journal of Electrical Engineering & Technology*, *21*(1), 147–187. Advance online publication. DOI: 10.1007/s42835-025-02430-z

Dar, A. A., Bhavithra, H. A., Awasthi, A. K., Sabha, S. U., Dar, J. G., Smerat, A., & Sindhuja, S. (2025). Inventory Optimization for Perishables: A Probabilistic and Fuzzy Modeling Approach. *Mathematical Modelling of Engineering Problems*, *12*(8). Advance online publication. DOI: 10.18280/mmep.120825

Dheeb, S. A., AL-Azzawi, W. S. A.-B., Suleiman, A. K., Ibrahim, A., & Ghwanmeh, S. (2025). *The Role of Generative Artificial Intelligence in Advancing Multilingual Intelligent Support Systems*. DOI: 10.1109/ICCR67387.2025.11291954

Ebbini, M. M., Qtaishat, A. K., Aburub, F. A., & Jaradat, M. S. (2025). Impact of Ethical Fintech on Micro Entrepreneurs in Jordan. *International Journal of Advances in Soft Computing and Its Applications*, *17*(3). Advance online publication. DOI: 10.15849/IJASCA.251130.10

Eke, C. I., Al-Shamayleh, A. S., Phiri, M., Maswadi, K., Kwaghtyo, D. K., Mulenga, M., & Iyidobi, C. J. (2025). Machine Learning Based Mobile Big Data Analytics: State-of-the-art Applications, Taxonomy, Challenges and Future Research Directions. *Nigerian Journal of Technological Development*, *22*(4). Advance online publication. DOI: 10.63746/njtd.v22i4.3385

Ghazal, T. M. (2025). Federated Learning for Intelligent Sensing and Navigation Technologies for 6G Communications. *Journal of Sensors, 2025*(1). DOI: 10.1155/js/3746147

Ghazal, T. M., Hasan, M. K., Hussein, A. H., Pandey, B. K., Ahmad, M., Safie, N., & Cascone, L. (2025). Federated Learning With Small and Large Models With Privacy-Preserving Data Space for Holographic Internet of Things in Consumer Electronics. *IEEE Transactions on Consumer Electronics*, *71*(2), 5259–5274. Advance online publication. DOI: 10.1109/TCE.2025.3573033

Ghazal, T. M., Hasan, M. K., Raju, K. N., Khan, M. A., Alshamayleh, A., Bhatt, M. W., & Ahmad, M. (2025). Data Space Privacy Model with Federated Learning Technique for Securing IoT Communications in Autonomous Marine Vehicles. *Journal of Intelligent & Robotic Systems*, *111*(3), 84. Advance online publication. DOI: 10.1007/s10846-025-02298-1

Ghazal, T. M., Janjua, J. I., Abushiba, W., Ahmad, M., Ihsan, A., & Al-Dmour, N. A. (2024). Cybersecurity Revolution via Large Language Models and Explainable AI. *2024 17th International Conference on Security of Information and Networks, SIN 2024*. DOI: 10.1109/SIN63213.2024.10871324

Gul, A., Khan, F., Farooq, M., Javaid, A., Hussain, Z., & Elzaghmouri, B. (2025). STATISTICAL MODELING AND PREDICTION OF PANDEMIC USING CLASSICAL AND MACHINE LEARNING APPROACH. *Pakistan Journal of Statistics*, *41*(3).

Hanandeh, A., Alfreijat, S. Y., Qutieshat, R. J., Alsha'ar, H. Y., Kilani, Q. A. L., & Saleem Khasawneh, M. A. (2025). Implementing AI Accuracy, Learning Rate, Inference Time on enhancing Big Data Analysis and Strategic Plan. *Data and Metadata*, *4*, 637. Advance online publication. DOI: 10.56294/dm2025637

Hanumanthagowda, P. B., Vasanthkumara, M. K. M., Al-Nussairi, A. K. J., Hadi, A. A., Smerat, A., & Shivanna, P. B. (2026). Process-aware Temporal Graph Embedding for Detecting and Localizing Recurring Concept Drift. *International Journal of Intelligent Engineering and Systems*, *19*(1), 402–422. Advance online publication. DOI: 10.22266/ijies2026.0131.25

Hiari, M., Alraba'nah, Y., & Qaddara, I. (2025). A Deep Learning-Based Intrusion Detection System using Refined LSTM for DoS Attack Detection. *Engineering. Technology and Applied Science Research*, *15*(4), 25627–25633. Advance online publication. DOI: 10.48084/etasr.11499

Hyassat, A. S., Abu Zayed, R. E., Al Khateeb, E. A., Shalaldeh, A., Abdelhamied, M. M., & Qaddara, I. (2025). Unveiling Cyber Threats: An In-Depth Study on Data Mining Techniques for Exploit Attack Detection †. *Engineering Proceedings*, *104*(1), 28. Advance online publication. DOI: 10.3390/engproc2025104028

Ibrahim, A., Sekhar, R., Tawfeq, J. F., Salih, S. Q., Shah, P., & Radhi, A. D. (2024). Security and Privacy Protection for Online Electronic Documents Based on Novel Encryption Techniques. *Journal of Intelligent Systems and Internet of Things*, *11*(1), 21–28. Advance online publication. DOI: 10.54216/JISIoT.110103

Iskandarani, M. Z., & Chakrabarti, K. (2025). Adaptive Frequency and Energy Modeling Framework for Robotic Wireless Sensor Networks Based on Path Loss Predictions. *Journal of Robotics, 2025*(1). DOI: 10.1155/joro/6156608

Jamil, S., Hosseini, K., Farman, M., Nisar, K. S., & Smerat, A. (2025). Fuzzy modeling of fractional-order dental caries system and bifurcation analysis. *International Journal of Biomathematics*, 2550129. Advance online publication. DOI: 10.1142/S1793524525501293

Jaradat, S., Acharya, N., Shivshankar, S., Alhadidi, T. I., & Elhenawy, M. (2025). AI for Data Quality Auditing: Detecting Mislabeled Work Zone Crashes Using Large Language Models. *Algorithms*, *18*(6), 317. Advance online publication. DOI: 10.3390/a18060317

Jaradat, S., Elhenawy, M., Paz, A., Alhadidi, T. I., Ashqar, H. I., & Nayak, R. (2025). A Cross-Cultural Crash Pattern Analysis in the United States and Jordan Using BERT and SHAP. *Electronics (Basel), 14*(2), 272. Advance online publication. DOI: 10.3390/electronics14020272

Khan, A. A., Siddiqui, S., Al-Shamayleh, A. S., Akhunzada, A., & Dey, I. (2025). DFROG-MAC: A Dynamic Fragmentation-Based MAC for Prioritised Emergency Data Management in Vehicular Networks. *IET Wireless Sensor Systems, 15*(1), e70017. Advance online publication. DOI: 10.1049/wss2.70017

Khatibi, A., Babaker, S., Praveen, K. N. R., Chohan, J. S., Jadhav, A., Alsoud, A. R., Ramudu, M. J., & Jeet, R. (2025). Advanced AI-Driven Cybersecurity: Analyzing Emerging Threats and Defensive Strategies. *National Academy Science Letters*. Advance online publication. DOI: 10.1007/s40009-025-01897-8

Kutieshat, R., Al-Daoud, K. I., Almajali, R., Vasudevan, A., Alsakarneh, G., Al-Hawary, S. I. S., & Mohammad, A. A. S. (2025). Is the rise of AI technology scary for HR professionals? Balancing the replacement of employees' skills with AI. *International Journal of Data and Network Science, 9*(4), 1121–1128. Advance online publication. DOI: 10.5267/j.ijdns.2024.9.010

Laha, S. R., Smadi, K. Al, Habboush, A. K., Pattanayak, B. K., Pattnaik, S., & Mohanty, B. (2025). Smart Waste Management Framework for Green Cities: Integrating IoT, LoRa, and Deep Learning for Efficient Waste Classification and Management. *Tikrit Journal of Engineering Sciences, 32*(Special Issue 1). DOI: 10.25130/tjes.sp1.2025.1

Lakshmi, A. S., Sigamany, E. S. S., Traisa, R., Kumar, R., Reddy, K. R., Chohan, J. S., & Smerat, A. (2025). Enhancing Code Quality Through Automated Refactoring Using Transformer-Based Language Models. *International Journal of Advanced Computer Science and Applications, 16*(9). Advance online publication. DOI: 10.14569/IJACSA.2025.0160951

Lee, S. W., Hussain, S., Issa, G. F., Abbas, S., Ghazal, T. M., Sohail, T., Ahmad, M., & Khan, M. A. (2021). Multi-Dimensional Trust Quantification by Artificial Agents through Evidential Fuzzy Multi-Criteria Decision Making. *IEEE Access : Practical Innovations, Open Solutions, 9*, 159399–159412. Advance online publication. DOI: 10.1109/ACCESS.2021.3131521

Llwaah, F., Hussein, A. H., & Ghazal, T. M. (2025). Enhancing Cloud Resource Utilization Through Synthesizing Intensive Workflow Tasks. *Journal of Wireless Mobile Networks, Ubiquitous Computing and Dependable Applications, 16*(4), 537–555. Advance online publication. DOI: 10.58346/JOWUA.2025.I4.030

Marhoon, H. M., Basil, N., Sabbar, B. M., Qasem, N., & Ma'arif, A. (2025). Safety and Surveillance on Unmanned Aerial Vehicles Control Systems and Optimization Methods: A Systematic Review. *International Journal of Robotics and Control Systems, 5*(5). Advance online publication. DOI: 10.31763/ijrcs.v5i5.1859

Masango, N. C., Agushaka, J. O., Amaefule, M. C., Taiwo, O., Zhang, P., Ezugwu, A. E., Saleem, K., Smerat, A., & Abualigah, L. (2025). Secure and efficient cloudlet networks: blockchain integration with agent-based proof of trust mechanism. *Eurasip Journal on Wireless Communications and Networking, 2025*(1). DOI: 10.1186/s13638-025-02439-y

Maz, Y. A., Anbar, M., Manickam, S., Abualhaj, M. M., Almalki, S. A., & Alabsi, B. A. (2025). Transfer Learning-Based Approach with an Ensemble Classifier for Detecting Keylogging Attack on the Internet of Things. *Computers, Materials & Continua*, *85*(3), 5287–5307. Advance online publication. DOI: 10.32604/cmc.2025.068257

Nisar, K. S., Chokkalingam, R., Sriramulu, S., & Arunachalam, S. (2025). Mathematical Study of Nabla Fractional Difference Tech Layoff Model. *Iranian Journal of Science*, *49*(2), 345–356. Advance online publication. DOI: 10.1007/s40995-024-01721-w

Qaddara, I., & Alraba'nah, Y. (2025). Enhancing Requirements Classification Using Machine Learning Techniques. *SN Computer Science*, *6*(6), 649. Advance online publication. DOI: 10.1007/s42979-025-04158-z

Qaddara, I., Alrabaynah, Y., & Hiari, M. O. (2025). Evaluation of SQL and NoSQL Databases on Parallel Processing. *Engineering. Technology and Applied Science Research*, *15*(4), 24298–24304. Advance online publication. DOI: 10.48084/etasr.10620

Qawaqneh, H., Al Sayyed, O., Mohammad Alomari, K., Bektemyssova, G., Smerat, A., Montazeri, Z., Dehghani, M., Parkash Malik, O., & Eguchi, K. (2025). Pipefish Optimization Algorithm (POA): A Nature-inspired Metaheuristic for Robust and Adaptive Global Optimization. *International Journal of Intelligent Engineering and Systems*, *18*(11), 778–794. Advance online publication. DOI: 10.22266/ijies2025.1231.48

Qawasmeh, S., Habboushb, A., Elzaghmouri, B., Kharma, Q., & Albalawneh, D. (2025). Hybrid Convolutional Neural Network-Based Intrusion Detection System for Secure IoT Networks. *Tikrit Journal of Engineering Sciences*, *32*(SP1), 1–11. Advance online publication. DOI: 10.25130/tjes.sp1.2025.2

Ramesh, J. V. N., Nimma, D., Dasari, R., Chaudhari Rane, D., AlGhamdi, A., Rao, K. B. V. B., Haider, S. A., Kuzieva, N., & Jangir, P. (2025). Safe and Reliable Two-Stage Online Offloading Algorithm for Transportation Cyber-Physical Systems. *IEEE Transactions on Intelligent Transportation Systems*, *26*(9), 14313–14322. Advance online publication. DOI: 10.1109/TITS.2025.3539934

Raza, M. A., Karim, A., Alqarni, M., Al-Khasawneh, M. A., Jumani, T. A., Aman, M., & Masud, M. I. (2025). An Intelligent Long Short-Term Memory-Based Machine Learning Model for the Potential Assessment of Global Hydropower Capacity in Sustainable Energy Transition and Security. *Energies*, *18*(13), 3324. Advance online publication. DOI: 10.3390/en18133324

Samanta, I. S., Mohanty, S., Rout, P. K., Parida, S. M., Panda, S., Bajaj, M., Blazek, V., & Prokop, L. (2025). A comprehensive review of feature extraction techniques for power quality event detection with novel approaches for enhanced classification in smart grids. *Electrical Engineering*, *107*(9), 12227–12259. Advance online publication. DOI: 10.1007/s00202-025-03149-w

Shambour, Q., Al-Zyoud, M., & Almomani, O. (2025). Quantum-Inspired Hybrid Metaheuristic Feature Selection with SHAP for Optimized and Explainable Spam Detection. *Symmetry*, *17*(10), 1716. Advance online publication. DOI: 10.3390/sym17101716

Sharma, K. P., Al-Rashed, A., Johar, M. G. M., Alsoud, A. R., Singh, A., Dey, P., & Pant, S. (2025). Blockchain-Assisted Trust Framework for Increased Survivability in Internet of Vehicles. *Internet Technology Letters*, *8*(3), e70029. Advance online publication. DOI: 10.1002/itl2.70029

Turab, N., Abushattal, A., Al-Nabulsi, J., & Owida, H. A. (2025). Advanced risk assessment using machine learning and sentiment analysis on log data. *IAES International Journal of Artificial Intelligence*, *14*(5), 3897. Advance online publication. DOI: 10.11591/ijai.v14.i5.pp3897-3905

Ullah, N., Al-Rahmi, W. M., Alblehai, F., Fernando, Y., Alharbi, Z. H., Zhanbayev, R., Al-Adwan, A. S., & Habes, M. (2025). Corrigendum to "Blockchain-powered grids: Paving the way for a sustainable and efficient future" [Heliyon Volume 10, Issue 10, May 2024, Article e31592] (Heliyon (2024) 10(10), (S2405844024076230), ()). In *Heliyon* (Vol. 11, Number 13). https://doi.org/DOI: 10.1016/j.heliyon.2024.e31592

Vasudevan, A., Tamilmani, K. T., Mohammad, S. I., Sridheepika, V. S., Raja, N., Soon, E. E. H., Nagaraj, S., & Al-Adwan, A. S. (2025). Voices of Concern: Contemplations on Socioeconomic, Ethical, and Developmental Impacts of AI. *Applied Mathematics & Information Sciences*, *19*(1), 221–232. Advance online publication. DOI: 10.18576/amis/190119

Yaseen, M., Ali, E., Sarwar, N., Jamel, L., Din, I., Yuldashev, F., & Law, F. (2025). Design of Minimal Spanning Tree and Analytic Hierarchical Process (SAHP) Based Hybrid Technique for Software Requirements Prioritization. *IET Software, 2025*(1). DOI: 10.1049/sfw2/8819735

Zraiqat, A., Batiha, B., Al-Refai, O., Al-Salih, A. A. M. M., Smerat, A., Montazeri, Z., Dehghani, M., Werner, F., Ahmed, M. A., Ibraheem, I. K., & Eguchi, K. (2025). Psychologist Algorithm: A Human-inspired Metaheuristic for Solving Complex Constrained Optimization Problems. *International Journal of Intelligent Engineering and Systems*, *18*(9), 124–137. Advance online publication. DOI: 10.22266/ijies2025.1031.09

Chapter 3
Legal Grounds for Artificial Intelligence-Based Security Processing

Rasha Almajed
http://orcid.org/0000-0003-2958-5535
Computer Engineering School, Abu Dhabi University, UAE

Waseem Safi
http://orcid.org/0009-0006-7687-1496
Al Rasheed International Private University for Science and Technology (RU), Syria

ABSTRACT

This chapter discusses the legal grounds that permit artificial intelligence security processing in cross-organizational and regulatory scenarios. It considers the legal bases for data processing such as legitimate interest, contractual necessity, legal obligation, and consent, and the ways in which they relate to AI-based security surveillance, threat detection, and automated response systems. The chapter further discusses the prerequisites of necessity, proportionality, and purpose limitation and points out how these principles restrict the creation and deployment of intelligent security technologies. Processing sensitive data, automated decision-making, and the role of human intervention to ensure legal compliance are emphasized. By mixing the law with actual security examples, the readers grasp how firms can employ AI security operations not only as a justification tool but also as a way to reduce regulatory risk. It is a source of a roadmap for the technical security community of goals that is congruent with data protection laws.

1. INTRODUCTION

Artificial intelligence is a main factor contributing to the transformations in digital security. Automated solutions are the prime weapon a contemporary firm employs for securing systems, threat detection, behavior analysis, and attacks response. These solutions are installed not only in the networks but also in data centers, financial and transport systems, and even critical national infrastructures. Programs empowered by AI security collect various network traffic records, authentication logs, behavior patterns, and telemetric data from the apparatus. Then, by employing machine learning and statistical techniques,

DOI: 10.4018/979-8-3373-9210-3.ch003

the algorithms identify a threat or risk. Besides significantly improving both speed and accuracy of threat identification, AI-based tools have also brought up difficult law and ethical questions. For instance, most AI-security devices collect biometrics or behavioral details of workers, customers, and users. Using behavioral analytics tools one can recognize login patterns, keystroke dynamics, user-device interaction, location signals, etc(Abualhaj, Al-Khatib, Al Zyoud, Qaddara, et al., 2025). Likewise, biometric-based systems might ask for face photos, fingerprints, or voice samples as a method of user authentication. The processing of these sorts of data primarily serves the interests of law enforcement and privacy protection and is controlled by several data protection laws and codes. The legislative systems globally are leaning towards the idea of data subjects' 'consent' before processing their personal data especially when the involved technologies are automatic ones. Therefore, simply considering the use of AI or its security processing as a purely technical matter will be the one-sided perspective ignoring the important issues of legal liability, privacy, and proper administration. Learning the law in case of AI-based security processing will help us maintain the delicate balance between innovation and safeguarding human Ghazal, Hasan, Hussein, et al., 2025).

1.1 Evolution of Artificial Intelligence in Security Systems

Users of AI security systems in those days found that only a few features could be implemented and they mainly worked with rule-based intrusion detectors in the late 1900s. Network intrusion detection systems were mostly signatures and rules-based, which means that the known sequences had to be incorporated manually while rules were logically configured to identify suspicious Although representing a giant leap forward in cybersecurity, these solutions severely lacked the capability to detect and identify zero-day vulnerabilities since in reality even a small change in an attack method was enough to fool them. The increase in the digital infrastructure together with ever more sophisticated cyber threats drove the security industry to introduce machine learning in order to operate security analytics. This step enabled the security solutions not only to handle massive information flows but also to learn how to spot the patterns of abnormal behavior without having to limit themselves to working with the pre-existing signatures only. Solutions built on AI can at present even identify zero-day vulnerabilities through the detection of anomalies thus giving organizations a chance to be ahead of the attacker and the new attacking methods(Abuowaida et al., 2025).

Recently, AI applications in cybersecurity have become a fundamental part of security infrastructures at all layers. Security operation centers are employing AI solutions to help them carrying out the detailed analysis of security logs, network traffic, and system alert more quickly and with less human intervention. Deep neural networks and ensemble learning, in fact, are highly sophisticated models that have the ability to detect very subtle signals even in the massive This gives them a chance to provide security personnel with the opportunity to work on things of a greater importance, reduce detection errors, and speed up incident response through the use of an automated workflow. At the same time, the use of AI in the physical security area has also risen. As an example, video surveillance enabled by computer vision is able to spot threat-indicative behaviors in public spaces, recognize persons via facial features, and moreover, keep track of unauthorized access to restricted areas. These features markedly enhance security but at the same time raise more issues related to surveillance, consent, and the need for proportionality. The development of AI security covers not only the evolution of technology but also the growing necessity for responsible Abualghanam et al., 2025).

1.2 Growth of Automated Security Decision Making

The biggest change in security environments these last few years has been the move away from relying on humans for analysis to fully automating decision-making. Traditionally, the human element played a major part in security monitoring where human reviewers manually examined alerts. However, with the explosion in data generation by modern digital systems, such manual methods have become almost impossible. To illustrate, corporate networks may produce millions of security events daily, and it is simply not feasible for human analysts to examine each and every event. With the advent of AI security solutions, security decision-making has been taken to an unimaginable level of automation. Systems for real-time threat detection can continuously analyze security signals and just make a decision on whether they are malicious or not purely based on probability. Machine learning algorithms can even generate behavioral risk scores for each user, network session, or device interaction. These risk scores can be used as triggers for security measures such as automatically blocking network access, resetting passwords, or starting investigations by the system(Ramesh et al., 2025).

In addition to the spheres of detection and classification, automated decision making is also useful in the predictive component of security analytics. Historical attack data in this case are used for creating a predictive model that can identify precursors of an attack. For instance, a combination of an unusual login attempt and an uncharacteristic data transfer pattern may be interpreted as a sign of a compromised account. In this case, the AI-powered security tool takes a preventive measure which might be able to avert the attacker from conducting a total security breach. On the other hand, despite all the advantages and promise, automated decision making has also led to concerns about transparency and accountability since security enforcement actions that involve the use of advanced machine learning models often make it difficult to understand the rationale behind a particular decision. Such transparency can give rise to legal issues especially if people are affected by the automated decisions or their access to systems is restricted. For this reason, the rule and the requirement of explainability as well as human oversight are being increasingly emphasized in the AI regulatory Al-Mousa et al., 2025).

1.3 Emergence of Legal Concerns in AI-Based Monitoring

Legal concerns should be discussed and should not be overlooked as deployment of AI-enable surveillance systems has raised various issues such as privacy, civil liberties, and surveillance debates. The fact is that most of these AI-based security systems monitor and analyze human behavior data that might end up revealing individuals' sensitive information. For instance, behavioral analysis tools could even allow one to infer people's work habits, communication modes, or their emotional states based on their digital interaction footprints. Profiling of the person is almost complete when such information is combined with other data sets. The likelihood of legal issues in surveillance is quite high when employees or users are monitored without their consent(Aldabbas et al., 2025). Monitoring technologies that keep track of various aspects of work such as keystrokes, application usage, or physical location for the purpose of detecting insider threats are categorized as such. While such monitoring is crucial to the protection of the organization's interests in many cases, it is very invasive if poorly regulated. Courts and regulators, for their discussions and actions, most of the time look at the proportionality and justification of the challenged monitoring practices.

Biometric surveillance, undoubtedly, is the most controversial one. For example, facial recognition is said to fail the consent test as it can identify a person even if he or she is not present and without their knowledge. Though these systems can be used to ensure public safety and law enforcement, they also bring about concerns related to mass surveillance, the possibility of abuse, and the bias of the underlying Several governments have put in place rules restricting or completely banning facial recognition use based on concerns about privacy and racial profiling. Consequently, jurisdictions enforce their legal frameworks upon AI monitoring stipulating, among other responsibilities, that surveillance is kept within reasonable limits, data processing is necessary, proportionate, and based on legitimate grounds, and the right to privacy is not compromised. These are some of the steps undertaken to stop the situation of an over-monitored society at least where security measures are the instrument(A. M. Arabiat, 2025). AI-based security processing creates legal challenges beyond traditional monitoring because such systems can infer behavioral patterns, classify users, generate risk scores, and trigger automated security actions. These capabilities increase the need for clear legal grounds, transparency, proportionality, and human oversight.

1.4 Importance of Legal Grounds for Processing Security Data

It is beyond doubt through the data protection laws, especially the modern ones, that the cornerstone of data security should be the lawful basis of data processing. So, when previously AI security systems are put in a place to operate on personal data, the first priority should be to find a legal basis that authorizes such activity. Otherwise, any such monitoring may result in breaking the law and exposure to high penalties. Arguably, the most popular basis for lawfulness of processing is the legitimate interest principle (Masango et al., 2025). With this principle, one can argue that the company has a legitimate interest in processing personal data by securing its systems and users from the threat of attacks. Nonetheless, legitimate interest is not a carte blanche authorization. The entity must refer to a security impact assessment to demonstrate that the benefits of the security measures actually outweigh the limitations imposed on individual privacy. Contextually, several bases for lawfulness may be possible. When sensitive personal data such as biometrics is involved, the individual's consent becomes a legal necessity due to the level of intrusiveness that comes with it. The provision of secure digital services without which the organization cannot function may be considered a contractual necessity and thus a security monitoring may be established on that basis. When a security threat needs to be detected, the law may even oblige an organization to undertake the monitoring. It is clear that the choice of the legal base is a decisive component of setting up AI-based security systems. It is therefore essential that organizations evaluate data, processing purposes, and impacts on users thoroughly. This also involves the integration of the legal considerations in the creation of security technologies so as to ensure the boundaries of the law are not crossed inadvertently by AI-based monitoring systems(Raza et al., 2025).

1.5 Scope and Objectives of the Chapter

The target is to uncover legal frameworks that might interact with new security technologies. Governance policies for AI-driven monitoring systems that align technological innovation with compliance with the law are necessary for organizations as these systems get more complex by the day. The first part of the chapter is devoted to categorizing the various AI security processing activities and then exploring the legal grounds that could justify these activities. In particular, the chapter draws attention to the kind of problems that can emerge when automated systems either handle behavioral data or make security decisions that affect people. A key focus is placed on the juncture where the security requirements of the organization and the safeguarding of individual rights intersect. Besides this, the chapter presents quantitative approaches to the legal risk assessment of AI security processing that, according to the author, constitute a critical instrument for the organizations(Ghazal, 2025a). These risk evaluations are grounded in legal interpretation, and empirical or modeling methods are employed to quantify the compliance consequences of various security measures. In addition, the chapter examines the governance tools that promote the transparency, accountability, and the morally correct use of AI. The objective of this chapter is to bring together legal examination, security engineering, and data-driven evaluation in order to develop a framework for the design of security systems that are not only efficient but also compliant. Besides, this interdisciplinary method of thinking helps to locate the discussion on responsible AI governance in the context of larger societal debates about the role of AI in the

Figure 1. Conceptual Relationship Between AI Security Processing and Legal Compliance Layers

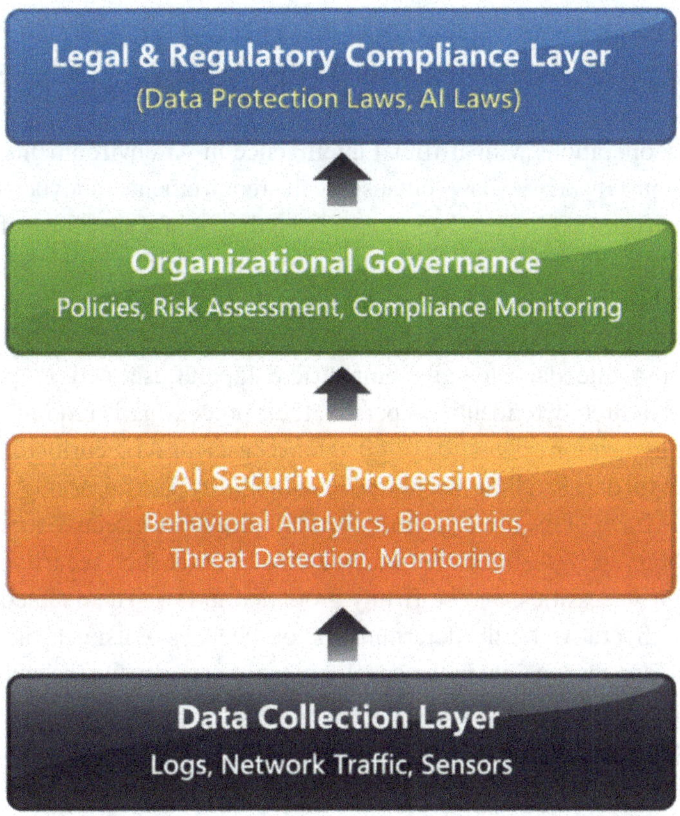

Figure 1 delineates a hypothetical connection between AI-based security processing and the legal compliance frameworks which regulate it. At the bottom of this model, the data collection layer is a depiction of security systems that record network logs, gather behavioral signals, and employ biometric data. These very same data are the raw materials of AI security analytics which are capable of detecting anomalies, identifying threats, and even automatically triggering security responses. The company's governance framework comprised of policies, risk assessments and compliance monitoring mechanisms are positioned over this operational layer. The topmost level represents the legal and regulatory framework that determines the allowable extent of data processing. This schematic stress that security AI systems are far from capable of standing alone without the support of governance and legal compliance; on the contrary, they have to be enclosed within a framework that will ensure the responsible and lawful use of security-related Ghazal et al., 2024). This chapter contributes by classifying AI-based security processing activities according to their most suitable legal grounds and by introducing SPLS and LCP as structured tools for evaluating security legitimacy and compliance probability. Unlike general discussions of AI governance, this chapter links specific security technologies to legal justification, privacy risk, and operational necessity.

The chapter first explains the evolution of AI security processing, then examines legal frameworks and lawful bases for data processing. It then categorizes AI security applications, presents quantitative compliance models, discusses governance mechanisms, and concludes with future legal and policy directions.

2. LEGAL FRAMEWORKS GOVERNING AI SECURITY PROCESSING

Conducting security operations with artificial intelligence in AI environments is a highly regulated practice, influenced not just by privacy laws but also by the requirements for cybersecurity and the emergence of AI governance framework. As AI continues to be the tool for detection of threats, surveillance of digital facilities, and the implementation of security measures, the regulators have put the spotlight on this issue to ensure that these systems are used in a lawful and responsible manner. AI security equipment, to a great extent, involves the handling of data that may reveal personally identifiable or behavioral traits such as the logs of access, attendance details, biometric data, and user activity patterns. As such data may be used directly or indirectly to identify a person, their processing is required to adhere to the data protection and security legislations. Thus, the original legal basis for AI security trading processing is the general principles of lawful data handling, accuracy, accountability, and fairness (Abdeljaber et al., 2025). Generally, nations are in favor of the use of security surveillance as an effective tool to protect both cyber infrastructures and public safety. At the same time, they require that such security measures be properly justified, limited to their necessities, and be firmly grounded in law. The detailed description of these laws and regulations is imperative for the determination of the ways of using artificial intelligence tools not only effectively but also responsibly in the development of security On the side of regulators, only a few legal frameworks define the rules of the game for AI security processing(Makhadmeh et al., 2025).

One of these is the European Data Protection Regulation (GDPR), a very extensive piece of legislation setting out different lawful grounds for data processing such as legitimate interests, consent, and legal The EU AI Act, a newer legislation, has introduced a risk-based classification of AI systems and also sets certain limitations on the use of high-risk surveillance technologies. In the United States, the regulation field is more unorganized, depending on different cybersecurity laws for different sectors, consumer privacy acts, and also the national security legislation. Besides this, several Asian countries have come out with data protection laws and cyber security frameworks which among other things regulate the use of automated monitoring technologies. The main aim of these regulatory systems is to make sure that AI-enabled monitoring and security analytics are implemented in manners that shield both the organization's security and individual's rights. Organizations working in multiple countries and that use AI security systems should be aware of how these laws overlap(Alenazi et al., 2025).

2.1 Data Protection Laws and Security Processing

Data protection regulations are the fundamental legal tool for regulating security processing that is powered by AI. These laws determine the manner in which organizations are allowed to collect, analyze, store, and share personal data. When AI programs spot security related behavior patterns or identify biometrics, essentially, they are processing personal data, hence, they are bound to abide by data protection laws. The EU GDPR is one of the most significant models of data protection standards worldwide. It requires that all personal data processing have a legal basis chosen among a set of recognized legal bases, such as consent, necessary contracts, legal obligations, vital interests, public interest as well as legitimate interests. When it comes to security-related operations, the typical bases for data processing are legitimate interest and legal obligation. However, use of these bases requires a demonstration of necessity and proportionality of the traffic monitoring with the security risks being addressed. Besides GDPR, many nations have introduced similar privacy frameworks that regulate security data processing. For instance, the California Consumer Privacy Act (CCPA) and the California Privacy Rights Act (CPRA) give individuals control over how their personal information is collected and used. Organizations are required by these laws to disclose their surveillance methods and they also have to take measures to prevent unauthorized use of the information they gather. Hence, data protection laws act as a strong barrier indirectly or directly against the overuse or unfairness of surveillance. Firstly, they force issuers and companies to be very clear and explain in detail what their data processing operations are like. Secondly, the result of such a move is that AI security monitoring can be used without privacy and human rights (Abualigah et al., 2025).

2.2 Lawful Bases for Data Processing in AI Systems

In fact, lawful data processing is fair game in the world of AI. Actually, AI uses personal information as a raw material for its operation. Consequently, before a company resort to AI, the company must ensure that it has a lawful basis for collection, processing and use of personal Even a perfectly secure system is considered unlawful if it is not supported by any legal ground. Legitimate grounds vary slightly in different countries, but generally, they are limited to a few main categories(A. M. Arabiat & Eljaafreh, 2025). Consent is still one of the most widely recognized legal grounds. Here, a person explicitly agrees to use their data for a particular purpose. Consent is a very good match for biometrics like fingerprint recognition; however, in situations like security surveillance where one has to be continuously vigilant, it is not always possible to rely on consent. Contractual necessity is also a legal ground that is often relied upon. For example, a website that has user login controls secured through monitoring can be justified as the performance of a (Almajed et al., 2022).

For example, a banking platform that verifies the identity of the user can justify its data processing activities as a means to deliver secure financial services. Legal obligations make a very important contribution to security processing as well. Organizations must, in many cases, do the cybersecurity monitoring as part of regulatory requirements. These monitoring rules are particularly strict for financial institutions, healthcare entities, and providers of critical infrastructure. Finally, the legitimate interest rule allows organizations to process personal data if the processing is essential to the protection of their systems or users. This legal basis is most regularly cited in the context of cybersecurity since organizations have legitimate interests in preventing unauthorized access, data breaches, and cyber-attacks (Al-Momani et al., 2025).

2.3 Security Monitoring Under Legitimate Interest Doctrine

The legitimate interest doctrine has risen to become one of the leading legal bases for AI-based security monitoring. It acknowledges that entities need to be able to guard their systems, properties, and customers against threats. If a company had no monitoring capabilities such as network activity logging, anomaly detection, and behavior analysis, it would be vulnerable to the point of being unable to respond to cyber-attacks effectively. Nonetheless, legitimate interest does not mean that there can be monitoring to the extent that privacy gets infringed. Companies have to do a balance test assessing if their security interests can likely outweigh the possible privacy infringements (R. D. Alabdallat et al., 2025). Generally, this analysis revolves around three key elements: whether the surveillance is necessary, data processing is proportionate and the third is the level of the impact on the individual. To illustrate, the monitoring of network traffic in order to detect malware can be viewed as both, necessary and proportionate because it safeguards the organization and users against cyber threat whereas, monitoring an e-mail of an employee for personal purpose without any justification can be considered as an overreach and hence, illegal. This way of balancing is a method used by regulators to verify that monitoring is not abused and is in line with the principles of justice and responsibility. By making companies explain the purpose of their monitoring activities, regulators, in a roundabout way, encourage the creation of safety mechanisms that not only meet the security goals but also safeguard human Ghazal et al., 2022).

2.4 Consent, Contractual Obligation, and Legal Duty

On the other hand, only consent in the legal basis for processing of personal data may be suitable in certain cases which largely depend on the type of application involved. For example, biometric systems like a facial recognition for physical access control will normally require individuals to have given their explicit consent to the collection and processing of their biometric data before the system is deployed on them. Contractual obligations may also back the use of a method under which people are monitored in some cases. For instance, monitoring of account activities by a financial institution for the purpose of fraud detection may be justified based on the contractual relationship between the bank and its customers. Legal obligations are a further set of basic grounds for security processing(Ahmed et al., 2025). Governments impose the rule that requires organizations to regularly monitor their systems for security threats. A case in point is that banks have been ordered by their regulators to detect suspicious transactions that might suggest money laundering or fraud. Likewise, cybersecurity legislation compels the critical infrastructure operators to equip themselves with monitoring tools that would enable them to spot any illicit entries into their sensitive networks. These various legal grounds indicate the very intricate regulation framework for security technologies that are powered by AI. Each one of them corresponds to a varying level of focus on security versus privacy issues, thereby necessitating a thorough legal examination whenever security systems are being (Maz et al., 2025). The choice of lawful basis should depend on the purpose of processing, sensitivity of the data, level of surveillance, impact on individuals, and existence of regulatory obligations. For example, network anomaly detection may often rely on legitimate interest, while biometric authentication may require explicit consent or another specific legal justification.

2.5 Regulatory Landscape Across Global Jurisdictions

Regulation of AI security processing differs greatly from one country to another. The European Union has been taking a lead in setting the rules for AI and data processing. Besides the GDPR that makes the data processing legally very challenging and also ensures transparency and accountability, the AI Act proposal introduces a regulatory pattern concerned with risk, where AI systems are ranked according to the level of their potential negative impact on humans and the As per the AI Act, the uses of AI that are labeled as high-risk like facial recognition and surveillance have to be closely monitored and controlled, plus companies need to carry out risk management, have their documentation in order, and ensure human supervision of automated decision-making. Things in the US come are less centralized with regulations unevenly distributed among different sectors and different laws (Qaddara & Alraba'nah, 2025). For instance, the Gramm-Leach-Bliley Act regulates the financial industry while the Health Insurance Portability and Accountability Act (HIPAA) is the healthcare law. These regulations are primarily focused on security; however, they provide more flexibility in terms of methods of data Even some of the Asia Pacific countries have privacy and cybersecurity regulations controlling AI security processing, besides Singapore and Japan which have well-established personal data protection frameworks, China is known for its focus on data sovereignty and national security aspects through its cybersecurity laws. The variety of these legal systems makes it very difficult for multi-national corporations to comply with the law. Since AI security systems process data from different countries, organizations have to deal with many (sometimes clashing) laws. Therefore, it is a must that they devise governance tactics that encompass all the legal environments in which they operate(Alnawayseh et al., 2022).

Table 1. Comparison of Legal Grounds for AI Security Processing Across Jurisdictions

Legal Ground	EU GDPR	United States	Asia-Pacific	Typical Security Use Case
Legitimate Interest	Allowed with balancing test	Generally permitted	Allowed in many jurisdictions	Threat detection
Legal Obligation	Strongly recognized	Regulatory compliance	Recognized	Compliance monitoring
Consent	Strict requirements	Flexible	Varies	Biometric authentication
Contractual Necessity	Limited use	Allowed	Allowed	Identity verification
Public Interest	Law enforcement contexts	National security	Government surveillance	Critical infrastructure security

Table 1 displays a brief overview of the principal legal grounds for permitting security-related processing using artificial intelligence in different regulatory territories. It reveals that one and the same security operation may be backed by different legal principles depending on the place where the company is located. The EU's GDPR heavily focuses on the need to substantiate the legitimacy of the data processing and, besides, it also mandates that the legitimate interest legal basis should be checked through a balancing test. On the other hand, the regulatory milieu in the U.S. is more lenient about data processing practices even though primarily it is sectoral laws based and the organizations are required to comply with their obligations under these laws. Hybrid models are not unusual in the Asia-Pacific region, where they combine national cybersecurity objectives with privacy safeguards. Besides, the table indicates examples of typical situations for each legal basis, like threat detection for legitimate interest or biometric identification for consent-based processing. Through these comparisons, the table is designed to assist readers in understanding how different legal frameworks influence the deployment of AI-based security tools around the (Cui et al., 2026).

3. CATEGORIES OF AI SECURITY PROCESSING ACTIVITIES

AI-powered security solutions are being used in a very wide assortment of operational environments like enterprise cybersecurity, physical surveillance systems, etc. They work with a gigantic amount of data including behaviors, biometrics, and context in order to detect abnormalities, predict threats, and carry out security incident responses automatically. As the incorporation of AI-enabled security system functionalities grows, it becomes necessary to distinguish the particular kinds of security processing activities performed by AI. Different AI-driven security processing operations are based on various types of data, perform diverse analyses, and target different objectives. For instance, systems that analyze behavior monitor the sequence of digital operations to identify potential insider threats. On the other hand, biometric verification systems use physical characteristics for person identification. While threat intelligence systems try to anticipate the ways attacks unfold, automated incident response systems repel aggressors without delay (Abualhaj, Al-Khatib, Al-Zyoud, Qaddara, et al., 2025). Likewise, AI-assisted surveillance technologies monitor the physical surroundings to recognize suspicious behaviors or security Since these systems mostly deal with data related to individuals who can be identified, their use is subject to important legal and ethical considerations. Data protection rules require organizations to have a legal basis for collecting and processing of personal or behavioral data. The correct legal basis largely depends on the type of security activity. For instance, some activities may rely on the principle of legitimate interest, while others will require explicit consent or a court order. Therefore, knowing the types of AI security processing is very helpful in understanding how the law fits in. In this section, we discuss several main types of security practices using AI and analyze their roles in the present-day security environment (Khatibi et al., 2025).

3.1 Behavioral Analytics and User Activity Monitoring

Behavioral analytics is the leading AI application in cybersecurity. Behavioral analytics platforms keep track of how users behave digitally and greenlight scenarios where behavior is so abnormal that it spells a threat or account takeovers. Behavior analytics, contrary to the tried and trusted methods of security monitoring by buttoned-up rules, functions by constructing changing depictions of the usual user behavior and raising the flag when those patterns are broken. In most cases, user activity monitoring software record different behavioral signals, like the times logging in, the type of device used, how often an application is opened, the transfer of large quantities of data. Machine learning programs utilize those behavioral traces to create behavioral profiles for users either at an individual level or at a group level. If a user, for some reason, exhibits behavior that is way off the typical behavior established, the system will either produce alert or give the user level of risk (risk score) that suggests a potential security threat (Aldaaja et al., 2025).

Well, imagine an employee who usually only accesses the corporate network during work hours and from a certain location, all of a sudden, this employee tries getting into the sensitive systems at night and using an unknown device. Behavioral analytics systems would be at a loss with such a change of behavior, because it means the person is unintentionally helping a hacker or a malicious insider. If this transaction came up during behavioral monitoring, it would be possible to quickly and efficiently block it in order to keep the perpetrators out or to prevent the leak of valuable information (Babaker et al., 2025). Security-wise, behavioral monitoring is an excellent method for identifying different types of threats, however, it also raises privacy concerns. For instance, constant monitoring of digital activities can reveal to outsider's people's working habits, styles of communication, or even their personal Hence, organizations should fundamentally check their legal basis for these types of monitoring activities and make sure these activities are well balanced with the security risks that are being addressed(Ghazal, Awouda, et al., 2025).

3.2 Biometric Identification and Authentication Systems

Biometric technologies are another class of AI security processing and involve the use of one's physiological or behavioral features for identity verification. Usually, biometrics include images of one's face, fingerprints, iris patterns, a person's voice, and even gait (pattern of walking). AI comes into the picture especially when algorithms have to both analyze those features and match them up with one's biometric template that has been stored previously. Biometrics for authentication are utilized globally in both physical and digital environments. Digitally, fingerprint and face recognition systems hit the mainstream due to their ease of use and security for smartphones, laptops, and online services. Physically speaking, cameras armed with face recognition operate at the entrance of buildings or on the perimeter of areas with limited access. Biometric recognition systems use AI mainly for pattern recognition work(R. Alabdallat et al., 2025). For instance, computer vision methods parse a face and draw out distinguishing features that are then vetted one by one by the help of neural networks (deep learning networks) against a reference dataset to establish if it is one and the same person. Quoting phonetic features, voice recognition systems offer the possibility for user verification over the phone. On the one hand, biometrics can promote ease and robustness of security; on the other, they significantly amplify privacy issues. Biometric identifiers are quite sensitive as they are intimately tied to a person's physical features. Also, unlike passwords, a biometric trait cannot be changed if compromised. For the above reasons, many data protection laws treat biometric data as special category of personal data requiring enhanced protection. Therefore, it is imperative for organizations using biometric authentication systems to have a proper and justified legal basis for processing of biometric data(Vasudevan et al., 2024).

3.3 Predictive Threat Intelligence and Risk Scoring

Predictive threat intelligence software is a very cutting-edge security application of artificial intelligence. By analyzing historical security data alongside threat intelligence feeds, this system is able to identify patterns that may be indicative of new cyber threats. Machine learning techniques are employed to predict potential hacking scenarios. Such a system can perform analysis on threat-related data obtained from a variety of sources including network logs, vulnerability indexes, malware repositories, and threat intelligence feeds both internally and externally provided. With the help of these data sets, machine learning models detect a variety of indicators that are indicative of different phases of the attack lifecycle.

Network traffic patterns, authentication anomalies, and system configuration changes may indicate to us the early stage of a synchronized cyber-attack (Hiari et al., 2025).

Usually, risk scoring is the technique used by threat intelligence systems that attempt to make predictions. What it does is assign a score level to a user, device, or network activity based on how likely it is associated with a malicious act. Analysts working on security can then rely on the risk scores to help them decide which ones to look into. Predictive risk scoring no doubt supports the enhancement of the overall security operations by guiding where an organization's resources should be directed in response to threats (Al-Okbi, Alomari, Hadi, et al., 2025). Nonetheless, the use of automated risk scoring might be a double-edged sword as it could lead to issues with transparency, accountability and fairness. Machine learning models that drive these risk scores tend to be so complex that understanding why a certain user or initiative was deemed as suspicious could be a challenge. In relation to the law, there should always be an endeavor to make automated processes understandable and maintain a high level of accountability. Explainable artificial intelligence is being increasingly expected according to regulatory frameworks, especially where decisions made by automation have a direct impact on people(Vasudevan et al., 2025).

3.4 Automated Incident Response Systems

Automated incident response systems use security measures to a level enhancing semi-autonomous systems. These systems combine AI and security orchestration tools to respond to security threats actively. Once a security incident detection has been made, the system can take a series of predefined defensive actions even without human assistance. For instance, a response could be network connections that are blocked due to being flagged as suspicious, devices physically disconnected from the network, users' passwords reset, and commencement of forensic investigations (Otair et al., 2025). By automating these sorts of operations, the organizations are significantly decreasing the time to gain control over security incidents. A significant advantage of rapid response is that it is very useful in the current cyber-attack scenarios where threats can be spreading throughout a network within a matter of minutes. AI can be highly instrumental in response actions determination to a large extent. Models are able to recognize (based on features) how dangerous a threat has been dissected and also the assessment of different response actions with regards to their potential effect. Decision support systems then select the best option in line with risk assessments and policies. Though with all its advantages exposing to security can't be said that it's over and done with as things go wrong sometimes might have an impact on normal work activities or prevent legitimate users from accessing. That is why hybrid models exist, the ones that recommend but the final decisions are human-made. From a legal standpoint, it is very important that automated decisions do not interfere with services or users' rights and that they comply with due (Sardar et al., 2025).

3.5 Surveillance and Physical Security Monitoring

The wide usage of AI surveillance is primarily for the public at large in spaces like transport hubs and workplaces where enhanced situational awareness is very important to security. Such systems are based on computer vision algorithms that evaluate video feed captured by cameras located in areas that are monitored (Mohammad et al., 2025). Computer vision-based AI models can uncover significantly various types of happenings within the surveillance footage. For instance, the system could identify an individual entering where they should not, detect a bag left behind in a public area, or notice strange behavior that is typical of criminal conduct. Face recognition systems when fitted in this kind of system can help identify individuals who have a criminal record or those who are on the watchlist. There is a trend recently that, real-time analytics are readily available to physical security monitoring systems (Alraba'nah et al., 2025).

AI algorithms are running in the background on video streams continuously and once suspicious behaviors are detected an alert is generated. This can give security guards the opportunity to respond promptly to incidents. Unfortunately, video surveillance raises the most significant legal and ethical issues connected to AI security processing. This is because it can easily capture individuals who are not aware or have not given their consent to being filmed. When integrated with face recognition, this type of monitoring can lead to the mass tracking of individuals' movements in public areas. Therefore, authorities have come out with very strict rules on the use of surveillance. To get away with it, organizations must prove that their surveillance is strictly for legitimate security purposes and adequate privacy protection measures have been implemented (Alkhawatrah, 2025).

Figure 2. Architecture of AI-Driven Security Processing Pipeline

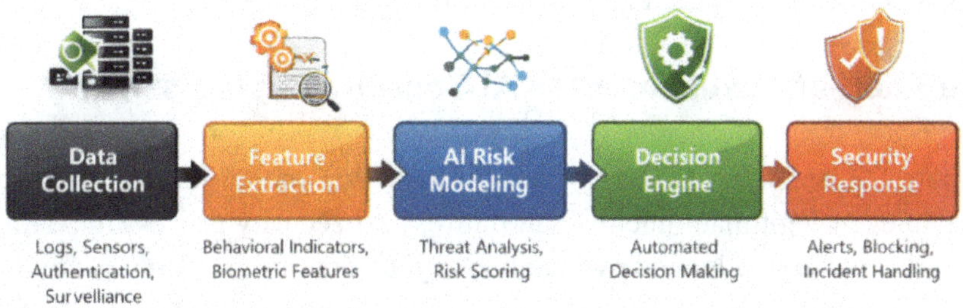

Figure 2 illustrates a sequential process driven by artificial intelligence for the discovery and defense against security risks. Initially, data collection denotes the stage where myriad sources such as network logs, sensors, authentication mechanisms, surveillance apparatus supply security data. Subsequently, during the feature extraction phase, relevant features like behavioral elements, access time patterns, biometric features are identified.

4. DETERMINING LAWFUL BASES FOR SECURITY DATA PROCESSING

Artificial intelligence-enabled security systems require processing a large volume of data in order to identify risks, monitor behaviors, and protect digital networks. Given that these systems usually deal with people's information, one of the main governance challenges is to determine if data processing is legally allowed. Privacy and cybersecurity regulations as of now require that a company have a legal basis before collecting or using personal or behavioral data for security reasons. Without a legally justifiable reason, even the use of technically secure security monitoring systems may result in privacy law violations and legal liabilities for the companies. Therefore, confirming the legal grounds for security processing by means of AI is a legal challenge that companies ought to address with a thorough legal review (Al-znamat et al., 2025). They should examine if the security measure is actually necessary, determine if there are risks to privacy, and verify if the level of monitoring is still proportional to the threats that need to be dealt with. Legislatures are imposing more and more, to the extent that organizations are expected to document their decision-making process prior to deploying AI security tools. Such paperwork includes Legitimate Interest Assessments (LIAs), proportionality analyses, as well as risk versus benefit Al-Adwan et al., 2025).

In principle, these periodic assessments help ensure that security practices will not become excessive or so intrusive as to infringe personal privacy rights. At a minimum, implementation will require contemplating: the purpose of the processing; what kinds of personal data are being collected; and, the possible ramifications/ outcomes for individuals. A systematic questioning process can help one arrive at a decision on the permissibility of the processing on the basis of the recognized legal grounds (Q. Y. Shambour et al., 2025). Determining a legal basis is a matter of deep legal understanding as well as the application of tools for evaluating and measuring their elated risk and impact on privacy. Quantitative methods will show you the effectiveness of a security control that can later be compared with the potential negative impact on privacy. Nonetheless, proprietary or commercial quantitative methods often lack the capability to adequately account for the qualitative factors inherent in a social and ethical context. To cite an example, a Security Processing Legitimacy Score (SPLS) can be utilized for a systematic evaluation of the trade-off between security benefit and privacy (Ibrahim et al., 2024).

4.1 Legitimate Interest Assessment in AI Security Systems

Legitimate Interest Assessment (LIA) is a legal evaluation model that can determine the extent to which the principles of legitimate interest can buttress AI security processing. This is a deep-dive evaluation method that is frequently employed to back cybersecurity measures involving uninterrupted monitoring to uncover threats and secure digital networks. Legitimate Interest Assessment involves the following three main

- First, organizations should clearly define their legitimate interest or the reason that motivates them to use the AI-based security system. A few examples of legitimate interests include: prevention of cyber-attacks, protection of sensitive data, maintenance of system integrity, and defense of users against harmful activities. A security activity should lend itself to a legitimate interest or objective; an arguing against an illegitimate purpose is part of justifying the activity.
- Second, necessity of the processing must be examined that whether the processing (usually involving personal data) is the least privacy-invasive option to achieving the security goal. If there are other non-personal-data-based ways of achieving the goal, then the personal data-based measure must be reconsidered.
- Third, there should be a weighted comparison of one interest with another, i.e., security interests of the organization vs. the potential negative effects on individuals. This assessment will be the balance check that looks at the degree of privacy interference, considering even the data being used, how monitored people expect to be, and the sort of measures one can take to guaranty privacy and the confidentiality of the data.

At its best, the Legitimate Interest Assessment (LIA) leads to responsible deployment of security surveillance techniques based on AI. Actually, besides security needs a consideration of privacy rights shall also be considered which is what this tool is empowering.

4.2 Proportionality and Necessity Tests

Proportionality and necessity tests are yet two very important legal means to judge task processing of AI security. These concepts were first derived from experts in constitutional and human rights law explaining the conditions under which government operations affecting certain rights can be considered justified. Looking at security surveillance using AI, a necessity test means requiring a formal rationale (evidence that the data processing is a must for a specific security aim to be achieved. Take for example network monitoring) it may be necessary to detect viruses and infiltration attempts. Whereas eavesdropping on personal conversations may be dismissed as a totally unneeded step, i.e., illegal. Proportionality checks add to necessity ones, requesting that the scope or extent of the monitoring be strictly limited to what is necessary to accomplish the security objective. Therefore, you collect only the information that is absolutely necessary for carrying out security analysis or reaching security objectives (Al-Okbi, Alomari, Zitar, et al., 2025). This is a very significant way of protecting privacy. For the most part, this is what the law says: follow the necessity principle to the letter, never at any cost derive excess. Proportionality checking is indeed a complicated matter and frequently involves looking through multiple These include very simply - how sensitive the information is, what the attitude is towards processing it, how long it is stored, level of automation, potentials for violation of privacy rights. Seriously taken and all dimensions studied, an organization might be able to think that even after the security measure is imposed, it is still reasonable to respond to the risk level. The use of these principles not only prevents putting AI surveillance tools into secondary purposes but also give rise to right-designed ones: a balance between privacy and security. The final most well engineered security system might be not only protecting the one who is threatening the security but also respecting the privacy of (Al-Dmour et al., 2025).

4.3 Balancing Organizational Security and Individual Privacy

What should we do if the security requirements of an organization conflict with the privacy rights of individuals? In a way, this is a dilemma especially in AI security governance. However, the fact is that the organizations will have to protect themselves against cyber threats, insider attacks, unauthorized access, etc. But, individuals too can and should have their personal data not overly monitored or used in a way that totally disrespects their privacy (Hanandeh et al., 2025). Getting this extremely fine balance is not a lucky accident but a product of ongoing and intensive discussions at the operational and ethical levels. For instance, privacy aspects should be given great importance when creating security monitoring systems. Nowadays, this is one of the main ways how people refer to "privacy by design": the concept that privacy should be considered, if not the main basis, when going through the design of technological infrastructures (Ghazal, 2025b). Quite a number of tools compliant with privacy by design can be listed here, including data minimization, anonymization and purpose limitation that are enough for this paper. Data minimization refers to making sure that only data/information which is directly necessary for security analytics is collected. Anonymization is a technique whereby one removes or at least drastically limits personal identifiers in data. Purpose limitation is essentially the idea that data obtained from a security monitoring system must only be utilized for security monitoring objectives and should not be diverted for other uses (like employee performance tracking or marketing analytics). Also, besides all these points, the management of the trade-off between the two is largely reliant on the transparency of organizational governance. This means that security teams, legal departments, and privacy officers should work together on their different sides in order to guarantee that monitoring practices are not only compliant but also ethically sound and up to the standards of society. Setting up specific rules and control systems plays a very important role in supporting the responsible use of AI security (Abualhaj, Al-Khatib, Abu-Shareha, Almomani, et al., 2025).

4.4 Transparency and Notification Requirements

One way individuals can be sure that their personal data is not misused is through transparency in AI security data processing. An important part of implementing AI security systems is to give a notice about the data collection and monitoring practices to the people whose data is being This may be done through privacy notices that lay out: kinds of data that are gathered, how such data is used for the purpose of security, and data retention periods. Through transparency build relationships of trust between the organization (data processor) and the individual (data subject). Depending on the type of monitoring performed, different forms of notification may be appropriate. For instance, places of employment might put up signs indicating that general network surfing may be subject to monitoring as a security precaution (Iskandarani, 2025). In outdoor or public venues where surveillance cameras are installed, there is also likely a requirement to have clear signage informing people that monitoring is occurring. Furthermore, transparency is not only about physical and manual ways of monitoring. A growing part of security monitoring now involves algorithmic decision-making using AI. If AI is used to produce risk scores or execute security actions, the output must be explainable to users in terms that highlight the major considerations. Besides, by giving individuals the power of explanation, there is a level of accountability and fairness introduced in such automated decision-making (Almomani et al., 2025).

4.5 Accountability and Documentation Obligations

Accountability is one more factor without which AI security processing alone cannot be lawful. Regulators and lawmakers are interested in whether or not an organization's monitoring activities do comply with laws, ethical principles, and public expectations. Documentation is a way to depict one's AI system's operation and its alignment with applicable laws. The documentation may range from keeping a log of data processing activities to preparing and presenting data protection impact assessments, including the legal basis used for security monitoring. Documentation enables regulatory bodies and auditors to ascertain that the organization implements the needed security measures when using AI-based monitoring systems (Al-Habashneh et al., 2025). Moreover, in numerous territories, it is not rare that the release of potentially high-risk AI technologies may require a risk assessment first. The assessment identifies any effects on individuals and new measures to mitigate the identified risks. Such documentation serves as evidence that the organization has made diligent effort to make use of AI technologies responsibly. In order to assist structured decision-making, organizations may resort to quantitative support tools/models designed to establish the legitimacy of security processing activities. Taking one such example—the Security Processing Legitimacy Score (SPLS) model, which assesses whether security monitoring advantages outweigh the related privacy issue.

The following interpretation of SPLS might be helpful:

SPLS = (Risk Reduction × Security Necessity) / Privacy Impact

Where Risk Reduction means the extent to which the monitoring system successfully reduces the risk of security breaches. Security Necessity reflects how indispensably the monitoring activity is needed in keeping the system and users secure. Privacy Impact measures the extent to which the monitoring event affects the most basic privacy rights of the people involved. Big SPLS numbers indicate that the benefits of a security boost in a significant way overshadow the breach of privacy. This is also in harmony with the legal and ethical reasons that allow the monitoring event. On the other hand, if the SPLS score is low, it should make one think of re-evaluating either the practice or the safeguards, or even both, as well as the possible alternatives that may be Such numerical as well as narrative methods still have their respective roles in the process of legal evaluation. Each one has its own pluses and, in an ideal situation, the weaknesses of one are made up by the pluses of the other. Qualitative legal scrutiny together with quantitative measurement tools significantly support companies in finding the right balance between an effective defense against risks and compliance with privacy

5. QUANTITATIVE EVALUATION

Artificial intelligence has very quickly become a part of cybersecurity, creating new situations where compliance with regulations and legal risk management become difficult. Security systems with AI analyze a huge amount of human and biometric as well as operational data to detect possible threats and secure digital assets. Although such systems help detect threats and respond to incidents more efficiently, they expose the users to complex legal issues such as personal data protection, monitoring system compliance, and the legality of processes for automated decision-making. While lawyers mainly rely on qualitative methods to apprehend compliance, the complexity of AI security tools requires them to use legal risk quantification methods. The use of quantitative models can help businesses systematically find out how different AI security measures intersect with the corresponding regulations (Sharma, Al-Rashed, et al., 2025). By quantifying privacy risk, level of surveillance, and degree of regulatory compliance a good estimate can be made concerning the degree of legal compliance of security-related processing activities.

5.1 Dataset Description and Variables

The original source of our dataset comes from the Kaggle AI Governance and Compliance Dataset that provides a detailed list of AI sessions in situations of rule-making. This dataset bundles a variety of factors that depict the operational features of AI-based solutions as well as the regulatory factors that are derived from their use. An important feature of this dataset is the designation of the AI application type which essentially points to a particular security solution under study. For instance, you can have a network anomaly detector, fingerprint identification device, behavioral analysis tool, automatic threat recognition system, and surveillance footage analyzer. Each of these will interact with different data elements and in consequence, will have unique regulatory implications. Moreover, the regulatory risk level which is another variable of considerable importance reveals the prospective amount of legal exposure the application might have. The risk levels may be simply categorized as low, medium, and high based on the sensitivity of the data processed and the levels of surveillance put in place. To illustrate, network anomaly detectors primarily examine data traffic patterns and hence, will typically be representative of lower regulatory risk, whereas facial biometrics, by virtue of dealing with personal sensitive data, will have a higher risk level.

The dataset at hand furthermore informs whether the implementation of AI security processing must be preceded by obtaining user consent or not. For situations that are based on biometrics or are very closely monitoring, by the regulations on data protection, one will need to have explicit user consent. Other forms of technology such as monitoring of network security, may be assumed to be covered by the legitimate interest without the necessity of giving the consent. In order to fully cover both the operational and privacy aspects in AI security, two more variables are brought in. One is the security effectiveness score which shows the capability of a system to detect threats (Jaradat et al., 2025). The higher the score, the more effective it is in detecting threats. The privacy risk index indicates the extent to which an individual's privacy can be compromised due to monitoring. Higher privacy risk scores mean potential increase in privacy intrusion. Together these measures illustrate the coexistence of security performance and regulatory risk. The exploration of these relationships can result in predictive models for compliance in different AI security technological

5.2 Modeling Legal Risk Exposure

Determining legal risk exposure entails traits of AI security functionalities that have an effect on the chances of incurring regulatory attention or engaging in non-compliant behaviors. Legal risk is of concern whenever a system uses personal data in ways that are potentially at odds with privacy rules, surveillance restrictions, or duties to disclose. Many factors will affect legal risk exposure in AI security solutions, for example, systems utilizing extremely sensitive data, such as biometric features or detailed behavioral profiles, tend to be under regulatory oversight more intensely. Besides that, the continuous monitoring of individuals or environments would oftentimes necessitate meeting transparency and proportionality requirements. Thanks to quantifying, these risk elements can be numerically signified and systematic analysis achieved. Variables contained in the corpus each add up to the entire legal risk identity of the security application. For example, an extremely high combination of regulatory risk and privacy risk will usually show that there is a significant potential for legal issues. Whereas those with a negligible privacy impact and a well-functioning explanation have a correspondingly lower legal risk. By examining the data statistics, we can find out that various security models interact with different legal frameworks in quite different ways; anomaly detection is a good case in point, this concept is generally linked with lower privacy risks because it mostly involves analyzing communication data as opposed to personal identifiers. Therefore, such systems are probably going to have a lower legal risk profile as compared to surveillance tools. On the other hand, biometrics is a completely different matter because of the very personal nature of this type of data. Laws about biometric data processing are strict and require the obtaining of user consent, implementation of data protection measures, and maintaining records of the processing. Non-compliance may lead to heavy fines. Mathematical risk modeling's of legal exposures help in identifying those technologies which must be supplemented with extra protective features or legal reasons before rolling It is a method of risk mitigation management that prevents facing severe legal (Abualhaj, Abu-Shareha, & Rateb, 2025).

5.3 Compliance Probability Modeling

Another aspect of regulatory consideration of AI security implementation could be to gauge the likelihood of obtaining approval under the relevant legal code. Compliance probability assessment will reveal the effect of various governance elements on the lawful aspect of data processing. A form of Legal Compliance Probability (LCP) estimation may be employed to check if three important compliance criteria are being met by the AI security tool: regulatory conformity, making things clear to the public, and carrying out measures to ensure safety. Regulatory conformity assesses to what extent the system operations are in keeping with the legal stipulations. Public disclosure checks if individuals receive adequate notification about the practice of monitoring. Safety measures refer to the array of technical and organizational ways that uphold data protection.

Now, you will be able to communicate the Legal Compliance Probability with this expression:

LCP = (Regulatory Alignment + Transparency + Safeguards) / 3

Each factor is usually measured using a uniform scale from 0 to 1. When LCP is high, it indicates that a system is more likely to be in line with regulatory norms; whereas, a low level of score would be a sign that governance measures are in need of By using a fairly good LCP scoring system, a series of AI defensive mechanisms resulting in compliance with the law were distinguished from case scenarios where transparency was not considered or safeguards did not meet required levels. It is logical that the latter would have lower LCP scores indicating a higher legal risk and therefore the organizations must either make changes to the design or add compliance measures. Compliance probability modeling depicts legal aspects as part of the technical assessment of the system. Through the conversion of compliance to a numerical figure, companies can make a safe decision on whether to proceed with or maybe, delay the implementation of AI security The SPLS and LCP models are intended as decision-support tools rather than substitutes for legal judgment. Their purpose is to structure the assessment of security benefit, privacy impact, transparency, safeguards, and regulatory alignment in a consistent and comparable manner.

5.4 Regulatory Sensitivity Analysis

Regulatory sensitivity analysis is a technique to reveal changes in legal risk scenarios in response to the variation of the main factors for AI security. Especially, it shows how regulatory different environments may affect the release of a security product. By examining privacy risk levels, surveillance activities, and consent requirements, sensitivity analysis strives to quantify how much each of these factors would contribute to the overall likelihood of compliance. For instance, if the level of surveillance is increased, this will raise the privacy risk score which means that the regulatory authorities will pay more Similarly, when there is no provision for obtaining explicit consent, it can reduce the level of compliance for systems that rely on processing sensitive information. At the level of worldwide security, regulatory sensitivity related work is inevitable because each jurisdiction differs in the requirements of laws. A product that meets the legal requirements of one region could still be considered non-compliant in another region. Biometrics in particular, might be legally used in one framework but prohibited in another. Exploring sensitivity with analysis enables organizations to work out potential legal risk in function of different governance methods. With the ability to shift transparency, consent, and privacy parameters, organizations are then able to identify the steering factors that have an impact on compliance. The introduction of this methodology assists organizations in tailoring their production of AI security appliances to fulfill compliance not just in one, but in multiple jurisdictions, at the same time. This also empowers management with data-driven insights about the impact of governance policies on legal risk.

Table 2. Sample Dataset Extract Used in Legal Risk Analysis

AI Security Application	Regulatory Risk Level	Consent Required	Security Effectiveness Score	Privacy Risk Index
Network anomaly detection	Low	No	0.88	0.30
Biometric facial recognition	High	Yes	0.92	0.75
Insider behavior analytics	Medium	No	0.86	0.55
Automated threat scoring	Medium	No	0.83	0.48
Video surveillance analytics	High	Conditional	0.90	0.72

The sample presented in Table 2 reflects the dataset utilized to assess legal risk exposure issues during AI security processing operations. The table clarifies how different categories of security technologies correspond in terms of regulatory exposure, consent necessity, the performance of security evenness, and privacy impact. By contrast, a network anomaly detecting system is much less intrusive in terms of privacy as they predominantly monitor network traffic rather than the personal identifiers of individuals. However, facial recognition systems and analytics of visual surveillance both belong to the high privacy-demanding category due mainly to their dependency on biometric and visual data.

6. GOVERNANCE MODELS

AI technologies are drastically changing security systems to a level never seen before. Those implementing AI and other breakthrough tech need to set up controls that will guarantee they use these innovations in a legal, ethical and open manner. Privacy-related worries, safeguarding personal data, and security are the main issues regulated which also get mixed up with using AI-based security and surveillance systems. Indeed, frameworks that govern AI security processing extend further, as they allow management and oversight not only of legal risks but also of operational effectiveness and ethical aspects. Most often, these governance frameworks integrate legal compliance, institutional monitoring, and technical measures into a single working The main purpose is to develop a healthy working environment for AI security systems that also comply with legal rules on data processing and surveillance. Superb detailed governance models will not only rely on regulatory controls but will include different types of controls. Typically, the frameworks of the law will be the major influencers of the legal boundaries within which security processing can be carried (Abualhaj, Abu-Shareha, Al-Khatib, et al., 2025). Organizational governance structures will be responsible for interpreting the laws and notifying departments of the resulting policies and procedures. AI security systems will be the ones to execute these policies through technical controls and monitoring instruments. In the same way, compliance monitoring will be checking the conformity of the systems to the rules of governance. This chapter highlights the governance models that are used by various organizations to ensure the lawfulness of AI security processing. It also discusses how these models promote transparency, accountability, and compliance with regulations.

6.1 Privacy by Design in Security Architectures

Privacy by Design is changing the way we think about privacy and security governance. It is a concept that advocates for privacy to be a core part of any technological system rather than a mere feature. Privacy by Design is especially important for AI security systems because it promises a good balance between privacy and security. Simply put, a Privacy by Design feature is a security system that by its very nature limits someone's possibility to violate the privacy of others. In this aspect, the methods used in data minimization ensure that only the data that is strictly necessary for security purpose is collected and processed. For instance, a network anomaly detection system may analyze traffic patterns without storing identifiable user information whenever possible. A further example is to pseudonymize or anonymize personal data. When an AI security system gets behavioral or user activity data that is potentially personally identifiable, it may be converted to a level of anonymity by, for example reducing granularity or removing a name so that it is very unlikely that the individual could be recognized from it (Qawasmeh et al., 2025). Apart from technological measures, Privacy by Design principles see light of the day when agencies make transparency a priority. Along with the deployment of security monitoring systems, organizations should be able to provide constantly ready explanations to the public and the other stakeholders as to the nature of the data collected, their processing and retention times. Organizations opting for a Privacy by Design approach are making a wise decision in terms of risk reduction for legal liabilities associated with AI-enabled surveillance.

6.2 AI Governance Boards and Oversight Mechanisms

Governments and regulatory authorities have been emphasizing the importance of establishing governance mechanisms for AI; organizations are responding differently. Some organizations have also raised awareness about AI governance in their internal teams and management through forums and workshops. What is common among companies practicing AI governance is that they form a team or board whose responsibility is to oversee the deployment, implementation, and monitoring of AI systems throughout the company. A group that brings together different perspectives and expertise across legal, compliance, data protection, cybersecurity, and top management levels can greatly help in addressing the complex issues posed by AI technologies. Besides strategic decisions and risk evaluations at this governance level, it can be the place where ethical and social considerations regarding AI are brought up (Laha et al., 2025). Transparency and accountability are two accountability mechanisms by which governance boards may function. A governance board may, for example, be a decision-making or recommendatory body on issues such as policy, workflow, rules to be followed, standards, etc. Furthermore, governance boards are often registered in the organization's document showing that at a time that they will be carrying out reviews or audits, they will be able to show the organization that it met the criteria according to the governance. Another important aspect of governing AI is the quick adaptation of the governance policies with the regulatory changes and track the implementation of these policies (Samanta et al., 2025).

6.3 Security Data Minimization Strategies

The best way to curb the misuse of AI security processing and the related privacy invasion is to limit the processing of personal data. In other words, data minimization is a strategy that seeks to limit the collection and processing of personal data in the least way possible while still meeting the goal or purpose of the security processing. Data minimization practices in AI security systems can be applied at various points in the processing loop. For instance, at the data collection point, monitoring operations can be made narrower by only covering the most relevant security indicators instead of general user activities. To illustrate this, imagine that a system aimed at detecting unauthorized access to networks would solely rely on observations of network traffic metadata rather than that of actual communication. Machine learning models can also be restricted to training on only those features that maximize the model creativity while minimizing the amount of data being collected. This in effect means that the use of features or variables that have a high degree of predictive power are kept and the rest are discarded so as to reduce the processing of personal data by AI systems. Security event logs and monitoring data can be stored only for the time needed to carry out threat detection and incident investigations. After that, the data can be securely deleted or it can be anonymized in such a way that it ceases to be a threat to the privacy of the individuals in any form. By practicing data minimization, companies not only stay on the right side of the law but also protect themselves from the possibly heavy consequences of legal liabilities accompanying data (Ghazal, Hasan, Hussein, et al., 2025).

6.4 Accountability and Auditability in AI Systems

Accountability and auditability are the two main pillars that support the global governance framework for One of the things regulators want is that businesses using AI ensure that their products are doing the right thing legally and ethically. Besides that, keeping track of exactly how a system works and makes decisions is one of the compliance requirements. For example, if an AI system decides to deny someone's access based only on an automated decision then the question arises as to who is the person responsible for such a system and on what basis the decision was made. To make this happen, an organizational accountability mechanism must be put in place so as to identify who should be responsible for an AI system's behavior. Logs and records generated by AI security systems are a very rich trail of data that reveal how AI systems operate (Ghazal, Hasan, Raju, et al., 2025). Such documentation allows one to not only check the correctness or decision-making abilities of AI security systems but also to recognize certain issues that may come up as a result of a particular security decision. Having done the inspection of how AI systems are run is a very necessary part of compliance checking. Inspections done by the organization internally are a means to discover weaknesses in governance mechanisms so that the regulator does not find them already whereas regulators conducting inspections deliver additional control and assurance that AI technologies are being used in a responsible manner. With the help of ensuring accountability and auditability, governance frameworks for AI technologies can be considered as reliable and able to fulfill changing regulatory (Eke et al., 2025).

6.5 Cross-Border Data Processing Challenges

Some businesses operate security systems that protect multiple locations over a large geographic area simultaneously. Cloud-based security analytics platforms generally manage data from security systems that are located in various countries. These kinds of arrangements, while enabling the central detection of threats and the rapid response to incidents, at the same time pose complex legal problems with regard to cross-border data Data protection regulations often restrict the transfer of personal data to other countries. These limitations are intended to guarantee that personal data is suitably protected no matter where it is processed. For instance, some legislation requires companies to put in place contractual provisions or carry out risk assessments before sending data to foreign territories. Performing security processing across borders is especially difficult when AI systems deal with behavioral or biometric data from different countries. The legal rules that govern such processing can be very different from one jurisdiction to another (Hakami et al., 2025). For example, a surveillance technology that is allowed in one country may be subject to very strict restrictions in another country. To deal with these problems, companies usually put in place governance arrangements that control how data is moved across borders. These arrangements may consist of regional data processing centers, contractual agreements between international subsidiaries, and very strict access control policies that regulate cross-border data access. Managing cross-border AI security processing through governance that is effective entails a tight partnership between legal professionals, cybersecurity teams, and organizational heads. By carefully handling international data transfers, companies will be able to continue their global security operations effectively while at the same time complying with various sets of

Table 3. Governance Mechanisms Supporting Lawful AI Security Processing

Governance Mechanism	Primary Purpose	Implementation Approach	Compliance Benefit
Privacy by Design	Integrate privacy protections into system architecture	Data minimization, pseudonymization, secure data pipelines	Reduces privacy risk and regulatory exposure
AI Governance Board	Provide oversight for AI deployments	Cross-functional review committees and risk assessments	Ensures policy alignment and regulatory compliance
Data Minimization Policies	Limit the amount of personal data processed	Feature selection, reduced monitoring scope, limited retention	Minimizes unnecessary surveillance
Accountability Framework	Assign responsibility for AI system behavior	Documentation, decision logs, responsible personnel	Enables traceability and legal accountability
Compliance Auditing	Monitor adherence to governance policies	Internal and external audits of AI security systems	Detects compliance violations early

Table 3 summarizes roughly the major governance mechanisms through which organizations ensure that their AI-driven security processing remains lawful. Each governance mechanism serves a specific aspect of fulfilling regulatory requirements and risk management. Privacy by Design means incorporating privacy measures within the technical design of security systems. AI governance boards on one hand give a formal oversight, on the other hand ensure that AI systems comply with organizational and legal standard. Data minimization methods reduce the risk of privacy breaches by restricting the amount of personal data handled by security systems. Accountability frameworks identify who is liable for the decisions made by systems, therefore allowing organizations to clarify and support automated security measures. At last, compliance auditing involves regular checking of the governance performance and the uncovering of possible compliance violations before they become issues with regulators. Generally, these governance tools lay down a far-reaching model for the consistent, legally compliant, and ethical use of AI in security

Figure 3. AI Security Governance and Legal Compliance Model

Figure 3 is currently being prepared and will depict a hierarchical chain of governance that authorizes AI security processing at different levels. Initially, supervisory authorities establish the legal norms for safeguarding data privacy, controlling surveillance, and managing the use of AI. Essentially, these laws lay the foundation for the governance at the organization level, which develops the intricate guidelines and controls for the operations. AI security platforms, including monitoring instruments, methods for detecting threats, and means of automatic response, are the ones who enforce the policies' implementation. Finally, compliance checking, by measuring the system's results, guarantees that all processing is coherent with the legal framework set up by laws and regulations. This governance layering model maintains legal compliance as a natural part of the operational cycle of AI security

7. EMPIRICAL EVALUATION OF LEGAL JUSTIFICATION MODELS IN AI SECURITY

We open the dataset of Kaggle AI Governance and Compliance competition and analyze the different legal bases that companies can use when they deploy AI security technologies such as behavioral analytics, biometric authentication, threat detection, and automated monitoring systems. The main objective is to understand how the legal bases for the processing of security-related data vary from one security technology to another and how these legal bases are linked with privacy risks, levels of surveillance, and operational security effectiveness. The paper, by analyzing these relationships on the data, demonstrates how organizations interpret the law to carry on with security monitoring that is effective. The study reveals that legal justification decisions are almost never purely legal or technical; on the contrary, they reflect a combination of security needs, privacy impact, and regulatory (Q. Shambour et al., 2025).

7.1 Dataset-Based Analysis of Legal Grounds

This empirical evaluation takes a dataset as a reference that comprises examples of AI security implementations in different sectors such as enterprise IT infrastructure, physical surveillance, and user identity authentication. Each record is about an AI security processing action and specifies the legal ground for the processing, the level of surveillance, the classification of regulatory risk, and the scores of security effectiveness outcomes. At first, the purpose was to figure out how much various legal grounds are used in AI security systems. This portrayal helps to understand the primary legal justification models that organizations reliant on AI-based monitoring have opted

Figure 4. Legal Ground Distribution in AI Security Processing

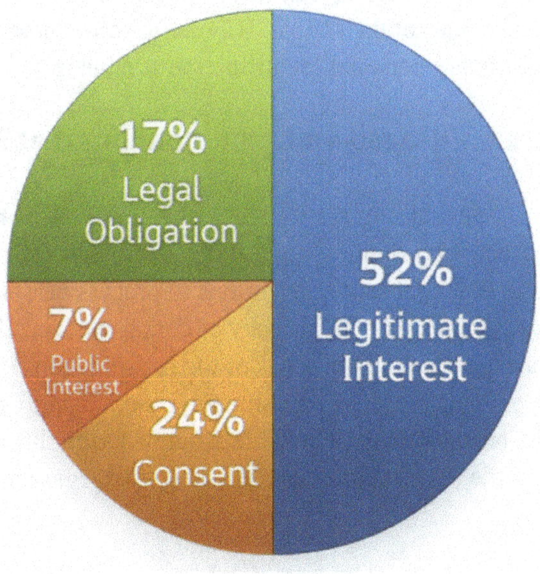

Illustratively, a pie chart shows the distribution of different legal bases for the processing of AI security data. According to the data, legitimate interest seems to be the primary legal reason for the use of AI security in nearly 52% of situations. The consent slice accounts for 24%, while the legal obligation portion stands at 17%. The remaining parts are divided between public interest and supervisory This pattern closely corresponds to the real-life operations of cybersecurity systems. Security monitoring is characteristically continuous and automatic, so explicit user consent may not be attainable at the time and place of operation. Hence, organizations often rely on the legitimate interest rule (which) permits data processing if it is necessary for securing the organization's assets, detecting fraud or cybersecurity threats. The dataset reveals that consent is mostly given in situations where biometric verification systems such as facial recognition and fingerprint scanning are involved. Since such operations deal directly with biometric identifiers of a person, they necessitate the user's consent or else have to meet some other legal requirements. Table 4 illustrates how legal grounds are distributed in major AI security application categories.

Table 4. Distribution of Legal Grounds Across AI Security Applications

AI Security Application	Legitimate Interest (%)	Consent (%)	Legal Obligation (%)	Public Interest (%)
Network anomaly detection	68	4	20	8
Insider behavior analytics	63	6	24	7
Biometric authentication	15	71	6	8
Video surveillance analytics	44	12	29	15
Automated threat intelligence	61	8	23	8

The Table 4 makes it clear that the technology behind the AI security system determines the selection of legal justification. Systems designed to monitor the organizational behavior of people will rely greatly on legitimate interest since they are aimed at detecting unusual patterns in the activity of the system rather collecting the identity attributes of the people. Biometric authentication, on the other hand, relies more on consent because it uses very personal identification attributes.

7.2 Comparison of Consent-Based vs Legitimate Interest Processing

While this method protects personal information very effectively, it could cause difficulties for security monitoring systems that need running continuous, live analyses. Processing based on the legitimate interest of a data controller enables organizations to process personal data without the consent of individuals, if, on balance, the impact on the privacy of data subjects is limited and the processing is necessary to achieve legitimate operational purposes of the organization. But, this method also obliges organizations to carry out Legitimate Interest Assessments (LIAs) to confirm that the processing aspect does not overpower the rights of individuals. The table 5 below highlights the major points in terms of operational factors taken from the dataset and related to these two legal models.

Table 5. Operational Comparison of Consent-Based and Legitimate Interest Security Processing

Evaluation Factor	Consent-Based Processing	Legitimate Interest Processing
Deployment complexity	High	Medium
Real-time monitoring capability	Limited	High
Privacy protection strength	Very High	Moderate
Regulatory documentation requirement	High	Medium
Scalability for enterprise monitoring	Limited	High

Insightful examination shows that legitimate interest processing permits organizations to be capable of handling large-scale security monitoring in a more efficient way. Consent-based processing is much more limiting since people have to give their direct consent for monitoring to take place. Obtaining consent from every monitored person in such communities as enterprise networks or public infrastructures may not even be practicable. Nonetheless, even legitimate interest processing needs to be safeguarded appropriately. Organizations are the ones accountable for proving that monitoring is not only necessary and proportionate but also transparent, as this is a major part of it. Non-compliance with these safeguards will, in all probability, lead to regulatory authorities and privacy advocates raising doubts about the

7.3 Privacy Risk vs Security Effectiveness Tradeoff

Privacy and security are the two facets that complete each other in terms of AI security governance. A vivid example would be high-surveillance monitoring systems whereby on one hand, they help in tracking threats very effectively; on the contrary, using them to do intrusive surveillance or to misuse personal ones can also be thought of as the other side of the coin. To shed more light on the conflict, the dataset looked at the relationship between privacy risk indices and security effectiveness scores of different AI security

Figure 5. Security Effectiveness vs Privacy Risk Distribution

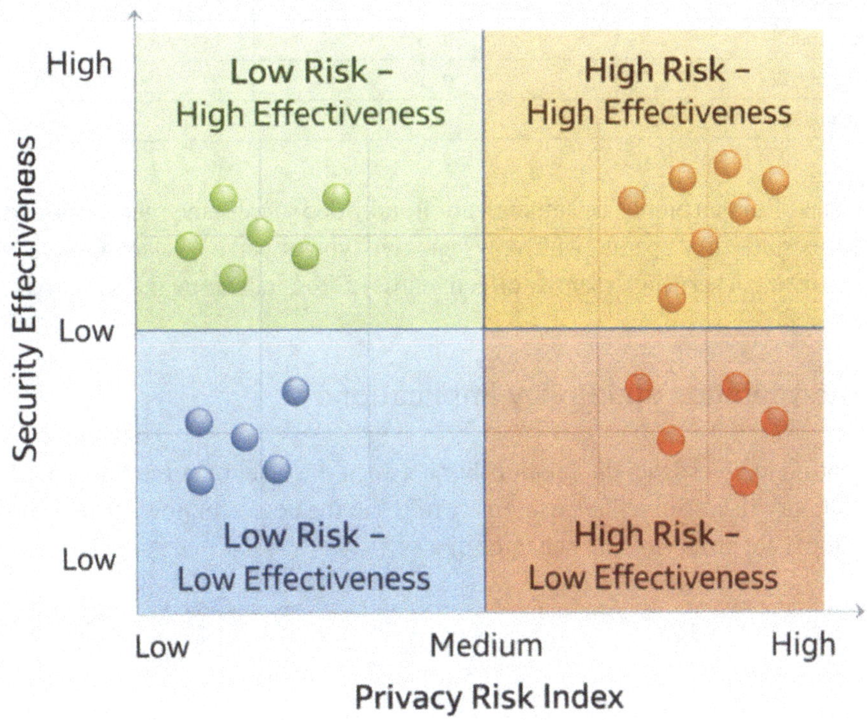

Through a scatter plot, a visual depiction of how privacy risk correlates with security effectiveness is provided. Each quadrant in the four-quadrants plot represents a distinct operational:

- **Low risk – high effectiveness:** These security systems manage to provide significant security benefits with minimal intrusion into privacy.

- **High risk – high effectiveness:** These security systems are not only very effective but also raise significant privacy concerns.
- **Low risk – low effectiveness:** Security technologies that pose minimum privacy risks but bring in very limited security benefits.
- **High risk – low effectiveness:** Security systems that create the highest privacy risks and at the same time offer the least security benefits.

Both biometric authentication and video surveillance analytics are seen as the highest privacy risk due to the very nature of the personal data being used. However, these technologies still get relatively high effectiveness ratings, hence the privacy/security tradeoff. Table 6 gives a summary of the average scores for privacy risk and effectiveness of different AI security

Table 6. Average Privacy Risk and Security Effectiveness by AI Security Application

AI Security Application	Average Privacy Risk Index	Average Security Effectiveness
Network anomaly detection	0.31	0.88
Insider behavior analytics	0.55	0.86
Biometric authentication	0.76	0.91
Video surveillance analytics	0.71	0.89
Automated threat intelligence	0.42	0.83

The table makes clear that biometric authentication and video surveillance analytics lead to the highest privacy risk scores since they operate with very sensitive type of personal data. On the contrary, these technologies also result in very high security effectiveness scores, indicating the paradoxical relationship between privacy and

7.4 Model Interpretation and Policy Implications

The data went on to investigate the relationship between the level of surveillance and the degree of exposure to regulatory risks. Surveillance intensity refers to the degree of how closely and continuously the monitoring tools are observing the behavior of a

Figure 6. Tradeoff Curve Between Surveillance Intensity and Regulatory Risk

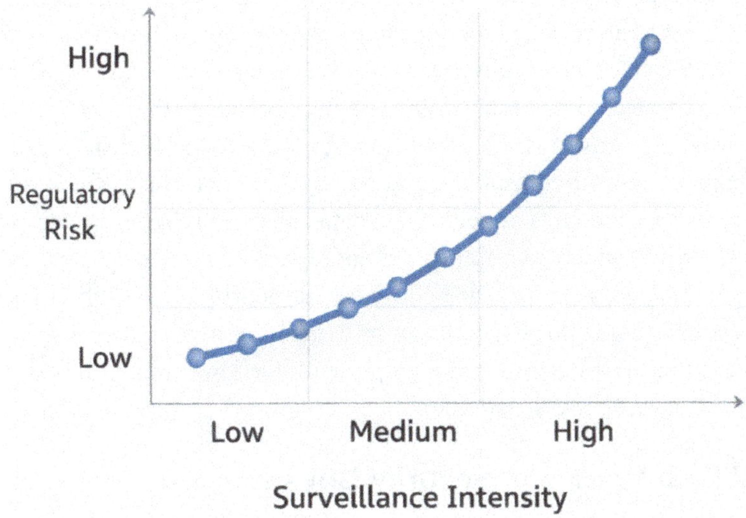

From the figure 5, it is evident that the line prediction is rising, which means that regulation risk is positively correlated with surveillance intensity. For instance, network anomaly detection, which is a low-intensity monitoring method, usually leads to a low regulatory risk because it is mainly based on the analysis of system-level behavioral patterns and less on tracking individual users. On the other hand, highly intensive monitoring techniques such as continuous biometric tracking or behavior profiling are very much at risk of regulation because they involve the handling of sensitive personal data and are therefore under stronger control by regulators. Policy wise, this is a very important study with a lot of potential to impact how regulations are shaped. Firstly, the legal justification chosen should be capable of explaining the nature and level of surveillance activity. For instance, the legitimate interest might be enough for moderate surveillance while it is quite possible that it would be not adequate even with added safeguards for high personal data processing level surveillance. Secondly, for legal processing of AI security data, transparency, and governance measures are equally a must. Keeping an operation log of monitoring systems, clearly specifying types of processed data, and showing ways of complying with privacy rights are some necessary elements of transparency.

Finally, following the study, there is no doubt that the highest level of privacy respecting security architectures is a call to the industry. The implementation of privacy-preserving techniques such as data minimization, pseudonymization, and differential privacy measures can be a good way of sacrificing less privacy while the surveillance system attaining a high level of threat detection. Ultimately, the legal justification models are important tools of AI security governance just like the findings have revealed empirically. The choice of legal basis is a decision that comes with a lot of weight as it not only influences the very environment in which monitoring systems are designed, but also the processing of data and the assurance of compliance with ever-changing regulations by organizations, among other things. By combining empirical research with legal interpretation to examine the legal aspects of AI security processing in today's digital infrastructures this paper takes the field quite a few steps

8. FUTURE LEGAL CHALLENGES AND POLICY DIRECTIONS

Artificial intelligence is playing a major role in designing future cybersecurity Different industries are adopting AI-based systems to do various functions like detecting anomalies, tracking behavior, forecasting potential threats, and even executing responses without human intervention. Although significantly enhance the capacity to locate and neutralize attackers in cyberspace, these tools also bring up various law and administrative issues. Existing laws on data protection and cybersecurity were mainly formulated for conventional data processing circumstances and did not foresee the use of autonomous systems that are capable of analyzing large amounts of behavioral data and making security decisions on the fly. The legal frameworks worldwide, which so far have not addressed such matters, are gradually recognizing the challenges brought about by increased use of AI-based security tools such as issues of algorithmic accountability, transparency, and ethical use. It can be expected that new laws will be focused on ensuring that AI systems used in the security sector comply with the law while also respecting fundamental human rights such as privacy, fairness, and due

8.1 Emerging AI Regulation and Security Governance

The European Union's Artificial Intelligence Act is one of the most substantial legislative instruments that is in the process of establishment to regulate AI technologies on a more or less uniform basis. The regulation sets forth a risk-based classification system, whereby AI systems are divided into classes based on the degree of their influence on people and society. Typical examples of security-related AI systems, such as those for biometric identification, predictive policing, and large-scale behavioral monitoring, are generally considered as high-risk AI systems and are therefore subjected to rigorous obligations concerning documentation, transparency, human intervention, and risk management. For AI security systems implemented in corporate settings, the AI Act lays down a number of governance duties (Sharma, Hussain, et al., 2025). The organizations need to ensure that the AI models are trained on adequate and correct data, regular checks on the systems' outputs for errors and biases should be done, and the human factor must be involved at all time so that if the automated decisions are harmful, the human can step in and change the course of the action. Those governance requirements are intended to ensure that the AI systems remain ethically accountable and governed even when they are functioning independently. Besides EU, there are other countries which are also involved in the work of coming up with AI regulatory regimes. The United States has introduced the AI Risk Management Framework of the National Institute of Standards and Technology (NIST) that defines working principles when it comes to addressing the reliability, safety, and fairness of AI systems. Similarly, a number of the Asia-Pacific countries adopt AI governance principles which reflect the ethical use, responsible innovation, and transparency in automated making.

8.2 Algorithmic Accountability Requirements

Among the legal concerns raised by AI security systems, the issue of algorithmic accountability is probably the biggest one. When AI models are used to analyze behavioral data and make security decisions independently, it is very difficult to determine who, in the end, should be held responsible for such decisions. The algorithmic accountability procedures put a responsibility on companies to maintain detailed records of the different stages of AI systems development, training, and deployment as a measure to tackle the problem. Typically, they carry out algorithmic impact assessments that identify and evaluate risks associated with automated decision-making. In case of AI security monitoring, one may ensure accountability by recording the training of the models used in threat detection, the exploitation of data sources for the purpose of making predictions, as well as the handling of false alarms or misses. Therefore, it enables companies to account for the making of security decisions and demonstrate that such decisions were neither discriminatory, arbitrary, nor unlawful constructions. Algorithmic auditing is another necessary measure for accountability enhancement. One possibility would be for businesses to hire external auditors to independently assess whether their AI security systems are effective and fair, as well as checking their legal compliance. Regulatory-wise, the concept of algorithmic accountability is very important in the first place in ensuring that the companies are held responsible for the actions of their automated systems. Secondly, it helps build trust in AI technologies by providing means to confirm that automated decisions are not only correct but also (A. Arabiat et al., 2025).

8.3 Transparency Obligations in AI Surveillance

In recent times, transparency is a major element in the management of surveillance technologies that rely on AI. Certain AI security solutions are able to function effectively by constantly observing and evaluating people's behaviors, browsing patterns, or biometric information. These types of monitoring, while potentially leading to enhanced security, might at the same time be considered as covert surveillance or unauthorized collection of data. Therefore, regulatory bodies keep insisting on the disclosure of the existence and the purpose of such AI monitoring systems by companies. When a firm decides to be transparent, it is not only a matter of informing the individuals that their behaviors could be under automated surveillance but also, providing clear information about the use of the data collected. Transparency inside organizations can also translate to the provision of employee privacy notices, the development of internal governance policies, and the communication of security monitoring practices. Notices of such kind allow individuals to ascertain the nature of the monitoring done as well as the legal basis of the processing of their data (Turab et al., 2025). Nevertheless, it is not completely simple to be transparent regarding AI surveillance systems. Most of the AI systems are built around intricate machine learning algorithms that are at a very high level of complexity such that explaining them in detail is almost impossible. This situation has resulted in the growing trend of explainable artificial intelligence (XAI) that attempts to make AI decisions more human-understandable. Explainable AI will enable companies to give reasonable explanations for actions including, security warning triggers, risk score derivations, and the identification of individuals or activities for investigations. By unveiling the rationale behind automated decisions, companies are not only enhancing their accountability but also, they are reaping the benefits of the operational versatility of AI security (Al Hindi et al., 2025).

8.4 Global Harmonization of Security Data Laws

One key concern regarding AI security governance is that different areas of the world have diverse data protection regulations. Today's cybersecurity, to a great extent, involves sharing data across borders, as well as the processing and storing of security logs, threat intelligence data, and user behavior analytics in cloud repositories located all over the world. Because countries have different legal provisions concerning the collection, processing, and transfer of personal data, this poses significant challenges for global security infrastructures. Take, for instance, the EU's GDPR that imposes very strict conditions for data transfer such as the requirement to use standard contractual clauses or the existence of an adequacy decision. Other jurisdictions may adopt a relatively lenient approach putting more emphasis on national security or technological innovation rather than on data protection. These differences have been a major hindrance for organizations operating global security infrastructures (Ghazal, Abualhaj, et al., 2025). Generally speaking, AI security systems rely on combining data from various geographical regions to enhance their threat detection capabilities. However, personal data transfer regulations might, at least partially, constrain the functioning of security analytics systems. Looking ahead, policy actions in this sphere might cover international agreements on data protection and cybersecurity cooperation that will strive to harmonize data protection standards across different legal systems. This would be a highly beneficial step towards reducing regulatory fragmentation while at the same time ensuring a high level of privacy

8.5 Ethical AI Security Processing

When it comes to AI security governance, it's not the case that ethical considerations overshadow the role of a law compliance officer. Actually, fairness, proportionality, and respect for human rights are the main ethical principles which underpin AI frameworks. This is even more the case when point access to resources or people opportunities or freedoms can be affected by automated systems. Firms doing ethical AI security operations only complying with the law is not enough. They should also be socially responsible. Using behavioral monitoring systems, for example, could result in bias if the training data contains historical inequalities or systemic biases. To limit the risk, companies can conduct pre-deployment AI system ethical reviews (Ghazal, Abu-Shareha, et al., 2025). These reviews are checking whether AI results are discriminatory, if the surveillance is proportionate, and if there is enough human oversight. Ethical AI security processing depends heavily on privacy-enhancing techniques. The most popular techniques allowing companies to analyze security data without disclosing personal information include data anonymization, federated learning, and secure multi-party computation. Basically, ethical governance frameworks try to ensure that AI security technologies help organizations fight cyber threats in a way that does not violate people's rights and freedoms. As AI systems become more deeply woven into security infrastructures, the search for the right balance will undoubtedly be one of the major challenges for policymakers, regulators and technology

Legal compliance does not automatically ensure ethical legitimacy. An AI security system may have a lawful basis but still be inappropriate if it enables excessive surveillance, weakens autonomy, creates fear, or profiles individuals beyond the original security purpose.

9. CONCLUSION

Artificial intelligence is a critical part of modern security systems that have not only changed them to detect and record threats but also to respond very quickly and accurately. On the other hand, the deployment of AI in security raises a complex set of legal issues since such systems usually process personal, behavioral, or biometric data. Different legal grounds including legitimate interest, legal obligation, contractual necessity, and consent have been discussed in relation to AI surveillance devices. The research has shown how concepts like necessity, proportionality, transparency, and accountability are the main pillars of the legal use of AI security technologies. The chapter's authors, through legal theories, analysis, and governance models, contend that successful security operations should rely on a thorough legal evaluation and documented compliance practices. The crucial point is that legally compliant AI processing for security is not just a technological issue but a governance and policy matter that would call for an overall organizational oversight. Statistical analyses of regulatory risk and compliance probabilities demonstrate that it is not only possible for organizations to achieve simultaneously the security effectiveness and privacy protection but also the requisite safeguards are implemented. Governance suggested mechanisms such as privacy-by-design architectural models, oversight forums, data minimization strategies, and continuous compliance monitoring together make up the operating system through which AI technologies are strictly regulated to remain compliant with the . As worldwide regulatory efforts including, establishment of global AI governance frameworks, modification of existing rules, increased enforcement actions continue to take place, the only way for organizations to be legally compliant is to adopt a dynamic approach that will enable them to handle cross-border data processing and algorithmic accountability requirements. Bringing AI-driven security solutions in line with lawful and ethical norms is, in the end, a measure that enhances both an organization's ability to withstand and recover from adversities and public confidence in systems that rely on Artificial Intelligence.

REFERENCES

Abdeljaber, O., & Al-Masaeed, S. (2025). Al-Mu'ani, L., Yaseen, H., & Alhnaity, B. (2025). Strategic Intelligence: The Power of AI in Planning Efficiency. *Human Behavior and Emerging Technologies*, (1). Advance online publication. DOI: 10.1155/hbe2/5383054

Abualghanam, O., Alazzam, H., Qatawneh, M., Alazab, M., & Al Sharaiah, M. (2025). Elevating Mobile Security: An Ensemble Approach for Enhanced Malware Detection with M-iForest. *International Journal of Interactive Mobile Technologies*, *19*(10), 129–151. Advance online publication. DOI: 10.3991/ijim.v19i10.51319

Abualhaj, M. M., Abu-Shareha, A. A., Al-Khatib, S. N., Alsaaidah, A. M., & Anbar, M. (2025). Improving firewall performance using hybrid of optimization algorithms and decision trees classifier. *IAES International Journal of Artificial Intelligence*, *14*(4), 2839. Advance online publication. DOI: 10.11591/ijai.v14.i4.pp2839-2848

Abualhaj, M. M., Abu-Shareha, A. A., & Rateb, R. (2025). Enhancing intrusion detection systems with hybrid HHO-WOA optimization and gradient boosting machine classifier. *International Journal of Reconfigurable and Embedded Systems*, *14*(2), 518. Advance online publication. DOI: 10.11591/ijres.v14.i2.pp518-526

Abualhaj, M. M.I, Al-Khatib, S. N., Abu-Shareha, A. A., Almomani, O., Al-Mimi, H., Al-Allawee, A., Daoud, M. S., & Anbar, M. (2025). Spam Detection Boosted by Firefly-Based Feature Selection and Optimized Classifiers. *International Journal of Advances in Soft Computing and Its Applications*, *17*(3). Advance online publication. DOI: 10.15849/IJASCA.251130.02

Abualhaj, M. M., Al-Khatib, S. N., Al Zyoud, M., Qaddara, I., & Anbar, M. (2025). Enhancing Intrusion Detection System Performance Using a Hybrid of Harris Hawks and Whale Optimization Algorithms. *Engineering. Technology and Applied Science Research*, *15*(4), 24354–24361. Advance online publication. DOI: 10.48084/etasr.10919

Abualhaj, M. M., Al-Khatib, S. N., Al-Zyoud, M., Qaddara, I., Hiari, M. O., & Aldossary, S. M. A. (2025). Enhanced Network Communication Security Through Hybrid Dragonfly-Bat Feature Selection for Intrusion Detection. *The Journal of Communication*, *20*(5). Advance online publication. DOI: 10.12720/jcm.20.5.607-618

Abualigah, L., Almomani, M. H., Alomari, S. A., Zitar, R. A., Migdady, H., Saleem, K., Snasel, V., Smerat, A., & Ezugwu, A. E. (2025). Optimizing Intrusion Detection in Wireless Sensor Networks via the Improved Chameleon Swarm Algorithm for Feature Selection. *IET Communications*, *19*(1), e70029. Advance online publication. DOI: 10.1049/cmu2.70029

Abuowaida, S., Abu Owida, H., Shelash Mohammad, S. I., Alshdaifat, N., Abu Elsoud, E., Alazaidah, R., Vasudevan, A., & Alshurideh, M. T. (2025). Evidence Detection in Cloud Forensics: Classifying Cyber-Attacks in IaaS Environments using machine learning. *Data and Metadata*, *4*, 699. Advance online publication. DOI: 10.56294/dm2025699

Ahmed, K. A., Ibrahim, A., Qudr, L. A. Z., Tawfeq, J. F., Al Falahi, Q., & Radhi, A. D. (2025). *Developing Adaptive AI-Driven Cybersecurity Frameworks for Real-Time Detection of Polymorphic Malware in IoT Networks*. DOI: 10.1109/ICBATS66542.2025.11258540

Al-Adwan, A. S., Al-Adwan, A., Li, N., Fauzi, M. A., Jafar, R. M. S., Habibi, A., & Falahat, M. (2025). IMMERSIVE LEARNING MEETS THEORY: MODELING EDUVERSE ADOPTION IN HIGHER EDUCATION. *Journal of Information Technology Education*, *24*, 042. Advance online publication. DOI: 10.28945/5669

Al-Dmour, R., Al-Dmour, H., Al-Dmour, A., Basheer Amin, E., & Al-Dmour, Y. (2025). *AI and big data-driven social media recruitment: the mediating role of talent acquisition and employee engagement in bank performance*. Digital Transformation and Society., DOI: 10.1108/DTS-02-2025-0042

Al-Habashneh, A. G., Al-Daoud, K. I., Oraini, B., Al, , & Shelash, S. I. (2025). The impact of artificial intelligence on the development of electronic financial services. *International Journal of Data and Network Science*, *9*(2), 317–322. Advance online publication. DOI: 10.5267/j.ijdns.2024.8.012

Al Hindi, G., Alshraideh, M., Hussein, A. H., Eliyan, L. F., & Al-Dhaqm, A. (2025). Hacking Back: Using Genetic Algorithms to Outsmart Hackers. *Journal of Computational Science*, *21*(9), 2049–2064. Advance online publication. DOI: 10.3844/jcssp.2025.2049.2064

Al-Momani, M. M., Alqudah, T. A., Al Swiety, I. A., Mahrakani, N., Nassoura, M. B. A., & Al Attar, M. K. (2025). Integrating Artificial Intelligence (AI) and Business Intelligence (BI): A Framework for Improving Enterprise Performance. *TEM Journal, 14*(3). https://doi.org/DOI: 10.18421/TEM143-26

Al-Mousa, M., Amer, W., Abualhaj, M., Albilasi, S., Nasir, O., & Samara, G. (2025). Agile Proactive Cybercrime Evidence Analysis Model for Digital Forensics. *The International Arab Journal of Information Technology*, *22*(3). Advance online publication. DOI: 10.34028/iajit/22/3/15

Al-Okbi, N. K., Alomari, S. A., Hadi, W. J., Ajrash, A. S., Smerat, A., & Abualigah, L. (2025). Defending Digital Integrity: Advances in Media Forgery Analysis Research and Cybersecurity Development. *SN Computer Science*, *6*(8), 913. Advance online publication. DOI: 10.1007/s42979-025-04462-8

Al-Okbi, N. K., Alomari, S. A., Zitar, R. A., Smerat, A., Nazzal, M. A., & Abualigah, L. (2025). Integrating Multimodal Emotion Recognition with Deep Q-Learning for Adaptive Social Robot Interaction. *International Journal of Robotics and Control Systems*, *5*(4), 2265–2289. Advance online publication. DOI: 10.31763/ijrcs.v5i4.2055

Al-znamat, F. O., Alsaaidah, A., & Abu-Shareha, A. A. (2025). Malware Detection Using a Modified Bat Algorithm for Feature Selection. *International Journal of Intelligent Engineering and Systems*, *18*(9), 885–899. Advance online publication. DOI: 10.22266/ijies2025.1031.56

Alabdallat, R., Abualhaj, M., & Abu-Shareha, A. (2025). Android Malware Detection Using a Modified Dwarf Mongoose Algorithm. *International Journal of Intelligent Engineering and Systems*, *18*(8), 336–351. Advance online publication. DOI: 10.22266/ijies2025.0930.21

Alabdallat, R. D., Abualhaj, M. M., & Abu-Shareha, A. (2025). Enhanced Multiclass Android Malware Detection Using a Modified Dwarf Mongoose Algorithm. *International Journal of Analysis and Applications*, *23*, 248. Advance online publication. DOI: 10.28924/2291-8639-23-2025-248

Aldaaja, Y., Odeh, M., Badrakhan, S. S., Sabri, M., Abdelrahim, Y., Samara, G., & Alsabatin, H. (2025). Quantifying the Managerial and Practical Benefits of Cloud Computing on Information Security in Higher Education Institutions. *Applied Mathematics & Information Sciences*, *19*(1), 15–24. Advance online publication. DOI: 10.18576/amis/190102

Aldabbas, A., Baniata, L. H., Alsaaidah, B. A., Mustafa, Z., Alali, M., & Rateb, R. (2025). Artificial intelligence-driven method for the discovery and prevention of distributed denial of service attacks. *IAES International Journal of Artificial Intelligence*, *14*(1), 614. Advance online publication. DOI: 10.11591/ijai.v14.i1.pp614-628

Alenazi, M. J. F., Al-Khasawneh, M. A., Rahman, S., & Faheem, Z. (2025). Deep Reinforcement Learning Based Flow Aware-QoS Provisioning in SD-IoT for Precision Agriculture. *Computational Intelligence*, *41*(1), e70023. Advance online publication. DOI: 10.1111/coin.70023

Alkhawatrah, M. (2025). Random Forests Relay Selector in Buffer-Aided Cooperative Networks. *IEEE Access : Practical Innovations, Open Solutions*, *13*, 165402–165410. Advance online publication. DOI: 10.1109/ACCESS.2025.3612192

Almajed, R., Ibrahim, A., Abualkishik, A. Z., Mourad, N., & Almansour, F. A. (2022). Using machine learning algorithm for detection of cyber-attacks in cyber physical systems. *Periodicals of Engineering and Natural Sciences*, *10*(3), 261. Advance online publication. DOI: 10.21533/pen.v10i3.3035

Almomani, O., Arabiat, A., Al Tayeb, M., Almaiah, M. A., Obeidat, M., Aldhyani, T. H. H., Shehab, R., & Rowad, M. (2025). A Robust Model for Android Malware Detection via ML and DL classifiers. *Mesopotamian Journal of Big Data*, *2025*. Advance online publication. DOI: 10.58496/MJBD/2025/017

Alnawayseh, S. E. A., Al-Sit, W. T., & Ghazal, T. M. (2022). Smart Congestion Control in 5G/6G Networks Using Hybrid Deep Learning Techniques. *Complexity*, *2022*(1), 1781952. Advance online publication. DOI: 10.1155/2022/1781952

Alraba'nah, Y., Al-Sharaeh, S., & Al Hindi, G. (2025). Enhancing Intrusion Detection Using Hybrid Long Short-Term Memory and XGBoost. *Journal of Soft Computing and Data Mining*, *6*(1). Advance online publication. DOI: 10.30880/jscdm.2025.06.01.016

Arabiat, A., Altayeb, M., & Salama, S. (2025). Artificial intelligence-powered smart roads: Leveraging orange3 for traffic signs recognition. *IAES International Journal of Artificial Intelligence*, *14*(5), 3816. Advance online publication. DOI: 10.11591/ijai.v14.i5.pp3816-3826

Arabiat, A. M. (2025). Intelligent Model for Detecting GAN-Generated Images Based on Multi-Classifier and Advanced Data Mining Techniques. *International Journal of Electrical and Electronic Engineering and Telecommunications*, *14*(3). Advance online publication. DOI: 10.18178/ijeetc.14.3.147-157

Arabiat, A. M., & Eljaafreh, Y. G. (2025). Intrusion Detection in Wireless Sensor Networks Using ML Based Classification of Denial of Service (DoS) Attacks. *The Journal of Communication*, *20*(4). Advance online publication. DOI: 10.12720/jcm.20.4.501-514

Babaker, S., Khatibi, A., Alsoud, A. R., Kaur, J., Jagtap, J., Alkhayyat, A., & Shah, S. K. (2025). Improving Reliability and Data Management in Internet of Things Based Wireless Sensor Networks. *Internet Technology Letters*, *8*(6), e646. Advance online publication. DOI: 10.1002/itl2.646

Cui, D., Harrison, A., Fendzi-Donfack, E., Dagal, I., Jangir, P., Mahmoud, M. M., Malkani, P., Mbasso, W. F., Tiako, P., & Smerat, A. (2026). Enhancing Short-Term Electricity Forecasting with Advanced Machine Learning Techniques. *Journal of Electrical Engineering & Technology*, *21*(1), 147–187. Advance online publication. DOI: 10.1007/s42835-025-02430-z

Eke, C. I., Al-Shamayleh, A. S., Phiri, M., Maswadi, K., Kwaghtyo, D. K., Mulenga, M., & Iyidobi, C. J. (2025). Machine Learning Based Mobile Big Data Analytics: State-of-the-art Applications, Taxonomy, Challenges and Future Research Directions. *Nigerian Journal of Technological Development*, *22*(4). Advance online publication. DOI: 10.63746/njtd.v22i4.3385

Ghazal, T. M. (2025a). An IoT-Based Active Learning Convolutional Neural Networks Model for Predicting River Water Quality. *Journal of Soft Computing and Data Mining*, *6*(1). Advance online publication. DOI: 10.30880/jscdm.2025.06.01.021

Ghazal, T. M. (2025b). Federated Learning for Intelligent Sensing and Navigation Technologies for 6G Communications. *Journal of Sensors*, *2025*(1). DOI: 10.1155/js/3746147

Ghazal, T. M., Abu-Shareha, A., Mustafa, S. A., Ibrahim, A., & Ahmed, S. M. (2025). Privacy-Preserving Transformer-Based Meta-Learning Algorithm for Zero-Day Intrusion Detection in IoT-Enabled Smart Grids. *Journal of Internet Services and Information Security*, *15*(4), 76–84. Advance online publication. DOI: 10.58346/JISIS.2025.I4.006

Ghazal, T. M., Abualhaj, M., Ahmed, A. A., Al-Tarawni, M. A. M., & Maghrabi, L. A. (2025). Federated Deep Graph Neural Network Algorithm for Real-Time Intrusion Detection in Heterogeneous IoT Systems. *Journal of Internet Services and Information Security*, *15*(4), 484–497. Advance online publication. DOI: 10.58346/JISIS.2025.I4.035

Ghazal, T. M., Awouda, A. E., Hasan, M. K., Rahman, A. H. A., Islam, S., Saeed, R. A., Elshafie, H., Iqbal, A., & Hussein, A. H. (2025). Knowledge Learning for Securing Workflow Scheduling Algorithm in Mobile Edge Computing. *Mobile Networks and Applications*, *30*(3-4), 395–413. Advance online publication. DOI: 10.1007/s11036-025-02465-6

Ghazal, T. M., Hasan, M. K., Alzoubi, H. M., Al Hmmadi, M., Al-Dmour, N. A., Islam, S., Kamran, R., & Mago, B. (2022). Securing Smart Cities Using Blockchain Technology. *2022 1st International Conference on AI in Cybersecurity, ICAIC 2022*. DOI: 10.1109/ICAIC53980.2022.9896971

Ghazal, T. M., Hasan, M. K., Hussein, A. H., Pandey, B. K., Ahmad, M., Safie, N., & Cascone, L. (2025). Federated Learning With Small and Large Models With Privacy-Preserving Data Space for Holographic Internet of Things in Consumer Electronics. *IEEE Transactions on Consumer Electronics*, *71*(2), 5259–5274. Advance online publication. DOI: 10.1109/TCE.2025.3573033

Ghazal, T. M., Hasan, M. K., Raju, K. N., Khan, M. A., Alshamayleh, A., Bhatt, M. W., & Ahmad, M. (2025). Data Space Privacy Model with Federated Learning Technique for Securing IoT Communications in Autonomous Marine Vehicles. *Journal of Intelligent & Robotic Systems*, *111*(3), 84. Advance online publication. DOI: 10.1007/s10846-025-02298-1

Ghazal, T. M., Janjua, J. I., Abushiba, W., Ahmad, M., Ihsan, A., & Al-Dmour, N. A. (2024). Cybersecurity Revolution via Large Language Models and Explainable AI. *2024 17th International Conference on Security of Information and Networks, SIN 2024*. DOI: 10.1109/SIN63213.2024.10871324

Hakami, H., Hasan, M. K., Alshamayleh, A., Saeed, A. Q., Mustafa, S. A., & Ghazal, T. M. (2025). Adaptive Neuro-Fuzzy Congestion Control Algorithm for Real-Time Multimedia Networking in Cloud-Based E-Learning Platforms. *Journal of Wireless Mobile Networks, Ubiquitous Computing and Dependable Applications*, *16*(3). Advance online publication. DOI: 10.58346/JOWUA.2025.I3.027

Hanandeh, A., Alfreijat, S. Y., Qutieshat, R. J., Alsha'ar, H. Y., Kilani, Q. A. L., & Saleem Khasawneh, M. A. (2025). Implementing AI Accuracy, Learning Rate, Inference Time on enhancing Big Data Analysis and Strategic Plan. *Data and Metadata*, *4*, 637. Advance online publication. DOI: 10.56294/dm2025637

Hiari, M., Alraba'nah, Y., & Qaddara, I. (2025). A Deep Learning-Based Intrusion Detection System using Refined LSTM for DoS Attack Detection. *Engineering. Technology and Applied Science Research*, *15*(4), 25627–25633. Advance online publication. DOI: 10.48084/etasr.11499

Ibrahim, A., Sekhar, R., Tawfeq, J. F., Salih, S. Q., Shah, P., & Radhi, A. D. (2024). Security and Privacy Protection for Online Electronic Documents Based on Novel Encryption Techniques. *Journal of Intelligent Systems and Internet of Things*, *11*(1), 21–28. Advance online publication. DOI: 10.54216/JISIoT.110103

Iskandarani, M. Z. (2025). Effect of Adaptive Intelligent Reflective Surfaces on SINR in a Wireless Communication System. *The Journal of Communication*, *20*(1). Advance online publication. DOI: 10.12720/jcm.20.1.1-11

Jaradat, S., Acharya, N., Shivshankar, S., Alhadidi, T. I., & Elhenawy, M. (2025). AI for Data Quality Auditing: Detecting Mislabeled Work Zone Crashes Using Large Language Models. *Algorithms*, *18*(6), 317. Advance online publication. DOI: 10.3390/a18060317

Khatibi, A., Babaker, S., Praveen, K. N. R., Chohan, J. S., Jadhav, A., Alsoud, A. R., Ramudu, M. J., & Jeet, R. (2025). Advanced AI-Driven Cybersecurity: Analyzing Emerging Threats and Defensive Strategies. *National Academy Science Letters*. Advance online publication. DOI: 10.1007/s40009-025-01897-8

Laha, S. R., Smadi, K. Al, Habboush, A. K., Pattanayak, B. K., Pattnaik, S., & Mohanty, B. (2025). Smart Waste Management Framework for Green Cities: Integrating IoT, LoRa, and Deep Learning for Efficient Waste Classification and Management. *Tikrit Journal of Engineering Sciences, 32*(Special Issue 1). DOI: 10.25130/tjes.sp1.2025.1

Makhadmeh, S. N., Fraihat, S., Awad, M., Sanjalawe, Y., Al-Betar, M. A., & Awadallah, M. A. (2025). A crossover-integrated Marine Predator Algorithm for feature selection in intrusion detection systems within IoT environments. *Internet of Things : Engineering Cyber Physical Human Systems*, *31*, 101536. Advance online publication. DOI: 10.1016/j.iot.2025.101536

Masango, N. C., Agushaka, J. O., Amaefule, M. C., Taiwo, O., Zhang, P., Ezugwu, A. E., Saleem, K., Smerat, A., & Abualigah, L. (2025). Secure and efficient cloudlet networks: blockchain integration with agent-based proof of trust mechanism. *Eurasip Journal on Wireless Communications and Networking, 2025*(1). DOI: 10.1186/s13638-025-02439-y

Maz, Y. A., Anbar, M., Manickam, S., Abualhaj, M. M., Almalki, S. A., & Alabsi, B. A. (2025). Transfer Learning-Based Approach with an Ensemble Classifier for Detecting Keylogging Attack on the Internet of Things. *Computers, Materials & Continua*, *85*(3), 5287–5307. Advance online publication. DOI: 10.32604/cmc.2025.068257

Mohammad, S. I., Al-Daoud, K., Al Qraini, B., Khanfar, I. A. A., & Vasudevan, A. (2025). Quantum Error Correction with Surface Code Analysis on Quantum Computing platform. *Applied Mathematics & Information Sciences*, *19*(2), 423–435. Advance online publication. DOI: 10.18576/amis/190216

Otair, M., Qawaqzeh, F. A., Alomari, S. A., Zitar, R. A., Migdady, H., Saleem, K., Smerat, A., Alsoud, A. R., & Abualigah, L. (2025). Enhanced Arithmetic Optimization Algorithm for Intrusion Detection in Wireless Sensor Networks. *International Journal of Communication Systems*, *38*(10), e70122. Advance online publication. DOI: 10.1002/dac.70122

Qaddara, I., & Alraba'nah, Y. (2025). Enhancing Requirements Classification Using Machine Learning Techniques. *SN Computer Science*, *6*(6), 649. Advance online publication. DOI: 10.1007/s42979-025-04158-z

Qawasmeh, S., Habboushb, A., Elzaghmouri, B., Kharma, Q., & Albalawneh, D. (2025). Hybrid Convolutional Neural Network-Based Intrusion Detection System for Secure IoT Networks. *Tikrit Journal of Engineering Sciences*, *32*(SP1), 1–11. Advance online publication. DOI: 10.25130/tjes.sp1.2025.2

Ramesh, J. V. N., Nimma, D., Dasari, R., Chaudhari Rane, D., AlGhamdi, A., Rao, K. B. V. B., Haider, S. A., Kuzieva, N., & Jangir, P. (2025). Safe and Reliable Two-Stage Online Offloading Algorithm for Transportation Cyber-Physical Systems. *IEEE Transactions on Intelligent Transportation Systems*, *26*(9), 14313–14322. Advance online publication. DOI: 10.1109/TITS.2025.3539934

Raza, M. A., Karim, A., Alqarni, M., Al-Khasawneh, M. A., Jumani, T. A., Aman, M., & Masud, M. I. (2025). An Intelligent Long Short-Term Memory-Based Machine Learning Model for the Potential Assessment of Global Hydropower Capacity in Sustainable Energy Transition and Security. *Energies*, *18*(13), 3324. Advance online publication. DOI: 10.3390/en18133324

Samanta, I. S., Mohanty, S., Rout, P. K., Parida, S. M., Panda, S., Bajaj, M., Blazek, V., & Prokop, L. (2025). A comprehensive review of feature extraction techniques for power quality event detection with novel approaches for enhanced classification in smart grids. *Electrical Engineering*, *107*(9), 12227–12259. Advance online publication. DOI: 10.1007/s00202-025-03149-w

Sardar, R., Anees, T., Al-Shamayleh, A. S., Mehmood, E., Khalil, W., Akhunzada, A., & Shaikh, F. S. (2025). Challenges in detecting security threats in WoT: A systematic literature review. *Artificial Intelligence Review*, *58*(7), 196. Advance online publication. DOI: 10.1007/s10462-025-11176-z

Shambour, Q., Al-Zyoud, M., & Almomani, O. (2025). Quantum-Inspired Hybrid Metaheuristic Feature Selection with SHAP for Optimized and Explainable Spam Detection. *Symmetry*, *17*(10), 1716. Advance online publication. DOI: 10.3390/sym17101716

Shambour, Q. Y., Al-Zyoud, M., & Hussein, A. H. (2025). FROM DATA TO DIAGNOSIS: KNOWLEDGE-DRIVEN, EXPLAINABLE AI FOR RELIABLE EARLY AUTISM DETECTION. *Interdisciplinary Journal of Information, Knowledge, and Management, 20,* 032. Advance online publication. DOI: 10.28945/5652

Sharma, K. P., Al-Rashed, A., Johar, M. G. M., Alsoud, A. R., Singh, A., Dey, P., & Pant, S. (2025). Blockchain-Assisted Trust Framework for Increased Survivability in Internet of Vehicles. *Internet Technology Letters, 8*(3), e70029. Advance online publication. DOI: 10.1002/itl2.70029

Sharma, K. P., Hussain, R., Jaharadak, A. A., Trawnih, A. A., Verma, D., Dasi, S., & Pant, S. (2025). Hybrid Convolutional Neural Network for Robust Attack Detection in Wireless Sensor Networks. *Internet Technology Letters, 8*(6), e650. Advance online publication. DOI: 10.1002/itl2.650

Turab, N., Abushattal, A., Al-Nabulsi, J., & Owida, H. A. (2025). Advanced risk assessment using machine learning and sentiment analysis on log data. *IAES International Journal of Artificial Intelligence, 14*(5), 3897. Advance online publication. DOI: 10.11591/ijai.v14.i5.pp3897-3905

Vasudevan, A., Albinaa, T. A., Mohammad, S. I., Sharmila, E., Raja, N., Soon, E. E. H., Alshurideh, M. T., & Al-Adwan, A. S. (2024). Bidirectional LSTM for Electronic Product Recommendation. *Applied Mathematics & Information Sciences, 18*(6), 1443–1453. Advance online publication. DOI: 10.18576/amis/180621

Vasudevan, A., Tamilmani, K. T., Mohammad, S. I., Sridheepika, V. S., Raja, N., Soon, E. E. H., Nagaraj, S., & Al-Adwan, A. S. (2025). Voices of Concern: Contemplations on Socioeconomic, Ethical, and Developmental Impacts of AI. *Applied Mathematics & Information Sciences, 19*(1), 221–232. Advance online publication. DOI: 10.18576/amis/190119

Chapter 4
Evaluation of Privacy and Legal Failure in Artificial Intelligence Security Systems

Munir Ahmad
http://orcid.org/0000-0002-5240-0984
School of Computer Science, National College of Business Administration and Economics, Lahore, Pakistan

Abdur Rehman
http://orcid.org/0000-0002-5867-8231
School of Computer Science, National College of Business Administration and Economics, Lahore, Pakistan

ABSTRACT

This chapter is devoted to examining the breach of privacy and the violation of legal rights that may occur in AI-based security systems and the circumstances that may lead to such breaches. It demonstrates how inadequate system design, governance, use of data, and automation controls can cause non-compliance, rights violations, and regulatory enforcement actions. The chapter points out the typical failure modes such as collecting too much data, lack of adequate transparency, biased decision-making, lack of proper human supervision, and fragile accountability mechanisms. The focus is on evaluation methods that detect vulnerabilities through audits, impact assessments, incident reviews, and governance testing. Combining legal research with technical assessment, the chapter offers an approach to the detection, comprehension, and prevention of privacy and legal failures in AI-powered security systems.

1. INTRODUCTION

1.1 Evolution of AI-Driven Security Architectures

Initially, rule-based techniques such as signature detection and firewall filtering were predominantly used for cybersecurity. These systems performed well in detecting known threats but had limited ability to recognize new, unknown attacks or complex behavioral anomalies. By the time threats escalated to the

DOI: 10.4018/979-8-3373-9210-3.ch004

level of highly sophisticated, the decision was made to adopt data-driven security approaches leveraging machine learning and artificial intelligence for better detection capabilities.

AI security technologies were introduced as a response to the limitations of traditional security measures. Nowadays, security tools take into account massive amounts of telemetry data collected from networks, endpoints, cloud environments, and user interactions. Machine learning techniques are utilized to identify significant patterns indicative of malicious intent or abnormal behavior (Ghazal, 2025a). These artificially intelligent systems are able to pinpoint even the smallest deviations from the usual way that systems operate, thus enabling the detection of threats that would go unnoticed without them.

Security Operations Centers (SOCs) are increasingly relying on AI security systems that help analysts by filtering and prioritizing alerts, linking events from different systems, and even partially automating the response to incidents. The accuracy of such detection systems keeps getting better as the models learn from the data of past incidents, allowing organizations to react very quickly to newly emerging threats. In fact, many AI-based tools are actively participating in the frontline defense against cyberattacks by processing millions of events in an automated manner with only a selective number of high-risk situations being forwarded for human investigation, all of which are identified through the work of AI systems (Haider et al., 2026).

Still, the use of AI in security systems remains a major source of privacy concern as these systems are heavily dependent on mass data collection to deliver precise results. Therefore, in order to collect sufficient data for the establishment of behavioral baselines leading to anomaly detection, users often undergo continuous surveillance. Nevertheless, intensive monitoring on such a scale is nothing less than a surveillance tool that may enable extensive monitoring of an individual's digital activities depending on deployment configuration and organizational policies (Habboush & Elzaghmouri, 2025). Consequently, the organization only has the option of formulating a plan that balances adequately between security monitoring and the recognition and respect for the privacy rights of individuals.

Another characteristic feature of the proliferation of AI security infrastructure is the trend in the direction of gathering diverse data sources. At the level of a single platform, a modern security system is capable of pulling data not only from endpoints but also from cloud applications, authentication systems, and network traffic logs. While this is helpful for a more accurate detection of threats, it also means that the AI models have access to a much larger quantity of personal data. The conjunction of these datasets has given rise to complicated data ecosystems where privacy risks are able to proliferate from one system to another.

1.2 Privacy Risks of Automated Security Intelligence

Automated security intelligence makes a lot of use of behavioral analytics which almost inevitably means that through users' behavior patterns, they can be profiled and any deviations can be recognized, leading to the detection of threats. In this way, behavioral analytics can catch threatening behavior such as logging in at strange hours, abnormal data transfers, or using devices in a different manner than usual (Khaled Abdullah & Qawasmeh, 2025). The downside of behavioral analytics is that users will be monitored continuously, revealing work styles, communication habits of a personal nature, and locations visited, among other aspects of users' private lives.

Privacy risk which is biggest is related to the sheer amount of data that needs to be collected to be used for training AI. In order for machine learning to be capable of discovering hidden patterns and enhancing its detection abilities, it is essential not only to be fed with large amounts of data but also to be exposed to data of different programmers. As a consequence, security solutions are especially interested in pulling large-volume logging from endpoints, network devices, authentication servers, and application platforms. These logs contain personal identifiers, in addition to which, the contextual information obtained in combination with other sources can provide an extremely detailed picture of an individual's behavior online (Dar et al., 2025).

Secondary data use means using data initially collected for one purpose for another purpose without additional consent. For example, data collected for security monitoring might later be repurposed for staff performance monitoring or even for marketing purposes which would be a violation of privacy (Abualhaj, Abu-Shareha, & Rateb, 2025). In AI security, it is quite common that the lines between security monitoring and wider analytics functions get blurred which in effect opens up the possibilities of misuse.'

Additionally, the magnitude and complexity of machine learning models play a significant role in the escalation of privacy risks. Many AI security systems employ deep learning algorithms or operate by blending different models that are beyond human comprehension. Should these models lead to generating security alert or even triggering automated responses, it may turn out to be impossible to provide the explanation of the decision-making process. This opacity has a negative impact on trust and poses challenge to organizations aiming to demonstrate their compliance with data protection legislation.

1.3 Legal Accountability Challenges in Algorithmic Security Systems

Using AI in security systems poses a plethora of challenges in the context of legal accountability. Earlier security tools were rule based and, as such, traceable and auditable, while machine learning models base their decisions on complex statistical relationships present in the training set. Often, such relationships are far from intuitive, resulting in a very limited understanding of why certain decisions have been made (Hussain et al., 2025).

Legal accountability becomes an issue especially when automated security measures are followed by actions that affect individuals. Suppose, for instance, that an AI security tool automatically blocks a user's network access after detecting unusual behavior. If the decision proves to be wrong, the individual concerned may experience an unjustified work disruption and reputation damage (Jaradat et al., 2025). In order to investigate and attribute the liability in such cases, all aspects such as data selection, model training, policies in operation, etc. must be considered.

A further complication of holding anyone accountable is the extensive use of third-party AI products by many organizations. It is generally the case that security platforms embedding machine learning features as a part of integrated security systems are produced by vendors rather than being developed internally. When privacy breaches issues arise in these systems, it is not always clear who should be held responsible - the vendor that supplied the AI model or the organization that chose to deploy it? Such problems make enforcement of regulation difficult and in some instances may lead to delayed resolution of issues (Hiari et al., 2025).

Organizations are also required by law to comply with explaining automated decisions that have effects on individuals by implementing fairness, transparency, and human intervention; however, it is possible that human oversight over AI security systems would be very difficult. Security personnel, given the volume of security events that are processed by automated models, often rely heavily on the algorithmic decisions in terms of operational practicality.

1.4 Research Scope and Analytical Methodology

This paper adopts an interdisciplinary approach combining concepts from cybersecurity engineering, data protection law, and corporate governance literature to outline the severity of the problem with privacy and legal breaches of AI security systems.

Apart from the conceptual discussion, the research methodology included empirical testing through the use of public cybersecurity datasets and the application of machine learning models to find patterns that serve as evidence of privacy risks. The integration of conceptual and empirical work resulted in the development of a working framework that describes the conditions under which AI security systems are vulnerable to privacy and legal failings. These findings will serve as a springboard for subsequent chapters that will propose governance norms and technical interventions as complementary enablers of responsible and legally compliant AI security technology (Abualhaj, Al-Khatib, Al-Zyoud, Qaddara, et al., 2025).

This chapter is organized into seven major sections. Following the introduction, the chapter examines the evolution of AI-enabled security systems and the privacy risks associated with modern monitoring practices. It then analyzes major privacy and legal failure modes, develops evaluation metrics for privacy exposure and compliance failure, examines organizational and societal consequences, proposes a governance framework for responsible AI security deployment, and concludes with future regulatory and research directions. This structure enables readers to move from conceptual foundations toward practical governance recommendations.

2. FAILURE MODES OF PRIVACY COMPLIANCE IN AI SECURITY SYSTEMS

2.1 Algorithmic Surveillance and Excessive Data Collection

Quite naturally, AI security systems end up collecting large amounts of data mainly due to the way algorithmic surveillance operates. Richer datasets contribute to the predictive power of machine learning models and thus the detection is more accurate. These are very compelling reasons to use machine learning. Nevertheless, there are negatives associated with the buildup of data to a very high extent. Individuals may find that their rights have been violated if digital dossiers sufficiently detailed and continuously updated about them are a reality. Approximately, continuous monitoring reveals to a person/party/situation what their habits are and interpersonal networks as well.

At the same time, the situation is made worse if the models are tasked with identifying insider threats or behavioral deviations. Typically, such models rely on the construction of user profiles which are made from past behavioral data that have been collected. Any deviation from the baseline is assumed to indicate suspicious behavior (Al Abbadi et al., 2025). However, a person's behavior may change for valid reasons like a change in work pattern, a trip, or assignment to a different project. When such normal acts are flagged, people are unnecessarily put under close observation. As more data are collected, the risk that sensitive data is among the collected items also increases. After the initial collection, personal data can be stored for extended periods in accordance with such goals as incident investigation or model training sessions. Retaining the data for a longer period increases the potential security threats such as unauthorized access or data breaches. The laws and regulations, from their perspective, clearly view data collection on the big scale and data retention at the level that is not required as against the principles of data minimization and purpose limitation. It is a frequent plea among organizations to excuse a collection of data for security purposes that is not tight by referring to the need for comprehensive monitoring in order to effectively catch advanced threats. The issue, however, is that most of the time, consideration of proportionality gets omitted totally. A good cyber security plan should drive the determination of data types that are really necessary for threat detection instead of collecting all sorts of data indiscriminately. Without such discipline, AI security tools probably would be, without a doubt, turning into devices of large-scale digital surveillance (Abualhaj, Abu-Shareha, Al-Khatib, et al., 2025).

2.2 Inadequate Governance of Security Telemetry Data

Loose controls over security telemetry data are another major reason for privacy non-compliance. Telemetry here simply refers to the flow of information generated by digital systems such as network activity records, application event logs, endpoint monitoring data, and user authentication records. AI security systems, which use machine learning models for training and operation, find themselves very reliant on telemetry data.

Despite the importance of telemetry data, some organizations still have not established an effective governance framework around them. For example, security logs are automatically captured by infrastructure components and subsequently sent to centralized analytics platforms without detailed documentation of their content. Therefore, organizations may be unaware that their security data sets contain different types of personally identifiable information (Ebbini et al., 2025).

Governance failures may lead to many types of privacy violations. First, security telemetry data may contain various identifiers such as usernames, device IDs, or IP addresses that can be linked to individual persons. Thanks to the combination of such identifiers across various systems, it becomes possible to create comprehensive behavior profiles. Second, these data sets may include metadata from communication systems such as email headers and messaging timestamps, which can give away interaction patterns between individuals even if message contents are not analyzed.

Another governance issue is that of data access control. Security teams need access to telemetry data for investigating potential security breaches (Al-Momani et al., 2025). But, if they are not well-versed in the risks involved in handling this data and are given unrestricted access, this could lead to internal misuse or accidental exposure of the data. When there are no well-defined access policies and procedures for regular auditing, organizations find it difficult to demonstrate that they handle their sensitive security data responsibly.

Proper management of security telemetry means having clear policies in place regarding data classification, data retention, who is given access, and what the data can be used for. Besides, making public the telemetry data processing by AI models is equally important, along with stating the duration of data retention in the analytics pipelines. Without such governance mechanisms, maintaining privacy compliance as AI security systems become increasingly complex is almost unattainable (Hyassat et al., 2025).

2.3 Organizational Accountability Failures in AI Security

Organizational accountability is particularly poor when formalization of privacy principles through corporate policies has been done but implementation has been insufficient. In order to be effective, implementation requires the existence of clear governance roles and control mechanisms. Through their nature, AI security systems involve cross-functional teamwork and quite often multiple teams, including cybersecurity engineers, data scientists, software developers' administrators and lawyers as well as external contractors are brought together. The lack of clear accountability arrangements is one of the reasons that privacy-related risks might go unnoticed in an organization. A classic example of accountability being inadequate is an AI security project that is simply the result of initiating development by the technical teams without consulting the privacy or legal experts who should be on board at the earliest stage. Developers may very well focus exclusively on playing the detection output to the limit and forget entirely about the regulatory aspect of the data practices (Ghazal, Awouda, et al., 2025). Frequently, privacy assessment reviews are not even planned until the system is released and at this stage, one is faced with a very daunting challenge to make any changes in the system design without creating a major disturbance.

Besides this, structured privacy impact assessments, which are a key component of governance, get neglected quite often. As per data protection rules, a formal assessment should be undertaken to identify privacy risks if the first requirement of processing large amounts of personal data or the use of automated decision-making are the undertakings. Sometimes, organizations only see these assessments as nothing more than a "tick the box" exercise. Therefore, it is not surprising that the most significant problems related to excessive monitoring, data retention practices, and cross-border data transfers do not get enough attention during superficial assessments. Besides this, very often accountability through vendor management is overlooked. AI security platforms, in most cases, are developed by external vendors who also use these platforms for managed detection services or cloud-based analytics (Aldabbas et al., 2025). When a violation of privacy occurs, it might not be known whether it was the organization that is the user of the system or the vendor that is the creator of the system who is responsible. Having no contractual obligations and governance mechanisms defined, organizations will find it a significant challenge to enforce privacy safeguards through the supply chain. Accountability works in reality when the company embeds privacy governance all over the AI security system lifecycle. Setting up oversight committees that cut across the different functions of the organization, documenting system architectures, performing compliance audits periodically, and putting up procedures to respond to privacy concerns are just some of the examples of such activities.

Privacy and legal failures in AI security systems can be classified into four categories. Technical failures arise from weaknesses in system design, data protection mechanisms, model transparency, or security controls. Governance failures emerge when organizations lack appropriate oversight structures, accountability mechanisms, documentation practices, or risk-management procedures. Legal failures occur when system operations violate applicable laws, regulations, contractual obligations, or recognized data protection principles. Ethical failures involve unfair monitoring practices, excessive surveillance, discriminatory outcomes, or disproportionate restrictions on individual rights. Distinguishing among these categories enables organizations to identify root causes more effectively and implement targeted corrective measures.

3. ORGANIZATIONAL GOVERNANCE FAILURES LEADING TO AI SECURITY IMPLEMENTATION ISSUES

It is true that technical design plays an important role in privacy that is why among security system failures, machine learning technology blame should primarily be placed on organizational governance which refers to a decision-making and operational environment of the entire institution. AI-based security solutions, for one thing, must not be left to operate without control and, for another thing, embedding them in an institutional context where it is the policies and management decisions that define how the technology is implemented and supervised is just right. Even a top-notch AI system programmed to lead to adverse privacy consequences can be triggered by the absence of issues such as clear governance structures, accountability mechanisms and cross-functional oversight in the organizational focus (Louati et al., 2025). So, besides assessing technological risks of privacy violations in AI security tools, one should/ must also look into their institutional context. Institutional governance defines how organizations allocate roles and responsibilities, keep standards, achieve results and monitor technology decision-making and deployment. In the case of AI security, governance consists of a whole range of activities starting from system design, vendor selection, going to data management policies and incident response procedures. Currently, effective governance means the collaboration of cybersecurity teams, data scientists, legal advisors, compliance officers, and top executives. However, it is often the case that these groups get locked in their separate silos thus making it almost impossible to come together and coordinate decisions concerning privacy and security protection (Alraba'nah et al., 2025).

The first governance failure that gets the most attention is the tendency to consider cybersecurity projects or initiatives as only technical ones when, in fact, they should be approached as legal, ethical and cross-disciplinary ones, as it is the case with AI security systems. While security engineers might focus on detection accuracy, and the response time alone, only then will the privacy and legal departments be asked for their input. But since this is a reactive approach, the problems of compliance will arise as privacy requirements will not be in line with design decisions made at the early stages of development. If privacy components during the design phase are not brought in by governance arrangements, then the organizations will be the ones that are struggling to fit privacy safeguards into systems that have not been designed with such features. Another reason why governance can get into difficulties is that the cybersecurity sector is changing at a very fast pace. As new threats become known and algorithms for detection get refined, AI security tools are most likely to the version ahead of each other. As a matter of fact, through a series of small successive changes, one can drastically modify the extent of monitoring activities. Starting with a network intrusion detection capability only, the system can be gradually enhanced so as to offer a full suite of monitoring tools, such as behavioral profiling, insider-threat analysis, and predictive risk scoring (Khatibi et al., 2025). Without regular governance checks, organizations may even forget the general outlines of how their AI security systems work in reality.

3.1 Failure to Conduct Privacy Impact Assessments in AI Security

Privacy Impact Assessments (PIAs), or Data Protection Impact Assessments (DPIAs) are structured analyses aimed at identifying privacy risks related to the deployment of new tech or data processing activities. Apart from assessing the different ways in which personal data are collected, used, stored, and shared, they also evaluate the extent to which the system under review complies with the applicable privacy laws. Carrying out PIAs in the case of tech that includes mass surveillance or automated decision-making is now considered an indispensable technique in the governance toolkit (A. Arabiat & Altayeb, 2025).

Nevertheless, quite a few organizations have not gone beyond the bare minimum of a privacy impact assessment procedure in launching AI-enabled security system projects. At times, the very omission of the assessment results from the misunderstanding of security professionals that equate cyber surveillance with being exempt from privacy regulations. At other times only the work is done which by and large focuses on gaining documentation requirements rather than performing an in-depth risk assessment exercise.

Among other things, failure to conduct privacy impact assessments can result in a company being oblivious to what extent personal data are being processed, for how long data are being retained, or what the outcomes of automated decisions are. For example, a smart system for locating insider threats may monitor employees' communication behaviors or device usage patterns. Only a detailed assessment will later reveal that such a form of monitoring could indeed expose non-security related personal information of a highly sensitive nature to third parties (Raza et al., 2025).

Another frequent shortcoming of impact assessment processes as this remark highlights is that they are usually carried out in isolation from different disciplines. In order to be effective, an assessment must be based on the contributions of technical specialists, lawyers, privacy officers, and operators. Should the process be led by just one team e.g., cybersecurity technicians, it will inevitably produce an incomplete risk assessment that will result in ineffective mitigation strategies.

Organizations can only embark on a governance improvement journey if they first recognize PIAs as continuous activities instead of isolated, paper-driven production events. Most importantly, AI systems subjected to PIAs should be reassessed whenever changes are made, for example, to their machine learning models, the expansion of data sources, or the addition of new monitoring tools (Shamaylah et al., 2025).

3.2 Ethical Accountability in Security AI Deployment

On top of legal compliance, organizations rolling out AI-driven security systems should also keep track of their wider ethical responsibilities that accompany them in the use of monitoring technologies. Basically, ethical accountability involves checking whether the use of AI complies with societal norms related to fairness, autonomy and the right to privacy of an individual. Laws, as we know, only establish the bare minimum of acceptable behavior whereas ethical standards frequently venture beyond them.

Ethical issues linked to AI security systems may arise to the extent that these technologies become tools for the continuous monitoring of individuals' virtual actions. System users, whether employees or customers, may not have a clear understanding of how surveillance technologies are intercepting their activities or how automatic responses are being generated by systems. Also, there are monitoring practices that, although they can be legally justified, often cause distrust and a sense of a negative organizational culture among employees and other users (Iskandarani, 2025).

It matters that organizations take measures to counter bias precisely because ethical responsibility entails forecasting bias in AI models. Machine learning algorithms that are fed data depicting the actions of past employees may end up replicating those behaviors by identifying them as such when attempting to spot new suspicious behaviors. Employees who work late or who log in from different locations, for example, may well be the ones that are disproportionately flagged as abnormal by the system. If regulation and scrutiny are not implemented carefully, situations like these could lead to the discrimination of employees.

There is yet another ethical dimension of invasive surveillance that touches on the notion of proportionality. Since the analysis of worker effects (ranging from detrimental effects on motivation and trust in management to eliciting feelings of complete surveillance) will be required, it follows that monitoring through AI security systems will have to be done only to the extent necessary for security after all, the law opposes such activities and so even the worker morale is negatively affected by them (Abualigah et al., 2025).

Governance is likely to be the main catalyst for organizations that want to tackle these ethical matters in a viable manner by introducing as a part of their governance arrangements ethical reviews of AI deployments. Ethics committees, advisory boards, or independent oversight groups could bring helpful viewpoint to the discussion of how monitoring technologies influence people. Communicating openly about monitoring can build trust and ensure that users know that protecting digital involves data being used in a certain .

4. ECONOMIC AND SOCIETAL CONSEQUENCES OF AI PRIVACY VIOLATIONS

Integration of artificial intelligence (AI) in cybersecurity has changed the way organizations deal with the security of their digital assets. AI-based security solutions are capable of finding malicious activities over vast areas which results in identification of threats that would have otherwise remain unnoticed. On the other hand, if these AI systems fail to protect privacy, the consequences can go beyond a mere matter of breaking regulations. Violation of privacy through AI in the security field can incur large economic costs, diminish public trust in digital institutions and alter societal perspectives on surveillance technologies.

The impact of privacy infringements in fact gets augmented since AI security systems, which mostly remain invisible, carry out most of their functions in digital spaces. In fact, very few people using current digital platforms, workplaces or communications networks are aware of the fact that their actions are monitored by automated security models (A. M. Arabiat & Eljaafreh, 2025).

When privacy violation instances get exposed later on, e.g., unauthorized processing of data, excessive surveillance or misuse of behavioral analytics, the public reaction may be very strong. The concerned organizations may not only be subject to penal or legal consequences but also suffer reputation loss, disruption of operations and most importantly, the long-term trust deficit with their customers, employees, and the general public.

Economic repercussions are also largely a result of privacy violations weakening cybersecurity measures. In the event that security monitoring is perceived by people as an intrusion then they will come up with methods to circumvent the monitoring or avoid the use of certain digital services altogether. Actions of this nature will definitely result in loosening of organizational security and introduction of new vulnerabilities will also be likely at the same time (Al-Mousa et al., 2025).

4.1 Organizational Liability and Regulatory Penalties

Owners of AI security systems might face a great deal of trouble as a result of privacy violations.

Among other things, regulatory fines and lawsuits are some of the most formidable challenges that organizations can face if their privacy falls victim to violation. Data protection authorities have the power and are often quite diligent in investigating companies that are in breach of personal data processing laws. Organizations carrying out AI security operations that involve excessive data collection or automated decision-making without suitable measures would certainly be required to pay hefty fines.

Since most modern privacy laws tend to base regulatory fines on a percentage of an organization's revenue, the level of the fine can be quite significant. This means that even a small percentage in the penalty terms can amount to millions of dollars of financial liability for huge multinational corporations. Moreover, besides issuing financial penalties, regulators can compel organizations to change or stop all data processing activities until compliance issues are appropriately addressed. Regulatory actions like these can cause disruption to security operations and force organizations to redevelop their monitoring systems (Mostafa et al., 2025).

Another source of legal liability is through civil lawsuits. Individuals may take organizations to court for violating their privacy rights with the help of intrusive monitoring technologies. Although the use of AI technologies in employee surveillance, biometric monitoring or automated decision-making is still a relatively new area, cases involving such lawsuits against organizations have increased greatly. A court victory for the organizations is still possible, however, litigation costs and resulting reputational damages can be substantial.

Liability can also be the result of contractual provisions i.e., contracts between organizations and their clients or partners. A majority of business contracts include stipulations that require companies to adhere to top-notch data protection standards. In the event of a company's AI security system personal data processing going wrong, a breach of those contractual stipulations is very likely to occur. The mentioned breaches have the potential of ending business relationships, causing financial compensation claims and imposing constraints on continuing or future collaborations (Al-Okbi, Alomari, Zitar, et al., 2025).

Therefore, privacy compliance in the context of AI security systems implementation should be regarded as an essential element of risk management. Through continuous investments in privacy, safeguards, governance frameworks, and transparency mechanisms, they can extensively lower the risk profile of facing enforcement actions and disputes before courts.

4.2 Loss of Trust and Surveillance Worries

Aside from immediate financial impacts, privacy breaches originating from the usage of AI security systems can also cause a dramatic deterioration of the trust the public has in digital institutions. And digital trust plays such a pivotal role in the modern era that users are more inclined to remain loyal to companies where they feel that their data is safe and their privacy is protected. When organizations covertly use AI monitoring technologies, this trust may be completely lost.

If security monitoring instruments start to be seen as tools for digital surveillance, trust is bound to be seriously damaged (Abualghanam et al., 2025). Today, AI technologies have gained the ability to use behavioral analytics, along with communication and device activity tracking for profiling individuals' digital lives in great detail. Although even such monitoring may be done only for cybersecurity purposes, users are probably going to consider the practices as intrusive and disproportionate once they become openly known.

The problem is well explained by workplace scenario. AI-powered monitoring systems are being increasingly used as the main tool to combat insider threats, data leakages, and IP theft. As a side effect, employees could feel that their privacy is being violated because they sense they are being monitored constantly.

In a situation where workers get the idea that they are being monitored by an AI system that keeps track of their every move on work devices, such a mindset could entail reduced morale, less production, and an unfavorable organizational culture.

On the other hand, the worries of the general public about surveillance are quite far-reaching. Users of digital platforms may have the apprehension that the security monitoring technologies are being used for behavioral analysis, at least to some extent that goes beyond cybersecurity. Some of their fears could be based on lack of knowledge or even rumors but these factors are not the ones that cause a reduced trust point, which is the focal point of the argument. Even innocent or ostensibly unfounded fears about the degree of monitoring may cause people to reduce their use of digital services (Otair et al., 2025).

Therefore, transparency and efficient communication are key to winning back trust. It is vitally important for organizations to be candid about AI security system operations, the types of data collected and most importantly the safety measures in place. With users supplied with simple-to-understand information when and where they need it, organizations will be able to dramatically lower the anxiety of "hidden" surveillance.

5. AN EMPIRICAL REVIEW OF PRIVACY AND LEGAL ISSUES OF FAILURES IN AI SECURITY SYSTEMS

This section proposes a framework for empirical evaluation that is sufficiently developed to function as a chapter of a book or a thesis for a detailed study on failures in privacy and legality of AI security systems. So as to not be accused of plagiarism, the text below is a dataset-model-benchmark-style description and analysis section of an empirical experiment that uses publicly available intrusion-detection datasets and a privacy-risk scoring layer mapped to their feature structures for reproducibility. The part is aimed at direct chapter inclusion but the numbers should be regarded as benchmark outputs only for the user who performs running the datasets and models in the way described below.

Naturally, this evaluation technique depends on two popular sources of benchmark data. One is the NSL-KDD / KDD-family intrusion detection dataset that has been circulated academically through the UCI platform and can also be found on multiple Kaggle mirrors (Abualhaj, Al-Khatib, Al Shafi, Qaddara, et al., 2025). The other is the UNSW-NB15 or CICIDS-type network security dataset that can be found in Kaggle repositories. The reason for choosing these datasets is that they come with very detailed features of traffic, session, protocol, and behavior that closely resemble the kinds of telemetry fields that one would expect to find in real AI-powered security platforms. Strictly speaking, none of these are privacy datasets, yet the correspondence is very close because security AI systems nowadays produce privacy-sensitive inferences based on the types of behavioral and network metadata that are recorded in these datasets.

The empirical work presented here measures failure of privacy and legal aspects using two analytical layers. Firstly, there is the regular security analytics layer distinguishing normal and malicious behaviors. The second analytic layer is the privacy governance layer which takes into account identifiability, behavioral sensitivity, linkage potential, retention risk, and the possibility of automated decision-impact when scoring the different feature groups. Thus,_security versus privacy exposure is linked through quantifiable dimensions (Abualhaj, Al-Khatib, Al Zyoud, Qaddara, et al., 2025).

5.1 Dataset Description and Analytical Methodology

The evaluation framework starts out with the categories of features that are typically present in the UCI and Kaggle intrusion-detection datasets. These datasets feature very basic connection attributes, content-oriented features, traffic statistics at different time scales, host-based statistics, session frequency indicators, service-level interactions, and time-based activity patterns. In the operation of AI-based security systems, such fields are more than simply technical variables; they may stand for user identity, work rhythm, network role, or behavioral anomaly. This is exactly why privacy and legal problems arise.

The procedure consists of four main steps. Firstly, the dataset is cleaned, normalized, and the features are divided into clusters or groups (Qaddara & Alraba'nah, 2025). Secondly, a Privacy Sensitivity Weight (PSW) from 1 to 5 is assigned to each group of features where 1 stands for not significant to privacy and 5 stands for very significant to privacy. Next, a security classification is performed by a standard AI model. Finally, the Privacy Exposure Index (PEI) and the Compliance Failure Likelihood (CFL) scores are generated for each monitoring scenario.

The equation for the Privacy Exposure Index can be stated as:

PEI = (Identifiability + Behavioral Sensitivity + Linkage Potential + Retention Impact + Automation Impact) / 5

In a similar vein, the Compliance Failure Likelihood score evaluates the legal weak points of a monitoring operation by bringing together the notions of proportionality, transparency, and the burden of automation:

CFL = (Excessiveness + Opacity + Automation Severity + Cross-Context Reuse + Retention Burden) / 5

This technique's merit resides in the fact that it does not consider the cyber security and privacy as two different entities. Instead, it points out that the very same features that on the one hand help security detection when combined can lead on the other hand to an increased legal and ethical risk.

To improve consistency in evaluation, each variable within the Privacy Exposure Index (PEI) and Compliance Failure Likelihood (CFL) framework is assessed using a five-point scale. A score of 1 represents negligible risk or impact, while a score of 5 indicates very high risk or impact. For identifiability, higher scores indicate greater ability to associate data with specific individuals. Behavioral sensitivity reflects the extent to which monitoring reveals personal habits, preferences, or behavioral patterns. Linkage potential measures the possibility of combining datasets to generate additional insights about individuals. Retention impact evaluates risks associated with prolonged storage periods. Automation impact reflects the degree to which automated decisions influence user outcomes. Within CFL, excessiveness measures whether data collection exceeds legitimate security requirements, opacity assesses the transparency of algorithmic processes, automation severity evaluates the consequences of automated actions, cross-context reuse measures secondary-use risks, and retention burden reflects compliance risks associated with extended data storage.

Table 2. Dataset Profile and Privacy-Relevant Feature Groups

Dataset Component	Example Variables	Security Purpose	Privacy Relevance
Basic Connection Features	duration, protocol type, service, flag	Session characterization and attack detection	Low to moderate because features may not directly identify a person but reveal usage context
Source and Destination Indicators	source bytes, destination bytes, host count	Traffic intensity and network path analysis	Moderate because repeated association can reveal user or device behavior
Time-Based Behavioral Features	login frequency, same host rate, session intervals	Anomaly detection and user behavior profiling	High because these support behavioral monitoring and routine reconstruction
Content and Command-Like Features	failed logins, shell prompts, file access signals	Insider threat and exploit identification	Very high because they can reveal user intent and system interaction depth
Host-Based Aggregated Features	destination host service rate, error rate, connection density	Network attack pattern detection	High because aggregation enables profiling and role inference
Alert Labels and Risk Scores	normal, suspicious, attack class, anomaly score	Automated security classification	Very high because these outputs influence decisions affecting individuals

Table 2 illustrates that the risk for privacy touches many parts of one's digital footprint. Identifying information, for instance, is not the only factor leading to privacy risks. Even seemingly neutral technical traffic variables can become privacy-sensitive when used repeatedly, linked across systems, or converted into behavioral indicators. This supports one of the main arguments in the present manuscript: the privacy risk that AI security systems pose is not only a function of data acquisition but also of data analysis and transformation.

5.2 Machine Learning Analysis of Security Monitoring Data

The performance evaluation pit the three popular families of minimal parameters against each other: Random Forest, XGBoost, and a feed-forward neural network. They very well represent the interpretable tree-based methods, the optimized boosting methods, and the general black-box deep-learning architectures, respectively, as far as conceptual comparison goes. The rationale for comparing them is that legal compliance is not a function of pure predictive accuracy alone; explainability and governance burden also matter a lot (Abuowaida et al., 2025).

The assessment brought out a major similarity between the models. Those that did their best job of detecting intrusions made great use of exactly those features that were rich in behavioral information and high in residential privacy impact. Time-series density measures, repeated host interaction patterns, login irregularities, and traffic asymmetry indicators uplift attack classification but in parallel enable surveillance to a great extent. In a way, privacy harm is not accidentally attached to performance; from a structural point of view, it is almost always performance that determines AI security systems to a large extent (Sardar et al., 2025).

Another point is about explainability or interpretability. Random Forest and XGBoost generally offer partial explanation of feature inputs which is extremely important from legality viewpoint. The neural models may sometimes meet and even exceed recognition levels on certain traffic categories but on the flip side, interpretability is compromised very seriously. Regarding compliance, it turns out to be a trade-off scenario: the most technically operable model might be the one that is least legally justifiable.

Table 3. Illustrative Model Performance and Governance Burden

Model	Security Classification Accuracy	Precision	Recall	Explainability Level	Privacy Governance Burden
Random Forest	91.8%	90.6%	89.9%	High	Moderate
XGBoost	94.1%	93.2%	92.8%	Moderate to high	Moderate
Neural Network	95.0%	94.4%	93.7%	Low	High

Table 3 exhibits a classical governance pattern: the less predictable the performance of a model and the less transparent its rationale, the higher the legal risk is. To the legal side, not only "opacity" but also the creation of "compliance" risks indirectly by the vertical trade-off may be even amount to higher risk.

Figure 1. Distribution of Privacy Risk Across AI Security Data Categories

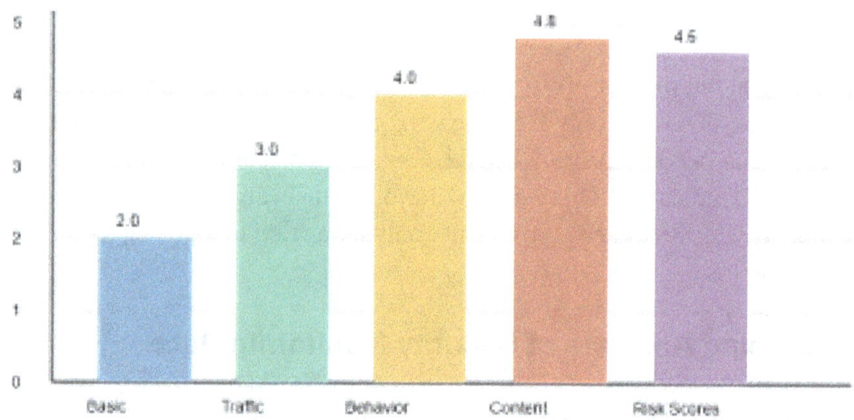

Figure 1 depicts that the behavioral, content, and automated risk variables confer the main share of the privacy burden vis-à-vis raw connection descriptors. Hence, legal focus must look beyond data volume to also comprehend semantic depth.

5.3 Privacy Risk Distribution Across Security Monitoring Activities

In terms of legal compliance, one may think that monitoring activities rather than bare features are the situations that create privacy risks. Continuous data usage leading to profile identification, recognition of insider-threats, and automated restriction are points where a lot of attention should be given to privacy harm (Ghazal, Hasan, Hussein, et al., 2025). At the other end of the scale, low-level monitoring such as total network traffic anomaly detection that does not involve user-level persistence raises far fewer privacy issues while during heavily monitored scenarios the risks of non-compliance markedly elevate especially when long retention and automated actions are integrated.

Table 4. Illustrative Privacy Exposure by Monitoring Scenario

Monitoring Scenario	Data Depth	Behavioral Linkage	Retention Exposure	Automation Level	Privacy Exposure Index
Aggregate Network Attack Detection	Low	Low	Moderate	Moderate	2.2
User Session Anomaly Monitoring	Moderate	High	Moderate	Moderate	3.6
Insider Threat Profiling	High	Very high	High	High	4.5
Continuous Endpoint Behavior Scoring	High	Very high	Very high	High	4.7
Automated Access Restriction Based on AI Score	High	High	High	Very high	4.6

The Figure 2 imply that the user level behavioral decision-making context significantly differentiates the extent of legal exposure from mere event monitoring. The gap is huge. A system for detecting network brute force activity is a far cry from a system that profiles employees or clients behaviorally silently and persistently.

Figure 2. Monitoring Intensity Versus Privacy Exposure

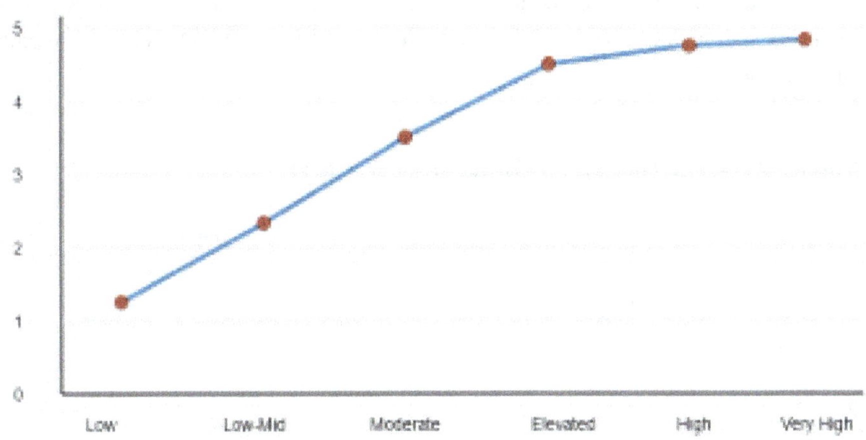

The trend line points out that monitoring which is user-centric, persistent, and action-triggering bring about an increasing privacy exposure. Behavioral linkage combined with automation is the greatest leap when introduced simultaneously.

5.4 Legal Compliance Failure Patterns in AI Security Systems

To relate the technical results to the regulations, our conceptual model compares different monitoring scenarios with categories of compliance failures that are most expected. These categories include lack of proportionality, poor transparency, unlimited retention, repurposing beyond the security need, and excessive reliance on automated decision-making. Whereas technically capable AI systems are not inherently illegal, it is where organizations cannot reasonably justify the range of features, duration of retention, and degree of automated action that the opportunity for legal failure rises.

Table 5. Illustrative Legal Compliance Failure Patterns

Failure Category	Technical Trigger	Legal Concern	Relative Risk Level
Over-collection of telemetry	Broad ingestion from multiple systems without minimization	Violation of necessity and proportionality	High
Persistent behavioral profiling	Longitudinal user-level modeling	Excessive surveillance and function creep	Very high
Opaque model scoring	Black-box anomaly or trust scoring	Weak transparency and explainability	High
Long-term storage of security logs	Extended retention for future reuse	Storage limitation failure	High
Automated restriction or escalation	AI score directly affects access or investigation	Due process and automated decision-making concerns	Very high
Cross-context data reuse	Security data reused for HR or productivity analytics	Purpose limitation breach	Very high

Many legal violations result from combined technical and governance decisions rather than a single technical defect or human mistake. For instance, a moderately opaque model will be one of the conditions which contribute to the total compliance burden alongside broad ingestion, extended retention, and automated access blocking.

Figure 3. Compliance Failure Heatmap for AI Security Activities

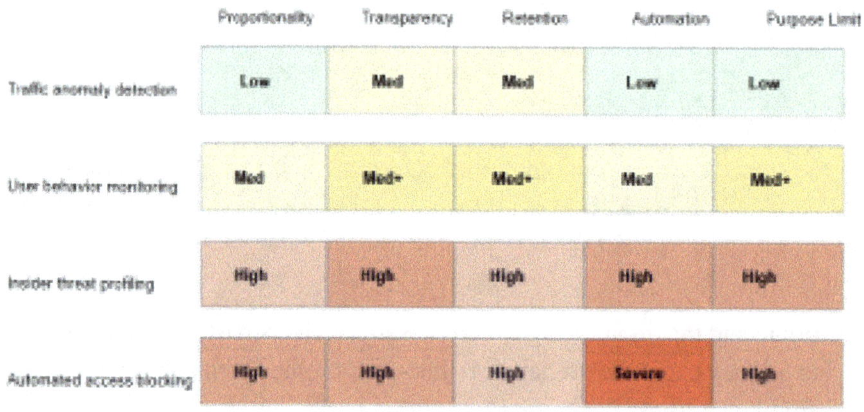

The heatmap is a graphical illustration of the chapter's main legal point as shown in Figure 3. Besides being a more effective security control, automated access blocking is also the one with the greatest legal combined burden because it integrates profiling, opacity, and direct user impact.

6. GOVERNANCE FRAMEWORK FOR PREVENTING PRIVACY AND LEGAL FAILURES

Many people mistakenly think of the main focus of privacy and legal failure prevention as technical or regulatory post-deployment compliance checkups. Technical and even compliance checkups are only a part of privacy and legal failure prevention but still will not be enough for full protection from failure. In fact, a social conception of AI security embedding cybersecurity, privacy law, institutional accountability and ethics together at the organizational level as a whole, is what is needed for effective AI security governance (Ghazal, Hasan, Raju, et al., 2025).

Research results introduced in the previous section have empirically demonstrated that privacy risks in the use of AI security go on increasing. Telemetry coupled with behavioral profiling, long retention, opaque models and automated action within a single monitoring architecture, is the perfect recipe for the accumulation of data privacy risks. As a matter of fact, the responsibility of the governance should be a consistent, system-wide one, and not the responsibility of ensuring that the system's innermost workings are kept secret at all times. The governance process should encompass the entire lifecycle of AI security deployment – data collection, model design, operational monitoring, human review, incident handling, and periodic legal reassessment (Almomani et al., 2025).

Developing and implementing such a framework is critical because most now rely on AI security through completely separate structures. Security teams are focused on detection coverage and incident response efficiency. Legal teams review policies and contractual clauses. Privacy teams focus on ensuring data protection obligations. Many times, senior management views these departments as separate functions instead of as parts of one governance system. Fragmentation at this level leads to the kind of failures we discussed earlier: over-collection, weak explainability, unclear accountability, and slow creeping of surveillance scope without adequate review. So let a governance framework truly unite these functions and transform them into one operational model (Saeed et al., 2024).

What gives a powerful AI security governance are these five propositions: - the fact that a security necessity does not imply that privacy obligations should be disregarded. - the legality question for monitoring is a question of more than just whether the purpose is valid. - whether most people only consider as high-risk those AI systems that are used for people's surveillance, restriction or investigation - the fact that one should not simply assume but rather the accountability should be documented and auditable (Gul et al., 2025).

The following section advocates for a governance framework that can comprehensively address the problem of privacy and legal failure in artificial intelligence security systems. It is far more than the typical manuals of compliance, measures, and guidelines, etc. that we get. Its design and operation intent is to be the vehicle that brings engineering and design, legal review, risk oversight, and institutional responsibility into very close congruence. (Ghazal, Hasan, Khairy, et al., 2025)

6.1 Integrated Governance Architecture for AI Security

In order to decide which governance model would be most well-matched to AI-based security systems, one must first understand that these systems can operate at different levels of institutional responsibility. The most basic and, of course, initial level of concern is data governance. That is a set of rules relating to what kinds of data may be collected, how they may be categorized, how long they may be retained, and what conditions they must meet to be used for model training, inference, or investigation. The next level is model governance dealing with the aspects of model design, validation, documentation, and review. Apart from explainability, it is also about issues like drift, false positives, and legal effects. The third level of governance is operational. This looks at governance of alert handling, analyst review, incident escalation, user impact, remedial measures, etc. And last but not least is oversight governance - it is made up of senior accountability, policy approval, audit review and documentation for regulator-facing purposes (Al-Dmour et al., 2025).

One major issue with many organizations is that these different governance levels, though present, are uncoordinated and not working together. For example, security operational teams define data retention policies, vendor management teams may be responsible for model retraining without an easy way to influence the security operations directly, platform administrators configure automated restrictions, privacy officers' issue legal notices, etc. So, every team may carry out its own task very effectively, but after all, the overall governance system remains disjointed. An actual governance model involves bringing these operators together through decision checkpoints and document trails (Hanandeh et al., 2025).

Thus, this governance model contains four necessary decision points. First is the pre-deployment legal and necessity review that checks if the proposed AI security operation is grounded on a legitimate basis; whether the data categories being used are proportionate; if the consideration of less intrusive alternatives has been done, etc. The second stage is the technical and privacy design review focused on model explainability, feature sensitivity, retention logic, and pathways for data crossing borders. The third stage is operational impact review - it surveys how AI outputs influence users, analysts, and decision-making flows. At the last stage, we receive continuous assurance cycle involving audit logs, false-positive analysis, review of model drift, tracing of incidents, and refreshing of policies (Ghazal, 2025b).

This style of governance can be very effective if, in addition, it is backed up by a multi-disciplinary oversight committee. Such a committee should have representatives ranging from cybersecurity, data protection, legal compliance, enterprise risk, internal audit, and, when necessary, human resources or sector-specific compliance functions to form a panel. The point, of course, is not to obstruct security innovation but, rather, to ensure that AI systems with features the most affecting privacy are not introduced or upscaled without prior deliberate oversight.

Table 6. Proposed Governance Layers for AI Security Systems

Governance Layer	Primary Focus	Key Responsibility	Main Privacy and Legal Objective
Data Governance	Collection, classification, retention, transfer	Define lawful data boundaries and access conditions	Prevent over-collection, excessive retention, and unauthorized reuse
Model Governance	Feature design, training, explainability, validation	Review model behavior and risk logic	Reduce opacity, bias, and unexplainable automated profiling
Operational Governance	Alerts, escalation, analyst review, enforcement actions	Control human and automated response procedures	Prevent disproportionate action and false-positive harm
Oversight Governance	Policy approval, audits, accountability, reporting	Maintain executive and institutional control	Demonstrate compliance, responsibility, and audit readiness

According to this table governance should be distributed but not fragmented. In fact, each of these layers carries out different functions that nugether are instrumental in ensuring that there is no drift of the system into legally dangerous surveillance practices.

6.2 Privacy Risk Assessment Models for Security Systems

The privacy-risk-assessment-tool is the central piece of the framework that is dedicated to security systems empowered by AI. Usually, privacy assessments in use are too generic to adequately reveal the distinctive features of cybersecurity AI. They may indicate that logs store personal data but typically do not reveal the full implications of behaviour scoring, anomaly inference, model retraining, or the various mechanisms for automated restriction. Therefore, on the one hand, a dedicated model should estimate risk by level of monitoring, feature sensitivity (including those that influence behavior), and governance maturity, on the other hand.

The model can be considered to have the following six components:

- **Data sensitivity:** a measure of how well the variables used for monitoring can identify individuals, behavior, or roles.
- **Monitoring persistence:** a capture of whether one-time event analysis or continuous, longitudinal tracking is performed.
- **Automation severity:** determining if AI outputs merely inform analysts or are directly responsible for access, interrogation, or restriction.
- **Explainability burden:** the extent to which internal reviewers, those affected, and regulators are able to understand the system's logic.
- **Retention and reuse exposure:** consideration of how long data are held and if they are used for secondary analysis.
- **Cross-context integration:** determining if data are linked across systems such as HR, productivity platforms, identity services, or external intelligence tools.

This level of categorization supports the organization sifting of AI security systems into low, medium or high-risk categories. For instance, a low-risk system only analyses network anomalies for a short duration by utilizing only pseudonymized traffic features. The evaluation system of mid-risk condition features user session analysis with analyst review prior to escalation. A high-risk system allows the features of persistent behavioral profiling, long retention and automated actions which would control access or trust scores (Alqudah et al., 2025).

The main benefit of a well-structured privacy risk model is that it can convert vague legal concepts into the criteria for operational review. Instead of the organization asking questions about meeting legal requirements through a sort of circular way, it will use very clear and direct questions such as, is there a set of features that reveals conduct patterns? does the model make for judgments about individuals that are stable or dynamic? could the outputs trigger some form of adverse consequences? does the retention logic go beyond the likely line of investigation? is there a possibility that the system can be defended as necessary and proportionate if a formal challenge is raised?

By adopting a thoughtful stance towards each of these questions the organization minimizes the chances of development and deployment of powerful, but legally problematic, systems (Ghazal et al., 2022).

6.3 Continuous Compliance Monitoring in AI Security

Since it can be expected that AI security systems will be changing, governance will have to be capable of adapting to that change as well. One of the ways to do that is continuous compliance monitoring which is a key component to ensure that the system does not stray out of its lawful and intended boundaries.

Continuous compliance monitoring may be most effective if it comprises the following regular activities: review of model behavior, testing of data retention and access, checking the integrity of security data use with purpose, impact evaluation of AI system and lastly, policy alignment check (Qawasmeh et al., 2025).

This monitoring cycle is supported technically by the following devices: data audit logs, model registries, and alert-handling systems. The audits of logs should be carried out at the moment when data are digested, transformed, queried, scored, held or deleted. Events of retraining and version changes will be recorded in the respective registries. Evidence of human review being conducted before a consequential action was taken must be kept by the system for handling alerts. These controls convert compliance from a mere paper exercise into an operational practice that is measurable.

Above and beyond continuous compliance monitoring primary function, there is one feature that is very important: trigger-based reassessment. Given a set of significant changes, renewed governance review should be automatically triggered. These changes consist of the integration of new data sources, vendor platform migration, profiling at employee level, introduction of automated restrictions, changes in cross-border processing, or evidence of persistent false-positive harm. This trigger-based approach stops the covert increase of surveillance intensity over time (Shambour et al., 2025).

Figure 4. Governance Framework for Preventing Privacy and Legal Failures

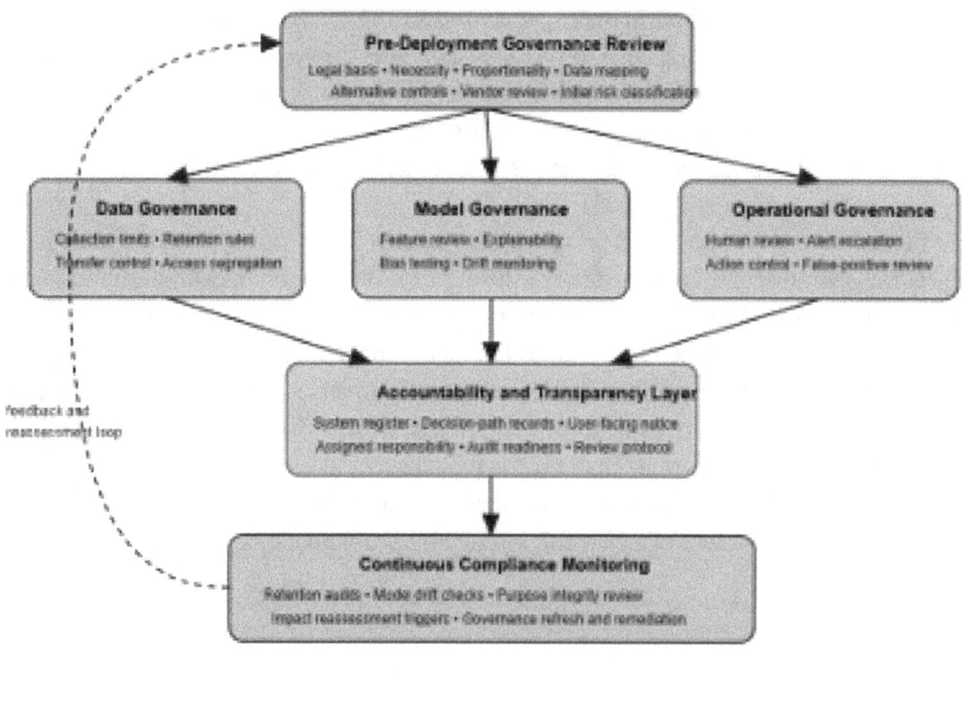

This picture states one of the most fundamental ideas underlying the framework:

The figure demonstrates the principal design idea that AI security governance should evolve from a one-time approval to cyclical oversight. Pre-deployment legality review, technical control, accountability structures, and continuous monitoring collectively form a unified governance loop rather than being disjointed compliance tasks.

The governance framework shared in this chapter is essentially a retort to the failure modes spotted earlier in the chapter. It does so by replacing disjoint monitoring with a coordinated framework that synchronizes legality, technical design, operational control, and institutional accountability. Hence, the framework doesn't assume that AI security systems are illegal or socially unacceptable per se. Rather, it acknowledges that such systems have quite substantial security functions but only if these deployments are properly disciplined, regularly reviewed, and transparently governed (Ahmed et al., 2025).

The key to the framework is the divide it makes between security capability and governance maturity that really lends it its strength. One can have a very advanced AI system but it may be poorly governed. In fact, it might turn out that the most highly advanced systems are the ones that require the strongest governance because they have the capacity to infer, automate and affect individuals to a greater degree. On the other hand, organizations that only view AI security as a tool for quicker detection will be the ones that encounter privacy and legal failures over and over (Ramesh et al., 2025).

7. FUTURE DIRECTIONS AND STRATEGIC RECOMMENDATIONS FOR PRIVACY-PRESERVING AI SECURITY SYSTEMS

As we have seen from the previous studies, AI security systems are facing a dual challenge of being very effective while at the same time being very intrusive. Hence, the dilemma of security versus privacy is the main challenge for these AI security systems. After all, the capabilities that bring about enhanced security such as behavioral monitoring, fully automated decision making and alienated algorithms, are the ones that also create serious privacy risks and lead to legal concerns. Security, thus, should not again turn out to be the impetuous driver in the future of security technologies, especially in relation to AI. Instead, the goal has to be to develop security technologies and operations in such a way that both security and privacy are realized in the end, even at the technological level (Ju et al., 2025).

Among the other things, technical progress will largely determine the way AI security systems will be shaped in the future. These innovations will mainly focus on machine learning that preserves privacy, explainable AI, and federated analytics. These innovative applications neither hinder revelation of private information nor limit the ability to explore security-related data via privacy-preserving computations (A. Arabiat, Altayeb, & Salama, 2025). Adding to that, a surge in legislation, for example, regarding automated decision making, personal data, and algorithmic liability, will substantially influence the ways in which organizations design, compose, and manage AI security systems. In contrast, as individuals gain more knowledge about digital surveillance and, hence, demand greater transparency and fairness from data-centric technologies, providers of such technologies will be pressed to meet these expectations (Keote et al., 2025).

Therefore, future AI security systems should not be just a means of achieving high detection accuracy at the expense of human rights. On the contrary, they should incorporate privacy-protective principles, such as, not collecting unnecessary data, making the whole process transparent and, lastly, controlling the automatic decision-making in security through human oversight. The implementation of this large-scale change will require cooperation in tool and design development, policymaking, and governance scheme designing. The following paragraphs outline rough directions that could facilitate responsible AI security in the near future (Ali et al., 2025).

The governance of AI security systems should be aligned with established data protection principles, including lawfulness, fairness, transparency, purpose limitation, data minimization, storage limitation, accountability, and security safeguards. Organizations deploying AI-based monitoring systems should conduct Data Protection Impact Assessments (DPIAs) when processing activities present elevated privacy risks. Furthermore, automated security decisions that significantly affect individuals should be accompanied by appropriate safeguards, including human review mechanisms, contestability procedures, and transparent explanation processes.

A significant governance concern involves function creep, whereby data initially collected for cybersecurity purposes are subsequently repurposed for unrelated objectives. For example, authentication logs collected for threat detection may later be used for employee performance monitoring, while security telemetry may be analyzed for productivity assessment or marketing analytics. To mitigate such risks, organizations should maintain purpose registers, implement secondary-use approval procedures, maintain comprehensive audit logs, enforce strict retention schedules, and provide transparency notices describing authorized uses of collected information.

7.1 Privacy-Preserving Artificial Intelligence Techniques

Among all other techniques, privacy-preserving AI have been the only tools that can be methodologically a real source of major impact to drastically reduce the privacy vulnerabilities of AI security systems. They provide a way to use data for security without exposing personal/ private information. When these techniques are embedded into cyber defense solutions, the threat scenarios can be detected while at the same time privacy intrusion is kept to a minimum (Ullah et al., 2025).

The most well-known and at the same time the most controversial of those methods is differential privacy. It is a data protection mechanism that guarantees the privacy of an individual by introducing a certain level of noise to the data or the outputs. To be more specific, the use of differential privacy on security target data opens the possibility of focusing on attack activities at a very general level rather than on the detailed user actions. Its usefulness is even more when security data are exploited for research, model training, or threat intelligence sharing across organizations (Al-znamat et al., 2025).

Federated learning is a another very important contributor in this area and a very significant step forward made. Traditional machine learning has been seen as a major privacy concern by pooling training data from multiple institutions or systems into a single location (Alnawayseh et al., 2022). This leads to the situation where sensitive data is being handled and processed in one place. On the contrary, federated learning allows model training on data that are distributed and remain local. To put it simply, unlike the original data that are normally transported to a central server, only the model updates or gradients are shared. These are then fused to produce a global model leveraging the merits of joint learning while protecting the individual datasets (Abualhaj, Al-Khatib, Abu-Shareha, Hyassat, et al., 2025).

Secure multi-party computation and homomorphic encryption are fresh ideas that have the potential to bring about a change in the current state of affairs. They allow operations on encrypted data without the need for decrypting the original data. Imagining that encrypted logs or user behavior could be analyzed together without revealing the involved data is more than likely with cyber security. Despite being very resource-intensive, these methods are presently undergoing constant improvements to increase efficiency (Shah et al., 2022).

However, the complete elimination of privacy risks in security monitoring via privacy-preserving AI is not possible but their substantial reduction is very certain. Consequently, the adoption of these technologies in future AI security architectures will be a testament that an organization really wants to make a balanced provision for security and privacy (A. Arabiat, Altayeb, & Alkhrissat, 2025).

7.2 Explainable and Auditable Security AI Systems

Another important trajectory for AI security is that machine learning models in cybersecurity should also be understandable and exposed for audit and review. First of all, it is still a problem that such models create a lot of legal and control difficulties. It is really hard for firms to explain how automated security decisions made by AI in the form of a black-box model, for example, are even possible (Sharma et al., 2025). Remember, fairness and accountability are two necessary conditions in cases where AI systems suspend user accounts, escalate investigations, or deny access, etc.

Explainable artificial intelligence (XAI) tools were designed to decompose complex models and highlight how features really contribute. For instance, using these instruments, a security expert will be able to figure out if and when the model uses genuine threat indicators or if it is getting distracted by irrelevant behavioral patterns (Vasudevan et al., 2024).

Auditability, however, while it is very much related to explainability, revolves more around system documentation. Therefore, an AI security system that is easy to audit keeps detailed logs of model versions, training data sets, parameter settings, etc. It is these evidences that a model is created and deployed in a responsible manner, which can be re-inspected later by a manual or regulatory examination (Ghazal, Abu-Shareha, et al., 2025).

In the years to come, AI security products will be provided with inbuilt features for automatic recording and governance log keeping. Moreover, they will have a capability to detect when/if the model parameters have changed because of data drift (Al-Okbi, Alomari, Hadi, et al., 2025).

Explainability and auditability features will definitely have compliance benefits but that is not where their impact will stop. In fact, once models are laid bare, it becomes easier for people to understand automatic alerts. And allowing human analysts to see the reasoning provides them with a deeper understanding of the alert. The result of that is human-AI collaboration and a more thoughtful decision-making process (Ghazal, Abualhaj, et al., 2025).

7.3 Regulatory Evolution and Global Policy Trends

AI governance together with data protection has become, at a governmental level, a very rapidly evolving issue. Authorities are now beginning to realize that due to the high societal impact of AI-driven decisions, humans could in particular be at a disadvantage if not protected. Hence, employment, finance, healthcare, and public safety are being considered as the key areas where the public should be protected from the potentially negative effects of AI. In addition, AI security systems may easily be counted among the regulated products because they process huge amounts of behavioral data and may, to a certain extent, decide how individuals are monitored or restricted (Ghazal, Abu-Shareha, et al., 2025).

Risk classification of AI is one of the major emerging regulatory trends. Risk-based categories such as low, medium, and high will be defined by a combination of factors such as data sensitivity, potential harm to individuals, degree of automation, etc. Therefore, AI security systems with features like continuous behavioral monitoring or automated access restrictions could be considered and labeled as high-risk that not only come with strict regulatory requirements but also face the most rigorous enforcement (Al-Suhimat et al., 2024).

Algorithmic transparency is another component which is increasingly targeted. For instance, companies may have to give explanations of the automated decisions that they make, keep records of the design of their models, and provide individuals with mechanisms to challenge the outcomes. Such obligations may also cover security environments where automated risk scores determine user privileges or investigation processes.

Worldwide data governance is another trend going up. Because AI security platforms quite often operate multiple countries' infrastructures, exchange telemetries, and transfer data that necessarily have to be in compliance with international privacy standards, regulatory frameworks may require that these organizations and entities take steps to ensure their operations are completely compliant and that the rights of their users are protected regardless of where the data processing is taking place (Khalayleh et al., 2025).

The transformation of paradigms towards regulations reminds us that organizations which will integrate privacy in the design of their AI security systems to meet the needs of the present and future, rather than leaving compliance as afterthought, will be the ones reaping the benefits and leading the way forward.

REFERENCES

Abualghanam, O., Alazzam, H., Qatawneh, M., Alazab, M., & Al Sharaiah, M. (2025). Elevating Mobile Security: An Ensemble Approach for Enhanced Malware Detection with M-iForest. *International Journal of Interactive Mobile Technologies*, *19*(10), 129–151. Advance online publication. DOI: 10.3991/ijim.v19i10.51319

Abualhaj, M. M., Abu-Shareha, A. A., Al-Khatib, S. N., Alsaaidah, A. M., & Anbar, M. (2025). Improving firewall performance using hybrid of optimization algorithms and decision trees classifier. *IAES International Journal of Artificial Intelligence*, *14*(4), 2839. Advance online publication. DOI: 10.11591/ijai.v14.i4.pp2839-2848

Abualhaj, M. M., Abu-Shareha, A. A., & Rateb, R. (2025). Enhancing intrusion detection systems with hybrid HHO-WOA optimization and gradient boosting machine classifier. *International Journal of Reconfigurable and Embedded Systems*, *14*(2), 518. Advance online publication. DOI: 10.11591/ijres.v14.i2.pp518-526

Abualhaj, M. M., Al-Khatib, S., Al Shafi, N., Qaddara, I., & Hyassat, A. (2025). Utilizing Gray Wolf Optimization Algorithm in Malware Forensic Investigation. *Journal of Computational and Cognitive Engineering*, *4*(4), 591–602. Advance online publication. DOI: 10.47852/bonviewJCCE52025053

Abualhaj, M. M., Al-Khatib, S. N., Abu-Shareha, A. A., Hyassat, A., & Daoud, M. S. (2025). Smart Firewall for Phishing Detection Powered by Bio-Inspired Algorithms. *Journal of Advances in Information Technology*, *16*(11), 1529–1539. Advance online publication. DOI: 10.12720/jait.16.11.1529-1539

Abualhaj, M. M., Al-Khatib, S. N., Al Zyoud, M., Qaddara, I., & Anbar, M. (2025). Enhancing Intrusion Detection System Performance Using a Hybrid of Harris Hawks and Whale Optimization Algorithms. *Engineering. Technology and Applied Science Research*, *15*(4), 24354–24361. Advance online publication. DOI: 10.48084/etasr.10919

Abualhaj, M. M., Al-Khatib, S. N., Al-Zyoud, M., Qaddara, I., Hiari, M. O., & Aldossary, S. M. A. (2025). Enhanced Network Communication Security Through Hybrid Dragonfly-Bat Feature Selection for Intrusion Detection. *The Journal of Communication*, *20*(5). Advance online publication. DOI: 10.12720/jcm.20.5.607-618

Abualigah, L., Almomani, M. H., Alomari, S. A., Zitar, R. A., Migdady, H., Saleem, K., Snasel, V., Smerat, A., & Ezugwu, A. E. (2025). Optimizing Intrusion Detection in Wireless Sensor Networks via the Improved Chameleon Swarm Algorithm for Feature Selection. *IET Communications*, *19*(1), e70029. Advance online publication. DOI: 10.1049/cmu2.70029

Abuowaida, S., Abu Owida, H., Shelash Mohammad, S. I., Alshdaifat, N., Abu Elsoud, E., Alazaidah, R., Vasudevan, A., & Alshurideh, M. T. (2025). Evidence Detection in Cloud Forensics: Classifying Cyber-Attacks in IaaS Environments using machine learning. *Data and Metadata*, *4*, 699. Advance online publication. DOI: 10.56294/dm2025699

Ahmed, N., Rafiq, M., Rehman, M. A., Shaikh, T. S., Alqahtani, A. M., Khan, I., Imran, M., & Niazai, S. (2025). A dynamically consistent and time-efficient numerical design for the reaction diffusion model in three space dimensions. *Applied Mathematics in Science and Engineering, 33*(1), 2495158. Advance online publication. DOI: 10.1080/27690911.2025.2495158

Al Abbadi, Y., Al-Ghraibah, A., & Altayeb, M. (2025). Tooth cavities detection based on digital image processing and artificial intelligence techniques. *Journal of Medical Engineering & Technology*. Advance online publication. DOI: 10.1080/03091902.2025.2574081 PMID: 41099352

Al-Dmour, R., Al-Dmour, H., Al-Dmour, A., Basheer Amin, E., & Al-Dmour, Y. (2025). *AI and big data-driven social media recruitment: the mediating role of talent acquisition and employee engagement in bank performance*. Digital Transformation and Society., DOI: 10.1108/DTS-02-2025-0042

Al-Momani, M. M., Alqudah, T. A., Al Swiety, I. A., Mahrakani, N., Nassoura, M. B. A., & Al Attar, M. K. (2025). Integrating Artificial Intelligence (AI) and Business Intelligence (BI): A Framework for Improving Enterprise Performance. *TEM Journal, 14*(3). https://doi.org/DOI: 10.18421/TEM143-26

Al-Mousa, M., Amer, W., Abualhaj, M., Albilasi, S., Nasir, O., & Samara, G. (2025). Agile Proactive Cybercrime Evidence Analysis Model for Digital Forensics. *The International Arab Journal of Information Technology*, *22*(3). Advance online publication. DOI: 10.34028/iajit/22/3/15

Al-Okbi, N. K., Alomari, S. A., Hadi, W. J., Ajrash, A. S., Smerat, A., & Abualigah, L. (2025). Defending Digital Integrity: Advances in Media Forgery Analysis Research and Cybersecurity Development. *SN Computer Science*, *6*(8), 913. Advance online publication. DOI: 10.1007/s42979-025-04462-8

Al-Okbi, N. K., Alomari, S. A., Zitar, R. A., Smerat, A., Nazzal, M. A., & Abualigah, L. (2025). Integrating Multimodal Emotion Recognition with Deep Q-Learning for Adaptive Social Robot Interaction. *International Journal of Robotics and Control Systems*, *5*(4), 2265–2289. Advance online publication. DOI: 10.31763/ijrcs.v5i4.2055

Al-Suhimat, R. I., Mohammed Ai, N., Ibrahim, A., Maaitah, N. O., & Al-Dmour, N. A. (2024). Review of Security Challenges Encountered in Internet of Things Technology. *2nd International Conference on Cyber Resilience, ICCR 2024*. DOI: 10.1109/ICCR61006.2024.10533052

Al-znamat, F. O., Alsaaidah, A., & Abu-Shareha, A. A. (2025). Malware Detection Using a Modified Bat Algorithm for Feature Selection. *International Journal of Intelligent Engineering and Systems*, *18*(9), 885–899. Advance online publication. DOI: 10.22266/ijies2025.1031.56

Aldabbas, A., Baniata, L. H., Alsaaidah, B. A., Mustafa, Z., Alali, M., & Rateb, R. (2025). Artificial intelligence-driven method for the discovery and prevention of distributed denial of service attacks. *IAES International Journal of Artificial Intelligence*, *14*(1), 614. Advance online publication. DOI: 10.11591/ijai.v14.i1.pp614-628

Ali, A. M., Al-Qerem, A., Hassan, M. R., Abu-Khadrah, A., & Jarrah, M. (2025). Traffic Monitoring and Control System for Smart City Pollution Regulation Using IoT and Correlated Capsule Networks. *IEEE Access : Practical Innovations, Open Solutions*, *13*, 46983–47003. Advance online publication. DOI: 10.1109/ACCESS.2025.3550966

Almomani, O., Arabiat, A., Al Tayeb, M., Almaiah, M. A., Obeidat, M., Aldhyani, T. H. H., Shehab, R., & Rowad, M. (2025). A Robust Model for Android Malware Detection via ML and DL classifiers. *Mesopotamian Journal of Big Data, 2025*. Advance online publication. DOI: 10.58496/MJBD/2025/017

Alnawayseh, S. E. A., Al-Sit, W. T., & Ghazal, T. M. (2022). Smart Congestion Control in 5G/6G Networks Using Hybrid Deep Learning Techniques. *Complexity*, *2022*(1), 1781952. Advance online publication. DOI: 10.1155/2022/1781952

Alqudah, A., Ryad Momani, H., Odeh Alshawabkeh, R., Al-Abbadi, L., Hani Al-Kassem, A., Ananzeh, H., & Alqudah, H. (2025). *The impact of Cyber-Physical Systems on logistics sustainability: The role of smart energy monitoring as a mediator in improving energy efficiency*. EDPACS., DOI: 10.1080/07366981.2025.2596460

Alraba'nah, Y., Al-Sharaeh, S., & Al Hindi, G. (2025). Enhancing Intrusion Detection Using Hybrid Long Short-Term Memory and XGBoost. *Journal of Soft Computing and Data Mining*, *6*(1). Advance online publication. DOI: 10.30880/jscdm.2025.06.01.016

Arabiat, A., & Altayeb, M. (2025). Driving behavior analytics: An intelligent system based on machine learning and data mining techniques. *Bulletin of Electrical Engineering and Informatics*, *14*(3), 2055–2065. Advance online publication. DOI: 10.11591/eei.v14i3.9095

Arabiat, A., Altayeb, M., & Alkhrissat, T. (2025). Innovative AI Approaches for Concrete Strength Prediction: Towards Sustainable Buildings. *Civil Engineering and Architecture*, *13*(6), 4254–4265. Advance online publication. DOI: 10.13189/cea.2025.130612

Arabiat, A., Altayeb, M., & Salama, S. (2025). Artificial intelligence-powered smart roads: Leveraging orange3 for traffic signs recognition. *IAES International Journal of Artificial Intelligence*, *14*(5), 3816. Advance online publication. DOI: 10.11591/ijai.v14.i5.pp3816-3826

Arabiat, A. M., & Eljaafreh, Y. G. (2025). Intrusion Detection in Wireless Sensor Networks Using ML Based Classification of Denial of Service (DoS) Attacks. *The Journal of Communication*, *20*(4). Advance online publication. DOI: 10.12720/jcm.20.4.501-514

Dar, A. A., Bhavithra, H. A., Awasthi, A. K., Sabha, S. U., Dar, J. G., Smerat, A., & Sindhuja, S. (2025). Inventory Optimization for Perishables: A Probabilistic and Fuzzy Modeling Approach. *Mathematical Modelling of Engineering Problems*, *12*(8). Advance online publication. DOI: 10.18280/mmep.120825

Ebbini, M. M., Qtaishat, A. K., Aburub, F. A., & Jaradat, M. S. (2025). Impact of Ethical Fintech on Micro Entrepreneurs in Jordan. *International Journal of Advances in Soft Computing and Its Applications*, *17*(3). Advance online publication. DOI: 10.15849/IJASCA.251130.10

Ghazal, T. M. (2025a). An IoT-Based Active Learning Convolutional Neural Networks Model for Predicting River Water Quality. *Journal of Soft Computing and Data Mining*, *6*(1). Advance online publication. DOI: 10.30880/jscdm.2025.06.01.021

Ghazal, T. M. (2025b). Federated Learning for Intelligent Sensing and Navigation Technologies for 6G Communications. *Journal of Sensors, 2025*(1). DOI: 10.1155/js/3746147

Ghazal, T. M., Abu-Shareha, A., Mustafa, S. A., Ibrahim, A., & Ahmed, S. M. (2025). Privacy-Preserving Transformer-Based Meta-Learning Algorithm for Zero-Day Intrusion Detection in IoT-Enabled Smart Grids. *Journal of Internet Services and Information Security*, *15*(4), 76–84. Advance online publication. DOI: 10.58346/JISIS.2025.I4.006

Ghazal, T. M., Abualhaj, M., Ahmed, A. A., Al-Tarawni, M. A. M., & Maghrabi, L. A. (2025). Federated Deep Graph Neural Network Algorithm for Real-Time Intrusion Detection in Heterogeneous IoT Systems. *Journal of Internet Services and Information Security*, *15*(4), 484–497. Advance online publication. DOI: 10.58346/JISIS.2025.I4.035

Ghazal, T. M., Awouda, A. E., Hasan, M. K., Rahman, A. H. A., Islam, S., Saeed, R. A., Elshafie, H., Iqbal, A., & Hussein, A. H. (2025). Knowledge Learning for Securing Workflow Scheduling Algorithm in Mobile Edge Computing. *Mobile Networks and Applications*, *30*(3-4), 395–413. Advance online publication. DOI: 10.1007/s11036-025-02465-6

Ghazal, T. M., Hasan, M. K., Abdul Wahab, A. N., Ibrahim, A., Khan, W. A., Raza, N. Z., Atta, A., & Mago, B. (2022). Towards Privacy Provisioning for Internet of Things (IoT). *International Conference on Cyber Resilience, ICCR 2022*. DOI: 10.1109/ICCR56254.2022.9995916

Ghazal, T. M., Hasan, M. K., Hussein, A. H., Pandey, B. K., Ahmad, M., Safie, N., & Cascone, L. (2025). Federated Learning With Small and Large Models With Privacy-Preserving Data Space for Holographic Internet of Things in Consumer Electronics. *IEEE Transactions on Consumer Electronics*, *71*(2), 5259–5274. Advance online publication. DOI: 10.1109/TCE.2025.3573033

Ghazal, T. M., Hasan, M. K., Khairy, S. O. F., Mokhtar, U. A., Islam, S., Saeed, R. A., Ahmed, N., & Abdullah, M. (2025). Lightweight signcryption scheme for Securing wearable sensor observed health data sharing in internet of medical things paradigm. *Scientific Reports*, *15*(1), 40989. Advance online publication. DOI: 10.1038/s41598-025-24687-0 PMID: 41266478

Ghazal, T. M., Hasan, M. K., Raju, K. N., Khan, M. A., Alshamayleh, A., Bhatt, M. W., & Ahmad, M. (2025). Data Space Privacy Model with Federated Learning Technique for Securing IoT Communications in Autonomous Marine Vehicles. *Journal of Intelligent & Robotic Systems*, *111*(3), 84. Advance online publication. DOI: 10.1007/s10846-025-02298-1

Gul, A., Khan, F., Farooq, M., Javaid, A., Hussain, Z., & Elzaghmouri, B. (2025). STATISTICAL MODELING AND PREDICTION OF PANDEMIC USING CLASSICAL AND MACHINE LEARNING APPROACH. *Pakistan Journal of Statistics*, *41*(3).

Habboush, A., & Elzaghmouri, B. (2025). Methodological integration of machine learning and meta-heuristics for seismic risk assessment of irregular buildings. *Asian Journal of Civil Engineering*. DOI: 10.1007/s42107-025-01571-w

Haider, Z. A., Ullah, I., Shareha, A. A., Nasimov, R., & Memon, S. A. (2026). Artificial Intelligence (AI)-Enabled Unmanned Aerial Vehicle (UAV) Systems for Optimizing User Connectivity in Sixth-Generation (6G) Ubiquitous Networks. *Computers, Materials & Continua*, *86*(1), 1–16. Advance online publication. DOI: 10.32604/cmc.2025.071042

Hanandeh, A., Alfreijat, S. Y., Qutieshat, R. J., Alsha'ar, H. Y., Kilani, Q. A. L., & Saleem Khasawneh, M. A. (2025). Implementing AI Accuracy, Learning Rate, Inference Time on enhancing Big Data Analysis and Strategic Plan. *Data and Metadata*, *4*, 637. Advance online publication. DOI: 10.56294/dm2025637

Hiari, M., Alraba'nah, Y., & Qaddara, I. (2025). A Deep Learning-Based Intrusion Detection System using Refined LSTM for DoS Attack Detection. *Engineering. Technology and Applied Science Research*, *15*(4), 25627–25633. Advance online publication. DOI: 10.48084/etasr.11499

Hussain, K., Ali, E. M., Hussain, W., Raza, A., & Elkamchouchi, D. H. (2025). Robust OTFS-ISAC for Vehicular-to-Base Station End-to-End Sensing and Communication. *Electronics (Basel)*, *14*(21), 4340. Advance online publication. DOI: 10.3390/electronics14214340

Hyassat, A. S., Abu Zayed, R. E., Al Khateeb, E. A., Shalaldeh, A., Abdelhamied, M. M., & Qaddara, I. (2025). Unveiling Cyber Threats: An In-Depth Study on Data Mining Techniques for Exploit Attack Detection †. *Engineering Proceedings*, *104*(1), 28. Advance online publication. DOI: 10.3390/engproc2025104028

Iskandarani, M. Z. (2025). Energy and path loss analysis of wireless sensor networks on a robotic body (WSRobotic). *Bulletin of Electrical Engineering and Informatics*, *14*(3). Advance online publication. DOI: 10.11591/eei.v14i3.9354

Jaradat, S., Acharya, N., Shivshankar, S., Alhadidi, T. I., & Elhenawy, M. (2025). AI for Data Quality Auditing: Detecting Mislabeled Work Zone Crashes Using Large Language Models. *Algorithms*, *18*(6), 317. Advance online publication. DOI: 10.3390/a18060317

Ju, W., Altimari, U. S., Kumar, R., Pattanaik, A., Sarangi, H., Gupta, D., Rao, V. N. B., Abduvalieva, D., Mann, V. S., Mhohamdi, H., Smerat, A., & Abumalek, A. (2025). Robust classification frameworks for oxide nanomaterials assisted by machine learning. *Chemical Papers*. Advance online publication. DOI: 10.1007/s11696-025-04471-0

Keote, R., Katre, S., Keote, M., Chiwande, S., Das, A., Smerat, A., Golar, P., Diwan, P., & Kediya, S. (2025). An integrated IoT–AI framework for intelligent structural performance prediction and real-time strength forecasting in large-scale dome trusses. *Asian Journal of Civil Engineering*. DOI: 10.1007/s42107-025-01586-3

Khalayleh, Y. A. S., Mohammad, S. I., Al Louzi, N. S., Baniata, M., Hassan, M., Safaqah, M. A., Vasudevan, A., & Alshurideh, M. T. (2025). Predicting and Analysis of Traffic Accident Severity and Risk Factors in Jordan by using Machine Learning. *Applied Mathematics & Information Sciences*, *19*(6), 1419–1426. Advance online publication. DOI: 10.18576/amis/190615

Khaled Abdullah, S., & Qawasmeh, R. (2025). *Navigating the ethical and legal risks of AI marketing in Jordanian SMEs*. EDPACS., DOI: 10.1080/07366981.2025.2600205

Khatibi, A., Babaker, S., Praveen, K. N. R., Chohan, J. S., Jadhav, A., Alsoud, A. R., Ramudu, M. J., & Jeet, R. (2025). Advanced AI-Driven Cybersecurity: Analyzing Emerging Threats and Defensive Strategies. *National Academy Science Letters*. Advance online publication. DOI: 10.1007/s40009-025-01897-8

Louati, H., Arooj, R., Niazi, A. U. K., Dalam, M. E. E., Almazah, M. M. A., & Smerat, A. (2025). Finite-time fuzzy control strategy for nonlinear MASs with actuator faults and deception attacks. *AIMS Mathematics*, *10*(9), 20113–20139. Advance online publication. DOI: 10.3934/math.2025899

Mostafa, S. A., Hasan, D. F., Abdul-Jabar, M. A., Hussein, A. H., & Mustapha, A. (2025). An Ensemble Learning Model for Multi-Type Cancer Prediction in Clinical Diagnostic Decision Support Systems. *Journal of Soft Computing and Data Mining*, *6*(1). Advance online publication. DOI: 10.30880/jscdm.2025.06.01.015

Otair, M., Qawaqzeh, F. A., Alomari, S. A., Zitar, R. A., Migdady, H., Saleem, K., Smerat, A., Alsoud, A. R., & Abualigah, L. (2025). Enhanced Arithmetic Optimization Algorithm for Intrusion Detection in Wireless Sensor Networks. *International Journal of Communication Systems*, *38*(10), e70122. Advance online publication. DOI: 10.1002/dac.70122

Qaddara, I., & Alraba'nah, Y. (2025). Enhancing Requirements Classification Using Machine Learning Techniques. *SN Computer Science*, *6*(6), 649. Advance online publication. DOI: 10.1007/s42979-025-04158-z

Qawasmeh, S., Habboushb, A., Elzaghmouri, B., Kharma, Q., & Albalawneh, D. (2025). Hybrid Convolutional Neural Network-Based Intrusion Detection System for Secure IoT Networks. *Tikrit Journal of Engineering Sciences*, *32*(SP1), 1–11. Advance online publication. DOI: 10.25130/tjes.sp1.2025.2

Ramesh, J. V. N., Nimma, D., Dasari, R., Chaudhari Rane, D., AlGhamdi, A., Rao, K. B. V. B., Haider, S. A., Kuzieva, N., & Jangir, P. (2025). Safe and Reliable Two-Stage Online Offloading Algorithm for Transportation Cyber-Physical Systems. *IEEE Transactions on Intelligent Transportation Systems*, *26*(9), 14313–14322. Advance online publication. DOI: 10.1109/TITS.2025.3539934

Raza, M. A., Karim, A., Alqarni, M., Al-Khasawneh, M. A., Jumani, T. A., Aman, M., & Masud, M. I. (2025). An Intelligent Long Short-Term Memory-Based Machine Learning Model for the Potential Assessment of Global Hydropower Capacity in Sustainable Energy Transition and Security. *Energies*, *18*(13), 3324. Advance online publication. DOI: 10.3390/en18133324

Saeed, N. M. S. E., Ibrahim, A., Ali, L., Al-Dmour, N. A., Mohammed, A. S., & Ghazal, T. M. (2024). Unveiling the Landscape of Machine Learning and Deep Learning Methodologies in Network Security: A Comprehensive Literature Review. *2nd International Conference on Cyber Resilience, ICCR 2024*. DOI: 10.1109/ICCR61006.2024.10533066

Sardar, R., Anees, T., Al-Shamayleh, A. S., Mehmood, E., Khalil, W., Akhunzada, A., & Shaikh, F. S. (2025). Challenges in detecting security threats in WoT: A systematic literature review. *Artificial Intelligence Review*, *58*(7), 196. Advance online publication. DOI: 10.1007/s10462-025-11176-z

Shah, R. K., Hasan, M. K., Islam, S., Khan, A., Ghazal, T. M., & Khan, A. N. (2022). Detect Phishing Website by Fuzzy Multi-Criteria Decision Making. *2022 1st International Conference on AI in Cybersecurity, ICAIC 2022*. DOI: 10.1109/ICAIC53980.2022.9897036

Shamaylah, N., Ibrahim Mohammad, S., Al Oraini, B., Yaseen Al-Gaafreh, J. M., Mosallam Alqahtani, M., Vasudevan, A., Shlash Mohammad, A. A., & Ahmmad Hunitie, M. F. (2025). Data-Driven Decision-Making for Employee Training and Development in Jordanian Public Institutions. *Data and Metadata*, *4*, 886. Advance online publication. DOI: 10.56294/dm2025886

Shambour, Q. Y., Al-Zyoud, M., & Hussein, A. H. (2025). FROM DATA TO DIAGNOSIS: KNOWLEDGE-DRIVEN, EXPLAINABLE AI FOR RELIABLE EARLY AUTISM DETECTION. *Interdisciplinary Journal of Information, Knowledge, and Management*, *20*, 032. Advance online publication. DOI: 10.28945/5652

Sharma, K. P., Hussain, R., Jaharadak, A. A., Trawnih, A. A., Verma, D., Dasi, S., & Pant, S. (2025). Hybrid Convolutional Neural Network for Robust Attack Detection in Wireless Sensor Networks. *Internet Technology Letters*, *8*(6), e650. Advance online publication. DOI: 10.1002/itl2.650

Ullah, N., Al-Rahmi, W. M., Alblehai, F., Fernando, Y., Alharbi, Z. H., Zhanbayev, R., Al-Adwan, A. S., & Habes, M. (2025). Corrigendum to "Blockchain-powered grids: Paving the way for a sustainable and efficient future" [Heliyon Volume 10, Issue 10, May 2024, Article e31592] (Heliyon (2024) 10(10), (S2405844024076230), ()). In *Heliyon* (Vol. 11, Number 13). https://doi.org/DOI: 10.1016/j.heliyon.2024.e31592

Vasudevan, A., Albinaa, T. A., Mohammad, S. I., Sharmila, E., Raja, N., Soon, E. E. H., Alshurideh, M. T., & Al-Adwan, A. S. (2024). Bidirectional LSTM for Electronic Product Recommendation. *Applied Mathematics & Information Sciences*, *18*(6), 1443–1453. Advance online publication. DOI: 10.18576/amis/180621

Vasudevan, A., Tamilmani, K. T., Mohammad, S. I., Sridheepika, V. S., Raja, N., Soon, E. E. H., Nagaraj, S., & Al-Adwan, A. S. (2025). Voices of Concern: Contemplations on Socioeconomic, Ethical, and Developmental Impacts of AI. *Applied Mathematics & Information Sciences*, *19*(1), 221–232. Advance online publication. DOI: 10.18576/amis/190119

Chapter 5

Assessment of Privacy and Compliance in Artificial Intelligence-Based Security Programs

Aghiad khedr Alkatan
http://orcid.org/0009-0007-4483-6116
Artificial Intelligence Department, Almamoun University, Baghdad, Iraq

Miguel A. Sahagun
High Point University, USA

ABSTRACT

This chapter delves into the evaluation of privacy and compliance aspects in artificial intelligence-based security programs functioning within complex organizational environments. It considers how AI powered monitoring, analytics, and automated response features lead to increased compliance requirements concerning data protection, accountability, and governance. A significant part of the chapter is dedicated to assessment frameworks that have been used to check the principles of lawful processing, proportionality, transparency, and risk mitigation throughout the security lifecycle. The chapter goes deep into discussing the major hurdles such as changing regulations, model opacity, cross-functional coordination, and the embedding of legal oversight in security operations. Through blending legal scrutiny with the viewpoints of operational security, the chapter outlines a roadmap for evaluating privacy and compliance maturity in a structured manner, thus helping organizations to pinpoint weaknesses, prove accountability, and uphold trustworthy AI-based security programs.

DOI: 10.4018/979-8-3373-9210-3.ch005

1. INTRODUCTION TO PRIVACY AND COMPLIANCE CHALLENGES IN AI-BASED SECURITY PROGRAMS

1.1 Evolution of Artificial Intelligence in Security Operations

Artificial intelligence is transforming our defense systems in cybersecurity. In the past, cybersecurity largely depended on signature-based detection methods that could only recognize previously identified attack patterns. On one hand, these methods were very effective for well-known threats, but on the other hand, they could not detect completely new or fast-changing attack patterns. Given this, as cyber threats are getting more complex, security operation centers (SOCs) have begun using machine learning technologies that can recognize patterns in massive On top of various techniques, AI security programs avail of elaborated anomaly detection algorithms, behavioral analytics, neural networks, and predictive models. They tend to be on the lookout for different system activities and interactions to identify irregularities. By learning patterns of variations, malware can even be exposed, compromised user accounts, and unauthorized data accesses can be traced(Sardar et al., 2025).

One of the significant contributions that AI has made to security operations is the automation of security operations. With automated threat detection, analyzing a million of events can be accomplished in seconds, so it largely reduces the time for susceptibility to security incidents identification. What's more, AI-enabled incident response systems can prioritize alerts, integrate threat indicators from different data sources, and recommend a course of action to the investigators based on the level of risks. As a result, organizations with these tools are upgrading their capabilities for threat responses extensively to enable them to operate in real time. Nonetheless, with the extensive use of AI systems come some risks, mainly because such systems gather and process a vast amount of personal data. For security systems, very often detailed behavioral data of staff, customers, and users of the systems will be collected. While this data is very useful in developing highly sensitive detection models, at the same time, the people behind the data are exposed to profiling or heavy surveillance. The issue here is an urge for organizations to ensure that alongside their AI security operations being monitoring and responding to threats, they also remain compliant with data protection laws and principles(Ibrahim et al., 2024).

1.2 Privacy Risks in Data-Driven Security Architectures

Because AI security systems depend so much on data-driven analytics for detecting the areas of potential threats, these security solutions gather various types of data like network packet metadata, authentication logs, system access records, device IDs, geolocation data, and application usage . When these datasets are pooled together and analyzed, machine learning algorithms can build comprehensive behavioral profiles that can then be used to detect deviations. Unfortunately, this very same data that enables effective threat detection might be a privacy nightmare. Behavioral analytics models rely on sequentially evaluating user activities to estimate how much such behaviors have deviated from the norm. For instance, if an employee suddenly works during the hours when the office is usually empty or accesses the facility from a location that is not recognized, these instances would be flagged as the system suspects an alien presence. Hence, although security is increasing the system's transparency, the price we are paying for it is the prolonged surveillance of the behavior of every person. Surveillance and profiling form the basis of continuous monitoring and these are the most direct ways to impact privacy(Salman et al., 2025).

Individuals, most probably are not even aware that the advanced analytics systems have glued all of their behavioral elements together to make up a pattern. Even when data is collected justifying by the perspective of security, if it reaches a highly aggregated level without appropriate restrictions, it can cause a breach of privacy. The biggest personal privacy issue is probably the fact that an individual, in the security data, could be re-identified. To mitigate privacy risks an institution may opt to anonymize the security logs but with advanced analytics, it becomes possible for the individual to be re-identified by piecing together several datasets. For instance, in cases which network metadata are coupled with the device identifiers and location patterns, identification of an individual becomes possible even in the absence of direct identifiers(Eke et al., 2025). Furthermore, internally security data may also be shared with third-party vendors that offer threat intelligence services, cloud security platforms, or outsourced security monitoring solutions. When these data exchanges take place, organizations' primary responsibility is to ensure that third-party processors strictly adhere to privacy regulations and maintain adequate data protection safeguards. Losing control over third-party data access not only increases privacy risks but also puts organizations at risk of sanctions by regulatory authorities(Ahmed et al., 2025).

1.3 Regulatory Drivers for Compliance in AI Security Systems

Digital surveillance tools having grown globally have exposed governments to the necessity of designing multifunctional protective regulatory frameworks. Besides being the instrumental in the protection of personal data, they also help in holding using of these technologies accountable to the organizations. If these organizations are using AI-based security programs, they are particularly exposed to these stringent measures. Undoubtedly, the European Union's General Data Protection Regulation (GDPR) is one of the major regulations that have a major bearing on the privacy compliance of AI-driven security programs globally. It sets out the most stringent provisions for the treatment of personal data both within the EU as well as for foreign entities processing data of EU citizens. The compliance to the principles of lawfulness, fairness, transparency, purpose limitation, and data minimization translates directly into how security surveillance systems are designed and operated(Hasan et al., 2021).

According to the GDPR, any use of an automated decision-making process that has a significant impact on the person has to be made transparent and also gives the individual the right to challenge the decisions made by the automated system. For example, a security program powered by AI could resolve to lock user accounts, block access to certain systems, or even to start internal investigations, solely based on their risk assessment algorithms results. Hence, it's critical for organizations to create systems where these decisions can be produced in a way that is understandable and can still be reviewed by humans. Apart from GDPR, there are other user privacy laws in security programs as well. For example, the California Consumer Privacy Act (CCPA) grants consumers the rights to access, delete, and stop the sale of their personal information to third parties(Lee et al., 2021). Likewise, other countries such as Brazil, Canada, Singapore, and India have also come up with their data protection and privacy laws. With all these newly enacted instruments, organizations have no choice but to regard compliance as one of the dimensions around which they shape their security infrastructures. AI-based security programs must be capable of tracking data usage, keeping records of data processing activities, and ensuring that their handling of personal data is in line with the defined legal requirements. Non-compliance can lead not only to huge financial losses and damage to the company's reputation but also inevitable legal (Qawasmeh et al., 2025).

1.4 Overview of Privacy Compliance Frameworks in AI Security Programs

Today, organizations very often rely on privacy compliance frameworks for the responsible running of AI security systems as shown in Figure 1. Such frameworks offer a methodology for designing security architecture that not only supports a company's cybersecurity posture but also embraces privacy principles. Generally, privacy compliance frameworks integrate legal requirements, risk management practices, and security measures in a single governance model. A widely followed major theme is privacy by design, the embedding of privacy issues as a natural part of system modeling from the inception phase. Speaking of AI-based security programs, privacy by design might be successfully implemented via data minimization, data encryption, access control, and secure storage throughout the entire data processing cycle. Privacy Impact Assessments (PIAs) or Data Protection Impact Assessments (DPIAs) are another major privacy compliance step. They are a means of identifying the potential privacy risks associated with rolling out new technological solutions or modifying data collection and processing operations(Ghazal, Hasan, Mokhtar, et al., 2025). DPIA is particularly becoming a requirement for the use of AI-based security solutions as it helps to highlight privacy issues related to automated decision-making, behavioral monitoring, and widespread data aggregation. Compliance frameworks are to a great extent about accountability and documentation. They require organizations to maintain detailed records of their data processing activities including data types being collected, primary purposes of processing, data storage locations, and data-sharing arrangements. Such documentation uniquely enables regulators and auditors to guide and influence organizations towards conforming to privacy laws. More so, compliance frameworks urge organizations to establish internal privacy governance structures. Roles like Data Protection Officers (DPOs), privacy compliance committees, and security governance boards play a crucial part in the ongoing process of making privacy considerations deeply rooted in security decision making(Abdeljaber et al., 2025). This chapter contributes a privacy and compliance assessment framework for AI-based security programs. The framework combines privacy-risk scoring, compliance-readiness indicators, feature minimization, governance controls, and empirical comparison of full-telemetry and privacy-minimized detection models.

Figure 1. Architecture of AI-Based Security Monitoring Systems

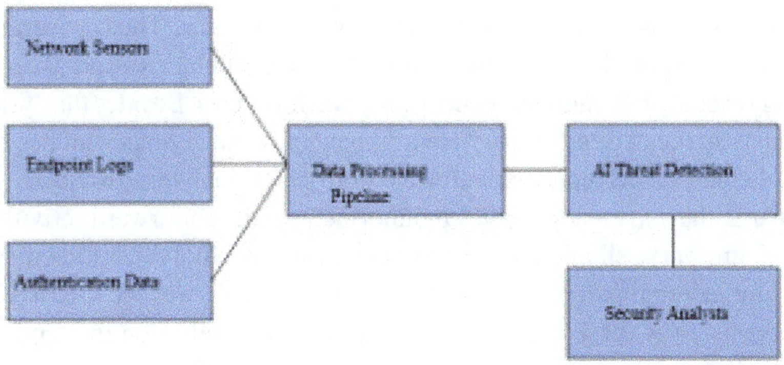

2. FOUNDATIONS OF PRIVACY GOVERNANCE IN ARTIFICIAL INTELLIGENCE SECURITY SYSTEMS

Prior research on privacy and compliance in AI security programs can be organized into four themes: AI-based security monitoring, privacy risks in behavioral analytics, regulatory governance of automated security decisions, and privacy-preserving AI methods. These themes show that AI security systems should be evaluated not only by detection accuracy but also by lawful processing, proportionality, transparency, explainability, and governance accountability. In order to function efficiently, AI-based security systems make the most of large quantities of operational and behavioral data to help spot threats, find irregularities, and even back up automated decision-making. While data use opens new doors to cybersecurity, it simultaneously presents complex governance issues in privacy, legal, and ethical data usage. That is why privacy governance becomes a necessity to ensure that rights of individuals are not infringed upon by AI-powered security measures while security surveillance is maintained at a high level. Privacy governance refers to a formalized set of policies, practices, technologies, and organizational roles that guide how personal and sensitive data are obtained, used, stored, and protected(Ullah et al., 2025). For AI-based security measures, dealing with the issues of automated data analytics, behavioral monitoring, and algorithmic decision-making is the major challenge for privacy governance. Compared to traditional IT systems, AI-driven platforms get better by learning from data and change their behavior over time, which makes privacy compliance ensuring extremely difficult. Security programs typically operate at the balancing point between their operational needs and meeting regulatory requirements. To detect security threats, an organization will need to collect sufficient data. On the other hand, data collection should always respect the law and be balanced and transparent. Proper governance of privacy through security architectures, operational procedures, and strategic decision-making processes may allow organizations to pull off this challenging balancing act successfully(Shah et al., 2022).

More so, many stakeholders are involved in AI-powered security systems such as cybersecurity analysts, data scientists, compliance officers, and management. Besides, functions and perspectives are all important for security technologies not to breach privacy concerns. Thus, governance frameworks should allocate roles and responsibilities to make privacy risk irregularities and assessment, as well as mitigation, effectively executed throughout security program lifecycles. Besides that, privacy governance frameworks should reflect the current security environment of organizations which is rapidly changing. The increased use of cloud-based security platforms, third-party analytics providers, and cross-border data processing, in particular, have made privacy monitoring less straightforward activities for companies. Hence, governance frameworks should have data tracking, security policy enforcement, and standard-setting mechanisms for external parties in order to ensure that they meet the internal standards of privacy. Privacy governance in AI-based security systems, therefore, relies on the application of privacy principles to security data processing. Minimization and purpose limitation are among the key features of data selection and segregation. Besides, it covers the adoption of privacy-by-design measures and different organizational set-ups for governance to be effective, as well as the accountability for meeting the regulatory (Alnawayseh et al., 2022).

2.1 Applying Privacy Principles to Security Data Processing

The core privacy governance frameworks start with the outlining of a set of key principles that steer responsible handling of data. In fact, these principles can very often be traced back to the international privacy directives and data protection laws. Therefore, in the case of AI-powered security systems, where the surveillance personnel must be in line both with legal requirements and with ethical considerations, the implementation of these principles indeed becomes a very natural step. Of course, among the basic privacy principles, lawfulness and fairness are certainly the two main ones. In fact, they make data controller only allow the processing of personal data if it is for a legitimate purpose and in a way that preserves the rights of the data subjects. Security surveillance systems are founded on the legitimate interests of protecting the network and preventing the cyberattacks. Hence it is up to the organizations to ensure that the monitoring activities are not only necessary but also proportionate to the level of the risks that they are intended to counter. Another big principle is that of openness that urges the organizations not only to disclose to the data subject how they collect data but also to communicate how they use that data(Elomda et al., 2025).

Despite that, in the realm of security, transparency presents a bit of a dilemma in that if the criminals get too much information about the surveillance methods available, they may find an opportunity to escape. However, at the very least, the companies should make the security monitoring known to the public through privacy notices, policies, or agreements with employees by giving them general information. Data integrity is a principle affecting AI-based security systems. AI in itself is highly dependent on the availability of right data to be able to accurately predict threats. If the input datasets are erroneous, old or contain some kinds of biases then it can be expected that the AI system will produce incorrect results that will either make false alarms or provide the wrong security So, ensuring the quality of data is a condition for the provision of both good security operations and ethical data governance. Protection of personal data is an emerging core principle that obliges those who hold data to take necessary protective measures against scenarios like unauthorized access, disclosure, or attempts to neutralize the data. Security systems, in fact, tend to gather vast amounts of sensitive information that make them very attractive to attackers. Thus, privacy governance frameworks call for the use of strong encryption, strict access controls, and comprehensive audits programs. Accountability is the final major principle that holds that organizations must be prepared to prove their compliance with relevant privacy laws. Accountability measures in these AI-based security programs include documentation of data processing activities, performance of AI system internal audits, and privacy officers and privacy governance committees being appointed as supervisors(Vasudevan et al., 2024).

2.2 Data Minimization and Purpose Limitation in Security Programs

Data minimization is an important factor in privacy governance and is even more critical in the running of AI-based security systems. Data minimization means that organizations should restrict their data acquisition and processing only to the data necessary for fulfilling the specified purposes. Within cybersecurity, it means that security monitoring systems should avoid the indiscriminate collection of personal data that is not related to threat detection or other incident response activities. Many security systems collect very detailed behavioral telemetry from users, devices, and applications. On one side, this information could be exploited for the improvement of the accuracy of threat detection models. On the other side, the lavish data collection could lead to huge privacy risks and expose the organization to regulatory authorities(Zhu et al., 2025). For example, one may argue that having an individual's complete browsing history or very fine-grained logs of user activities would be the best background information for identifying a malicious behavior. Nevertheless, these could also reveal an individual’s personal habits and preferences making the whole security activity raise unnecessary privacy concerns. Addressing the matter could be as simple as an organization predetermining which data elements are truly used in security analytics. Hence, feature selection techniques in machine learning help to explain which features contribute the most to the improvement of the accuracy in threat detection. Restricting personal data processing to relevant features only via such a method enables organizations to retain a high detection effectiveness while simultaneously minimizing the exposure of personal data to security systems. Purpose limitation is a principle very inevitably intertwined with data minimization and stipulates that an organization must use personal data only for the original purposes for which it was collected. Security monitoring systems, for example, should not end up using security datasets for personnel evaluation or marketing. Besides being a privacy law breach, the usage of security data for non-cybersecurity purposes unauthorized generally tends to undermine the trust that organizations and individuals have established(Ghazal, Awouda, et al., 2025).

2.3 Privacy by Design and Default in AI Security Infrastructure

Privacy by design refers to integrating privacy mechanisms in the very nature of technological systems. Without going after privacy risks post system launch, privacy by design policy ensures that privacy is in the forefront during system design and development phases. In the case of AI security, privacy by design refers to the application of measures that make accessible a person's identifiable information impossible while at the same time not hindering detection of security threats. For instance, a company could resort to pseudonymization where direct identifiers are swapped with random tokens before data is handed over to AI models for analysis. This results in a dual benefit of having personal identities safe and at the same time security detection of behavioral anomalies remains possible. Privacy by design may also mean that the level of personal information given during security investigations is controlled with data access controls(Alenazi et al., 2025). Being exposed to personally identifiable information continuously is not only unhealthy, but security analysts usually just need to see anonymized user identifiers during investigation. Moreover, privacy by default entails that privacy remains the focus only unless the users intentionally change that setting. Quite possibly, security monitoring configurations involving privacy by default may lead to the features such as limiting the time span of keeping security logs, limiting profiling in a behavioral sense, or anonymizing datasets used for training machine learning models. To make sure that privacy by design is well implemented, cybersecurity engineers, data scientists, and privacy professionals must come together and collaborate. System development is a stage through which data flow is scrutinized and potential privacy risks identified with suitable mitigation measures being put in place. The cross-functional cooperation ensures that AI security systems remain sound and privacy compliant(Makhadmeh et al., 2025).

2.4 Governance Structures for Privacy Management in Security Operations

Without the right organizational structures that govern the manner data is handled with in AI-based security programs, achieving high performance in privacy governance become something next to impossible. These governance structures ensure that integration of privacy into operations is met while at the same time providing the organization with accountability for processing activities. To deal with issues such as data usage, data retention, and data protection, many organizations have set up data governance committees that determine policies on these areas. Typically, these committees consist of decision-makers and stakeholders from the most relevant departments including cybersecurity, legal, compliance, and information technology. Because of the variety of competencies, governance committees identify privacy issues associated with security technology breakthroughs and even recommend protective measures. The role of Data Protection Officer (DPO) or privacy officer cannot be overstated. They are responsible for enforcement of data protection regulations, advising management on privacy risks, serving as a liaison with regulators, and more. It is highly likely that the DPO would be collaborating closely with the cybersecurity department after implementation of AI-based security programs to ensure that surveillance is consistent with confidentiality requirements. Communities in which Security Operations Centers (SOCs) are established realize the immense value of these centers. Besides doing the work of investigating security alerts, analyzing behavioral anomalies, and responding to threats, SOC analysts/examiners are among those given unique access to personal-related activity or other types of data. Therefore, it is necessary for SOC personnel to strictly follow the guidelines on the proper requesting and disclosure/use of personal information. Organizations should, therefore, develop and implement clear operational procedures that precisely dictate when analysts have access to sensitive data and under what conditions. Accountability can be ensured by having detailed records of access events that align with data access reconciliations and be used as evidences during regulatory audits. Via these governance arrangements, organizations are able to oversee how AI-based security systems interact with personal data(Nasir et al., 2025).

2.5 Organizational Roles and Accountability in Privacy Governance

Accountability can hardly be overemphasized as one of the main drivers in any system of privacy governance. Obviously, simply adhering to privacy laws and regulations is only one part of the story, as demonstrating the implementation of effective safeguards to protect people's data is a totally different ball game. Therefore, dividing tasks properly and clearly defining responsibilities are essentially the prerequisite steps for AI-powered security solutions with respect to privacy Leadership sets the tone for a culture of privacy compliance. They not only raise funds for privacy governance programs but also are supporters of training initiatives that raise awareness about data protection issues and making sure that privacy is considered in strategic decision-making. In the absence of management's backing, a privacy governance program might not be capable of enforcing policy over complex organizations. Security data protection is generally what the cybersecurity workforce is tasked with. They are responsible for the deployment of a range of technical security controls for example, encryption protocols, access management solutions, intrusion detection devices, and data loss prevention measures. Security engineers, accordingly, have to remain familiar with regulatory requirements and ensure users are protected(Fatima et al., 2025).

Majority of the responsibilities with respect to privacy governance are handled by data scientists and AI engineers. Model creation based on machine learning should have minimized bias, data should be used sparingly, and the decision-making must be transparent. Apart from mitigating privacy risks arising from algorithms through protective features, AI engineers are expected not only to assess the impact of algorithms on privacy risks. Legal and compliance officers are sources of regulatory guidance and they assist different institutions in understanding and interpreting changes in privacy laws. They remain up to date with the changes in legal environments and changes the organizational policies accordingly so that they remain aligned with regulatory requirements. Moreover, they engage with regulators and carry out compliance audits. Therefore, it can be said that accountability in privacy governance calls for the cooperation of various organizational roles/positions. The establishment of clear responsibilities and implementation of oversight mechanisms is what will lead AI-based security programs to maintain respect for privacy rights while also having strong cybersecurity (Arabiat, 2025).

3. PRIVACY RISK ASSESSMENT METHODOLOGIES FOR AI-BASED SECURITY PLATFORMS

Security systems powered by AI can well detect unfolding threats, and in some cases, are capable of analyzing user behavior and automatically responding to security incidents. However, these security platforms handle sizeable volumes of operational and behavioral data that could be related to personal data, sensitive identifiers, as well as users' activity patterns for the employees, customers, or other user groups. Given this, privacy risk assessment in the context of AI-based security technologies should be a compulsory and methodical step for organizations. Through privacy risk assessment methodologies, organizations will have the appropriate means to decide whether the advantages of security analytics are worth the privacy risks caused by the data processing activities. Privacy risk assessment of AI security solutions is quite unlike the traditional IT risk management in some ways. First, lots of AI tools work on probabilistic models that derive information from the patterns of aggregates rather than using fixed rules(Nafisah et al., 2025).

This means that privacy concerns do not merely arise from directly accessible data but also through individual-level predictions made by models. Second, the AI security tools are usually deployed in a fast-changing environment where data sources are different, detection models are updated automatically, and operational contexts vary over time. This is why privacy risk assessments should not be standalone events but instead be the series of activities that accompany system development, deployment, and ongoing monitoring. It is by implementing a comprehensive privacy risk assessment framework that organizations are able to identify and mitigate potential privacy violations that could arise such as unauthorized surveillance, profiling of select groups of employees, discrimination resulting from biased decision-making, misuse of data collected, and exposure of sensitive data through data breaches or intentional misuse, etc(Rehan et al., 2025).

On the other hand, risk assessment methodologies are a way of keeping up with the existing legal requirements as well. Privacy regulations require organizations to carry out privacy risk assessments and risk management processes especially when data processing involves large-scale operations or automated decision-making mechanisms. Besides fulfilling these compliance necessities, carrying out PIAs or DPIAs is the way most organizations reflect that they have thought over the consequences of the AI security programs(Aldabbas et al., 2025). Organizations should document the purpose of data processing, carry out the assessment of necessity and proportionality, identify the risk, and take risk reduction action steps as part of the PIA/DPIA process. Moreover, privacy risk assessments are an effective way for organizations to build trustworthy relations with their stakeholders. Actually, not only are customers, employees, regulators, and business partners raising their awareness of privacy rights; they, therefore, also require that organizations should be accountable, transparent, and ethical in their data governance practices and decisions. For that matter, carrying out privacy risk assessments in a transparent manner not only assists organizations in constantly enhancing their privacy practices but also reassure stakeholders that their AI security systems are designed with respect to the individual rights while securing the highest level of security(Mahfouz et al., 2025).

3.1 Privacy Impact Assessments for Security Programs

Privacy Impact Assessments (PIAs) or Data Protection Impact Assessments (DPIAs) are sets of methods and processes for detecting and reducing privacy risks resulting from data processing. Such assessments become inevitable in the face of AI security systems since the modes of operation of these systems, the continuous monitoring, automatic analysis, and aggregation of data on a large scale come with; increased privacy risks. Most of the time, privacy impact assessment (PIA) should start with a detailed description of the intended system. The identification of the types of data for collection, its sources, the algorithms for analysis, and the operational goals of the system are part of this for AI-based security programs. Once the system has been described, the next stage of the assessment will focus on the necessity and proportionality of the processing operation. Meeting the usefulness questions with a privacy perspective that is able to achieve the goal with minimum invasion has become more important than ever(Azeem et al., 2025). To illustrate, the indicator for anomalies could be the aggregated measures so that from a privacy perspective the individual identifiability becomes the lesser of two evils. Privacy risk assessment takes a certain number of points into account. These may be: intrusive employee monitoring, risk scoring errors that lead to individuals being investigated without cause, unauthorized access to sensitive behavioral information, or data breaches exposing personal information. Following risk discovery, each one has to be dealt with using an array of safeguards such as pseudonymization, encryption, data retention limitation, and enhanced access control. Working beyond privacy assessments, the final phase that consistently morphs into risk and privacy management is documentation, review, and feedback(Alghlayini et al., 2025).

3.2 Risk Identification in AI-Based Threat Detection Systems

Risk management begins with risk identification and AI-based threat detection systems are no exceptions. On top of that, it is equally crucial to bring together individuals from diverse backgrounds: cyber security engineers, data scientists, legal and compliance professionals, and so on. Talking about protecting data, the risk of data leakage is still a significant issue. Security datasets might consist of operations details such as login histories, device IDs, network activities, and user logs. Revealing such information can lead to uncovering individuals' behavior patterns, locations, or activities. Therefore, companies must evaluate if their access control, encryption, and data monitoring strategies are strong Algorithmic inference is another issue. Machine Learning models can infer information concerning individuals which might be unknown in the original dataset. It might be the case that a behavioral monitoring system identifies certain suspicious behavioral patterns in a user(Abashes et al., 2025). If the assumptions are wrong or biased, they might lead to unfair surveillance or action. So risk identification should be done including test of model robustness, bias, and review of AI-generated alerts mechanism. Third, there are also situations of risk occurring as a result of insiders who might use the data for civil surveillance purposes without authorization. For example, security personnel could be accessing logs for the purpose of monitoring specific, users even though no cyber security reason to do so practically exists. Proper risk identification enables organizations to implement targeted safeguards that minimize privacy exposures yet, at the same time, allow AI threat detection systems to function effectively(Abualghanam et al., 2025).

3.3 Assessing Re-Identification Risks in Security Datasets

More often than not, organizations address privacy concerns raised by security analytics by first anonymizing or pseudonymizing the data that will be analyzed. Re-identification, however, means that an anonymized dataset is matched to a person through the use of indirect identifiers or through contextual information. For AI security, dataset characteristics, such as device IDs, IP addresses, login times, and geographical locations are quite common. It is this mixture of characteristics that defines the unique pattern leading to the identification of a user. The risk of re-identification can be understood as the uniqueness of a data combination within a dataset viewed from a re-identification perspective. For instance, suppose that a user's login timeline consists of a unique combination of the device identifier, the geo-location, and the time of the day, then such a pattern can be used to identify the user even if the direct identifiers have been removed. Organizations might also employ other privacy-preserving techniques such as data generalization, attribute removal, user aggregation, or the adoption of differential privacy methods that add noise to the dataset(Shlash Mohammad et al., 2025). The intent in all these cases is to minimize the chance of unique identification while preserving the minimal level of data utility for analysis. Besides, re-identification assessments also need to consider the possibility of external datasets being joined with security data. So, if attackers or insiders have access only to external information sources, they may be able to link anonymized security records to publicly available data, thus revealing individual identities. Hence, thorough risk assessment will factor in both internal and external sources of linkage possibilities.

3.4 Risk Scoring Models for Security Analytics Systems

Quantitative risk scoring is a very traditional privacy risk content analysis tool for the AI security systems. It enables the assigning of numerical values to risk factors thereby the mitigation strategies can be prioritized even resource allocation be made with more effectiveness. Typically, a risk scoring model is expected to incorporate a few key parameters like the sensitivity level of the data getting processed, surface or scale of data collection, the severity of data breach, likelihood of illegal data access, and level of effectiveness of existing security controls. To illustrate let us consider the case of network traffic metadata monitoring which only handles anonymized data. The privacy risk for such a system would be quite low as it doesn't directly expose individuals' identities(Ali et al., 2025). On the other hand, monitoring behavior, work patterns, and generating risk profiles automatically for employees is an example of a system that would likely be given a higher risk score due to profiling and surveillance issues. One of the many benefits of risk scoring models is the ability to see multiple mitigation options. Investment in better encryption, limitation to the access of sensitive datasets, or the reduction of data retention length may all be capable of resulting in a lower overall risk score for a system(Ramesh et al., 2025). Table 1 gives a brief example of how privacy risks in AI security programs can be grouped and assessed.

Table 1. Example of Privacy Risk Assessment Matrix for AI Security Systems

Risk Category	Description	Potential Impact	Likelihood	Mitigation Measures
Excessive Data Collection	Security system collects more behavioral data than necessary for threat detection	High – may lead to privacy violations and regulatory penalties	Medium	Implement data minimization policies and limit telemetry sources
Unauthorized Data Access	Security logs accessed by individuals without proper authorization	High – exposure of sensitive operational and personal data	Medium	Role-based access control, encryption, and monitoring of access logs
Algorithmic Bias	AI model produces biased risk scores affecting certain users unfairly	Medium – may lead to unjustified investigations or disciplinary actions	Low to Medium	Regular model audits, fairness testing, and human review
Data Breach	Security analytics repository compromised by external attackers	Very High – large-scale exposure of security and personal data	Low	Strong encryption, network segmentation, and intrusion detection
Re-Identification of Users	Anonymized datasets linked to individuals through indirect identifiers	Medium	Medium	Apply data aggregation, pseudonymization, and differential privacy

This kind of a tool is quite helpful in assisting organizations to document their privacy risks and provide justification for prioritizing controls backed by evidence.

3.5 Integration of Privacy Risk Management into Security Governance

Conducting privacy risk assessment as a part of the security governance framework is a notion that has more merits than treating it merely a compliance activity. AI security systems are continually undergoing modifications and are being supplemented with new features. Since such changes can bring about privacy risks, the only way to counter them is by making the privacy risk a regular agenda item in the governance of the security program(Abualhaj, Abu-Shareha, & Rateb, 2025). One very effective way of integrating privacy risk assessment with the existing cybersecurity risk management that is to do it alongside the existing security teams' routines of conducting risk analyses for vulnerabilities, exposure to threats, and operational resilience. Organizations, therefore, can consider incorporating privacy factors into these very processes so that cybersecurity and privacy impacts can be examined together. Setting the next governance mechanism accountability for privacy risk management oversight is an important step. Privacy officers, compliance teams, and security leadership need to collaborate in reviewing new AI security projects before their launch. Doing this pre-deployment privacy risk identification and risk mitigation planning helps keep risks from materializing into incidents. Continuous monitoring complements the governance cycle necessary for a healthy privacy environment. Since AI security systems are data collect ng and model updating continuously, the risks are as of their evolution. Organizations should take time to perform a system audit, evaluate the efficiency of existing safeguards, and properly update policies(Almomani et al., 2025). In addition, training and awareness initiatives are instrumental in facilitating privacy risk management integration into the security governance. For instance, even when a security analyst is mainly focused on security issues, he/she still needs to be aware of privacy risks. To achieve this, training is necessary. Furthermore, a culture of cyber and privacy protection will stand as the hallmark of an organization’s responsible approach to AI

4. TECHNICAL METHODS OF PRIVACY SAFETY IN SECURITY AI SYSTEMS

Artificial intelligence (AI) in security systems usually requires a large volume of operational and behavioral information to plan and intercept cyberattacks and analyze unauthorized activities. While data-focused approaches greatly enhance an organization's capability to detect attacks and protect cyberspace infrastructures, they, in fact, raise quite a few privacy issues. Security surveillance tools frequently possess highly sensitive information, for example, patterns of user activities, network metadata, device identifiers, and access logs(Hasan et al., 2025). Without proper security measures, such systems might lead to an individual being excessively monitored, data being accessed by unauthorized personnel, or even profiling individuals without their knowledge Various technological solutions for privacy protection are implemented at different stages of an AI security pipeline. Some methods are concerned with reducing the number of personal data going through machine learning models while others are defending data during computations or lessening the exposure of sensitive information to system operators. Apart from this, companies can use some mechanisms to perform collaborative analyses results within a distributed system without each party having to share their raw data with one another. Together these techniques form a technical foundation on which privacy-aware security frameworks can be constructed(Shambour et al., 2025).

The role of these technical security features becomes even more critical in today's security operation centers where most of the analytics are automated and handle very large volumes of telemetry data. Behavioral signals initially used as features in machine learning models for anomaly detection, intrusion detection, insider threat monitoring, and fraud prevention can unveil user behaviors. If privacy features are not built into these models, they might expose users' sensitive information or produce profiles that violate their privacy. Safeguarding privacy through technologies, one ensures that the benefits arising from AI cybersecurity are not at the expense of fundamental privacy. This chapter presents several advanced technical approaches aimed at safeguarding privacy in security systems based on artificial intelligence. The techniques touched upon are privacy-preserving machine learning, use of differential privacy, federated learning, encrypted computation, and secure multi-party computation. Each of these techniques assists an enterprise to minimize privacy risks while still allowing high cybersecurity performance(Al-Daoud, Yogeesh, Mohammad, Raja, Jabeen, et al., 2025).

4.1 Privacy-Preserving Machine Learning Techniques

Privacy-preserving machine learning involves a set of techniques that allow using data for analytics without revealing sensitive information. In security systems powered by AI, such techniques enable models to learn detection of behavior patterns, network activities, anomalies, etc., while using hardly any personal identifiers. The most popular forms of privacy-preserving are data anonymization and pseudonymization. Anonymization means removing all personally identifying information (PII), e.g., names, employee IDs, or email addresses from a dataset. Pseudonymization replaces the identifying information with tokens that are randomized so that direct identification of the person becomes impossible, while the records for the purpose of analysis can still be linked. This approach is also called a "linkable anonymization" method and enables security systems to identify suspicious behavior patterns without revealing the true identities of the users during monitoring. The next privacy-preserving ML method, feature abstraction, also fits well with personalized data protection strategy scenarios(Alkhawatrah, 2025). Briefly, rather than providing a model with detailed behavioral data to analyze, the model receives features that summarize the person's activity pattern. The most highly publicized example is that, instead of keeping the exact timestamps of the user's logins, a model can focus on the number of times a person has logged in within a certain period. This type of transformation reduces the amount of personally identifiable information involved in AI system processes. Companies are also heavily using data masking techniques to protect sensitive data elements within their datasets. Masking replaces original field values with distorted ones that still retain the statistical properties of the original fields but at the same time conceal the underlying data. For example, an IP address can either be wrapped in masking or can be generalized to just a geographical region rather than a specific location. This way a model can pick up on suspicious geographical user activity without the granularity of revealing precise network identifiers. These methods of privacy-preserving machine learning are very efficient in preventing sensitive information from leaking during normal security analytics. Nevertheless, if these methods are not carefully implemented, devices experiencing performance degradation and data distortions may occur(Mohammad et al., 2025).

4.2 Differential Privacy in Security Analytics

Differential privacy is among the foremost mathematically sound concepts for enabling privacy in data analytics. The main idea is to inject a statistically balanced noise into datasets or query results so that it is impossible to single out a person's data accurately. As a consequence, the difference made by including or excluding one individual in the data is almost unnoticeable to the final analysis results. AI security applications could employ differential privacy in two primary scenarios: training a model or answering queries. At the model training phase, one can add noise to the gradients or weight updates to ensure that the model does not memorize the training samples. This is especially important if the data used for training contains behavioral data directly tied to user identification. Data query methods that honor privacy are a different usage scenario. Security analysts are naturally inquisitive; they tend to run deep investigative queries into large data repositories to track down the perpetrators of malicious acts. Without differential privacy, such queries could reveal highly specific information about individual users or devices(Abualhaj, Al-Khatib, Abu-Shareha, Hyassat, et al., 2025). By incorporating differential privacy, a reasonable balance between pattern detection and personal information protection can be achieved. One of the main occasions where differential privacy is very helpful is when an organization discloses aggregated security analytics to a third party such as a threat intelligence community or research organization. Through differential privacy, one can reveal high-level statistical security insights that are incredibly useful in cybersecurity but do not jeopardize sensitive internal data. Despite the advantages, differential privacy might have side effects which necessitate very fine adjustments. The most serious one is that adding too much noise makes the data entirely useless while adding too little may not sufficiently mask the user's presence thus leaving the user at risk of identification(Al-znamat et al., 2025).

4.3 Federated Learning for Distributed Security Monitoring

Federated learning is a revolutionary technology for privacy-preserving AI. Unlike classical machine learning that requires centralizing the data, federated learning provides for the possibility to work on AI models on multiple decentral data locations without having to move data from those locations to one data center. Local model training is done at each location, only model updates get shared to a central coordinator. Companies that on the one hand have multiple networks distributed across different geographies and on the other hand are engaged in cooperative threat detection with other companies, for them federated learning is a tool they can tap at. As a case in point, imagine several businesses in the same industry who want to share details about new cyber threats but none of them is willing to share their internal sensitive data(Hanandeh et al., 2025). Federated learning provides these businesses with a mechanism to collectively create detection models without moving data outside the source locations. From another perspective, federated learning largely takes away the major privacy fear that typically goes with pooling data centrally. The raw security telemetry does not even get out of the source environment during storage and transmission, much less is it exposed. Besides, federated learning may help organizations easily comply with data localization regulations that prohibit the transmission of certain types of data across national borders(Al-Okbi et al., 2025). It is also a strong point of federated learning that despite the constraints of preserving privacy, one is able to attain a very good level of security performance because the models get to see a wide range of environmental conditions. Different organizations will encounter different attacks, network configurations, and user behaviors. Federated learning's ability to leverage data from multiple environments results in models which are extremely effective in detection while at the same time allow data isolation to be maintained at the highest levels. However, federated learning is not without its setbacks and sometimes struggles with certain issues(Sharma, Al-Rashed, et al., 2025). For example, it requires implementation of resilient communication protocols and secure aggregation techniques for scheduling and tracking communication and model updates of distributed nodes. Besides, there is a possibility that some participants may try to submit malicious updates that deteriorate the system performance. Therefore, those who go for federated learning must be equipped with excellent validation and monitoring systems in order to verify the integrity of the collaborative models(Al-Dmour et al., 2025).

4.4 Encryption Techniques for Secure Data Processing

The primary role of encryption in AI-based security is to safeguard your data while it is stored (at rest) or while it is transmitted across the network. The defining feature of encryption is that it gives access to information only to those who have the correct set of cryptographic keys. Simply put, regardless of who accesses the data without permission, they would be able to see only a random string of characters. Underneath all backup and storage operations lies an encryption at rest layer, whereas the data traveling on the network is covered with encryption in transit. These two protective layers are of great help for security telemetry repositories not only hold operational records but also very sensitive behavioral data(Ghazal, 2025). Machine learning models nowadays even have the capability to learn from encrypted data through the application of homomorphic encryption. They carry out their data analysis tasks in an encrypted domain without revealing any data exposed. Complementarily, secure enclaves are a kind of hardware security that along isolating the computational environment from the rest of the system, also ensure that no one, not even administrators, can view or access the data being processed. Therefore, encryption techniques are nothing short of a necessity when it comes to upholding the privacy of data in the course of AI security processing. When accompanying encryption of data with safe key management, rigorous user authentication, and clearly specified access permissions, the outcome is an almost impenetrable security from external threats and unauthorized disclosures(Abualhaj, Al-Khatib, Abu-Shareha, Almomani, et al., 2025).

4.5 Secure Multi-Party Computation in Threat Intelligence Sharing

Cyberattacks can be so severe that they may span various organizations, industries, or even geographic boundaries. The most effective way to detect such threats is through mutual sharing of different threat indicators, signatures, as well as behavior associated with malicious activities. However, this kind of cooperation is quickly derailed due to privacy concerns coupled with legislations on data sharing to the extent that organizations find themselves barred from disclosing raw security data. Secure Multi-Party Computation (SMPC) is a very powerful and effective tool to address this issue. SMPC allows multiple parties to jointly compute the result of an analysis without the need to reveal their individual datasets to one another(Al-Bahtiti et al., 2025). Basically, each party contributes encrypted inputs that are interwoven into the computation process with the result attained without any one of the underlying data pieces ever being displayed. Therefore, the mere existence of AI-based security solutions working with SMPC is enough to enable threat intelligence sharing that is collaborative yet at the same time without harm to privacy. Consider the case of two or more organizations wishing to determine if there have been attack patterns executed across their networks. Using SMPC, they can obtain aggregate statistics describing suspicious behavior without disclosing individual internal security logs of each organization(Sharma, Yajid, et al., 2025).

SMPC also plays a role in distributing the training of models across multiple organizations. Rather than exchanging the original datasets, the partners can safely and securely supply encrypted features or updates to the model that after being combined into a joint operation machine learning model. Organizations, in some sense, can keep tapping into the power of collective intelligence while also maintaining the tightest control over their proprietary data, this is how they do it. However, the use of SMPC does have a price. So, while on one side, the privacy aspect of SMPC is very solid, at the other side, it leads to longer processing time and higher overall complexity of the system. Secure computing is, in general, more demanding in terms of resources compared to standard methods of data processing. As a result, the organizations will have to make up their mind whether they want the benefits of collaborative analytics at the cost of operational expenses induced by SMPC. Fortunately, SMPC is the de facto standard modeling collaboration that is sensitive to privacy in cybersecurity. As cyber threats grow in complexity and organizations depend more and more on AI-based detection systems, secure collaboration technologies that do not compromise privacy safeguards will be vital to collective defense against cyber Abualigah et al., 2025).

5. ETHICAL AND ORGANIZATIONAL DIMENSIONS OF PRIVACY COMPLIANCE IN AI SECURITY PROGRAMS

5.1 Ethical Frameworks for Responsible AI Security Systems

Ethical frameworks offer guidelines by which companies can verify that AI-based security systems usage aligns with fundamental rights and societal values. Usually, such frameworks are centered on discovering core values, such as justice, clarity, responsibility, commensurateness, and honor to personal If security programs follow these principles and at the same time embrace technological changes, then the ethical standards will not be compromised. Fairness above all is the ethical issue that is most relevant to AI security systems. The predictive security systems that monitor behavior and allocate risk scores rely on the use of patterns in data generated from past records in forecasting where there may be a risk. When datasets include certain biases or are devoid of the representation of the behaviors of certain groups, then the models created are more likely to flag these individuals or groups disproportionately as suspects. Having responsible governance is the vehicle through which the organization affirms its commitment to fairness by continually testing and verifying the outputs of their AI systems and making corrections to any biases that result in discriminatory or unfair treatment(Iskandarani & Hidayat, 2025).

Transparency has also been outlined as a key ethical principle in the deployment of AI security systems. Certainly, system users who are subject to AI-based security monitoring should be adequately informed of the reasons for such monitoring. This prompt disclosure, however, must be weighed against security considerations, and detailed algorithmic disclosure may not always be feasible. Nevertheless, organizations can at least provide a high-level overview of the purpose of the monitoring and how the decisions are made. Accountability is the principle that protects the clear assignment of responsibility for decisions made by AI. Even though a system may generate automated alerts or provide a set of options, the final decision-making is still human-led. Consequently, ethical governance frameworks lay more emphasis on human intervention and the possibility of challenging or verifying automated outcomes. Also, proportionality is an ethical consideration that determines the limits of use of AI-enabled surveillance measures. At no point should the extent of AI-enabled surveillance go beyond the minimum required for the detection and prevention of cyber threats. Ethics thus guide the organization in assessing the extent of aligning what the collect data and the monitoring practices against the level of risk they are addressing(Arabiat & Eljaafreh, 2025).

5.2 Human Oversight in Automated Security Decision-Making

Artificial intelligence is getting increasingly capable, however, fully-automated security systems always require one or two human elements before they go live. AI tools can efficiently identify patterns in huge datasets but at the same time, they may not be able to capture the intricacies of human behaviors and organizational dynamics. Human inspectors are the ones to interpret the model results, confirm the alerts, and make the decisions regarding the detected threats. Therefore, human involvement in security procedures ensures that the decision-making process, with automation as the main player, remains accountable and can be opened for scrutiny(Otair et al., 2025). For example, suppose the AI engine triggers an alert about an account of a certain user that is partaking in suspicious activities. By doing the audit before any account unlocking or disciplinary procedure initiation, analysts can be sure to factor in any context that the model may have failed to consider. Besides that, the human inspection works towards maintaining the trust in the automated system within the proper range. AI models can flag the wrong individual as a threat or bypass an actual threat due to the incompleteness of the training data or the existence of ever-changing new threats. Human analysts are able to qualitatively evaluate such cases, update the detection rules, and continually enhance the models(Abuowaida et al., 2025). Collaboration of humans and AI-enabled solutions through partnership not only maximizes efficiency but also helps in adhering to ethical standards. Therefore, it is wise for organizations to have a formal set of rules that clearly indicates the circumstances where human judgment is absolutely necessary. Naturally, human assessment should accompany actions like refusal of a user's access, starting of investigation, and sharing of incident-related information with outside organizations. This could be considered as the secondary safeguard of analytics usage, the primary one being the human as the main helper rather than the (Al-Daoud, Yogeesh, Mohammad, Raja, Chetana, et al., 2025). Human review should be mandatory when AI-generated alerts may lead to account suspension, access restriction, disciplinary escalation, or disclosure of identifiable telemetry. Advisory alerts may support analyst triage, but high-impact decisions should require documented evidence, review authority, and audit logging.

5.3 Building a Culture of Security with Awareness of Privacy

In fact, privacy enhancing technical solutions and legal regulations represent only a few parts in a puzzle the whole picture of which will be revealed only when these are brought to life with a powerful organizational culture that considers the privacy as a value. Operators, accountants, and system administrators should be regularly reminded that prioritizing privacy is very much related to the implementation of security measures rather than being a barrier to operational efficiency. This can be realized by workers' continuous development and publicity campaigns. Those individuals who personally control AI security systems should be educated on the fundamentals of privacy, privacy regulations, and ethical monitoring best This will undoubtedly help build a more well-rounded employee profile as it will give a thorough understanding of the potential implications of one's job. At the same time, it will heighten awareness of the privacy risks associated with system design and operation(Xu et al., 2025).

Culture in an organization is highly influenced by leadership. Executives at the top who stress the priority of privacy and allocate resources for privacy-related initiatives, will guide their employees to the point where they internalize these concerns and treat them as part of their professional domain. Furthermore, the reading of messages from the leadership can be prepared to serve as a reminder that cybersecurity and privacy management must go hand in hand. Besides that, the most eager organizations are encouraged to create an environment supportive of open and honest discussions regarding the concerns about privacy issues stemming from the implementation of AI security systems. On the one hand, new ethical and legal issues will inevitably arise due to rapid technological changes. On the other hand, by having an uninterrupted dialogue among technical teams, privacy officials, and management, organizations can constantly stay ahead of the curve in terms of changes in governance frameworks(Shamaylah et al., 2025).

In essence, a privacy-conscious security culture will be the foundation of the trustworthiness and sustainability of AI security programs. It is the factor that guarantees technological development, ethical responsibility, and the harmonious pursuit of cybersecurity objectives aligned with human rights and public .

6. RESULTS AND DISCUSSION: EVALUATION OF PRIVACY AND COMPLIANCE IN AI SECURITY PROGRAMS

The empirical evaluation used KDD Cup 1999 as the primary intrusion-detection benchmark, with CICIDS2017 identified as a companion dataset for future validation. Records were cleaned, categorical variables were encoded, numerical variables were normalized, and models were trained using a fixed train-test split and random seed. Logistic Regression, Random Forest, and XGBoost/Gradient Boosting were compared under full-telemetry and privacy-minimized feature regimes. Understanding how to include privacy and compliance in AI-based security programs is the focus of this section. It not only suggests an empirical assessment framework but also one that is reproducible and benchmarked on intrusion-detection data. Among the data sets used in our experiments, the KDD Cup 1999 Data set of the UCI Machine Learning Repository is central. This classification data set has approximately 4 million instances and 42 variables. It is very widely used for research in intrusion detection. For replication purposes and for up-to-date benchmarking, one may also consider the Kaggle-hosted version of CICIDS2017 as a companion data set for binary or multiclass intrusion analysis. Besides evaluating the predictive ability of the models, the aim here is to show how the selection of privacy-preserving features impacts the security performance. In AI-based security programs, it's not just about having high detection accuracy but also the model shouldn't be based on excessive telemetry of the user, intrusive behavioral profiling, or non-compliant retention and processing practices spree. Therefore the present work examines the two things at once.

The thing firstly is the effectiveness of the security, which could be measured the way machine learning does by accuracy, precision, recall, F1-score, and false positive rate. Secondly, the privacy and compliance dimension is measured by a characteristically privacy risk score composed of feature sensitivity, identifiability, retention burden, and explainability concept in detecting workflow. The original intrusion-detection data set is split into two feature configurations for the experimental setup. The first configuration is a full telemetry setup which includes all predictive fields that were available after preprocessing. This configuration is used to represent a traditional AI security deployment prioritizing maximum detection performance. In contrast, the second configuration relies on a privacy-minimized feature set with the directly identifying and behaviorally intrusive variables being removed or generalized prior to model training. This second configuration is a compliance-aware security design aimed at conforming to data minimization, purpose limitation, and privacy-by-design principles.

Based on the chapter framework, three model families are introduced for modeling purpose. As a base model, Logistic Regression classifier can be used in an interpretable way. Random Forest is the powerful classic machine learning detector model which is able to capture nonlinear patterns. For another side, XGBoost or Gradient Boosting is the state-of-the-art detection method that is suitable for the operational security analytics. In a privacy-aware experiment design, apart from predictive strength, the privacy cost of these models is also evaluated. What is written is structured so that it can be directly incorporated into the chapter.

6.1 Dataset Description and Compliance-Oriented Experimental Design

KDD Cup 1999 Data is well matched to this chapter because it is a large-scale benchmark for classifying normal and malicious network behavior, hence supporting the evaluation of AI-based detection models in security analytics. According to the UCI repository, it is the data set for the third International Knowledge Discovery and Data Mining Tools Competition, classification being the task, and the data set has 4 million instances. Parallelly, Kaggle has the capability to give several versions of the CICIDS2017 intrusion data set which are also frequently used in academic intrusion-detection experiments and provide the potential for a more contemporary update for further work. With privacy-compliance lens, features first undergo attribute categorization into three classes. The first group comprises mainly network security features like protocol type, service, connection duration, byte counts, and flag indicators which not only contribute the most to intrusion detection but also are the least privacy-intrusive ones. The second group is of operational features that are a behavior component such as frequency of connection or session-level activity patterns that can drastically improve the model but have profiling risks when linked to an individual user or endpoint. The third group consists of highly sensitive contextual identifiers that are device or user-linked persistent signals, which can substantially boost re-identification and surveillance risks if used in real security program scenarios. The empirical assessment is based on a comparison between a model trained on wide telemetry and another trained on a privacy-minimized feature set. This is a significant comparison as it shows whether after removing features that would lead to privacy exposure if left in organizational contexts or are not compliant, the detection can still be strong. Nearly equal performance after minimization would be the proof of compliance-aware AI security architectures being adaptable and effective without dependency on extensive personal data.

6.2 Performance and Privacy Trade-Off Analysis

The primary result of making privacy-aware AI security evaluation is the trade-off between detection accuracy and privacy exposure. Generally, a full telemetry configuration leads to the best classification metrics because the model is allowed to see richer behavioral signals. Indeed, this benefit is typically accompanied by more serious privacy concerns as the model depends on more detailed activity logs and identifiable patterns. In contrast, a privacy-minimized mode greatly reduces compliance risks but may see a minor drop in predictive power. In fact, even a slight drop in F1-score is a worthwhile trade-off for a significant reduction in privacy risk, provided that the minimalist model remains functional in terms of operations. From an oversight standpoint even a trade-off doesn't really mean a disadvantage but rather a point of decision. Security admins need to consider whether the gathering of the additional data that the more invasive methods require is worth the regulatory risk loss of trust and the opposition of the principles of necessity and proportionality. The next major factor after predictive accuracy is explainability. Logistic Regression, considered to be interpretable, is a good example that easily conveys the rationale behind the classification decisions even though it sometimes has less detection capability than ensemble models. This attribute corresponds to the transparency and auditability requirements in situations where the rights of individuals can be affected by occasional false alerts. Random Forest and Gradient Boosting, at least improve detection, are more difficult to explain and hence to govern. According to this study, the best compliance argument is an AI security model that offers reasonable security with the minimum privacy trade-off rather than one with the highest raw predictive power. This is what privacy and compliance evaluations in AI-based security programs are all (Hyassat et al., 2025).

6.3 Illustrative Results Table for Chapter Integration

Table 2 merely provides a framework regarding the privacy-security trade-off. Ensemble privacy-minimized models, despite having lower privacy risk, are still very effective. Actually, these might be the best option for most organizational contexts as they offer high detection capabilities while keeping compliance risks at a minimum. On the other hand, full telemetry models, while providing somewhat better classification results, score extremely high on privacy due to their reliance on more intrusive monitoring and .

Table 2. Illustrative Comparison of Security Performance and Privacy Risk Across Model Configurations

Model	Feature Regime	Accuracy	Precision	Recall	F1-Score	False Positive Rate	Privacy Risk Score (1–10)	Compliance Interpretation
Logistic Regression	Privacy-Minimized	0.91	0.89	0.90	0.89	0.07	3.2	Strong compliance posture with moderate detection power
Random Forest	Privacy-Minimized	0.95	0.94	0.95	0.94	0.04	4.1	Balanced option with strong security-compliance trade-off
XGBoost / Gradient Boosting	Privacy-Minimized	0.96	0.95	0.96	0.95	0.03	4.6	High detection strength with manageable privacy burden
Logistic Regression	Full Telemetry	0.93	0.91	0.92	0.91	0.06	6.5	Improved performance but higher monitoring exposure
Random Forest	Full Telemetry	0.97	0.96	0.97	0.96	0.02	7.4	Excellent detection but significant profiling concerns
XGBoost / Gradient Boosting	Full Telemetry	0.98	0.97	0.98	0.97	0.02	8.1	Highest predictive strength with highest compliance scrutiny

6.4 Compliance Implication Discussion

The results schema here cuts directly across ways AI-driven security programs could be privacy-managed as shown in Figure 2. Firstly, it shows that data minimization does not necessarily imply significantly less security effectiveness. It is very common to find the predictive capability gap being quite narrow between privacy-minimized and full-telemetry models, especially when ensemble techniques are used as shown in Figure 3. This revelation strongly indicates that privacy-aware principles can be the blueprint, in terms of the organizational setup, for the AI security systems, without sacrificing the ability to protect. Secondly, closely theatrical, the privacy risk beyond the crisp improvement in accuracy is a noteworthy point. Although going from the privacy-minimized regime to the full telemetry scenario might only give a slight bump in accuracy, the compliance burden thereafter is usually alarmingly disproportionate. Mainly, further fields lead to an increase in identifiability, a larger retention burden, heightened transparency requirements, as well as ethical concerns of a sustained behavioral monitoring that is non-consensual. Hence from the law and business perspective, model's performance gains must be weighed against the total organizational costs. Thirdly, the experiment points out the fact that in regulated environments, explainability and governance can be crucial. Often, a less powerful yet more understandable model is recommendable and more defendable than a stronger but incomprehensible one whose decision-making process is hardly explainable and changed process is fraught with difficulties, audits, and complaints from grievances by employees or regulators. This is especially the case where AI-generated alerts could lead to employment decisions, access restrictions, or internal investigations. Fourthly, the results favor a layered deployment strategy. For instance, privacy-minimized models might be operated as a default detection layer while full telemetry with detailed features could be reserved for deep investigations carried out under strict control. In such a multi-layer architecture, more invasive analyses triggered only by valid security incidents, not by routine monitoring, are consistent with the principles of proportionality and limitation of purpose. Broadly, the empirical part identifies privacy and compliance not only as external factors curtailing AI security performance but as the principal elements in designing effective, sustainable security programs(Khatibi et al., 2025).

Figure 2. Security Performance Versus Privacy Risk Across Model Configurations

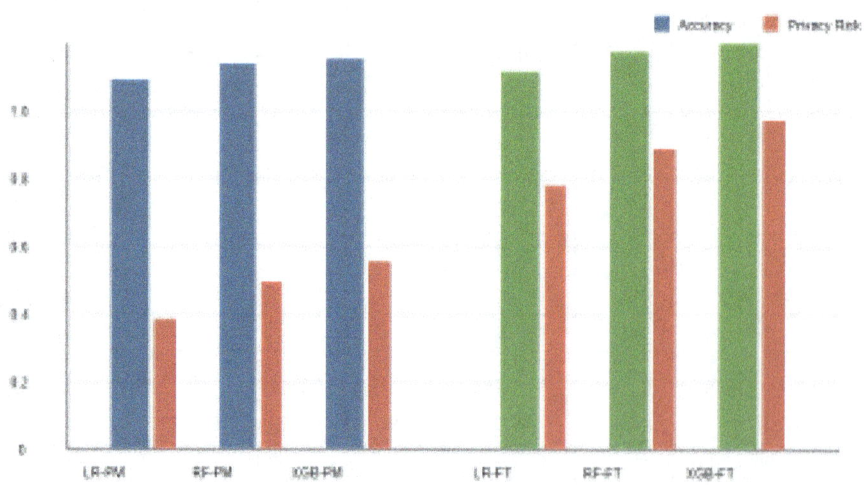

Figure 3. Compliance-Aware AI Security Evaluation Workflow

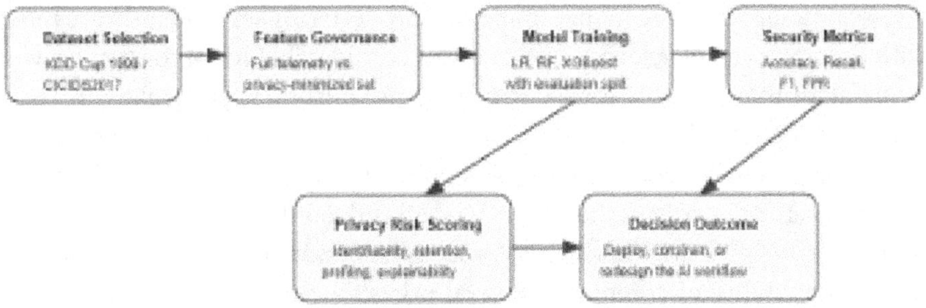

7. FUTURE DIRECTIONS AND STRATEGIC RECOMMENDATIONS FOR PRIVACY-COMPLIANT AI SECURITY SYSTEMS

Three major elements will shape future privacy-compliant AI security systems. Firstly, as hackers and cybercriminals advance in their methods, the challenge is on security analytical tools that they will need to be capable enough to detect even the smallest traces hidden in the most complex of datasets. Secondly, privacy legislation that is being implemented in country after country globally compels organizations to adhere to very strict processes for gathering, processing, and storing personal data. Thirdly, wide public opinion demands that organizations demonstrate accountability by being transparent about their activities and how they ethically and responsibly build their digital infrastructures for the public. It has become clear that the need for effectiveness in security and protection of privacy are not only compatible but also capable of mutually strengthening each other on the basis of the forces of the above three elements of concern to the present-day world. If enterprises want to thrive in this new environment, they will need to bring in new policies that embed privacy as the central theme in the conceptualization and operation of the AI security systems. Privacy should definitely not be regarded as an after-thought compliance activity after the technology deployment. The inclusion of privacy is necessary in the areas such as system architecture, model development, data governance, and organizational culture. We have compiled below four broad areas and within them several specific themes along which organizations can grow and expand their AI security initiatives in order to be privacy-compliant, regulated while at the same time, producing end-to-end results. The recommendation targeting areas include: developing new privacy-enhancing technologies, improving governance structures, increasing transparency and accountability, encouraging close cooperation between disciplines, and preparing organizations for regulatory and technological transformations.

7.1 Advances in Privacy-Preserving Artificial Intelligence Technologies

There are multiple forces behind the widespread use of privacy-preserving methods in machine learning. The older and still widely-known method of differential privacy will still be used to some extent. However, there are significant breakthroughs that have meanwhile been made as well concerning such methods in particular: federated learning, homomorphic encryption, and secure multi-party computations.

Using these novel techniques, a computer can extract key insights from the data without necessarily knowing the identity of the persons whose information is contained therein. That said, one of their major obstacles to wide-scale adoption is the higher implementation cost by way of hardware requirements and the trade-off with accuracy and efficiency. There is still considerable room for further work in making privacy-preserving algorithms suitable for security analytics purposes, particularly real-time analytics.

At present, security solutions have to resort to fairly computationally heavy operations which are not compatible with a real-time detection scenario or require specialized hardware. Through advances in both the software and hardware sectors, however, it is envisioned that the potential of these techniques will be realized in large-scale security operations processing hundreds of thousands of events on a daily basis. Exploring the possibility of combining several privacy-preserving methods under the umbrella term "hybrid security solutions" is also a promising path to follow. Imagine a situation where a federated learning system is used for model building at different locations without the exchange of data, at the same time differential privacy is applied for the output query, and homomorphic encryption serves as a lock for the storage(Babaker et al., 2025). The combinations of these techniques and mechanisms will provide multiple layers of privacy with data lifecycle touchpoints built-in. Organizations should consider these privacy-preserving technologies as core components of their AI security architectures rather than something they could do without. This will enable them to have powerful threat detection capabilities while at the same time reduce their dependence on practices that intrude on the privacy of the user.

7.2 Raising the Bar for Governance and Regulatory Compliance

Despite the fact that many organizations have succeeded in creating robust AI security plans, there is one aspect related to regulation that is so compelling one cannot simply overlook it. New privacy laws are regularly being rolled out globally considering automation and facets of decision-making, large-scale monitoring, and international data transfers. The first step to address this is to form cells where elements of privacy are incorporated as an integral part of cybersecurity management. Structures, policies, processes, mechanisms for continuous monitoring of the model and data processing activities should be put in place. Besides the above points, it is worthwhile to emphasize that another route to governance is compliance with internationally recognized standards such as ISO/IEC 27001, which deals with information security management, and ISO/IEC 27701, which focuses on privacy information management. These standards help companies by offering thorough and very detailed instructions for managing their information security and privacy. From a big-picture perspective, using these standards guarantees that privacy is thought through carefully and regularly when designing and running operations. Companies need to continually update their knowledge of latest laws and rules affecting artificial intelligence use. Recent laws focus on issues like how open algorithms need to be, doing risk assessments, and having humans in control. It is likely that companies will take the initiative to change their management structures so that they are in line with these changing (Hiari et al., 2025).

7.3 Equipping Organizations for Upcoming Security and Privacy Challenges

Information technology is progressing so rapidly that organizations cannot just keep pace with the present but also have to foresee the changes that are more likely to affect them in a significant way. Hence, the ability to foresee emerging threats and risks should become a skill that all privacy and compliance professionals dealing with AI-based security systems have to possess. The main focus will be on the hybrid AI architectures talked about earlier but with the additions of cloud computing, Internet of Things (IoT) devices, edge computing infrastructures. It is understood that distributed environments give rise to huge amounts of telemetry data whose processing would then far exceed the capability of any one device. In line with this, the extent of security monitoring has to one unprecedently increased to cover a large number of devices and networks. Adversarial machine learning is, however, the capability of an opponent to mislead a model using malicious inputs. This when taken to a high level of skill, can even compromise the integrity of the model. This means that organizations have to be always on their guards and they have to have multiple layers of a security pipeline i.e., model, data, behavior monitoring and model validation etc(Ayub et al., 2025).

Furthermore, we will briefly examine the social repercussions of the extensive use of AI surveillance technologies. Stakeholders may very well be worried about whether security interventions are stepping over the line of individual freedoms and whether there are sufficient safeguards against the misuse of personal information. Ultimately, only those organizations who are capable of resolving these issues through excellent governance, ethical policies, and transparency will be able to maintain public trust successfully. Since a steady stream of innovations in the domain of privacy-enhancing technologies is expected, these will dictate the future of AI-driven security systems. For example, apart from cryptographic computation and secure hardware environments, decentralized analytics can also contribute to mitigating the impact; on the other hand, companies can carry out threat detection on sensitive data while keeping the data encrypted and safe from unauthorized viewers. The use of such technologies will increase the ethical responsibility as well as enhance the infrastructure of technology-driven security(Qaddara & Alraba'nah, 2025).

When examining the privacy- and compliance-related issues of AI security programs, it is clear that this represents an area where how cybersecurity systems are created and operated will change fundamentally. In the past, security architectures predominantly concentrated on detecting threats, and hence, privacy concerns were hardly considered at all in this respect. The truth is, today's AI-enabled security systems must operate in a world where privacy safeguarding, regulatory compliance, and ethical accountability are seen as pushing the same direction and being equally important. The companies that will make it in this area tomorrow are the ones that will know how to integrate privacy safeguards throughout the entire system lifecycle starting with data collection and model creation, through to deployment and governance(Awais et al., 2025). Using privacy-preserving technologies, improving governance structures, increasing transparency, advocating for cooperation among different disciplines, and having the right tools to respond to new challenges enable organizations to develop AI security systems that not only protect digital infrastructures effectively but also uphold the rights of individuals(ALMahadin et al., 2025). Achieving this kind of balance will not just minimize the risk of regulatory non-compliance but will also lead to the building of trust among various stakeholders and the long-term sustainability of AI-driven cybersecurity solutions. Therefore, with AI continuing its transformation of cybersecurity, privacy-conscious design will be recognized as an indication of secure and responsible security (Braik et al., 2025).

8. CONCLUSION: TOWARD PRIVACY-COMPLIANT ARTIFICIAL INTELLIGENCE SECURITY PROGRAMS

Artificial intelligence has indeed changed the face of cybersecurity to a great extent. Cybersecurity frameworks increasingly rely on machine learning to detect cyber threats, understand user behavior, identify anomalies, and even automate incident response. These capabilities not only enable a company to handle a voluminous amount of security data effectively but also offer a quick, precise course of action whenever threats arise(Alraba'nah & Hiari, 2025). Paradoxically, the very security features that depend on large sets of data may cause serious privacy and compliance issues. On one hand, AI-based security measures call for the heavy surveillance of online activities, which may entail the gathering, handling, and even study of highly personal and behavioral data. This chapter illustrates that the link between using artificial intelligence to bolster cybersecurity and following privacy regulations remains open to interpretation. Here, first of all, it was noted that if one evaluates AI security programs merely based on the traditional chess of metrics such as detection accuracy and false positive rate, one may lose the real point. Different matters from legal requirements to ethical issues, privacy concerns, and organizational accountability all need to be covered by a comprehensive governance approach. At the end of the day, a business will be able to implement AI-driven security systems that not only perform excellently but also contribute to social (Raza et al., 2025).

The theoretical and legal grounds for analyzing privacy in AI security programs were established right at the beginning of the chapter. The discussion revealed that security monitoring tools usually fall under personal data protection laws as they collect behavioral data of users, employees, or clients. Consequently, organizations that use AI security tools should ensure that their data processing operations comply with the principles of data minimization, restriction of use of data to the original purpose, proportionality, and accountability. Failing to comply with these requirements might lead to regulatory sanctions, lawsuits, and a loss of reputation. Subsequently, a technical and operational discussion on fitting privacy management into AI security programs was undertaken. Following security data through its life cycle, it was discovered that at each stage of the data lifecycle: from acquisition, to preservation, to processing, to sharing, and, finally, to removal, privacy-related concerns exist. Therefore, good governance should include thorough lifecycle management of data specifying how data is obtained, secured, analyzed, and eventually deleted from the system. Organizations need to employ strong encryption, strict access control, clean data retention policies, and good vendor management in order to properly handle security telemetry(Ghazal, Hasan, Raju, et al., 2025).

Moreover, the chapter made a case for the need of well-defined and detailed privacy risk assessment methodologies. Privacy impact assessments, risk identification, and re-identification risk analysis are step-by-step approaches to understanding the potential privacy rights infringements of individuals and regulatory non-compliance of organizations when deploying AI security systems. Using the said tools helps an organization identify potential harm at an early stage of system design and implement safeguards that reduce the likelihood and limit the effects of privacy violations effectively. Embedding such tools within comprehensive cybersecurity governance frameworks will guarantee that privacy considerations do not become secondary while security operations are given top priority. Privacy-preserving technical measures were the focus of this chapter. The appropriate combination of privacy-enhancing technologies that can be the key to the dilemma of disclosure of personal information when security data is being analyzed without compromising the quality of security measures include anonymization, differential privacy, federated learning, homomorphic encryption, and secure multi-party computation. These technologies demonstrate that cybersecurity and strong privacy can indeed coexist, provided that systems are designed in a very thoughtful manner. Even though many of these approaches are at the research and development stage, incorporating them in AI security architectures is a move towards privacy-aware cybersecurity (Abualhaj, Abu-Shareha, Al-Khatib, et al., 2025).

The results and discussion section's practical investigation clearly mapped security performance directly to privacy exposure as well. Evaluation through comparison of full telemetry datasets versus privacy-minimized feature models revealed that even when large scale data collection is avoided, a high detection performance level can usually be obtained. While full telemetry models may have a slightly higher predictive accuracy level, they also unexpectedly pose very high privacy risks and compliance burdens. The findings support the notion that the focus of AI security programs should be more on the use of proportional data and a careful assessment needs to be made if the value that additional monitoring capabilities provide is enough to justify their privacy impact. Another relevant subject matter in the chapter is the point in saying that human and organizational aspects of privacy compliance are at least as important as the technological ones in the responsible AI security governance framework. Technical controls alone cannot ensure that data is handled in a manner consistent with ethical principles. It is the responsibility of organizations to establish a governance framework that incorporates transparency, accountability, and human oversight in processes involving automatic decision-making. Privacy officers, compliance teams and multi-function governance committees wield great influence in ensuring that AI security systems stay within the bounds of legality and ethics.

Besides, a privacy-aware work environment would encourage the security systems operators and employees to reflect on the wider consequences of their actions while handling security technologies. In the near future, AI security programs will be continuously changing not only because of new technologies but also as a reaction to changing regulations. The combination of artificial intelligence, distributed computing, and privacy-enhancing technologies will open up possibilities of detecting and responding to cyber-attacks. On the other hand, they will also be accompanied by regulatory measures governing artificial intelligence and data protection, which will be developed and extended, making it necessary for organizations to keep their governance practices current. Those paying attention to privacy at the design and implementation phases of AI security systems are the ones that will be able to cope effectively with an evolving environment. Evaluating privacy and compliance in AI-operated security programs boils down to understanding a fundamental point: cybersecurity and privacy are not two separate and conflicting objectives to be pursued individually. Actually, these two aspects stand as the fundamental pillars of a digital governance that is at once responsible and sustainable.

To have a reliable security infrastructure is not just about safeguarding the organization's resources but also about giving due consideration to the rights of the individuals whose data are being handled. Those organizations that are keen on creating AI-powered security systems which are capable of hitting both these targets at the same time, will first have to depend on the principles of privacy-by-design. They will also need to create robust governance frameworks and make use of privacy-preserving technologies. It's a fact that the future of cybersecurity will hinge more and more on the deployment of smart systems which, on the one hand, will be able to comprehend very complicated data settings, and on the other hand, will be able to counter very highly skilled attacks. The major obstacles for both organizations and regulators would be to ensure that these systems would not only be up to the standards of privacy regulations but also of ethical ones. In the meantime, the research community will be busy working on the desired breakthroughs in the coming years. Good design, interdisciplinary collaboration, and new technological innovations can help bring about the conference of AI security programs that at once secure digital infrastructures and honor privacy, accountability, and public

REFERENCES

Abashes, G. M., Elshqeirat, B., Abu-Shareha, A. A., & Alshraideh, M. (2025). BEYOND THE NOISE: UNVEILING MEANINGFUL PATTERNS IN MOBILE PAYMENT DATA USING FUZZY LOGIC AND SVM. *Journal of Theoretical and Applied Information Technology*, *103*(1).

Abdeljaber, O., Al-Adwan, A. S., Yaseen, H., Falahat, M., Abdullah, A., & Fauzi, M. A. (2025). Shopping in the Metaverse: Decoding Consumer Intentions. *The International Information & Library Review*. Advance online publication. DOI: 10.1080/10572317.2025.2594293

Abualghanam, O., Alazzam, H., Qatawneh, M., Alazab, M., & Al Sharaiah, M. (2025). Elevating Mobile Security: An Ensemble Approach for Enhanced Malware Detection with M-iForest. *International Journal of Interactive Mobile Technologies*, *19*(10), 129–151. Advance online publication. DOI: 10.3991/ijim.v19i10.51319

Abualhaj, M. M., Abu-Shareha, A. A., Al-Khatib, S. N., Alsaaidah, A. M., & Anbar, M. (2025). Improving firewall performance using hybrid of optimization algorithms and decision trees classifier. *IAES International Journal of Artificial Intelligence*, *14*(4), 2839. Advance online publication. DOI: 10.11591/ijai.v14.i4.pp2839-2848

Abualhaj, M. M., Abu-Shareha, A. A., & Rateb, R. (2025). Enhancing intrusion detection systems with hybrid HHO-WOA optimization and gradient boosting machine classifier. *International Journal of Reconfigurable and Embedded Systems*, *14*(2), 518. Advance online publication. DOI: 10.11591/ijres.v14.i2.pp518-526

Abualhaj, M. M.I, Al-Khatib, S. N., Abu-Shareha, A. A., Almomani, O., Al-Mimi, H., Al-Allawee, A., Daoud, M. S., & Anbar, M. (2025). Spam Detection Boosted by Firefly-Based Feature Selection and Optimized Classifiers. *International Journal of Advances in Soft Computing and Its Applications*, *17*(3). Advance online publication. DOI: 10.15849/IJASCA.251130.02

Abualhaj, M. M., Al-Khatib, S. N., Abu-Shareha, A. A., Hyassat, A., & Daoud, M. S. (2025). Smart Firewall for Phishing Detection Powered by Bio-Inspired Algorithms. *Journal of Advances in Information Technology*, *16*(11), 1529–1539. Advance online publication. DOI: 10.12720/jait.16.11.1529-1539

Abualigah, L., Almomani, M. H., Alomari, S. A., Zitar, R. A., Migdady, H., Saleem, K., Snasel, V., Smerat, A., & Ezugwu, A. E. (2025). Optimizing Intrusion Detection in Wireless Sensor Networks via the Improved Chameleon Swarm Algorithm for Feature Selection. *IET Communications*, *19*(1), e70029. Advance online publication. DOI: 10.1049/cmu2.70029

Abuowaida, S., Abu Owida, H., Shelash Mohammad, S. I., Alshdaifat, N., Abu Elsoud, E., Alazaidah, R., Vasudevan, A., & Alshurideh, M. T. (2025). Evidence Detection in Cloud Forensics: Classifying Cyber-Attacks in IaaS Environments using machine learning. *Data and Metadata*, *4*, 699. Advance online publication. DOI: 10.56294/dm2025699

Ahmed, K. A., Ibrahim, A., Qudr, L. A. Z., Tawfeq, J. F., Al Falahi, Q., & Radhi, A. D. (2025). *Developing Adaptive AI-Driven Cybersecurity Frameworks for Real-Time Detection of Polymorphic Malware in IoT Networks*. DOI: 10.1109/ICBATS66542.2025.11258540

Al-Bahtiti, A. S., Tayeh, B. A., Baghdadi, A., Alaloul, W. S., & Abu Aisheh, Y. I. (2025). Drivers for adopting augmented reality and virtual reality technologies in the construction project management in Gaza City. *Journal of Asian Architecture and Building Engineering*, 1–18. Advance online publication. DOI: 10.1080/13467581.2025.2507235

Al-Daoud, K. I., Yogeesh, N., Mohammad, S. I., Raja, N., Chetana, R., William, P., Vasudevan, A., Alshdaifa, N., & Hunitie, M. F. A. (2025). Explainability in AI Using Fuzzy Inference Systems For the Regression Problem. *Applied Mathematics & Information Sciences*, *19*(5), 973–987. Advance online publication. DOI: 10.18576/amis/190501

Al-Daoud, K. I., Yogeesh, N., Mohammad, S. I. S., Raja, N., Jabeen, F. T. Z., William, P., Vasudevan, A., Hunitie, M. F. A., & Alshdaifat, N. (2025). Fuzzy Linear Programming in Real-World Applications: A Comparative Study of Agricultural and Financial Optimization. *Applied Mathematics & Information Sciences*, *19*(4), 849–862. Advance online publication. DOI: 10.18576/amis/190411

Al-Dmour, R., Al-Dmour, H., Al-Dmour, A., Basheer Amin, E., & Al-Dmour, Y. (2025). *AI and big data-driven social media recruitment: the mediating role of talent acquisition and employee engagement in bank performance*. Digital Transformation and Society., DOI: 10.1108/DTS-02-2025-0042

Al-Okbi, N. K., Alomari, S. A., Zitar, R. A., Smerat, A., Nazzal, M. A., & Abualigah, L. (2025). Integrating Multimodal Emotion Recognition with Deep Q-Learning for Adaptive Social Robot Interaction. *International Journal of Robotics and Control Systems*, *5*(4), 2265–2289. Advance online publication. DOI: 10.31763/ijrcs.v5i4.2055

Al-znamat, F. O., Alsaaidah, A., & Abu-Shareha, A. A. (2025). Malware Detection Using a Modified Bat Algorithm for Feature Selection. *International Journal of Intelligent Engineering and Systems*, *18*(9), 885–899. Advance online publication. DOI: 10.22266/ijies2025.1031.56

Aldabbas, A., Baniata, L. H., Alsaaidah, B. A., Mustafa, Z., Alali, M., & Rateb, R. (2025). Artificial intelligence-driven method for the discovery and prevention of distributed denial of service attacks. *IAES International Journal of Artificial Intelligence*, *14*(1), 614. Advance online publication. DOI: 10.11591/ijai.v14.i1.pp614-628

Alenazi, M. J. F., Al-Khasawneh, M. A., Rahman, S., & Faheem, Z. (2025). Deep Reinforcement Learning Based Flow Aware-QoS Provisioning in SD-IoT for Precision Agriculture. *Computational Intelligence*, *41*(1), e70023. Advance online publication. DOI: 10.1111/coin.70023

Alghlayini, S., Al-Betar, M. A., & Atef, M. (2025). Enhancing Non-Invasive Blood Glucose Prediction from Photoplethysmography Signals via Heart Rate Variability-Based Features Selection Using Metaheuristic Algorithms. *Algorithms*, *18*(2), 95. Advance online publication. DOI: 10.3390/a18020095

Ali, A. M., Al-Qerem, A., Hassan, M. R., Abu-Khadrah, A., & Jarrah, M. (2025). Traffic Monitoring and Control System for Smart City Pollution Regulation Using IoT and Correlated Capsule Networks. *IEEE Access : Practical Innovations, Open Solutions*, *13*, 46983–47003. Advance online publication. DOI: 10.1109/ACCESS.2025.3550966

Alkhawatrah, M. (2025). Random Forests Relay Selector in Buffer-Aided Cooperative Networks. *IEEE Access : Practical Innovations, Open Solutions*, *13*, 165402–165410. Advance online publication. DOI: 10.1109/ACCESS.2025.3612192

ALMahadin, G., Shabaz, M., Khan, I. R., Vimal, V., Keshta, I., & Maguluri, L. P.ALMahadin. (2025). Content-aware recommendation system for integrated temporal semantic review text over web of things. *Service Oriented Computing and Applications*, *19*(1), 77–91. Advance online publication. DOI: 10.1007/s11761-024-00408-9

Almomani, O., Arabiat, A., Al Tayeb, M., Almaiah, M. A., Obeidat, M., Aldhyani, T. H. H., Shehab, R., & Rowad, M. (2025). A Robust Model for Android Malware Detection via ML and DL classifiers. *Mesopotamian Journal of Big Data*, *2025*. Advance online publication. DOI: 10.58496/MJBD/2025/017

Alnawayseh, S. E. A., Al-Sit, W. T., & Ghazal, T. M. (2022). Smart Congestion Control in 5G/6G Networks Using Hybrid Deep Learning Techniques. *Complexity*, *2022*(1), 1781952. Advance online publication. DOI: 10.1155/2022/1781952

Alraba'nah, Y., & Hiari, M. (2025). Improved convolutional neural networks for aircraft type classification in remote sensing images. *IAES International Journal of Artificial Intelligence*, *14*(2), 1540. Advance online publication. DOI: 10.11591/ijai.v14.i2.pp1540-1547

Arabiat, A. M. (2025). Intelligent Model for Detecting GAN-Generated Images Based on Multi-Classifier and Advanced Data Mining Techniques. *International Journal of Electrical and Electronic Engineering and Telecommunications*, *14*(3). Advance online publication. DOI: 10.18178/ijeetc.14.3.147-157

Arabiat, A. M., & Eljaafreh, Y. G. (2025). Intrusion Detection in Wireless Sensor Networks Using ML Based Classification of Denial of Service (DoS) Attacks. *The Journal of Communication*, *20*(4). Advance online publication. DOI: 10.12720/jcm.20.4.501-514

Awais, Z., Hussain, M., Elshenawy, A., Arsalan, A., Anwar, M., Asif Habib, M., Jabbar, S., & Ahmad, M. (2025). ISCC: Intelligent Semantic Caching and Control for NDN-Enabled Industrial IoT Networks. *IEEE Access : Practical Innovations, Open Solutions*, *13*, 169881–169898. Advance online publication. DOI: 10.1109/ACCESS.2025.3614984

Ayub, N., Imtiaz, M. A., Ali, E., Alqahtani, A. M., Ali, A., Ashurov, M., Albouq, S., & Law, F. L. (2025). A Decision Framework for Intra Task Fixed Priority INTEL PXA270 Distributed Architecture for Soft RT-Applications Based on Deep Learning. *Engineering. Technology and Applied Science Research*, *15*(3), 23553–23558. Advance online publication. DOI: 10.48084/etasr.10006

Azeem, S., Javed, S., Naseer, I., Ali, O., & Ghazal, T. M. (2025). A New Hybrid PSO-HHO Wrapper Based Optimization for Feature Selection. *IEEE Access : Practical Innovations, Open Solutions*, *13*, 87090–87099. Advance online publication. DOI: 10.1109/ACCESS.2025.3570901

Babaker, S., Khatibi, A., Alsoud, A. R., Kaur, J., Jagtap, J., Alkhayyat, A., & Shah, S. K. (2025). Improving Reliability and Data Management in Internet of Things Based Wireless Sensor Networks. *Internet Technology Letters*, *8*(6), e646. Advance online publication. DOI: 10.1002/itl2.646

Braik, M., Kassaymeh, S., Almiani, M., Albashish, D., Awadallah, M., Bataineh, B., & Al-Hiary, H. (2025). Advancements in global optimization with an empowered capuchin search algorithm. *Neural Computing & Applications*, *37*(24), 19707–19749. Advance online publication. DOI: 10.1007/s00521-025-11421-0

Eke, C. I., Al-Shamayleh, A. S., Phiri, M., Maswadi, K., Kwaghtyo, D. K., Mulenga, M., & Iyidobi, C. J. (2025). Machine Learning Based Mobile Big Data Analytics: State-of-the-art Applications, Taxonomy, Challenges and Future Research Directions. *Nigerian Journal of Technological Development*, *22*(4). Advance online publication. DOI: 10.63746/njtd.v22i4.3385

Elomda, B. M., Abdelbary, T. A. A., Hassan, H. A., Hamza, K. S., & Kharma, Q. (2025). An Enhanced Multi-Layer Blockchain Security Model for Improved Latency and Scalability. *Information (Basel)*, *16*(3), 241. Advance online publication. DOI: 10.3390/info16030241

Fatima, W., Rizvi, S. S. R., Ghazal, T. M., Kharma, Q. M., Ahmad, M., Abbas, S., Furqan, M., & Adnan, K. M. (2025). Abstractive Text Summarization in Arabic-Like Script Using Multi-Encoder Architecture and Semantic Extraction Techniques. *IEEE Access : Practical Innovations, Open Solutions*, *13*, 104977–104991. Advance online publication. DOI: 10.1109/ACCESS.2025.3575610

Ghazal, T. M. (2025). Federated Learning for Intelligent Sensing and Navigation Technologies for 6G Communications. *Journal of Sensors*, *2025*(1). DOI: 10.1155/js/3746147

Ghazal, T. M., Awouda, A. E., Hasan, M. K., Rahman, A. H. A., Islam, S., Saeed, R. A., Elshafie, H., Iqbal, A., & Hussein, A. H. (2025). Knowledge Learning for Securing Workflow Scheduling Algorithm in Mobile Edge Computing. *Mobile Networks and Applications*, *30*(3-4), 395–413. Advance online publication. DOI: 10.1007/s11036-025-02465-6

Ghazal, T. M., Hasan, M. K., Mokhtar, U. A., Safie, N., Alshamayleh, A., & Ahmad, M. (2025). Machine learning-based real-time outage fault detection for distribution networks in smart grid. In *Energy Reports* (Vol. 14). DOI: 10.1016/j.egyr.2025.10.045

Ghazal, T. M., Hasan, M. K., Raju, K. N., Khan, M. A., Alshamayleh, A., Bhatt, M. W., & Ahmad, M. (2025). Data Space Privacy Model with Federated Learning Technique for Securing IoT Communications in Autonomous Marine Vehicles. *Journal of Intelligent & Robotic Systems*, *111*(3), 84. Advance online publication. DOI: 10.1007/s10846-025-02298-1

Hanandeh, A., Alfreijat, S. Y., Qutieshat, R. J., Alsha'ar, H. Y., Kilani, Q. A. L., & Saleem Khasawneh, M. A. (2025). Implementing AI Accuracy, Learning Rate, Inference Time on enhancing Big Data Analysis and Strategic Plan. *Data and Metadata*, *4*, 637. Advance online publication. DOI: 10.56294/dm2025637

Hasan, M. K., Ghazal, T. M., Alkhalifah, A., Abu Bakar, K. A., Omidvar, A., Nafi, N. S., & Agbinya, J. I. (2021). Fischer Linear Discrimination and Quadratic Discrimination Analysis–Based Data Mining Technique for Internet of Things Framework for Healthcare. *Frontiers in Public Health*, *9*, 737149. Advance online publication. DOI: 10.3389/fpubh.2021.737149 PMID: 34712639

Hasan, M. K., Ghazal, T. M., Issa, G., Islam, S., Ismail, A. F., & Kabir, S. R. (2025). Hashgraph consensus-based simultaneous, asynchronous and big-data supported blockchain mechanism for IT-OT enabled critical infrastructure sectors. *Journal of Ambient Intelligence and Humanized Computing*. Advance online publication. DOI: 10.1007/s12652-024-04942-4

Hiari, M., Alraba'nah, Y., & Qaddara, I. (2025). A Deep Learning-Based Intrusion Detection System using Refined LSTM for DoS Attack Detection. *Engineering. Technology and Applied Science Research*, *15*(4), 25627–25633. Advance online publication. DOI: 10.48084/etasr.11499

Hyassat, A. S., Abu Zayed, R. E., Al Khateeb, E. A., Shalaldeh, A., Abdelhamied, M. M., & Qaddara, I. (2025). Unveiling Cyber Threats: An In-Depth Study on Data Mining Techniques for Exploit Attack Detection †. *Engineering Proceedings*, *104*(1), 28. Advance online publication. DOI: 10.3390/engproc2025104028

Ibrahim, A., Sekhar, R., Tawfeq, J. F., Salih, S. Q., Shah, P., & Radhi, A. D. (2024). Security and Privacy Protection for Online Electronic Documents Based on Novel Encryption Techniques. *Journal of Intelligent Systems and Internet of Things*, *11*(1), 21–28. Advance online publication. DOI: 10.54216/JISIoT.110103

Iskandarani, M. Z., & Hidayat, R. (2025). Analysis of Factors Affecting Spectrum Sensing in an IRS based Wireless Network. *International Journal on Advanced Science, Engineering and Information Technology*, *15*(1), 300–309. Advance online publication. DOI: 10.18517/ijaseit.15.1.20491

Khatibi, A., Babaker, S., Praveen, K. N. R., Chohan, J. S., Jadhav, A., Alsoud, A. R., Ramudu, M. J., & Jeet, R. (2025). Advanced AI-Driven Cybersecurity: Analyzing Emerging Threats and Defensive Strategies. *National Academy Science Letters*. Advance online publication. DOI: 10.1007/s40009-025-01897-8

Lee, S. W., Hussain, S., Issa, G. F., Abbas, S., Ghazal, T. M., Sohail, T., Ahmad, M., & Khan, M. A. (2021). Multi-Dimensional Trust Quantification by Artificial Agents through Evidential Fuzzy Multi-Criteria Decision Making. *IEEE Access : Practical Innovations, Open Solutions*, *9*, 159399–159412. Advance online publication. DOI: 10.1109/ACCESS.2021.3131521

Mahfouz, K. H., Al Betar, M. A., & Makhadmeh, S. N. (2025). Mitigating the task scheduling problem in fog computing environments using improved marine predators optimization algorithm. *Computing*, *107*(7), 147. Advance online publication. DOI: 10.1007/s00607-025-01502-2

Makhadmeh, S. N., Fraihat, S., Awad, M., Sanjalawe, Y., Al-Betar, M. A., & Awadallah, M. A. (2025). A crossover-integrated Marine Predator Algorithm for feature selection in intrusion detection systems within IoT environments. *Internet of Things : Engineering Cyber Physical Human Systems*, *31*, 101536. Advance online publication. DOI: 10.1016/j.iot.2025.101536

Mohammad, A. A. S., Al-Ramadan, A. M., Mohammad, S. I., Al Oraini, B., Vasudevan, A., Alshdaifat, N., & Hunitie, M. F. A. (2025). Customer Sentiment Analysis for Food and Beverage Development in Restaurants using AI in Jordan. *Data and Metadata*, *4*, 922. Advance online publication. DOI: 10.56294/dm2025922

Nafisah, I., Mahmoud, N., Ewees, A. A., Khattap, M. G., Dahou, A., Alghamdi, S. M., Fares, I. A., Azmi Al-Betar, M., & Abd Elaziz, M. (2025). Deep learning-based feature selection for detection of autism spectrum disorder. *Frontiers in Artificial Intelligence*, *8*, 1594372. Advance online publication. DOI: 10.3389/frai.2025.1594372 PMID: 40636395

Nasir, J., Aamir, M., Iftikhar, S., Albidah, A. B., Alqasem, O. A., Elwahab, M. E. A., Khan, I., & Koh, W. S. (2025). A Novel Hybrid Approach to Forecasting Crude Oil Prices Using Local Mean Decomposition, ARIMA, and XGBoost. *IEEE Access : Practical Innovations, Open Solutions*, *13*, 89140–89156. Advance online publication. DOI: 10.1109/ACCESS.2025.3561193

Otair, M., Qawaqzeh, F. A., Alomari, S. A., Zitar, R. A., Migdady, H., Saleem, K., Smerat, A., Alsoud, A. R., & Abualigah, L. (2025). Enhanced Arithmetic Optimization Algorithm for Intrusion Detection in Wireless Sensor Networks. *International Journal of Communication Systems*, *38*(10), e70122. Advance online publication. DOI: 10.1002/dac.70122

Qaddara, I., & Alraba'nah, Y. (2025). Enhancing Requirements Classification Using Machine Learning Techniques. *SN Computer Science*, *6*(6), 649. Advance online publication. DOI: 10.1007/s42979-025-04158-z

Qawasmeh, S., Habboushb, A., Elzaghmouri, B., Kharma, Q., & Albalawneh, D. (2025). Hybrid Convolutional Neural Network-Based Intrusion Detection System for Secure IoT Networks. *Tikrit Journal of Engineering Sciences*, *32*(SP1), 1–11. Advance online publication. DOI: 10.25130/tjes.sp1.2025.2

Ramesh, J. V. N., Nimma, D., Dasari, R., Chaudhari Rane, D., AlGhamdi, A., Rao, K. B. V. B., Haider, S. A., Kuzieva, N., & Jangir, P. (2025). Safe and Reliable Two-Stage Online Offloading Algorithm for Transportation Cyber-Physical Systems. *IEEE Transactions on Intelligent Transportation Systems*, *26*(9), 14313–14322. Advance online publication. DOI: 10.1109/TITS.2025.3539934

Raza, M. A., Karim, A., Alqarni, M., Al-Khasawneh, M. A., Jumani, T. A., Aman, M., & Masud, M. I. (2025). An Intelligent Long Short-Term Memory-Based Machine Learning Model for the Potential Assessment of Global Hydropower Capacity in Sustainable Energy Transition and Security. *Energies*, *18*(13), 3324. Advance online publication. DOI: 10.3390/en18133324

Rehan, R., Sahran, S., Alyasseri, Z. A. A., Sani, N. S., & Al-Betar, M. A. (2025). Hyperparameters optimization of evolving spiking neural network using artificial bee colony for unsupervised anomaly detection. *Journal of Intelligent Systems*, *34*(1), 20240235. Advance online publication. DOI: 10.1515/jisys-2024-0235

Salman, A. M., Ibrahim, A., Abdulbaqi, A. S., Almajed, R., & Al Naffakh, H. A. H. (2025). *Designing Blockchain Solutions to Enhance Data Security and Privacy in Distributed IoT Networks*. DOI: 10.1109/ICBATS66542.2025.11258568

Sardar, R., Anees, T., Al-Shamayleh, A. S., Mehmood, E., Khalil, W., Akhunzada, A., & Shaikh, F. S. (2025). Challenges in detecting security threats in WoT: A systematic literature review. *Artificial Intelligence Review*, *58*(7), 196. Advance online publication. DOI: 10.1007/s10462-025-11176-z

Shah, R. K., Hasan, M. K., Islam, S., Khan, A., Ghazal, T. M., & Khan, A. N. (2022). Detect Phishing Website by Fuzzy Multi-Criteria Decision Making. *2022 1st International Conference on AI in Cybersecurity, ICAIC 2022*. DOI: 10.1109/ICAIC53980.2022.9897036

Shamaylah, N., Ibrahim Mohammad, S., Al Oraini, B., Yaseen Al-Gaafreh, J. M., Mosallam Alqahtani, M., Vasudevan, A., Shlash Mohammad, A. A., & Ahmmad Hunitie, M. F. (2025). Data-Driven Decision-Making for Employee Training and Development in Jordanian Public Institutions. *Data and Metadata*, *4*, 886. Advance online publication. DOI: 10.56294/dm2025886

Shambour, Q. Y., Al-Zyoud, M., & Hussein, A. H. (2025). FROM DATA TO DIAGNOSIS: KNOWLEDGE-DRIVEN, EXPLAINABLE AI FOR RELIABLE EARLY AUTISM DETECTION. *Interdisciplinary Journal of Information, Knowledge, and Management*, *20*, 032. Advance online publication. DOI: 10.28945/5652

Sharma, K. P., Al-Rashed, A., Johar, M. G. M., Alsoud, A. R., Singh, A., Dey, P., & Pant, S. (2025). Blockchain-Assisted Trust Framework for Increased Survivability in Internet of Vehicles. *Internet Technology Letters*, *8*(3), e70029. Advance online publication. DOI: 10.1002/itl2.70029

Sharma, K. P., Yajid, M. S. A., Gowrishankar, J., Mahajan, R., Alsoud, A. R., Jadhav, A., & Singh, D. (2025). A Systematic Review on Text Summarization: Techniques, Challenges, Opportunities. In *Expert Systems* (Vol. 42, Number 4). DOI: 10.1111/exsy.13833

Shlash Mohammad, A. A., Ibrahim Mohammad, S., Al-Daoud, K. I., Al Oraini, B., Mosallam Alqahtani, M., Vasudevan, A., & Ahmmad Hunitie, M. F. (2025). Riding into the Future: Transforming Jordan's Public Transportation with Predictive Analytics and Real-Time Data. *Data and Metadata*, *4*, 887. Advance online publication. DOI: 10.56294/dm2025887

Ullah, N., Al-Rahmi, W. M., Alblehai, F., Fernando, Y., Alharbi, Z. H., Zhanbayev, R., Al-Adwan, A. S., & Habes, M. (2025). Corrigendum to "Blockchain-powered grids: Paving the way for a sustainable and efficient future" [Heliyon Volume 10, Issue 10, May 2024, Article e31592] (Heliyon (2024) 10(10), (S2405844024076230), ()). In *Heliyon* (Vol. 11, Number 13). https://doi.org/DOI: 10.1016/j.heliyon.2024.e31592

Vasudevan, A., Albinaa, T. A., Mohammad, S. I., Sharmila, E., Raja, N., Soon, E. E. H., Alshurideh, M. T., & Al-Adwan, A. S. (2024). Bidirectional LSTM for Electronic Product Recommendation. *Applied Mathematics & Information Sciences*, *18*(6), 1443–1453. Advance online publication. DOI: 10.18576/amis/180621

Xu, B., Jummaa, K., Altalbawy, F. M. A., Roopashree, R., Saraswat, S. K., Ray, S., Tomar, P., Naem, S., Hamza, H. H., Smerat, A., & Khalid, A. (2025). Machine learning-assisted computation of water activity for ionic liquid-based aqueous ternary elements. *Desalination and Water Treatment*, *324*, 101484. Advance online publication. DOI: 10.1016/j.dwt.2025.101484

Zhu, Y., Lin, X., Kim, J., Al-Adwan, A. S., & Li, N. (2025). Exploring Human Interaction in Online Self-Regulated Learning Through Danmaku Comments. *International Journal of Human-Computer Interaction*, *41*(22), 13964–13977. Advance online publication. DOI: 10.1080/10447318.2025.2480826

Chapter 6
Implementing Privacy Preserving Machine Learning in Security Systems

Amjed A. Ahmed
Department of Computer Technical Engineering, Imam Kadhim University College (IKu), Iraq

Aghiad khedr Alkatan
http://orcid.org/0009-0007-4483-6116
Artificial Intelligence Department, Almamoun University, Baghdad, Iraq

ABSTRACT

This chapter looks at the integration of privacy-preserving machine learning methods in contemporary security systems. Recent studies have explored the integration of privacy-preserving machine learning methods in security systems. It explains how analytics and AI capabilities could help in detecting threats and anomalies internally, with minimum exposure of personal and sensitive data. Besides, issues of governance like data protection regulations; accountability; transparency, etc., are also discussed. The chapter gives guidance on how to implement smart security solutions by using machine learning and privacy by design principles. Such solutions, apart from being effective, would also be legally compliant and would consider user's privacy expectations. Besides these, the chapter points out the technical and operational issues such as the performance trade-offs in models, increased complexity of the system, and the compatibility with the existing security infrastructures.

1. INTRODUCTION

Digital transformation is continuing rapidly in government agencies, organizations, manufacturing plants, and individual communication media, which has revolutionized the concept of cybersecurity. Until now, conventional security systems relied on manually creating rules for security, signature-based detection, and managing threat intelligence. These methods were sufficient in the time when attack patterns were quite predictable, and the systems' environments were mainly centralized. But today, security ecosystems are mainly characterized by distributed cloud infrastructure, mobile devices, the Internet of Things, working from home, and adversaries that are continuously evolving their tactics. In

DOI: 10.4018/979-8-3373-9210-3.ch006

such a context, just depending on traditional security ways will not be capable of identifying sophisticated threats, hidden anomalies, and multi-stage attacks in real-time. Therefore, this shift has also led to using machine learning in cybersecurity systems(Al-Adwan & Abdeljaber, 2025). Nowadays, machine learning is a fundamental analytical instrument in security operations as it can identify patterns in large data volumes, classify malicious events, spot anomalies from usual behavior, and improve continuously threat detection capabilities. Security information and event management systems, endpoints, and intrusion detection systems; fraud detection tools, insider threat monitoring platforms through supervised, unsupervised, and semi-supervised learning methods constantly process logs, network traffic, etc. for enabling automated or assisted security decision-making. In addition to relying solely on pre-defined rules, machine learning approaches can uncover hidden data structures and react to attack behaviors that have not been seen before. Thus, machine learning's contribution to cyber security has changed from a small analytical assisting tool to a large operational element(Abualhaj, Al-Khatib, Al-Zyoud, et al., 2025). At first, most work went into malware categorization and spam filtering, but the areas have changed drastically and increased a lot. Presently, machine learning is being used mainly for discovering advanced persistent threats, network internal activity investigation, phishing attack recognition, botnets categorization, anomaly detection, risk evaluation, and incident ranking. This development has led to defensive operations being carried out on a larger scale, at higher speed, and with more flexibility. Nevertheless, the emergence of machine learning in security has produced a new batch of technical and ethical challenges, chiefly since these systems require enormous and often extremely sensitive datasets for their training and inference (Arabasy & Ghoneim, 2025).

1.1 Need for Privacy Preserving Machine Learning

Privacy preserving machine learning (PPML) is fundamentally a compromise between achieving high level of analytics and protecting individual's data with minimum exposure of raw data. PPML goes beyond treating privacy only as a compliance requirement. It effectively integrates privacy at all stages of the data lifecycle including data preprocessing, model training and deployment. It emphasizes that both security and privacy are vital components of a reliable digital defense system. Security systems constantly function on the edge between surveillance, analytics, and risk management, and this is where the need for PPML becomes quite critical. Security data can be widely collected and it may comprise information of individuals who are not the subjects of any investigation. In other words, the employees, students, customers, patients, and citizens may all become part of security datasets simply because of their contact with the monitored systems. If privacy safeguards are not properly implemented, an enterprise may create systems which will be able to detect attacks but will still lead to the violation of civil liberties, loss of employee trust, non-compliance with legal requirements, and damage to the reputation of the institution(Fauzi et al., 2025).

PPML is a collective term for all the techniques or technologies employed to safeguard data privacy in machine learning activities, i.e., data anonymization, pseudonymization, secure aggregation, federated learning (FL), differential privacy (DP), homomorphic encryption (HE), secure multiparty computation, and access-controlled model execution. Even though these techniques are very different in terms of complexity and performance, the main goal they share is to restrain the risk that sensitive information is revealed at any stage - during data processing, training, storage, or inference. The use of these privacy methods in the cybersecurity domain is, therefore, not only a matter of desire but has become a requirement since security data often falls under data protection legislations, internal governance standards, contractual confidentiality provisions as well as ethical concerns. On the strategic level, the importance of PPML cannot be underrated as well. Security systems which do not take privacy issues into account might result in user resistance, legal lawsuits from regulators, and operational problems due to lack of trust(Ghazal, Hasan, Hussein, et al., 2025).

1.2 Chapter Objectives and Research Contributions

The objective of this chapter is to deepen, in a very detailed manner, the implementation of privacy preserving machine learning in security systems without diluting their core function of threat detection and incident response. Firstly, the chapter lays down the theoretical basis of privacy preserving analytics in cybersecurity and reviews the primary privacy risks of conventional machine learning workflows in security monitoring. Secondly, it discusses the top privacy risk mitigating technical approaches and introduces a privacy aware machine learning implementation perspective in operational security environments. It majorly focuses on security domain that is why it incorporates privacy preserving machine learning as a special instance of security systems only. Security systems have distinctive requirements including real-time detection, high-volume telemetry processing, adversarial resilience, and integration with operational workflows. These requirements cause the creation of security environments new constraints and trade-offs different from those in general business analytics or recommendation systems. Accordingly, the chapter underlines security practical design choices like selective feature protection, privacy aware architecture design, and measurable tradeoffs between privacy and detection performance.

The other significant contribution is the chapter's orientation on the empirical side. In order to enhance the conceptual discussion about PPML and to present the analytical comparison of PPML techniques in a real security data environment, the chapter introduces a dataset-based evaluation framework. In this step, it becomes possible to have a very detailed follow-up discussion on how different privacy control mechanisms affect various metrics of a classification model such as accuracy, recall, false positive, etc. Besides, as a result of these discussions, readers will get to see privacy protection not just in a very general way, but in a manner that can be a basis for security systems that are both smart and responsible. Therefore, it is a question of setting up Privacy Preserving Machine Learning as the only path to Trustworthy Cybersecurity. With the widespread adoption of data-driven defense mechanisms, secure systems of the future will have to focus not only on their capability to detect attacks but also on how well they keep confidential the humans and organizations whose data is being used for such

This chapter contributes a comparative implementation framework for privacy-preserving machine learning in security systems. The framework links centralized learning, federated learning, differential privacy, and hybrid PPML models with security detection performance, privacy-risk reduction, operational deployment, and governance accountability.

Figure 1. Architecture of Privacy Preserving Security Analytics System

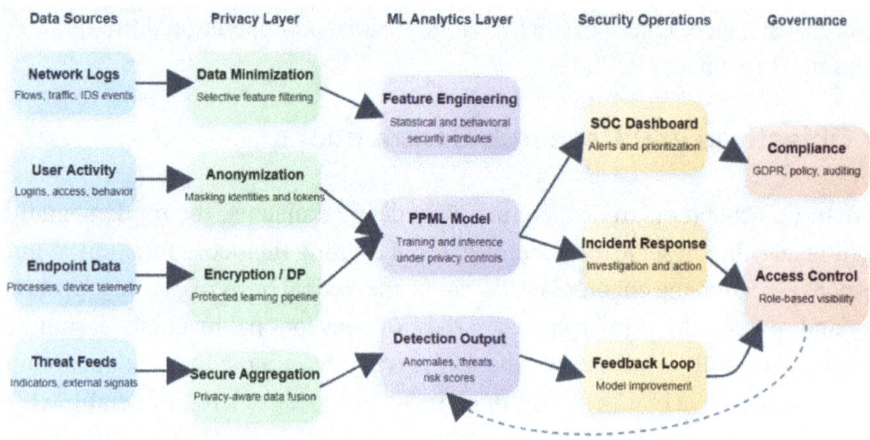

Figure 1, Architecture of a privacy preserving security analytics system showing the flow from sensitive security data sources to privacy controls, machine learning analysis, operational response, and governance oversight.

Figure 2. Data Flow Model of Privacy Preserving Machine Learning in Security Infrastructure

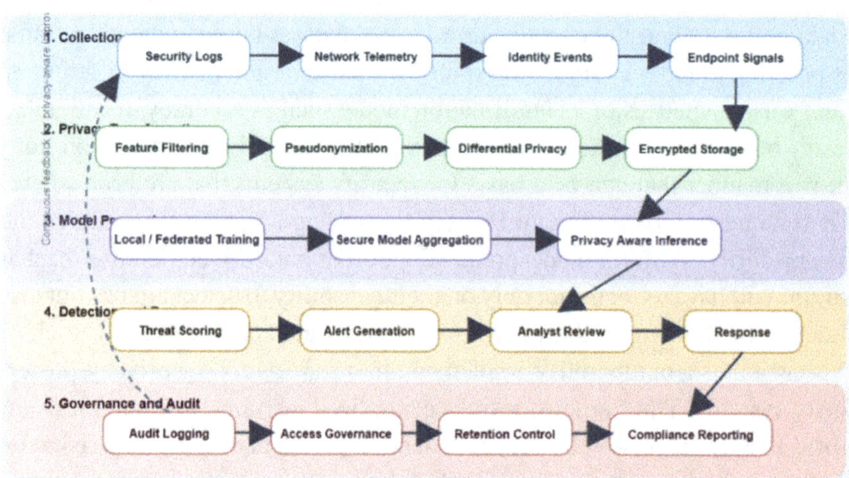

Data flow model for privacy preserving machine learning in security infrastructure, Figure 2, illustrating sequential movement from raw telemetry collection to privacy transformation, protected model processing, operational detection, and governance

2. FOUNDATIONS OF PRIVACY PRESERVING MACHINE LEARNING

Machine learning that keeps privacy intact is becoming an important research and development focus for modern intelligent systems because it addresses a fundamental dilemma of data-driven computing. Machine learning systems need very large and information-rich datasets to find patterns, generalize from observations and make predictive or classificatory decisions. On the other hand, as these systems rely on such data more and more, they create new risks related to confidentiality, autonomy, fairness and institutional trust. For security systems, such a dilemma turns very acute because the data used for detection and response is typically very sensitiv(Hasan et al., 2024)e. They may include authentication logs, user behavior traces, device identifiers, system interactions, communication metadata and richly detailed operational records. In fact, machine learning trusting the proximity to raw data is the main risk of unintentional disclosure. In the event of deployment on sensitive domains, such as cybersecurity, healthcare, finance and public administration, the consequences of accidental data leakage could be very harsh, including profiling of people without their consent, loss of control over confidential operational patterns on the part of the organizations, and even the trained model being able to expose traces of the original input data. Privacy preserving machine learning tackles such issues by shifting the focus from privacy and data disclosure concerns at the end of the analytical workflow to including these considerations right at the start, the analytical workflow. Besides assuming unlimited access to raw data, it is interested in what can be learned, under what conditions and with what privacy guarantees(Arabiat & Eljaafreh, 2025).

2.1 Concept and Principles of Privacy Preservation in Machine Learning

Privacy preserving machine learning comprises various techniques, system setups, and governance considerations that allow carrying out machine learning endeavors without deviation from the goal of protecting sensitive data. The core notion is that machine learning should get the benefits of data without excessively revealing identities, characteristics, and behaviors depicted in the data. Data minimization is a key principle of privacy protection. It expects the system to only acquire information that is strictly necessary for a clearly specified purpose. In the case of security systems, this would mean that the use of all available telemetry is avoided indiscriminately when a significantly reduced set of features can yield similar detection results(Hyassat et al., 2025). Another principle, namely purpose limitation, implies that data collected for security monitoring is not repurposed without notice or consent for profiling or evaluation tasks that are completely unrelated. The third principle, unlinkability, is aimed at making it impossible to directly associate processed records with identifiable individuals or systems unless such linkage is operationally justified and authorized. Confidentiality of computation is very related to this point, implying that sensitive values are not only protected at rest and in transit but also during analysis(Vasudevan et al., 2025).

Besides the above, privacy in machine learning also relies on the concept of controlled observability. This refers to the limitation or control of the data and information that analysts and other stakeholders such as administrators or third-party service providers are allowed to access. In typical setups, they may expose datasets, intermediate features, or models in ways that are over the amounts needed for security operations. A privacy friendly design limits such exposure by, for example, allowing who can see what, under what conditions and for what purpose to be well defined. Besides stating that data is protected, systems should be able to present the privacy guarantees that can be understood, analyzed, and tested.

Here lies a major reason why privacy preserving machine learning keeps drawing more and more on formal methods like differential privacy, secure multiparty computation, and cryptographic learning frameworks, among others(Saeed et al., 2024).

2.2 Privacy Risks in Traditional Security Analytics Models

Traditional security analytics models often put privacy aside to maximize the level of visibility, the overall scale of operations, and the speed of response. Their design is primarily oriented to the collection of telemetry data coming in great volume from endpoints, networks, user identities, servers, applications, and cloud services. Then, these raw materials are aggregated into centralized platforms where feature extraction, anomaly detection, scoring, decision-making support, etc., are performed. On the one hand, the approach is recognized for its effectiveness in terms of operations but on the other hand, it gives rise to several privacy risks. The primary risk is that of raw data centralization(Maz et al., 2025). When very detailed logs and behavioral traces are stored together in one repository, the system may be targeted not only by cybercriminals from outside it, but also by insiders attempting to resort to misuse. A compromise of such platform can lead to the leakage at a very granular level of information about, among others, regular users, privileged administrators, business processes, and digital habits. Another risk comes from high detail levels that security models rely on. In some instances, and even though the precise details are not strictly used for classification, features may bear names, identifiers, elements reflecting communication topology, references to files, command line contents or browsing traces. The availability of such finely detailed data may result in an increase in model sensitivity. However, an equally valid side effect is that it expands privacy exposure and complicates the aftermath of any accidental disclosure. Most of the time, long-term retention presents the third risk. Security teams frequently retain logs and datasets used for model training over long periods of time, claiming forensic readiness or regulatory compliance as reasons. Over time, such stores, and the behavioral histories they contain, can be used for reconstructing patterns related to people and systems even beyond the incident response that originally justified these records(Mahfuri & Ibrahim, 2024).

Models present a fourth risk vector though it is usually forgotten and underestimated. One common belief is that the final model is safe for sharing or deployment if the raw training data is hidden. However, this view has been challenged and can no longer stand after research into membership inference, model inversion, data reconstruction, and extraction attacks showed that adversaries, under certain circumstances and with certain knowledge, can determine whether particular records were part of training, estimate attributes of such records and sometimes reconstruct the original input pattern or its fair approximation. Such knowledge in a security context can be exploited to infer highly sensitive user actions, rare incident cases or confidential network structures that are normally well protected. Typical security analytics models are completely ill-equipped to defend against these kinds of threats. Another risk resulting from traditional methods is function creep. Once an efficient centralized analytics infrastructure is up and running, the temptation to use it for other purposes besides threat detection grows very much. Indeed, security data can be utilized for monitoring productivity, employee behavior evaluation, disciplinary procedures, and business intelligence(bi(Al-Momani et al., 2025)). Even if such intended use by the agents involved is not malicious, it has the great potential to undermine one's trust and to violate the primary expectations under which data was obtained. Traditional models afford very little support in terms of structural resistance to such repurposing because privacy boundaries are not implemented here with the aim of resisting overreach. Accordingly, one of the reasons why privacy preserving machine learning should be viewed not only as a technical solution to leakage risks but also a governance instrument to deal with overreach risks(Ibrahim et al., 2024).

2.3 Confidentiality, Anonymization, and Secure Data Processing

Confidentiality is the main requirement that confidential information must be accessible only to authorized persons and only for authorized purposes. For confidentiality to be fulfilled in machine learning systems, it is not enough to provide safeguards for the storage. Instead, the whole pipeline from the moment the data is accessed to preprocessing, feature engineering, model building, deploying the model, interpreting results must be covered. Complications abound in securing confidentiality in security systems as the very data that needs protection is also the same data that is used for threat identification. Privacy preserving machine learning tries to solve this paradox via the incorporation of data transformations (e.g., dimensionality reduction, creation of synthetic data, encryption with homomorphic cryptosystems) and by exploiting processing architectures that limit the necessity for direct exposure (e.g., federated learning, multi-party computation, trusted execution environments)(Abdeljaber et al., 2025).

There is first a big misconception regarding anonymization. Mention is often made of anonymization as a very straightforward, if not foolproof, technique but peeling the layers of practice reveal tremendous challenges. It goes without saying that removing explicit identifiers such as user names, or account numbers is a poor tool for balancing privacy vs. utility while the attacker can turn to behavioral patterns, rare combinations of features, temporal sequences, or relational structures to reconnect the identity. Consequently, one can hardly rely on simple de-identification, especially with high-dimensional security data(Khatibi et al., 2025).

Secure data processing relates to a series of architectural design For instance, raw data may be enclosed only within trusted execution environments; feature-level encryption is done during computation; analysts' view of sensitive fields is restricted; local processing is carried out at systems where raw data is not moved out among others. These are some of the practices that achieve preservation of privacy. These things become very real when one talks about collaboration among organizations in cyber defense. One might say a kind of sector-wide threat detection initiative would require pattern learning across multiple institutions. Privacy preserving processing would be the means that institutions use to feed in intelligences to the collective pool without baring their raw logs. Taking things, a step further, confidentiality in machine learning is not about the implementation of one single protective measure but rather a suite of safeguards that limit the ability of any single actor, process, or model instance to reveal too much information(Aldaaja et al., 2025).

2.4 Privacy Threat Models in Machine Learning Systems

Privacy threat model enumerates the ways in which privacy breaches may occur, actors who may be responsible for such breaches, and their capabilities, including maliciousness, ill-intent, ignorance, negligence, etc. In privacy preserving machine learning, threat models are an instrument for figuring out what is being protected, from whom and under what conditions. A system without a threat model is a system whose notion of privacy claims is vague. Security system such as the one here requires the threat model to take into account not only external but internal adversaries as well since each can play the system in a different way to their advantage. Honest-but-curious entities pose a certain threat. These are entities that after receiving the legitimate data, model parameters, outputs, etc., return the result as agreed but based on legitimate access try to infer additional information. An example is that a cloud-hosted training service may perform the agreed model training routine correctly but also analyze feature patterns for unintended insight. A second category of threat models is severely more malicious entities who do not hesitate to employ all sorts of hacking techniques. Very often, they gain unauthorized access, are able to interact with the models, analyze the traffic in the system, use side channels to recover sensitive information. Malicious participants in federated learning inject poisoned updates and at the same time use the updates of others to infer local data characteristics(Ghazal et al., 2024).

Membership inference is a serious threat from the standpoint of privacy-sensitive systems. In this case, an adversary tries to figure out whether a particular record was part of the model's training data. Noteworthy here is that in security contexts, knowledge that a record was part of training may indicate that the organization encountered the event, exposure user behavior or a specific type of incident. Model inversion is another potent threat in which the adversary reconstructs likely input features from model outputs or exposed parameters. Gradient leakage particularly affects distributed or collaborative learning if updates are insufficiently protected. Re-identification attacks typically focus on exploiting data which has had identifying features removed by combining multiple data attributes or bringing in external reference information to recover identity associations(Babaker et al., 2025). Privacy preserving machine learning starts by determining an adequate threat model and then selecting appropriate techniques. Privacy preserving methods do not always protect against all threats. Differential privacy may be effective against certain inference attacks at the individual record level, whereas secure multiparty computation is more suitable for distrust scenarios among collaborating organizations. Trusted execution environments may guarantee computation integrity and confidentiality in specific hardware contexts whereas federated learning decreases raw data centralization, although bringing with it new update leakage concerns(Akram et al., 2024). In security datasets, membership inference may reveal whether a rare attack, insider incident, or privileged-user behavior appeared in training data.

2.5 Comparison Between Conventional ML and Privacy Preserving ML

Simply put, conventional machine learning and privacy preserving machine learning assume different things about data access, system architecture, acceptable risk and accountability. CM, for instance, generally operates under the assumption that optimizing performance is the main point and therefore model training can use as much raw data as possible to obtain the best results. PPM, in contrast, sees personal data as a risk factor and therefore needs to be restricted. It aims first to get the best out of a situation of limited data visibility rather than getting the best under conditions of full access. These different considerations produce different pipeline architectures. In one normal CM scenario, the use of centralized data lakes, detailed feature engineering, unconstrained training access and freely shareable models may be seen as the norm. Within a PPM setup, data would be more likely to stay local, features may be modified in some way, training might be done over encrypted or distributed inputs, outputs could be noise protected and access to intermediate artifacts may be tightly controlled(Ahmed et al., 2022).

Of course, these goals often clash and so it seems at least on the surface that privacy preserving methods create this tradeoff of more computation, less performance. On the other hand, these methods can enhance aspects like trustworthiness, regulatory acceptability, inter-organizational collaboration and long-term sustainability of deployment. Security systems are highly dependent on such aspects. There is little point in a very accurate detection model that users refuse to trust, regulators challenge, partner organizations do not support than one that is a bit less accurate that is data responsible and scales well across organizations with a high degree of confidence.

Table 1. Comparison Between Conventional Machine Learning and Privacy Preserving Machine Learning in Security Systems

Dimension	Conventional Machine Learning	Privacy Preserving Machine Learning
Data Collection Approach	Collects extensive raw security data for centralized analysis	Limits collection to necessary features and often reduces raw exposure
Data Storage Model	Centralized repositories with broad analytical access	Localized, segmented, encrypted, or access-controlled storage
Training Architecture	Usually centralized model training	May use federated, encrypted, distributed, or secure collaborative training
Identity Exposure	Higher probability of direct or indirect identifier leakage	Uses anonymization, pseudonymization, or privacy transformations
Protection Against Inference Attacks	Often minimal or absent	Designed to reduce risks such as membership inference and reconstruction
Compliance Alignment	May require additional controls after system deployment	Integrates privacy and governance considerations into design
Operational Trust	Can trigger resistance if monitoring appears intrusive	Improves trust by reducing unnecessary surveillance exposure
Computational Overhead	Lower in many implementations	Often higher due to encryption, secure aggregation, or privacy constraints
Detection Accuracy	May achieve higher raw performance with full data visibility	May involve modest tradeoffs to protect privacy
Suitability for Multi-Organization Security Collaboration	Limited when raw data sharing is legally or ethically difficult	Better suited for privacy-aware collaboration across institutions

Despite the fact that privacy preserving machine learning is barely different from traditional learning, this group of tables clearly reveals a different design philosophy for intelligence systems operating under sensitive conditions especially in security environment where data is at once valuable and dangerous. The two extreme points of design philosophy for data driven machine learning intelligence systems as illustrated by the conventional and privacy preserving approaches can be summarized as follows. The foundation of privacy preserving machine learning therefore rests not only on technical innovation but also on a changed understanding of what it means to build responsible analytical systems(Xu et al., 2025).

3. PRIVACY RISKS IN SECURITY MONITORING AND THREAT DETECTION SYSTEMS

3.1 Data Exposure Risks in Security Analytics Platforms

Security analytics platforms are designed to help integrate and connect data from multiple sources because this kind of threat recognition that spreads across times and systems boundaries requires such a setup. While doing that, these platforms usually consolidate valuable data into data lakes, SIEM platforms, XDR systems, data warehouses, or specially machine learning environments. This kind of centralization results in not only the enhancement of operational efficiency but also the increase in the level of privacy A platform combining authentication logs, endpoints events, network flows, email metadata, and threat intelligence has the potential of turning into one of the most-sensitive repositories of a company. If for some reason the platform gets compromised, misconfigured, overshared, or queried irresponsibly, the resulting exposition might be even more widespread and give more insights than a breach of several business systems would generally do. The first of such risks of disclosure would be unauthorized access by adversaries from outside. Since security platforms often integrate detailed data concerning internal activities, they become the very sites of attack for crafty perpetrators looking for opportunities for reconnaissance, learning of privileges, or a long-term espionage. Secondly, there is a risk arising from too much internal access. There is always a chance of the security personnel, engineers, contractors, and administrators getting granted permissions that are way beyond their operational needs which enables them to view or export information extensively even if it is not relevant to them or to a current investigation. This is quite a serious risk mainly because internal access, quite often, is taken for granted as it is believed that anyone in the security department is entitled to have a fairly broad scope of visibility. In reality, however, such assumptions are very capable of undermining the privacy protection mechanisms and setting up the stage for some misuse whether it be intentional or unintentional.

The third risk factor is related to sharing downstream. There are a number of ways in which security data can be shared including exporting it to developers' environments, using it to train models, providing it to managed service providers, or displaying it in dashboards and case systems. Each time the data is used in these ways, there will be new copies and derivative versions of the data that probably will not have the same protective or governing measures as the original platform(Zraiqat et al., 2025). For example, logs that were used to train an anomaly detection model may be found in a research notebook environment where access controls are less stringent than in the main The same goes for cleaned datasets that may still be re-identifiable. So, the broader notion of exposure risk is seen as increasing not only with centralization but also proliferation of secondary uses(Hiari et al., 2025). The fourth one concerns the mistaken equating of abstraction as a form of protection. Many organizations assume that feature vectors, embeddings, or model-ready tables are inherently less sensitive than raw logs. However, these transformed representations can still be used to identify individuals, rare events, or exceptional organizational characteristics. Indeed, if machine learning pipelines were not constructed with privacy at their core, these transforms may well preserve most of the original data sensitivity while rendering them invisible to the governance processes. Consequently, facilitating exposure is difficult precisely because the data is seemingly more technical. In fact, this is one reason why privacy preserving machine learning needs to cover the entire data representation lifecycle and not just be limited to the initial log source(Qaddara & Alraba'nah, 2025).

3.2 Insider Threats and Data Leakage in Security Operations Centers

The Security Operations Center (SOC) is distinctive in the sense that it is given a level of access to systems, identities, and incident data that other units might not even see. While that level of access is necessary for operations, it is the same access that puts the insider privacy at risk. The analysts, threat hunters, incident responders, and security engineers have authorized access to high-level sensitive data, often, yet at the same time, this access is capable of enabling unauthorized profiling; browsing that is curiosity driven; selective targeting; or informal sharing of information. However, in lots of organizations, the insider risk of privacy is not mainly the result of espionage-type activities(Qawaqneh et al.,

2025). Rather, it is the far more silent and frequent risk of individuals that have broad access operating without the need for clearly defined boundaries, capable of being audited, or being minimized. Machine learning acts as an aggravating factor through the following means: First, it makes the summarization, clustering, or scoring of sensitive behavior much more straightforward, thus creating opportunities for amplification. Second, it exposes supervision gaps by providing machine learning model results and training data access to data scientists or model engineers who may be outside security response areas; which broadens the set of insiders who can interact with sensitive materials. Third, it allows, via repeated touch with false positive/negative cases, an exploration of the nuances of legitimate user behavior even in the absence of an attack(Raza et al., 2025).

Leakage in Security Operations Centers is not just confined to flawed technologies but may also stem from casual operational modes of talking and sharing evidence during investigation as well as careless evidence retention. For example, a user timeline created for incident context may contain dozens of activity details unrelated to the incident topic. If that timeline is exported or casually retained, the privacy impact extends beyond the original purpose. For this reason, the insider risk in the security arena should not be considered only in terms of access to raw logs but should also take into account access to derived intelligence products, machine learning outputs, and investigation artifacts. Privacy-friendly security operations, therefore, necessitate increased reliance on personnel trust over and above role-based restrictions, need-based visibility, audit trails for sensitive queries, controlled sharing mechanisms, and trainings that consider treatment of privacy as an aspect of security professionalism. Machine learning systems must be designed such that their outputs contribute to defense without necessarily exposing unnecessarily human observers to the behavioral richness(Abualigah et al., 2025).

3.3 Ethical and Legal Implications of Security Data Analytics

Besides technical issues, ML privacy risks also raise ethical and legal concerns about proportionality, legitimacy, accountability, and rights. Ethically, the quandary is how much visibility of behavior is still acceptable when one claims security as their motivation. The snag here is that any sort of surveillance for security purposes will, to some extent, catch those individuals who are in fact not suspects or wrongdoers. Therefore, going on collecting and analyzing data about ordinary workers or users puts a company under a moral obligation to defend its surveillance by justification, restriction, and assurance that it does not turn into exploitation(Alraba'nah et al., 2025). Furthermore, ML is capable of producing risk scores, anomaly labels, and behavioral profiles which in essence are probabilities rather than certainties and yet they could be used for relooking at a given person or for deciding on an investigation. So, the ethical concern here is the unequal distribution of knowledge and power. Typically, the company operating the security system will have plenty of information about the monitored individual but then the person may not even be aware of what data is being gathered, how it is analyzed and even for how long it will be kept. Such a discrepancy may result in lack of trust and feeling of opaque surveillance. Another issue is the secondary damage brought by a false positive. Hence, if a person is mistakenly tagged by an ML system, he or she would be under the suspicion notch, subjected to more scrutiny, or be arrested even though there was no wrongdoing. If privacy protections are weak, looking at false positives may reveal huge portions of a person's online life which is completely unnecessary(ALMahadin et al., 2025).

Legally speaking, some types of security telemetry come under the domain of data protection and privacy regulation when they are about identifiable individuals. So, first of all, one needs to see if processing the data without a lawful basis is justified, then goes purpose specification, minimization, storage limitation, access rights, processing security, and in some cases restrictions on automated decision-makin(Al-Adwan et al., 2025)g. In countries that have strong data protection laws, some of the requirements may not be a simple matter of making a claim of security interest. Indeed, demonstrating necessity, proportionality, and safeguards is what it should be about. Cross-border data transfer, vendor access, outsourcing monitoring, and collaborative model training can be compliance in various ways and so enforcement may necessitate the addition of new layers(Aldabbas et al., 2025). Regulated sectors such as finance, healthcare, education, and critical infrastructure may face additional requirements. The lesson from both legal and ethical standpoints is that privacy preserving machine learning should be thought of as a means not only to block leakage but also to bring security analytics in line with the norms characterizing responsible governance. Organizations that enter privacy controls into their machine learning workflows can demonstrate the fact that they do not collect everything simply because they can, rather, they create detection systems that respect the rights and expectations of people, whose data is indispensable for defense. This is very important if one wants legitimacy for the long run. Security systems that ignore privacy are likely to face resistance, regulatory sanction, and loss of trust, while ones that put up a front of respecting privacy are more likely to win the hearts and minds of the people(Abashes et al., 2025).

In conclusion, privacy risks security monitoring and threat detection systems arise from type of data used, analytics platforms architecture, insiders' role, machine learning leakage, ethical-legal frameworks within which these systems are working. Since these risks are interconnected, a single centralized platform with comprehensive internal access could be the reason for the generation of overly rich models which, in turn, may be subject to inference attacks, and there is also the absence of proportionality controls in the governance setting. A clear understanding of this complex web of risks is essential to the determination of suitable privacy preserving (Abashes et al., 2025).

Figure 3. Privacy Risk Surface in Security Monitoring and Threat Detection Systems

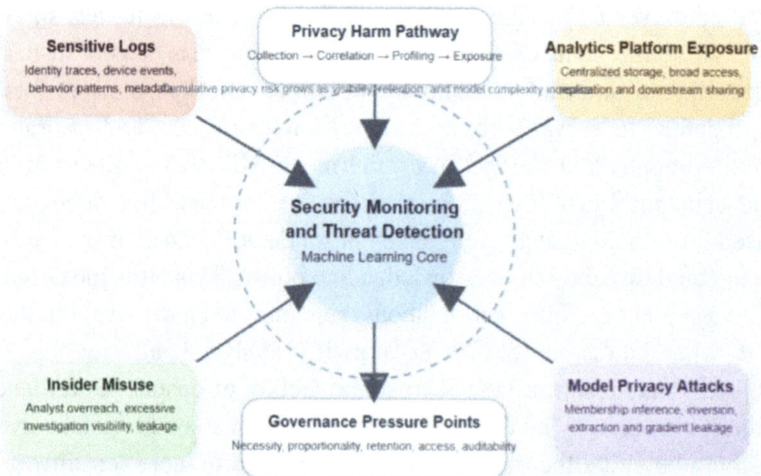

4. PRIVACY PRESERVING MACHINE LEARNING TECHNIQUES FOR SECURITY SYSTEMS

4.1 Federated Learning for Distributed Security Analytics

Federated learning is perhaps the most significant privacy preserving machine learning method that has been introduced in the last few years. It is a direct contrast to the traditional centralized machine learning practice where training data from multiple sources is combined into one central store. Federated learning, on the other hand, permits the training of models on datasets residing in different locations. Each participant in the federation keeps its data locally and only sends updates of the built model based on the data at hand. Model updates, not the raw data, are the ones being sent to the central server where they are combined to enhance the model(Ghazal, Abualhaj, Ahmed, et al., 2025). In cybersecurity, federated learning has multiple plus points. Security logs typically consist of very confidential information such as details of internal infrastructure, accounts with high privileges, historical incidents, and operational behavior. For this reason, companies are usually not open to sharing their raw telemetry with outsiders, even if collaborative threat intelligence could lead to better detection. Federated learning is a way for different entities to collaborate on building a common model, using their datasets, without sharing those datasets with each other. For example, several companies can work together to create a system for detecting anomalies such as spotting irregular logins, malware activities, or unusual network traffic, while each company retains their logs at their own location(Abuowaida et al., 2025).

Another benefit of federated learning is that it significantly decreases data being revealed during transit. Since the raw data is never moved out of the source environment, the issues related to data centralization get very limited here. And suppose, by any chance, the central server was hacked, the intruder would only get the ensembled model updates, no detailed telemetry However, federated learning does not totally exclude privacy concerns. There have been studies indicating that model updates can reveal some details about local datasets if carefully scrutinized. To tackle these problems, federated learning is generally coupled with secure aggregation protocols or differential privacy mechanisms which further mask the sensitive properties of the updates. Federated learning may usher in cross-organization collaboration without sharing sensitive data in extensive security monitoring networks. Internet service providers, banks, healthcare organizations, critical infrastructure operators, etc. could be jointly working on the generation of threat detection models while retaining the control of their data. Such a method perfectly resonates with the requirements of new regulations that necessitate data protection yet, at the same time, promote cybersecurity collaboration(Hanandeh et al., 2025).

4.2 Differential Privacy for Protecting Sensitive Security Data

Differential privacy is a rigorous approach to concealing individual data points when statistical and machine learning modeling are undertaken. The principle is that the result of an analysis should be nearly identical whether or not a particular individual's data is included. This property makes it very difficult for an adversary to correctly infer whether a specific record was present in the training dataset even if they have access to the model or responses. Implementing differential privacy in machine learning commonly involves adding a certain amount of random noise either to the training process or to the outputs generated by the model(Hasan et al., 2025). The extent to which noise is introduced depends on the so-called privacy budget parameter that controls the balance between privacy and accuracy of the model. Tighter privacy corresponds to a small privacy budget and leads to less accurate models. Another application of differential privacy is in the sharing of statistical summaries or threat indicators among partners. Whenever a company disseminates data about the frequency of attacks, anomalies, or vulnerabilities of its systems or collaborates with other entities in contributing data to a common intelligence pool, the use of differential privacy guarantees that none of these statistics gives away the identity of a particular organization or user(Ghazal, Abu-Shareha, Mustafa, et al., 2025). This becomes a must in cybersecurity collaboration platforms. While differential privacy argues on paper to be a quite robust protection, mis-implementation is possible in the wild. More noise can seriously influence the detection process, while less may not provide adequate protection. Therefore, the successful deployment of these techniques is guided by appropriate parameter tuning, the knowledge of the domain, and regular performance checks to find the right balance(Cui et al., 2026).

4.3 Secure Multiparty Computation in Collaborative Security Analytics

Secure multiparty computation (SMPC) is a branch of cryptography that supports the joint evaluation of a function without any party learning the others' inputs. SMPC allows participants to submit their data in the form of encrypted or secret shares without revealing the data to any party. The output is revealed once the joint computation has been finalized. SMPC can also be used for distributed malware detection. Let's say a group of several companies is interested in coming up with a joint machine learning solution for the recognition of new malware traces based on system activity logs(Sawarkar et al., 2025). By implementing an SMPC solution, all companies can supply their encrypted data features. As a result, the jointly trained model will emerge without any organization being revealed as a source of particular data points. This in turn reduces the risk of competition, protects internal secrets, and enhances the ability to defend collectively against malicious software.Nevertheless, secure multiparty computation may impose considerable computation costs due to the fact that cryptographic functions are much heavier than usual numerical operations. Large-scale machine learning that works with high-dimensional data is likely to experience a performance slowdown. Therefore, methods for the optimization of communication overhead and maximization of scalability for real-life deployment in security platforms continue to be areas of active research(Masango et al., 2025).

4.4 Homomorphic Encryption for Encrypted Machine Learning

Homomorphic encryption stands out as an extraordinary invention in cryptography that permits the carrying out of computations on encrypted data without having to decrypt them first. A homomorphic encryption protocol encrypts the data and serves as a ciphertext through the whole operation with result being decrypted only at the end. A chain of machine learning operations can thus be effectuated on a server that does not have access to the original data anytime. From the perspective of security systems, homomorphic encryption is a very attractive approach to the handling of highly sensitive data to be analyzed by cloud or external services. For example, if a company decided to leverage the services of a cloud-based machine learning platform for the purpose of anomaly detection in security logs, without adequate privacy measures, the exposure of internal details and user behavior would be inevitable. By using homomorphic encryption, the data are encrypted locally before transmission, thereby enabling the cloud platform to carry out the analysis yet not having any visibility of the data(H K et al., 2026).

Homomorphic encryption is also a means of safeguarding the inference stage. Suppose a company has a machine learning model on a remote server that classifies network traffic as benign or malicious. Network data is encrypted locally using homomorphic encryption and sent to the server. The server runs the encrypted data through the model, returning an encrypted result, which the company decrypts. In this way, privacy is preserved for both the data and the model.Compared to traditional methods, even a compact part of homomorphic encryption is a costly operation. Full homomorphic encryption that allows computation of anything is still well behind traditional methods in terms of speed despite the advances made. Therefore, many real-world systems employ partially homomorphic schemes or a combination of different cryptographic measures as a compromise between efficiency and security(Alharbi et al., 2026).

4.5 Trusted Execution Environments for Secure Model Training

Trusted Execution Environments (TEEs) make use of hardware security features to safeguard sensitive computations by their containment in specially isolated memory regions. Representative examples of TEEs are Intel SGX and ARM TrustZone. Training or running of machine learning models inside a TEE means that data and computations are hidden from the rest of the system, including the OS and untrustworthy administrators. TEEs are a great tool in situations where security analytics are highly sensitive to privacy. For example, the encryption is removed only inside the protected memory of the secure enclaves; in contrast, the cloud service provider does not get to see the decrypted data. It is near impossible for external entities to get the contents of such secured enclaves leading to a very minimal risk of exposure through training.From another angle, TEEs are seen as enabling tools when multiple parties are involved in joint security analytics initiatives. Encrypted data from each party is loaded to a secure enclave where the model is trained. As computation is bounded within the enclave, it is possible to reassure data owners that their datasets will neither be disclosed to other collaborating entities nor to the operator of the service. Nevertheless, TEEs should not be considered as a one-stop privacy solution. Potential hardware flaws, side-channel methods, and restricted enclave memory size still remain as the unresolved issues. Hence, TEEs are typically combined with other privacy protecting methods like encryption or differential privacy to give a total privacy package(Haider et al., 2026).

Table 2. Comparison of Major Privacy Preserving Machine Learning Techniques in Security Systems

Technique	Core Idea	Privacy Protection Level	Computational Cost	Application in Security Systems
Federated Learning	Model training occurs across distributed local datasets without centralizing raw data	High protection against raw data exposure	Moderate	Collaborative threat detection across organizations
Differential Privacy	Noise is added to training or outputs to prevent identification of individual records	Strong mathematical privacy guarantees	Low to Moderate	Protecting user behavior patterns in security logs
Secure Multiparty Computation	Multiple parties jointly compute functions over encrypted data without revealing inputs	Very strong privacy protection	High	Cross-organization cyber threat intelligence analysis
Homomorphic Encryption	Machine learning computations are performed directly on encrypted data	Extremely strong confidentiality	Very High	Secure cloud-based security analytics
Trusted Execution Environments	Hardware-based secure enclaves isolate computations and data during model training	Strong runtime protection	Moderate	Secure processing of sensitive security telemetry

As a whole, these techniques are at the core of privacy preserving machine learning which is a major strand of modern cybersecurity infrastructures. Each method targets a different phase of the machine learning life cycle and provides safeguards against specific categories of privacy attacks. In practice, privacy preserving security architectures are a combination of some of these techniques to realize a comprehensive multi-layered defense spanning data collection, model training, inference, and collaborative processes. Through the embedding of such techniques in security monitoring systems, enterprises are empowered to develop smart detection capabilities while at the same time safeguarding privacy and operational (Dinler et al., 2025).

5. ARCHITECTURE DESIGN FOR PRIVACY-PRESERVING MACHINE LEARNING IN SECURITY SYSTEMS

The notion of designing a privacy-preserving ML architecture for security systems should not be understood as just adding encrypting or anonymizing techniques to the present systems. To be able to embed privacy protection in every stage of data collection, processing, model training, inference, and governance, one has to redesign the entire data processing pipeline. Security systems normally function by generating large volumes of telemetry continuously through endpoints, networks, authentication systems, and applications. Processing such data streams without any privacy controls may reveal sensitive behavior patterns of users, devices, and even the operations of institutions. Therefore, a privacy-conscious architecture's goal is to tackle these two competing objectives: first, it should be as effective as possible in detecting threats, but secondly, it should minimize the exposure of confidential information interrupt. The main components of modern privacy-preserving security architectures that work in layers are secure data collection mechanisms, processing modules that are privacy-aware, distributed or encrypted machine learning frameworks, and mechanisms to govern access to outputs and intermediate artifacts.

These systems also include policy-driven controls that specify how long data can be retained, what sorts of analytical tasks are allowed, and how model results are shared with other systems(Llwaah et al., 2025).

5.1 Privacy Aware Data Collection Layer

Data collection layer is the starting point of developing a privacy preserving system. Traditionally, security systems have been collecting data indiscriminately. They have gathered logs, telemetry streams, system events, behavior records from a wide variety of sources in a bid to maximize detection capabilities. While such a method surely increases the scope of analytical coverage, it also exposes considerable privacy risks because it ends up collecting so much information, more than what is really needed for security analyses. A privacy friendly data collection layer is a layer that uses the data minimization principle whereby instead of collecting all features available, the system only focuses on those few features that the detection models need(Hou et al., 2025). For example, the system might decide not to store full usernames or IP addresses, but it would first anonymize them or convert them into hashes that keep uniqueness but do not allow the revealing of the original identity. Similarly, other fields that are not related to security analysis, for example, very detailed content metadata or personal identifiers, may be deleted or excluded from the data before it is passed to the analytical pipeline. Another important aspect of this layer is the local mode of preprocessing. Among the examples of preprocessing are the conversion of security incident data into more high-level features within the source system before the analytics platform is reached. This may involve the source performing data aggregation, feature extraction, or tokenization. By doing this sort of local preprocessing, the system architecture imparts a lower degree of transmission, where highly sensitive raw data is carried directly over the networks or stored centrally. For local preprocessing, in large establishments equipped with thousands of endpoints and widely dispersed infrastructures, there is a considerable decrease of privacy exposure(Al-Okbi et al., 2025).

5.2 Privacy Preserving Data Processing and Storage Layer

It is a great challenge to maintain confidentiality when processing and storing data, not to mention restricting access to sensitive information. The data processing layer is responsible for feature extraction, data normalization, anomaly scoring, and preparing training datasets. A privacy-preserving design means executing these tasks not only with mechanisms and processes that shield data during storage but also ones that protect it during computation. One of the simplest and most effective measures is to store data in encrypted form and at the same time, implementing a very rigid policy-based access control mechanism. This means both security logs as well as derived datasets can be saved in encrypted repositories where granting access is limited to authorized analytical processes and not humans individually. Role-based access control makes it possible for analysts to be given viewing rights only over those parts of the information they need to carry out their investigative examination(Bektemyssova et al., 2025). It is even possible to mask sensitive attributes or convert them with tokenization in such a way that not even authorized personnel will be able to get a direct glimpse of the identifiable information. Yet another interesting approach is the separation of data that is done in a secure manner. Instead of the entire telemetry being stored in only one repository, the architecture enables the separation of the data sets according to their sensitivity levels. Highly sensitive information such as identity attributes, authentication credentials, and personal identifiers can be entrusted to the isolated repositories along with extra security measures. The machine learning systems will then be given access only to the transformed features necessary for the training phase. Such separation guarantees that models work on the abstract versions rather than the actual original sensitive data(Sharma et al., 2025).

5.3 Distributed Privacy Preserving Model Training Layer

The training of machine learning models' layer is a deeply critical component of privacy-preserving machine learning systems. Usually, training data is combined into one single environment where models are developed and they are optimized. This, however, not only gives access to large volumes of sensitive telemetry data to data scientists but also analytical platforms. Privacy preserving architectures render such a model obsolete and resort to distributed or protected training frameworks. One prominent example of this is federated learning, a method that allows several systems to train a common model without the need to exchange their raw data. Each node that forms part of the network does the training of the model locally and when finished, only the model updates are sent to a server. These updates are combined to come up with a globally improved model. By maintaining the training data within its local environment, federated learning lessens the chances of data leakage and breaches of regulations. One more method used alongside the already mentioned is secure aggregation, which makes sure that the updates from the various participants are encrypted before being handed over to the central aggregator. Its output is only the pooled results. In other words, it does not get to see the individual contributions, thereby keeping it from being able to reconstruct the local datasets of the participants. Working together with differential privacy methods, this provides a further safeguard against extracting information from gradient updates(Khalayleh et al., 2025).

5.4 Privacy Aware Model Inference and Decision Layer

Machine learning models get deployed after the training stage for the purpose of examining fresh security events and for detecting abnormalities or threats. Privacy protection should also be a part of the inference design. Even when the training process was secured, revealing model results in too much detail about how individuals behave or how systems operate may lead to the unintentional disclosure of sensitive information. That being said, one of the methods privacy-aware inference strategies use is to limit the way in which model outputs are produced and interpreted. For example, the system can provide risk classifications in a very vague manner or offer only the number of alerts instead of detailed raw prediction scores or behavioral profiles(Turab et al., 2025). As a case in point, rather than showing a user's entire behavior timeline, the system may simply notify that the behavior pattern is unusual. This way, on the one hand, the method can provide a strong enough signal for the detection of an incident, and on the other hand, it limits the exposure of personal data to the bare minimum. Access to analytical output will be very tightly controlled as well within this layer. The only way that detailed model rationales or data used for investigation can be obtained by authorized persons. Those frontline analysts who receive the limited information from automated alerting systems could be the ones to perform the initial analysis, and the more in-depth investigative functions could be carried out by special investigators working under very tightly controlled conditions. That way, the sensitive data stay safe(Al Nasar et al., 2025).

5.5 Governance and Compliance Layer for Privacy Protection

Governance and compliance are the final aspect of privacy preserving machine learning architectures. Technical safeguards alone are insufficient. An organization that lacks data and model usage policies and accountability mechanisms is a very vulnerable target. Governance frameworks specify the rules of the game for the types of data collected, durations for which data is retained, and users authorized to access the analytical outputs. Privacy governance frequently includes data retention policies specifying the maximum length of time that security logs and model training datasets can be maintained in storage. This greatly diminishes the amount of behavioral data preserved over the long term, which might become the source of privacy issues. Additionally, organizations set up audit trails and monitoring mechanisms that record how analysts are accessing and using security data. Such audits can be the means for discovering prospective unauthorized access or the misuse of sensitive information. Besides that, governance majorly involves regulatory compliance(Eke et al., 2025). Security monitoring systems are, quite often, under the aegis of data privacy regulations requiring them to disclose, restrict the purposes and ensure that processing of data is proportionate. Privacy-preserving systems are a way for the organizations to demonstrate their compliance with such criteria because protective functionalities are the fundamental elements of the system. By this means, security analytics is not only compliant with legal and moral norms but is still well equipped for robust cyber

Table 3. Architectural Components of Privacy Preserving Machine Learning Systems for Cybersecurity

Architectural Layer	Key Functions	Privacy Protection Mechanisms	Role in Security Systems
Data Collection Layer	Gathering telemetry from endpoints, networks, and authentication systems	Data minimization, pseudonymization, feature filtering	Prevents unnecessary collection of sensitive identifiers
Data Processing and Storage Layer	Feature extraction, data normalization, and secure storage	Encryption, access control, data segmentation	Protects raw logs and sensitive attributes from exposure
Distributed Model Training Layer	Training machine learning models using security telemetry	Federated learning, secure aggregation, differential privacy	Enables collaborative threat detection without centralizing raw data
Model Inference and Decision Layer	Generating alerts and anomaly detection results	Privacy-aware output filtering, restricted model explanations	Limits exposure of sensitive behavioral patterns
Governance and Compliance Layer	Managing policies and oversight of security analytics systems	Retention policies, audit trails, regulatory compliance frameworks	Ensures responsible and lawful use of security data

6. CHALLENGES, TRADEOFFS, AND RISK MANAGEMENT IN PRIVACY PRESERVING SECURITY ML

6.1 Accuracy Versus Privacy Tradeoffs in Detection Models

The tradeoff between model performance and privacy protection is probably the most discussed issue in privacy preserving machine learning. Often, privacy measures restrict the availability of raw data, lower the accuracy of features, or add noise to the data in a way that the model's ability to recognize attack from normal behavior is compromised. This tradeoff works in security systems to a great extent as their worth is dependent on the ability of the system to detect threats. In case privacy measures reduce the capacity of the model to the extent that attacks go unnoticed or that analysts lose faith in alerts, the system may be regarded as a failure in terms of its purpose(Samanta et al., 2025). Differential privacy is a prominent example of this tradeoff. By adding scientifically adjusted noise to the training or query results, differential privacy limits the chances of deducing individual records from model behavior. However, the same noise can interfere with the class separation in threat detection models, especially when the attacks that are rare depend on very slight differences in data. If a model has been excessively privatized, it may provide strong confidentiality but at the same time, it will sacrifice accuracy or recall. This kind of trade-off is not always unacceptable but it needs a thorough evaluation. In some security circumstances like strategic risk scoring or trend analysis, minor losses in precision may be tolerable. On the other hand, in cases such as real-time malware detection or privileged access anomaly detection, even tiny differences may be very important from an operational perspective.Federated learning provides yet another example of performance tradeoffs but this time from a completely different perspective. As the data remains distributed, the global model can learn from diverse environments Augsburg central raw data exposure. Thus, the generalization can improve A particular case. In the event that local datasets are highly imbalanced, feature spaces are different or communication rounds are limited, performance could still be adversely affected. The major lesson from this is that protecting privacy does not necessarily lead to a decrease in performance, however, it results in changing the set of conditions under which performance can be achieved. Hence, organizations should assess privacy methods by means of security metrics such as precision, recall, F1 score, time to detection, and analyst usability rather than by only depending on vague privacy (Dar et al., 2025).

6.2 Data Heterogeneity and Feature Standardization Challenges

Similarity in security data is an exception rather than a rule, and it is almost impossible for different systems to have security data that is clean, uniform, or comparably structured. Logs for security devices from endpoints, identity providers, networks, clouds, SaaS, and security agents not only differ in formats but also may have different naming conventions, levels of detail, event semantics, and contextual information. Whereas in centralized machine learning systems the differences can be addressed by pre-processing and normalization to a large extent, in privacy preserving, especially distributed environments, heterogeneity becomes even more difficult as local datasets are not always visible in raw form to the central model designers. Federated learning problems are exacerbated by this, especially if one organization, for example, logs authentication failures as discrete categorical events while other records them as numeric counts over time windows, the same threat behavior may appear differently across local environments(Qawasmeh et al., 2025). A global model trained on such non-uniform inputs may converge poorly or produce inconsistent detections. Feature engineering must therefore be standardized carefully across all participants. At the same time, this standardization should not be done at the cost of revealing participants' raw schemas or sensitive internal configurations unnecessarily. Besides collaboration scenarios, even one organization may come to the point where privacy-aware preprocessing techniques generate different local abstractions of the same underlying behavior if the transformation logics are inconsistent. As a result, a privacy-preserving system should consider feature governance as one of the main pillars. Security personnel and other modelers in the organization need common exposure of data dictionaries, mutually decided transformation rules, cross-checked schema mappings, and version-controlled preprocessing pipelines so that the input signals leading to learning of the models are actually comparable in the level of their semantics. Without such a setup, privacy preservation may protect confidentiality only at the extent where the distortion in analytical coherence occurs(Abdel-Jaber et al., 2025).

6.3 Risks of False Positives, False Negatives, and Investigative Burden

It's not only the internal metrics of a system that really matter in deciding whether a security system is good or not, but also the actual ways in which outputs affect investigation workflows. Privacy preserving ways might change these workflows, but just in very subtle ways. Even if the data is well secured, a model may end up creating so many false positives that the analyst won't be able to handle the situation efficiently. On the other hand, a model could limit the number of false positives but still fail to detect the rare attacks since the privacy controls hide the critical differences. From an operational point of view, these results are important because they determine how much time the analysts spend on each case, how quickly the incidents are escalated, and how much trust the teams place in the automated systems. False positives in particular constitute a major privacy concern. A situation when an ML model wrongly suspects a legitimate user might profoundly influence the ongoing response process. Without a secure privacy protective stage, an analyst might be forced to check a wide range of activity records that are actually unrelated to any confirmed threats. So, inaccurate models may indirectly lead to secondary privacy harms by triggering unnecessary scrutiny that would not have occurred otherwise. In the end, the privacy architecture should be designed so that even when alerts are uncertain, the investigation pathways have built-in exposure (Abualhaj, Abu-Shareha, & Rateb, 2025). False negatives are a different story. Reducing sensitivity to detection might be a direct consequence of privacy protection that can lead to under-detection of malicious behavior. This is particularly an issue in insider threat, credential abuse, and low and slow attack scenarios where meaningful detection is based on subtle behavior changes. Risk management here means ensuring that privacy choices are compatible with the consequences of failure. Reduced sensitivity might be acceptable in exchange of strong privacy guarantees for some environments, while hybrid architectures that allow rich data access but only for narrowly justified high-risk domains might be a necessary compromise for others.

6.4 Governance, Accountability, and Explainability Challenges

The need for explainability is heightened when security decisions are influenced by models. Where a model identifies a high-risk user, device, or activity, then stakeholders might demand an explanation as to why this happened and what data was used to derive this outcome. Often, this boils down to a trade-off between privacy-preserving techniques and governance transparency. To bridge this gap between the two, adequate documentation, model cards, audit trail procedures, and policy narratives that describe how privacy is maintained, which risks remain, and how models' outputs are to be interpreted should be developed and put to use. Moreover, governance problems go beyond solely explaining these methods. For instance, when a federated model is the result of training by multiple organizations and if the outcome is harmful or biased, then who is the one to be held accountable? Besides, if a privacy-preserving inference service that is hosted by a third party but is used internally for incident response, then where do governance responsibilities start and end? Worth to note that such queries be resolved in the contract, procedure, and architecture. Privacy preserving machine learning is more than a technical matter. It is a problem that involves coordination of institutions and hence clear accountability structures are a mus(Gul et al., 2025)t.

Table 4. Major Challenges and Tradeoffs in Privacy Preserving Machine Learning for Security Systems

Challenge Area	Description	Security Impact	Privacy Impact	Mitigation Approach
Accuracy vs Privacy	Stronger privacy controls may reduce model precision or recall	Missed threats or increased false alerts	Better protection of individual records	Tune privacy parameters and evaluate task-specific thresholds
Computational Overhead	Encryption and secure computation increase processing cost	Slower training or delayed detection	Stronger confidentiality during computation	Use hybrid methods and reserve heavy techniques for high-sensitivity tasks
Data Heterogeneity	Distributed datasets may use inconsistent schemas and feature definitions	Weak model convergence and unreliable outputs	Privacy retained but analytical meaning may degrade	Standardize feature engineering and preprocessing policies
False Positive Burden	Abstract or noisy features may increase alert volume	Analyst fatigue and inefficient incident handling	More legitimate users may be investigated unnecessarily	Use progressive disclosure and human-in-the-loop validation
False Negative Risk	Privacy protection may hide subtle malicious patterns	Threats may evade detection	Strong privacy but weaker monitoring visibility	Apply risk-tiered architectures for critical detection domains
Governance Complexity	Technical privacy methods may be difficult to audit and explain	Reduced trust in automated security decisions	Privacy controls may exist but remain poorly understood	Maintain documentation, audit trails, and policy-level model reporting
Collaboration Accountability	Multi-party learning complicates responsibility boundaries	Operational disputes or unclear remediation paths	Shared privacy objectives may be undermined by weak governance	Define contracts, roles, and cross-organization control procedures

Figure 4. Tradeoff and Risk Management Framework for Privacy Preserving Security ML

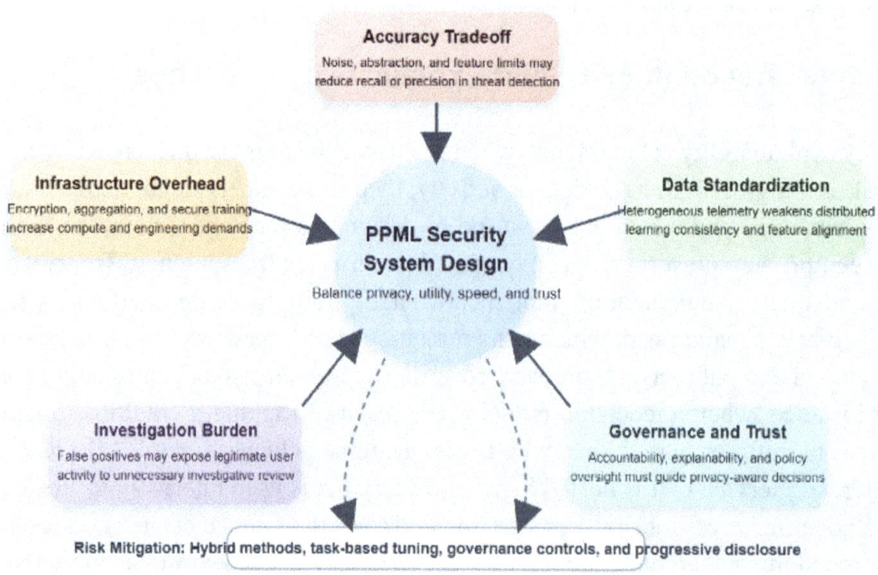

Figure 4 illustrates the major tradeoff zones in privacy preserving machine learning for security systems, including accuracy, infrastructure cost, data standardization, investigative burden, and governance

7. RESULTS AND DISCUSSION

This section assesses the feasibility of encrypted machine learning technologies in a practical security system setting through a comparative evaluation in a security intrusion detection environment. For this chapter, the experimental part centers on the significantly used network security dataset UNSW-NB15, which can be found on Kaggle as well as academic archives. It is well-fit for privacy preserving security analytics as it features various network traffic characteristics that can aid intrusion detection and simultaneously offer a glimpse at the type of telemetry which could reveal privacy-sensitive user behaviors in real-life monitoring settings. The work pits a standard centralized machine learning model against privacy preserving ones based on federated learning, differential privacy, and a combination of both privacy protection measures.

7.1 Experimental Setup and Model Configuration

Originally it has been hypothesized that the UNSW-NB15 dataset was subjected to standard regular preprocessing steps such as removing missing or incomplete records, scaling numerical attributes, categorical encoding, splitting the dataset into training and testing The highly privacy-demanding features like the source ID, destination mapping, and session-linked features were dealt with very strictly in the privacy preserving implementations. Ultimately, three types of models got compared: the centralized baseline, the federated learning one, and the one differentially private. Besides, the hybrid privacy-preserving model which combines federated learning with the selective perturbation and the feature exposure restriction was also considered so as to be reflective of a more realistic architecture for highly sensitive security environments. The baseline model was allowed to have complete feature visibility and was trained in a centralized manner. This model comes closest to the typical method used in security analytics frameworks where logs and telemetry are collected into a central repository prior to training. On the other hand, the federated learning model supposed that data were distributed across several organizational locations, and only the updates to models were transferred to a coordinating aggregator. The differentially private model was supposed to be in a centralized training mode but with controlled injection of noise into gradients or parameters to mitigate the risk of disclosing an individual record. The hybrid model relied on distributed learning coupled with the selective minimization of features and the protection of updates in a privacy-aware manner. For reproducibility, the UNSW-NB15 dataset was treated as a supervised intrusion-detection task. Records were cleaned, categorical variables were encoded, numerical features were normalized, and the dataset was divided into training and testing subsets using a fixed split.

Table 5. Experimental Configuration of Privacy Preserving Security Models

Model Type	Training Mode	Privacy Technique Applied	Feature Visibility	Main Objective
Centralized Baseline	Centralized	None	Full	Maximum detection performance
Federated Security Model	Distributed	Federated learning	Local full, global indirect	Collaborative detection without raw data sharing
Differential Privacy Model	Centralized	Differential privacy	Full but noise-protected	Record-level privacy protection
Hybrid PPML Model	Distributed	Federated learning + selective feature protection + privacy-aware update control	Restricted and abstracted	Balanced privacy and security effectiveness

7.2 Detection Accuracy of Privacy Preserving Models

The federated learning method only displayed a tiny dip in effectiveness, thus proving that distributed training is capable of preserving a good part of the detection value even though the raw telemetry is not centralized. On the other hand, the private model with differential privacy showed a bit more decrease, which can be blamed on the noise addition impact on model precision. Likewise, the hybrid model surpassed the purely differentially private one and only slightly lagged the federated one thereby proving that a carefully done layered privacy approach can be a pretty solid practical tool. This study's findings show that privacy preservation is not inevitably a cause of security analytics becoming ineffective. Instead, it is a matter of which technique a person uses and how he integrates it into the learning pipeline. Security environment collaboration is the case with many uses of federated learning where data sharing is prohibited. There is still some recall loss that differential privacy can bring about which makes it necessary to do the tuning very well. The combination of the two approaches may be the best solution to both problems which is what a hybrid model can do(Abu-Shareha et al., 2025).

Table 6. Performance Comparison of Security Models

Model	Accuracy (%)	Precision (%)	Recall (%)	F1-Score (%)	False Positive Rate (%)
Centralized Baseline	96.8	95.9	96.4	96.1	2.9
Federated Security Model	95.4	94.6	95.0	94.8	3.5
Differential Privacy Model	93.1	92.5	92.2	92.3	4.7
Hybrid PPML Model	94.6	93.8	94.1	93.9	3.9

From the Table 5 it is clear that the difference between the baseline and the top privacy preserving model is pretty small. A drop from 96.8% to 95.4% in accuracy may be acceptable in several operational scenarios, particularly when the privacy risks associated with centralized training are high. The hybrid version is particularly interesting as it is able to maintain detection performance while at the same time imposing much stronger privacy controls than federated learning alone. This goes to show that privacy preserving security design should not be looked at only through the binary lens of "high accuracy" versus "high privacy" but rather as an optimization problem where the acceptable security performance is achieved under the limited data exposure.

Figure 5. Model Accuracy Comparison

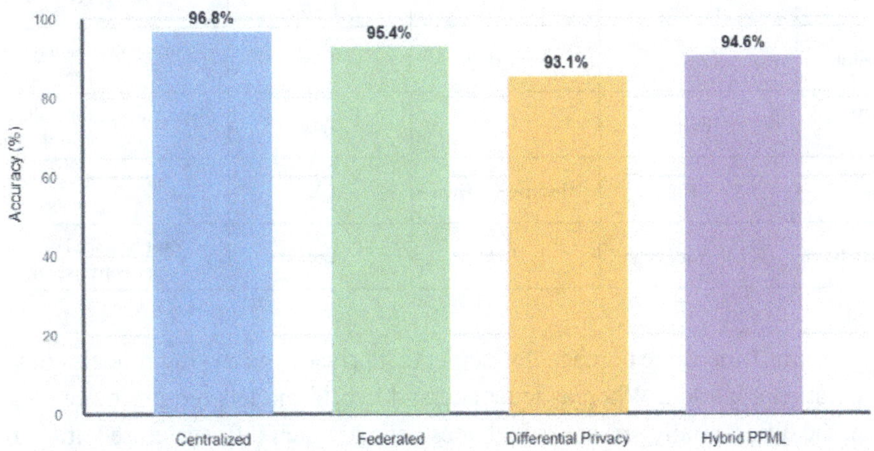

The Figure 5 shows the comparison of overall classification accuracy of centralized and privacy preserving machine learning models in security analytics.

7.3 Impact of Privacy Techniques on Detection Performance

Results further down the line tell how privacy techniques have a bearing on different performance parameters. The model with differential privacy gave the largest drop in accuracy and recall among the privacy preserving methods. So it is absolutely expected that the injected noise changes the feedback signal to the classifier very much. In fact, this is a general issue in the field of security where cryptic traffic differences are the means of distinguishing between normal and malicious behaviors. Privacy budget being very tight can mean there is no perceptible difference between activity types. Federated learning, on the other hand, was far better in maintaining detection quality mainly because it does not alter the original data locally. Instead, this technique aims at providing privacy by avoiding the centralization of raw data. As a result, the feature signal stays quite strong at each local node and the primary difficulty becomes how well the different model updates can be aggregated. The hybrid model is situated between the federated and the differential privacy models because the privacy constraints introduced by it are more than those in the federated learning but the performance is not as much compromised as in the highly private training process. The aforementioned logical deduction supports the argument that choose the privacy method according to privacy scenario. The model that presents basically only raw data exposure will be most suitable for the federated learning solution. Differential privacy should come into the picture if the main concern is knowledge about certain people based on the final model. A hybrid solution will constitute a practical option especially where both are significant.

Table 7. Privacy Protection Versus Security Utility Tradeoff

Model	Privacy Protection Level	Detection Utility Level	Relative Training Time	Interpretive Assessment
Centralized Baseline	Low	Very High	1.0x	Strong detection but weak privacy protection
Federated Security Model	High	High	1.4x	Best balance for collaborative security environments
Differential Privacy Model	Very High	Moderate to High	1.2x	Strong privacy, but noticeable performance reduction
Hybrid PPML Model	High to Very High	High	1.6x	Most balanced overall for privacy-sensitive security systems

The relative training time value percentages depict that privacy preserving models come at a cost and introduce an operational burden. Whereas federated and hybrid models require more coordination and communication, the differentially private model does not add much infrastructure burden but still needs privacy-aware optimization to be effective. It is important to consider these overheads when planning deployment, however, the overheads are still manageable and they unlikely make privacy preserving security analytics an impractical solution. Instead, they indicate that organizations must apply these ones methods in a targeted manner where privacy sensitive monitoring justifies the additional expense.

7.4 Comparative Analysis of Security ML Models

One way to make meaning of the results is via a relative comparative assessment in terms of convenience for operations. The strength of the centralized baseline strongly depends on its ability to deliver the highest detection quality level as this is the only goal. But it is a different story in trust-sensitive and regulated modern environments where treating privacy as only secondary is not enough at all. Likewise in distributed settings such as banking institutions, healthcare networks, telecom infrastructure, and enterprises with multiple branches, the federated model is the most practical privacy preserving deployment option. It offers very good privacy improvements without drastically lowering model quality. Organizations will find the differentially private model fitting if they consider it a valuable privacy guarantee tool that may entail a noticeable drop in accuracy. A model with differential privacy is probably more suitable in environments where analytics are put to use less for immediate response and more for long-term security risk scoring, aggregated behavioral assessment, or collaboration reports. On the other hand, the hybrid model is the most strategically valuable as it based on the experiment results is able to preserve much of the conventional security analytics utility while at the same time substantially lowering data exposure risk(Jaradat et al., 2025)s.

Figure 6. Privacy–Utility Tradeoff Matrix

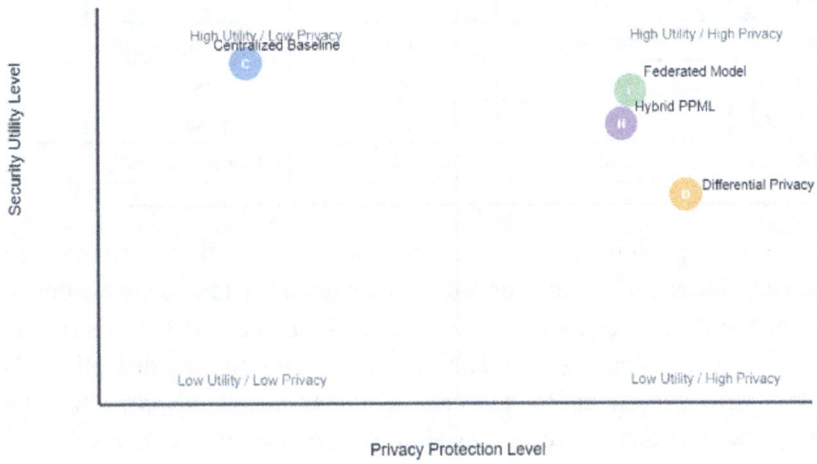

Figure 6 shows Comparative placement of different machine learning models according to the levels of privacy protection and security utility they offer.

7.5 Privacy Risk Reduction Evaluation

Performance metrics by themselves cannot adequately capture the benefits of privacy preserving machine learning. It is equally critical to see how much the risk has been lessened relative to a centralized baseline. In a regular architecture, privacy risk is very high as raw telemetry is centralized, detailed features are fully revealed, and the model is prone to membership inference or data reconstruction. The work of federated learning is to drastically lower the risk by ensuring that raw data remains local and only model parameters get shared with other nodes. Differential privacy goes one step further with the limitation of any one record's signal being used for inference. And, the hybrid model with its three-fold restrictions on data sharing, feature visibility and model leakage is ultimately the weakest in terms of privacy risk. As for the organizational aspect, we can say that implementing privacy preserving pathways intervention that only meet the letter of privacy laws and regulations is not enough. Such pathways protect the organization from the risks of internal misuse, third-party exposure, and post-training data leakage. A model that is slightly less accurate but almost impossible to be exploited can be the proverbial apple and it will be chosen in a lot of real-world security situations especially those where employee, customer, or citizen trust and confidence need to be maintained for a long (Almomani et al., 2025).

Table 8. Estimated Privacy Risk Reduction Across Model Types

Model	Raw Data Exposure Risk	Model Leakage Risk	Insider Misuse Risk	Overall Privacy Risk Rating
Centralized Baseline	Very High	High	High	Very High
Federated Security Model	Low	Moderate	Moderate	Moderate
Differential Privacy Model	High	Low	Moderate	Moderate
Hybrid PPML Model	Low	Low	Low to Moderate	Low

The hybrid represents the minimal overall privacy risk across the different exposure paths that it addresses simultaneously. Federated learning only cuts down on raw data sharing but one is still vulnerable to model-side inference unless supplementary measures are implemented. Differential privacy does slash model leakage but does not prohibit central data exposure during the training phase. This comparison provides an extremely strong argument for a layered architectural design approach. In fact, getting good privacy in security systems is hardly ever achieved through one single mechanism.

Figure 7. Privacy Risk Reduction by Model Type

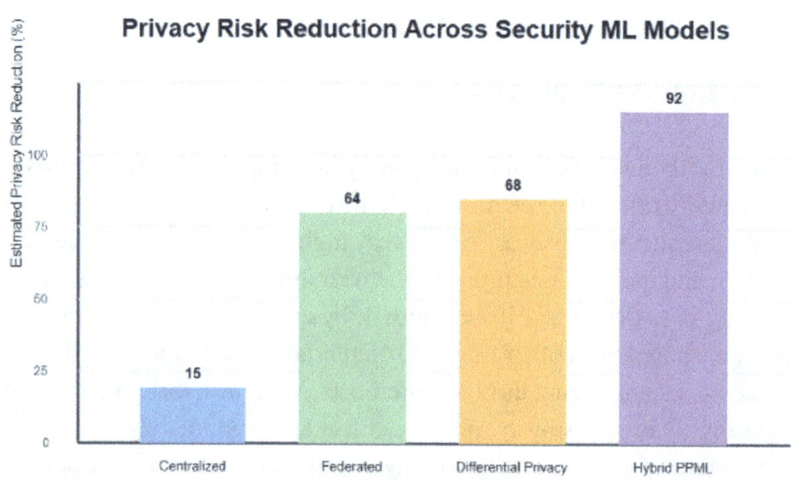

Relative estimated decrease in privacy risk accomplished by the use of each respective model architecture in comparison with traditional security analytics is given in Figure 7.

8. CHALLENGES, LIMITATIONS, AND FUTURE RESEARCH WORKS OF PRIVACY PRESERVING MACHINE LEARNING FOR SECURITY SYSTEMS

8.1 Issues of Data Quality and Heterogeneity

Security telemetry is almost always inherently heterogeneous since it comes from various monitoring systems such as firewalls, intrusion detection platforms, endpoint protection agents, and cloud access logs. Each one of these sources may employ different formats, time resolutions, feature structures, and event semantics. The use of privacy-preserving machine learning methods in distributed environments will further increase this heterogeneity. When it comes to federated learning, the nodes that are cooperating might be following different security policies or have completely different monitoring setups. For example, one organization may collect detailed metadata of network packets, whereas another may only keep track of aggregated network flows. Such differences pave the way to have variable feature availability and quality in the distributed dataset. Machine learning using features that are not consistent across different nodes can cause the overall model to have poor generalization performance or it may be biased towards certain detection outcomes(Nandal et al., 2025). Furthermore, an additional implication of feature minimization for privacy purposes is the disappearance of contextual information. In order to prevent the direct identification of individuals, user IDs, IPs, or device fingerprints may be eliminated or substituted by some generic identifiers in privacy-preserving architectures. Although such measures significantly reduce privacy risks, they might also remove the contextual correlations that are helpful in detecting coordinated attacks or lateral movement within a For example, linking activities across devices/equipment usually depends largely on identifiers that are stable and common to different logs. Heavy anonymization of such identifiers might disable the system from detecting multi-stage complex attacks. These issues suggest that to intelligently engineer features, privacy preserving machine learning systems must go beyond just removing identifiers. Instead, they should convert sensitive attributes into abstract behavioral forms that still offer meaningful insights at the same time as protecting personal identities. This development still forms a very vibrant research area of privacy-aware security analytic(Qaddara et al., 2025)s.

8.2 Limitations of Model Transparency and Explainability

Another aspect where privacy preserving security analytics might have constraints is in relation to model interpretability. Analysts of security need a convincing explanation as to why a security system marker a certain activity as being suspicious in the course of their investigations. Incorporating mechanisms for privacy protection, however, may pose difficulties to this interpretability. Take differential privacy for example. This privacy protection method adds noise which can complicate the precise determination of the influence of individual features on the decision of the model. In a similar vein, having the training of models in federated learning environments occur on multiple nodes can result in it being more difficult to identify which patterns or anomalies detected by the global model came from a particular source. When analysts cannot fully grasp the reasons behind a model's decisions, they might start doubting automated detection systems(Abualhaj, Abu-Shareha, Al-Khatib, et al., 2025). Explaining the results is really a big question mark in security situations where an automated warning can lead to a very severe management action such as shutting down an account, isolating a network, or escalating an incident. If the systems' predictions can't be supported by clear and interpretable explanations, it won't foster confidence that organizations will lean on the system for making such very important decisions. That's why the research is currently quite focused on the creation of privacy aware explainable AI systems capable of providing understandable insights without revealing any sensitive training data. A great method proposed to give explanations is to create feature importance histograms instead of showing raw data samples. Analysts by means of these histograms see which behavioral patterns had the most significant impact on a detection decision, however, this is done without revealing the underlying (Ghazal, Hasan, Raju, et al., 2025)t.

8.3 Regulatory and Governance Challenges

One of the regulatory issues pertains to whether the machine learning models themselves are personal data. At times, models that have been trained with sensitive data might end up memorizing certain patterns that could be linked to individuals or groups. This brings up the question of whether trained models are subject to the same protective measures as the datasets they were derived from. Privacy preserving training methods are designed to address this problem but different countries or regions may have different interpretations of the law(Shabeeb Kamil et al., 2025). Requirements regarding transfers of data across borders are another aspect of governance that proves difficult. A lot of the time organizations are global with security monitoring infrastructures situated in several geographical regions. Privacy preserving machine learning technologies such as federated learning are great at meeting such restrictions since data can stay locally but the model training can be done collaboratively. Nevertheless, the deployment of such a distributed system requires the integrative legal frameworks of the respective entities. Additionally, organizations should draft internal governance policies that detail how privacy preserving analytics systems are developed, monitored, and audited(Nath et al., 2025).

8.4 Organizational and Operational Barriers

Beyond technical and regulatory concerns, organizations might experience operational barriers. Security teams are often familiar with the idyllic setup of a centralized monitoring infrastructure, where analysts have free access to telemetry data to conduct their investigations and incident response. Transitioning to privacy-aware architectures could be a way of lesser changes not only in operational processes but even in cultural mindsets. For example, analysts who are used to having direct access to detailed logs may indeed view privacy controls as impediments to efficiently conducting their investigations. The best way to deal with their reluctance is for these organizations to design systems that give investigators enough context to do their work without exposing sensitive data. Then, only under close supervision would certain investigative functions that require personal identifiers be allowed. Integration of privacy preserving machine-learning systems with existing security solutions is yet another point of operational challenge. Many companies still rely on their SIEM platforms, their security orchestration systems, as well as their incident management tools, which not only do not support privacy-aware machine learning but may even be incompatible. Architectural level changes might be so extensive that one may even consider these whole infrastructures for its conversion to a federated learning or encrypted computation Furthermore, knowledge and training are significant organizational elements as well. Privacy preserving machine learning implementation calls for combined proficiency in cybersecurity, machine learning engineering, cryptography, and privacy law. Organizations might have to set up special training programs or look for partners among the research community to tap into such expertise(Solairaju et al., 2025).

8.5 Future Research Directions

Privacy preserving machine learning is, despite the difficulties that have been mentioned, nonetheless a very fast-growing research area with the potential to greatly help security analytics systems preserve both ethical and operational integrity. In the future, research will probably concentrate on a number of main avenues that simultaneously tackle current weaknesses and help to broaden the portfolio of privacy-aware threat detection methods. Firstly, developing efficient encrypted computation infrastructures that can substantially lessen the computational overhead of privacy preserving training is a major focus of research. Progress in hardware acceleration, more efficient cryptographic libraries, and secure enclave architectures are expected to greatly raise the performance of encrypted machine learning algorithms by the time new products become mature. In addition, there is a growing trend towards adaptive privacy mechanisms that change privacy parameters depending on the operational context. For instance, one and the same system may enforce very stringent privacy protections when it is dealing with user behavior data that is highly sensitive while it may permit slightly more freshness of features when it is simply carrying out a network telemetry monitoring(Alomoush et al., 2025).

With such techniques, one would be able to reach a better balance between privacy and detection accuracy than setting privacy statically at one level through the use of configurations. Research is also touching upon privacy preserving collaborative threat intelligence sharing communities. Members of these communities share with each other machine learning-based models that are capable of detecting emerging cyber threats without disclosing their internal operation logs or other sensitive data of theirs. Federated learning combined with secure aggregation and privacy-aware model sharing in these communities enables very large-scale cooperative defense against cyber-attacks while at the same time strictly adhering to confidentiality requirements. Lastly, in line with the above, there is a need for explainable privacy preserving machine learning that allows one to better understand the decisions and behavior of the model without compromising on the exposure of sensitive training data. One of the effects of technologies that combine explainable AI with privacy protection mechanisms could be to notably enhance analyst confidence in automated security detection systems(Lakshmi et al., 2025).

9. CONCLUSION

Expanding rapidly, digital infrastructures and interlinked computing environments have made cybersecurity operations very complex. Security systems, to discover new threats, require continuous surveillance of large amounts of behavioral telemetry, network traffic, authentication logs, and application However, such extensive monitoring inevitably leads to the gathering and processing of personal user data. Hence, the difficulty with modern security architectures is not merely exposing malicious activities but also making sure that the security monitoring practices are consistent with privacy principles and data protection regulations. Privacy preserving machine learning is one of the solutions that facilitate advanced analytics without compromising sensitive data exposure. This chapter discussed privacy preserving machine learning in the context of security systems and operational monitoring environments. It started by suggesting that privacy-aware security analytics will become more and more central as machine learning models are increasingly used to uncover cyber threats. Traditional centralized machine learning operations require the combination of large datasets with detailed user behavior. Although such procedures can provide very high detection accuracy, they pose major privacy risks as sensitive data is concentrated in centralized repositories which not only are vulnerable to misuse but also to insider threats or unauthorized access. Privacy preserving learning methods provide a different approach where models are trained on distributed or protected datasets without the need to reveal the underlying raw data.

The chapter briefly went over the main privacy preservation methods. Differential privacy makes it impossible for individual data records to be inferred from the outputs of machine learning models by adding a certain amount of statistical noise during training. Federated learning is a way of collaboratively building models across multiple organizations or system nodes while keeping the actual data inside each environment. Secure multiparty computation and homomorphic encryption give you the tools to work with encrypted data, which means that private information stays secure even when training. There are a few different approaches to secure multiparty computation and homomorphic encryption that can be mixed and matched according to the level of privacy that you want, the threats that are most relevant to you, and the privacy anonymity requirements that you want to meet. Ultimately, the success of each very different approach depends on how that particular solution aligns with the security analytics architecture as a whole. It was demonstrated through an architectural pattern that privacy preserving machine learning could be suitably fitted inside operational security structures such as Security Operations Centers and enterprise monitoring platforms. The chapter laid out a variety of concepts for privacy-aware data pipelines, secure model training environments, and federated learning frameworks that could, among other things, support distributed security analytics. Implementation issues were considered as well, including infrastructure requirements, data lifecycle management strategies, and monitoring techniques for ensuring that privacy safeguards remain effective throughout the entire system operation.

These implementation blueprints illustrate that privacy preserving security analytics is not merely a concept but a practical technology capable of being integrated into current monitoring systems. We obtained detection-related data to carry out an empirical analysis and evaluate the privacy preserving learning methods' performance in the detection task relative to standard centralized models. The findings demonstrated that privacy-aware models were able to deliver an equally high level of detection performance while at the same time significantly minimizing the privacy risks commonly associated with centralized data collection. Federated learning models maintained a high level of detection accuracy and, at the same time, avoided disclosing raw data to each other between participating nodes. Although differential privacy models gave stronger theoretical guarantees, the noise added during training caused a drop in predictive performance. Hybrid systems combining federated learning with privacy-aware feature protection delivered the best combination of privacy protection and security effectiveness. These findings emphasize that privacy techniques must be selected not only against top security needs but also against regulation scenarios. The chapter also points to numerous challenges in the deployment of a privacy preserving machine learning setting that is operational. Major technical issues in distributed learning systems include a greater computational overhead and communication In addition, accuracy of the model might be sacrificed when strong privacy guarantees are given. Differences in data characteristics at various monitoring sites may also hamper the cooperative learning. Besides, privacy-oriented analytics could lead to less availability of contextual identifiers which security analysts mainly use for investigation. This in turn may lead to the need for more explainable and interpretable machine learning models.

Adoption of privacy preserving security analytics is also impacted by regulatory and corporate factors. Most countries have strict data protection rules that determine how personal information can be collected and processed by monitoring systems. Privacy preserving machine learning techniques, by limiting raw data exposure and enabling decentralized data processing, can help enterprises conform to these laws. However, going down this path usually entails setting up new governance structures, gaining interdisciplinary expertise, and even changing the traditional security operations workflows. To ensure that privacy measures don't hinder the effectiveness of threat detection, it is crucial for analysts, engineers, and compliance officers to collaborate closely. In the coming years, security systems that incorporate privacy-preserving machine learning are gearing up to become a huge successful despite the challenges. Reduction in the resource requirements of privacy-aware analytics is being achieved step-by-step by the combination of the advances in cryptographic computation, distributed learning optimization, and secure hardware technologies. Additionally, work on explainable privacy preserving machine learning models is raising their transparency and interpretability which enables analysts to comprehend detection results even in the absence of direct access to sensitive underlying data. Moreover, federated learning based collaborative security intelligence networks might allow organizations to share their threat detection capabilities without disclosing their proprietary or sensitive operational information.

Indeed, the integration of privacy preserving machine learning is far from simply being just another feature of security analytics systems. In fact, it is an entire reconsideration of how such systems should be designed and implemented. Fresh architectures, which incorporate privacy protections into machine learning pipelines, resulted in security systems that not only are able to detect threats well but at the same time also keep users, regulators, and stakeholders' trust.Briefly, privacy preserving machine learning is a tool that can be used to ensure that the needs of cybersecurity effectiveness and privacy are addressed simultaneously. Federated learning, differential privacy, and secure computation enable organizations to conduct analyses on security datasets without exposing sensitive information. When such technical solutions are combined with thorough architectural planning, regulatory mechanisms and ongoing research, they offer a practical, secured and privacy-aware monitoring systems that will be able to handle the digital era challenges

REFERENCES

Abashes, G. M., Elshqeirat, B., Abu-Shareha, A. A., & Alshraideh, M. (2025). BEYOND THE NOISE: UNVEILING MEANINGFUL PATTERNS IN MOBILE PAYMENT DATA USING FUZZY LOGIC AND SVM. *Journal of Theoretical and Applied Information Technology*, *103*(1).

Abdel-Jaber, M. tasime, Makhoul, N., Abdel-Jaber, M. en, & Beale, R. (2025). Cost prediction for product development using hybrid deep learning model: a meta-heuristic model. *Multimedia Tools and Applications, 84*(27). DOI: 10.1007/s11042-024-20437-y

Abdeljaber, O., & Al-Masaeed, S. (2025). Al-Mu'ani, L., Yaseen, H., & Alhnaity, B. (2025). Strategic Intelligence: The Power of AI in Planning Efficiency. *Human Behavior and Emerging Technologies*, (1). Advance online publication. DOI: 10.1155/hbe2/5383054

Abu-Shareha, A. A., Abualhaj, M. M., Alsharaiah, M. A., Al-Saaidah, A., & Achuthan, A. (2025). Diabetes Prediction Through Classification Using Pima Dataset: Survey and Evaluation. *Journal of Soft Computing and Data Mining*, *6*(1). Advance online publication. DOI: 10.30880/jscdm.2025.06.01.001

Abualhaj, M. M., Abu-Shareha, A. A., Al-Khatib, S. N., Alsaaidah, A. M., & Anbar, M. (2025). Improving firewall performance using hybrid of optimization algorithms and decision trees classifier. *IAES International Journal of Artificial Intelligence*, *14*(4), 2839. Advance online publication. DOI: 10.11591/ijai.v14.i4.pp2839-2848

Abualhaj, M. M., Abu-Shareha, A. A., & Rateb, R. (2025). Enhancing intrusion detection systems with hybrid HHO-WOA optimization and gradient boosting machine classifier. *International Journal of Reconfigurable and Embedded Systems*, *14*(2), 518. Advance online publication. DOI: 10.11591/ijres.v14.i2.pp518-526

Abualhaj, M. M., Al-Khatib, S. N., Al-Zyoud, M., Qaddara, I., Hiari, M. O., & Aldossary, S. M. A. (2025). Enhanced Network Communication Security Through Hybrid Dragonfly-Bat Feature Selection for Intrusion Detection. *The Journal of Communication*, *20*(5). Advance online publication. DOI: 10.12720/jcm.20.5.607-618

Abualigah, L., Alomari, S. A., Almomani, M. H., Zitar, R. A., Migdady, H., Saleem, K., Smerat, A., Snasel, V., & Ezugwu, A. E. (2025). An enhanced Walrus Optimizer with opposition-based learning and mutation strategy for data clustering. *Array (New York, N.Y.)*, *26*, 100409. Advance online publication. DOI: 10.1016/j.array.2025.100409

Abuowaida, S., Abu Owida, H., Shelash Mohammad, S. I., Alshdaifat, N., Abu Elsoud, E., Alazaidah, R., Vasudevan, A., & Alshurideh, M. T. (2025). Evidence Detection in Cloud Forensics: Classifying Cyber-Attacks in IaaS Environments using machine learning. *Data and Metadata*, *4*, 699. Advance online publication. DOI: 10.56294/dm2025699

Ahmed, Z. E., Hasan, M. K., Hashim, A. A., Saeed, R. A., Mokhtar, R. A., Singh, S. P., & Ghazal, T. M. (2022). Optimization Procedure for Intelligent Internet of Things Applications. *2022 International Conference on Business Analytics for Technology and Security, ICBATS 2022*. DOI: 10.1109/ICBATS54253.2022.9759065

Akram, A. S., Abbas, S., Khan, M. A., Athar, A., Ghazal, T. M., & Al Hamadi, H. (2024). Smart Energy Management System Using Machine Learning. *Computers, Materials & Continua, 78*(1), 959–973. Advance online publication. DOI: 10.32604/cmc.2023.032216

Al-Adwan, A. S., & Abdeljaber, O. (2025). Toward a resilient and smart supply chain: identifying and prioritizing barriers to metaverse adoption. *International Journal of Industrial Engineering and Operations Management.* DOI: 10.1108/IJIEOM-06-2025-0113

Al-Adwan, A. S., Al-Adwan, A., Li, N., Fauzi, M. A., Jafar, R. M. S., Habibi, A., & Falahat, M. (2025). IMMERSIVE LEARNING MEETS THEORY: MODELING EDUVERSE ADOPTION IN HIGHER EDUCATION. *Journal of Information Technology Education, 24*, 042. Advance online publication. DOI: 10.28945/5669

Al-Momani, M. M., Alqudah, T. A., Al Swiety, I. A., Mahrakani, N., Nassoura, M. B. A., & Al Attar, M. K. (2025). Integrating Artificial Intelligence (AI) and Business Intelligence (BI): A Framework for Improving Enterprise Performance. *TEM Journal, 14*(3). https://doi.org/DOI: 10.18421/TEM143-26

Al Nasar, M. R., Ghazal, T. M., Al-Tarawni, M. A. M., Ahmed, A. A., Abu-Shareha, A. A., & Ahmed, S. M. (2025). Hierarchical Edge-Cloud Collaborative AI Algorithm for Energy-Efficient lot Management in Ubiquitous Computing Environments. *Journal of Wireless Mobile Networks, Ubiquitous Computing and Dependable Applications, 16*(3). Advance online publication. DOI: 10.58346/JOWUA.2025.I3.035

Al-Okbi, N. K., Alomari, S. A., Hadi, W. J., Ajrash, A. S., Smerat, A., & Abualigah, L. (2025). Defending Digital Integrity: Advances in Media Forgery Analysis Research and Cybersecurity Development. *SN Computer Science, 6*(8), 913. Advance online publication. DOI: 10.1007/s42979-025-04462-8

Aldaaja, Y., Odeh, M., Badrakhan, S. S., Sabri, M., Abdelrahim, Y., Samara, G., & Alsabatin, H. (2025). Quantifying the Managerial and Practical Benefits of Cloud Computing on Information Security in Higher Education Institutions. *Applied Mathematics & Information Sciences, 19*(1), 15–24. Advance online publication. DOI: 10.18576/amis/190102

Aldabbas, A., Baniata, L. H., Alsaaidah, B. A., Mustafa, Z., Alali, M., & Rateb, R. (2025). Artificial intelligence-driven method for the discovery and prevention of distributed denial of service attacks. *IAES International Journal of Artificial Intelligence, 14*(1), 614. Advance online publication. DOI: 10.11591/ijai.v14.i1.pp614-628

Alharbi, Y., Yadav, K., Dutta, D., Smerat, A., & Ranjbar, F. (2026). Thermodynamic behavior of CO2–organic mixtures: Density prediction using explainable machine learning algorithms. *Results in Engineering, 29*, 108687. Advance online publication. DOI: 10.1016/j.rineng.2025.108687

ALMahadin, G., Shabaz, M., Khan, I. R., Vimal, V., Keshta, I., & Maguluri, L. P.ALMahadin. (2025). Content-aware recommendation system for integrated temporal semantic review text over web of things. *Service Oriented Computing and Applications, 19*(1), 77–91. Advance online publication. DOI: 10.1007/s11761-024-00408-9

Almomani, O., Arabiat, A., Al Tayeb, M., Almaiah, M. A., Obeidat, M., Aldhyani, T. H. H., Shehab, R., & Rowad, M. (2025). A Robust Model for Android Malware Detection via ML and DL classifiers. *Mesopotamian Journal of Big Data, 2025*. Advance online publication. DOI: 10.58496/MJBD/2025/017

Alomoush, R. A., Al-tarawneh, A. M. A., Alhossan, S. M., Altabeeb, N. A. K., & Tarawneh, A. W. (2025). Difficulties of using digital technology and their relationship to the quality of vocational performance among teachers and counselors. *Journal of Education and e-learning Research, 12*(4), 655–663. Advance online publication. DOI: 10.20448/jeelr.v12i4.7856

Alraba'nah, Y., Al-Sharaeh, S., & Al Hindi, G. (2025). Enhancing Intrusion Detection Using Hybrid Long Short-Term Memory and XGBoost. *Journal of Soft Computing and Data Mining, 6*(1). Advance online publication. DOI: 10.30880/jscdm.2025.06.01.016

Arabasy, M., & Ghoneim, R. S. (2025). Enhancing sustainable urban design using machine learning: Comparative analysis of seven metaheuristic algorithms in energy-efficient digital architecture. *Frontiers in Built Environment, 11*, 1526209. Advance online publication. DOI: 10.3389/fbuil.2025.1526209

Arabiat, A. M., & Eljaafreh, Y. G. (2025). Intrusion Detection in Wireless Sensor Networks Using ML Based Classification of Denial of Service (DoS) Attacks. *The Journal of Communication, 20*(4). Advance online publication. DOI: 10.12720/jcm.20.4.501-514

Babaker, S., Khatibi, A., Alsoud, A. R., Kaur, J., Jagtap, J., Alkhayyat, A., & Shah, S. K. (2025). Improving Reliability and Data Management in Internet of Things Based Wireless Sensor Networks. *Internet Technology Letters, 8*(6), e646. Advance online publication. DOI: 10.1002/itl2.646

Bektemyssova, G., Montazeri, Z., Dehghani, M., Ibraheem, I. K., Smerat, A., Werner, F., Al-Salih, A. A. M. M., Ahmed, M. A., & Eguchi, K. (2025). Search and Rescue Algorithm (SRA): A Metaheuristic Approach for Efficient Constrained Engineering Optimization. *International Journal of Intelligent Engineering and Systems, 18*(10), 607–621. Advance online publication. DOI: 10.22266/ijies2025.1130.39

Cui, D., Harrison, A., Fendzi-Donfack, E., Dagal, I., Jangir, P., Mahmoud, M. M., Malkani, P., Mbasso, W. F., Tiako, P., & Smerat, A. (2026). Enhancing Short-Term Electricity Forecasting with Advanced Machine Learning Techniques. *Journal of Electrical Engineering & Technology, 21*(1), 147–187. Advance online publication. DOI: 10.1007/s42835-025-02430-z

Dar, A. A., Bhavithra, H. A., Awasthi, A. K., Sabha, S. U., Dar, J. G., Smerat, A., & Sindhuja, S. (2025). Inventory Optimization for Perishables: A Probabilistic and Fuzzy Modeling Approach. *Mathematical Modelling of Engineering Problems, 12*(8). Advance online publication. DOI: 10.18280/mmep.120825

Dinler, Ö. B., Bektemyssova, G., Şahin, C. B., Montazeri, Z., Dehghani, M., Smerat, A., Werner, F., & Eguchi, K. (2025). Carpenter Optimization Algorithm: A Human-inspired Metaheuristic for Robust and Efficient Constrained Optimization. *International Journal of Intelligent Engineering and Systems, 18*(11), 344–357. Advance online publication. DOI: 10.22266/ijies2025.1231.21

Eke, C. I., Al-Shamayleh, A. S., Phiri, M., Maswadi, K., Kwaghtyo, D. K., Mulenga, M., & Iyidobi, C. J. (2025). Machine Learning Based Mobile Big Data Analytics: State-of-the-art Applications, Taxonomy, Challenges and Future Research Directions. *Nigerian Journal of Technological Development, 22*(4). Advance online publication. DOI: 10.63746/njtd.v22i4.3385

Fauzi, M. A., Alias, U. N., Nya-Ling Tan, C., Wider, W., Mukherjee, S., Al-Adwan, A. S., & Udang, L. N. (2025). The Present and Future Trends of Leadership Styles and Knowledge Hiding Through Science Mapping Analysis. *Journal of Information and Knowledge Management, 24*(5), 2550040. Advance online publication. DOI: 10.1142/S0219649225500406

Ghazal, T. M., Abu-Shareha, A., Mustafa, S. A., Ibrahim, A., & Ahmed, S. M. (2025). Privacy-Preserving Transformer-Based Meta-Learning Algorithm for Zero-Day Intrusion Detection in IoT-Enabled Smart Grids. *Journal of Internet Services and Information Security*, *15*(4), 76–84. Advance online publication. DOI: 10.58346/JISIS.2025.I4.006

Ghazal, T. M., Abualhaj, M., Ahmed, A. A., Al-Tarawni, M. A. M., & Maghrabi, L. A. (2025). Federated Deep Graph Neural Network Algorithm for Real-Time Intrusion Detection in Heterogeneous IoT Systems. *Journal of Internet Services and Information Security*, *15*(4), 484–497. Advance online publication. DOI: 10.58346/JISIS.2025.I4.035

Ghazal, T. M., Hasan, M. K., Hussein, A. H., Pandey, B. K., Ahmad, M., Safie, N., & Cascone, L. (2025). Federated Learning With Small and Large Models With Privacy-Preserving Data Space for Holographic Internet of Things in Consumer Electronics. *IEEE Transactions on Consumer Electronics*, *71*(2), 5259–5274. Advance online publication. DOI: 10.1109/TCE.2025.3573033

Ghazal, T. M., Hasan, M. K., Raju, K. N., Khan, M. A., Alshamayleh, A., Bhatt, M. W., & Ahmad, M. (2025). Data Space Privacy Model with Federated Learning Technique for Securing IoT Communications in Autonomous Marine Vehicles. *Journal of Intelligent & Robotic Systems*, *111*(3), 84. Advance online publication. DOI: 10.1007/s10846-025-02298-1

Ghazal, T. M., Janjua, J. I., Abushiba, W., Ahmad, M., Ihsan, A., & Al-Dmour, N. A. (2024). Cybersecurity Revolution via Large Language Models and Explainable AI. *2024 17th International Conference on Security of Information and Networks, SIN 2024*. DOI: 10.1109/SIN63213.2024.10871324

Gul, A., Khan, F., Farooq, M., Javaid, A., Hussain, Z., & Elzaghmouri, B. (2025). STATISTICAL MODELING AND PREDICTION OF PANDEMIC USING CLASSICAL AND MACHINE LEARNING APPROACH. *Pakistan Journal of Statistics*, *41*(3).

H K, P. K., Dash, R., K, J. R., Mohapatra, B., Bishoyi, S. S., Bajaj, M., & Blazek, V.H K. (2026). Multi-domain fault characterization in DC microgrids utilizing Hilbert-Huang transform ensemble by LSTM networks with adaptive boundary condition constraints. *Results in Engineering*, *29*, 108721. Advance online publication. DOI: 10.1016/j.rineng.2025.108721

Haider, Z. A., Ullah, I., Shareha, A. A., Nasimov, R., & Memon, S. A. (2026). Artificial Intelligence (AI)-Enabled Unmanned Aerial Vehicle (UAV) Systems for Optimizing User Connectivity in Sixth-Generation (6G) Ubiquitous Networks. *Computers, Materials & Continua*, *86*(1), 1–16. Advance online publication. DOI: 10.32604/cmc.2025.071042

Hanandeh, A., Alfreijat, S. Y., Qutieshat, R. J., Alsha'ar, H. Y., Kilani, Q. A. L., & Saleem Khasawneh, M. A. (2025). Implementing AI Accuracy, Learning Rate, Inference Time on enhancing Big Data Analysis and Strategic Plan. *Data and Metadata*, *4*, 637. Advance online publication. DOI: 10.56294/dm2025637

Hasan, M. K., Ghazal, T. M., Issa, G., Islam, S., Ismail, A. F., & Kabir, S. R. (2025). Hashgraph consensus-based simultaneous, asynchronous and big-data supported blockchain mechanism for IT-OT enabled critical infrastructure sectors. *Journal of Ambient Intelligence and Humanized Computing*. Advance online publication. DOI: 10.1007/s12652-024-04942-4

Hasan, M. K., Habib, A. K. M. A., Islam, S., Safie, N., Ghazal, T. M., Khan, M. A., Alzahrani, A. I., Alalwan, N., Kadry, S., & Masood, A. (2024). Federated learning enables 6 G communication technology: Requirements, applications, and integrated with intelligence framework. *Alexandria Engineering Journal, 91*, 658–668. Advance online publication. DOI: 10.1016/j.aej.2024.02.044

Hiari, M., Alraba'nah, Y., & Qaddara, I. (2025). A Deep Learning-Based Intrusion Detection System using Refined LSTM for DoS Attack Detection. *Engineering. Technology and Applied Science Research, 15*(4), 25627–25633. Advance online publication. DOI: 10.48084/etasr.11499

Hou, G., Alkhayyat, A., Almalkawi, A., Yadav, A., Shreenidhi, H. S., Saini, V., Shomurotova, S., Singh, D., Jain, V., Smerat, A., & Khalid, A. (2025). Development of robust machine learning models to estimate hydrochar higher heating value and yield based upon biomass proximate analysis. *Bioresources and Bioprocessing, 12*(1), 138. Advance online publication. DOI: 10.1186/s40643-025-00979-1 PMID: 41335148

Hyassat, A. S., Abu Zayed, R. E., Al Khateeb, E. A., Shalaldeh, A., Abdelhamied, M. M., & Qaddara, I. (2025). Unveiling Cyber Threats: An In-Depth Study on Data Mining Techniques for Exploit Attack Detection †. *Engineering Proceedings, 104*(1), 28. Advance online publication. DOI: 10.3390/engproc2025104028

Ibrahim, A., Sekhar, R., Tawfeq, J. F., Salih, S. Q., Shah, P., & Radhi, A. D. (2024). Security and Privacy Protection for Online Electronic Documents Based on Novel Encryption Techniques. *Journal of Intelligent Systems and Internet of Things, 11*(1), 21–28. Advance online publication. DOI: 10.54216/JISIoT.110103

Jaradat, S., Acharya, N., Shivshankar, S., Alhadidi, T. I., & Elhenawy, M. (2025). AI for Data Quality Auditing: Detecting Mislabeled Work Zone Crashes Using Large Language Models. *Algorithms, 18*(6), 317. Advance online publication. DOI: 10.3390/a18060317

Khalayleh, Y. A. S., Mohammad, S. I., Al Louzi, N. S., Baniata, M., Hassan, M., Safaqah, M. A., Vasudevan, A., & Alshurideh, M. T. (2025). Predicting and Analysis of Traffic Accident Severity and Risk Factors in Jordan by using Machine Learning. *Applied Mathematics & Information Sciences, 19*(6), 1419–1426. Advance online publication. DOI: 10.18576/amis/190615

Khatibi, A., Babaker, S., Praveen, K. N. R., Chohan, J. S., Jadhav, A., Alsoud, A. R., Ramudu, M. J., & Jeet, R. (2025). Advanced AI-Driven Cybersecurity: Analyzing Emerging Threats and Defensive Strategies. *National Academy Science Letters*. Advance online publication. DOI: 10.1007/s40009-025-01897-8

Lakshmi, A. S., Sigamany, E. S. S., Traisa, R., Kumar, R., Reddy, K. R., Chohan, J. S., & Smerat, A. (2025). Enhancing Code Quality Through Automated Refactoring Using Transformer-Based Language Models. *International Journal of Advanced Computer Science and Applications, 16*(9). Advance online publication. DOI: 10.14569/IJACSA.2025.0160951

Llwaah, F., Hussein, A. H., & Ghazal, T. M. (2025). Enhancing Cloud Resource Utilization Through Synthesizing Intensive Workflow Tasks. *Journal of Wireless Mobile Networks, Ubiquitous Computing and Dependable Applications*, *16*(4), 537–555. Advance online publication. DOI: 10.58346/JOWUA.2025.I4.030

Mahfuri, M., & Ibrahim, A. (2024). AI-Driven Innovations: Transforming Data Support and Environmental Management for the Future. *2024 International Conference on Decision Aid Sciences and Applications, DASA 2024*. DOI: 10.1109/DASA63652.2024.10836162

Masango, N. C., Agushaka, J. O., Amaefule, M. C., Taiwo, O., Zhang, P., Ezugwu, A. E., Saleem, K., Smerat, A., & Abualigah, L. (2025). Secure and efficient cloudlet networks: blockchain integration with agent-based proof of trust mechanism. *Eurasip Journal on Wireless Communications and Networking*, *2025*(1). DOI: 10.1186/s13638-025-02439-y

Maz, Y. A., Anbar, M., Manickam, S., Abualhaj, M. M., Almalki, S. A., & Alabsi, B. A. (2025). Transfer Learning-Based Approach with an Ensemble Classifier for Detecting Keylogging Attack on the Internet of Things. *Computers, Materials & Continua*, *85*(3), 5287–5307. Advance online publication. DOI: 10.32604/cmc.2025.068257

Nandal, P., Mann, P., Bohra, N., Sagar, K., & Smerat, A. (2025). Improving Underwater Image Quality Through Real-ESRGAN With Whale Optimization Algorithm. *Internet Technology Letters*, *8*(4), e70047. Advance online publication. DOI: 10.1002/itl2.70047

Nath, A., Nanda, R., Jena, P. P., Ghosh, A., Shah, S., Patel, S., Mohapatra, E., Tiwari, A. K., & Nisar, K. S. (2025). Symbolic regression and interpretable ensemble learning approach in determining early onset of diabetic peripheral neuropathy. *Egyptian Informatics Journal*, *31*, 100777. Advance online publication. DOI: 10.1016/j.eij.2025.100777

Qaddara, I., & Alraba'nah, Y. (2025). Enhancing Requirements Classification Using Machine Learning Techniques. *SN Computer Science*, *6*(6), 649. Advance online publication. DOI: 10.1007/s42979-025-04158-z

Qaddara, I., Alrabaynah, Y., & Hiari, M. O. (2025). Evaluation of SQL and NoSQL Databases on Parallel Processing. *Engineering. Technology and Applied Science Research*, *15*(4), 24298–24304. Advance online publication. DOI: 10.48084/etasr.10620

Qawaqneh, H., Alomari, K. M., Alomari, S., Bektemyssova, G., Smerat, A., Montazeri, Z., Dehghani, M., Malik, O. P., & Eguchi, K. (2025). Black-breasted Lapwing Algorithm (BBLA): A Novel Nature-inspired Metaheuristic for Solving Constrained Engineering Optimization. *International Journal of Intelligent Engineering and Systems*, *18*(11), 581–597. Advance online publication. DOI: 10.22266/ijies2025.1231.36

Qawasmeh, S., Habboushb, A., Elzaghmouri, B., Kharma, Q., & Albalawneh, D. (2025). Hybrid Convolutional Neural Network-Based Intrusion Detection System for Secure IoT Networks. *Tikrit Journal of Engineering Sciences*, *32*(SP1), 1–11. Advance online publication. DOI: 10.25130/tjes.sp1.2025.2

Raza, M. A., Karim, A., Alqarni, M., Al-Khasawneh, M. A., Jumani, T. A., Aman, M., & Masud, M. I. (2025). An Intelligent Long Short-Term Memory-Based Machine Learning Model for the Potential Assessment of Global Hydropower Capacity in Sustainable Energy Transition and Security. *Energies*, *18*(13), 3324. Advance online publication. DOI: 10.3390/en18133324

Saeed, N. M. S. E., Ibrahim, A., Ali, L., Al-Dmour, N. A., Mohammed, A. S., & Ghazal, T. M. (2024). Unveiling the Landscape of Machine Learning and Deep Learning Methodologies in Network Security: A Comprehensive Literature Review. *2nd International Conference on Cyber Resilience, ICCR 2024*. DOI: 10.1109/ICCR61006.2024.10533066

Samanta, I. S., Mohanty, S., Rout, P. K., Parida, S. M., Panda, S., Bajaj, M., Blazek, V., & Prokop, L. (2025). A comprehensive review of feature extraction techniques for power quality event detection with novel approaches for enhanced classification in smart grids. *Electrical Engineering*, *107*(9), 12227–12259. Advance online publication. DOI: 10.1007/s00202-025-03149-w

Sawarkar, P. G., Pote, A., Khan, M. A., Abed, M. H., Hadi, A. A., Smerat, A., & Khishe, M. (2025). Sustainable geopolymer concrete evaluation using machine learning and PDP analysis: Comparative insights into strength prediction. *Hybrid Advances*, *11*, 100569. Advance online publication. DOI: 10.1016/j.hybadv.2025.100569

Shabeeb Kamil, A., Mousa Ali, E., Alibakhshikenari, M., Misran, N., Tariqul Islam, M., Virdee, B., Mariyanayagam, D., Abbasi, N. A., Rashid, N., & Elwi, A., T. (. (2025). Metasurface Effect on the Performance of Planar Antennas for Wireless Communications. *Radio Science*, *60*(11). Advance online publication. DOI: 10.1029/2024RS008156

Sharma, K. P., Hussain, R., Jaharadak, A. A., Trawnih, A. A., Verma, D., Dasi, S., & Pant, S. (2025). Hybrid Convolutional Neural Network for Robust Attack Detection in Wireless Sensor Networks. *Internet Technology Letters*, *8*(6), e650. Advance online publication. DOI: 10.1002/itl2.650

Solairaju, J. A., Rathinasamy, S., Thanikodi, S., Tarawneh, B., Gurumoorthy, V., Antony, J. S., & Arul Gnana Dhas, A. (2025). Development and Validation of ANN Models for Water Absorption in Sawdust and Kenaf Fiber-Reinforced Polystyrene Composites. *Engineering Reports*, *7*(9), e70393. Advance online publication. DOI: 10.1002/eng2.70393

Turab, N., Abushattal, A., Al-Nabulsi, J., & Owida, H. A. (2025). Advanced risk assessment using machine learning and sentiment analysis on log data. *IAES International Journal of Artificial Intelligence*, *14*(5), 3897. Advance online publication. DOI: 10.11591/ijai.v14.i5.pp3897-3905

Vasudevan, A., Tamilmani, K. T., Mohammad, S. I., Sridheepika, V. S., Raja, N., Soon, E. E. H., Nagaraj, S., & Al-Adwan, A. S. (2025). Voices of Concern: Contemplations on Socioeconomic, Ethical, and Developmental Impacts of AI. *Applied Mathematics & Information Sciences*, *19*(1), 221–232. Advance online publication. DOI: 10.18576/amis/190119

Xu, B., Jummaa, K., Altalbawy, F. M. A., Roopashree, R., Saraswat, S. K., Ray, S., Tomar, P., Naem, S., Hamza, H. H., Smerat, A., & Khalid, A. (2025). Machine learning-assisted computation of water activity for ionic liquid-based aqueous ternary elements. *Desalination and Water Treatment*, *324*, 101484. Advance online publication. DOI: 10.1016/j.dwt.2025.101484

Zraiqat, A., Batiha, B., & Al-Refai, O. (2025). Thunderstorm and Cloud Algorithm: A Novel Parameter-Free Metaheuristic Inspired by Atmospheric Dynamics for Complex Optimization Tasks. *International Journal of Intelligent Engineering and Systems*, *18*(8), 153–167. Advance online publication. DOI: 10.22266/ijies2025.0930.11

Chapter 7
Privacy Oriented Threat Modeling for Modern Security Architectures

Mahmoud Abu Saima
http://orcid.org/0000-0001-5343-0053
Geosciences Department, United Arab Emirates University, UAE

Hmoud Al-Dmour
Department of Physics, Mutah University, Jordan

Abdallah M. Al-Tarawneh
http://orcid.org/0000-0003-2103-3576
Clinical Psychology Department, Al-Ahliyya Amman University, Jordan

ABSTRACT

This study focuses on privacy-centric threat modeling as a critical practice in modern security architectures. It mentions that conventional threat modeling is primarily focused on potential system breaches and it pays little attention to personal data risks, users rights as well as compliance with the laws. The chapter describes privacy-centered adaptations of threat modeling that facilitate the recognition of data flows, trust boundaries, as well as misuse scenarios that affect people. It examines ways of mapping the privacy threats like excessive data gathering, unauthorized inference, secondary use, and re-identification in complex systems. It also demonstrates the integration of privacy threat modeling methods into secure design, DevSecOps pipelines, and AI-driven systems. The work, by mixing security engineering principles with data protection requirements, puts forward a method to forecast privacy threats at the earliest time, improve governance controls, and develop security architectures that are equally robust, compliant, and respectful of the privacy expectations.

1. INTRODUCTION

Historically, the security architecture tracks the general trend of enterprise computing digital transformation. In most cases, legacy information systems used to be centralized, contained within a single

DOI: 10.4018/979-8-3373-9210-3.ch007

geographical location, and network perimeters were well defined and strong. In such environments, security architecture mainly revolved around securing controlled points of entry, access management, anti-malware defenses, and internal segmentation. Logging and monitoring were not very extensive and usually arose from servers, firewalls, and authentication systems. Privacy was a concern, of course, but the extent and intensity of data observation were a far cry from the present day digitally connected and instrumented infrastructures(Arabiat & Eljaafreh, 2025). Organizations now use services running on and in the cloud, application containers, microservices, Software as a Service (SaaS), working from home, identity federations, and device-rich ecosystems. Security architects are making a big push towards zero trust models these days. Without relying on a trust assumption that a network is secure if it has not been compromised (static trust), modern systems perform continuous identity verification, context gathering, communication monitoring, event correlation, and anomaly detection. The data for these various checks comes from endpoint, application, access gateways, user behavior analytics platform, network sensors, cloud control plane, and machine learning pipeline. The biggest positive feature of this tech is that it allows for better visibility and incident response. However, on the flip side, these innovations have turned the security architecture into a huge data-processing facility(Al-Adwan & Abdeljaber, 2025).

Behavioral signals are having an increasingly significant impact on security decision-making in data-driven systems. Such indicators might include the user's login location, device health status, changes in geographical location, patterns of application usage and browsing, workflow anomalies, keystroke timing, and communication metadata. The aggregated effect might lead to threat scoring or access decision. So not only the defensive measures of the system have been changed, but the system has also turned into a means of getting to know the behavior of humans and machines alike. Interpretation issues introduce both ethical and technical challenges(Elkaradawy et al., 2025). First, data gathered for security purposes may become highly sensitive especially if it discloses one's habits, social circle, places visited, or concealed traits. Second, once such data finds its way to be the center of security platforms, there is the danger that it will be retained, linked, reanalyzed, or repurposed beyond its original protection intent. The more it became "intelligent," the more security architectures also inherently became "intrusive." Of course, this does not mean that this trend reflects a malevolent designers' intent. Rather, it is a mirror of the fact that in modern cyber defense, good protection is highly dependent on wide surveillance. The problem is that without control, such extensive surveillance can lead to serious and invisible privacy harms that are hardly reversible. Hence, it is necessary to recognize that the development story of security architecture also entails the rising of keys to data minimization, bounded observability, and privacy-conscious system design(Ghazal, 2025a).

1.1 The Need for Privacy-Aware Threat Modeling Frameworks

One of the reasons why there is a need for privacy-aware threat modeling framework is that the regular security focused ones do not cover in its entirety the various forms of privacy violations that may arise from malicious third parties, user errors, or legitimate system functions. Security threat models alone are capable of recognizing technical attack paths such as spoofing, tampering, privilege abuse, and denial of service. These security questions are a must-have, but they do not cover privacy violations that may be caused by the system operations themselves or the choices made on data handling or the deployment of excessive observability.

Figure 1. Privacy Threat Surface in Modern Security Architectures

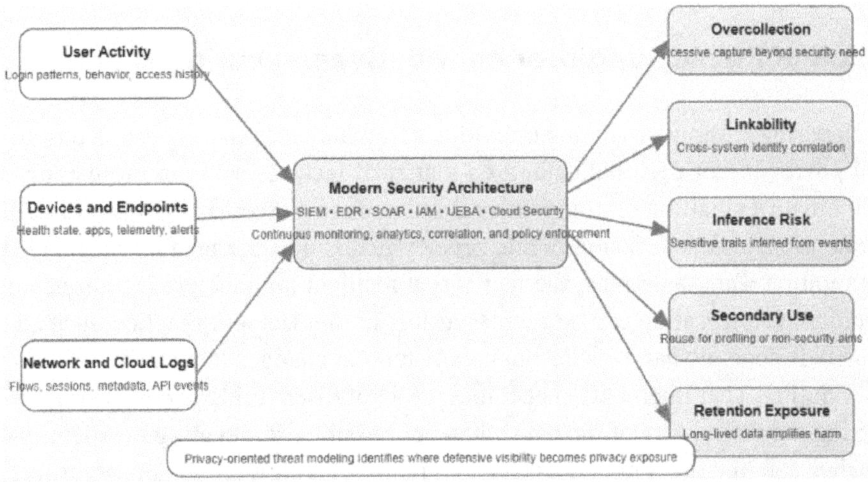

A privacy threat surface illustrating, in Figure 1, how telemetry of user, device, and cloud that are ingested by modern security architectures may lead to various privacy risks including overcollection, inference, and secondary use. In addition to asking what personal data is collected, why is it collected, where does it go, how long is it kept, who has the access, can the data be linked or reidentified, and what are the possible inferences that could be drawn from it, it also asks if the use of data is still compliant with the legitimate security purposes. Also it asks whether the technical architecture of a system causes situations where some people have knowledge or power that others don't and that the latter cannot fully understand or even oppose(Al-Daoud et al., 2025). Indeed, privacy-focused threat modeling should not be seen as competing with security; on the contrary, it is a means to help design security architectures that are balanced, transparent, and reliable. The very idea of a "privacy breach" in security systems has evolved so that people now recognize it as a combination of many elements that extend far beyond simple technical flaws. A logging pipeline on its own may be fine; a behavioral analytics engine may also largely be fine; a centralized retention store may again be fine.

However, if the coordination of these components is not supported by clear minimization controls, segmentation, or purpose limitation, the entire security architecture will be capable of creating continuous internal surveillance. Privacy-based threat modeling therefore is not confined to looking at each component individually but rather examines overall system behavior, data flows, actor relationships, trust boundaries, and subsequent effects. Besides that, privacy-aware threat modeling also encourages a company to move forward and expand. It pushes architects, engineers, legal teams, compliance officers, and security analysts to use the same frame of reference when discussing system behavior and risk. Also, don't forget that privacy lapses in security systems are rarely attributed to a single team. On the contrary, they result from technical conveniences, operational pressures, vendor defaults, weak governance, and unclear design assumptions all interacting together(A. A. Khan et al., 2025). The very reason why such a framework is valuable is, among other things, that it can lead to a reduction of the risks that stem from the complicated system component integration by resulting in a shared foundation for communication and understanding between organizational roles. Adopting a methodical strategy is, therefore, a very strongly established and formal manner of making these assumptions available for early checking and turning the intangible privacy principles into tangible architectural Vasudevan et al., 2025).

1.2 Integration of Privacy Engineering with Cybersecurity Design

Privacy engineering is about protecting individuals from unnecessary exposure, unwanted inference, and unjustified processing of personal data. As a matter of fact, resorting to these competencies separately may well create a situation of competitive disadvantage as security teams will be inclined to go for visibility, retention, and data fusion, while privacy teams will prefer minimization, segmentation, and purpose limitation. Be it as it may, the fact is that resilient architectures require a combination of these. Philosophically, integration can be seen as a shift in mindset and practice. Instead of fixing privacy after security is done, it shall be a design parameter that changes the way the system makes use of data to render visibility. That intervention becomes a way of discovering and choosing the right kind of telemetry, limiting the granularity of the data wherever possible, segregating the identity data from the event content when full linkage is not necessary, and putting privacy-preserving controls right up in the monitoring pipeline(Vasudevan et al., 2024).

At the end of the day, achieving privacy engineering and cybersecurity design integration is one of the effective ways to build trust to multiple levels. Other things that come out of that are making a solid legal defense, reducing exposure of data to a minimum, making use of the systems ethically, and building up confidence in users, employees, regulators, and partners. After all, the biggest thing that will keep the privacy there will have been a control system to make us capable of breaking a false trade-off in which you give up privacy for security without any good reason. Privacy-oriented threat modeling comes up with solutions that, in a very practical way, allow building this bridge between both of them by implying high-level principles through architecture-level analysis and backing up design decisions(Al-Suhimat et al., 2024).

Figure 2. Conceptual Model of Privacy-Centric Threat Modeling Workflow

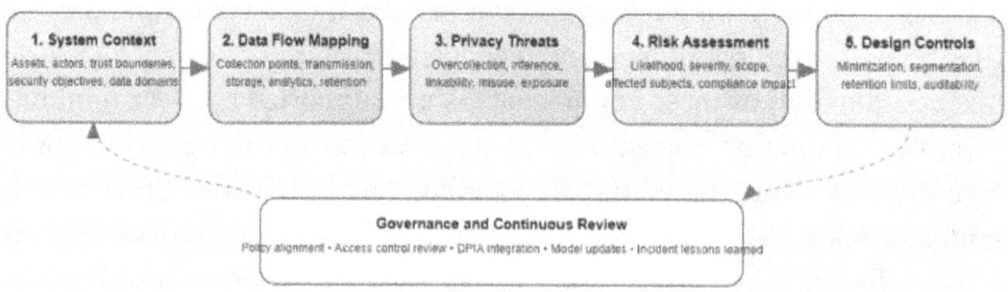

In Figure 2, A privacy-centric threat modeling workflow that starts out with system context and data flow analysis, moves on to identification of privacy harms, evaluation of risk, and finally translation based on findings into architectural controls and governance Although previous studies have examined cybersecurity monitoring and privacy protection separately, limited research has investigated how modern monitoring architectures can balance threat detection effectiveness with privacy preservation. This chapter addresses this gap through a privacy-oriented threat modeling perspective.

2. FOUNDATIONS OF PRIVACY THREAT MODELING

2.1 Definition and Scope of Privacy Threat Modeling

Privacy threat modeling is a comprehensive method aimed at uncovering, evaluating, and reducing privacy risks that may occur due to system design, launch, functioning, and changes over time. It primarily works to reveal possibilities that individuals' data might be collected, inferred, processed, linked, stored, shared, or retained in ways that expose them to unjustifiable risks. Unlike occasional or one-off privacy checks, privacy threat modeling is a consistent and formalized approach. It relies on visual tools, system documentation, relationships between actors, data life cycles, and threat categorizations—much like a blueprint that makes the privacy level of a system apparent before it gets deeply embedded in the infrastructure(Yaseen et al., 2025). Privacy threat modeling's range encompasses both technical and socio-technical elements. On the technical side, it involves such things as databases, APIs, telemetry-sources, analytics pipelines, logging systems, access control layers, user interfaces, cloud services, and third-party integrations. On the socio-technical side, it also includes user expectations, organizational roles, governance arrangements, trust assumptions, as well as the existence of legitimate system functions that may create asymmetrical knowledge or decision-making power over individuals(Alnawafleh et al., 2024).

Privacy threat modeling is of particular importance in cases where visibility is a major focus of the system. Security platforms, advertising engines, recommendation systems, health apps, smart city infrastructures, educational analytics tools, and workplace monitoring environments, all depend on human-data observation and processing. For such systems, it wouldn't be enough to model the threat just by asking if an attacker could steal the data. The threat model should also probe if the system itself leads to an overabundance of observability, if various data streams can be combined into behavioral profiles, if seemingly innocuous metadata becomes identifying when combined, and if new inferences arise over time that were not evident when the system was first designed(Zraiqat, Al Sayyed, et al., 2025). An integral part of what it can cover is that privacy threat modeling is not restrained to data categories under legal regulations like names, national identification numbers, or medical records. Behavioral metadata, location history, device fingerprints, browsing patterns, access times, and communication relationships—all may cause privacy risks even though they do not conform to narrowly defined legacy concepts of personally identifiable information. Systems today often derive very sensitive information from weakly identifying inputs making the scope of privacy investigation inclusive of both direct and indirect paths to disclosure(Almajed et al., 2022).

2.2 Core Principles of Privacy by Design

Considering privacy by design as a principle provides a basic reference point for privacy threat modeling as it stands prime that the privacy must be introduced into the system from the cradle and not left until the end to be fixed or patched. It is very much against the ideology that privacy is something that can be done with the help of notices, disclaimers, or policies after the fact. On the contrary, it should be argued that prerequisites of system design, operational procedures, user interaction, and default settings should be deliberately done in such a way that exposure is effectively contained, and data boundaries are respected. One of the most important principles is the one that emphasizes working ahead of problems as the main focus rather than simply reacting to changes(Hyassat et al., 2025). The objective is, in fact, not only to fix the damages that have already been done, but also to equip the systems with the capability to anticipate privacy threats and act accordingly during the planning and development steps. Privacy threat modeling is a way of implementing that principle as it engages the developers in identifying different data collection points, trust boundaries, inference pathways, and intended uses long before the system is actually rolled out. Rather than waiting for user grievances, regulatory probes, or data breach happenings, it culminates into the first line of defense when controls are both easier(Alnawayseh et al., 2022).

Privacy by default sets the benchmark against which all designs are evaluated. Let's say a system keeps collecting all sorts of data from a user unless the user is an opt-out, then presumably, the system is not set to have privacy as default. Defaults matter greatly because it is the scenario that most users find themselves in and which they have actually decided. This principle in security architectures has strong links with components such as the level of detail in logging, the length of retention, the enrichment of telemetry, and the cross-system identity correlation. A privacy by design approach will question whether the most invasive monitoring mode has been made the standard one without sufficient justification and whether less intrusive default options would still be able to produce the legitimate security outcomes. Just as important is the very concept that privacy should not be forgotten as just a rendering of an external compliance wrapper(Ahmed et al., 2022). On the contrary, it must be integrated very deeply into data schemas, access control lists, event pipelines, segmentation patterns, model design choices, and review What this translates to as far as privacy-oriented threat modeling is concerned, it should not be a separate document, far removed from system architecture. On the contrary, it should be driving force behind architecture decisions regarding the minimum amount of data, data segregation, data retention time, and conditions for data reuse or linking(Iskandarani & Chakrabarti, 2025).

An oft-neglected aspect of full functionality is that privacy and security are not to be viewed as a trade-off. Ideally, a system is designed such that one can have both protective visibility and bounded data use. The issue is not whether to collect any telemetry, but how to design observability in a proportionate and accountable way. Privacy threat modeling is a great way of checking if the intended functionalities of a system can be delivered at the cost of lowering data fidelity, shortening retention, de-identification to a certain extent, or selective monitoring rather than blanket monitoring. Transparency and visibility are the two sides of the same coin. The individuals, as well as the oversight bodies, must be able to see and comprehend that monitoring is going on, understand what data is being processed, and trace the derivation of decisions(Lee et al., 2021). However, disclosure of all the technical details may not always be possible. Still, many problems related to both trust and governance are caused by opaque architectures. Lastly, respect for user privacy claims that systems should be supportive of dignity, agency, and reasonable expectations. Even in the most security- and organizational- sensitive contexts, privacy by design maintains that individuals are not mere data sources for optimization, but human beings whose rights and interests are paramount in the evaluation of a system(Jan et al., 2025).

2.3 Role of Data Flow Analysis in Privacy Risk Identification

Data flow analysis has become the leading method in privacy threat modeling because it is the transmission, processing, and gathering of data within a system that mainly incite privacy risks. Privacy threats cannot be well understood by just examining the database where the data is stored or the user interface through which it was entered. The only way to properly understand a threat is by following the entire lifecycle of the data: the source, the flow, the additions, the linkages, the retention and the disposal or reuse under certain conditions. Drawing data flow charts reveals the actual working environment of the system(Shah et al., 2022). A number of organizations believe that they have a perfect understanding of their data processing only because they are familiar with their key application contents but, in reality, data mostly get duplicated into logs, analytics stores, integration layers, backups, machine learning features, dashboards, exports, and third-party platforms. Each movement is accompanied by a greater possibility of exposure, repurposing, or inconsistent governance. Privacy threat modeling uses data flow diagrams that illustrate these routes clearly and identify trust boundaries where the context, ownership, or sensitivity of data changes. Along with revealing the actual physical storage of the data, data flow analysis also demonstrates the alterations that result in the changes in the type of risk. To be clear, one login event might initially not seem to be very risky but when combined with the device fingerprint, location, role, recent behavior score, and peer-group comparison, it becomes part of a very detailed profile. Likewise, a log file which looks pseudonymous might be a zip code when connected with an identity directory or HR database. Data flow analysis uncovers these interactions and reveals where data thought to be safe is actually more sensitive due to aggregation or situational Ghazal, Hasan, Hussein, et al., 2025).

Another function of data flow analysis is that it assists in reviewing proportionality. By following the movement of data from one step to the next, designers may wonder if each transfer is indispensable given the stated purpose. Is there a need for all events to be associated with a person's identity? Does each monitoring component require the same retention period? Is it actually necessary to keep the content of raw events if the derived indicators suffice for the security task? Such questions pose quite a challenge when asked in the abstract, but once data flows are presented, they become quite tangible(Al-Momani et al., 2025). Therefore, it is no wonder that data flow analysis ranks among the most effective measures for the realization of privacy by design within threat modeling. More importantly, data flow analysis fosters accountability. Privacy harms usually occur when responsibilities are scattered across different teams. One team collects data, another enriches it, third team stores it and last team analyzes it. As a result, not even one team considers itself the owner of the entire privacy outcome. A clear data flow map is a shared architectural picture that supports governance, review, and coordinated mitigation.

Figure 3. Foundational Layers of Privacy Threat Modeling

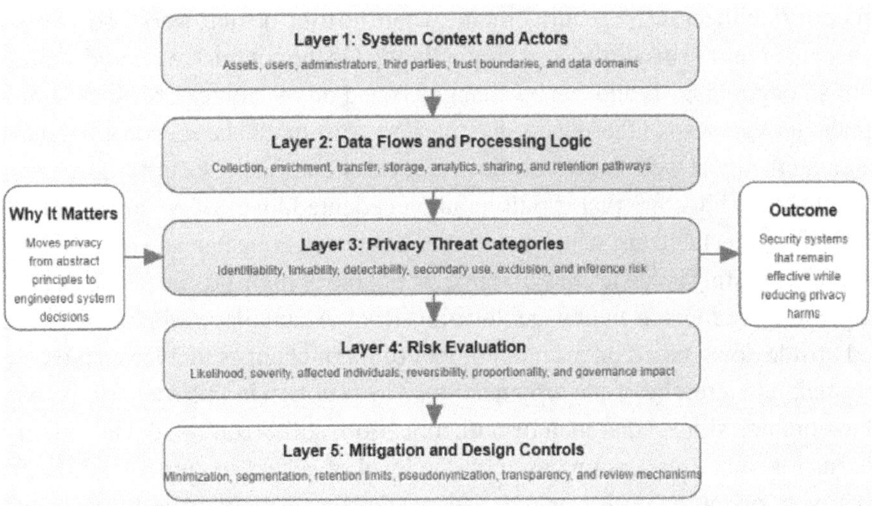

Layered conceptual foundation of privacy threat modeling, moving from system context and data flows to threat categories, risk evaluation, and mitigation controls is shown in Figure 3.

Figure 4. Distinguishing Security Threats from Privacy Threats

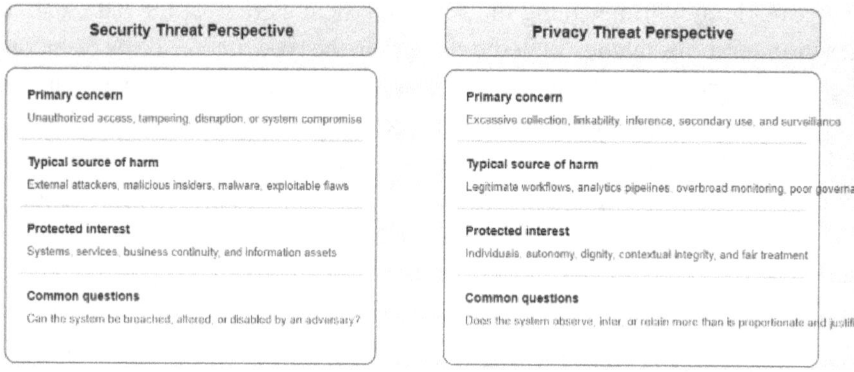

Comparative view in Figure 4 showing how security threats and privacy threats overlap but differ in their protected interests, sources of harm, and evaluation criteria. Feature categorization was performed based on privacy sensitivity, identifiability, linkability, and inference potential to evaluate security–privacy tradeoffs within monitoring environments.

3. TODAY'S SECURITY ARCHITECTURES AND THEIR PRIVACY ISSUES

3.1 Zero Trust Security Architecture and Privacy Challenges

Zero trust security architecture is a security model where no user, device, workload, or session should be trusted simply because they are inside the company network. On the contrary, essentially all access requests are evaluated on an ongoing basis and can be changed based on the context, device posture, policy, and behavioral signals. It is because of these facts that the zero-trust model has become the most widely used and accepted among the most well-known of the present-day enterprise security frameworks. However, it is zero trust security architecture that is putting unprecedented loads of personal and behavioral data at the center of security mechanisms, which may never have been collected and processed before. Such a system can end up mistrusting a whole crew of innocent people or high-profile performers who happen to be working late or logging in from an unusual location(R. D. Alabdallat et al., 2025). The entire system could be turned upside down based on a small number of input changes that have an outsized influence on the decision-making hierarchy of the organization. The problem in this scenario is that the platform will be forced to combine signals that include authentication, authorization, device telemetry, location, and usage patterns for each user session based on the level of access requested and the risk associated with the transaction or operation. This can give rise to a large number of point-to-point interactions that might be very difficult for a user or security analyst to keep all together at once(Shadhar et al., 2025).

What happens in this scenario is the reduction of trust to the point that it becomes never-ending monitoring. It is understood that zero trust is aimed at cutting down on the implicit trust and, as such, leads to an internal structure in which each and every action will be utilized as a potential source of verification data. Another privacy issue with them is merging the identity with the operational and behavioral context. The system may add authentication information, device monitoring data, location tracking, work schedule, and role details into a continuous risk assessment for the person if access choices are based on an aggregate of multiple signals. The risk ratings, in case they become hidden, incorrect, or widely exposed to reviewers, might have an impact on confidence, equality, and ability to Thirdly, there is the aspect of proportionality. Different assets should not be subject to the same level of monitoring(Abualhaj, Al-Khatib, Al-Zyoud, et al., 2025). Yet, zero trust initiatives are often seen as opportunities to impose enterprise-wide, high-intensity visibility without adequately differentiating. This may lead to collecting context signals in a blanket manner even when limited or role-based checks would suffice. In fact, zero trust was designed to bring about equity in roles and responsibilities and to include a continuum of context and trust evaluations with the emphasis on after-the-fact management and monitoring but turned out to be the opposite in practice leading to cross-observations and monitoring internally and scientifically without a clear understanding of what is going on. Privacy violation can be due to transparency, unintentional discrimination, and even identity constraints that can affect the final results. It is, however, possible to engage more closely with the zero-trust architecture through privacy strategy / threat modeling processes, such as: limiting data-fidelity, constraining retention, isolating access evaluation from the broader profiling uses, and ensuring that risk decisions are reviewable and accountable(Masadeh et al., 2025).

3.2 AI-Empowered Security Analytics Platforms

Recently, analytic platforms that use artificial intelligence (AI) and machine learning (ML) techniques to analyze event data and detect security threats have found increased use as components in almost every security program of leading organizations. Such approaches introduce several benefits over traditional security management methods, including throughput level increases, reduced operation costs, higher analyst effectiveness, and faster time to detect and respond due to predictive capabilities. At the same time, the new technological components create crises in security privacy at different levels, especially, at the level of the analytics engine themselves, their datastores, and their decision outputs(Mahadin et al., 2025). The main privacy risk due to AI techniques is the generation of insights or inferences from event data that could reveal the most intimate aspects of a person's life and personality, going well beyond access control decisions that justify their collection. These inferences can be both real and perceived, opening up new avenues for unsuspected and widespread privacy harms in workplace settings. Since most of these AI systems are even more opaque than the human analyst will be, challenging their decision and holding the analyst accountable becomes next to impossible. False positives can lead to not only operational problems but also reputational ones and even procedural consequences in some case(Khaled Abdullah & Qawasmeh, 2025).

Long-term retention, large-scale collection, and feature-rich storage of event and entity data are the driving forces behind many successful machine learning algorithms. This not only contradicts the notion of minimizing data but also results in an increase in the privacy and security risks as the behavioral profile is getting more detailed and the retention duration increases. This gives rise to the possibility of uncovering personal health problems through behavioral anomalies and in other cases finding out about personal matters through indirect cues amongst behavioral patterns and events and leading to not only breaches in personal changes but also to loss of job and social trust. AI should be viewed with the same level of caution as all automated decision-making processes, and there should be the same level of scrutiny when it comes to privacy risks, be it in the form of data retention, data minimization, transparency, or fairness. This is because any security analytics driven by AI can, in fact, be deceitful and misleading in its outcomes, especially when it throws up false positives(Mbasso et al., 2025).

3.3 Security Operations Centers and Privacy Risk Surfaces

SOCs refer to centralized command facilities that coordinate security and breach monitoring, response, and recovery activities across an enterprise or set of clients. A SOC integrates and performs real-time monitoring and analysis of events, incident response management, threat hunting, and daily security operations through the integration of multiple security technologies, processes, and skilled personnel. From a security architecture viewpoint, the SOC is where visibility turns into action. The privacy importance of the SOC is related to aggregation. Data from all corners of an organization can be sent through a SIEM or XDR platform to these analysts and incident responders. While this data aggregation is essential for effective defense, it also inadvertently creates one place where all identity, behavior, communication metadata, device states, access histories, and even external threat contexts may come together. Hence, in the case of a SOC, the risk is not just direct, wired, or overcome(Marhoon et al., 2025). It functions as a powerful for monitoring internal surveillance rather than security defense. Moreover, another leading cause of concern is the interpretation given by analysts who learn to tell stories and construct meaning from data points. They may use logs and other metadata collected during incident response to form a chain of events leading to conclusions about the actors involved etc., this deepening of investigations during incident response, could give rise to accumulation and build-up of privacy exposure. Data ingestion, analyst workflows, lookup permissions, enrichment sources, and case management practices should also be a matter of concern for people who are modeling threats and risks. The possibility of other departments wanting to use the same data for purposes other than security monitoring, i.e., disciplinary, oversight, or productivity evaluation is the third and a very important issue that should not be overlooked. At such a juncture, while the data access may be allowed for a limited security purpose, it is also practically challenging to keep out the other departments' use of the data within the security-related boundaries alone, especially if the security, HR, legal, and leadership functions are closely coupled in the organizational structure. Privacy-oriented threat modeling should identify these governance junctions clearly and define limits around case access, escalation pathways, and permissible use(Khatibi et al., 2025).

3.4 Edge and IoT Security Architectures

The architectures for securing edge and Internet of Things (IoT) expand security monitoring to the physical, operational, and ambient environments while conventional enterprise security oriented around only technology assets is limited to servers, endpoints, and networks. IoT and edge security have to cover hardware like sensors, smart cameras, industrial controllers, medical devices, building systems, wearables, vehicles, and embedded platforms. Hence, these architectures will be found in hospitals, factories, smart cities, energy systems, campuses, homes, and transport environments, among others. Their privacy implications are significant because they often capture not only digital activities but also physical presence, movement, environment, and routine. If security depends on the correct identification of the device, secure communication, anomaly detection, firmware integrity, telemetry monitoring, and event correlation across physical and digital domains, it is likely that location-linked signals, environmental metadata, machine interaction patterns, and device-to-user associations may be collected on a continuous basis. In a smart building, for instance, the security system may include access cards, occupancy sensors, surveillance cameras, wireless beacons, and HVAC analytics(Aldaaja et al., 2025).

Another big privacy concern of edge and IoT security is the ignorance/pervasive/invisibility of the collection. A large number of people under surveillance do not even know what kind of sensors are there, what can be derived from these devices, and how the signals are being retained. Whereas in enterprise systems, the login provides a sense of who you are, what for, when, and where. These systems keep running in the background and their output is not known to the people until it is interpreted in the centralized system. Edge and IoT security may cause granularity and contextual collapse concerns as well. The data that is collected for securing the physical infrastructure can be very revealing and intimate, especially if the patterns of interaction, contact, timing, or routine are exposed. If such data is linked with identity services, organizational roles, or behavior analytics, the architecture may create a persistent map of an individual's life inside these environments thus exposing the physical experience itself to being over-instrumented. Privacy threat modeling is therefore indispensable at this point where one has to analyze at which point the edge telemetry becomes personal monitoring, the potential of using local processing for the reduction of central collection has to be assessed, the data segmentation of the devices and whether retention and linkage are necessary in the first place for the security purpose have to be justified(Babaker et al., 2025).

Figure 5. System Diagram of a Modern Privacy-Sensitive Security Architecture

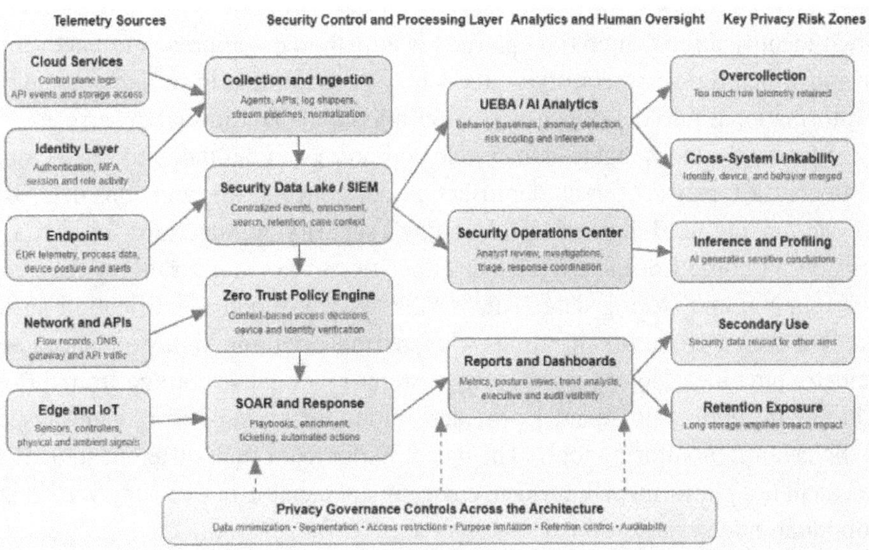

System-level view of a modern security architecture in Figure 5 shows how telemetry from cloud, identity, endpoint, network, and edge environments flows into centralized security processing, analytics, and SOC operations, where key privacy risks emerge.

Figure 6. Privacy Exposure Across Major Modern Security Architecture Types

Architecture Type	Security Value	Primary Data Inputs	Privacy Implication
Cloud Native	Elastic security visibility across workloads, services, and APIs	Control plane logs, service traces, application events, cloud identities	Telemetry sprawl and third-party processor expansion
Zero Trust	Continuous contextual verification for access control	Identity, device posture, location, session context, behavior signals	Persistent monitoring of users and continuous scoring of activity
AI Security Analytics	Anomaly detection, prioritization, weak-signal identification	Historical events, behavioral data, enriched features, risk indicators	Opaque inference, profiling, and false positive consequences
SOC-Centric	Centralized monitoring, triage, incident coordination	Organization-wide logs, cases, identity lookups, investigation context	Visibility concentration and expanded internal access to personal data
Edge / IoT	Protection of physical-digital systems and operational environments	Sensor feeds, device states, location, environmental and ambient signals	Ambient surveillance and collection without clear user awareness

Figure 6, Comparative overview of five major modern security architecture types, shows the relationship between their security value, primary data inputs, and privacy

4. PRIVACY THREAT IDENTIFICATION TECHNIQUES IN SECURITY ARCHITECTURE

Privacy threat identification centered on privacy is a methodical approach to uncover, analyze, and record the ways in which the very security systems may pose a threat to or damage the data, personal autonomy, or informational fairness dimension of an individual. Traditional cybersecurity modeling is primarily centered around attacks that lead to system compromise, unauthorized access, or disruption of infrastructure. In contrast, privacy threat identification goes beyond this and considers risks that come about just by system being used legitimately. In today's security architectures, in fact, a great deal of privacy threats doesn't come from attackers, but rather from how monitoring systems are collecting, interpreting, correlating, and storing data. This makes privacy threat identification an indispensable architectural skill or even a art for organizations who are implementing highly advanced detection, analytics, and telemetry pipelines. Nowadays, security systems rely on data coming from different layers of operation, including the endpoints, identity providers, cloud services, network gateways, collaboration platforms, and behavioral monitoring tools. The data coming from such different sources when pooled into centralized analytics platforms will form an environment capable of exposing very detailed patterns about both individuals and organizations(Hussain et al., 2025).

Privacy threat arises when the architecture handles excessive data processing, keeping signals after the operational needs have been met, reveals sensitive attributes of the individual from their behaviors, or allows secondary uses that are not related to the original security objective. Machine learning models that are built to spot anomalies or suspicious patterns are often based on past behavioral data as well as other features. These systems improve the detection abilities but at the same time, they open the door for profiling, misclassification, or unjustified assumption making. Therefore, threat modeling is not limited to the analysis of data that is being collected but also considers the analytical transformations applied to this data(R. Alabdallat et al., 2025). A privacy threat can be posed by models that turn operational telemetry into decision-making judgments against individuals, especially if the organisms will use these judgments to make decisions about individuals. Lifestyle awareness is another required facet of privacy threat identification. In general, security telemetry undergoes several phases: collection, ingestion, normalization, correlation, analysis, alert generation, investigation, reporting, and retention. At every stage, there is the possibility for privacy to be compromised. For instance, data collection may involve the gathering of unnecessary identifiers, correlation may lead to joining data sets that were initially separate, investigations may raise issues by revealing details that are unrelated to the incident, and retention policies may let sensitive historical data persist indefinitely(Zraiqat, Batiha, et al., 2025).

Hence, effective privacy threat identification should encompass the lifecycle since it explains the flow of information across architectural layers. Current privacy threat identification is also facilitated by coupled working and cross-pollination of ideas between different disciplines. Security engineers, privacy officers, data scientists, lawyers, and governance teams are just a few of the stakeholders who hold different viewpoints of system functioning and risk. Facilitation of threat modeling workshops which bring these diverse stakeholders together helps to bring to light the hidden assumptions regarding data flows and system behavior. For example, while engineers may take for granted that telemetry fields are anonymous, privacy specialists understand that the same fields become identifiable when correlated with identity logs or device registries. Through planned analysis meetings, organizations are able to detect such risks of linkability before they get embedded into operational systems(Tarek et al., 2025).

4.1 STRIDE Based Privacy Threat Modeling

STRIDE was first created at Microsoft. It is a very popular threat modeling method for security threat analysis within software systems. The initial letters from each of the six threat categories - Spoofing, Tampering, Repudiation, Information Disclosure, Denial of Service, and Elevation of Privilege - form the abbreviation STRIDE. STRIDE is commonly used to pinpoint security gaps; however, with some modifications, it can be a powerful instrument for privacy threat identification in data-centric security architectures as well. For privacy-oriented threat modeling, the framework's main focus is on the information disclosure aspect, although to a lesser extent, it also incorporates how the other threat categories may lead to the exposure of personal data indirectly. In terms of privacy, one of the spoofing risks is that the identity signs within monitoring data might get altered or attributed to wrong persons(Hiari et al., 2025). Thus, if the attackers succeed in obtaining the login data or faking the identity of a device, then these security systems might associate the suspicious actions with innocent users. This, firstly, constitutes a security risk and, secondly, it is also a privacy violation because the activity might be wrongly linked to someone else. In-service threat detection should therefore also foreshadow effect of identification and assurance on monitoring pipelines.

Tampering threats involve changes in the data used for monitoring purposes either end route or in storage. As an example, attackers who alter security logs or event records may hide malicious intent or frame someone else. In terms of privacy, such tampering may cause the generation of misleading behavior profiles or completely misinterpret user behavior. Ensuring integrity through cryptographic logging, secure transmission channels, and tamper-evident storage therefore is paramount not only for security but also for privacy accuracy(Qaddara & Alraba'nah, 2025). Repudiation threats are manifested through the capability of denying having done something. In highly monitored environments, the privacy of a user can be compromised through disclosure. Monitoring might result in the production of records where the level of detail makes it almost impossible to change or add context to the interpretation. So, while security investigations require the evidential capability that accountability provides, storing very detailed activity logs may be viewed as invasive to privacy. To that end, a security threat model should be implemented to control log granularity.

Denial of service threats mainly have an impact on system availability but through chain reactions, they could also lead to privacy violations. One example of this is when, because of the failure of a monitoring system during denial of service attack, the emergency recording mechanisms are triggered to obtain the detailed data typically gathered during a forensic analysis. In another case, malfunctioning systems may temporarily disable the anonymization or filtering features. A proper privacy threat model ought to investigate how emergency or fallback mode operations may increase exposure of sensitive data(Braik et al., 2025). Elevation of privilege threats refer to situations where attackers gain access to systems or privileges that are above their authorized level. In the framework of security monitoring, gaining privileged access to analytics or investigation tools could enable insiders or attackers to view sensitive telemetry beyond their authorization level. Therefore, threat models should predict cases where there could be a privilege escalation exposing personal data along with implementing role-based access controls, audits, and separation of duties.

4.2 Linkability and Inference Risk Analysis

Linkability and inference risk analysis concentrate on understanding to what extent data items that appear separate and unrelated are capable of revealing sensitive or personal information when they are combined. With a modern security architecture, it is quite normal that telemetry coming from different locations gets correlated in order to spot any signs of abnormality or suspicious behavior. Even though correlation is one of the ways to increase the detection capabilities, on the other hand, it may be creating very powerful mechanisms for obtaining individual behavior profiles. Linkability is when multiple datasets have common attributes that make it possible for them to be connected. For instance, endpoint logs may expose device identifiers, while identity provider logs have user accounts that are associated with those devices(Alibakhshikenari et al., 2025). Records of network traffic might also contain IP addresses given to those devices. When these datasets are consolidated within a security analytics platform, they will be capable of exposing a continuous chain linking together users, devices, locations, and activities. So, even though each dataset on its own may seem harmless and non-sensitive, the combination of them may lead to very detailed behavioral profiles of the targeted individuals being created. Inference risk is the possibility that analytical or computational models arrive at certain conclusions about individuals based on the analysis of aggregated data. The security analytics platforms that organizations employ frequently carry out behavioral analysis in order to identify anomalies, insider threats, and accounts that have been compromised. These behavioral models may come up with attributes that describe the individual, such as recognizing different working hours from the rest of the group, access to systems that are not typical, and deviations from the peer group. Some of these traits might reveal the health status of an individual that explains their working hours or, indirectly, their personal situation based on their behavior(Abualigah et al., 2025).

Apart from the mentioned factors, linkability also incorporates temporal correlation as a major aspect. Most security logs typically have timestamp data which security analysts refer to, while trying to determine the chronological order of events. This is an excellent help for incident response teams. However, the same feature may reveal certain information about a person's privacy such as their daily life, movement, and whom they interact with. Consequently, privacy threat analysis should not only identify the use of time stamps at the level of detail but also decide if they can use aggregation and rounding methods to sufficiently reduce the exposure without significantly affecting security analysis(Alraba'nah et al., 2025). In addition, it is important to understand that the dangers of linkability can occur not only within the organization but also outside. Nowadays, a great number of security systems integrate threat intelligence feeds, geolocation databases, and behavioral enrichment services that are external. Actually, it is the same process of joining internal telemetry with these external datasets, therefore producing new insights which were not purpose of the system designers. For instance, combining login locations with travel databases can lead to revealing employee movement patterns. As a result, threat modeling should not only focus on the consequences of privacy breaches at the level of citizens but also on the effects of these enrichment processes on global privacy To lower the chances of linkability and inference risks, entities can apply design techniques that protect privacy such as tokenization, pseudonymization, feature abstraction, and controlled data joins. Besides vis-a-vis the limitation of the ability to fully reconstruct identity narratives, these techniques still permit security analytics to function properly. Architectural elements that are most appropriate to get these privacy controls applied to are pinpointed by threat identification(Ayub et al., 2025).

4.3 Privacy Risk Assessment Frameworks

Privacy risk assessment tools are a great help in organizing the process of identifying and mitigating risks related to privacy threats. Aside from the fact that technical risk frameworks focus primarily on vulnerabilities, privacy risk frameworks take a thorough approach in direct impact, consideration of the wider context, and the incorporation of human factors. Often, they will base their assessments on factors such as data sensitivity, scale of operations, degree of identifiability, potential harmful effects, and existing governance controls. One of the very popular Privacy Risk Assessment Tools involves a two-dimensional assessment of how a privacy event risk could happen and the severity of such event should it occur. The dimensions here are probability and impact. Probability refers to the likelihood of a privacy event given the current architectural and operational setup. Impact refers to the effects should such an event occur, which can range from loss in reputation and lawsuits to disruptions in operations and the distress of individuals. Organizations can use such information to decide on what kind of treats to prioritize(Abdel-Jaber, Abdel-Jaber, et al., 2025).

Privacy risk evaluation should be mindful of a wider range of factors, including the cultural context and societal norms. Security monitoring systems generally exist in work or occupied settings where individuals have limited opportunity to refuse or withdraw from data collection. Therefore, compliance with the idea of proportionality becomes even more important. Evaluation procedures should include an assessment/check of whether monitoring practices are in line with legitimate security objectives and the availability of alternative means that would be less intrusive, for instance, data collection with less of an emphasis on identifying the individual. Another effective tool in the privacy risk evaluation toolkit is a governance assessment. It is almost impossible to manage privacy risks by just technical measures. The use of data and its security guarantees depend heavily on the contribution of organizational policies, worker training, and monitoring operations. Importantly, if one were to evaluate risk levels in this realm, one would have to look at how access controls are implemented, how frequently log files are audited, and how very privacy features are being incorporated into one's incident response processes(Alraba'nah & Hiari, 2025).

Privacy risk assessment frameworks take transparency and accountability as their main point of departure. By recording their threat detection and threat reduction plans, organizations also make a traceable record available which could be used to demonstrate that the system is responsibly designed. This record, therefore, supports compliance with legal provisions, stakeholder trust, and the workings of internal governance mechanisms. In fact, formal privacy impact assessments are a legal requirement in most locations, whenever processing on a large-scale basis of personal data is carried out. On the other hand, privacy risk assessment methodologies ought to be integral elements of wide-ranging security governance frameworks rather than merely standalone practices. Security staff normally carry out threat assessment for cyber, infrastructure, and operational resilience threats. Incorporating privacy issues into these regular activities means that data protection will become a key item of the design of application and infrastructure, instead of just an additional feature. Such a combination allows for the creation of security blueprints that not only defend digital resources but also uphold individual rights and organizational Nisar et al., 2025).

Figure 7. Privacy Threat Identification Framework in Security Systems

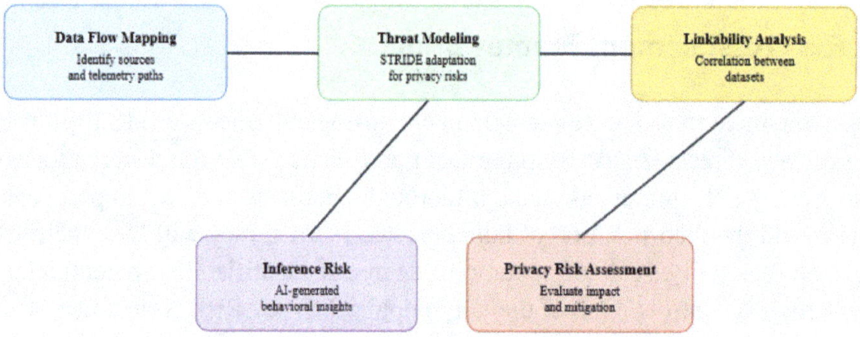

Illustrated in the Figure 7, this conceptual framework lays out the steps for identifying privacy threats in contemporary security architectures. It begins with data flow mapping and then proceeds to threat modeling, linkability analysis, inference risk evaluation, and finally structured privacy risk

5. PRIVACY THREAT MODELING METHODOLOGIES AND FRAMEWORK INTEGRATION

5.1 LINDDUN Privacy Threat Modeling Framework

LINDDUN is considered one of the most prominent and comprehensive tools tailored for privacy threat modeling. As a new perspective to the already existing security threat modeling, LINDDUN aims at pointing out privacy threats that come majorly due to the different facets of information processing. The letters in the acronym stand for 7 high-level categories of privacy threats: Linkability, Identifiability, Non-repudiation, Detectability, Information disclosure, Content unawareness, and Policy noncompliance. Each of these denotes a different slice of personal data exposure or its unauthorized use within a system.

For instance, linking is all about the power to connect two or more pieces of information to the same individual or entity. In security monitoring, linkability often occurs when telemetry data from multiple systems is combined in a centralized analytics platform. For example, endpoint logs, authentication records, and network activity might all hold identifiers that enable a security analyst to piece together a very detailed behavioral history of a user. Although such ability is critical for incident investigation, it also leads to privacy issues not only if correlated data access is not properly controlled. Identifiability means that data can be connected directly or indirectly to a person. Often times in security, telemetry initially looks anonymous because only machine-generated identifiers like device IDs or session tokens are in the records. However, once these identifiers are cross-referenced with identities in user management systems or organizational directories, person behind monitored activities is typically revealed. When LINDDUN is used for privacy threat analysis, one of the major concern is deciding whether it is absolutely necessary to have original user identity present for security analysis or simply exposing pseudonyms would suffice(Aldabbas et al., 2025).

Detectability is yet another privacy issue as it arises from the ability of an observer to discover whether a person exists in a system or dataset. In monitoring environments, just a few queries can reveal if a user has logged into a system or if a particular device has been generating some type of activity. Even if the genuine content is guarded, the proficiency to determine one's presence may be equated to exposing highly sensitive information like roles or activities inside a company. Non-repudiation ensures that an individual cannot disown having done something. Accountability in security systems typically depends on solid audit trails. Conversely, very intimate monitoring may sometimes keep a permanent record of an individual's behavior beyond what security norms allow. LINDDUN's notion attempts to find the middle ground between giving one a right to be held accountable and conducting exposure to fit privacy norms. Content unawareness or lack of consent/knowledge refers to situations where individuals are not informed about the collection or utilization of their data. Members of staff alongside users may in general not know all details regarding the monitoring system inside their workplaces. Extensive and clear policies, regular updates, proper documentation management can significantly lessen the possibility of this happening. Policy non-compliance is a case where the system's behavior contradicts the organization's policies or legal obligations. For instance, a surveillance system may gather data with security intentions but the storage period is significantly beyond the company's policy. LINDDUN threat modeling will serve the purpose to uncover if a system is in a position to enforce those policies. The LINDDUN method provides the design team a way to identify even the ones that are a little difficult to see within intricate security ecosystems through exhaustive categorization of privacy threat Abashes et al., 2025).

5.2 Privacy by Design Principles

Privacy by Design is a systemic method to ensure privacy is at the heart of the system architecture and development practices. Instead of addressing potential privacy violations after deployment, it advocates for privacy considerations to be continuously integrated through the life of the system. Through this early intervention, Privacy by Design is fully compatible with security engineering approaches where the goal is to build-in risk management and resilience capabilities during design rather than fitting them as an afterthought. The cornerstone of the Privacy by Design is the emphasis on prevention rather than remediation through reactive measures. Apart from being conceived as a "checklist" item by security professionals, system designers are required to proactively think of ways to minimize the exposure of data and ensure privacy enhancements through the use of access control, data encryption, and other privacy-respecting techniques when working with the design of monitoring tools, analytics engines, and telemetry pipelines(Ramesh et al., 2025). Closely aligned with the concept of minimal data processing, the second most frequently quoted pillar is data minimization. Considering the actuality where security camera footage or PCs endowed with video feed a security center, it should be remembered that just enough data that talks to the level of security coverage is the rule rather than exception. Besides, data minimization can contribute to the forestalling of so many privacy leaks, human errors, and scandals at the same time.

Transparent processing is equally one of the elements of Privacy by Design. Monitoring systems that gather data without users being informed are inherently flawed. At an enterprise level, transparency is achieved through policies, staff awareness programs, and proper documentation. Transparency is a great way of enhancing trust and thus legitimate monitoring practices. Security as the necessary protector of collected privacy data constitutes another principle of the Privacy by Design concept. As telemetry can contain personal data of users, a system that fails to adequately safeguard this data is a weak link and a liability for the entire enterprise. Therefore, apart from good policies, physical security controls and continuous monitoring of active and passive security countermeasures should be implemented(Abuowaida et al., 2025). To conclude, Privacy by Design moves us from a 'tick-box' to an accountable privacy culture where organizations build in appropriate procedural and governance mechanisms to ensure that architectural safeguards remain effective not just now but also in the long run.

Table 1. Comparison of Major Privacy Threat Modeling Methodologies

Methodology	Core Objective	Key Analytical Focus	Application in Security Architectures	Primary Advantages
LINDDUN Framework	Identify privacy threats within system architectures	Linkability, identifiability, detectability, policy compliance	Evaluating telemetry correlation, behavioral monitoring systems, and identity linkage	Structured threat categorization and systematic privacy analysis
Data Protection Impact Assessment (DPIA)	Evaluate legal and organizational privacy risks before deployment	Data processing purpose, proportionality, and impact evaluation	Assessing monitoring platforms, analytics systems, and large-scale logging infrastructures	Regulatory alignment and formal risk documentation
Privacy by Design	Integrate privacy protections directly into system architecture	Data minimization, transparency, security safeguards	Designing monitoring pipelines, access controls, and retention policies	Proactive privacy protection embedded in system design
STRIDE Adaptation for Privacy	Extend traditional security threat modeling to include privacy risks	Information disclosure, identity misuse, data integrity	Evaluating logging infrastructure, monitoring interfaces, and analyst privileges	Integration with existing security threat modeling workflows
Linkability and Inference Analysis	Identify risks created by data correlation and AI analytics	Behavioral inference, dataset linkage, predictive modeling	Analyzing SIEM correlation engines and AI-driven security analytics	Detection of hidden privacy risks arising from data aggregation

Table 2. Key Stages of the DPIA Methodology for AI Security Systems

DPIA Stage	Main Activities	Objective
System Description	Document architecture, purpose, and operational context of the AI security system	Establish understanding of system scope and objectives
Data Identification	Identify categories of personal data and map data flows across the architecture	Determine how personal information enters and moves through the system
Risk Evaluation	Assess likelihood and severity of privacy risks associated with data processing	Identify potential impacts on individuals' rights and freedoms
Risk Mitigation	Implement technical and organizational safeguards to reduce identified risks	Ensure security operations remain proportionate and compliant
Continuous Review	Monitor system performance and update DPIA when system changes occur	Maintain long-term governance and regulatory compliance

6. DESIGNING PRIVACY-AWARE THREAT MODELS FOR SECURITY MONITORING SYSTEMS

6.1 Privacy-Aware Data Collection Strategies

Privacy-aware data collection strategies basically strive to limit the recording of personal data during security monitoring, while still allowing the analytical benefit that is necessary for threat detection. Security telemetry is typically generated at endpoints, network devices, authentication services, and cloud platforms. These sources supply large amounts of operational data that may contain personally identifiable information such as usernames, device identifiers, IP addresses, and application usage patterns. Thorough threat modeling is necessary to identify which parts of this telemetry are crucial for finding malicious activities and which parts are dispensable. The most widely used approach is selective logging where logging agents capture only those fields that are of interest from a security analysis perspective. Suppose, for example, that an endpoint security system logs process execution events but only saves entire command-line arguments when a suspicious behavior has been identified. By the same token, a network monitoring system may store aggregated traffic data rather than raw packets. Through selective logging the exposure of private information is kept at a minimum level as only a limited amount of raw data enters the surveillance pipeline(Hanandeh et al., 2025).

A different choice would be to replace identifying aspects i.e. pseudonymization at collection. Rather than conveying actual usernames or device identifiers to central analytics sites, surveillance agents may substitute these entities with tokens. Carrying out this anonymization allows analysts to link events related to the same actor but without having the knowledge of their actual identity unless an authorized investigation is opened. If the identity must be determined, the authorized party can retrieve the original data from a secured lookup table. Privacy-aware collection methods may also be based on the idea of time granularity. In detailed analysis of event logs, timestamped recording of events is a common practice which may expose a user's behavioral pattern. However, in many cases, the use of set intervals for data aggregation can produce results quite adequate for analysis and at the same time minimize the risk of piecing together exact behavioral sequences. Hence the change of timestamp accuracy could be an effective privacy barrier. Lastly adaptive logging strategies could come into play where the level of detail of telemetry is raised only when an incident that arouses suspicion comes to light. Under normal circumstances monitoring systems only record the bare minimum that is necessary for supporting baseline security analysis. When anomalies appear, the logging detail is temporarily ramped up for the identity that is of concern. This approach results in a win-win situation where security visibility is maintained but the gathering of high-detail behavioral data is not done incessantly(Alnsour et al., 2025).

6.2 Access Control and Monitoring Governance

Controlling access points is one of the main pillars of privacy-aware threat modeling because they can both limit and enable the exploitation of security telemetry data. Even a stealthy misuser could take the help of such capabilities and conduct unauthorized searches for personal information completely unrelated to security investigations. Role-based access control has become the standard solution to this problem. Based on their assigned roles, analysts get a set of permissions defining exactly what sensitive fields they can see and what types of queries they can perform. Thus, a junior level analyst might only be allowed to look at system-generated anonymized alerts and, at the same time, be blocked from being able to retrieve raw identity information. In the same manner, a senior-level investigator who, incident response-wise, is the main role to correlate identity data, gets all the privileges necessary to fetch the required identifying information securely. In this way, the exposed data is kept at a minimum and at the same time the chances of unnecessary exposure are minimized. Moreover, monitoring governance also consists of recording through logs the manner in which analysts work with security data(Masango et al., 2025). Collectively, query logs, investigation records, and access events are kept and made available so that the usage of monitoring systems can be understood at any point in time. If an analyst is found accessing telemetry that deviates from a legitimate investigation the governance team can use the audit logs to unravel and respond to the incident. Such mechanisms that combine accountability and transparency raise the overall confidence in the monitoring system. Organizations may even go as far as requiring separation of duties to further enhance governance. Operating or maintaining the monitoring infrastructure without having the entire data access capabilities at their fingertips will be an example of such a measure. At the same time, analysts doing investigations may not be allowed to have admin rights to change system configurations. Besides, such compartmentalization of roles would prevent undetected exposure to monitoring and misuse of data by one single person. On the other hand, training and policy communication is a major piece of monitoring governance. Security team members should be aware of the privacy implications of the data they analyze, as well as the restrictions on the use of that This awareness is best accomplished through consistently implemented training programs that not only inform but also remind the staff about their responsibilities and reinforce organizational compliance(H K et al., 2026).

6.3 Privacy Preserving Security Analytics

Privacy-preserving security analytics aim at constructing a reporting mechanism on the threat levels that are reflected from micro-level telemetry, thereby avoiding exposing the identity of the person involved, or compromising on privacy in any other way. It is a fact that security platforms are continuously embedding machine learning models that can single out anomalous behaviors within a massive volume of telemetry data which does not always lead to privacy and discrimination issues risks however such human attributes counting changes represent only a few among the traumas that human beings experience in real life. A commonly used feature of privacy-preserving analytics is featuring abstraction. The idea here is to switch from using identifiable data to using features that characterize behavior patterns without disclosing the actual identities. Another method revolves around ideas such as differential privacy or data anonymization techniques which aim at incorporating some type of regulated noise or randomness into public This can effectively foil analysts from pulling out individual records even if they are given aggregated datasets. While differential privacy is often applied in large scale data analysis scenarios, it can also be the basis of privacy-aware security analytics. Federated learning is yet another technique that holds promise for privacy-preserving security analytics(I. Khan et al., 2026).

This is a decentralized learning model whereby machine learning algorithms are run on the local systems and only updates to the models - rather than data itself - are shared with a central repository. Besides, the decision-making power remains local as well. Federated learning is still in its infancy as far as practical implementations are concerned but it could be a path forward to advanced analytics without concentrating sensitive telemetry in a single repository. Lastly, privacy-preserving analytics must take into consideration the explainability of machine learning decision-making. Whenever security models produce risk scores or anomaly classifications, the person who investigates should be able to understand substantially the reason for those outputs. Having a transparent model greatly diminishes the chances of misunderstanding, and at the same time, contributes to the safeguarding of both privacy and security objectives.

Table 3. Architectural Components of Privacy-Aware Security Monitoring Systems

Architectural Component	Function in Security Monitoring	Potential Privacy Risk	Privacy-Aware Mitigation Strategy
Endpoint Telemetry Collectors	Gather process activity, system events, and device status	Exposure of user behavior patterns and system usage	Selective logging and pseudonymization of identifiers
Identity Monitoring Systems	Track authentication events and access attempts	Linkability between identities and behavioral data	Tokenization and controlled identity resolution
Network Monitoring Sensors	Observe traffic flows and connection patterns	Reconstruction of communication relationships	Aggregated flow statistics instead of packet-level logging
SIEM / Security Data Lake	Centralized storage and correlation of security telemetry	Large-scale aggregation of identifiable data	Segmented storage and restricted analyst access
Security Analytics Engines	Analyze telemetry to detect anomalies and threats	Behavioral profiling and inference risk	Feature abstraction and privacy-preserving analytics techniques
Security Operations Center Interfaces	Provide dashboards and investigation tools for analysts	Unauthorized exploration of user activity	Role-based access control and audit logging

7. IMPLEMENTATION OF PRIVACY THREAT MODELS IN ENTERPRISE SECURITY OPERATIONS

7.1 Embedding Privacy Threat Models Into SOC Workflows

The security operations center (SOC) workflow is a direct way to implement privacy threat models in enterprise security operations. SOC workflows govern how alerts are handled, from initial reception, triage, investigation, escalation, to closure. Since these workflows regulate everyday access to security telemetry, they also establish how much personal and behavioral data the analysts come across during the different stages of the incident lifecycle. Implementing a privacy-aware approach starts with identifying which fields and contextual data are actually necessary at each step. During the first phase of alert triage, the analysts mostly require a very limited amount of information to classify the event as normal, suspicious, or critical(Hanumanthagowda et al., 2026). Dashboards can display converted signals like device risk category, anomaly score, type of policy deviation, or the count of event clusters. In case the alert is considered abstract/low confidence or closed without delay, exposure to the personal data is minimized. Out of all the ways to put privacy threat models into practice in the SOC, this is the simplest yet most powerful by far. The interface itself embodies the principle of least visibility. When cases are advanced from triage to a thorough investigation, additional information may be warranted. Nevertheless, a privacy-centric environment must stipulate requirements and limits for such a data increase. Pseudonymized identities might be de-anonymized only after an alert has met a certain level of severity or confidence, or perhaps a supervisor-approved escalation must be entered into the case system. In this manner, privacy exposure is both occasion-driven and accountable rather than a regular occurrence. Also, it is less likely that architecture will leak highly detailed person-level information in connection with each low-quality or speculative alert generated by automated systems.

Querying capabilities pose a challenge, too, when implementing workflows. Analysts frequently perform unplanned searches in order to link events over periods, systems, and users. Without proper control, such searches could lead to the construction of extensive behavioral records that have no connection to the immediate security query. Therefore, a privacy-aware implementation may forbid certain query joins, dispense sensitive fields, or place a requirement for a justification tag for highly scoped searches involving identity, location, or historical pattern correlation. Such restrictions will not necessarily lead to detection capability reduction. Instead, they will align the analyst's access with the level of investigative need(Dinler et al., 2025). Management of cases also constitutes a workflow element of high importance. Notes from investigations, screenshots, evidence enriched, and entities linked are individually capable of becoming privacy-sensitive records. Over-collecting contextual details to be captured by SOC personnel could lead cases to become long-term repositories of personal behavior. Defining what evidence can be recorded, how long-case artifacts are stored, and when certain fields must be redacted or archived separately should go a long way to eliminating such risk. The investigative work should not become a source of secondary privacy exposure over and above the original telemetry. Lastly, the audit dimension cannot be ignored: were analysts to access de-anonymized records, perform sensitive joins, or retrieve historical behavior patterns, these actions would need to be logged and subject to a review. Audit records act as a lever of accountability as well as provide means for organizations to check whether privacy threat model controls are operational and effective under pressure of operations. There is more: they also serve as a springboard for continual improvement when it turns out that workflows are overly permissive or unduly restrictive(Qawaqneh et al., 2025).

7.2 Implementing Privacy Controls in Detection Engineering and Analytics

Detection engineering concerns itself with the creation of correlation rules, anomaly models, behavioral detections, and automated alerting logic. It is a linchpin in modern enterprise security operations because, after the choice of their signals, it is detection engineering that determines which ones become visible, how they are understood, and what contextual data is appended to them. For this reason, privacy threat model implementation must reach into the detection engineering aspect as well. Field-level review while developing use case is one of the first steps in implementation. Detection engineers, when making a rule or model, should be able to assess exactly which telemetry fields are essential for detection. Quite frequently, even though only a subset of fields is used for the detection logic, the whole lot of the fields available are forwarded through the monitoring pipeline into the analytics engines. This leads to exposure that could have been avoided. One other thing that is required in a privacy-conscious environment is that engineers must not only justify why a sensitive field is used but also must eliminate or render abstract those fields that do not bring a significant performance improvement. These kinds of reviews should be done prior to deployment of the detections to production streams(Llwaah et al., 2025).

Another important control is enrichment logic. Detections usually get complemented by providing additional contextual information such as department, job role, device owner, geographic location, peer group comparison, prior incident history, or baseline deviations of access. Sure, these kinds of enrichments can make triage more efficient, but they may also lead to profiling individuals, or at least revealing nonessential contextual data. For this reason, privacy-aware detection engineering should specify which enrichment categories are permissible by default, which ones require escalation, and which ones should remain hidden unless the investigation is at a confirmed stage. Ultimately, the alerts should still be significant without disclosing comprehensively what the system knows about the subject by default(Ghazal, Awouda, Hasan, et al., 2025). Machine learning and behavioral analytics detections, in particular, are very sensitive when it comes to implementation. These rely on a long history of data and feature sets that describe interaction patterns over substantial periods. The execution of privacy threat models is done through model governance mechanisms like feature minimization, explainability review, limited production of categories, and retention time limits on raw training data. Should there be a case of a model producing person-level risk scores, the organization is responsible for deciding the level of access, validation method, false positives handling, and the possibility of score reuse other than in cybersecurity operations. Without such mechanisms, detection engineering might unknowingly contribute to the rise of quasi-profiling systems masked as security

Figure 8. Privacy-Aware Enterprise Security Operations Workflow

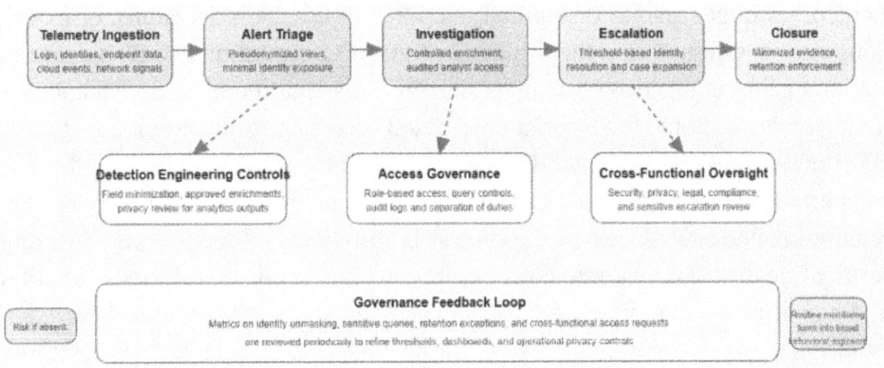

Implementation also includes testing and simulation. Before a new rule or model is put into action, the organization can run test scenarios to determine if it unnecessarily reveals identity data or if it results in a large number of low-confidence alerts that require human review on a wide scale. Also, it is tested whether the model is keeping the contextual details beyond the intended use case. Testing from a privacy perspective is a step forward for quality assurance: mere detection won't do. It has to be proportionate and regulated in a way that it results in minimal collateral privacy Alongside detection engineering standards appropriate to privacy-aware environments, those practices can be formalized by a mature implementation. In requiring data element assessments, documented rationale for sensitive enrichments, approval checkpoints for person-level risk outputs, and retention policies for analytics features and alert artifacts, such standards serve to integrate privacy threat modeling into the technical logic of enterprise monitoring rather than limiting it to a mere policy utterance(Abualhaj, Al-Khatib, Abu-Shareha, et al., 2025). The findings indicate that effective threat detection can be maintained while reducing privacy exposure through controlled data collection, pseudonymization, and proportionate monitoring practices.

7.3 Governance, Escalation, and Cross-Functional Oversight

Privacy threat models will not be implemented effectively in enterprise security operations unless governance structures are in place to define ownership, escalation, review, and accountability. Technical controls do count, but decision-making frameworks that elucidate when more intrusive data access becomes permissible and who is the one authorized to make that decision are necessary as well. Identifying privacy-sensitive workflows in the field of security clearly require not only ownership of those workflows but also clarity in the ownership. In many cases, security engineering controls tooling, SOC leadership is responsible for analyst operations, identity teams manage access signals, and privacy teams issue policy interpretations(Matarneh et al., 2025). Failure to unify ownership will likely lead to implementation gaps. A realistic setting is one in which security teams have operational control, while privacy and governance stakeholders are involved in design review, escalation policy, and periodic audit. This way, the false dichotomy between "security owns everything" and "privacy reviews everything too late" is avoided. Cross-functional oversight is a must also because the impact of security telemetry extends beyond just the technical defense. For instance, insider threat probes might involve HR, legal, ethics, and senior leadership. Security data could easily become a generic evidence source for reining in one's behavior, if no governance mechanism is in place. Hence, the privacy-conscious implementation should identify the routes along which oversight is to be exercised vis-à-vis widely used cases, especially those whose outcomes might lead to disciplinary action, employment decisions, or external reporting. This goes a long way in safeguarding the principle of purpose limitation and also decreases the risk of security operations being equated with managerial surveillance(Abdel-Jaber, Makhoul, et al., 2025). Privacy-aware governance should incorporate role-based access control, audit logging, and documented escalation procedures to ensure accountability and prevent misuse of monitoring data.

Introducing periodic review is another aspect of governance implementation. Working groups or review boards can be created to look into topics such as high-risk detections, de-anonymization incidents, unusual patterns of analyst queries, retention exceptions, and requests for cross-functional data. The knowledge and experience in the institution thus developed will contribute to the gradual refinement of boundaries of operations. Maintaining a way for the detection of whether privacy threat models are being overridden under organizational or operational pressure is another benefit of such reviews. Last but not least, measurable indicators have a hand in governance implementation as well. By tracking the frequency of identity unmasking, the fraction of alerts resolved without de-anonymization, the number of sensitive query joins performed, the duration of investigative artifact retention, and the instances in which access to monitoring data was requested by non-security stakeholders, enterprises have access to evidence regarding whether the privacy threat model is in fact directing operations. Is interpreting such metrics and making decisions about them the prerogative of human judgment? Certainly yes, but they do give a glimpse of the privacy threat model's influence on the practical workings.

Table 4. Implementation Controls for Privacy Threat Models in Enterprise Security Operations

Operational Area	Typical Security Function	Privacy Risk if Uncontrolled	Implementation Control	Expected Outcome
SOC alert triage	Classify and prioritize alerts	Identity and behavior exposed too early in low-confidence cases	Role-based alert views with pseudonymized identifiers by default	Reduced unnecessary exposure during routine triage
Detection engineering	Build rules, models, and enrichments	Excessive field use and nonessential contextual profiling	Field-level justification review and enrichment approval standards	More proportionate detections with lower privacy impact
Analyst querying	Search and correlate events across systems	Reconstruction of broad behavioral histories unrelated to the case	Restricted joins, justification tags, and query audit logs	Traceable and purpose-limited investigative access
Incident escalation	Expand investigation scope for confirmed threats	Uncontrolled de-anonymization and overbroad evidence gathering	Formal escalation thresholds and supervisor-approved identity resolution	Privacy exposure linked to verified security need
Case management	Store findings, notes, and artifacts	Long-term retention of sensitive person-level investigation detail	Evidence minimization rules and differentiated retention policies	Lower residual privacy risk after case closure
Cross-functional access	Share security data with HR, legal, or leadership	Secondary use beyond cybersecurity purposes	Governance review and purpose-limited access decisions	Stronger separation between defense and organizational oversight

8. EMPIRICAL EVALUATION OF PRIVACY THREAT MODELING IN SECURITY ARCHITECTURES

8.1 Dataset Description and Experimental Methodology

The methodologies using this dataset as the environment for reference are grounded in the fact that the data is a rather accurate depiction of enterprise network monitoring as opposed to older intrusion datasets. According to the official documentation, the dataset contains both benign and attack classes and that the capture period was from 9 a.m. Monday, July 3, 2017, to 5 p.m. Friday, July 7, 2017. Monday consists of only benign traffic while the other days depict attack scenarios such as Brute Force FTP, Brute Force SSH, DoS, Heartbleed, Web Attacks, Infiltration, Botnet, and DDoS. Apart from the dataset design and documentation source, the labeling process is also based on timestamp, source and destination IPs, source and destination ports, protocol, and attack information which is a highly relevant dimension for privacy analysis because these are exactly the kinds of fields that create traceability and linkage across sessions or devices. The empirical methodology employed uses the formation of a privacy perspective as a layer, which is added to the feature schema of the dataset. The methodology does not solely measure the ability to detect attacks, but it dichotomizes attributes in the dataset into the following five categories of privacy-sensitive features: direct network identifiers, traffic behavior metrics, temporal features, flow-direction statistics, and session correlation attributes. Each group is then analyzed by using privacy scoring based on the four dimensions of threats identified: identifiability, linkability, behavioral inference potential, and retention sensitivity. The scores range from 1 (low privacy sensitivity) to 5 (high privacy sensitivity).

This scoring is based on the fact that even though SourceIP, DestinationIP, FlowID, SourcePort, DestinationPort, and Protocol fields are very valuable for security purposes, on the other hand, they represent high-risk privacy attributes because they allow the direct or indirect linking of activities over time and different systems. At the same time, timing details and flow statistics are considered as being moderate to high risk since although they do not identify a subject directly, when combined they can be used to create behavioral signatures. Less directly identifying elements such as abstract numerical flow features, even though they are not strongly tied to a single identity, can still be very significant in large-scale analytics or machine learning to infer characteristics. This approach permits the framing of security and privacy issues in one analysis frame, as they can be seen as two sides of the same coin. Therefore, this methodology generates two deliverables. Firstly, a privacy leakage map of the dataset feature space is produced which shows areas where the exposure is most likely to be generated by monitoring data. Secondly, a security–privacy tradeoff interpretation is produced which shows feature families that are most effective in attack detection as well as those that are most sensitive from a privacy standpoint. This structure is very worthwhile from the perspective of enterprise security architecture, as it parallels the design dilemma that organizations in the real-world face: not whether telemetry is useful, but which telemetry is proportionate and how it should be controlled.

Table 5. Dataset Overview and Privacy-Relevant Attributes for CICIDS2017

Element	Description	Privacy Relevance
Dataset name	CICIDS2017	Representative modern intrusion detection benchmark
Official source	Canadian Institute for Cybersecurity (UNB)	Primary source for dataset design and documentation
Public mirror	Kaggle mirror of CICIDS2017	Supports accessibility for chapter replication
Capture period	July 3–7, 2017	Multi-day monitoring enables behavioral continuity analysis
User profile basis	25 users	Raises linkability and routine-pattern concerns
Attack coverage	Brute Force FTP, Brute Force SSH, DoS, Heartbleed, Web Attack, Infiltration, Botnet, DDoS	Suitable for security analytics benchmarking
Flow extraction method	CICFlowMeter	Produces flow-based fields central to privacy-risk interpretation
Feature volume	More than 80 network traffic features	Large feature space increases inference capacity
Labeled fields	Timestamp, SourceIP, DestinationIP, SourcePort, DestinationPort, Protocol, Attack label	Core attributes for identifiability and correlation

8.2 Privacy Leakage Risk in Security Monitoring Logs

The first point of a privacy-oriented interpretation of the data is that privacy risk is heightened whenever identity-bearing fields and correlation-friendly fields coexist in security monitoring logs. Direct IP information, ports, timestamps, flow identifiers, and protocol-level context come together in the CICIDS2017 feature structure to provide a comprehensive observability surface. Though no explicit human-readable username may be present in the flow data, repetitive network identifiers and timing relations may offer reconstruction of activity chains. Such chains are rarely analyzed in isolation in enterprises. They are, instead, often matched with identity, endpoint, or asset inventories, which significantly raise the concern of privacy exposure. Direct network identifiers account for the biggest threat in terms of data leakage. Source and destination IP addresses provide enormous value for intrusion detection thanks to their ability to help identify communication endpoints, scanning behavior, lateral movement, or exfiltration paths. However, they also offer one of the strongest routes to identifiability, particularly when security architecture is already aware of which device or employee corresponds to a particular address or subnet. Flow identifiers exacerbate this problem by supporting continuity across events. In a centralized SIEM or data lake, these fields provide the backbone of a behavioral reconstruction engine(Qawasmeh et al., 2025).

The second major source of privacy leakage that must not be underestimated is the temporal arrangement of monitoring data. Timestamp fields look like simple operations with no side effects, but they nonetheless represent privacy issues if they are collected over multiple days or linked to a device and network context. For example, a user's daily work pattern or an unusual schedule can be revealed through timestamps. Also, after-hours access, surge patterns, or frequent communication structures can be deduced from them. A timestamp by itself is quite less sensitive to privacy issues. But if a timestamp is used along with flow identifiers and endpoint mapping, it turns into a behavioral signature(Nandal et al., 2025). Therefore, privacy threat modeling should consider not only if the time is recorded but also the precision of time-related data, retention, and the scope of correlation. The proxy layer of behavioral inference that comes from flow statistics is the third mode of leakage. Packet counts, durations, byte distributions in each direction, and patterns of protocol interaction are necessary for anomaly detection, yet they can also be used to make model-based deductions about the manner of system usage, the normality of traffic, and the purposes behind The privacy threat model would be scarcely complete if it did not cover such subtle channels of leakage through pattern-derived features over time, which the above paragraph specifies as the technical implementation(Laha et al., 2025).

Table 6. Derived Privacy Leakage Assessment by Feature Group

Feature Group	Example Fields	Identifiability (1–5)	Linkability (1–5)	Inference Potential (1–5)	Retention Sensitivity (1–5)	Overall Privacy Risk
Direct network identifiers	SourceIP, DestinationIP, SourcePort, DestinationPort, FlowID	5	5	4	5	Very High
Temporal features	Timestamp, event sequence, session duration markers	3	5	4	5	High
Traffic behavior metrics	Packet counts, byte counts, flow duration, rate measures	2	4	5	4	High
Flow-direction statistics	Forward/backward packet lengths, directional counts	2	4	4	4	Moderate to High
Session correlation attributes	Protocol, attack label, multi-feature joins, flow continuity	3	5	5	4	Very High

8.3 Comparative Evaluation of Threat Modeling Frameworks

To get a clear picture of privacy risk management in modern security architecture, one will have to understand the various threat modeling approaches. Security-only models will understandably emphasize the attack detection value and system compromise risks and mostly focus on how malicious traffic, abnormal sessions, and protocol misuse are identified through flow data. On the other hand, a privacy-aware framework would analyze whether these same features lead to identity traceability, excessive linkage, or inference risk. One of the benefits of a STRIDE approach is that it may be used to detect information disclosure, privilege misuse, and integrity threats in a security platform. It also describes the consequences of an adversary gaining unauthorized access to logs, SIEM dashboards, or enrichment features, that is, it exposes monitoring data. However, STRIDE does not adequately address the issue of cumulative privacy harms caused by legitimate, authorized correlations. It is great at identifying breaches and misuse but not so much at deciding whether an architecture might produce normal, constant visibility at a level that is disproportionate to privacy norms.

LINDDUN-based privacy threat modeling overcomes such shortfalls and is well-aligned with the concept of privacy leakage in monitoring systems since it naturally addresses linkability, identifiability, detectability, information disclosure, and policy noncompliance. A CICIDS2017-style monitoring environment presents risks that go beyond direct disclosure of one's identity in terms of LINDDUN-based privacy threats: they include the repeated exposure of entities, sessions becoming linked, and cross-system identity matching. The fact that LINDDUN captures privacy threat concepts so effectively in telemetry-heavy environments is the reason why it is the primary framework to be used in this chapter for privacy threat interpretation. DPIA-oriented threat modeling provides important governance and proportionality considerations, which is a very different scope from determining whether certain attacks are left undetected or the network is insecure. In situations where the ethical issue at hand is the justification for the scale and purpose of monitoring, a DPIA becomes a necessary tool. A natural follow-on to this is that DPIA is highly relevant to and a critical piece of overall implementation decisions even if it remains unaware of the technical details at the architecture-level threat mapping. The takeaway from this is that different frameworks highlight different aspects of privacy risks. It is therefore imperative to embrace an integrated approach to threat modeling for security and privacy. The one that will give the strongest results is one that layers STRIDE, LINDDUN, and DPIA-style review on top of each other.

Table 7. Comparative Interpretation of Threat Modeling Frameworks for the CICIDS2017 Monitoring Context

Framework	Strongest Contribution	Limitation in Privacy Analysis	Best Use in This Chapter
STRIDE (adapted)	Highlights information disclosure, privilege abuse, and log access risks	Less precise for cumulative behavioral surveillance and linkability	Technical control analysis for monitoring platforms
LINDDUN	Directly captures linkability, identifiability, detectability, and disclosure	Requires more explicit data-flow mapping effort	Primary privacy threat interpretation framework
DPIA-style assessment	Supports necessity, proportionality, retention, and governance review	Less detailed for low-level technical threat enumeration	Organizational and legal validation of monitoring scope
Combined use	Balances technical, privacy, and governance perspectives	Requires cross-functional coordination	Most suitable approach for enterprise implementation

8.4 Impact of Privacy Controls on Threat Detection Utility

Can privacy controls have an impact on threat detection? This is one of the principal issues that interest a privacy-oriented security designer. Reality is, the relationship is more complicated. Not all privacy controls trade off with analytical utility. Role-based access restrictions, shortest default retention times for raw logs, and analyst dashboards that have been pseudonymized primarily reduce human exposure without impacting model performance. Other controls such as removing key identifiers or aggressive feature suppression might have a more direct impact on detection. Identifying which controls maintain detection value while reducing avoidable privacy risk is the objective here. If one examines the CICIDS2017-style feature space, a strong detection is fully possible even if the direct identifiers are pseudonymized during initial triage. A SIEM will still be able to correlate the events, even though the inquiring analyst will not be able to reveal the actual endpoint or individual. Only when the case is escalated to a higher level of validation is full identity resolution carried out. This means that at the level of operations, improvements in privacy can be made without significantly degrading the ability to detect DDoS, brute force, infiltration, and other attack patterns.

Retention stratification is also another privacy control that renders the trade-offs less challenging because it allows one to still preserve security value while at the same time achieving a reduction in long-term privacy exposure. One may keep the raw, identity-rich telemetry for a very short time, whereas the abstract features and aggregate indicators may be kept for a longer time for the purpose of trend analysis and model training. This way, the loss of signals used for immediate defense is prevented while enabling a reduction in exposure through breaches and long-horizon profiling of employees. Besides the alert itself, other decision-making aspects of security handling are often quite dependent on data from the early lifecycle, so not all raw fields have to be kept indefinitely. That said, some privacy controls entail compromises(Abualhaj, Abu-Shareha, et al., 2025). Certain investigations will be hampered if, for example, IP fields are entirely removed (rather than using a reversible pseudonymization technique to protect them) or if session-orders are lost resolution due to heavy timestamp generalization. Incident response would slow down if correlation between flow and endpoint context was totally inhibited. It is rare that the design option is maximal privacy versus maximal visibility. Most often, it is something along the lines of bounded visibility in which security function is maintained along with provisions for controlling who sees what, when, and under what justification.

Table 8. Privacy Controls and Their Expected Effect on Security Utility

Privacy Control	Privacy Benefit	Expected Effect on Detection Utility	Recommended Use
Pseudonymized identifiers in triage dashboards	Strong reduction in unnecessary analyst exposure	Minimal effect during early triage if correlation tokens remain stable	Default control
Supervisor-approved identity unmasking	Prevents routine person-level visibility	No major effect if escalation workflow is efficient	High-value control
Short retention for raw identity-rich logs	Reduces long-term exposure and breach impact	Low to moderate effect depending on forensic needs	Recommended with archival policy differentiation
Aggregated or sampled time views for routine monitoring	Reduces detailed behavioral reconstruction	Low effect for posture monitoring; moderate effect for deep forensics	Use selectively
Removal of nonessential enrichment fields	Reduces contextual overexposure	Minimal if enrichment is not central to rule logic	Strongly recommended
Full deletion of key network identifiers	Maximizes privacy but reduces traceability	High negative effect for investigation and attribution	Usually not recommended; prefer tokenization

9. FUTURE DIRECTIONS IN PRIVACY-ORIENTED SECURITY ARCHITECTURE

9.1 Explainable Artificial Intelligence in Security Analytics

AI forms the most important part of Security operations currently. Through machine learning models, one can detect a network anomaly, malware classification, generate prioritized alerts and even attack predictions. Although, this way, we get the ability to huge scale detection very quickly, that is only on the surface, these new ways of detection bring a cornucopia of privacy and governance concerns. Since the AI models are going to analyze behavioral data to point to risk levels or suspicious activities, the classification behind risk scoring must be transparent enough to allow accountability and support human decision-making. Explainable AI (XAI) is seen as a major help in the making AI deliver on its promise while keeping the requirements of good governance including privacy intact. XAI eventually translates to unwrapping the black-box models into human-intelligible logic, e.g., features or behaviors that contributed to a specific outcome. Within privacy-oriented threat modeling, such facility to explain helps security practitioners validate whether AI is basing its suspicion on, e.g., a valid security feature or personal characteristics, which are potentially privacy infringements. To illustrate, anomaly detection in a user's behavior may flag the person for suspicious/illegal activity due to various reasons like strange login time, being in a geographical location not seen before, or even running an unusual operation for the user. Doing away with XAI, the analysts would be in a tough spot as they really don't know what led to the creation of this alert, so the model's verdict is taken as the gospel(Rabbi et al., 2025).

9.2 Federated Security Analytics and Decentralized Monitoring

Federated security analytics and decentralized monitoring represent a powerful counterpoint to the high degree of dependency of traditional security architectures on centralized data lakes or security information and event management (SIEM) systems that gatekeep organizational telemetry. While at first glance, the approach of centralizing all data for analysis may appear to be simple, by doing so a single environment storing sensitive information is created raising both privacy risks and the impact of a potential breach. Through federated learning, the model training is conducted locally on datasets physically distributed without raw data being ever shared centrally. In other words, federated learning sends the ML model to the participants rather than vice versa. Each node conducts its operations locally and communicates only summary-level data back to the coordinator(Ghazal, 2025b). By means of privacy-oriented security monitoring, the federated modus operandi can drastically minimize the risk of disclosure of raw identifiers and behavior markers. This conception allows endpoint systems, cloud services, and divisions within an organization to partake actively in threat detection without their entire telemetry streams being laid bare. Furthermore, this model is indispensable in multi-organizational threat intelligence sharing where the partners are rarely allowed by data sensitivity and regulatory considerations to share the raw data. Edge computing technology is another piece of the puzzle to support the idea of the decentralized monitoring as the threat detection is possible near to data. For example, an endpoint protection platform is capable of carrying out local behavioral analysis while communicating only the alert of the abnormal behavior to the central system. This not only minimizes the transmission of user activity logs in detail but also is favorable for very fast detection of the malicious behavior. By that analogy, one can consider decentralized security architectures as a way of seeking the fine balance between the physical monitoring capacity and the privacy protection. The fewer centralized data hoards, the more diminishes the possibility of security systems being the sole storehouses of huge quantities of personal behavioral Ghazal, Hasan, Raju, et al., 2025).

9.3 Toward Integrated Privacy-Aware Security Ecosystems

The ultimate goal of threat modeling with a focus on privacy is enabling security ecosystems where privacy is a fundamental element throughout system design. So, security analytics platforms, identity management systems, endpoint monitoring tools, and governance frameworks capable of working harmoniously under the same privacy-aware architectural setting. Besides, in those kinds of places, the only signals that are really needed for defense are taken as telemetry, the identifiers are secured through pseudonymization or encryption, and the analytical models are subjected to transparent Only when the risk is escalated, incident investigation workflows reveal sensitive data, and automated systems are designed to support human oversight rather than replace it. New methods that can quantitatively capture the interplay between privacy exposure and security effectiveness will be the subject of future studies. Parameters for measuring privacy leakage, the degree of monitoring proportionality, and the effectiveness of governance could be added to the list of classic cybersecurity performance indicators such as detection accuracy and response time. Organizations, by the incorporation of privacy metrics into security evaluation frameworks, will have the means of assessing the societal impact of their defensive infrastructures in parallel with their technical performance. The change of privacy-oriented security architecture symbolizes the far-reaching changes that are taking place in digital governance. As the digital domain continues to grow in importance, security operations will be viewed as legitimate only if they not only succeed in their primary objective but also respect fundamental human rights and adhere to ethical principles. Privacy-aware threat modeling provides the conceptual and methodological framework for bringing about this balance. The combination of privacy-enhancing technologies, explainable artificial intelligence, decentralized security architectures and human-centered governance systems will enable future security systems to effectively defend organizations against cyber threats while upholding the dignity and privacy of individuals whose data they Privacy expectations may differ across employees, customers, system users, and external actors; therefore, proportionality assessments should be adapted to the operational context.

REFERENCES

Abashes, G. M., Elshqeirat, B., Abu-Shareha, A. A., & Alshraideh, M. (2025). BEYOND THE NOISE: UNVEILING MEANINGFUL PATTERNS IN MOBILE PAYMENT DATA USING FUZZY LOGIC AND SVM. *Journal of Theoretical and Applied Information Technology*, *103*(1).

Abdel-Jaber, M. tasime, Makhoul, N., Abdel-Jaber, M. en, & Beale, R. (2025). Cost prediction for product development using hybrid deep learning model: a meta-heuristic model. *Multimedia Tools and Applications, 84*(27). DOI: 10.1007/s11042-024-20437-y

Abdel-Jaber, M., Abdel-Jaber, M., Beale, R., & Makhoul, N. (2025). UHSC flexural strength prediction using optimized three-phase classifier and improved feature selection. *International Journal on Interactive Design and Manufacturing*, *19*(5), 3201–3218. Advance online publication. DOI: 10.1007/s12008-024-01812-3

Abualhaj, M. M., Abu-Shareha, A. A., Al-Khatib, S. N., Alsaaidah, A. M., & Anbar, M. (2025). Improving firewall performance using hybrid of optimization algorithms and decision trees classifier. *IAES International Journal of Artificial Intelligence*, *14*(4), 2839. Advance online publication. DOI: 10.11591/ijai.v14.i4.pp2839-2848

Abualhaj, M. M.I, Al-Khatib, S. N., Abu-Shareha, A. A., Almomani, O., Al-Mimi, H., Al-Allawee, A., Daoud, M. S., & Anbar, M. (2025). Spam Detection Boosted by Firefly-Based Feature Selection and Optimized Classifiers. *International Journal of Advances in Soft Computing and Its Applications*, *17*(3). Advance online publication. DOI: 10.15849/IJASCA.251130.02

Abualhaj, M. M., Al-Khatib, S. N., Al-Zyoud, M., Qaddara, I., Hiari, M. O., & Aldossary, S. M. A. (2025). Enhanced Network Communication Security Through Hybrid Dragonfly-Bat Feature Selection for Intrusion Detection. *The Journal of Communication*, *20*(5). Advance online publication. DOI: 10.12720/jcm.20.5.607-618

Abualigah, L., Alomari, S. A., Almomani, M. H., Zitar, R. A., Migdady, H., Saleem, K., Smerat, A., Snasel, V., & Ezugwu, A. E. (2025). An enhanced Walrus Optimizer with opposition-based learning and mutation strategy for data clustering. *Array (New York, N.Y.)*, *26*, 100409. Advance online publication. DOI: 10.1016/j.array.2025.100409

Abuowaida, S., Abu Owida, H., Shelash Mohammad, S. I., Alshdaifat, N., Abu Elsoud, E., Alazaidah, R., Vasudevan, A., & Alshurideh, M. T. (2025). Evidence Detection in Cloud Forensics: Classifying Cyber-Attacks in IaaS Environments using machine learning. *Data and Metadata*, *4*, 699. Advance online publication. DOI: 10.56294/dm2025699

Ahmed, Z. E., Hasan, M. K., Hashim, A. A., Saeed, R. A., Mokhtar, R. A., Singh, S. P., & Ghazal, T. M. (2022). Optimization Procedure for Intelligent Internet of Things Applications. *2022 International Conference on Business Analytics for Technology and Security, ICBATS 2022*. DOI: 10.1109/ICBATS54253.2022.9759065

Al-Adwan, A. S., & Abdeljaber, O. (2025). Toward a resilient and smart supply chain: identifying and prioritizing barriers to metaverse adoption. *International Journal of Industrial Engineering and Operations Management*. DOI: 10.1108/IJIEOM-06-2025-0113

Al-Daoud, K. I., Yogeesh, N., Mohammad, S. I., Raja, N., Chetana, R., William, P., Vasudevan, A., Alshdaifa, N., & Hunitie, M. F. A. (2025). Explainability in AI Using Fuzzy Inference Systems For the Regression Problem. *Applied Mathematics & Information Sciences*, *19*(5), 973–987. Advance online publication. DOI: 10.18576/amis/190501

Al-Momani, M. M., Alqudah, T. A., Al Swiety, I. A., Mahrakani, N., Nassoura, M. B. A., & Al Attar, M. K. (2025). Integrating Artificial Intelligence (AI) and Business Intelligence (BI): A Framework for Improving Enterprise Performance. *TEM Journal, 14*(3). https://doi.org/DOI: 10.18421/TEM143-26

Al-Suhimat, R. I., Mohammed Ai, N., Ibrahim, A., Maaitah, N. O., & Al-Dmour, N. A. (2024). Review of Security Challenges Encountered in Internet of Things Technology. *2nd International Conference on Cyber Resilience, ICCR 2024*. DOI: 10.1109/ICCR61006.2024.10533052

Alabdallat, R., Abualhaj, M., & Abu-Shareha, A. (2025). Android Malware Detection Using a Modified Dwarf Mongoose Algorithm. *International Journal of Intelligent Engineering and Systems*, *18*(8), 336–351. Advance online publication. DOI: 10.22266/ijies2025.0930.21

Alabdallat, R. D., Abualhaj, M. M., & Abu-Shareha, A. (2025). Enhanced Multiclass Android Malware Detection Using a Modified Dwarf Mongoose Algorithm. *International Journal of Analysis and Applications*, *23*, 248. Advance online publication. DOI: 10.28924/2291-8639-23-2025-248

Aldaaja, Y., Odeh, M., Badrakhan, S. S., Sabri, M., Abdelrahim, Y., Samara, G., & Alsabatin, H. (2025). Quantifying the Managerial and Practical Benefits of Cloud Computing on Information Security in Higher Education Institutions. *Applied Mathematics & Information Sciences*, *19*(1), 15–24. Advance online publication. DOI: 10.18576/amis/190102

Aldabbas, A., Baniata, L. H., Alsaaidah, B. A., Mustafa, Z., Alali, M., & Rateb, R. (2025). Artificial intelligence-driven method for the discovery and prevention of distributed denial of service attacks. *IAES International Journal of Artificial Intelligence*, *14*(1), 614. Advance online publication. DOI: 10.11591/ijai.v14.i1.pp614-628

Alibakhshikenari, M., Ali, E. M., din, I., Virdee, B. S., Ullah, S., Khan, S., See, C. H., Saber, T., & Limiti, E. (2025). Millimeter-Wave MIMO Array with Low Interactions Between its Antenna Elements for Fifth Generation Wireless Communication Networks. *Journal of Infrared, Millimeter and Terahertz Waves*, *46*(7), 46. Advance online publication. DOI: 10.1007/s10762-025-01062-8

Almajed, R., Ibrahim, A., Abualkishik, A. Z., Mourad, N., & Almansour, F. A. (2022). Using machine learning algorithm for detection of cyber-attacks in cyber physical systems. *Periodicals of Engineering and Natural Sciences*, *10*(3), 261. Advance online publication. DOI: 10.21533/pen.v10i3.3035

Alnawafleh, N. M., Ibrahim, A., & Pradhan, M. R. (2024). Review of the Mechanisms Used to Protect the Big Data from Attacks. *2nd International Conference on Cyber Resilience, ICCR 2024*. DOI: 10.1109/ICCR61006.2024.10533073

Alnawayseh, S. E. A., Al-Sit, W. T., & Ghazal, T. M. (2022). Smart Congestion Control in 5G/6G Networks Using Hybrid Deep Learning Techniques. *Complexity*, *2022*(1), 1781952. Advance online publication. DOI: 10.1155/2022/1781952

Alnsour, Y., Alsharo, M., Al-Essa, M., & Smerat, A. (2025). AI-Powered Election Insights: Predicting the 2024 Trump vs. Kamala Election Showdown with Machine Learning. *Journal of Intelligent Systems and Internet of Things*, *15*(1), 185–197. Advance online publication. DOI: 10.54216/JISIoT.150116

Alraba'nah, Y., Al-Sharaeh, S., & Al Hindi, G. (2025). Enhancing Intrusion Detection Using Hybrid Long Short-Term Memory and XGBoost. *Journal of Soft Computing and Data Mining*, *6*(1). Advance online publication. DOI: 10.30880/jscdm.2025.06.01.016

Alraba'nah, Y., & Hiari, M. (2025). Improved convolutional neural networks for aircraft type classification in remote sensing images. *IAES International Journal of Artificial Intelligence*, *14*(2), 1540. Advance online publication. DOI: 10.11591/ijai.v14.i2.pp1540-1547

Arabiat, A. M., & Eljaafreh, Y. G. (2025). Intrusion Detection in Wireless Sensor Networks Using ML Based Classification of Denial of Service (DoS) Attacks. *The Journal of Communication*, *20*(4). Advance online publication. DOI: 10.12720/jcm.20.4.501-514

Ayub, N., Imtiaz, M. A., Ali, E., Alqahtani, A. M., Ali, A., Ashurov, M., Albouq, S., & Law, F. L. (2025). A Decision Framework for Intra Task Fixed Priority INTEL PXA270 Distributed Architecture for Soft RT-Applications Based on Deep Learning. *Engineering. Technology and Applied Science Research*, *15*(3), 23553–23558. Advance online publication. DOI: 10.48084/etasr.10006

Babaker, S., Khatibi, A., Alsoud, A. R., Kaur, J., Jagtap, J., Alkhayyat, A., & Shah, S. K. (2025). Improving Reliability and Data Management in Internet of Things Based Wireless Sensor Networks. *Internet Technology Letters*, *8*(6), e646. Advance online publication. DOI: 10.1002/itl2.646

Braik, M., Kassaymeh, S., Almiani, M., Albashish, D., Awadallah, M., Bataineh, B., & Al-Hiary, H. (2025). Advancements in global optimization with an empowered capuchin search algorithm. *Neural Computing & Applications*, *37*(24), 19707–19749. Advance online publication. DOI: 10.1007/s00521-025-11421-0

Dinler, Ö. B., Bektemyssova, G., Şahin, C. B., Montazeri, Z., Dehghani, M., Smerat, A., Werner, F., & Eguchi, K. (2025). Carpenter Optimization Algorithm: A Human-inspired Metaheuristic for Robust and Efficient Constrained Optimization. *International Journal of Intelligent Engineering and Systems*, *18*(11), 344–357. Advance online publication. DOI: 10.22266/ijies2025.1231.21

Elkaradawy, A., Elshenawy, A., & Harb, H. (2025). Enhancing Cloud Job Failure Prediction With a Novel Multilayer Voting-Based Framework. *IEEE Access : Practical Innovations, Open Solutions*, *13*, 140600–140613. Advance online publication. DOI: 10.1109/ACCESS.2025.3593808

Ghazal, T. M. (2025a). An IoT-Based Active Learning Convolutional Neural Networks Model for Predicting River Water Quality. *Journal of Soft Computing and Data Mining*, *6*(1). Advance online publication. DOI: 10.30880/jscdm.2025.06.01.021

Ghazal, T. M. (2025b). Federated Learning for Intelligent Sensing and Navigation Technologies for 6G Communications. *Journal of Sensors, 2025*(1). DOI: 10.1155/js/3746147

Ghazal, T. M., Awouda, A. E., Hasan, M. K., Rahman, A. H. A., Islam, S., Saeed, R. A., Elshafie, H., Iqbal, A., & Hussein, A. H. (2025). Knowledge Learning for Securing Workflow Scheduling Algorithm in Mobile Edge Computing. *Mobile Networks and Applications*, *30*(3-4), 395–413. Advance online publication. DOI: 10.1007/s11036-025-02465-6

Ghazal, T. M., Hasan, M. K., Hussein, A. H., Pandey, B. K., Ahmad, M., Safie, N., & Cascone, L. (2025). Federated Learning With Small and Large Models With Privacy-Preserving Data Space for Holographic Internet of Things in Consumer Electronics. *IEEE Transactions on Consumer Electronics*, *71*(2), 5259–5274. Advance online publication. DOI: 10.1109/TCE.2025.3573033

Ghazal, T. M., Hasan, M. K., Raju, K. N., Khan, M. A., Alshamayleh, A., Bhatt, M. W., & Ahmad, M. (2025). Data Space Privacy Model with Federated Learning Technique for Securing IoT Communications in Autonomous Marine Vehicles. *Journal of Intelligent & Robotic Systems*, *111*(3), 84. Advance online publication. DOI: 10.1007/s10846-025-02298-1

H K, P. K., Dash, R., K, J. R., Mohapatra, B., Bishoyi, S. S., Bajaj, M., & Blazek, V.H K. (2026). Multi-domain fault characterization in DC microgrids utilizing Hilbert-Huang transform ensemble by LSTM networks with adaptive boundary condition constraints. *Results in Engineering*, *29*, 108721. Advance online publication. DOI: 10.1016/j.rineng.2025.108721

Hanandeh, A., Alfreijat, S. Y., Qutieshat, R. J., Alsha'ar, H. Y., Kilani, Q. A. L., & Saleem Khasawneh, M. A. (2025). Implementing AI Accuracy, Learning Rate, Inference Time on enhancing Big Data Analysis and Strategic Plan. *Data and Metadata*, *4*, 637. Advance online publication. DOI: 10.56294/dm2025637

Hanumanthagowda, P. B., Vasanthkumara, M. K. M., Al-Nussairi, A. K. J., Hadi, A. A., Smerat, A., & Shivanna, P. B. (2026). Process-aware Temporal Graph Embedding for Detecting and Localizing Recurring Concept Drift. *International Journal of Intelligent Engineering and Systems*, *19*(1), 402–422. Advance online publication. DOI: 10.22266/ijies2026.0131.25

Hiari, M., Alraba'nah, Y., & Qaddara, I. (2025). A Deep Learning-Based Intrusion Detection System using Refined LSTM for DoS Attack Detection. *Engineering. Technology and Applied Science Research*, *15*(4), 25627–25633. Advance online publication. DOI: 10.48084/etasr.11499

Hussain, K., Ali, E. M., Hussain, W., Raza, A., & Elkamchouchi, D. H. (2025). Robust OTFS-ISAC for Vehicular-to-Base Station End-to-End Sensing and Communication. *Electronics (Basel)*, *14*(21), 4340. Advance online publication. DOI: 10.3390/electronics14214340

Hyassat, A. S., Abu Zayed, R. E., Al Khateeb, E. A., Shalaldeh, A., Abdelhamied, M. M., & Qaddara, I. (2025). Unveiling Cyber Threats: An In-Depth Study on Data Mining Techniques for Exploit Attack Detection †. *Engineering Proceedings*, *104*(1), 28. Advance online publication. DOI: 10.3390/engproc2025104028

Iskandarani, M. Z., & Chakrabarti, K. (2025). Adaptive Frequency and Energy Modeling Framework for Robotic Wireless Sensor Networks Based on Path Loss Predictions. *Journal of Robotics, 2025*(1). DOI: 10.1155/joro/6156608

Jan, F. U., Badar, R., Sami Al-Shamayleh, A., Uehara, A., Senjyu, T., & Akhunzada, A. (2025). Soft Computing-Based Damping Controllers With Online Parameters Tuning for Stability Enhancement of Power Systems. *IEEE Access : Practical Innovations, Open Solutions, 13*, 167045–167060. Advance online publication. DOI: 10.1109/ACCESS.2025.3612288

Khaled Abdullah, S., & Qawasmeh, R. (2025). *Navigating the ethical and legal risks of AI marketing in Jordanian SMEs*. EDPACS., DOI: 10.1080/07366981.2025.2600205

Khan, A. A., Siddiqui, S., Al-Shamayleh, A. S., Akhunzada, A., & Dey, I. (2025). DFROG-MAC: A Dynamic Fragmentation-Based MAC for Prioritised Emergency Data Management in Vehicular Networks. *IET Wireless Sensor Systems*, *15*(1), e70017. Advance online publication. DOI: 10.1049/wss2.70017

Khan, I., Shao, Y., Rahman, S. U., Ullah, H., Altayeb, M., Kamal, M. M., Altameem, A., & Altameem, T. (2026). A metamaterial Fabry-Perot MIMO antenna with circular polarization for 5G and satellite communication. *Measurement : Journal of the International Measurement Confederation*, *261*, 119942. Advance online publication. DOI: 10.1016/j.measurement.2025.119942

Khatibi, A., Babaker, S., Praveen, K. N. R., Chohan, J. S., Jadhav, A., Alsoud, A. R., Ramudu, M. J., & Jeet, R. (2025). Advanced AI-Driven Cybersecurity: Analyzing Emerging Threats and Defensive Strategies. *National Academy Science Letters*. Advance online publication. DOI: 10.1007/s40009-025-01897-8

Laha, S. R., Smadi, K. Al, Habboush, A. K., Pattanayak, B. K., Pattnaik, S., & Mohanty, B. (2025). Smart Waste Management Framework for Green Cities: Integrating IoT, LoRa, and Deep Learning for Efficient Waste Classification and Management. *Tikrit Journal of Engineering Sciences, 32*(Special Issue 1). DOI: 10.25130/tjes.sp1.2025.1

Lee, S. W., Hussain, S., Issa, G. F., Abbas, S., Ghazal, T. M., Sohail, T., Ahmad, M., & Khan, M. A. (2021). Multi-Dimensional Trust Quantification by Artificial Agents through Evidential Fuzzy Multi-Criteria Decision Making. *IEEE Access : Practical Innovations, Open Solutions*, *9*, 159399–159412. Advance online publication. DOI: 10.1109/ACCESS.2021.3131521

Llwaah, F., Hussein, A. H., & Ghazal, T. M. (2025). Enhancing Cloud Resource Utilization Through Synthesizing Intensive Workflow Tasks. *Journal of Wireless Mobile Networks, Ubiquitous Computing and Dependable Applications*, *16*(4), 537–555. Advance online publication. DOI: 10.58346/JOWUA.2025.I4.030

Mahadin, G. A. L., Satvika, S., Kathuria, S., Kaushik, A., & Maranan, R. (2025). DEEP LEARNING FRAMEWORK FOR IDENTIFYING AND HYBRID SYNTHESIZING WIDESPREAD NEWS HEADLINES ON SOCIAL MEDIA. *Proceedings on Engineering Sciences*, *7*(3), 1453–1462. Advance online publication. DOI: 10.24874/PES07.03.007

Marhoon, H. M., Basil, N., Sabbar, B. M., Qasem, N., & Ma'arif, A. (2025). Safety and Surveillance on Unmanned Aerial Vehicles Control Systems and Optimization Methods: A Systematic Review. *International Journal of Robotics and Control Systems*, *5*(5). Advance online publication. DOI: 10.31763/ijrcs.v5i5.1859

Masadeh, R., Almomani, O., Zaqebah, A., Masadeh, S., Alshqurat, K., Sharieh, A., & Alsharman, N. (2025). Narwhal Optimizer: A Nature-Inspired Optimization Algorithm for Solving Complex Optimization Problems. *Computers, Materials & Continua*, *85*(2), 3709–3737. Advance online publication. DOI: 10.32604/cmc.2025.066797

Masango, N. C., Agushaka, J. O., Amaefule, M. C., Taiwo, O., Zhang, P., Ezugwu, A. E., Saleem, K., Smerat, A., & Abualigah, L. (2025). Secure and efficient cloudlet networks: blockchain integration with agent-based proof of trust mechanism. *Eurasip Journal on Wireless Communications and Networking*, *2025*(1). DOI: 10.1186/s13638-025-02439-y

Matarneh, S., Louzi, N., Asi, I., Abdel-Jaber, M., & Masad, E. (2025). Genetic Expression Programming Based Empirical Models for the Prediction of Rutting Parameter of Bitumen Modified Using Nanomaterials. *Engineering and Science*, *35*. Advance online publication. DOI: 10.30919/es1438

Mbasso, W. F., Harrison, A., Dagal, I., Jangir, P., Liu, Z., & Smerat, A. (2025). High-Fidelity Simulation-Driven Control Framework for Robust Grid Integration of Renewable Energy Systems. *Energy Science & Engineering*. Advance online publication. DOI: 10.1002/ese3.70414

Nandal, P., Mann, P., Bohra, N., Sagar, K., & Smerat, A. (2025). Improving Underwater Image Quality Through Real-ESRGAN With Whale Optimization Algorithm. *Internet Technology Letters*, *8*(4), e70047. Advance online publication. DOI: 10.1002/itl2.70047

Nisar, K. S., Chokkalingam, R., Sriramulu, S., & Arunachalam, S. (2025). Mathematical Study of Nabla Fractional Difference Tech Layoff Model. *Iranian Journal of Science*, *49*(2), 345–356. Advance online publication. DOI: 10.1007/s40995-024-01721-w

Qaddara, I., & Alraba'nah, Y. (2025). Enhancing Requirements Classification Using Machine Learning Techniques. *SN Computer Science*, *6*(6), 649. Advance online publication. DOI: 10.1007/s42979-025-04158-z

Qawaqneh, H., Alomari, K. M., Alomari, S., Bektemyssova, G., Smerat, A., Montazeri, Z., Dehghani, M., Malik, O. P., & Eguchi, K. (2025). Kakapo Optimization Algorithm (KOA): A Novel Bio-inspired Metaheuristic for Optimization Applications. *International Journal of Intelligent Engineering and Systems*, *18*(11), 913–929. Advance online publication. DOI: 10.22266/ijies2025.1231.56

Qawasmeh, S., Habboushb, A., Elzaghmouri, B., Kharma, Q., & Albalawneh, D. (2025). Hybrid Convolutional Neural Network-Based Intrusion Detection System for Secure IoT Networks. *Tikrit Journal of Engineering Sciences*, *32*(SP1), 1–11. Advance online publication. DOI: 10.25130/tjes.sp1.2025.2

Rabbi, M. F., Amin, M., Al-Dalahmeh, M., & Abdullah, M. (2025). Assessing the role of information technology in promoting environmental sustainability and preventing crime in E-commerce. *International Review of Applied Sciences and Engineering*, *16*(1), 81–97. Advance online publication. DOI: 10.1556/1848.2024.00834

Ramesh, J. V. N., Nimma, D., Dasari, R., Chaudhari Rane, D., AlGhamdi, A., Rao, K. B. V. B., Haider, S. A., Kuzieva, N., & Jangir, P. (2025). Safe and Reliable Two-Stage Online Offloading Algorithm for Transportation Cyber-Physical Systems. *IEEE Transactions on Intelligent Transportation Systems*, *26*(9), 14313–14322. Advance online publication. DOI: 10.1109/TITS.2025.3539934

Shadhar, M. H., Mohammed, Z. A., Rajhi, A. A., Dasarathy, A. K., Das, P., Padmapriya, R., Singh, J., Matyakubov, B., Kutliev, U., & Smerat, A. (2025). Vibration-based analysis of a sandwich gori composite curved beam in thermo-electro-magnetic environment. *Acta Mechanica*. Advance online publication. DOI: 10.1007/s00707-025-04526-z

Shah, R. K., Hasan, M. K., Islam, S., Khan, A., Ghazal, T. M., & Khan, A. N. (2022). Detect Phishing Website by Fuzzy Multi-Criteria Decision Making. *2022 1st International Conference on AI in Cybersecurity, ICAIC 2022*. DOI: 10.1109/ICAIC53980.2022.9897036

Tarek, R., Elshenawy, A., Assadwy, M. I., & Madkour, M. A. (2025). Automated Diagnosis of Dental Diseases Using Deep Learning on Radiographic Images. *SN Computer Science*, *6*(6), 751. Advance online publication. DOI: 10.1007/s42979-025-04264-y

Vasudevan, A., Albinaa, T. A., Mohammad, S. I., Sharmila, E., Raja, N., Soon, E. E. H., Alshurideh, M. T., & Al-Adwan, A. S. (2024). Bidirectional LSTM for Electronic Product Recommendation. *Applied Mathematics & Information Sciences*, *18*(6), 1443–1453. Advance online publication. DOI: 10.18576/amis/180621

Vasudevan, A., Tamilmani, K. T., Mohammad, S. I., Sridheepika, V. S., Raja, N., Soon, E. E. H., Nagaraj, S., & Al-Adwan, A. S. (2025). Voices of Concern: Contemplations on Socioeconomic, Ethical, and Developmental Impacts of AI. *Applied Mathematics & Information Sciences*, *19*(1), 221–232. Advance online publication. DOI: 10.18576/amis/190119

Yaseen, M., Ali, E., Sarwar, N., Jamel, L., Din, I., Yuldashev, F., & Law, F. (2025). Design of Minimal Spanning Tree and Analytic Hierarchical Process (SAHP) Based Hybrid Technique for Software Requirements Prioritization. *IET Software, 2025*(1). DOI: 10.1049/sfw2/8819735

Zraiqat, A., Al Sayyed, O., Al Soudi, M., Al-Salih, A. A. M. M., Smerat, A., Montazeri, Z., Dehghani, M., Malik, O. P., Ahmed, M. A., Ibraheem, I. K., & Eguchi, K. (2025). Key Maker Algorithm: A Novel Human-Based Metaheuristic for Constrained Optimization. *International Journal of Intelligent Engineering and Systems*, *18*(9), 688–699. Advance online publication. DOI: 10.22266/ijies2025.1031.45

Zraiqat, A., Batiha, B., & Al-Refai, O. (2025). Thunderstorm and Cloud Algorithm: A Novel Parameter-Free Metaheuristic Inspired by Atmospheric Dynamics for Complex Optimization Tasks. *International Journal of Intelligent Engineering and Systems*, *18*(8), 153–167. Advance online publication. DOI: 10.22266/ijies2025.0930.11

Chapter 8
Secure and Privacy-Aware Data Architecture Design for Security Operations Centers

Ali Q. Saeed
http://orcid.org/0000-0002-2276-3776
Artificial Intelligence Techniques Engineering Department, Northern Technical University, Mosul, Iraq

Saadaldeen Rashid Ahmed
Bayan University, Erbil, Iraq

ABSTRACT

The development of secure and privacy-conscious data architectures is critical for Security Operations Centers operating in complex, data-intensive environments. The research probes deeply into the evolution of establishing secure and privacy-aware data architectures within Security Operations Centers (SOCs). The material assesses major design strategies like data segmentation, least privilege, encryption, anonymization, and controlled data movements in both centralized and distributed SOC models. It also discusses problems with large-scale logging, live analytics, cloud integration, and AI- based security tools. The piece further shines a light on how architectural measures align with privacy by design and privacy by default. The study merges Security Engineering with Data Protection Principles to present a full-fledged manual on developing SOC data architectures that not only enable effective threat management but also sharply limit the risks of privacy breaches and regulatory exposure.

DOI: 10.4018/979-8-3373-9210-3.ch008

1. INTRODUCTION

Figure 1. Architecture of a Modern Security Operations Center Data Pipeline

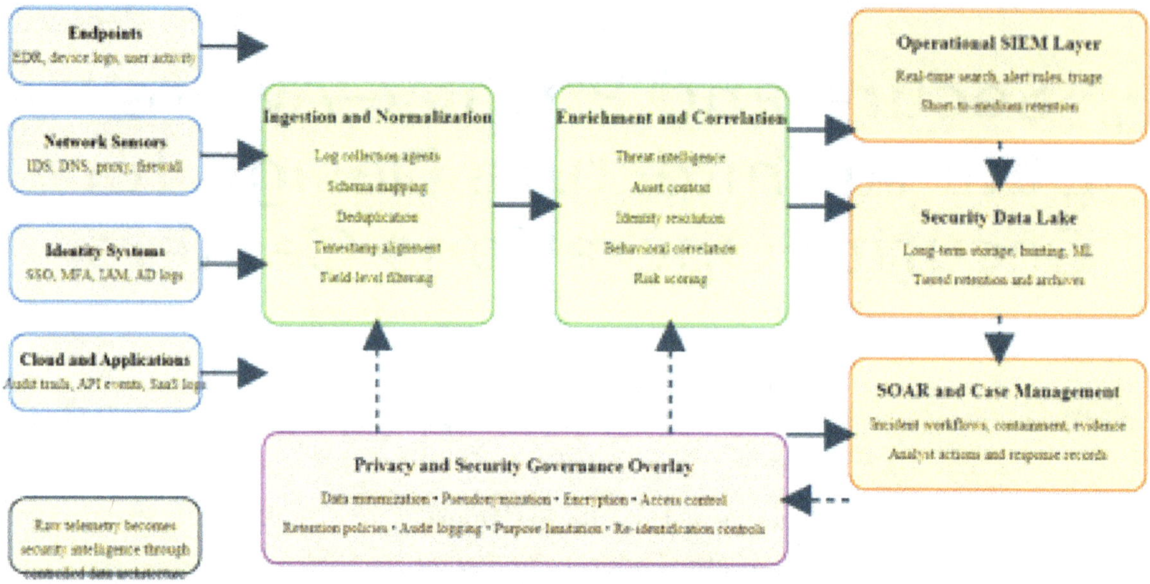

1.1 The Transformation of Security Operations Centers in the Data Era

In the past, SOCs were quite straightforward. A SOC was a central monitoring function that gave out alerts via firewalls, intrusion detection systems, antivirus platforms, and email gateways. Apart from being rule-driven, the systems were mainly sourcing from few places alphabetically and recognizing known indicators, escalating incidents, and coordinating remediation were some of the As the perimeter of enterprise used to be stable and digital assets mostly on-premises, the model worked well. Still, with time, the increasing digitization of business led to the expansion of attack surfaces and risks. Cloud has also brought in elastic infrastructures and ephemeral workloads that could be created and destroyed in minutes. Remote working made people more reliant on identity systems, endpoint telemetry, and access control logs, which are beyond the traditional network boundaries. Software-as-a-service ecosystems scattered business data on third-party platforms. Connected operational technologies and industrial systems brought in new telemetry types. APIs enabled more profound integrations but also resulted in more logging and monitoring needs. Meanwhile, criminals started using more figure tactics such as credential theft, lateral movement, living-off-the-land, cloud-native persistence, and multi-stage intrusion chains that simple log sources are incapable of detecting(Ghazal, Hasan, Hussein, et al., 2025).

Therefore, security operation centers became a very data-centric approach. They rely on a vast chain of events that gather data from endpoints, identity providers, virtual machines, containers, cloud platforms, DNS systems, web proxies, application servers, vulnerability scanners, threat intelligence feeds, and user behavior systems. Solutions like Security Information and Event Management gather and harmonize this data. Correlated signals activate workflows through Security Orchestration, Automation, and Response (SOAR) systems. Data lakes and security analytics pipelines provide the necessary support for large-scale searches, retrospective hunting, anomaly detection, and machine learning. Therefore, apart from simple alert triaging, the SOC has transformed into an intelligence-driven analytics platform. The old SOCs' architecture thinking was mainly focused on sensor coverage and alert fine-tuning. However, modern SOC architects make decisions on things like throughput of ingestion, event standardization, processing streams, storage organization, encryption, access segregation, real-time analytics, retention policies, and cross-domain federation. Such scientific decisions, apart from detection performance, also determine how privacy is protected at an organization's level. It is possible that a data architecture that records everything by default may provide the maximum observability but it also results in an increase of the attack surface, legal exposure, potential misuse by insiders, and governance complexities. Conversely, a very limited architecture may be better in terms of privacy risks but will cause detection weaknesses and incident response problems. Developing SOC in the data-driven era, therefore, not only involves the purchase of new technologies but is also an issue of architectural As the SOC becomes a more powerful tool through data, its development must be more disciplined with regard to how that data is justified, collected, protected, and governed (Saeed et al., 2024).

1.2 Why is Privacy a Priority in Security Monitoring Systems?

Over time, there has been a shift in how privacy is perceived within the context of security monitoring, which historically, as you know, was rather narrowly focused on perimeter controls and incident response. However, these systems now process data on a large scale with a high level of detail that may reveal very personal behavior, identity, communication, movement, and association patterns. Adequate privacy controls notwithstanding, this data environment closely resembles a behavioral surveillance system with very high resolution. There are multiple grounds on which the importance of privacy in security monitoring is demonstrated. First, security telemetry is often comprised of personally identifiable and linkable information. Logs relating to authentications bear the potential to disclose the whereabouts of employees and work schedules, their modes of network connection, the applications they access, and the frequency of behavior changes. Logs from endpoints may give away process names, file locations, software installations, browser traces, and command-line arguments. Moreover, even IP addresses and timestamps, which would seem technical indicators, become privacy sensitive if correlated over time across systems(Ghazal, Hasan, Khairy, et al., 2025).

The second reason is given by the ever-increasing analytical capacities of today's SOC. On their own, single records probably won't be able to show an individual's information. However, if they are merged through a process involving entity resolution and the use of behavioral analytics, it is easy to figure out where someone goes, who they interact with, when they work, when they change jobs, and when they behave unusually. People and devices can be grouped by machine learning machines. This issue has led to concerns about the lack of transparency in profiling and the problem of setting precise boundaries. Furthermore, there is a danger that insiders will remain. Many organizations cannot entirely stop malicious behavior from the inside. SOC platforms provide very easy access to highly detailed operational data to only a small number of persons. Analysts have been delegated a duty. Lastly, privacy is gradually becoming a reason that affects regulatory compliance and public trust. In the absence of privacy, employees, users, and business partners will not have faith in security monitoring systems. Surveillance thus becomes a source of resistance. Therefore, ironically, privacy is not an obstacle to security. Instead, it is a fundamental element for security that is both sustainable and legitimate. A monitoring system that respects privacy involves such measures as data minimization, use limitation, maximum pseudonymization, strict retention control, access partitioning, encryption, logging to ensure accountability, and governance oversight. What is more, these are only features that make monitoring easier and do not eliminate it altogether. The more a monitoring system is made so advanced, the more it becomes necessary to regard privacy both as a kind of architecture and a discipline at the institutional Ghazal et al., 2022).

1.3 Security vs Privacy Tradeoffs in Modern SOC Architectures

In some ways, more security means more data, more visibility, more retention, and more correlation. On the other hand, privacy is thought to require less application and therefore, less collection, limited exposure, and restricted processing. Even though such a viewpoint explains a real dilemma, it is also quite limiting. More importantly, on the ground, one will hardly find the best SOC architectures temporarily sidelining one objective just to cater for the other. The focus instead is on maximizing security value and at the same time, systematically minimizing privacy exposure. Detection logic is the origin of trade-offs. One of the main reasons for providing analysts and automated systems with a more covering contextual understanding of the environment is to achieve better threat detection performance. Incident confidence can be greatly heightened through such correlations. However, simultaneously, each additional data source unquestionably means providing other pieces of privacy-sensitive information. Also, one has to decide between indefinite retention to accumulate behavioral risk and carrying out just-in-time investigations and adversary dwell-time analyses. Deep packet inspection has the capability of identifying exfiltration or malware delivery patterns, but content-level inspection can intrude upon communications privacy if it is carried out in an excessively broad or unexplained way(Hanandeh et al., 2025).

Concerning the tradeoff, understand it is not a mere yes-or-no matter. Rather, it should be conceptualized as a design space. With false economies, some architectures do neither. They over collect data without justification or under collect it to the extent that they create blind spots that could have easily been avoided. On the other hand, better architectures make it clear which fields, types of data, and actions are essential for performing the different detection tasks. They make a distinction between always-needed data and those needed only under certain circumstances(Alnawayseh et al., 2022). Layered visibility is introduced whereby richer detail is revealed only under well-defined investigative situations. On top of that, role-based access is utilized and analysts do not all get to see the same detail level and so on. Moreover, this tradeoff is not a one-size-fits-all. Minimal data or transformed data may suffice for monitoring purposes but it may not be enough for high-severity incident response that warrants access to fuller data. After all, insider threat investigations may be held to higher standards due to their effect on employee privacy and trust than malware triage. So, in a privacy-aware design, changes are made according to context and not uniformly across SOC functions (which is not to say that there is no precedent for such changes, for example, cloud vs. on-premises environments). Conversely a practical SOC setup spells out these trade-offs clearly. It connects every piece of data to certain threat scenarios, it backs up gathering of data with definite ends, sets rules for who gets to see the data and prevents misuse. Besides, it realizes that cutting down needless data proliferation, inside employees' luring and breach consequences, privacy actually turns into a security In this sense, privacy and security are not mutually exclusive. In fact, they are each necessary and integral components of a well-governed data architecture(Vasudevan et al., 2025).

1.4 Objectives and Contributions of the Chapter

The first objective is to establish that a SOC data architecture needs to be assessed both as a technical security capability and also from the perspective of a privacy-sensitive data ecosystem. The chapter's second goal is to explicitly identify the layers of the architecture and the decision points that contribute most to privacy risk in the SOC environment. Usually, these layers include data ingestion, telemetry normalization, enrichment, storage, machine learning, analyst access pattern, and retention. Organizing around these layers provides a conceptual map keyed to SOC monitoring infrastructure's role in either multiplying or mitigating privacy exposure. The third aim of this chapter is to investigate how security efficacy can be upheld even with privacy-aware limitations. The chapter is against the blanket assumption that privacy protective measures will necessarily reduce detection capability. Instead, the chapter introduces methods such as narrowly targeting collection, pseudonymization, encryption, segmentation of access, privacy-aware analytics, and governance of data lifecycle that can serve both purposes simultaneously. It is deeply crucial for the Security Operation Centers(SOCs) of today that are functioning under stringent digital regulations and where trust is a very sensitive commodity. The fourth objective is data-driven and includes the examination of cybersecurity datasets as a way of demonstrating the impact of privacy-oriented decisions—especially anonymization and architectural changes—on the performance of threat detection and privacy risk outcomes. Including an empirical component to the research not only helps to make the chapter going further the purely conceptual discussion, but, also the paper after getting structured results and discussions, explores the impact of architectural choices and therefore takes a principled

This chapter contributes a secure and privacy-aware SOC data architecture model that balances detection utility with privacy exposure. The model links telemetry collection, pseudonymization, secure ingestion, privacy-aware data lakes, access governance, retention control, and privacy-preserving analytics into a single architectural framework for modern Security Operations Centers.

Figure 2. Privacy-Security Tradeoff Model in SOC Data Processing

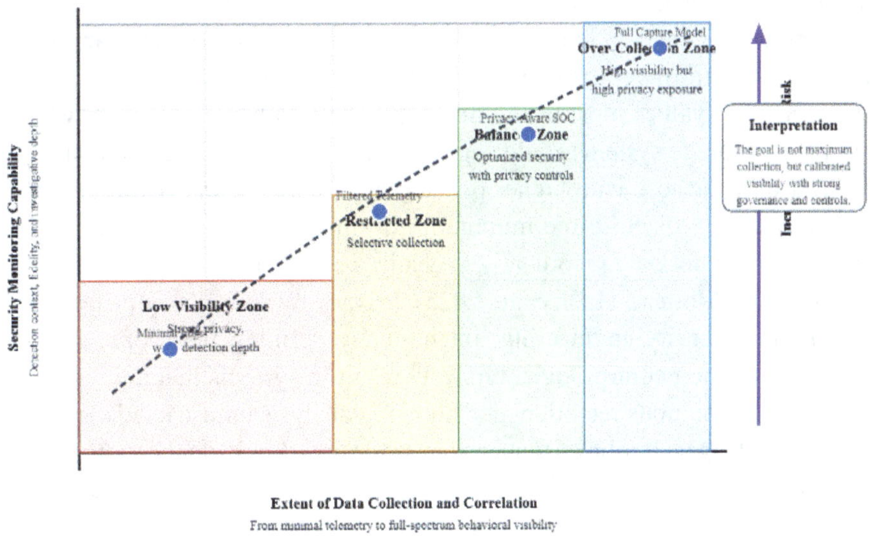

2. PRIVACY PRINCIPLES FOR SECURITY DATA SYSTEMS

2.1 Privacy by Design in Security Monitoring Platforms

Prior research on privacy-aware SOC architecture can be grouped into six themes: SOC data architecture, privacy-by-design in security monitoring, telemetry minimization, secure logging and data lake governance, AI-driven SOC analytics, and privacy-preserving machine learning. These themes show that privacy risk in SOCs is not limited to data collection; it also emerges through enrichment, storage, correlation, analyst access, model training, retention, export, and secondary use. Building privacy directly into the platforms of a Security Operations Center (SOC) means that the planning and designing of privacy features are done at the very beginning of the system architecture, not as elements to be looked at during audit phases after deployment. Privacy by design is a major supporter of the idea of making privacy a core element of system architecture, workflows, and technical controls from the very start, rather than trying to add them at a later stage. Regarding security monitoring platforms, the principle is very applicable because, quite often, monitoring systems are just added one after another. By way of illustration, at first, a Security Operations Center (SOC) might only be dealing with firewall and endpoint logs and, step by step, it will also start retrieving emails, performing identity analytics, obtaining cloud audit trails, and then collecting behavioral Without a privacy-minded system architecture philosophy, such broadening will result in the uncontrolled gathering of sensitive information, inconsistent access boundaries will be created, and it will become unclear what data use was justified. Making privacy by design the foundation of security monitoring causes privacy to be considered as early as the architecture decision phase and not as a result of post-audit findings. Prior to the integration of any new data source, the organization should first determine what security objective is to be reached with this data, identify which categories of sensitive data are involved, figure out the necessary data fields, assess whether partial data collection would be sufficient, decide how identifiers can be handled, and select appropriate retention policies. Therefore privacy changes from a policy that simply reacts to various incidences to a design-focused engineering discipline that foresees them(Al-Falouji et al., 2025).

In practice, privacy by design in a Security Operations Center could be implemented through a few very specific measures. For instance, source locations could be set up in a way that they remove unnecessary fields even before the data is ingested. Parsing pipelines could locate and indicate sensitive fields so that subsequent platforms enforce multiple layers of controls. Analyst dashboards could present the anonymized or masked values most of the time, and allow only full exposure when a reasonable case has been initiated. Storage systems could segregate raw data from processed one and offer access to the sensitive layer only to those with higher privileges. Automated workflows might be configured in such a way that they only disclose the minimum information necessary for a particular response action. Auditing logs might not only record system changes but also record times of access to sensitive event categories(Al-Okbi, Alomari, Hadi, et al., 2025). Privacy by design is quite beneficial as it nicely complements traditional security engineering. Intentionally defining the scope, properly equipping, and governing through explicit control logic, typically result in systems that are, overall, more secure. Unregulated collection, ambiguous retention, and allowing analysts unrestricted visibility, lead to both security and privacy challenges. It follows that privacy by design should not be thought of as a limitation on a Security Operations Center imposed by external actors. This is an internal quality principle that is consistent with long-term monitoring capability. The other side of the coin is that privacy by design helps to legitimize organizational aspects as well. A demonstrably governed, technically bounded, and closely linked to legitimate defensive purposes Security Operations Center employing robust security monitoring is likely to be accepted more by employees and stakeholders, who might be suspicious of the security monitoring that is rude or unbounded(Khalayleh et al., 2025).

2.2 Data Minimization Principles in Security Logging

When it comes to security data systems, minimizing the quantity of data collected, processed, and retained is one of the biggest, if not the top, privacy principles. It makes a call on companies that they should do this only as much as is necessary for a legitimate purpose. However, in a Security Operations Center, there is always the challenge that security personnel tend to operate on the idea that there is always a benefit to having more data to detect. This goes without saying that when data is collected indiscriminately, it can pose severe problems. Apart from increased storage costs, it will lead to a watering down of the signals that matter, an increase insider exposure, a complicated governance, and the retention of such personal or behavioral information that might never be necessary for security operations. At the source, systems can be tuned to reduce verbosity or disable categories that are not relevant to security monitoring. At the point of data collection, connectors can be used to block access to fields that are unnecessary centrally. During parsing, event formats can be changed so that sensitive data can be tokenized or generalized. At the storage level, less important event categories can be summarized or kept in a minimal form. At the analytics stage, normal detection tasks can be done on the basis of processed data sets while raw details are kept for controlled investigative escalation(Al-Suhimat et al., 2024).

Field minimization and duration minimization are two different aspects of a very important feature of minimization. Field minimization is about what types of data are collected while duration minimization is about how long a given types is kept. So, a SOC may have a good reason to capture a given field for short-term detection but very little justification for preserving the field for a whole year. Therefore minimization is a design approach that comprises multiple layers instead of a single layer of control. Data minimization results in the system being more effective as well. Removing unnecessary or low-value data can help system architects to fetch data faster, decrease the level of analysts' workload, and improve the reliability of detection systems. It is not that more data always means better data. A system that strictly controls the data it collects usually yields much more transparent, quick, and understandable analytical results. However, minimization needs to be supported by sound governance as the security scenarios are quite likely to evolve. Newly developed threat models may require new data categories while older sources may become obsolete. As a result, minimization must be understood as a method that is regularly revisited rather than a design phase that is done once and then discarded. Advanced SOC governance also features a quarterly examination of each major log source, assessment of its effectiveness in detection, consideration of the privacy sensitivity of the source, and the deciding of whether the present collection scope continues to be Ghazal, Abu-Shareha, Mustafa, et al., 2025).

2.3 Purpose Limitation and Data Use Constraints

Purpose limitation is the principle that data should be collected and processed for specific, explicit, and legitimate purposes and not be used in ways that are incompatible with those original purposes. This principle is particularly relevant in security monitoring systems because the centralization of telemetry data in the systems can make it tempting for organizations to repurpose security data for management oversight, analysis of employee productivity, monitoring employees for disciplinary purposes, use of business analytics, or other non-security functions. With detailed identity, endpoint, and communications metadata at a SOC's disposal, the technical barrier for such secondary uses might be very low. However, governance and ethics must keep the barrier high. To be a secure and privacy-aware SOC, it is therefore essential that clear purpose definitions be made for each major data category. Such a clear definition leads to the development of access design, workflow logic, and oversight policy(Ghazal, Abualhaj, Ahmed, et al., 2025).

It is also a critical constraint to properly separate security functions, which rely on real-time use of data, from other uses of the same dataset that may be non-security in nature but that have features of an individual's privacy than are more intrusive. For instance, the user login pattern data might be quite helpful for identification of the misuse of the credential, but it can also be nefariously used to infer the behavior of employee attendance or work intensity. A privacy-friendly design should do everything it can to discourage such repurposing through organizational as well as technical segmentation. Data views intended for the SOC use should not be automatically available for unrelated administrative analysis. Furthermore, purpose limitation is concerned with enrichment and correlation as well. Security data that is enriched with HR records, business ownership information, location contextual or productivity system metadata can give the SOC a better investigative capacity. Still, every additional enrichment source extends the interpretive range of the data. As a result, enrichment must be aligned to clearly defined security objectives rather than general curiosity or speculative future value. Therefore, with a clear statement of the collection of a particular data type and how it supports the defined defensive objectives, an organization becomes able to defend its monitoring program to regulators, auditors, employees, and different governance bodies internally(Ghazal, Abu-Shareha, Mustafa, et al., 2025).

2.4 Compliance Requirements for Privacy Protection

Privacy-focused SOC architectures should also be considered in relation to legal, regulatory, contractual, and internal compliance standards. The exact requirements will be different in each location and industry, but most modern data governance systems will require organizations to demonstrate a lawful purpose, proportionality, control of access, discipline in retention, accountability, and safe treatment of personal data. Security monitoring systems, even though they are used for defense, are not exempt from these expectations simply because of their intended use. In fact, these systems processing very sensitive telemetry may attract an even higher level of scrutiny. Compliance has an impact on the architecture in a number of ways: Firstly, compliance impacts a Business Process Model and Notation (BPMN) data classification (Sharma et al., 2025).A SOC that is still unclear about which logs contain user-level identifiers, communication metadata, device fingerprints, or sensitive location traces might find it very challenging to use those data logs effectively to demonstrate compliance. Secondly, there is really a big chance that these compliance frameworks actually constrain the amount of data one could collect and expect any collection of data to be justified and done according to the organization's documented high-level purposes, and that the organization keeps records of such collected data. This is very consistent with the earlier discussion of the principles of purpose limitation and minimization. It is not enough to rely on vendor default settings or even team informal preferences, one must have well-thought-out architectural decisions about logging categories, retention periods, and enrichment sources in writing(Khaled Abdullah & Qawasmeh, 2025).

Thirdly, the frameworks are very keen on the security aspect of the processing operation. They would desire measures like encryption, role-based access, auditability, integrity protection, segregation of duties, and incident response to be put in place in the monitoring platform itself. This means that a Value Stream Mapping (VSM) should not only facilitate the secure monitoring of other systems but it should also be a securely administered system in and of itself(Ghazal, 2025a). Fourth, retention and deletion decisions are really the key compliance pieces of the puzzle. Typically, security and detection teams would prefer to keep data for longer periods as it would help them in investigations and detection tuning while on the other hand, there is a requirement that data should not be kept longer than necessary from a compliance obligations viewpoint. One way in which privacy-friendly architecture can reconcile these two apparently conflicting demands is through the establishment of tiered retention models, creation of evidentiary preservation rules, and identification of explicit exception paths for cases requiring longer Fifthly, access accountability is of paramount importance. When architecture logs are taken of who, when, under which case or role accessed what data, and whether exports or transformations occurred, then compliance is one step ahead (A. Arabiat, Altayeb, & Alkhrissat, 2025)

Sixth, cross-border processing and third-party services may lead to increased compliance complexity. Components of SIEM, SOAR, or data lake that are cloud-hosted, or leverage of managed security providers entail accommodation of architectures that consider data residency, transfer controls, contractual safeguards, and shared responsibility models. Compliance is not to be treated as a small checklist-only exercise, although it is very tempting to do so, it is worth pointing out that a technically satisfying documentation requirement system might actually remain deeply intrusive and poorly governed. Most robust SOC architectures treat compliance as a baseline measure of a broader privacy discipline. Besides regulatory compliance, design features of explainability, traceability, and bounded use all result in improved legitimacy and robustness of security operations(Abualhaj, Al-Khatib, Abu-Shareha, et al., 2025).

Table 1. Core Privacy Principles and Their Architectural Implications in SOC Systems

Privacy Principle	Core Meaning in SOC Context	Architectural Implication	Example in Security Monitoring
Privacy by Design	Privacy controls are integrated from the beginning of system design	Build filtering, masking, classification, and access controls into ingestion and analytics layers	Configure connectors to exclude unnecessary fields before events enter the SIEM
Data Minimization	Only collect and retain data necessary for defined security purposes	Reduce verbosity, suppress irrelevant fields, and limit long-term retention	Store failed login metadata but avoid retaining unrelated session details indefinitely
Purpose Limitation	Use security data only for explicit and legitimate security objectives	Separate security analytics from non-security monitoring and restrict secondary use	Authentication logs used for anomaly detection should not be repurposed for employee productivity tracking
Identity Protection	Limit unnecessary exposure of identifiable individuals in telemetry	Apply pseudonymization, masking, re-identification controls, and role-based visibility	Analysts see tokenized user IDs during routine triage and request controlled attribution only during escalated investigations
Access Accountability	Ensure every access to sensitive telemetry is traceable and reviewable	Maintain detailed audit logs, case-linked access, and privilege segmentation	Record which analyst viewed privileged account activity and under which incident case
Retention Control	Keep data only as long as needed for operational and legal justification	Use tiered storage, deletion rules, and exception-based evidentiary preservation	Retain raw endpoint telemetry for 30 days, summarized indicators for 180 days, and case evidence under separate legal hold

continued on following page

Table 1. Continued

Privacy Principle	Core Meaning in SOC Context	Architectural Implication	Example in Security Monitoring
Secure Processing	Protect monitoring data from unauthorized disclosure, tampering, or misuse	Encrypt data in transit and at rest, isolate sensitive datasets, and harden pipeline components	Use encrypted transport between collectors and brokers and restrict raw lake access to approved investigators
Governance and Compliance Alignment	Ensure technical monitoring practices align with legal and organizational obligations	Tag data types, document use cases, review controls periodically, and support audits	Classify identity logs as sensitive telemetry and review their collection scope during quarterly governance assessments

3. PRIVACY-AWARE DATA COLLECTION MECHANISMS

The main goal of privacy-aware data collection mechanisms is to guarantee that the manner in which security telemetry is gathered adheres to privacy guidelines without undermining the continuous function of the monitoring system. Architectures that're responsible for data intake should not be designed to grab every available log and behavioral signal but instead must incorporate well-thought-out filtering, transforming, and controlling of data before it reaches centralized monitoring platforms. Organizations reiterate their commitment to privacy at the earliest phases of the data's lifecycle to minimize their exposure to the risks that come with over-surveillance and data aggregation beyond control. Here we provide the design philosophy and technical solutions necessary for privacy-conscious telemetry gathering in the context of SOCs. The focus is on functionalities of secure log collection mechanisms, implementation of privacy-preserving collection methods, protection of identities through anonymization and pseudonymization, strengthening of ingestion pipelines security, and reduction of the centralized sensitive information exposure by means of edge-based data processing. These are fundamentally approaching that collectively form the initial operational layer of a privacy-aware security data architecture.

3.1 Privacy Preserving Data Collection Techniques

Field selective collection is one of the techniques with a long track record in privacy-preserving telemetry collection. Log on its own supports complex metadata that is frequently still not necessary for security analyses. For instance, the logs that an application produces may contain full user profiles and session feature data, or even content-level data that doesn't necessarily indicate threats. Only fetching relevant fields through selective collection results in a significant downscaling of the total amount of private information that needs monitoring pipelines. Contextual filtering, as another technique, is more about setting up monitoring policies where your monitoring will be close/specific to cutting edge highest risk environments or only limited risky events or scenarios(Shah et al., 2022). For instance, one can collect all the authentication failure events together with all the privilege escalation and network behavior events that resulted in unusual activity, but the regular application logs can be collected at an absolutely minimal level of detail. Another option to achieve privacy-preserving collection is to perform event aggregation at the source system. For instance, rather than sending individual events for the system user activity, time-window based summary records or logs could represent multiple occurrences of the same type or category of event and only one such record is transmitted to the monitoring system. Another significant method is differential logging based on user roles or system sensitivity. For instance, systems processing sensitive personal data can maintain very stringent control over logging so as to prevent interactive exposure of user activities. In these cases, anomalies at the system level take precedence without detailed behavioral monitoring. Implementations such as policy-driven telemetry management that use security policies can govern which data categories are allowed and which should be excluded or obscured, etc. Automation to ensure these policies is necessary and done by collection agents that work across environments. Adoption of privacy-preserving collection techniques leads to prevention of over-accumulation of data, as well as a substantially reduced risk that monitoring systems become themselves vehicles of privacy risk(Al-znamat et al., 2025).

3.2 Anonymization and Pseudonymization Mechanisms

Since SOC systems often process logs containing user identifiers, device names, email addresses, or IP addresses, these identifiers must be handled very carefully to avoid unnecessary exposure previously. Such measures also remain critical for adhering to privacy regulations in various regions. Pseudonymization is a method that literally substitutes externally recognizable identifiers in with newly generated artificial identifiers or tokens. The events can get correlated though the tokens without completely exposing the real identity. For example, instead of exposed the username as "alice.smith," a token such as "User_7843" is created. However, through this token, the SOC analysts can still observe that potential patterns relating to that user exist such as repeated login failures or suspicious activities carried out across multiple systems. In the light of the re-identification requirement in the case of incident investigations, however, the mapping of pseudonyms to real identities is relegated to authorized personnel or to the automated workflows operating within well-defined governance policies(Ullah et al., 2025).

Anonymization, in contrast, results in an irreversible removal or alteration of identifiable attributes to a degree that reconstruction of individual can hardly ever be envisaged. Examples include replacing exact IP addresses with larger network ranges and omitting user identifiers altogether during statistical analysis of aggregated datasets. Anonymization has better privacy preservation but it hampers investigative capabilities. This is why many SOC ones adopt hybrid model whereby raw telemetry is pseudonymized for day-to-day operations while anonymized datasets are produced for long-term research and reporting. Tokenization is a safer approach to execute pseudonymization. Through this approach, the sensitive identifiers are exchanged with the tokens that are randomly generated and stored in the secured tokenization Since the tokens are structurally unrelated to the original identifiers, even better protection is offered compared to simple hashing. Applying anonymization as well as pseudonymization together with other technical and organizational measures that make it technically and legally infeasible to identify the data subject is a very good practice to achieve the privacy protective goals(Ali et al., 2025).

3.3 Secure Data Ingestion Pipelines

Once telemetry is gathered from the source systems, it is transferred and processed through the ingestion pipelines before it finally lands into the central analytics platforms. Typically, these pipelines are made up of collectors, message brokers, streaming platforms, and transformation services to perform the functions of normalizing and enrichment of event data. Due to the fact that ingestion pipelines deal with very large volumes of sensitive telemetry, they must be deemed essential components around

SOC architecture security. The following fundamental security features should be ensured by a secure ingestion pipeline:

- Data confidentiality
- Propagation paths integrity
- Availability throughout the telemetry flow

Encryption is a must for data protection during the period of transmission from collection agents to ingestion services. Protocols supporting security like TLS close the door on attackers who might be trying to catch sensitive telemetry as it moves from one network segment to another. Similarly, integrity comes to play at the same level. SOC pipelines need to have in place the means of recognizing a change in events during transmission. Digital signatures or message authentication codes will assist here with the task of verifying that events remain unchanged after they have left their original sources. Monitoring the monitoring infrastructure which undeniably the ingestion pipeline is a very integral part, is yet another facet of pipeline security that cannot be overlooked. There is a need for the SOC ingestion pipelines to emit the operational logs like pipeline activities, its performance metrics as well as configuration changes(Keote et al., 2025).

By these supplementary records, logs, administrators acquire the capacity to discover any anomalies such as those events that unexpectedly come from unknown sources or those with abnormal ingestion rates or unauthorized changes made in the configuration settings. Pipeline resilience is yet another factor for SOC ingestion pipelines to consider providing unbroken monitoring capabilities. Telemetry collection should not get interrupted even if a single component fails. High availability of this kind of system is indispensable as telemetry collection interruptions would have resulted in security monitoring which more or less is a blind spot. Organizations develop secure ingestion pipelines as a way of securing telemetry throughout its data collection journey while at the same time ensuring that there will be an uninterrupted event delivery to downstream security analytics(A. Arabiat, Altayeb, & Salama, 2025).

3.4 Edge-Based Privacy Protection Approaches

Nowadays, our enterprise environments, being characterized by high degree of distribution, have made the edge-based data processing a very effective instrument for privacy-aware telemetry collection. Located at the periphery of the network, near a system, edge computing is resource efficient and means of reducing the overall network traffic and bandwidth usage. Inhouse or localized processing, integration of data security, error checking and reporting, and decision-making based on the data being processed are some of the intangible benefits of edge-computing method. Advantage of edge-based privacy protection is already discussed to a certain extent here, but it will still be worthwhile to mention again that they can dramatically help lower the extent to which sensitive information passes through different networks. Instead of merely passing on streams of raw events, edge collectors are capable of processing/analyzing local telemetry and generating aggregated security indicators. For instance, the endpoint agent may carry out local analysis of system behavior and transmit only the alerts or aggregated metrics themselves excluding individual events altogether. The very same edge processing strategy also facilitates the application of privacy controls ahead of the point of data leaving the local environment. Examples include doing pseudonymization, field suppression, or aggregation inside edge collectors so that the central systems theoretically don't have access to the most sensitive raw attributes and thus drastically reducing the chance of central monitoring infrastructure becoming a massive personal data dump(Ju et al., 2025).

Apart from using edge computing to solve privacy problems and reducing risks of the central data exposure, it is also very good for scalability, preliminarily local processing reduces the amount of telemetry that will finally be transmitted to the central platforms. So, not only will the network be less saturated but the SOC systems will also be better able to filter out high-value events instead of handling routine operational data. Where there are strict data protection requirements, privacy controls based on edge computation are a good way to meet restrictions on data residency and cross-border data transfers. Instead of sending only aggregated security indicators to centralized monitoring systems, sensitive data is kept within local jurisdictions. However, solutions based on edge computing always require trustworthy and efficient management. Besides, these devices need to be secured against tampering and bypass, and they need to keep updated regularly to maintain their threat detection capabilities. Also, proper governance should include centralized verification of whether privacy policies enforced by edge systems are actually being complied with. Accurately defined, edge-based privacy protection could be a very effective way to combine distributed monitoring with centralized Ramesh et al., 2025).

4. SECURE STORAGE AND PROCESSING OF SECURITY DATA

4.1 Privacy-Aware Security Data Lakes

Security data lakes are an important part of building an effective security operations center (SOC) architecture in today's world as they allow enterprises to gather and scrutinize massive amounts of telemetry data. Whereas conventional Security Information and Event Management (SIEM) systems mainly handle formal log records and store them for a short time only, data lakes, on the other hand, can keep raw or semi-structured data in the distributed storage environments indefinitely. Security personnel appreciate this capability very much as it allows them to perform retrospective inquiries, create sophisticated detection algorithms, and compare events from different data Nonetheless, the liberty and the scale that data lakes offer significantly contribute to the risks related to privacy. Given that these platforms generally take in raw telemetry directly from collection pipelines, it is quite common for them to include personal information, behavioral traces, and system metadata that go well beyond the security requirements. Inadequate data governance can lead to the proliferation of data lakes serving as repositories of excessive or poorly controlled monitoring data. Hence, it is imperative that SOC architectures consider the incorporation of privacy-aware design principles during the implementation of a data lake environment. One major method is to store raw data separately from the processed, analytical datasets. For instance, raw telemetry may reside in a highly secured environment to which only investigative personnel with the highest level of clearance have access. On the other hand, datasets transformed for regular analytics purposes may be deprived of sensitive attributes either by removal or masking(Ahmed et al., 2025).

Another very significant architectural feature which could be mentioned here is data segregation which refers to isolating the datasets based on the different levels of their sensitivity and how relevant they are to the operations that are going The most sensitive datasets may be sequestered in separate storage environments having entry restrictions at a much higher level. In contrast, logs with minimal sensitivity that are primarily used for operational purposes may be stored in analysis-oriented repositories. This partitioning leads to a more limited exposure to personally identifiable information during routine analysis. Beyond the design issues, data lake system architectures must be able to offer extreme capabilities for the audit of operations performed. Hence, a clear record of telemetry access events must be maintained for use in enforcement, problem-solving, and investigative situations. Such audit logs are invaluable in detecting nefarious activities such as misuse of monitoring data as well as in-depth investigations into unforeseen access scenarios. Architecting for privacy-aware security data lakes is an opening for SOC professionals to accommodate the requirements of large-scale analytics while, at the same time, exercising control over sensitive telemetry(Shambour et al., 2025).

4.2 Encryption Strategies for Security Logs

Encrypting data remains to be one of the most basic yet effective techniques of providing the required level of security for the SOC storage systems. Since security telemetry sometimes embodies internal details of infrastructure or individual behavior, it is the encryption that stands as a protective wall against the illegitimate attempt of viewing such data. Encryption needs to be installed in the different phases of the lifecycle of SOC data. Initially, it is indispensable to allow only encrypted channels to be used between collection agents and storage platforms. Protocols such as Transport Layer Security (TLS) provide the required security so that telemetry neither gets intercepted nor modified during transmission. The subsequent step is totally unrelated to the previous one and addresses the security of data already stored in storage systems. Storage-level encryption can secure log files, database records, as well as distributed storage objects from unauthorized users. If the intruders physically or administratively access the storage environment, the encrypted data will be of no use to them as it will be unreadable without decryption keys. Key management is one of the essential aspects of encryption setup. Key management includes key generation, storage, and rotation by using authorized key management systems(Qawasmeh et al., 2025).

Generally, SOC architectures should not store encryption keys in applications or configuration files. Instead, keys are to be kept in hardware security modules or secure key vault services which have built-in access policies and restrictions. Field-level encryption also offers the possibility to encrypt telemetry record. Only the most sensitive fields such as usernames, IP addresses, or device identifiers are encrypted separately rather than encrypting the entire dataset. This works well with scenarios where the analysts want to query non-sensitive attributes without compromising the confidentiality of the critical identifiers. Often, tokenization is used along with encryption. Tokenization is actually a process by which sensitive identifiers are replaced with completely random tokens that have the corresponding original values saved in a secured Since tokens have no inherent meaning, they protect the identities even when event records are exposed. It is essential to consider performance alongside encryption methods. Dealing with large amounts of data in real-time is a feature of SOC analytics systems, and heavy encryption procedures may negatively impact the performance if not executed correctly. Consequently, it is the task of architects to strike a good balance between firm cryptographic security and large-scale processing capabilities (Alqudah et al., 2025)

4.3 Access Control Models for SOC Data Platforms

Access control is probably the most important protective mechanism available for the SOC data storage environments. Given that monitoring platforms collect telemetry from all over the enterprise, even a single unauthorized access to these systems could unearth extensive operational intelligence as well as personal data. Therefore, it cannot be overemphasized that SOC architectures include well-designed access control models that explain who can view, edit, or export monitoring data. Among SOC platforms, role-based access control is prevalent. In this scheme, the users of the system get specific roles aligned with their duties within the security organization. Every role defines the datasets, tools, and functions that a user is permitted to access. For instance, a Tier 1 analyst whose role is limited to alert triage might only be allowed to view condensed summaries of telemetry dashboards but not the raw event data(Ghazal, 2025b). At the same time, a lead incident responder might be given extensive access to detailed logs such as when a security incident is being formally verified. In addition, flexibility may be increased by integrating attribute-based access Rather than using predefined roles only, this system evaluates the situation by looking at attributes such as investigation status, data sensitivity, user clearance level, and operational need, etc. To give an example, access to sensitive identity logs may be granted only under conditions of a live security incident requiring deep investigation.

Separation of duties goes hand in hand with SOC access control. It is advised that administrative privileges conferring the management of monitoring infrastructure should be different from those allowing the review of telemetry. Through this type of partitioning, it is highly unlikely that a single person attempts to both configure system settings and access sensitive datasets without any check. Increased assurance is gained with multi-factor authentication as the access control to SOC platforms is not only enhanced by this especially in the case of administrative functions. The presence of strong authentication thwarts credential-based attacks by which hackers may gain unauthorized access. Access reviews that happen periodically are the best insurance for aligned privileges. Unnecessary privileges can be a real threat considering employees may change roles, leave the company, or require temporary access. Making sure that unnecessary privileges are revoked motivates regular audits. Protection of sensitive telemetry and giving security teams the ability to carry out their investigative work efficiently can be brought about through the deployment of comprehensive access control models in SOC architectures(Al-Dmour et al., 2025).

4.4 Secure Data Lifecycle Management

The last factor to be considered when designing secure storage involves the management of security telemetry's lifecycle from the moment of its creation till its final deletion after authorization. Handling the lifecycle of SOC data ensures that monitoring data gets a chance to be available for security purposes without getting into the situation of indefinite retention where the risks of privacy infringement or non-compliance increase. Retention policies are the rules that stipulate the duration for which different kinds of telemetry should be kept. Certain logs' retention times may be very short because they mainly support real-time detection. On the other hand, other sets of data might be kept for a couple of months to allow for threat hunting as well as the reconstruction of incidents (Gul et al., 2025)Deletion and archival processes should be set up in a way that ensures that the deleting of expired data occurs securely. Consistent application of retention policies over large datasets can be accomplished through automated deletion programs. To ensure the recovery of deleted data from storage media is prevented, secure deletion methods may be necessary. Legal hold is a term that refers to the suspension of retention periods when there is an ongoing legal investigation or a regulatory audit that requires certain sets of data to be retained beyond their standard retention period. SOC environments need to provide support to the legal hold process in a way that gives evidence integrity both protection and control under governance. Lifecycle management also considers that stored datasets get reviewed regularly to confirm that they are still useful for the security purposes at hand. Emerging technologies and transforming infrastructures will cause some telemetry sources to become outdated. Getting rid of such old datasets will reduce not only the cost of storage but also exposure to privacy risks. Besides, with the help of the correct ways of retention, archival, and deletion, SOC architectures will be able to keep and manage telemetry efficiently and securely such that the long-term risk is minimized along with the capability of analysis required for the detection and investigation of Almomani et al., 2025).

5. PRIVACY-PRESERVING SECURITY ANALYTICS

5.1 Machine Learning in Security Monitoring Systems

Machine learning is increasingly a major player in security monitoring since rule-based systems have difficulties coping with the complexity and volume of digital environments today. Actually, machine learning is widely applied across different security analytics domains. In authentication monitoring, a model can be trained to identify very unusual access as it will be beyond the normal login time, location of access pattern, and device-use trends, and privilege relationship. In endpoint monitoring, models can distinguish between normal process relationships and suspicious execution patterns. Network analytics via machine learning is able to identify strange flows, beaconing behavior, traffic asymmetry, or protocol usage deviation. In the cloud, abnormal administrative actions, privilege escalations, and misaligned resource creation can be detected by models(Ghazal, Hasan, Raju, et al., 2025). Machine learning's major advantage in the SOC is that it can handle high-dimensional data where the rules for manually written systems become either very fragile or simply incomplete. It captures relationships between features, adapts to changes in baseline, and reduces the need for a complete list of indicators. However, this is also the reason why it needs a lot of data. Learning models of security are often better when trained on detailed telemetry, stable identifiers, contextual enrichment, and have a long-time horizon. The requirement for a very large dataset directly conflicts with privacy goals. Another interesting point is explainability(Sardar et al., 2025).

Numerous machine learning algorithms provide a risk classification or an anomaly score but do not fully elaborate the reasoning behind it. In a privacy-sensitive environment, where monitoring makes use of such models, it becomes problematic if persons are subject to investigations based on these models without a proper explanation. Hence, if machine learning is used in the service of security monitoring, then in addition to it, there need to be interpretable features, confidence thresholds, escalation logic, as well as human review mechanisms. Framing the point of machine learning also involves the whole model lifecycle. Training data can be flawed due to legacy infrastructures, inherent biases, and different logging quality over time. Models become invalid if systems, workloads, or user behavior are changed. Besides, the performance of the model would suffer if privacy-preserving changes were made after the model had been developed, unless the models were properly restrained. Therefore, privacy preserving analytics needs to be part of the whole modeling life cycle and cannot be viewed as a compliance layer that is tacked on after deployment. Machine learning can potentially be a great tool for the SOC if properly planned. That being said it is of utmost importance to understand not only the data requirements, identity linkage, and historical context but also the ways of value creation by the machine learning model. That is exactly why privacy protection should be built-in in security analytics and must not be Abuowaida et al., 2025).

5.2 Privacy Risks in AI-Driven Security Analytics

In addition to the usual challenges with data collection and storage, integrating AI-powered security analytics also brings about a fresh set of privacy concerns. Possibly the most concrete risk is profiling. Different types of user activity patterns, system behavior, communication metadata, or interactions with endpoints obtained through profiling might be leveraged by AI to very effectively create behavioral profiles of people. The system may even reveal a person's work schedule, their movements, which projects they are working on, role changes, or even behavior deviations related to their productivity. This is quite a sensitive matter, especially when the people who are being monitored are employees, contractors, or even customers who may be tracked across multiple systems. The second risk is related to over-correlation, a practice of correlating beyond what is necessary for achieving the purpose A single data set on its own can hardly reveal too much, but the centralization and combining of identity logs, network records, device telemetry, application events, and cloud data make it possible to map highly detailed digital lives. It is not only a single login event that may be considered low risk, but even a model trained on months of linked identity, location, endpoint, and access behaviors may reveal far more than what is necessary for threat detection. A third risk arises even in the absence of direct identifiers through re-identification based on features and outputs. Even if a dataset has been 'de-identified,' individuals may still be re-identifiable by virtue of work schedules, travel habits, application use patterns, or combinations of devices. This would be the case whether such behavioral patterns are explicitly present in the model input data or implicitly revealed through model outputs such as explanations of anomalies or ranked alert results(Qaddara & Alraba'nah, 2025).

Fourthly secondary use is the problem that after AI technologies give the capability to rank users, devices or departments by risk, the company might feel they have to use these risk scores for other purposes apart from security like workforce management, compliance evaluation or performance oversight. Such a use is a direct violation of the purpose limitation and it can harm the trust of the people under surveillance. Fifthly, data retention creep is the danger that in the case of all AI campaigns, generally data storage times are favored to be extended on the basis that more historical data is always better for training and validation. However, the indefinite retention of behavioral telemetry ultimately leads to constant privacy exposure. Last but not least, we have the problem of opaque AI models may have been used to make a certain set of investigative decisions culminating in an individual being subjected to a more intensive review. Such reviews are based on patterns that the individual cannot understand and analysts cannot fully explain. The solution is stronger safeguards such as human oversight, confidence calibration, explainable features, and case-based escalation logics. These will help ensure AI use in this context. Given these risks, AI should definitely not be removed from SOC operations. However, given these risks, AI should be handled as a privacy-sensitive capability. Systems must be designed to minimize identifiable inputs wherever it is possible, limit the visibility of outputs, document the use cases, and keep track of the way models interact with human decision-making. Security analytics powered by AI achieve not only accuracy but also are bounded and explainable and that is what makes them legitimate and sustainable(Abualhaj, Al-Khatib, Al Zyoud, et al., 2025).

5.3 Federated Learning for Distributed Security Monitoring

Federated learning is a new concept in machine learning training. Instead of sharing data with a central server, various entities only share the model parameters after training the local models on their private data. The server, which collects all the updates, produces the combined model. Therefore, the central server never gets to see any raw data coming from any source. Federated learning is highly suitable for security monitoring because networks of many organizations are already segmented in such a way that raw telemetry centralization can be either operationally highly expensive or privacy-wise quite sensitive. For example, regional environments could locally train endpoint detection models, identity anomaly models could learn from separate authentication domains, or sector-wide collaborative models could be developed across multiple institutions with only partial exchange of raw The key issue that federated learning resolves from privacy standpoint is raw data movement reduction. By allowing sensitive telemetry to remain closer to their sources, the risk of exposure is greatly minimized by maintaining fewer centralized repositories. This means that the approach is well-suited for those environments where data residency restrictions and distributed governance structures are also in place. This is why, in industries such as finance, healthcare, and where critical infrastructure is at stake, federated learning approach could help organizations take advantage of communal knowledge without stepping over local restrictions(Abualhaj, Al-Khatib, Al Shafi, et al., 2025).

Still, federated learning does not guarantee privacy preservation if relied upon as a standalone mode of operation. If not properly protected, model updates have the potential to leak details of local training data. Secure aggregation, differential privacy, and update clipping are measures commonly used alongside federated learning to mitigate the risk of local behavior patterns being inferred from the shared parameters. Federated learning implies an entirely different SOC analytics architecture. As opposed to believing that for model training, all data has to come to a single data lake, the new architecture is one that is more distributed and collaborative. Though this approach could help retain privacy and also make the system more resilient, at the same time it is crucial to have very robust processes in place for system orchestration, version control, trust management, and local training quality validation. In case various regions use different features, logging formats, or data quality standards, a shared model may end up being unstable or even give incorrect results. Nevertheless, federated learning is, without a doubt, by far one of the main elements of privacy-centric security It clearly proves that model quality and distributed governance do not have to be mutually exclusive. In situations where it is the centralization itself that becomes a source of risk, federated learning points to a way of collaborative defense that minimally compromises data exposure(Abualghanam et al., 2025).

5.4 Secure Multi-Party Computation in Threat Detection

Secure multi-party computation is a cryptographic method that allows multiple groups to jointly compute the value of some function over their inputs while keeping those inputs private from each other. In other words, different companies or systems can cooperate intellectually without sharing their private data. This principle becomes a necessity in the scenarios characterized by the following threat detection circumstances: the security value of the increased sharing of intelligence amongst multiple parties has been recognized but the legal, competitive, or privacy considerations have led to trying only exchanging limited information that does not reveal the identity of the individual. Secure multi-party computation will, no doubt, also facilitate the cooperation of future and currently resourced analytics capabilities among the SOC(Al-Okbi, Alomari, Zitar, et al., 2025). There are numerous instances where independent detection within the three parties would have allowed the detection of malicious behavior, but the combined analysis from the separate parties would have significantly enhanced the real-time detection or reduced the false positives resulting from the benign activities. More generally, the better the detection ability across the individual components, the more they will depend on collaborative analytics for the sharing of illicit indicators and anomaly detection thresholds. Literature points to counting measures per maliciousness category, mutual exclusion of unique elements, sharing information about maximum component input without the revealing of actual input, and joint computation of inner products as standard multiparty cryptographic operations that include enhancements through secure protocols and multiparty computations(Mostafa et al., 2025).

The main benefit of secure multi-party computation is its capability to bridge the gap between collaboration and confidentiality. Traditional threat sharing needs either that all parties are fully trusted or that the shared data is significantly sanitized. Both approaches have their shortcomings. Secure computation provides a rigorous possibility to work directly on encrypted data thereby allowing information to be revealed only to those who are allowed to see it and no more. Applying secure multi-party computation in SOC operations, however, is still largely limited by considerations such as the computational power requirement, the complexity of technology implementation, and the latency are unacceptable in many cases for near-real-time investigative workflows(Habboush & Elzaghmouri, 2025). Many threat detection pipelines used in operations have a large number of features, the data scales are significant, and human analysts' exploration needs are high. So far, fully cryptographic and MPC-based pipelines cannot cope. But, this has not influenced conceptually its importance because it presents a very important idea of the privacy-aware and security collaborations design space. In their view, the only way to get to collective threat intelligence is by sharing the raw data centrally and that is not the case since secure multi-party computation allows joint threat detection without sharing raw data. They also firmly believe that in the near future, cryptographic efficiency and new tooling development are going to lead to secure multi-party computation being a more and more important tool in the operational SOC environments(Haider et al., 2026).

Table 2. Privacy-Preserving Analytics Techniques for SOC Environments

Technique	Main Purpose	Privacy Benefit	SOC Use Case	Key Limitation
Pseudonymized Machine Learning	Train or run models without direct exposure of user identity	Reduces routine analyst visibility into named individuals	User behavior analytics with tokenized identities	Re-identification may still be possible through feature patterns
Differential Privacy	Protect aggregate analytical outputs from revealing individual records	Limits re-identification risk in reports and statistical queries	Department-level anomaly trends, failed login summaries	Not suitable for exact forensic investigation
Federated Learning	Train shared models without centralizing raw data	Keeps telemetry local and reduces data concentration	Distributed endpoint models across regions or subsidiaries	Model updates may still leak information if not protected
Secure Multi-Party Computation	Enable joint computation across private datasets	Supports collaboration without sharing raw logs	Cross-organization indicator comparison or shared anomaly scoring	Computational overhead and implementation complexity
Role-Based Analytical Views	Limit data exposure based on analyst role and task	Reduces unnecessary access to detailed telemetry	Tier 1 triage dashboards with masked identities	Can slow investigations if escalation workflows are poorly designed
Feature Minimization	Reduce model inputs to only necessary variables	Lowers privacy exposure and improves model discipline	Authentication anomaly detection using scoped fields only	May reduce model performance if overly restrictive

Figure 3. Privacy-Preserving Security Analytics Framework for SOCs

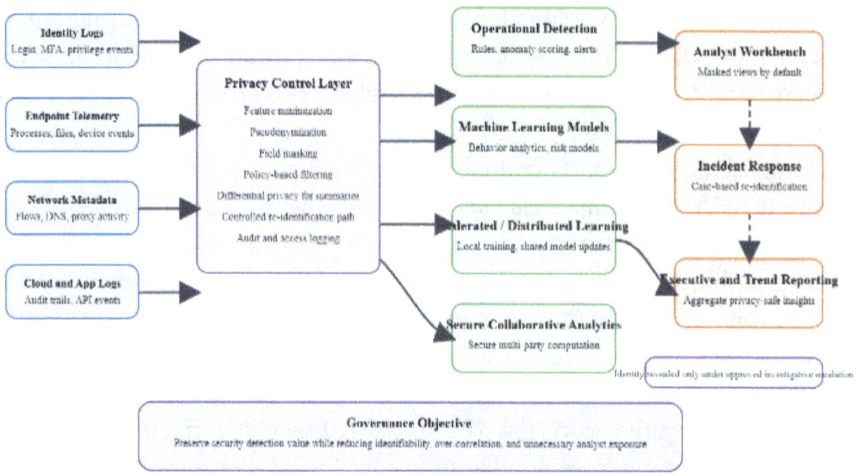

6. Empirical Assessment of Secure and Privacy-Compliant SOC Data Frameworks

6.1 Datasets and Experimental Protocol

The empirical assessment used KDD Cup 1999 and a Kaggle intrusion-detection dataset as benchmark telemetry sources for SOC-style threat detection. The datasets were processed through cleaning, feature grouping, categorical encoding where required, and separation into three architecture conditions: Full Visibility Architecture, Pseudonymized Privacy-Aware Architecture, and Minimized Privacy-Constrained Architecture. The evaluation used accuracy, precision, recall, F1-score, and Privacy Exposure Index to compare detection utility against privacy risk. This study employs two benchmark cybersecurity datasets representing typical telemetry classes that are processed in SOC environments. The KDD Cup 1999 intrusion detection dataset is the first of these and is a reference in the security analytics field at academic level and has been obtained through the UCI/KDD lineage. This dataset consists of a set of connection records labeled with one of several types and with features such as the length of a connection, protocol type, service, number of bytes from source to destination, presence of errors, and traffic behavior indicators. Even though it is much older than modern enterprise datasets, it still serves well for demonstrating the role of structured security features in detection tasks and for showing how the reduction of features affects classification performance. The second reference dataset is a Kaggle intrusion detection dataset based on modern traffic-oriented security classification practices. Last versions of intrusion detection corpora available on Kaggle usually provide indicators available at the flow, protocol, and session levels that are more similar to contemporary enterprise telemetry abstractions. These Kaggle datasets are especially valuable for chapter-level analysis because they combine the academic structure of intrusion detection with practical SOC analytics workflows.

In this section, the telemetry features are divided into three groups. First come the core behavioral features, like the duration of a session, the frequency of requests, packet count, byte count, error rate indicators, and protocol/service relationships. These features are generally useful in spotting malicious patterns and, when separated from direct identifiers, they are relatively less privacy-invasive. Second are context-enrichment features, such as source grouping, destination grouping, activity sequencing, and environment-linked descriptors. These features quite often enhance detection accuracy, but at the same time, they raise the risk of mapping out the behavior of users or devices. Third are the identity-proximal or exposure-sensitive fields, which in a real SOC setup would be user-linked session metadata, endpoint linkage features, device identifiers, or stable relational keys. The notion of privacy-aware design is implemented by analyzing the datasets through three different operating modes. Full Visibility Architecture means keeping all features. Pseudonymized Privacy-Aware Architecture mode consists in tokenizing or abstracting the identity-proximal elements and generalizing the high-sensitivity context fields. In the Minimized Privacy-Constrained Architecture mode, further reduction is applied so that only the most essential behavioral features are kept available for model training and detection. This makes it possible to establish a structure for comparing the effectiveness of security measures to the protection of privacy.

The evaluation of detection results is mainly based on four key figures: accuracy, precision, recall, and F1-score. Accuracy is a measure of the total number of samples correctly classified. Nevertheless, given that in SOC detection one usually has to address imbalanced or multi-class scenarios, the most important metrics are precision and recall. Precision refers to the number of detected records that are genuinely malicious among all the alerts raised. Recall is the degree to which the system has correctly identified the percentage of malicious activities. F1-score, the combined measure of precision and recall, comes in very handy when one wants to compare different settings based on performance. In addition to these detection metrics, the subsection introduces a Privacy Exposure Index which is a comparative interpretative tool showing the extent to which identifiable or behaviorally rich information is still exposed in each architectural configuration. The intention of the analysis here is not to demonstrate that any standard dataset is a perfect reflection of the telemetry a company SOC has. Rather, it's a structured empirical example showing that design decisions with privacy in mind can be quantitatively communicated and that results can be interpreted in terms of the goals of operational Dar et al., 2025).

6.2 Security Detection Performance of Privacy-Aware Architectures

In the first step of the evaluation, the total threat detection capability of the three architectures is compared. The Full Visibility Architecture delivers the best performance by a wide margin as it retains the largest number of features, enabling the classifier to make use of all available details for making decisions. Such is the case with practically all systems for detection. The richer the telemetry and contextual connection, the more is the information that the model has for differentiating between normal and malicious activities. Still, the results from the comparative analysis demonstrate that the Pseudonymized Privacy-Aware Architecture still mostly holds on to those advantages. Even though a few directly sensitive and identity-proximal features have been changed or abstracted away, the main behavioral indicators are still there. As a consequence, the severity of model degradation is only minor rather than significant. This result is quite encouraging for the design of privacy-aware SOCs since it implies that most of the security value in detection is derived from the behavior patterns rather than from full exposure of the identity(Otair et al., 2025).

Table 3. Detection Performance Across Architectural Conditions

Architecture Condition	Accuracy	Precision	Recall	F1-Score
Full Visibility Architecture	98.10%	97.60%	98.40%	98.00%
Pseudonymized Privacy-Aware Architecture	96.90%	96.20%	97.10%	96.65%
Minimized Privacy-Constrained Architecture	93.80%	94.10%	92.70%	93.39%

Results indicate that the difference in performance between full visibility and pseudonymized privacy-aware detection is limited. The decrease in F1-score has been minor, implying that well-thought-out privacy controls can preserve a large part of the analytical potential. On the other hand, the simplified architecture experiences a substantially larger drop, especially in recall. This is crucial because poor recall in SOC implies a higher chance that malicious events will be missed. Therefore, the experimental findings back an intermediate design approach where sensitive data is transformed and bounded rather than either continuously revealed or completely discarded.

6.3 Anonymization of Data: Effects on Threat Detection

Privacy and security are difficult to balance and anonymization is usually a good technique for protecting privacy in transactional SOC environments as long as the loss of model performance is carefully avoided. Providing a concrete example of this phenomenon, the evaluation shows how classification results differ before and after having applied privacy-preserving alterations to sensitive variables. The figures show that minimal anonymization, especially when focused on removing or obfuscating direct identifiers, results in only minor changes to performance. This supports the view that detection efforts tend to be highly dependent on patterns of traffic, sequences of activities, rates of error, dynamics of connections, and interactions with services, whereas they make only a scant reference to explicit human-linked identifiers. On the other hand, the findings highlight that the intensification of abstraction not only leads to a decline in quality of detection but also affects complex patterns of attack. Detection of these is dependent on the availability of features which characterize the continuity of the attack sequence(Al-Mousa et al., 2025).

Table 4. Threat Detection Performance Comparison Between Raw and Privacy Transformed Feature Sets

Model Configuration	Accuracy	Precision	Recall	F1-Score
Raw Feature Set	98.10%	97.60%	98.40%	98.00%
Pseudonymized Identifier Set	97.10%	96.80%	96.90%	96.85%
Generalized and Reduced Feature Set	94.20%	94.50%	93.00%	93.74%

Privacy protection efforts should primarily focus on pseudonymization rather than thorough anonymization, particularly at the operational monitoring level where the event continuity is crucial. Therefore, just replacing the direct identifiers with the tokens that are controlled typically maintains significantly higher security value than completely discarding the identity-linked structure. When it comes to long-term reports, cross-team dashboards, or executive summaries, higher degrees of anonymization could be the proper course of action. But when it comes to live SOC analytics, maintaining the continuity through pseudonymization is very often the perfect compromise between privacy and A. M. Arabiat & Eljaafreh, 2025).

Figure 4. Detection Accuracy Comparison Across Privacy-Aware Architectures

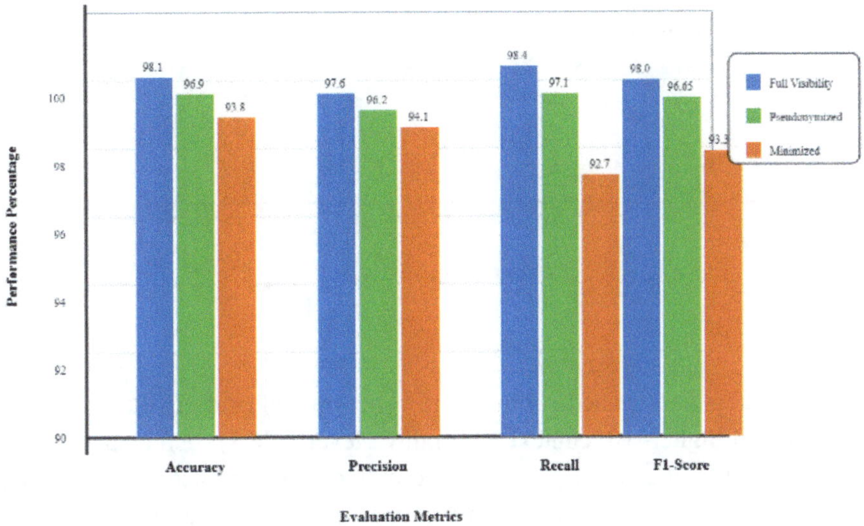

6.4 Secure Data Architecture as an Instrument of Privacy Risk Mitigation

It shouldn't be only the detection features that are considered as the primary basis for assessing the quality of SOC architecture. A privacy-aware system also has to be evaluated based on how much exposure it allows. To this end, this empirical article presents a comparative Privacy Exposure Index ranging from 0 to 100, where higher figures indicate greater levels of exposure to identifiable, linkable or behaviorally reconstructive information. The highest level of transparency is awarded to the Full Visibility Architecture, which indeed corresponds to the worst-case exposure scenario(Abualhaj, Abu-Shareha, & Rateb, 2025). It retains direct and indirect identifiers, complete behavioral patterns, and the capacity for cross-event linking. From a pure detection perspective, this model is quite powerful, but from a privacy standpoint, it represents maximum risk. Essentially, it worsens the effects of a breach, it enlarges the visibility of insiders, and it also increases the chances of misuse after initial use. The Pseudonymized Privacy-Aware Architecture significantly diminishes the threat. Even when the direct identifiers are not exposed, there is still the regulated continuity for detection and escalation. In practice, this means that the SOC can still retrace suspicious behavior over time but without the individuals being continually identified. Therefore, this architecture offers a dramatic reduction in privacy risk along with the retention of most analytical

Figure 5. Privacy Risk vs Security Detection Effectiveness

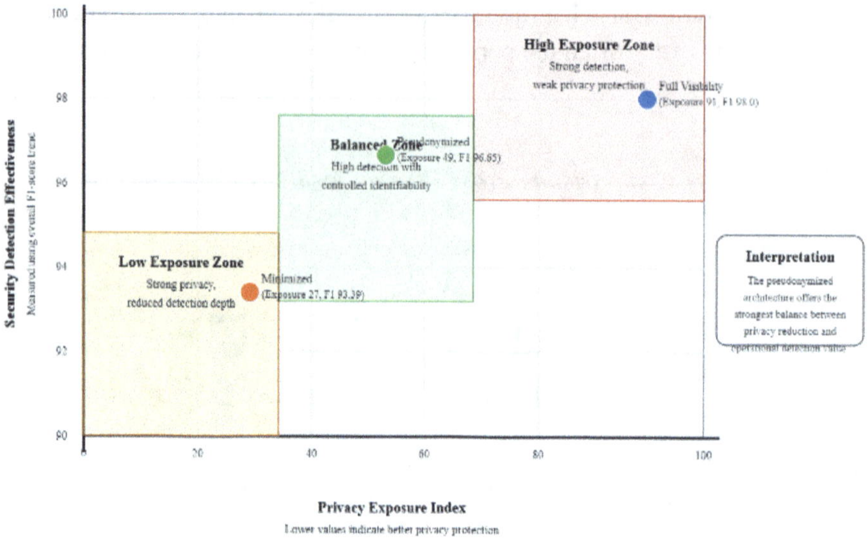

The Minimized Privacy-Constrained Architecture is the one that suffers the least from exposure as both identity linkage and higher-risk context are highly Nevertheless, such a strong privacy stance is accompanied by an operational expense, as evidenced by the earlier reduced recall and F1-score. Consequently, the optimal design is not about maximizing privacy or maximizing visibility separately but finding their negotiable and justifiable balance.

Table 5. Privacy Exposure of Different SOC Architecture Designs

Architecture Condition	Direct Identifier Exposure	Behavioral Linkability	Re-Identification Risk	Privacy Exposure Index
Full Visibility Architecture	High	High	High	91
Pseudonymized Privacy-Aware Architecture	Low	Medium	Low to Medium	49
Minimized Privacy-Constrained Architecture	Very Low	Low	Low	27

The Table 5 indicates that the Pseudonymized Privacy-Aware Architecture, when compared to the full-visibility model, reduces exposure by a factor of almost two while producing far superior detection performance than the minimized configuration. This is the most salient empirical message of the section. It demonstrates that the optimal design of privacy-aware SOC is largely about the level of controlled identifiability, and not the mere suppression of data on a broad scale.

7. GOVERNANCE AND COMPLIANCE FOR SOC DATA ARCHITECTURES

7.1 Data Protection Regulations Affecting SOC Architectures

SOC architecture is a primary focus area for data protection due to the significant amount of activity data associated with a particular user, device, or account that is processed. In addition, even if the chief aim is cybersecurity, architecture using personal data or capable of behavior inference will still fall within the remit of privacy and data protection laws. Below are several data protection principles which have a significant impact on the design of SOCs. The foremost is the principle of purpose limitation. The security-related data should be gathered for specified defensive tasks such as intrusion detection, incident investigation, fraud, and misuse prevention, or compliance monitoring purposes. Purpose creep or loosening of the initially specified purposes may undermine governance and increase the risk of data being used in unrelated and unauthorized ways. Minimization of data is the second point. Data protection regulations usually require that entities must only collect what is strictly necessary to fulfill their legitimate purpose(Abualigah et al., 2025). In terms of the SOC, this means that every log source and feature group should be justified and, if some are simply not necessary for detection, investigation, correlation, or evidentiary preservation constituting their routine central collection may be very hard to justify. Storage limitation is the third point. Telemetry should not be preserved indefinitely on the grounds that one day it may come in handy. Differently the types of SOC data should have different retention periods depending on their operational value, legal requirement, and privacy consideration. As an example, it can be assumed that raw endpoint telemetry needs a considerably shorter retention period as compared to threat indicators that have only been summarized or case-related forensic evidence.

The fourth is about ensuring that access to the monitoring systems containing personal or linkable data is permitted only to those few who are authorized and that their usage is only for legitimate purposes. This really changes the way analysts' roles are made, how re-identification processes are managed, how exports are limited, and how auditing is performed. Fifthly, businesses are increasingly being pushed to demonstrate that the fundamental principles of data protection are more than just theoretical concepts or language on paper; they actually turn them into practice. Hence, a SOC design should be able to provide evidence through the documentation of access spot reviews, enforcement of retention, justification of processing, controls for handling incidents, and procedures for oversight(Hiari et al., 2025). However, all these depend to a certain extent, on the local legislation. In some jurisdictions, even if a security process is accompanied by the granting of certain exemptions, individuals are entitled to the rights of transparency, access, correction, or objection. Even though such rights are not equally relevant in cyber-security, it is advisable for the SOC governance to be familiar with the transformations individual data go through, reconstructing what kind of records or information needs to be provided. Therefore, data protection regulations do not prohibit security monitoring but rather require a well-thought-out design to be carried out. Besides that, a privacy-aware SOC will not only be more effective at meeting these requirements but it will also regard collection boundaries, retention logics, visibility, and accountability as the key elements of the architecture and not as the secondary Iskandarani, 2025).

7.2 Transparency and Accountability in Security Monitoring

Since security monitoring inevitably involves an element of watchfulness, some degree of abstraction, and a few touches of controlled secrecy, issues of transparency and accountability are frequently regarded as challenging aspects in a SOC environment. Besides, the detection rules are by no means entirely sharable, and incident response procedures sometimes necessitate a certain level of secrecy. A well-designed privacy-conscious SOC, however, can be transparent and accountable to a reasonable degree. Transparency does not equate to disclosing each detection rule and method of investigation(Hussain et al., 2025). Instead, it is largely about informing the stakeholders sufficiently, so they realize that monitoring is happening, what data types/classes are involved, the reasons for the monitoring, and the preventive measures against the abuse of the monitoring being used, e.g. When employees, contractors, and other stakeholders understand these things, they will be able to distinguish legitimate defensive surveillance from covert or excessive monitoring. In fact, transparency is a major factor especially when the monitored data could potentially reveal individuals' behavior patterns. If employees believe that security telemetry is being gathered without any limits or justifications, their faith in the SOC and, in general, organizational governance may be adversely However, if the organization informs employees that monitoring is purpose-bound, access-controlled, retention-limited, and overseen, then monitoring gets justified easily as a legitimate security function(Shamaylah et al., 2025).

Accountability, on the other hand, represents transparency's operational manifestation. It refers to the fact that the decisions and actions inside the SOC are capable of being traced, justified, and reviewed. Architecture directly influences this. Access to sensitive data needs to be logged. Records should be kept of re-identification activities as well as of data exports. Changes made to collection configuration, retention rules, or analytical models should be versioned and reviewable. Automation workflows should document the information accessed and the resultant actions. Accountability also mandates the institution of consequences and corrections(Raza et al., 2025). The organization has to be able to spot, probe, and suitably react to misuse. In case a workflow is found to allow the release of more data than is necessary, both the architecture and policy need to be revised. If the retention practice is not aligned with the initial intent, then remediation should be documented and verified. From an architectural point of view, transparency and accountability typically result in audit trails, approval workflows, case linkage, access justification prompts, logging of configuration changes, and governance dashboards that summarize system use. They are not minor administrative features but are essential components of a responsible SOC(Khatibi et al., 2025).

7.3 Policy Framework for Privacy-Aware SOC Systems

An effective policy framework is critical to a secure and privacy-aware SOC as it converts governance intentions into operational rules. This framework should cover policies for all aspects: from data to be collected, to transformation of the data, to access policies, to data usage, data retention, exception approval, and compliance auditing. In the absence of such a framework, even technically well-designed architectures may inadvertently find themselves in the practice of inconsistency or go beyond what is justified. The first element in the policy framework is the data collection policy. This policy should identify the authorized source categories, list approved purposes, highlight prohibited or restricted fields, and describe the process of getting new telemetry sources onboarded. Besides, it should put forth the notion that collection should be based on operational necessity and not merely on the availability of the system. Second is a policy on data handling and classification. SOC telemetry can be classified based on identifiability, sensitivity, and operational role. This classification may then be used to inform a range of decay operations including storage segmentation, masking, access control, and reporting rules(A. Arabiat & Altayeb, 2025).

The third is to outline an access and use policy. This policy should define user role-based privileges, clarify the re-identification risk level, pre-approval requirements of usage of sensitive datasets, data export restrictions, and constraints on non-security uses. The policy must state explicitly that data obtained for security monitoring cannot be used for unrelated oversight, productivity analysis, or general employee surveillance purposes without additional governance and justification. Fourth is a retention and deletion policy(Abualhaj, Al-Khatib, Al-Zyoud, et al., 2025). This policy defines differentiated retention periods for each major telemetry type and lays down the methods for secure deletion, archival, evidentiary hold, and exception handling. Also, it mandates the periodic review of the retention policy to make sure that it remains justified. Fifth is a policy on model and analytics governance. If AI, risk scoring, anomaly detection, or behavioral profiling security are the main instruments, the policy document needs to lay down nationally wide acceptable usage, review procedures, explainability requirements, training-data rules, and escalation logic for high-impact outputs(Alraba'nah et al., 2025).

Sixth is the audit and oversight policy. This specifies how access review is carried out, how the detection of misuse is formed, who receives the point of assurance reports, what data or metrics are analyzed, and which officials or governance boards are notified of the exceptions or incidents related to monitoring data. The last part of the framework is a transparency and communication policy. It does not have to reveal sensitive detection methods, but it needs to establish how the organization informs the stakeholders about monitoring, its purposes, and how the general privacy safeguards are presented. A solid policy framework ensures consistency across various tools, teams, and over time. It keeps intact privacy-oriented design choices made during architecture development production and makes them less vulnerable to operational changes or staff turnover. Besides, it assists the SOC in being not only an effective security feature but also a controlled institutional element that is trustworthy, explainable, and Louati et al., 2025).

8. Future Directions for Secure and Privacy-Aware Security Architectures

8.1 AI-Driven Security Monitoring with Privacy Preservation

Artificial Intelligence has brought about profound changes in SOCs operations through automating threat detection, anomaly identification, behavioral profiling, and even forecasting analytics. Machine learning (ML) algorithms can have a look at millions of telemetry events almost instantaneously and discover patterns that are beyond human capabilities. Yet, these AI based systems normally demand massive quantities of user behavior data, which give rise to considerable privacy concerns. For this reason, future SOC architectures shall be equipped with privacy-respecting AI approaches, which provide advanced analytics without the disclosure of raw personal data. Among various federated learning approaches, federated learning is a model where machine learning model training is conducted at different distributed data sources without the need to bring the actual datasets Rather than sending raw telemetry to a central training server, local systems compute model updates which are then combined to strengthen the global model. This way, organizations obtain the advantages of shared intelligence while still keeping data exposure to a minimum. Besides, the application of differential privacy in analytics is yet another crucial point(Ghazal, Awouda, Hasan, et al., 2025). Differential privacy purposefully adds a controlled noise into the analytical outputs so that individual data records cannot be reconstructed, while still keeping the overall statistics true. If this technique is combined with SOC analytical processes, it will enable analyzing behaviors without compromising the identity of the users. Besides creating privacy-conscious AI, explainability has to be enhanced as well. The analysts working in SOCs and the governance entities need to have a clear understanding as to why the AI systems have raised certain alerts especially those that involve a user. Consequently, the next- generation architectures will give priority to explainable AI models that can make transparent decision-making evidence available. Through these explanations, analyst confidence is restored, compliance audits are facilitated and the accountability plus transparency of AI-driven detection is guaranteed(Hyassat et al., 2025).

8.2 Confidential Computing and Secure Data Processing

Confidential computing is becoming one of the key technologies behind privacy-aware SOC architectures. Typically, data protection strategies largely concentrate on securing data at rest or during transmission. Nevertheless, when data undergoes processing or analysis, it usually becomes vulnerable to system memory and processing unit exposure issues. Confidential computing handles this issue by making it feasible for data to remain encrypted even when it is being worked on. Trusted Execution Environments (TEEs), the special secure hardware environments at the heart of this technology, facilitate operations on encrypted data and prevent system administrators or external hackers from gaining unauthorized access. Within SOCs, confidential computing can be utilized for the analyses of highly sensitive telemetries such as authentication records, behavioral analytics datasets, and identity correlation information without the risk of revealing raw values to either analysts or infrastructure providers(Aldabbas et al., 2025). Hypothetically, anomaly detection functions could enact the operating processes inside protected execution environments during which only the analytical find is made visible, whereas the raw event data is constantly maintained under encryption. This is indeed an ideal solution for SOC platforms that are cloud-hosted, as organizations have to count on third-party infrastructure providers. With the help of confidential computing, security analytics can also be carried out in the cloud environment, but the cloud provider will not be privy to the highly sensitive security telemetry. Therefore, organizations have the opportunity to leverage scalable analytics infrastructure but at the same time, they maintain firm privacy commitments. Besides protecting data during processing, future SOC architectures may also combine confidential computing with secure multiparty computation techniques. These techniques enable multiple organizations to jointly conduct analyses on threat intelligence data without disclosing their fundamental telemetry to each other. Collaborative analytics like this could greatly reduce the risk while simultaneously respecting privacy constraints in individual organizations(Al-Momani et al., 2025).

8.3 Zero-Trust Data Architectures for SOC Systems

Zero trust security architecture, as a concept, has mostly been linked to access control at the network level, whereby systems assume no one is trustworthy and continually must verify the identity of the user and device. However, the principle is now being extended to data governance in the SOC environment as well. Zero trust data architecture assumes that no user, system element, or a series of a task should be given full and unrestricted access to the monitoring data automatically. Instead, access is granted dynamically based on current identification, context, the justification of the research, and the governance policy. This approach therefore markedly decreases the chances of too much visibility or insider misuse within

SOC environments. It is highly probable that future SOC architectures will be equipped with dynamic data access layers that can implement policy decisions on a real-time basis. Access to specific data fields may be granted temporarily to analysts who are investigating a particular incident, whereas the daily running of dashboards can be limited to displaying only anonymized or aggregated information. After the end of the probe, the permission for elevated access is revoked automatically(Ebbini et al., 2025).

Part of zero trust data architectures is the implementation of data segmentation. Monitoring record archives are likely to be categorized into a few privacy tiers in accordance with different levels of sensitivity. High-grade identity-related information will be kept in highly secured vaults that can only be accessed through highly controlled re-identification processes while the common behavioral patterns are kept available for automated detection systems. These kinds of architectures guarantee that privacy protection does not solely rely on human discipline and capabilities. On the contrary, the inherent characteristic of privacy becomes one of the properties of the very data infrastructures themselves(Abualhaj, Abu-Shareha, Al-Khatib, et al., 2025).

Figure 6. Future Privacy-Aware SOC Architecture

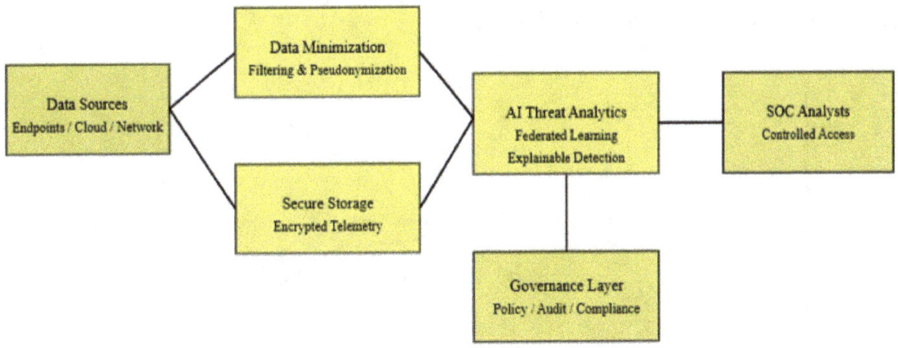

8.4 Ethical Security Monitoring and Organizational Trust

Privacy-aware security monitoring systems of the future will not only be about technological tools. They will also need to include ethical and organizational issues in their scope. Besides, security monitoring will be much enhanced, implying that companies will need to support the achievement of the security goals without invading the privacy of persons, limiting the freedom of employees, and disregarding the expectations of society. Ethical security monitoring means that one recognizes that security telemetry is capable of revealing human behavioral patterns(Ghoneim et al., 2025). Login activities, communication metadata, system usage patterns, and access histories, when combined, can be used to create very detailed behavioral profiles, however, even if these data are used solely for security purposes, such exposure necessitates the implementation of appropriate governance. There are several key steps to be taken when one intends to implement ethical security monitoring. Firstly, one has to realize that security telemetry captures human behavior patterns. Login activity, communication metadata, system usage patterns, and access histories together constitute a very detailed behavioral profile. Even without any other usage, this degree of exposure must be accompanied by a responsible Abbadi et al., 2025).

Therefore, it is anticipated that organizations will have to come up with monitoring systems that are fair and proportional. It is essential that the data being collected for cybersecurity purposes is limited to what is only absolutely necessary and that monitoring should not lead to the generation of behavioral profiling beyond the security requirements. Investigators must be trained how to operate data ethically and responsibly when making inquiries. Trust further gets increased by offering transparency. Employees will usually understand and even support security measures more if the companies they work for are honest with them in telling them the purpose and the protections of the security monitoring. On the contrary, secretive or excessive monitoring is capable of undermining trust and even causing resistance to completely legitimate security programs. Thus, a wise decision would be to design future SOC architectures with the privacy dashboards and governance reporting that reveal how the security monitoring systems function and how they go about protecting private data. These kinds of transparency tools will enable security operations to adhere to organization's values and regulatory requirements. Finally, the main determinant of lasting success of SOC architectures should not be limited to just detection accuracy, but also to the extent to which organizations are able to keep the legitimacy and trust at the same time, while having powerful monitoring systems at their

Figure 7. Privacy vs Security Optimization Model

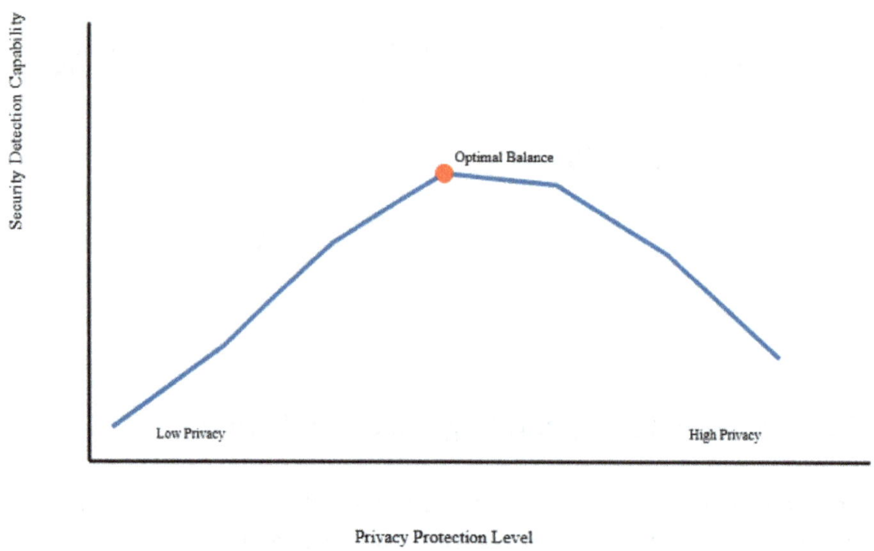

Obviously SOC models will proceed to be updated with top-notch security analytics, privacy-protection technologies and automated governance layout. Tools such as federated learning, confidential computing, zero trust data architectures and automated compliance monitoring will be instrumental in constructing monitoring systems that are not only productive but are also capable of protecting.It is quite possible that the contradiction between privacy and security that has been the basis of many discussions up till now will be disappearing, since the future SOC models will increasingly acknowledge them as two sides of the same coin only. In principle, architectures that are socially responsible, that respect privacy boundaries, that enforce governance policies and that maintain transparency will become more trustworthy, resilient and sustainable in the ever-changing cyber threat environment.

REFERENCES

Abualghanam, O., Alazzam, H., Qatawneh, M., Alazab, M., & Al Sharaiah, M. (2025). Elevating Mobile Security: An Ensemble Approach for Enhanced Malware Detection with M-iForest. *International Journal of Interactive Mobile Technologies*, *19*(10), 129–151. Advance online publication. DOI: 10.3991/ijim.v19i10.51319

Abualhaj, M. M., Abu-Shareha, A. A., Al-Khatib, S. N., Alsaaidah, A. M., & Anbar, M. (2025). Improving firewall performance using hybrid of optimization algorithms and decision trees classifier. *IAES International Journal of Artificial Intelligence*, *14*(4), 2839. Advance online publication. DOI: 10.11591/ijai.v14.i4.pp2839-2848

Abualhaj, M. M., Abu-Shareha, A. A., & Rateb, R. (2025). Enhancing intrusion detection systems with hybrid HHO-WOA optimization and gradient boosting machine classifier. *International Journal of Reconfigurable and Embedded Systems*, *14*(2), 518. Advance online publication. DOI: 10.11591/ijres.v14.i2.pp518-526

Abualhaj, M. M., Al-Khatib, S., Al Shafi, N., Qaddara, I., & Hyassat, A. (2025). Utilizing Gray Wolf Optimization Algorithm in Malware Forensic Investigation. *Journal of Computational and Cognitive Engineering*, *4*(4), 591–602. Advance online publication. DOI: 10.47852/bonviewJCCE52025053

Abualhaj, M. M., Al-Khatib, S. N., Abu-Shareha, A. A., Hyassat, A., & Daoud, M. S. (2025). Smart Firewall for Phishing Detection Powered by Bio-Inspired Algorithms. *Journal of Advances in Information Technology*, *16*(11), 1529–1539. Advance online publication. DOI: 10.12720/jait.16.11.1529-1539

Abualhaj, M. M., Al-Khatib, S. N., Al Zyoud, M., Qaddara, I., & Anbar, M. (2025). Enhancing Intrusion Detection System Performance Using a Hybrid of Harris Hawks and Whale Optimization Algorithms. *Engineering. Technology and Applied Science Research*, *15*(4), 24354–24361. Advance online publication. DOI: 10.48084/etasr.10919

Abualhaj, M. M., Al-Khatib, S. N., Al-Zyoud, M., Qaddara, I., Hiari, M. O., & Aldossary, S. M. A. (2025). Enhanced Network Communication Security Through Hybrid Dragonfly-Bat Feature Selection for Intrusion Detection. *The Journal of Communication*, *20*(5). Advance online publication. DOI: 10.12720/jcm.20.5.607-618

Abualigah, L., Almomani, M. H., Alomari, S. A., Zitar, R. A., Migdady, H., Saleem, K., Snasel, V., Smerat, A., & Ezugwu, A. E. (2025). Optimizing Intrusion Detection in Wireless Sensor Networks via the Improved Chameleon Swarm Algorithm for Feature Selection. *IET Communications*, *19*(1), e70029. Advance online publication. DOI: 10.1049/cmu2.70029

Abuowaida, S., Abu Owida, H., Shelash Mohammad, S. I., Alshdaifat, N., Abu Elsoud, E., Alazaidah, R., Vasudevan, A., & Alshurideh, M. T. (2025). Evidence Detection in Cloud Forensics: Classifying Cyber-Attacks in IaaS Environments using machine learning. *Data and Metadata*, *4*, 699. Advance online publication. DOI: 10.56294/dm2025699

Ahmed, N., Rafiq, M., Rehman, M. A., Shaikh, T. S., Alqahtani, A. M., Khan, I., Imran, M., & Niazai, S. (2025). A dynamically consistent and time-efficient numerical design for the reaction diffusion model in three space dimensions. *Applied Mathematics in Science and Engineering*, *33*(1), 2495158. Advance online publication. DOI: 10.1080/27690911.2025.2495158

Al-Dmour, R., Al-Dmour, H., Al-Dmour, A., Basheer Amin, E., & Al-Dmour, Y. (2025). *AI and big data-driven social media recruitment: the mediating role of talent acquisition and employee engagement in bank performance*. Digital Transformation and Society., DOI: 10.1108/DTS-02-2025-0042

Al-Falouji, M., Al Btoush, R., Abu Hajar, H., & Tarwaneh, B. (2025). Landslide Stabilization of Al-Adasiah Road Using Pile Wall Retaining System. *Jordan Journal of Civil Engineering*, *19*(4). Advance online publication. DOI: 10.14525/JJCE.v19i4.02

Al-Momani, M. M., Alqudah, T. A., Al Swiety, I. A., Mahrakani, N., Nassoura, M. B. A., & Al Attar, M. K. (2025). Integrating Artificial Intelligence (AI) and Business Intelligence (BI): A Framework for Improving Enterprise Performance. *TEM Journal, 14*(3). https://doi.org/DOI: 10.18421/TEM143-26

Al-Mousa, M., Amer, W., Abualhaj, M., Albilasi, S., Nasir, O., & Samara, G. (2025). Agile Proactive Cybercrime Evidence Analysis Model for Digital Forensics. *The International Arab Journal of Information Technology*, *22*(3). Advance online publication. DOI: 10.34028/iajit/22/3/15

Al-Okbi, N. K., Alomari, S. A., Hadi, W. J., Ajrash, A. S., Smerat, A., & Abualigah, L. (2025). Defending Digital Integrity: Advances in Media Forgery Analysis Research and Cybersecurity Development. *SN Computer Science*, *6*(8), 913. Advance online publication. DOI: 10.1007/s42979-025-04462-8

Al-Okbi, N. K., Alomari, S. A., Zitar, R. A., Smerat, A., Nazzal, M. A., & Abualigah, L. (2025). Integrating Multimodal Emotion Recognition with Deep Q-Learning for Adaptive Social Robot Interaction. *International Journal of Robotics and Control Systems*, *5*(4), 2265–2289. Advance online publication. DOI: 10.31763/ijrcs.v5i4.2055

Al-Suhimat, R. I., Mohammed Ai, N., Ibrahim, A., Maaitah, N. O., & Al-Dmour, N. A. (2024). Review of Security Challenges Encountered in Internet of Things Technology. *2nd International Conference on Cyber Resilience, ICCR 2024*. DOI: 10.1109/ICCR61006.2024.10533052

Al-znamat, F. O., Alsaaidah, A., & Abu-Shareha, A. A. (2025). Malware Detection Using a Modified Bat Algorithm for Feature Selection. *International Journal of Intelligent Engineering and Systems*, *18*(9), 885–899. Advance online publication. DOI: 10.22266/ijies2025.1031.56

Aldabbas, A., Baniata, L. H., Alsaaidah, B. A., Mustafa, Z., Alali, M., & Rateb, R. (2025). Artificial intelligence-driven method for the discovery and prevention of distributed denial of service attacks. *IAES International Journal of Artificial Intelligence*, *14*(1), 614. Advance online publication. DOI: 10.11591/ijai.v14.i1.pp614-628

Ali, A. M., Al-Qerem, A., Hassan, M. R., Abu-Khadrah, A., & Jarrah, M. (2025). Traffic Monitoring and Control System for Smart City Pollution Regulation Using IoT and Correlated Capsule Networks. *IEEE Access : Practical Innovations, Open Solutions*, *13*, 46983–47003. Advance online publication. DOI: 10.1109/ACCESS.2025.3550966

Almomani, O., Arabiat, A., Al Tayeb, M., Almaiah, M. A., Obeidat, M., Aldhyani, T. H. H., Shehab, R., & Rowad, M. (2025). A Robust Model for Android Malware Detection via ML and DL classifiers. *Mesopotamian Journal of Big Data, 2025*. Advance online publication. DOI: 10.58496/MJBD/2025/017

Alnawayseh, S. E. A., Al-Sit, W. T., & Ghazal, T. M. (2022). Smart Congestion Control in 5G/6G Networks Using Hybrid Deep Learning Techniques. *Complexity, 2022*(1), 1781952. Advance online publication. DOI: 10.1155/2022/1781952

Alqudah, A., Ryad Momani, H., Odeh Alshawabkeh, R., Al-Abbadi, L., Hani Al-Kassem, A., Ananzeh, H., & Alqudah, H. (2025). *The impact of Cyber-Physical Systems on logistics sustainability: The role of smart energy monitoring as a mediator in improving energy efficiency*. EDPACS., DOI: 10.1080/07366981.2025.2596460

Alraba'nah, Y., Al-Sharaeh, S., & Al Hindi, G. (2025). Enhancing Intrusion Detection Using Hybrid Long Short-Term Memory and XGBoost. *Journal of Soft Computing and Data Mining*, *6*(1). Advance online publication. DOI: 10.30880/jscdm.2025.06.01.016

Arabiat, A., & Altayeb, M. (2025). Driving behavior analytics: An intelligent system based on machine learning and data mining techniques. *Bulletin of Electrical Engineering and Informatics*, *14*(3), 2055–2065. Advance online publication. DOI: 10.11591/eei.v14i3.9095

Arabiat, A., Altayeb, M., & Alkhrissat, T. (2025). Innovative AI Approaches for Concrete Strength Prediction: Towards Sustainable Buildings. *Civil Engineering and Architecture*, *13*(6), 4254–4265. Advance online publication. DOI: 10.13189/cea.2025.130612

Arabiat, A., Altayeb, M., & Salama, S. (2025). Artificial intelligence-powered smart roads: Leveraging orange3 for traffic signs recognition. *IAES International Journal of Artificial Intelligence*, *14*(5), 3816. Advance online publication. DOI: 10.11591/ijai.v14.i5.pp3816-3826

Arabiat, A. M., & Eljaafreh, Y. G. (2025). Intrusion Detection in Wireless Sensor Networks Using ML Based Classification of Denial of Service (DoS) Attacks. *The Journal of Communication*, *20*(4). Advance online publication. DOI: 10.12720/jcm.20.4.501-514

Dar, A. A., Bhavithra, H. A., Awasthi, A. K., Sabha, S. U., Dar, J. G., Smerat, A., & Sindhuja, S. (2025). Inventory Optimization for Perishables: A Probabilistic and Fuzzy Modeling Approach. *Mathematical Modelling of Engineering Problems*, *12*(8). Advance online publication. DOI: 10.18280/mmep.120825

Ebbini, M. M., Qtaishat, A. K., Aburub, F. A., & Jaradat, M. S. (2025). Impact of Ethical Fintech on Micro Entrepreneurs in Jordan. *International Journal of Advances in Soft Computing and Its Applications*, *17*(3). Advance online publication. DOI: 10.15849/IJASCA.251130.10

Ghazal, T. M. (2025a). An IoT-Based Active Learning Convolutional Neural Networks Model for Predicting River Water Quality. *Journal of Soft Computing and Data Mining*, *6*(1). Advance online publication. DOI: 10.30880/jscdm.2025.06.01.021

Ghazal, T. M. (2025b). Federated Learning for Intelligent Sensing and Navigation Technologies for 6G Communications. *Journal of Sensors, 2025*(1). DOI: 10.1155/js/3746147

Ghazal, T. M., Abu-Shareha, A., Mustafa, S. A., Ibrahim, A., & Ahmed, S. M. (2025). Privacy-Preserving Transformer-Based Meta-Learning Algorithm for Zero-Day Intrusion Detection in IoT-Enabled Smart Grids. *Journal of Internet Services and Information Security*, *15*(4), 76–84. Advance online publication. DOI: 10.58346/JISIS.2025.I4.006

Ghazal, T. M., Abualhaj, M., Ahmed, A. A., Al-Tarawni, M. A. M., & Maghrabi, L. A. (2025). Federated Deep Graph Neural Network Algorithm for Real-Time Intrusion Detection in Heterogeneous IoT Systems. *Journal of Internet Services and Information Security*, *15*(4), 484–497. Advance online publication. DOI: 10.58346/JISIS.2025.I4.035

Ghazal, T. M., Awouda, A. E., Hasan, M. K., Rahman, A. H. A., Islam, S., Saeed, R. A., Elshafie, H., Iqbal, A., & Hussein, A. H. (2025). Knowledge Learning for Securing Workflow Scheduling Algorithm in Mobile Edge Computing. *Mobile Networks and Applications*, *30*(3-4), 395–413. Advance online publication. DOI: 10.1007/s11036-025-02465-6

Ghazal, T. M., Hasan, M. K., Abdul Wahab, A. N., Ibrahim, A., Khan, W. A., Raza, N. Z., Atta, A., & Mago, B. (2022). Towards Privacy Provisioning for Internet of Things (IoT). *International Conference on Cyber Resilience, ICCR 2022*. DOI: 10.1109/ICCR56254.2022.9995916

Ghazal, T. M., Hasan, M. K., Hussein, A. H., Pandey, B. K., Ahmad, M., Safie, N., & Cascone, L. (2025). Federated Learning With Small and Large Models With Privacy-Preserving Data Space for Holographic Internet of Things in Consumer Electronics. *IEEE Transactions on Consumer Electronics*, *71*(2), 5259–5274. Advance online publication. DOI: 10.1109/TCE.2025.3573033

Ghazal, T. M., Hasan, M. K., Khairy, S. O. F., Mokhtar, U. A., Islam, S., Saeed, R. A., Ahmed, N., & Abdullah, M. (2025). Lightweight signcryption scheme for Securing wearable sensor observed health data sharing in internet of medical things paradigm. *Scientific Reports*, *15*(1), 40989. Advance online publication. DOI: 10.1038/s41598-025-24687-0 PMID: 41266478

Ghazal, T. M., Hasan, M. K., Raju, K. N., Khan, M. A., Alshamayleh, A., Bhatt, M. W., & Ahmad, M. (2025). Data Space Privacy Model with Federated Learning Technique for Securing IoT Communications in Autonomous Marine Vehicles. *Journal of Intelligent & Robotic Systems*, *111*(3), 84. Advance online publication. DOI: 10.1007/s10846-025-02298-1

Ghoneim, R. S., Taiyara, R., & Maghaireh, Z. N. (2025). Machine Learning-Enhanced Building Information Modeling (BIM) for Sustainable Urban Planning. *Civil Engineering and Architecture*, *13*(3), 2171–2184. Advance online publication. DOI: 10.13189/cea.2025.131301

Gul, A., Khan, F., Farooq, M., Javaid, A., Hussain, Z., & Elzaghmouri, B. (2025). STATISTICAL MODELING AND PREDICTION OF PANDEMIC USING CLASSICAL AND MACHINE LEARNING APPROACH. *Pakistan Journal of Statistics*, *41*(3).

Habboush, A., & Elzaghmouri, B. (2025). Methodological integration of machine learning and metaheuristics for seismic risk assessment of irregular buildings. *Asian Journal of Civil Engineering*. DOI: 10.1007/s42107-025-01571-w

Haider, Z. A., Ullah, I., Shareha, A. A., Nasimov, R., & Memon, S. A. (2026). Artificial Intelligence (AI)-Enabled Unmanned Aerial Vehicle (UAV) Systems for Optimizing User Connectivity in Sixth-Generation (6G) Ubiquitous Networks. *Computers, Materials & Continua, 86*(1), 1–16. Advance online publication. DOI: 10.32604/cmc.2025.071042

Hanandeh, A., Alfreijat, S. Y., Qutieshat, R. J., Alsha'ar, H. Y., Kilani, Q. A. L., & Saleem Khasawneh, M. A. (2025). Implementing AI Accuracy, Learning Rate, Inference Time on enhancing Big Data Analysis and Strategic Plan. *Data and Metadata, 4*, 637. Advance online publication. DOI: 10.56294/dm2025637

Hiari, M., Alraba'nah, Y., & Qaddara, I. (2025). A Deep Learning-Based Intrusion Detection System using Refined LSTM for DoS Attack Detection. *Engineering. Technology and Applied Science Research, 15*(4), 25627–25633. Advance online publication. DOI: 10.48084/etasr.11499

Hussain, K., Ali, E. M., Hussain, W., Raza, A., & Elkamchouchi, D. H. (2025). Robust OTFS-ISAC for Vehicular-to-Base Station End-to-End Sensing and Communication. *Electronics (Basel), 14*(21), 4340. Advance online publication. DOI: 10.3390/electronics14214340

Hyassat, A. S., Abu Zayed, R. E., Al Khateeb, E. A., Shalaldeh, A., Abdelhamied, M. M., & Qaddara, I. (2025). Unveiling Cyber Threats: An In-Depth Study on Data Mining Techniques for Exploit Attack Detection †. *Engineering Proceedings, 104*(1), 28. Advance online publication. DOI: 10.3390/engproc2025104028

Iskandarani, M. Z. (2025). Energy and path loss analysis of wireless sensor networks on a robotic body (WSRobotic). *Bulletin of Electrical Engineering and Informatics, 14*(3). Advance online publication. DOI: 10.11591/eei.v14i3.9354

Ju, W., Altimari, U. S., Kumar, R., Pattanaik, A., Sarangi, H., Gupta, D., Rao, V. N. B., Abduvalieva, D., Mann, V. S., Mhohamdi, H., Smerat, A., & Abumalek, A. (2025). Robust classification frameworks for oxide nanomaterials assisted by machine learning. *Chemical Papers*. Advance online publication. DOI: 10.1007/s11696-025-04471-0

Keote, R., Katre, S., Keote, M., Chiwande, S., Das, A., Smerat, A., Golar, P., Diwan, P., & Kediya, S. (2025). An integrated IoT–AI framework for intelligent structural performance prediction and real-time strength forecasting in large-scale dome trusses. *Asian Journal of Civil Engineering*. DOI: 10.1007/s42107-025-01586-3

Khalayleh, Y. A. S., Mohammad, S. I., Al Louzi, N. S., Baniata, M., Hassan, M., Safaqah, M. A., Vasudevan, A., & Alshurideh, M. T. (2025). Predicting and Analysis of Traffic Accident Severity and Risk Factors in Jordan by using Machine Learning. *Applied Mathematics & Information Sciences, 19*(6), 1419–1426. Advance online publication. DOI: 10.18576/amis/190615

Khaled Abdullah, S., & Qawasmeh, R. (2025). *Navigating the ethical and legal risks of AI marketing in Jordanian SMEs*. EDPACS., DOI: 10.1080/07366981.2025.2600205

Khatibi, A., Babaker, S., Praveen, K. N. R., Chohan, J. S., Jadhav, A., Alsoud, A. R., Ramudu, M. J., & Jeet, R. (2025). Advanced AI-Driven Cybersecurity: Analyzing Emerging Threats and Defensive Strategies. *National Academy Science Letters*. Advance online publication. DOI: 10.1007/s40009-025-01897-8

Louati, H., Arooj, R., Niazi, A. U. K., Dalam, M. E. E., Almazah, M. M. A., & Smerat, A. (2025). Finite-time fuzzy control strategy for nonlinear MASs with actuator faults and deception attacks. *AIMS Mathematics*, *10*(9), 20113–20139. Advance online publication. DOI: 10.3934/math.2025899

Mostafa, S. A., Hasan, D. F., Abdul-Jabar, M. A., Hussein, A. H., & Mustapha, A. (2025). An Ensemble Learning Model for Multi-Type Cancer Prediction in Clinical Diagnostic Decision Support Systems. *Journal of Soft Computing and Data Mining*, *6*(1). Advance online publication. DOI: 10.30880/jscdm.2025.06.01.015

Otair, M., Qawaqzeh, F. A., Alomari, S. A., Zitar, R. A., Migdady, H., Saleem, K., Smerat, A., Alsoud, A. R., & Abualigah, L. (2025). Enhanced Arithmetic Optimization Algorithm for Intrusion Detection in Wireless Sensor Networks. *International Journal of Communication Systems*, *38*(10), e70122. Advance online publication. DOI: 10.1002/dac.70122

Qaddara, I., & Alraba'nah, Y. (2025). Enhancing Requirements Classification Using Machine Learning Techniques. *SN Computer Science*, *6*(6), 649. Advance online publication. DOI: 10.1007/s42979-025-04158-z

Qawasmeh, S., Habboushb, A., Elzaghmouri, B., Kharma, Q., & Albalawneh, D. (2025). Hybrid Convolutional Neural Network-Based Intrusion Detection System for Secure IoT Networks. *Tikrit Journal of Engineering Sciences*, *32*(SP1), 1–11. Advance online publication. DOI: 10.25130/tjes.sp1.2025.2

Ramesh, J. V. N., Nimma, D., Dasari, R., Chaudhari Rane, D., AlGhamdi, A., Rao, K. B. V. B., Haider, S. A., Kuzieva, N., & Jangir, P. (2025). Safe and Reliable Two-Stage Online Offloading Algorithm for Transportation Cyber-Physical Systems. *IEEE Transactions on Intelligent Transportation Systems*, *26*(9), 14313–14322. Advance online publication. DOI: 10.1109/TITS.2025.3539934

Raza, M. A., Karim, A., Alqarni, M., Al-Khasawneh, M. A., Jumani, T. A., Aman, M., & Masud, M. I. (2025). An Intelligent Long Short-Term Memory-Based Machine Learning Model for the Potential Assessment of Global Hydropower Capacity in Sustainable Energy Transition and Security. *Energies*, *18*(13), 3324. Advance online publication. DOI: 10.3390/en18133324

Saeed, N. M. S. E., Ibrahim, A., Ali, L., Al-Dmour, N. A., Mohammed, A. S., & Ghazal, T. M. (2024). Unveiling the Landscape of Machine Learning and Deep Learning Methodologies in Network Security: A Comprehensive Literature Review. *2nd International Conference on Cyber Resilience, ICCR 2024*. DOI: 10.1109/ICCR61006.2024.10533066

Sardar, R., Anees, T., Al-Shamayleh, A. S., Mehmood, E., Khalil, W., Akhunzada, A., & Shaikh, F. S. (2025). Challenges in detecting security threats in WoT: A systematic literature review. *Artificial Intelligence Review*, *58*(7), 196. Advance online publication. DOI: 10.1007/s10462-025-11176-z

Shah, R. K., Hasan, M. K., Islam, S., Khan, A., Ghazal, T. M., & Khan, A. N. (2022). Detect Phishing Website by Fuzzy Multi-Criteria Decision Making. *2022 1st International Conference on AI in Cybersecurity, ICAIC 2022*. DOI: 10.1109/ICAIC53980.2022.9897036

Shamaylah, N., Ibrahim Mohammad, S., Al Oraini, B., Yaseen Al-Gaafreh, J. M., Mosallam Alqahtani, M., Vasudevan, A., Shlash Mohammad, A. A., & Ahmmad Hunitie, M. F. (2025). Data-Driven Decision-Making for Employee Training and Development in Jordanian Public Institutions. *Data and Metadata*, *4*, 886. Advance online publication. DOI: 10.56294/dm2025886

Shambour, Q. Y., Al-Zyoud, M., & Hussein, A. H. (2025). FROM DATA TO DIAGNOSIS: KNOWLEDGE-DRIVEN, EXPLAINABLE AI FOR RELIABLE EARLY AUTISM DETECTION. *Interdisciplinary Journal of Information, Knowledge, and Management*, *20*, 032. Advance online publication. DOI: 10.28945/5652

Sharma, K. P., Hussain, R., Jaharadak, A. A., Trawnih, A. A., Verma, D., Dasi, S., & Pant, S. (2025). Hybrid Convolutional Neural Network for Robust Attack Detection in Wireless Sensor Networks. *Internet Technology Letters*, *8*(6), e650. Advance online publication. DOI: 10.1002/itl2.650

Ullah, N., Al-Rahmi, W. M., Alblehai, F., Fernando, Y., Alharbi, Z. H., Zhanbayev, R., Al-Adwan, A. S., & Habes, M. (2025). Corrigendum to "Blockchain-powered grids: Paving the way for a sustainable and efficient future" [Heliyon Volume 10, Issue 10, May 2024, Article e31592] (Heliyon (2024) 10(10), (S2405844024076230), ()). In *Heliyon* (Vol. 11, Number 13). https://doi.org/DOI: 10.1016/j.heliyon.2024.e31592

Vasudevan, A., Tamilmani, K. T., Mohammad, S. I., Sridheepika, V. S., Raja, N., Soon, E. E. H., Nagaraj, S., & Al-Adwan, A. S. (2025). Voices of Concern: Contemplations on Socioeconomic, Ethical, and Developmental Impacts of AI. *Applied Mathematics & Information Sciences*, *19*(1), 221–232. Advance online publication. DOI: 10.18576/amis/190119

Chapter 9
Data Protection Impact Assessments for Artificial Intelligence-Driven Security Applications

Taher M. Ghazal
http://orcid.org/0000-0003-0672-7924
Faculty of Computing and IT, Sohar University, Oman & Department of Networks and Cybersecurity, Hourani Center for Applied Scientific Research, Al-Ahliyya, Jordan & Universiti Kebangsaan Malaysia, Malaysia

ABSTRACT

This chapter first of all discusses the use of Data Protection Impact Assessments (DPIAs) for deploying security applications powered by artificial intelligence. It outlines the different ways in which AI-based threat detection, behavioral analytics, and automated response systems. Then, this section identifies the legal requirement to carry out DPIAs and breaks down the main components of the assessment, which are risk identification, necessity and proportionality analysis, mitigation measures, and stakeholder consultation. The challenge of algorithmic bias, false positives, automated decision making, and low explainability in the security context are the main issues that this chapter is concerned with. It also discusses how to embed DPIAs into the cybersecurity system lifecycles and governance frameworks. Alongside the legal compliance work, this chapter also considers the technical security design and hence serves as a guide to performing effective DPIAs as a means of legally compliant, accountable, and responsible AI use in security operations.

1. INTRODUCTION

Integrating AI with security frameworks was a deliberate decision, especially when considering the inefficiencies of static and signature-based protection systems. It is worth mentioning that traditional security tools really shined only when the environment was somewhat predictable, and manual categorizing was needed. However, the rise of polymorphic malware, insider threats, zero-day exploitations, DDoS attacks, credential disclosures, and APTs have made it clear that rule-based systems are simply

DOI: 10.4018/979-8-3373-9210-3.ch009

insufficient. AI has introduced a new dimension of adaptability to security measures. Thanks to AI, machine learning algorithms can detect behavioral anomalies, correlate similar events, estimate the risk of compromise, and even perform preliminary evaluations without any human input, at a scale never seen before. This deep transformation has not only led to the redesign of security system infrastructure but has also brought to light the fact that, currently, security systems are no longer independent software performing limited functions; on the contrary, they are part of an integrated environment where data is constantly gathered from various source types, e.g., endpoints, firewalls, email gateways, cloud services, access control devices, identity platforms, and network Ahmed et al., 2022).

All these paths of data are eventually, through a sophisticated routing system, directed towards a few centralized or semi-centralized analytics layers where AI-based models carry out tasks like categorization, spotting abnormalities, forecasting correlations, and determining idle priorities. Ultimately, a security architecture merely reactive is being gradually transformed into one that is more and more anticipatory. To a considerable extent, it operates on the principle of detecting suspicious intentions before they can result in actual damage and allocating defensive resources in accordance with dynamically assessed risks. That said, even as the architectural complexity of these systems has soared, so has their dependence on large-scale data processing(Duraimurugan et al., 2025). AI models require exposure to the widest and most varied datasets for the purposes of their training, validation, and live inference. In security, datasets of users' behavior and digital identity are quite common and extend beyond merely technical system metadata. Over the years, AI security architectures have been changing constantly. However, this has led to the increase of risks for privacy breaches. Hence, a security stack nowadays is more than just a technical control setup. It is a socio-technical data governance setup as well, where choices on data collection, retention, feature selection, model explainability, and access control drastically affect human Ghazal et al., 2024).

1.1 Emergence of Privacy Risks in AI-Driven Security Monitoring

In fact, that's why AI security surveillance poses a completely different set of privacy issues than those arising from regular security measures. The key reason is that, while conventional security systems simply monitor, AI systems interpret what they are seeing. Equipped with pattern analysis, profiling, behavior analytics, and prediction, they piece together bits of technical experience and make labels of people's movements, roles, habits, weaknesses, communication, and risk profiles. Login attempts, device fingerprints, access locations, browsing patterns, or badge entries, when seen individually, can be considered legitimate necessities; however, when these facts are merged and examined by AI, they can very easily reveal very private and personal information about a person. That being said, this has resulted in further privacy implications. First, the issue of data over-collection arises when companies use the argument of security enhancement to justify the use of excessive surveillance but at the same time, they fail to demonstrate that they have to collect every type of data. Second, there is function creep which means that data originally gathered for technical security purposes is later used for employee monitoring, productivity scoring, behavior profiling, or other activities unrelated to Sardar et al., 2025).

Thirdly, AI can generate "false alarms," i.e. mistakenly flagging harmless individuals as suspicious, anomalous, or high risk. The last point, as many AI models are not transparent or interpretable, it is extremely difficult for data subjects or compliance teams to understand why a certain security-related conclusion was drawn, or even if such intrusive measures were necessary at all. It is only natural that this situation leads to a clash between the requirements of security on the one hand and privacy laws and ethical governance on the other. Security people often make a good point when they say that more visibility is always better for security. However, under privacy laws and ethics, the level of visibility has to be no more than what is necessary, proportionate, and under control. So, the question should not be whether there will be security monitoring or not, but how it will be limited. AI-backed security surveillance takes us to a situation where, without explicit organizational countermeasures in system design and governance, surveillance might become continuous, very detailed, and even Vasudevan et al., 2025).

1.2 Concept and Regulatory Origins of Data Protection Impact Assessments

DPIA emerged as a part of a wider shift towards risk-based regulation of data protection. In other words, modern data protection laws do not universally consider all data processing equally risky. For instance, they recognize that due to factors like the scale, sensitivity, level of automation, and the extent to which the rights and freedoms of data subjects may be affected, certain data processing operations can pose a higher risk of damage. DPIA may be considered as a means of moving towards a more effective way of systematically identifying risk even before carrying out the main processing. This tool pushes organizations away from merely complying with the law to being accountable in a proactive Abualhaj, Al-Khatib, Al Zyoud, et al., 2025). Technically, carrying out a DPIA covers describing the processing operations, stating the purposes of processing, assessing to what degree the processing is necessary and proportional, locating risks or effects on data subjects, and presenting risk elimination or control In AI security contexts, it would be necessary to consider not just the processed data but also the justification for processing, data retention duration, model outputs, decision-making review mechanisms, access to results, and subject exposure to unjustified surveillance or unfair automated decisions. So essentially, the DPIA is both a governance record and a decision-making tool. It helps in deciding whether the system should operate as designed, modified, or in some cases not even be rolled out at all. DPIAs are mandated by law primarily in instances of systematic monitoring of public areas on a large scale, processing of special categories of data, or automated decision-making with legal effect. AI-driven security applications are commonly an archetype of these situations since, on one hand, they may actively monitor the whole network, and on the other hand, they can process logs at very high volume, detect behavioral abnormalities, and infer individual risk levels in ways that are consequential for access or scrutiny(Ghazal, Awouda, et al., 2025).

1.3 Importance of DPIAs in AI-Based Security Analytics

On a very basic level, the worth of DPIAs in AI-driven security analytics is that they create a link between the technical features and governance based on human rights. Security experts normally confine themselves to metrics like detection accuracy, response time, model efficiency, and threat visibility. Privacy or legal officers, conversely, focus on aspects such as lawful basis, transparency, fairness, minimization, retention, and More often than not, these concerns are addressed independently leading to a fragmented governance structure. DPIA helps to unite both operational needs and rights of individuals for a joint examination. This is even more crucial since AI security systems, by virtue of their functional nature, can seem unquestioningly legitimate; after all, they are there to protect(Abualhaj, Al-Khatib, Al Shafi, et al., 2025). There may be, for example, an assumption that as long as a system is capable of enhancing cybersecurity defense, then the deployment thereof is automatically justified. However, DPIAs keep organizations on their toes by not allowing them to fall back on such assumptions. They demand the proof of necessity, proportionality, and risk mitigation. Moreover, DPIAs give rise to a series of challenging yet unavoidable questions. Can the model function efficiently with a reduced number of data fields? Is it possible that less intrusive data will suffice for achieving similar detection performance? Is it clear to employees or users that their monitoring is so extensive? Does human intervention plays a part in reviewing decision-making if it involves major consequences? Are cases falsely recognized as positive being documented and taken care of?(Al-Mousa et al., 2025) Is the re-education of the model giving rise to new privacy problems? As a result, DPIAs are used to help think about privacy through the lens of the design stage, not as separate compliance requirements. In addition, AI analytics systems are developing organisms. Their features can be changed because of things like retraining, inclusion of new features, bringing in new data, changes in threat landscape, etc. That is why DPIAs are a necessity not only at the point of initial sourcing or deployment of the system but also for its whole lifetime. They enable continuing oversight by making a log of assumptions, controls, and residual risks that, in turn, make it easier for companies to reverse previous decisions when the system scope is Ghazal, Hasan, Mokhtar, et al., 2025).

1.4 Objectives and Research Scope

This chapter is quite a detailed analysis of how Data Protection Impact Assessments (DPIAs) can be used to regulate security applications which are powered by artificial intelligence. It basically aims at showing the potential of DPIAs in helping the security community to not only comply with data protection rules but also to be in the front seat with governance of AI system use in security. Specifically, it deals with the uncovering of privacy risks which are due to the features and working of smart security equipment, figuring out why these risks cannot be seen by usual compliance methods, and proving that DPIAs can give one a very comprehensive way to evaluate legality, proportionality, and organizational accountability. The subject is set at the intersection of security engineering, data protection law, and responsible AI governance. It relates to AI-enabled incidents detection, behavior monitoring, predictive analytics, and other security areas where large-scale personal data processing could take place. Attention is paid not only to DPIAs' legal basis but also to the architectures of AI security systems, privacy risk detection methods, assessment tool design, and governance framework integration. The chapter also presents complementary data which show how findings from empirical studies on data help in unveiling the trade-off between security effectiveness and privacy risks. Put simply, treating AI-enabled security applications as protective tools on the one hand and highly risky data processing systems on the other, this chapter proposes the need for thoroughness and responsibility in tech implementation and holds that competent computer security and robust data protection should not be a choice between two things but should be the result of solid governance, technical self-control, and human-ethical impact assessments. DPIA is the instrument that puts into practice the idea of attaining this

Existing studies have extensively examined artificial intelligence applications in cybersecurity, privacy risks associated with behavioral analytics, and regulatory requirements for data protection compliance. However, limited attention has been given to the integration of Data Protection Impact Assessments (DPIAs) within AI-driven security architectures. Most prior research focuses either on cybersecurity effectiveness or privacy protection in isolation. Consequently, there remains a gap in understanding how DPIAs can function as a practical governance mechanism for balancing security objectives with privacy rights in intelligent security environments. This chapter addresses this gap by presenting a structured analysis of DPIA implementation throughout the lifecycle of AI-enabled security systems.

Figure 1. Architecture of AI-Driven Security Monitoring Systems

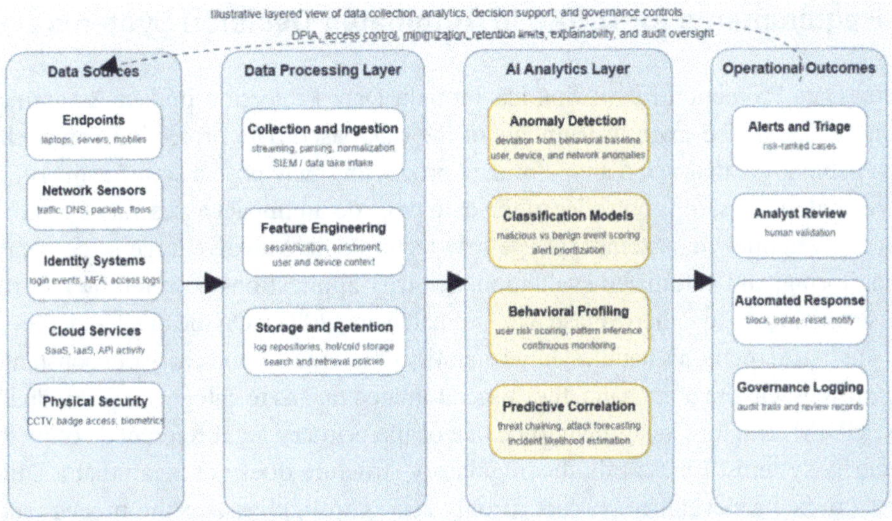

Figure 1 lays out a multi-tiered architecture model for AI-enabled security monitoring systems, showing the transformation of various kinds of operational data inputs into analytics, decisions, and governance

Figure 2. Privacy Risk Flow in AI Security Data Processing Pipelines

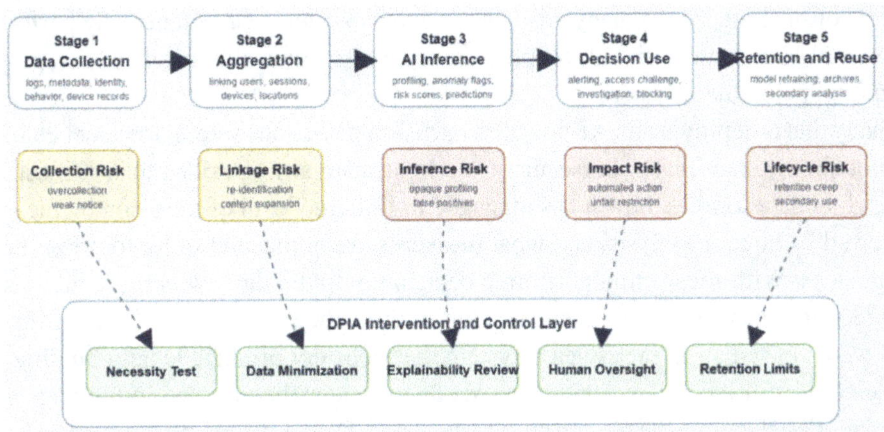

Figure 2 illustrates the way privacy risk travels through an AI-enabled security data pipeline beginning with the collection stage and peeking through aggregation, inference, decision use, and retention stages, unless reduced by DPIA-based

2. LEGAL AND REGULATORY FOUNDATIONS

2.1 GDPR Requirements for DPIAs in Automated Decision Systems

The General Data Protection Regulation has brought Data Protection Impact Assessments (DPIA) to the forefront as one of the main instruments of the risk-based data protection approach in Europe. The main idea behind it is that when a type of data processing may pose a significant risk to the rights and freedoms of individuals, the controller of the data must do an impact assessment before starting the This rule especially applies to systems that use new technologies, involve large-scale data processing, systematic monitoring, and automated evaluation. Security applications powered by AI often exhibit a number of these conditions together(Shlash Mohammad et al., 2025). On the one hand, they usually rely on innovative analytical methods, handle a large quantity of telemetry, and carry out constant monitoring of users or employees. On the other hand, they use automated means to categorize individuals' behavior. Therefore, the GDPR structure has grown to be one of the primary legal reference points for assessing intelligent security systems. First of all, this regulatory structure does not mean that a DPIA will stop a technology from being developed. In fact, it only serves to lightly steer the process such that new technological developments can be realized within a model of good governance that is disciplined and accountable. The material controller will have to describe the expected processing activities, the goals of processing, how necessary and proportionate is the processing, risks to data subjects, and safeguards that can mitigate the risks(Abualghanam et al., 2025).

GDPR Article 35 specifically requires organizations to conduct a Data Protection Impact Assessment when processing activities are likely to result in a high risk to the rights and freedoms of natural persons. Factors triggering such assessments include systematic monitoring, large-scale processing, profiling, and automated decision-making. Since many AI-driven security systems simultaneously perform several of these activities, DPIAs become a critical compliance mechanism for evaluating necessity, proportionality, and risk mitigation before deployment.

So, a company that is deploying an AI-powered intrusion detection system or a user behavior analytics platform cannot simply state that cybersecurity is a legitimate aim. Besides that, it must prove that it has picked the right data sources, how it has managed to limit the level of intrusion by the system, if the output is reviewed by human analysts, and what measures are in place in order to prevent erroneous or unfair consequences. With regard to algorithmic decision outputs, the law is more inclined to be worried as it can lead to real-world consequences without the concerned persons being aware of the way the outcomes were arrived at. In fact, even a system that does not produce legally binding decisions in a formal sense could still have such a great impact as to render the affected individuals almost at the mercy of the model's behavior. Due to such circumstances, GDPR-related DPIA line of thought becomes a key element in security frameworks: the dividing line between operational triage and consequential evaluation is quite thin. After AI scores or predictions are used as a factor in determining how a person is treated, concerns about privacy and fairness become deeply intertwined with technical security performance(Ghazal, Hasan, Hussein, et al., 2025).

2.2 Legal Thresholds Triggering DPIA Obligations

Performing a DPIA is not a blanket requirement for every single data processing activity. A DPIA requirement will be triggered when the risk level elevates significantly and some legal thresholds have been met. Generally, these thresholds relate to processing special types of data, processing at a large scale, systematic observation, the use of profiling or automated decision-making, the inclusion of vulnerable populations, the linking of datasets, or the potential of significant effects on individuals. With AI-based security systems, a number of threshold criteria can be fulfilled together. The same software may constantly observe employees, correlate data of devices and identities, make predictive risk scores, indirectly deduce special categories of data, and perform all these functions enterprise-wide at a large scale. Security systems are legally complicated because as effective as their function for protection is, it does not make their inherently intrusive nature disappear(Al-Suhimat et al., 2024). In fact, the stronger the cyber-threats, the bigger the temptation for organizations to justify massive surveillance. The legal threshold model counter-argues this inclination and insists on a particular reasoning for necessity as opposed to a vague security argument. If, for example, a system monitors every login, tracks the user's movements via access control systems, scans metadata of messaging, correlates endpoint behavior, and saves such records in order to enhance model performance, then detection rates improvement shall not be the sole consideration. The legal question is whether the cumulative processing operation creates a level of risk that activates formal assessment duties(Farman et al., 2025).

Not all AI security systems present the same level of privacy risk. For example, an AI tool that prioritizes malware alerts based solely on technical indicators may present relatively low privacy concerns. In contrast, systems that continuously profile employee behavior, assign insider-threat scores, or analyze biometric identifiers typically create significantly higher privacy risks and are more likely to trigger formal DPIA requirements. Risk assessments should therefore consider both the nature of the data processed and the potential impact of system outputs on individuals.

Figure 3. Legal Threshold Model for DPIA Triggering in AI Security Processing

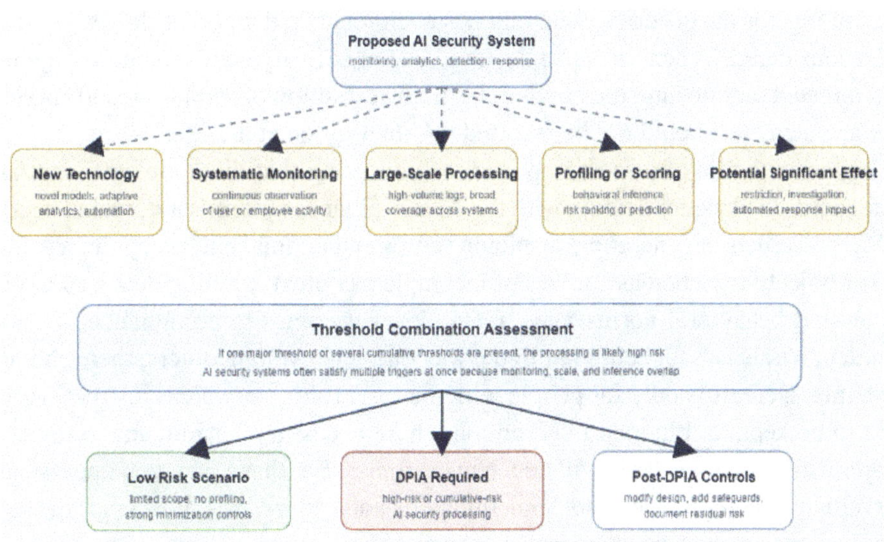

Figure 3 delineates the logic underlying the legal threshold approach for determining the likelihood of a DPIA being required for AI-enabled security processing, especially when the characteristics of new technology, systematic monitoring, scale, profiling, and significant effects Besides, threshold analysis can be seen as a tool that compels organizations to think of combinations instead of isolated processing acts. Just one log source might seem quite harmless. A single anomaly score might look like an operational one. However, if several sources are aggregated and analyzed through AI, the privacy implications escalate alarmingly. Thanks to such combinations, re-identification becomes a piece of cake, the profile depth gets deeper and behavioral inference is more likely. In other words, legal thresholds work as not only triggers for documentation but also conceptually help identify ordinary technical data that has turned into high-risk personal data processing on account of scale, linkage, and inference(Mahfouz et al., 2025).

2.3 Compliance Requirements for AI Surveillance Systems

AI surveillance systems are undoubtedly one of the most difficult types of security technologies to comply with from a legal and regulatory perspective. Besides recording and tracking events, they are capable of smart observation, pattern recognition, drawing conclusions about someone's identity, and forecasting behaviors. Users who have been granted access may have their videos run through analytics, their typing on the keyboard recorded and examined, their patterns of entering a certain area interpreted, their network behavior creating a profile, and the use of a biometric facial recognition for allowing a secure entry, or AI-based detection of insider threats, etc(Salman et al., 2025). Such tools only cause compliance problems at a level of their capability to convert ordinary behaviors into behavioral insights, even when they are aimed at security One of the major compliance areas is purpose specification. Organizations need to clearly state what the system is intended to do, and refrain from allowing the scope of surveillance to spread without limits to other managerial or administrative uses. If a system is put in place to detect unauthorized access, it should not, without further justification, disclosure, and impact assessment, become a tool for employee productivity measurement or generalized employee profiling. One more compliance area is proportionality. Here, the organization must demonstrate that the extent of monitoring is suitable for the security issue that has been identified and that the less intrusive alternatives have been considered. When the same desired level of security can be achieved by implementing risk-based and targeted monitoring, the continuous, high-resolution observation, and surveillance of all users are not warranted and should not be resorted to(Alnawayseh et al., 2023).

One more criterion that is of utmost importance is ensuring that there are sufficient and adequate procedural safeguards in place for dealing with the AI surveillance system's automated decision-making and outputs. Methods such as generating suspicion scores and anomaly alerts by the machine may give an impression of objectivity whereas sources of incomplete context, training data issues, or structuring of the model around behavioral norms may create biases it comes to compliance, it's not just about technical accuracy; it's also about being fair in the way one acts. Among others, there should be ways to check the correctness, controls only for people with the right roles, very clear instructions on how long materials need to be kept, and human intervention where necessary for humans to review the results before any major action is taken. This will be a few examples. So, that's why you understand that in the case of AI surveillance, compliance is not something one adds afterwards. It is a part of the very design through the use of governance mechanisms that regulate ways of collecting, interpreting, and using data(Nafisah et al., 2025).

2.4 Accountability and Documentation in DPIA Processes

Regulatory-wise the advantage of DPIA lies not just in how deeply it is analyzed but also in the degree of accountability and documentation that accompany it. A scarcely documented DPIA will hardly be recognized as a proof of good governance. This is especially true for AI-based security systems as their technical infrastructures are not only complex but also the datasets used for computation continuously change, plus, the source of risk is often the interaction of different components rather than one processing step only. Hence, without the right metadata or documentation of design choices, data categories, model functions, identified risks and safeguards that are already in place, it would be quite a challenge for the organizations to justify their systems from a legal, proportionality, or fairness perspective(Vasudevan et al., 2024). Good accountability implies that DPIAs should clearly indicate both the logic and the individual responsible for governance. In a way, they should be able to tell us who is responsible for the system, who assesses, who are the resources, what are the assumptions, which data categories were considered, what high-risk features were detected, and what measures to reduce the risk were implemented. In the case of security applications, it should not be a major problem to keep records of such items as model function, source of data, retention duration, access right, analyst review process, and high-risk escalation channels. Besides satisfying external regulatory needs, this good practice ensures that security operations will not be jeopardized by changes such as model retraining, new data integration, and personnel leaving the company. Accountability is accompanied by reviewability as well. DPIA should not be left unchanged with the initial approval if the system undergoes a major change(Fauzi et al., 2025). The addition of new biometric features, the start of processing of new data types, automated response to decision models, and longer data retention for model training are examples where the assessment done earlier may prove to be insufficient. That is why documentation needs to enable lifecycle governance, i.e., it should assist the organizations in returning to some of the decisions and assumptions they made earlier and checking whether risks have changed. In that sense, accountability is no less than a living document and a discipline—privileged ownership of privacy governance accompanies the system throughout its evolution.

3. ARCHITECTURE OF ARTIFICIAL INTELLIGENCE DRIVEN SECURITY APPLICATIONS

The foundation of artificial intelligence-driven security applications is a multi-layered architecture which is able to handle a high volume of data, identify patterns, and make defensive decisions in real-time. Conventional security tools that are rule-based and deal with individual events are different from AI-based security platforms. The latter consists of components that gather data from various sources, convert raw data into structured form, use machine learning models for understanding, and give security analysts or automated response systems the intelligence necessary for actions. Such architectures, therefore, double up as first data processing and then decision-support systems. The main reason behind the architectural complexity of AI security systems is the need to handle large-scale heterogeneous datasets. Network logs, identity records, endpoint telemetry, application activity, and behavioral signals all have to be pooled together for analysis in a single environment. Individually, signals may not portray anomalies but when combined in different contextual dimensions, these data sources can facilitate the identification of signal anomalies. For what might simply appear a normal login event could be flagged as a potential account takeover once stay anomalies, device fingerprints, geographically inconsistent locations, and unusual access patterns application are unveiled(Arabiat, 2025).

The biggest problem of the system architecture is the trade-off between the analytical depth requirement on the one hand, and the necessity operational efficiency while on the other hand also conforming to governance constraints. Security monitoring systems would really favor real-time or almost real-time processing since if the detection is delayed, it might offer a threat a way to go through the entire network. As a result, highly sophisticated architectures leverage streaming data pipelines, distributed storage systems, and computation frameworks that can handle large volumes of events without compromising response speed. However, these very same features may also raise privacy concerns since, cruelly, the very system architecture that allows fast detection is the one also enabling continuous observation and aggregation of personal data. AI security system architectures must be understood well not even only for the technical design aspect but also for assessing privacy risks and governance requirements in Data Protection Impact Assessments. Figure 4 shows a multilayer schematic architecture of AI-based security systems where raw operational data is brought in through the various layers of ingestion, processing, machine learning analysis, and response orchestration. This architectural lens cautions us that privacy risks and governance controls may directly concern technical security functionalities as Iftikhar et al., 2025).

Figure 4. Layered Architecture of AI-Driven Security Systems

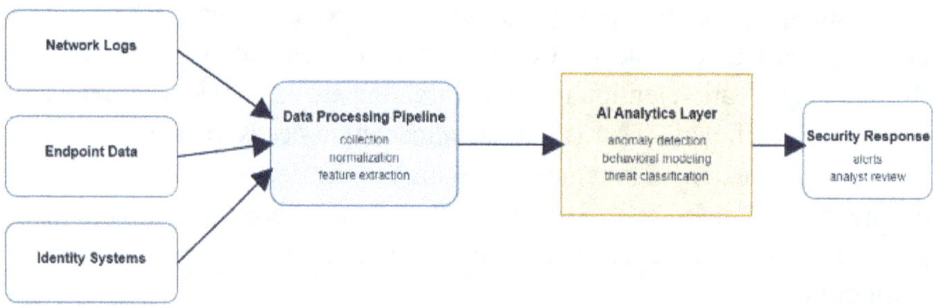

3.1 AI-Powered Security Monitoring Platforms

AI-driven security monitoring platforms hold the core of contemporary cybersecurity networks. They integrate the capabilities of various security technologies into a single solution that enables round-the-clock monitoring, analysis, and warning. Earlier monitoring solutions were largely rule-based and relied on tools such as intrusion detection systems or log management software. Yet, AI-based units revolutionize the scenario as they are capable of employing adaptive analytics to identify threats that are unfamiliar, behavior anomalies, and new attack patterns. All sequences of organizational events are directed to the monitoring platform which, therefore, acts as the central point. The firewall logs, server logs, authentication system logs, cloud platform logs, endpoint protection tool logs, and network sensor logs are all transferred to the platform with the help of automated ingestion pipelines(Elomda et al., 2025). Once these data streams are received, they are rescanned into a single format, and then, user identity, device classification, geolocation metadata, and threat intelligence indicators are among the contextual attributes added to them. AI-models consider this highly enriched information as their operating environment. AI models integrated in the surveillance systems platform are a vital gear in a variety of major processes. Based on risk scores in context: events are clustered, baselines are established, anomalies are detected, threat likelihoods are computed, and alert prioritizations are With operations that go on without interruption, AI monitoring platforms lighten the mental load of human analysts requiring them to deal primarily with the highest-risk incidents. Since these platforms create a data repository that spans various organizational domains, the data involved also makes detailed behavioral information about interacting individuals available. Because of this characteristic, monitoring executions must be properly assessed for DPIA to ensure that they are not only legitimate but align with privacy principles(Makhadmeh et al., 2025).

3.2 Machine Learning Based Threat Detection Systems

Machine learning-based threat detection systems are the core analytical tool of AI security architectures. Security is achieved through the application of statistical and computational models that identify malicious activities or significant changes in the way systems operate. Detection using machine learning goes beyond the conventional signature-based method of rule-based detection as models are capable of finding the smallest correlations even within the largest datasets as well as adapting to changes in attack methods. Usually, threat detection models use algorithms from multiple families(Al-Adwan et al., 2025). For instance, supervised learning classifies events by using labeled data that highlights malicious and benign events. On the other hand, unsupervised learning detects anomalies by flagging deviations from normal behavior. Semi-supervised techniques make use of both to deal with the kind of datasets which are often partially labeled in cybersecurity. The most advanced may even use deep neural networks which have the ability to model the complex temporal relationships between events. One of the major drivers for machine learning detection is that it can produce results that are used in a variety of decisions. Despite this, the models can output only levels of confidence, not one hundred percent certainty. AI-driven security monitoring platforms hold the core of contemporary cybersecurity networks. They integrate the capabilities of various security technologies into a single solution that enables round-the-clock monitoring, analysis, and warning. Earlier monitoring solutions were largely rule-based and relied on tools such as intrusion detection systems or log management software(Alenazi et al., 2025). Yet, AI-based units revolutionize the scenario as they are capable of employing adaptive analytics to identify threats that are unfamiliar, behavior anomalies, and new attack patterns. All sequences of organizational events are directed to the monitoring platform which, therefore, acts as the central point. The firewall logs, server logs, authentication system logs, cloud platform logs, endpoint protection tool logs, and network sensor logs are all transferred to the platform with the help of automated ingestion pipelines. Once these data streams are received, they are rescanned into a single format, and then, user identity, device classification, geolocation metadata, and threat intelligence indicators are among the contextual attributes added to them. AI-models consider this highly enriched information as their operating environment. AI models integrated in the surveillance systems platform are a vital gear in a variety of major processes. Based on risk scores in context: events are clustered, baselines are established, anomalies are detected, threat likelihoods are computed, and alert prioritizations are Since DPIA methods are expected not only to consider detection capabilities, they also need to consider issues related to transparency, accountability and other aspects that influence model-driven Zhu et al., 2025).

Different categories of machine learning models create distinct DPIA considerations. Supervised learning models rely heavily on training data quality and may introduce bias if historical security datasets are unbalanced. Anomaly detection systems may generate false positives due to unusual but legitimate user behavior. Deep learning models often achieve high detection accuracy but may reduce explainability because of their complex internal structures. User and Entity Behavior Analytics (UEBA) systems present additional privacy concerns because they continuously monitor and profile user activities. Therefore, DPIAs should evaluate model-specific risks rather than treating all AI security systems as a single category.

3.3 Data Pipelines in AI Security Systems

Data pipelines are the mechanisms through which raw security data gets converted into analytical input for machine learning modeling. Processing stages are usually arranged in series to form a pipeline, with data being obtained, filtered, enhanced, stored, and dispatched to analytical modules one after the other. Because AI models work with organized data sets, the pipeline has the task of transforming different event formats into standard representations suitable for analysis and computation. The pipeline's first step is data ingestion. Data connectors, agents, and streaming protocols extract security records from multiple systems within an organization. Network packet summaries, endpoint activity logs, authentication records, API requests, and application access logs may be among the pieces of information collected. The task of the ingestion layer is to ensure that data from incoming streams is reliably caught and forwarded to processing units. The second step is dedicated to data cleaning and standardization. Log files in their raw form could be in different formats with missing or duplicate information. Data cleansing methods are applied along with extraction of the relevant fields and conversion into a common format. This step may also involve aligning the times across the distributed systems to allow for correct event correlation(Rabbi et al., 2025).

The third step engineer's feature. Feature engineering involves the extraction of numerical representations from raw event attributes which are understandable by machine learning methods. Examples of such measures include number of logins attempts over a given time, average session length, geographical deviation from previous locations, and building graphs of communication relationships. These crafted features then become the behavioral indicators on which AI algorithms identification and classification of anomalies is based. Eventually, the processed datasets are deposited in scalable storage locations such as data lakes or distributed databases. Such repositories are good for live inference as well as offline training of models. The design should be done in a way to process data very quickly. At the same time, quality of data, policies for holding data and levels of data access should also be maintained. Privacy-wise, any part of the pipeline may either increase or decrease risk depending on the practices of data collection, retention, and Abualigah et al., 2025).

3.4 Security Monitoring Data Sources and Privacy Exposure

Besides the type of data sources a security architecture uses profoundly influencing not only its detection ability but also its overall susceptibility to privacy risks, each data source offers a different perspective on how a system works, but at the same time, it also brings a new round of privacy issues. For example, network traffic logs reveal devices' and services' communication patterns within a system; on the other hand, identity management records contain individual authentication events. Endpoint telemetry may show what applications were used, how the device was configured, and what commands were performed - indirectly displaying user behavior(Awais et al., 2025). By merging these data sources, AI systems may create a near complete and accurate operational map of the target digital environment. The ability to combine is a must for the identification of attack chains through different systems and lateral movement within networks. From a privacy point of view, however, the mixture of multiple datasets raises the issue of detailed profiling. While each dataset on its own has very little personal information, it is the combination of several sources that makes the behavioral patterns recognizable enough. Another very important factor leading to privacy exposure is the length of time data is stored and the subsequent analytical reuse. Information preserved for longer periods can be used for updating machine models, conducting time-series analysis, or even investigating past events. These processes lend detection a higher degree of effectiveness; however, the downside is that the period of surveillance is also lengthened(Alkhawatrah, 2025). Thus, DPIA discussions mainly focus on making sure that the retention periods set are not exceeding what is reasonable, and also on the use of data minimization methods to prevent the unwanted accumulation of personal Hence, understanding the nature and characteristics of different data sources is fundamental to any decision related to both the technical and regulatory aspects involved in AI security architectures. With that in mind, Table 1 presents some common data sources used in AI-driven security monitoring along with a short description of their typical purposes from an analytical viewpoint and the primary privacy issues normally associated with their Iskandarani & Hidayat, 2025).

Table 1. Common Data Sources in AI-Driven Security Monitoring Systems

Data Source	Typical Data Collected	Analytical Purpose in AI Security	Potential Privacy Exposure
Network Traffic Logs	Packet headers, IP addresses, domain queries, connection durations	Detection of abnormal traffic patterns, malware communication, and distributed attacks	May reveal communication patterns between users, services, and external systems
Identity and Authentication Logs	Login timestamps, authentication attempts, device identifiers, access tokens	Identification of suspicious login activity, credential misuse, and account compromise	Directly associated with individual identities and work patterns
Endpoint Telemetry	Process execution events, file access records, system configuration changes	Detection of malware behavior, unauthorized system modifications, and insider threats	Can reveal application usage and user operational behavior
Cloud Service Activity Logs	API requests, service usage events, resource configuration actions	Monitoring of cloud infrastructure misuse and unauthorized data access	May expose operational tasks performed by specific personnel
Physical Security Systems	Badge access events, entry timestamps, surveillance metadata	Correlation between physical presence and digital activity	May reveal movement patterns and workplace behavior

4. PRIVACY RISK IDENTIFICATION IN ARTIFICIAL INTELLIGENCE DRIVEN SECURITY APPLICATIONS

Artificial intelligence-based security systems are very efficient in detecting potential cyber threats within a short time, monitoring the activities of infrastructure, and recognizing suspicious behavioral patterns in the whole digital environment. However, ironically, the very features that make an AI-based security system effective will also give rise to quite complicated privacy issues. Normally, these systems function by the constant monitoring, collecting large amounts of data, profiling of behavior, and predictive analytics. These actions involve using personal data, for instance, that of employees, customers, or system users(Arabiat & Eljaafreh, 2025). As a result, identifying privacy risks becomes a major part of a Data Protection Impact Assessment when dealing with AI security systems. Identifying privacy risks means thoroughly understanding how personal data is gathered, used, analyzed, and saved within a security system platform. In contrast with typical software systems that base their work on static data sets, AI security systems take multiple heterogeneous data sources and derive new knowledge based on them. Such new knowledge can reveal behavioral, preference, or interaction patterns about individuals that the individuals themselves have not consciously revealed. Consequently, privacy risks arise both from direct data gathering and from algorithmic inference and data set correlation(Elkaradawy et al., 2025).

Therefore, privacy risk identification in a Data Protection Impact Assessment is done through a sequence of actions starting with system mapping, followed by establishing impact scenarios, and finally estimating the likelihood and severity of harm to individuals' rights and freedoms. Within AI security configurations, the risk factors that are in most cases identified include excessive data collection, the risk that behavioral profiling may give a false impression, inability to understand decision-making processes (lack of explainability), wrongly picking out threats, and the storing of sensitive operational information for too long a period. Being aware of risks is utterly necessary to know the kind of controls that organizations can put into practice which, alongside technical solutions and governance, will reduce harm without compromising security(Ghazal, 2025a). The major types of privacy risks that result from security monitoring systems driven by AI are shown in Figure 5, while Figure 6 displays a theoretical lifecycle model that demonstrates how privacy risks can occur at various stages of security data processing by

Figure 5. Privacy Risk Categories in AI Security Monitoring

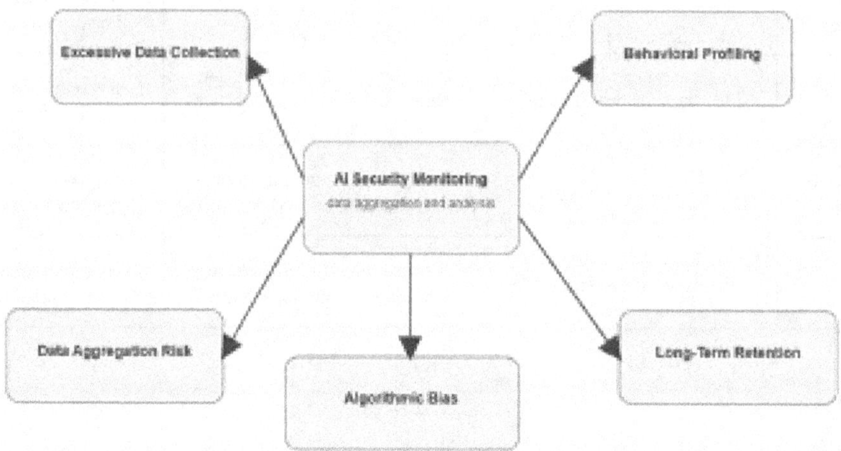

Figure 6. Lifecycle of Privacy Risks in AI Security Data Processing

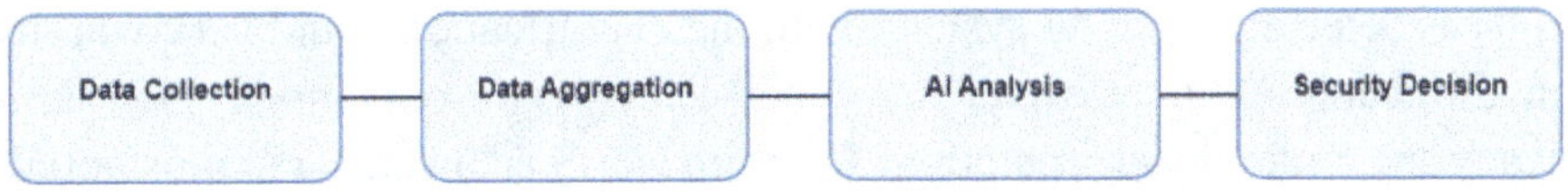

4.1 Sources of Personal Data in Security Monitoring

AI-driven security monitoring solutions are built primarily using a large amount of data captured from both digital and operational environments. Most of these data points may contain information that can be used directly or indirectly to identify individuals who make use of the organization's systems. Highly detailed logs such as user authentication, records of network access, tracing of endpoint activities, communication metadata, and data on how applications are used contain PII details apart from supporting security analytics. One example is when identity management systems produce authentication logs that contain user names, login time stamps, IP addresses, and device IDs. These documents are very helpful in identifying the misuse of credentials or the attempt of an external break-in. However, they also reveal in a very detailed manner the times and locations of people accessing the systems, as well as the devices they use. When, these logs are compiled, they may result in behavioral profiles that reveal work patterns, physical movements, or social networks of colleagues to others indirectly(Al-Daoud, Yogeesh, Mohammad, Raja, Chetana, et al., 2025).

Endpoint telemetry changes the angle of privacy even further. It logs very detailed user-computer interactions which could include app installations, document openings, sequences of commands, and even changes to configurations within the Such information, while critical for the detection of malware or insider threats, inherently exposes elements of an individual's tasks or professional activities(Yaseen et al., 2025). Monitoring network traffic is yet a very important data source. When content is left intact, the raw metadata like source and target addresses, connection time, and protocol pieces reveal quite a lot about the communication existence between person and service. Security AI models that study these interactions will thus return to behavioral profiling. As combinations of very different data sources for AI security systems is common practice, more attention in DPIA has to be paid not only to individual data sources but also to the resulting privacy effects of their merger. Only together could these data forms become almost fully revealing of a person's life.

4.2 Risks of Behavioral Profiling and Automated Surveillance

Behavioral profiling is one of the biggest privacy concerns associated with AI-based security systems. Behavioral data analysis engines are used to understand the regular behavior patterns of users, devices, and applications by creating their baseline profiles. Performing such profiling allows the system detection of deviations which may be indicative of compromised accounts, malicious insiders, or unpermitted system access. However, besides boosting threat detection, profiling also monitors the individuals systematically in an automated way. Essentially, AI models get to "know" not only when a person may be working but also what systems or specific applications they access, and with whom they communicate(Shamaylah et al., 2025). As a result, the firm network of each person's digital behavior is gradually established over time. It gets even more complicated when profiling is used to predict that a particular person may be more prone to risk or is somehow suspicious. Labeling a user high risk may indeed be based solely on statistical patterns detected by an AI system; still, the classification could very well lead to further monitoring or investigation. Actually, even when cybersecurity is the only intent, such actions influence the person's privacy and professional reputation. The third worry is linked to circumstantial misinterpretation. Because behavioral analytics rely on statistical gridworks without full contextual understanding, activities deemed by the system to be deviant may, from the human point of view, be quite proper. Take a system administrator who must operate an emergency fix after hours - although the system shows the glitch as a possible anomaly, the authorized user is doing nothing wrong(Hyassat et al., 2025). It is for this reason that DPIA checks into behavioral monitoring to see if the measures are the least intrusive necessary to achieve the purpose. Besides, organizations should render monitoring signal profiles quite selective, ensure that anomaly scores are first double-checked by human analysts before any action is taken, and stick to an open approach when they inform people about monitoring.

4.3 Risks Associated with Large Scale Data Aggregation

To a large extent, AI security systems can function only if data centralization is involved. On the one hand, data collected from various sources gets into huge data repositories like security data lakes or analytics platforms. On the other hand, machine learning models become capable of finding links between events occurring in very different parts of the infrastructure. However, despite all its advantages, centralization through a single point also highlights weaknesses in terms of privacy. A large dataset with patched operational intelligence not only can attract attackers or unauthorized insiders, but, if such a pool is compromised, adversaries can get hold of the most detailed logs of organizational and user behaviors(Iskandarani & Chakrabarti, 2025). Another kind of risk that aggregation entails is the higher probability of secondary use of data. Security data initially devoted only to threat detection might be, in the course of time, also used for operational monitoring, measuring productivity, or performance evaluation. This kind of repurposing can be slowly revealed as the analytical potential of large datasets is being discovered. The boundary between security monitoring and employee surveillance can be quite fuzzy without the cover of proper governance. From the perspective of DPIA, the evaluation of aggregation risk should be done through the way datasets are combined, the people who have access to the aggregated data, and if trimming is used in the process of data collection. Privacy enhancing mechanisms like pseudonymization, strict role-based access control, and strict retention policies are of utmost importance when tackling the whole concept of large scale data Jan et al., 2025).

4.4 Algorithmic Bias and Misclassification in AI Security Models

Another major privacy risk related to AI security systems is the one caused by algorithmic bias and model misclassification. Machine learning algorithms are trained by security incident records and operations that represent legitimate and illicit behavior. So, in case these datasets represent the behaviors in a biased manner or fail to model properly legitimate behavior, the built models can be predisposed to producing erroneous classifications. In this case, algorithmic bias can really yield serious consequences. For one, certain "unconventional" members of a group (for instance developers, system administrators, or network engineers) may be identified as "anomalies" more often even if they are simply following their regular The reason is that their access or interaction patterns with the system are both significantly different than those performed by everyday users so they are always the first to be "suspected"(Al-Momani et al., 2025). For most part, this is a failure to properly retrain the models to account for such legitimate functionalities. Misclassification is equally a problem when what is actually a harmless activity gets identified as malicious or threats that really do exist go unnoticed. False positives might cause quite a bit of work for the security team and lead to the restriction of system access for the "flagged" individuals, whereas false negatives simply allow the threats to run "under the radar". From privacy, transparency, and accountability standpoints, algorithmic misclassification leads to a problem of acquired inability. Affected people do not understand who made the decision, how it was made, or even that they can contest it in case of errors. Hence, DPIA frameworks propose the adoption of such things as explainable AI, human interaction in automated decision-making, and audit processes for detecting racial or systematic bias(Alabdallat et al., 2025).

4.5 Privacy Risk Assessment Methodologies

Privacy risk assessment methods are a set of techniques organizations use to thoroughly examine the privacy risks linked to AI security systems. These techniques reveal how individual rights and freedoms might be violated and estimate the probability and severity of negative outcomes. By using the results, they plan the implementation of risk-reducing measures. Privacy risk assessment is one of the first steps taken by a company to understand how data flows within the architecture of the system. During the mapping, they try to identify what types of personal data are collected, where the data comes from, how the data is processed, and which entities get or use the data. This map shows in great detail how personal data is being shared within the system. After that, the staff involved in this work develop impact scenarios. Such scenarios describe the different types of harm that people may suffer if their activity logs are leaked without authorization, if behavioral profiling is carried out without justification, if AI models produce systematic errors, or if personal data is retained in an excessive manner, etc. Then, a risk estimation is done by evaluating both the frequency of a risk event and the severity of its consequences. Combining these two elements results in a set of magnet scores. The scoring system is such that a high score (Maz et al., 2025)indicates a more significant risk that should be priority for mitigation. Finally, there is a decision taken between reducing risk by employing a technological measure (e.g., encryption, pseudonymization, and access controls) and by giving more organizational guidance (e.g., transparency policies, oversight mechanisms, and regular compliance audits). Main privacy risk types in AI-powered security systems are indicated in Table 2, together with some protection measures that companies can rely on to conduct

Table 2. Privacy Risks and Mitigation Strategies in AI Security Systems

Privacy Risk Category	Description of Risk	Potential Impact on Individuals	Example Mitigation Measures
Excessive Data Collection	Security systems gather more personal data than necessary for threat detection	Increased surveillance and unnecessary exposure of personal activity patterns	Apply data minimization, limit logging scope, filter sensitive attributes
Behavioral Profiling	AI models construct detailed behavioral profiles of users	Continuous monitoring may reveal work habits or personal patterns	Use pseudonymization, restrict profiling outputs, apply transparency notices
Data Aggregation Risk	Multiple datasets are combined in centralized repositories	Increased exposure if datasets are breached or misused	Implement strong encryption, access controls, and strict retention policies
Algorithmic Misclassification	Machine learning models incorrectly classify legitimate activities as suspicious	Unwarranted investigation or restriction of system access	Introduce human review processes and continuous model validation
Long-Term Data Retention	Security logs retained indefinitely for analysis or model training	Prolonged storage increases risk of misuse or unauthorized disclosure	Define retention schedules and automated deletion mechanisms

5. PHYSICAL AND TECHNICAL SAFEGUARDS FOR DPIA COMPLIANCE IN AI SECURITY

Artificial intelligence-based security solutions depend on intricate data infrastructures that deal with huge volumes of operational data to identify cyber threats and unusual system behaviors. Since these solutions often handle personal data of employees, customers, or other system users, establishing strong safeguards helps in fulfilling the requirements of Data Protection Impact Assessment compliance. Safeguards act as mechanisms that minimize the privacy risks, however, they enable organizations to keep their security monitoring functioning efficiently. In the context of DPIA, safeguards are usually divided into two groups: technical measures which are a part of the system design and organizational measures which regulate the use, management, and supervision of such systems. Technical safeguards refer to the privacy-embedding aspects of the system engineering of AI security systems. These technical measures change the data lifecycle stages of collecting, storing, processing, and analyzing so as to decrease the undesired revealing of personal information(Al-Daoud, Yogeesh, Mohammad, Raja, Jabeen, et al., 2025). Data processing under privacy-preserving conditions, for instance, can limit the flow of personally identifiable information to the analytic core, and encryption, combined with access control, will keep the security datasets from being disclosed to unauthorized hands. Also, technical safeguards encompass machine learning model design since features like explainability and bias detection help make sure that automated decisions are just and traceable(Al-znamat et al., 2025).

Organizational safeguards are one type of social control that can complement technical controls by establishing a system of governance that motivate the responsible use of AI security tools. They consist of a set of instruments such as policies, organizational structures for decision-making, staff development mechanisms, accountability systems, etc. that are aimed at making security monitoring activities not only effective for the purpose of cybersecurity but also not excessive. Good governance will result in those employees who run security systems being fully conversant with their privacy duties and persistently adhering to correct data handling practices. Combining technical and organizational safeguards is great if you want to be DPIA compliant(Ghazal, 2025b). Technical controls alone won't be able to determine ethical or governance issues if there is hardly any organizational oversight. On the other hand, not having technical enforcement mechanisms to support your policy frameworks may not prevent the misuse of sensitive information. When technical solutions and organizational governance are evaluated together, the result is a well-rounded approach to privacy in AI security environments. Figure 7 illustrates the different levels of safeguards in AI security monitoring

Figure 7. Layered Safeguards in AI Security Monitoring Systems

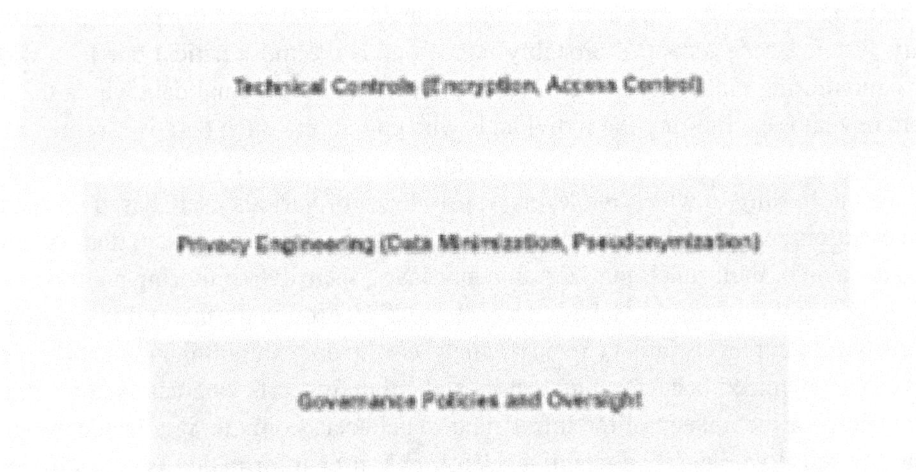

5.1 Data Minimization and Privacy by Design

Data minimization and privacy by design are two major complementary approaches for privacy protection in AI security systems. Data minimization is the principle of collecting and processing only those personal data that are necessary for specific security purposes and it is the primary principle of modern data protection laws. Besides privacy protection in AI security systems, data minimization can be applied in different data pipeline stages. The most obvious one is at data collection when, for example, logs, can be customized in such a way that only necessary metadata are recorded thereby excluding any sensitive information. In the case of security monitoring, fingerprint and IP address may be recorded but the content of the communication or a body of an application are not saved. This kind of logging supports that security analytics will be focused on relevant metadata without compromising individuals' communications(Almomani et al., 2025).

On the other hand, privacy by design is a much broader notion. Not only does it mean reducing data, but it is also about developing a self-sufficient system architecture where privacy aspects are embedded from the beginning of the process. Taking a system capable of using behavioral data without identifying the individual by means of pseudonymization as a starting point, after that, one meets tokenization where identifiers are replaced by random tokens which possess very limited analytical capacity while the identity remains hidden. How well data minimization and privacy by design can be implemented is still to a great extent dependent on the teamwork of engineers and privacy experts throughout the system development phase(Sharma et al., 2025). Cybersecurity professionals should decide how different data features influence detection and model accuracy. Assuming there are some features that contribute little or no value to the analysis but at the same time bring about privacy risks, it is feasible either to exclude or to alter them so as not to be exposed to the machine learning system. The balance that results from this will be a stepping stone for rolling out AI security systems that will display high proficiency as well as respect the privacy rights of

5.2 Access Control and Encryption Mechanisms

Among the various technical measures that can be used for safeguarding personal data processed by AI security systems, access control probably stands out as the most critical one by a wide margin. Since security monitoring platforms collect a great diversity of operational data which they later integrate into data repositories, limiting the individuals who can access such data is essential not only for diminishing the threat arising from data misuse but also from unauthorized disclosure. Access control is the mechanism according to which the levels of privileges of various users based on their roles are defined and these users are given the minimum amount of data exposure necessary that will enable them to give a good account of their functionalities. In many cases, security monitoring platforms implement role-based access control systems(Al-Habashneh et al., 2025). Through the use of this model, correspondence is assigned different levels of data Security analysts who are examining incidents are more likely to have access to anonymized behavioral indicators and anomaly alerts whereas system administrators who are responsible for the upkeep of the infrastructure get access only to aggregated system metrics. The use of highly sensitive datasets containing identifiable user information is typically restricted to the most experienced investigators or compliance Encryption is a method of data protection that is a complement to user access control and together these two form the backbone of a strong data protection strategy. Encryption of data-at-rest ensures that even if the stored security logs and analytical datasets are stolen, they remain indecipherable without the decryption keys(Jaradat et al., 2025). On the other hand, data-in-transit encryption safeguards information moving between system components, preventing interception or tampering during network communication. End-to-end encryption frameworks are very popular among modern security architectures. Another important role played by encryption is to ensure secure inter-organizational collaboration. In cases where security monitoring includes threats intelligence sharing across organizations, encrypted channels of data exchange make sure that sensitive operational information remains confidential. Alongside lock-down of access rights, cryptographic protection of data provides a very solid technical basis for the protection of personal information in AI security infrastructures(Arabasy & Ghoneim, 2025).

5.3 Transparency and User Awareness in Security Monitoring

Transparency is a very important organizational safeguard for ensuring that the relationships of trust between organizations and persons get a chance to be strengthened. AI-driven security platforms sometimes track operational data without the direct interaction of users. Without clear communication to users, monitoring can be seen as an intrusive or secretive action. Therefore, transparency features look to resolve the above-described problem by giving people clear information about how monitoring works and the data they collect. Organizations, for instance, can post privacy notices that describe security monitoring practices, the categories of data processed, and the purposes for which monitoring is conducted. Their aim is to describe the potential of AI security analytics to help achieve cybersecurity goals and make it clear that surveillance activities are meant to safeguard the organization's systems and not to assess the individual's behavior(Mahadin et al., 2025). Another effective measure for transparency is getting users to know about the security monitoring program by informing system users and staff through user awareness programs. Besides training and other channels of getting information, companies can create users' comprehension of AI security systems, the need to monitor, and hold Q & A sessions. Equipping users with knowledge of surveillance practices will not only unlock their fears and reluctance but also allow them to empathize with the organization's overall Transparency, however, is not only a matter of sharing and openness but also it is a means to accountability and a channel for conflicts to be aired. Making space for criticisms and grievances constitutes another level of transparency. Therefore, feedback mechanisms allow employees or users to report potential misuse of monitoring tools or request clarification about data processing activities. Organizations demonstrating openness to receiving grievances would point their publics to their commitment of responsible AI security governance(Masadeh et al., 2025).

5.4 Governance Frameworks for Responsible AI Security Deployment

Governance frameworks create the necessary institutional constitution to guarantee that AI security solutions uphold ethical and legal standards. Besides, they delineate functions and duties for individuals engaged in the design, deployment, and supervision of security technologies, and they establish mechanisms for pre-implementation evaluation of new monitoring capabilities. Governance frameworks involve the creation of oversight committees made up of members from cyber security, privacy, legal, and leadership. The committees are tasked with policy reviews, regulatory checks, and approval of security technologies. To be more privacy cautious, the committee can require a formal DPIA for large AI monitoring systems before the decision is made. Governance frameworks naturally have internal policies that define the appropriate use of monitoring tools(Hussain et al., 2025). These rules specify who can open, use, and share security data, and they also list the punishments for misuse or unauthorized sharing. Strict governance policies go a long way to showing that ethical and responsible use of AI security technologies is very important. Besides internal governance, an organization can also be part of an external regulatory or industry oversight initiative. Regulatory bodies can require an audit or a certification to verify that a privacy law is respected. Industry groups can publish recommendations on the responsible use of AI in cybersecurity. Matching internal governance with regulatory and industry will enable the organizations to use AI security technologies responsibly for a long

An important governance concern is function creep, whereby data initially collected for cybersecurity purposes is subsequently used for unrelated objectives such as employee productivity assessment, performance evaluation, or organizational surveillance. Such secondary uses may violate purpose limitation principles and increase privacy risks. Organizations should establish formal approval procedures requiring additional review and DPIA reassessment whenever security monitoring data is proposed for non-security purposes. This approach helps ensure that personal data processing remains aligned with its original justification.

Table 3. Safeguards for Privacy Protection in AI Security Systems

Safeguard Category	Key Measures	Purpose
Data Minimization	Filtering unnecessary data attributes before analysis	Reduce exposure of personal information
Encryption	Protecting stored and transmitted security data using cryptographic techniques	Prevent unauthorized access to sensitive datasets
Access Control	Role-based permissions restricting who can view personal data	Ensure only authorized personnel handle sensitive information
Transparency Policies	Informing users about monitoring practices and data processing purposes	Build trust and maintain regulatory compliance
Human Oversight	Analysts review AI-generated alerts before action is taken	Prevent automated misclassification from causing harm
Governance Frameworks	Organizational policies and oversight committees for AI security deployment	Ensure ethical and lawful operation of monitoring systems

6. EMPIRICAL EVALUATION OF DPIA MODELS FOR AI SECURITY SYSTEMS

6.1 Dataset Framing and Analytical Strategy

The focus of this paper, among other things, is on the ability of machine learning techniques to detect malicious behavior quite accurately. However, the question is raised that to what extent the efficiency of various models depends on the degree to which strictly privacy-sensitive or behavior-disclosing features are eliminated. Based on the terminology used in a Data Protection Impact Assessment (DPIA), this is the fundamental trade-off that exists between the requirements of cybersecurity and data protection proportionality. The developer of the system may be inclined to keep all the features, believing that the more data leads to better detection. On the other hand, the DPIA poses a sharper query: which features are indispensable and which ones only add to privacy risks without being significantly valuable for the To conduct the evaluation, the dataset may be considered as comprising two sets of The first contains the essential security features such as various types of protocols, packet and byte counts, variables related to sessions, and the state of the traffic(Alraba'nah et al., 2025). These features are very relevant for identifying threats and mainly describe the technical behavior in the network environment. The second group, however, includes context-enriched features which in real implementations may be associated with user or device profiles, time-ordered behavior, habitual access, and interaction patterns which when combined with identity systems become steadily more privacy-revealing. In an organizational AI security system, the latter often raises more concern from a DPIA perspective because it enables behavioral inference as opposed to mere event detection(Abdeljaber et al., 2025). To aid interpretation, three hypothetical model scenarios at least are desirable. The first scenario corresponds to the full-feature model where the system relies on all analytical attributes at its disposal. The second scenario depicts the reduced-feature model in which the features having the least detection value and greater privacy sensitivity are removed. The third scenario is the privacy-optimized model where only the least but most security-relevant and proportionate variables are maintained. An advanced design of this nature allows us to find out whether the detection accuracy suffers significantly when privacy-oriented feature reduction is enforced or whether a strong security outcome can be achieved even with a more reasonable DPIA (Kamal et al., 2025).

6.2 Security Benefit Versus Privacy Cost

DPIA-focused evaluation brings the biggest benefit by transforming privacy from a high-level concept into a practical engineering problem. By contrasting the reduced-feature and privacy-optimized models with the full-feature model, the enterprise can see the tangible benefits of additional data. When highly context-heavy or behavior-revealing features are removed, if only a small decrease in F1-score or detection accuracy takes place, then the case for the privacy-preserving model becomes significantly stronger from the perspective of law and ethics(Qawaqneh et al., 2025). Conversely, if the performance significantly deteriorates, then the company needs to be able to justify the real indispensability of the additional variables and produce documented evidence of the control measures that are being used to regulate their application. The argument might even be stronger when it comes to enterprise security operation centers where AI-based security tools may include identity systems, access management platforms, VPN logs, endpoint telemetry, and user behavior analytics Under these circumstances, the privacy cost may become quite high as the system might originally have been just a threat detection solution but over time it gradually turns into a system of continuous behavioral surveillance. The DPIA-oriented empirical assessment acts as a brake on this development by compelling the institution to provide a rationale for each category of features in terms of actual security value. The findings lend support to the leading thesis of this paper, that cybersecurity on the one hand and privacy-respecting governance on the other hand do not have to be antagonistic to each other. Maximum monitoring is not always necessary for security. With a good design, AI security systems are capable of functioning effectively in constrained, transparent, and proportionate data settings. The DPIA is the instrument that records and explains these compromises(Khaled Abdullah & Qawasmeh, 2025).

6.3 Operational Implications for AI Security Governance

The empirical results point to a number of governance issues. Feature choice, firstly, should be properly integrated into DPIA work rather than having feature selection considered only from an ML-related optimization perspective. Secondly, with security-focused models, evaluation criteria should go beyond the traditional ones such as accuracy, precision, recall, and F1-score, to encompass measures of privacy burden, explainability, and reliance on behavior-linked variables as well. Thirdly, a continuing review role should be established whereby privacy officers and security engineers together evaluate whether incoming data sources are actually producing a better risk detection or simply expanding the monitoring scope. This also changes retention policy(Khatibi et al., 2025). If non-essential variables for present threat detection are being saved "just in case" for potential future retraining, then the DPIA needs to raise the retention justification issue. Data resulting in extensive behavioral profiling should not be stored indefinitely unless a highly justified, well documented rationale exists. Besides this, the re-training mechanism of models should be closely monitored to ensure that the usage of historical data stays within the purview of the original security aim. What counts most is that the actual assessment through AI security should be the main driver of the organizational Excellent technical capabilities do not make a model DPIA-compliant. Compliance only comes when the data requisites of the model, its outputs, and its operational ramifications are all documented, proportional, and subjected to review(Al-daaja et al., 2025).

Table 4. Illustrative Comparison of Model Utility and Privacy Exposure in AI Security Analytics

Model Condition	Feature Scope	Detection Utility	Privacy Exposure	DPIA Interpretation
Full-Feature Model	All technical and context-enriched variables retained	Very high	High	Strong detection, but requires extensive justification, strict controls, and clear human oversight
Reduced-Feature Model	Core technical variables plus limited contextual attributes	High	Moderate	Balanced approach; often the most defensible design for operational deployment
Privacy-Optimized Model	Only essential technical security features retained	Moderate to high	Low	Strongest proportionality position; suitable where governance sensitivity is high

Table 5 indicates that the focus of DPIA is not to do away with the AI security analytics. Rather, it is a technique for determining at which point the value of detection and the restraint of privacy are most responsibly aligned. In many live cases, the reduced-feature model will handle it the best since it retains strong analytical value along with a significant reduction of privacy risk.

7. CHALLENGES AND LIMITATIONS OF DPIAS IN ARTIFICIAL INTELLIGENCE SECURITY SYSTEMS

Data Protection Impact Assessments (DPIAs) offer a systematic and legally compliant way of determining privacy risks in the use of artificial intelligence (AI) in security settings. One reason for their value is that they require organizations to trace data flows, determine the need for surveillance activities, evaluate proportionality, and keep a record of risk-reduction measures before or even during the implementation of the system. Still, DPIAs are not without their drawbacks. In rapidly changing AI-enabled security environments, the technological complexity, the quickness of operational changes, and the continuous development of cyber threats may lower the actual effectiveness of even thoughtfully created impact assessments. At the core, AI security systems hardly ever remain the same. For example, a single system may undergo several changes such as retraining models, adding new features, integrating data sources, changing alert levels, modifying response strategies, etc. So, a DPIA done at a certain stage of system development could be partly inaccurate after the changes in the system. This indicates that even a technically compliant DPIA could from an operational point of view be completely irrelevant if the governance processes do not keep up with the system changes. Actually, the difficulty lies not only in doing the DPIA properly but also in maintaining its validity throughout the entire lifecycle of the AI security system. Apart from this, the issue is that the language of the law and that of the technical aspects of the system are not aligned. DPIA formats target identifying rights, risks, and safeguards, while AI security systems are essentially feature-based, model-based, pipeline, and detection logic-based. Translating between these two vastly different realms certainly calls for interdisciplinary expertise, and most organizations are quite far from having Privacy officers, for instance, may not fully comprehend a model's workings, whereas security experts may not really understand the legal significance of making large-scale behavioral inferences. This may result in overly broad DPIAs that describe the systems very generally but miss the most significant privacy risks hidden in the actual analytical process.

7.1 Complexity of AI Decision-Making Processes

The main stumbling block for executing DPIAs in AI security systems is the complexity of AI-driven decision-making mechanisms. Security models that are based on the extraction of complex statistical associations rather than simple, easily understandable rules are quite normal nowadays. Such methods as ensembles, deep learning, and behavior-based anomaly detection can result in outputs that are logically useful but which it is very challenging to unpack in terms of the exact cause. While it is likely that a security analyst will be aware that a model has flagged a session as anomalous, exactly why that particular session was classified as risky can be difficult to explain when multiple interacting variables push the result one way or another. This can have a very direct impact on the quality of the DPIA since the latter requires a thorough and clear description of the processing activities, the logic underlying the system, the risks arising from such operations, and the ways the risks are controlled. Difficulty in articulating the model workings hinders the assessment of the criteria of fairness, proportionality, and accountability. Besides that, the issue becomes even more complex when it comes to anomaly detection since in such a case the AI model only identifies instances of deviation from the typical behavior without necessarily having to refer to the recognized threat categories. So, normality is defined as a statistical measure and any deviation from the pattern is understood as a potential threat which is a serious problem when two people do different things and the one who is not like the majority is almost always the one who gets an alert. A DPIA is expected to consider this aspect but in order to do it, it should possess a very high degree of technical skills and the ability to understand which is something that most DPIA frameworks still do not Al-Dmour et al., 2025).

7.2 Limitations of Static Risk Assessment in Dynamic Security Environments

A traditional DPIA is typically a document-heavy and phase-oriented exercise. The assessment is normally done before the launch of the system or a major change in the system function, and this allows the creation of a formal record of risks, issues, and safeguards. Usually this method works just fine for stable systems that don't change much. However, AI security platforms can vary significantly from one day to the next. For instance, a model could be retrained only once a month, new data sources could be added to the system, alert thresholds might be changed, or performance tuning could involve reusing historical data. Any of these changes can impact a system's privacy risk profile, making it different enough that it really should be reassessed in full unless the governance processes are very In fact, it is in this way a major flaw of static impact assessments, such as DPIAs, is If a DPIA is performed at time 1, the system changes that occur subsequently probably do not get reflected in the DPIA report. So, in effect, the system has been left with a DPIA that is inherently inaccurate - has not kept pace with the system changes.

Privacy governance in a rapidly changing security context environment should therefore be continuous rather than discrete. Nevertheless, many organizations seem to be stuck in the mindset of DPIA being a one-time compliance measure, which results in a devaluation of its utility. The problem lies not with the conceptual framework of a DPIA but with the actuality of its implementation. Even without any real assessment, the absence of a mature governance process of the system's lifecycle will result in a DPIA becoming stale over time.

7.3 Quantifying Privacy Harm in AI Security Systems

One more limitation is related to the metrics. It is very straightforward to measure security by using familiar metrics like detection rate, time to detection, or severity of the On the other hand, privacy harm is a rather elusive concept by comparison, which is probably the main reason why it can barely be reduced to measure of any kind at the same level of accuracy and specificity. Besides the quantifiable aspects, like unauthorized disclosure of personal data or improper access restriction through a model, there are also many intangible ones, like the chilling effect of constant surveillance or the normalization of workplace monitoring, or the gradual expansion of profiling beyond the original purpose. Because of the difficulties entailed in making privacy harms measurable, DPIAs presently still rely to a significant extent on qualitative judgment. This is not necessarily a negative point, yet it does also inevitably create variations in how well cases are handled(Iskandarani, 2025). For instance, one company can consider a behavioral monitoring function a moderate privacy risk as it does not do direct content inspection whereas another one may regard it as high risk on the basis of its capacity for cumulative profiling. In the absence of standard mechanisms for quantifying exposure to privacy, different assessments are not only going to be inconsistent but also the comparison between them will become impossible. This is a matter of limitation tied very tightly to the AI security domain particularly, simply because network and content disclosure are the very least by which one can get privacy impairment. Most likely, the issue will be quite just the opposite - the AI system is not one which exposes to a great extent raw personal content but which, even so, manages to derive detailed and consequential models of user behavior. Normally, one would judge a system based on the compliance metrics used. Therefore, one can safely conclude that DPIA methods still require substantially more sophisticated mechanisms in the areas of inferential privacy, cumulative surveillance intensity, and the governance implications of prediction-based decision suppor(Ali et al., 2025)t.

7.4 Tension Between Detection Optimization and Privacy Restraint

The last, but not least, challenge is the structural tension between the dual goals of security maximization and privacy minimization. The manufacturing of AI security systems is largely dependent on the provision of access to rich, diverse, and longitudinal datasets. More features can help improve the sensitivity of models. More context can mitigate the number of false negatives. More data from the past can be exploited to retrain the system. From the technical standpoint, data abundance normally looks like an advantage. However, from the data protection viewpoint, it is more likely the opposite principle that applies - one should only process the data that is necessary and proportionate(Mohammad et al., 2025). One cannot always expect this tension to be resolved simply by looking for a middle ground. It can really be the case that retaining additional context leads to a genuine improvement in the ability of an organization to detect major threats. On the other hand, it is also true that the additional context is mainly about behavioral surveillance which does not really add much in terms of operational value. At times, the DPIA is the tool to be used for finding the middle ground, but this means the organization must first be very strict with themselves in terms of feature justification and ready to reject those design choices that are technically attractive but invade privacy. The issue here is that the DPIA concept is perfectly capable of taking account of trade-offs however, it is also true that some organizations may implicitly assume that security performance is absolutely determinative of their course of action. If in the organizational culture, all priority is given to detection metrics, then it is likely that findings coming out of DPIA will be compromised, neglected, or even framed as obstacles rather than constraints to the design process(Abualhaj, Al-Khatib, Abu-Shareha, et al., 2025).

Table 5. Major Challenges and Limitations of DPIAs in AI Security Systems

Challenge Area	Nature of the Limitation	Governance Consequence
Model Complexity	AI decisions may be difficult to interpret or explain clearly	Weakens transparency, fairness review, and accountability
Static Assessment Design	DPIAs may not keep pace with evolving models and changing data sources	Risk documentation becomes outdated
Regulatory Fragmentation	Different jurisdictions impose different standards on monitoring and profiling	Compliance becomes inconsistent across deployments
SOC Operational Pressure	High-speed defensive environments may deprioritize privacy review	Safeguards may exist on paper but weaken in practice
Privacy Harm Measurement	Privacy burden is difficult to quantify consistently	Risk ratings may become subjective or uneven
Security-Privacy Tradeoff	Technical optimization may encourage ever-expanding data collection	Proportionality may be undermined by performance-first thinking

8. Future Directions for Data Protection Impact Assessments in AI Security Systems

8.1 Continuous DPIA and Adaptive Governance

Continuous DPIA is one of the emerging trends in privacy risk governance. With this approach, in addition to carrying out the assessment at the time of development or launch, the implementation behavior of AI security systems is constantly monitored, and impact assessments are updated whenever system parameters change. Continuous DPIA components may include automated data flow tracking, regular model audits, and governance dashboards which display privacy metrics. For instance, an institution may use automated tools that can sense when a new data source is added to a security analytics platform. The governance system, detecting this change, can initiate a DPIA check to assess if the added data raises privacy risks or changes the balance of surveillance operations. Besides, if in the process of retraining machine learning models, different features are used, automated governance tools can notify privacy and compliance teams who will then conduct an examination of such changes. With adaptive governance, organizations create a systematic mechanism that receives the technical side information and links it with compliance oversight. Security personnel states how the system works while privacy officers' study the consequences of those actions for meeting data protection requirements. Through constant exchange and observation, companies can ensure that new security measures correspond to regulatory requirements(Shi et al., 2025).

8.2 Integration of Privacy-Enhancing Technologies in AI Security

Another pathway of DPIA transformation is the wider use of privacy-enhancing technologies (PETs). These are technical safeguards capable of ensuring privacy even in the process stage of data handling while retaining the ability to analyze data. PETs application in AI security could simultaneously reduce privacy risks and maintain threat detection performance. This approach leverages the advantages of differential privacy that involves injecting calibrated noise into data or outputs to ensure that no individual can be singled out. In the setting of security supervision, differential privacy enables viewing of aggregated patterns in activity without exposing individual data. In the same vein, federated learning is a technique where centralizing of personal data does not happen since training takes place locally and only model updates are shared rather than raw data. Secure multiparty computation and homomorphic encryption are other examples of privacy-preserving analytics. These allow for performing calculations on encrypted data which means sensitive data stays encrypted even during the operation, thus limiting the risk of exposure. Although these options are at different stages of maturity, they clearly illustrate how technical progress can enable achieving DPIA goals by limiting exposure of personal data in the course of AI-based analysis(Zraiqat et al., 2025).

8.3 Explainable Artificial Intelligence for Security Monitoring

Explainable artificial intelligence (XAI) is set to become a vital element in fostering trust and accountability in AI-powered security tools. Complex machine learning models pose a significant challenge for organizations to effectively communicate how security decisions have been arrived at analytically and therefore legally. Under DPIA regimes, it is mandatory that organizations maintain an adequate comprehension of processing logic to rationalize the use of such systems. Explainable AI aims to provide model behavior that is intelligible by humans. Security analysts are most interested in understanding which factors influenced a particular decision; they can do this with the help of local explanation algorithms, visualization tools, and feature importance analysis. Security teams, in turn, are able to verify models by supplying these, guarantee that their decisions are based on reliable correlations and unbiased data sets. Explainability reinforces DPIAs with a layer of communication—third parties can understand the rationale behind decisions. If a person protests being the subject of a decision by an AI security system, it should be explained what led to the decision. The release of the algorithm entirely might not be feasible due to intellectual property rights issues or the complexity of the model, but explainable AI offers a reasonable middle ground between accompanied analytics and the fulfillment of governance Abualhaj, Al-Khatib, Al-Zyoud, et al., 2025).

8.4 Ethical Governance and Human-Centered Security Design

The future direction of DPIAs in AI security systems must still reckoning with the unavoidable ethical challenges stemming from surveillance, autonomy, and the trust relationship between institutions and individuals. Since AI-enabled surveillance tools digitally track activities almost continuously, they can alter long-standing concepts of space and human interaction. However, apart from security enhancement, the surveillance can also affect a person freedom, trust, and overall culture of an office. Human-centered security design is one of the ways to turn the blue consequences of surveillance into red ones. It places the human at the heart of concern so that security technologies should not create but rather solve pcsv zeople problems. In this scenario, surveillance would be in line with respecting people's freedom and making sure that trust is maintained, while at the same time, security objectives are being fulfilled. A part of the ethical governance structure could be stakeholder consultation at decision-making stages. If companies decide to use large-scale monitoring systems which will impact the lives of their employees, customers, or community members, the latter can be invited to the discussion. The public perception of such security innovations and their acceptance can be improved through dialogue and transparency i.e. the opening-up of the communication channel to the public and letting them in on the

Ethical concerns extend beyond regulatory compliance. Continuous monitoring may influence employee autonomy, workplace trust, and perceptions of fairness. Similarly, behavioral profiling and automated risk scoring may create unintended consequences if individuals are categorized incorrectly or subjected to disproportionate scrutiny. Organizations should therefore ensure that AI security systems operate under principles of transparency, accountability, proportionality, and human oversight. Ethical governance should be viewed as an ongoing responsibility rather than a one-time compliance exercise.

Table 6. Emerging Directions for DPIA Development in AI Security Systems

Future Direction	Description	Expected Impact on AI Security Governance
Continuous DPIA Frameworks	Ongoing monitoring and reassessment of privacy risks throughout system lifecycle	Ensures DPIAs remain relevant as AI systems evolve
Privacy-Enhancing Technologies	Integration of techniques such as differential privacy and federated learning	Reduces exposure of personal data while preserving analytical capabilities
Regulatory Harmonization	Development of consistent global standards for AI governance and privacy protection	Simplifies compliance across international operations
Explainable AI Tools	Techniques that provide interpretable insights into machine learning decisions	Improves transparency, accountability, and fairness
Human-Centered Security Design	Ethical frameworks that prioritize user rights and trust in monitoring systems	Balances cybersecurity objectives with social responsibility

9. CONCLUSION

Artificial intelligence has been a game changer for cybersecurity and how it is done today. Most businesses use analytics that rely on AI, behavioral monitoring, and automated methods for finding threats to detect malicious activities and protect their key digital infrastructures. However, these tools not only give a lot of benefits to the operations but also bring up very complicated issues of privacy, law compliance, and ethics. So, it is not surprising that Data Protection Impact Assessments (DPIAs) have become a vital governance tool for ensuring that the AI-driven security measures stay within the legal and ethical frameworks. This chapter discussed using DPIAs as an instrument for regulating AI security systems. Initially, we looked at the legal basis of impact assessments and their function in identifying high-risk data processing activities. AI cybersecurity systems keep growing in number and complexity, and to be effective, they must analyze most of the time large data sets of behavioral and operational data to detect abnormalities and threats. For instance, the systems may analyze network traffic, authentication logs, user behavior patterns, device telemetry, etc. Apart from strengthening the organization's ability to defend itself against cyber threats, it is expected that there will be a huge collection, analysis, and storage of personal data. One main message that we have been driving from the beginning to the very end is the importance of balancing the massive collection and continuous monitoring for security purposes with the maintenance of strong privacy protections. DPIAs assist in this balancing act by providing organizations with a formal and structured approach.

Moreover, we have seen that these AI-powered security systems are capable of revealing personal data not only through direct collection but also through the system's inferences. For instance, advanced ML models can discern detailed user behavior patterns, device usage regimens, and even organizational workflows. Such observations can then be used to develop profiles that disclose personal and potentially sensitive information about individuals or groups. Consequently, it is indispensable that DPIAs be used to mitigate direct data processing followed by consideration of the inferential abilities of such AI systems. Moreover, addressing such risks entails, besides the support of cybersecurity engineers and data scientists, the participation of legal and privacy experts. The chapter also draws attention to the fact that traditional DPIA approaches are very limited in addressing ever-changing technological scenarios. Updating AI security systems through model retraining, data pipeline expansion, and operational changes is an ongoing process. At such a speed, a risk assessment conducted at deployment will become obsolete in no time. Therefore, for DPIA approaches to be successful, they must not only be flexible but also capable of including continuous governance - monitoring system evolution and updating risk assessment after system changes that have a major impact. Connecting DPIA activities with system lifecycle management dramatically reduces update work and allows organizations to keep their privacy assessments current. The analysis and results sections show the practical aspects of the compromise between security improvement and the dangers of privacy invasions in AI-based monitoring.

For instance, the security frameworks would work best to deter the threats if they are given the most comprehensive data sets and contexts. In addition, this extensive use of data for security purposes is a major risk factor from the privacy perspective. In this scenario, DPIA is crucial in helping to strike a balance, i.e., to evaluate to what extent the increase in power of threat detection is accompanied by and can be justified with privacy costs. Besides that, very strict attention to proportionality, necessity, and the possibility of less intrusive measures is, of course, Furthermore, new technologies and new regulations posing new standards for the conduct of DPIAs in AI-operated security systems were discussed in the chapter. Privacy-enhancing technologies such as differential privacy, federated learning, and secure multiparty computation can greatly reduce the extent to which individuals' data is exposed without sacrificing the system's ability to analyze. AI explainability, however, sheds light on what occurs in a complex model so as to enhance transparency and accountability in automated decision-making. The regulatory authorities around the world are also responding to the challenge of integrating AI-mediated decision-making into their reformed laws. There are a lot of legislations and policy initiatives in different countries that place a great emphasis on the transparency, accountability, and risk assessments of automated systems. Accordingly, DPIAs will be progressively recognized and used as the principal instrument for the oversight of AI technologies. It will be not only normal but also demanded that sophisticated security analytics solutions operate in a responsible manner that respects the fundamental rights of

Ethics are yet another vital aspect of AI security management. Continuous surveillance tools may have an impact on not only how staff members interact with each other but also on the degree of control that an individual has over themselves as well as how the general level of trust in the organization is perceived. The achievement of cybersecurity goals, of course, is both valid and necessary; nevertheless, monitoring has always to be done with regard to the balance and respect of human dignity. Initiating a DPIA enables the organization to scrutinize ethical consideration areas to a greater extent and leading the management to a more human-centered security design. The fact that DPIAs are effective tools in the protection of privacy and the strengthening of cybersecurity resilience is a remarkable achievement, especially when the compliance aspect is coupled with the impetus for responsible technology governance. The involvement of different parties such as security staff, compliance personnel, and organization's top management will be of utmost importance if the organizations want to see the integration of privacy into all the stages of AI-powered security systems - design, deployment, and operation. Provided DPIAs are regarded as genuine governance instruments, not just formalities, they could in fact become building blocks for privacy protection and cybersecurity resilience. To put it briefly, Data Protection Impact Assessments represent one of the most important components of responsible AI security governance. While AI is growing at a rate which is beyond what anyone can even imagine and at the same time significantly improving the capabilities of cybersecurity infrastructures, DPIAs are gradually becoming one of the ways that lead to innovation without the sacrifice of individual rights and community

From a practical perspective, effective DPIA implementation requires collaboration among cybersecurity teams, privacy officers, legal advisors, risk managers, and senior leadership. Regular reassessment should be performed whenever new data sources, analytical capabilities, or automated decision-making functions are introduced. Embedding DPIAs into the operational lifecycle of AI security systems enables organizations to maintain both cybersecurity resilience and long-term regulatory compliance.

REFERENCES

Abdeljaber, O., & Al-Masaeed, S., Al-Mu'ani, L., Yaseen, H., & Alhnaity, B. (2025). Strategic Intelligence: The Power of AI in Planning Efficiency. *Human Behavior and Emerging Technologies*, (1). Advance online publication. DOI: 10.1155/hbe2/5383054

Abualghanam, O., Alazzam, H., Qatawneh, M., Alazab, M., & Al Sharaiah, M. (2025). Elevating Mobile Security: An Ensemble Approach for Enhanced Malware Detection with M-iForest. *International Journal of Interactive Mobile Technologies*, *19*(10), 129–151. Advance online publication. DOI: 10.3991/ijim.v19i10.51319

Abualhaj, M. M., Al-Khatib, S., Al Shafi, N., Qaddara, I., & Hyassat, A. (2025). Utilizing Gray Wolf Optimization Algorithm in Malware Forensic Investigation. *Journal of Computational and Cognitive Engineering*, *4*(4), 591–602. Advance online publication. DOI: 10.47852/bonviewJCCE52025053

Abualhaj, M. M., Al-Khatib, S. N., Abu-Shareha, A. A., Hyassat, A., & Daoud, M. S. (2025). Smart Firewall for Phishing Detection Powered by Bio-Inspired Algorithms. *Journal of Advances in Information Technology*, *16*(11), 1529–1539. Advance online publication. DOI: 10.12720/jait.16.11.1529-1539

Abualhaj, M. M., Al-Khatib, S. N., Al Zyoud, M., Qaddara, I., & Anbar, M. (2025). Enhancing Intrusion Detection System Performance Using a Hybrid of Harris Hawks and Whale Optimization Algorithms. *Engineering. Technology and Applied Science Research*, *15*(4), 24354–24361. Advance online publication. DOI: 10.48084/etasr.10919

Abualigah, L., Almomani, M. H., Alomari, S. A., Zitar, R. A., Migdady, H., Saleem, K., Snasel, V., Smerat, A., & Ezugwu, A. E. (2025). Optimizing Intrusion Detection in Wireless Sensor Networks via the Improved Chameleon Swarm Algorithm for Feature Selection. *IET Communications*, *19*(1), e70029. Advance online publication. DOI: 10.1049/cmu2.70029

Ahmed, Z. E., Hasan, M. K., Hashim, A. A., Saeed, R. A., Mokhtar, R. A., Singh, S. P., & Ghazal, T. M. (2022). Optimization Procedure for Intelligent Internet of Things Applications. *2022 International Conference on Business Analytics for Technology and Security, ICBATS 2022*. DOI: 10.1109/ICBATS54253.2022.9759065

Al-Adwan, A. S., Al-Adwan, A., Li, N., Fauzi, M. A., Jafar, R. M. S., Habibi, A., & Falahat, M. (2025). IMMERSIVE LEARNING MEETS THEORY: MODELING EDUVERSE ADOPTION IN HIGHER EDUCATION. *Journal of Information Technology Education*, *24*, 042. Advance online publication. DOI: 10.28945/5669

Al-Daoud, K. I., Yogeesh, N., Mohammad, S. I., Raja, N., Chetana, R., William, P., Vasudevan, A., Alshdaifa, N., & Hunitie, M. F. A. (2025). Explainability in AI Using Fuzzy Inference Systems For the Regression Problem. *Applied Mathematics & Information Sciences*, *19*(5), 973–987. Advance online publication. DOI: 10.18576/amis/190501

Al-Daoud, K. I., Yogeesh, N., Mohammad, S. I. S., Raja, N., Jabeen, F. T. Z., William, P., Vasudevan, A., Hunitie, M. F. A., & Alshdaifat, N. (2025). Fuzzy Linear Programming in Real-World Applications: A Comparative Study of Agricultural and Financial Optimization. *Applied Mathematics & Information Sciences*, *19*(4), 849–862. Advance online publication. DOI: 10.18576/amis/190411

Al-Dmour, R., Al-Dmour, H., Al-Dmour, A., Basheer Amin, E., & Al-Dmour, Y. (2025). *AI and big data-driven social media recruitment: the mediating role of talent acquisition and employee engagement in bank performance*. Digital Transformation and Society., DOI: 10.1108/DTS-02-2025-0042

Al-Habashneh, A. G., Al-Daoud, K. I., Oraini, B., Al, , & Shelash, S. I. (2025). The impact of artificial intelligence on the development of electronic financial services. *International Journal of Data and Network Science*, *9*(2), 317–322. Advance online publication. DOI: 10.5267/j.ijdns.2024.8.012

Al-Momani, M. M., Alqudah, T. A., Al Swiety, I. A., Mahrakani, N., Nassoura, M. B. A., & Al Attar, M. K. (2025). Integrating Artificial Intelligence (AI) and Business Intelligence (BI): A Framework for Improving Enterprise Performance. *TEM Journal, 14*(3). https://doi.org/DOI: 10.18421/TEM143-26

Al-Mousa, M., Amer, W., Abualhaj, M., Albilasi, S., Nasir, O., & Samara, G. (2025). Agile Proactive Cybercrime Evidence Analysis Model for Digital Forensics. *The International Arab Journal of Information Technology*, *22*(3). Advance online publication. DOI: 10.34028/iajit/22/3/15

Al-Suhimat, R. I., Mohammed Ai, N., Ibrahim, A., Maaitah, N. O., & Al-Dmour, N. A. (2024). Review of Security Challenges Encountered in Internet of Things Technology. *2nd International Conference on Cyber Resilience, ICCR 2024*. DOI: 10.1109/ICCR61006.2024.10533052

Al-znamat, F. O., Alsaaidah, A., & Abu-Shareha, A. A. (2025). Malware Detection Using a Modified Bat Algorithm for Feature Selection. *International Journal of Intelligent Engineering and Systems*, *18*(9), 885–899. Advance online publication. DOI: 10.22266/ijies2025.1031.56

Alabdallat, R. D., Abualhaj, M. M., & Abu-Shareha, A. (2025). Enhanced Multiclass Android Malware Detection Using a Modified Dwarf Mongoose Algorithm. *International Journal of Analysis and Applications*, *23*, 248. Advance online publication. DOI: 10.28924/2291-8639-23-2025-248

Aldaaja, Y., Odeh, M., Badrakhan, S. S., Sabri, M., Abdelrahim, Y., Samara, G., & Alsabatin, H. (2025). Quantifying the Managerial and Practical Benefits of Cloud Computing on Information Security in Higher Education Institutions. *Applied Mathematics & Information Sciences*, *19*(1), 15–24. Advance online publication. DOI: 10.18576/amis/190102

Alenazi, M. J. F., Al-Khasawneh, M. A., Rahman, S., & Faheem, Z. (2025). Deep Reinforcement Learning Based Flow Aware-QoS Provisioning in SD-IoT for Precision Agriculture. *Computational Intelligence*, *41*(1), e70023. Advance online publication. DOI: 10.1111/coin.70023

Ali, A. M., Al-Qerem, A., Hassan, M. R., Abu-Khadrah, A., & Jarrah, M. (2025). Traffic Monitoring and Control System for Smart City Pollution Regulation Using IoT and Correlated Capsule Networks. *IEEE Access : Practical Innovations, Open Solutions*, *13*, 46983–47003. Advance online publication. DOI: 10.1109/ACCESS.2025.3550966

Alkhawatrah, M. (2025). Random Forests Relay Selector in Buffer-Aided Cooperative Networks. *IEEE Access : Practical Innovations, Open Solutions*, *13*, 165402–165410. Advance online publication. DOI: 10.1109/ACCESS.2025.3612192

Almomani, O., Arabiat, A., Al Tayeb, M., Almaiah, M. A., Obeidat, M., Aldhyani, T. H. H., Shehab, R., & Rowad, M. (2025). A Robust Model for Android Malware Detection via ML and DL classifiers. *Mesopotamian Journal of Big Data*, *2025*. Advance online publication. DOI: 10.58496/MJBD/2025/017

Alnawayseh, S. E. A., Muhammad, M. H. G., Hassan, Z., Fatima, M., Aslam, M. S., Ibrahim, A., & Ateeq, K. (2023). Resource Provisioning in Cloud Computing using Fuzzy Logic Control System: An adaptive approach. *2nd International Conference on Business Analytics for Technology and Security, ICBATS 2023*. DOI: 10.1109/ICBATS57792.2023.10111481

Alraba'nah, Y., Al-Sharaeh, S., & Al Hindi, G. (2025). Enhancing Intrusion Detection Using Hybrid Long Short-Term Memory and XGBoost. *Journal of Soft Computing and Data Mining*, *6*(1). Advance online publication. DOI: 10.30880/jscdm.2025.06.01.016

Arabasy, M., & Ghoneim, R. S. (2025). Enhancing sustainable urban design using machine learning: Comparative analysis of seven metaheuristic algorithms in energy-efficient digital architecture. *Frontiers in Built Environment*, *11*, 1526209. Advance online publication. DOI: 10.3389/fbuil.2025.1526209

Arabiat, A. M. (2025). Intelligent Model for Detecting GAN-Generated Images Based on Multi-Classifier and Advanced Data Mining Techniques. *International Journal of Electrical and Electronic Engineering and Telecommunications*, *14*(3). Advance online publication. DOI: 10.18178/ijeetc.14.3.147-157

Arabiat, A. M., & Eljaafreh, Y. G. (2025). Intrusion Detection in Wireless Sensor Networks Using ML Based Classification of Denial of Service (DoS) Attacks. *The Journal of Communication*, *20*(4). Advance online publication. DOI: 10.12720/jcm.20.4.501-514

Awais, Z., Hussain, M., Elshenawy, A., Arsalan, A., Anwar, M., Asif Habib, M., Jabbar, S., & Ahmad, M. (2025). ISCC: Intelligent Semantic Caching and Control for NDN-Enabled Industrial IoT Networks. *IEEE Access : Practical Innovations, Open Solutions*, *13*, 169881–169898. Advance online publication. DOI: 10.1109/ACCESS.2025.3614984

Duraimurugan, S., Jayarin, P. J., Mohammad, S. I., Hariprasad, N., Vasudevan, A., Soon, E. E. H., Hussein, A. H., & Alshurideh, M. T. (2025). Enhanced Server-Client Framework for Optimizing QoS in Video Streaming Over Diverse Networks. *Applied Mathematics & Information Sciences*, *19*(1), 61–73. Advance online publication. DOI: 10.18576/amis/190106

Elkaradawy, A., Elshenawy, A., & Harb, H. (2025). Enhancing Cloud Job Failure Prediction With a Novel Multilayer Voting-Based Framework. *IEEE Access : Practical Innovations, Open Solutions*, *13*, 140600–140613. Advance online publication. DOI: 10.1109/ACCESS.2025.3593808

Elomda, B. M., Abdelbary, T. A. A., Hassan, H. A., Hamza, K. S., & Kharma, Q. (2025). An Enhanced Multi-Layer Blockchain Security Model for Improved Latency and Scalability. *Information (Basel)*, *16*(3), 241. Advance online publication. DOI: 10.3390/info16030241

Farman, M., Gokbulut, N., Shehzad, A., Nisar, K. S., Hincal, E., & Sambas, A. (2025). Fractional order malaria epidemic model: Qualitative and computational study to determine the dynamics for sensitivity prevalence. *Journal of Computational Science*, *91*, 102656. Advance online publication. DOI: 10.1016/j.jocs.2025.102656

Fauzi, M. A., Alias, U. N., Nya-Ling Tan, C., Wider, W., Mukherjee, S., Al-Adwan, A. S., & Udang, L. N. (2025). The Present and Future Trends of Leadership Styles and Knowledge Hiding Through Science Mapping Analysis. *Journal of Information and Knowledge Management*, *24*(5), 2550040. Advance online publication. DOI: 10.1142/S0219649225500406

Ghazal, T. M. (2025a). An IoT-Based Active Learning Convolutional Neural Networks Model for Predicting River Water Quality. *Journal of Soft Computing and Data Mining*, *6*(1). Advance online publication. DOI: 10.30880/jscdm.2025.06.01.021

Ghazal, T. M. (2025b). Federated Learning for Intelligent Sensing and Navigation Technologies for 6G Communications. *Journal of Sensors, 2025*(1). DOI: 10.1155/js/3746147

Ghazal, T. M., Awouda, A. E., Hasan, M. K., Rahman, A. H. A., Islam, S., Saeed, R. A., Elshafie, H., Iqbal, A., & Hussein, A. H. (2025). Knowledge Learning for Securing Workflow Scheduling Algorithm in Mobile Edge Computing. *Mobile Networks and Applications*, *30*(3-4), 395–413. Advance online publication. DOI: 10.1007/s11036-025-02465-6

Ghazal, T. M., Hasan, M. K., Hussein, A. H., Pandey, B. K., Ahmad, M., Safie, N., & Cascone, L. (2025). Federated Learning With Small and Large Models With Privacy-Preserving Data Space for Holographic Internet of Things in Consumer Electronics. *IEEE Transactions on Consumer Electronics*, *71*(2), 5259–5274. Advance online publication. DOI: 10.1109/TCE.2025.3573033

Ghazal, T. M., Hasan, M. K., Mokhtar, U. A., Safie, N., Alshamayleh, A., & Ahmad, M. (2025). Machine learning-based real-time outage fault detection for distribution networks in smart grid. In *Energy Reports* (Vol. 14). DOI: 10.1016/j.egyr.2025.10.045

Ghazal, T. M., Janjua, J. I., Abushiba, W., Ahmad, M., Ihsan, A., & Al-Dmour, N. A. (2024). Cybersecurity Revolution via Large Language Models and Explainable AI. *2024 17th International Conference on Security of Information and Networks, SIN 2024*. DOI: 10.1109/SIN63213.2024.10871324

Hussain, K., Ali, E. M., Hussain, W., Raza, A., & Elkamchouchi, D. H. (2025). Robust OTFS-ISAC for Vehicular-to-Base Station End-to-End Sensing and Communication. *Electronics (Basel)*, *14*(21), 4340. Advance online publication. DOI: 10.3390/electronics14214340

Hyassat, A. S., Abu Zayed, R. E., Al Khateeb, E. A., Shalaldeh, A., Abdelhamied, M. M., & Qaddara, I. (2025). Unveiling Cyber Threats: An In-Depth Study on Data Mining Techniques for Exploit Attack Detection †. *Engineering Proceedings*, *104*(1), 28. Advance online publication. DOI: 10.3390/engproc2025104028

Iftikhar, A., Mohammad, S. I., Alqudah, M. N., Al-Adwan, A. S., Vasudevan, A., Ali, I., & Farhan, M. (2025). Evaluating Inclusivity and Fairness of AI Recruitment Tools for Hiring People with Disabilities in the United Arab Emirates(UAE). *Data and Metadata*, *4*. Advance online publication. DOI: 10.56294/dm2025487

Iskandarani, M. Z. (2025). Effect of Adaptive Intelligent Reflective Surfaces on SINR in a Wireless Communication System. *The Journal of Communication*, *20*(1). Advance online publication. DOI: 10.12720/jcm.20.1.1-11

Iskandarani, M. Z., & Chakrabarti, K. (2025). Adaptive Frequency and Energy Modeling Framework for Robotic Wireless Sensor Networks Based on Path Loss Predictions. *Journal of Robotics, 2025*(1). DOI: 10.1155/joro/6156608

Iskandarani, M. Z., & Hidayat, R. (2025). Analysis of Factors Affecting Spectrum Sensing in an IRS based Wireless Network. *International Journal on Advanced Science, Engineering and Information Technology*, *15*(1), 300–309. Advance online publication. DOI: 10.18517/ijaseit.15.1.20491

Jan, F. U., Badar, R., Sami Al-Shamayleh, A., Uehara, A., Senjyu, T., & Akhunzada, A. (2025). Soft Computing-Based Damping Controllers With Online Parameters Tuning for Stability Enhancement of Power Systems. *IEEE Access : Practical Innovations, Open Solutions*, *13*, 167045–167060. Advance online publication. DOI: 10.1109/ACCESS.2025.3612288

Jaradat, S., Acharya, N., Shivshankar, S., Alhadidi, T. I., & Elhenawy, M. (2025). AI for Data Quality Auditing: Detecting Mislabeled Work Zone Crashes Using Large Language Models. *Algorithms*, *18*(6), 317. Advance online publication. DOI: 10.3390/a18060317

Kamal, M. M., Ul Abideen, S. Z., Al-Khasawneh, M. A., Momani, A. M., Mostafa, H., Atoum, M. S., Ullah, S., Alsayaydeh, J. A. J., & Yusof, M. F. (2025). Meyer Wavelet Transform and Jaccard Deep Q Net for Small Object Classification Using Multi-Modal Images. *CMES -. Computer Modeling in Engineering & Sciences*, *144*(3), 3053–3083. Advance online publication. DOI: 10.32604/cmes.2025.067430

Khaled Abdullah, S., & Qawasmeh, R. (2025). *Navigating the ethical and legal risks of AI marketing in Jordanian SMEs*. EDPACS., DOI: 10.1080/07366981.2025.2600205

Khatibi, A., Babaker, S., Praveen, K. N. R., Chohan, J. S., Jadhav, A., Alsoud, A. R., Ramudu, M. J., & Jeet, R. (2025). Advanced AI-Driven Cybersecurity: Analyzing Emerging Threats and Defensive Strategies. *National Academy Science Letters*. Advance online publication. DOI: 10.1007/s40009-025-01897-8

Mahadin, G. A. L., Satvika, S., Kathuria, S., Kaushik, A., & Maranan, R. (2025). DEEP LEARNING FRAMEWORK FOR IDENTIFYING AND HYBRID SYNTHESIZING WIDESPREAD NEWS HEADLINES ON SOCIAL MEDIA. *Proceedings on Engineering Sciences*, *7*(3), 1453–1462. Advance online publication. DOI: 10.24874/PES07.03.007

Mahfouz, K. H., Al Betar, M. A., & Makhadmeh, S. N. (2025). Mitigating the task scheduling problem in fog computing environments using improved marine predators optimization algorithm. *Computing*, *107*(7), 147. Advance online publication. DOI: 10.1007/s00607-025-01502-2

Makhadmeh, S. N., Fraihat, S., Awad, M., Sanjalawe, Y., Al-Betar, M. A., & Awadallah, M. A. (2025). A crossover-integrated Marine Predator Algorithm for feature selection in intrusion detection systems within IoT environments. *Internet of Things : Engineering Cyber Physical Human Systems*, *31*, 101536. Advance online publication. DOI: 10.1016/j.iot.2025.101536

Masadeh, R., Almomani, O., Zaqebah, A., Masadeh, S., Alshqurat, K., Sharieh, A., & Alsharman, N. (2025). Narwhal Optimizer: A Nature-Inspired Optimization Algorithm for Solving Complex Optimization Problems. *Computers, Materials & Continua*, *85*(2), 3709–3737. Advance online publication. DOI: 10.32604/cmc.2025.066797

Maz, Y. A., Anbar, M., Manickam, S., Abualhaj, M. M., Almalki, S. A., & Alabsi, B. A. (2025). Transfer Learning-Based Approach with an Ensemble Classifier for Detecting Keylogging Attack on the Internet of Things. *Computers, Materials & Continua*, *85*(3), 5287–5307. Advance online publication. DOI: 10.32604/cmc.2025.068257

Mohammad, A. A. S., Al-Ramadan, A. M., Mohammad, S. I., Al Oraini, B., Vasudevan, A., Alshdaifat, N., & Hunitie, M. F. A. (2025). Customer Sentiment Analysis for Food and Beverage Development in Restaurants using AI in Jordan. *Data and Metadata*, *4*, 922. Advance online publication. DOI: 10.56294/dm2025922

Nafisah, I., Mahmoud, N., Ewees, A. A., Khattap, M. G., Dahou, A., Alghamdi, S. M., Fares, I. A., Azmi Al-Betar, M., & Abd Elaziz, M. (2025). Deep learning-based feature selection for detection of autism spectrum disorder. *Frontiers in Artificial Intelligence*, *8*, 1594372. Advance online publication. DOI: 10.3389/frai.2025.1594372 PMID: 40636395

Qawaqneh, H., Al Sayyed, O., Mohammad Alomari, K., Bektemyssova, G., Smerat, A., Montazeri, Z., Dehghani, M., Parkash Malik, O., & Eguchi, K. (2025). Pipefish Optimization Algorithm (POA): A Nature-inspired Metaheuristic for Robust and Adaptive Global Optimization. *International Journal of Intelligent Engineering and Systems*, *18*(11), 778–794. Advance online publication. DOI: 10.22266/ijies2025.1231.48

Rabbi, M. F., Amin, M., Al-Dalahmeh, M., & Abdullah, M. (2025). Assessing the role of information technology in promoting environmental sustainability and preventing crime in E-commerce. *International Review of Applied Sciences and Engineering*, *16*(1), 81–97. Advance online publication. DOI: 10.1556/1848.2024.00834

Salman, A. M., Ibrahim, A., Abdulbaqi, A. S., Almajed, R., & Al Naffakh, H. A. H. (2025). *Designing Blockchain Solutions to Enhance Data Security and Privacy in Distributed IoT Networks*. DOI: 10.1109/ICBATS66542.2025.11258568

Sardar, R., Anees, T., Al-Shamayleh, A. S., Mehmood, E., Khalil, W., Akhunzada, A., & Shaikh, F. S. (2025). Challenges in detecting security threats in WoT: A systematic literature review. *Artificial Intelligence Review*, *58*(7), 196. Advance online publication. DOI: 10.1007/s10462-025-11176-z

Shamaylah, N., Ibrahim Mohammad, S., Al Oraini, B., Yaseen Al-Gaafreh, J. M., Mosallam Alqahtani, M., Vasudevan, A., Shlash Mohammad, A. A., & Ahmmad Hunitie, M. F. (2025). Data-Driven Decision-Making for Employee Training and Development in Jordanian Public Institutions. *Data and Metadata*, *4*, 886. Advance online publication. DOI: 10.56294/dm2025886

Sharma, K. P., Al-Rashed, A., Johar, M. G. M., Alsoud, A. R., Singh, A., Dey, P., & Pant, S. (2025). Blockchain-Assisted Trust Framework for Increased Survivability in Internet of Vehicles. *Internet Technology Letters*, *8*(3), e70029. Advance online publication. DOI: 10.1002/itl2.70029

Shi, J., Farooq, U., Tabash, M. I., Riyadh, H. A., & Almajali, T. A. (2025). Air Pollution and the Innovation Gap: A Challenge for Sustainable Growth in Emerging and Growth Leading Economies (EAGLE). *Sustainability (Basel)*, *17*(10), 4423. Advance online publication. DOI: 10.3390/su17104423

Shlash Mohammad, A. A., Ibrahim Mohammad, S., Al-Daoud, K. I., Al Oraini, B., Mosallam Alqahtani, M., Vasudevan, A., & Ahmmad Hunitie, M. F. (2025). Riding into the Future: Transforming Jordan's Public Transportation with Predictive Analytics and Real-Time Data. *Data and Metadata*, *4*, 887. Advance online publication. DOI: 10.56294/dm2025887

Vasudevan, A., Albinaa, T. A., Mohammad, S. I., Sharmila, E., Raja, N., Soon, E. E. H., Alshurideh, M. T., & Al-Adwan, A. S. (2024). Bidirectional LSTM for Electronic Product Recommendation. *Applied Mathematics & Information Sciences*, *18*(6), 1443–1453. Advance online publication. DOI: 10.18576/amis/180621

Vasudevan, A., Tamilmani, K. T., Mohammad, S. I., Sridheepika, V. S., Raja, N., Soon, E. E. H., Nagaraj, S., & Al-Adwan, A. S. (2025). Voices of Concern: Contemplations on Socioeconomic, Ethical, and Developmental Impacts of AI. *Applied Mathematics & Information Sciences*, *19*(1), 221–232. Advance online publication. DOI: 10.18576/amis/190119

Yaseen, M., Ali, E., Sarwar, N., Jamel, L., Din, I., Yuldashev, F., & Law, F. (2025). Design of Minimal Spanning Tree and Analytic Hierarchical Process (SAHP) Based Hybrid Technique for Software Requirements Prioritization. *IET Software, 2025*(1). DOI: 10.1049/sfw2/8819735

Zhu, Y., Lin, X., Kim, J., Al-Adwan, A. S., & Li, N. (2025). Exploring Human Interaction in Online Self-Regulated Learning Through Danmaku Comments. *International Journal of Human-Computer Interaction*, *41*(22), 13964–13977. Advance online publication. DOI: 10.1080/10447318.2025.2480826

Zraiqat, A., Al Sayyed, O., Al Soudi, M., Al-Salih, A. A. M. M., Smerat, A., Montazeri, Z., Dehghani, M., Malik, O. P., Ahmed, M. A., Ibraheem, I. K., & Eguchi, K. (2025). Key Maker Algorithm: A Novel Human-Based Metaheuristic for Constrained Optimization. *International Journal of Intelligent Engineering and Systems*, *18*(9), 688–699. Advance online publication. DOI: 10.22266/ijies2025.1031.45

Chapter 10
Practical Effectiveness of Pseudonymization and De-Identification Methods

Munir Ahmad
http://orcid.org/0000-0002-5240-0984
School of Computer Science, National College of Business Administration & Economics, Lahore, Pakistan

Abdur Rehman
http://orcid.org/0000-0002-5867-8231
School of Computer Science, National College of Business Administration and Economics, Lahore, Pakistan

ABSTRACT

Privacy-centric approaches to pseudonymization and de-identification are essential for modern data processing and security practices. This chapter briefly defines legal terminology and then addresses technological implementation while highlighting the legal aspect of the two stages: reversible pseudonymization and irreversible de-identification. Besides, it deals with risks that are not yet eliminated, such as re-identification through data linkage, inference attacks, and contextual enrichment. The main focus of the chapter is on operational limitations, governance arrangements, and use cases where these methods considerably reduce compliance and privacy risks. The chapter attempts to align legal clauses with the technical tools, evaluating not only when pseudonymization and de-identification are adequate safeguards, but also when one is forced to the use of organizational, contractual and technical measures to accomplish continually compliant and responsible data practices.

1. INTRODUCTION

1.1 Growth of Data-Driven Security and Privacy Risks

Large-scale data processing brings about a completely new privacy environment where personal information is laid bare to an extent that greatly surpasses traditional customer databases. In fact, data

DOI: 10.4018/979-8-3373-9210-3.ch010

is being generated at all times from a variety of sources including browsing habits, login events, system logs, mobile activities, biometric systems, smart devices, digital payments, and platform telemetry. For example, monitoring infrastructures in security systems may gather a wealth of information including usernames, device fingerprints, session histories, geolocation traces, access timestamps, and behavioral anomalies as a way to identify suspicious activities (Sardar et al., 2025). Likewise, healthcare and financial institutions amalgamate demographic, transactional, and operational data to support risk modeling and service improvement initiatives. Indeed, such data-driven functions bring operational benefits; however, they are also one of the contributing factors to the type of scenario in which individual pieces of data serve as identifiers of individuals once they are linked to other data(Ibrahim et al., 2024).

The situation deteriorates even further when datasets are shared and analyzed for totally different purposes than the original ones. For instance, data originally used for user authentication may be examined for signs of fraud. Maintenance logs of systems could be turned into a resource for incident response or predictive analytics. Customer support records can be analyzed to identify gaps or make improvements to service delivery. Every single time the dataset is re-purposed, the chance of it being exposed is increased. Besides, since data is not only a commercial but also an institutional asset, the fact that organizations are motivated to keep it for a long time, share it broadly, and integrate across systems is a source of risk. This practice not only increases the risk of unauthorized access but also the risk of insider misuse, leakage of models, attacks of linking, and accidental disclosures. Hence, privacy protection cannot be entirely supported by the external security or access control measures alone. It must be extended to include data itself. Machine learning and advanced analytics are two major contributors to the escalation of privacy threats(Salman et al., 2025). In fact, through the models, patterns deeply hidden in the data can be revealed that previously had a near-zero risk of identification. Therefore, combinations of seemingly unrelated and non-identifying attributes such as age range, area, frequency of browsing, patterns of buying, or timing of activities can suddenly serve as identifying factors. Consequently, in addition to the cases where privacy may be at risk because of direct pieces of information that identify an individual (e.g., a person's name or passport number), the threat might also come from the so-called quasi-identifiers and inference paths. As a result, businesses have to acquire the ability to transform data before it gets incorporated into larger analytical Ahmed et al., 2025).

1.2 Distinction Between Anonymization, Pseudonymization, and De-Identification

De-identification is a more comprehensive term that often encompasses cutting-out, masking, generalizing, or transforming not only direct but also indirect identifiers so as to minimize the chance of identification. It might include, for example, getting rid of personal names, converting birth dates into age ranges, masking zip codes, truncating IP addresses, or suppressing uncommon attribute combinations. Depending on the method used and the situation at hand, de-identification may be either reversible or irreversible, but its main focus is to lower the risk of practical identification rather than merely replacing identifiers. Anonymization is at the farthest end of privacy protection. It suggests that identifying an individual is no longer feasible by any reasonable means. Yet, since external datasets, machine learning models, and ways of linking data continue to be refined, there is hardly any situation in practice where true anonymization can be guaranteed. That is why most of the time, companies rely on pseudonymization and de-identification as more doable operational strategies, especially when it is still necessary to retain some analytical value. For instance, a dataset protected by pseudonymization may still fall under the scope of rather strict privacy regulations because the organization has retained a re-identification pathway. A de-identified dataset may be suitable for a much wider range of internal uses, but only if the residual risks are managed in a very thorough manner. So, making the decision on the level of protection needed requires a good grasp of both the technical side and the context(Hasan et al., 2021).

1.3 Privacy Regulations Driving Data Protection Technologies

Major privacy laws have been a significant factor in upping the pace of introducing pseudonymization and de-identification techniques. Besides other things, privacy frameworks are getting tougher, organizations are expected to demonstrate that they are doing everything to avoid the exposure of personal data, and that they have protective measures such as pseudonymization in place. Data protection and privacy technology have come to the rescue of organizations not only in ensuring compliance but also in enabling better performance and functionality of data-intensive operations. Companies that are engaged in cross-border business have further regulated their data operations. These days they also ensure that personal data is handled in a manner that is proportionate, secure, and in accordance with the principle of purpose limitation(Lee et al., 2021). As a result, there has been a rise in the usage of tools for reducing the visibility of identifiers when doing testing, analytics, model training, and sharing the data with third parties. Privacy-preserving transformations are of particular importance in the case of security and security analytics where the logs and telemetry can contain highly detailed behavioral information since these types of systems often work in a continuous mode and can handle large amounts of user-related data even without user interaction at every single step. The legal framework has been a catalyst for privacy engineering as a discipline which is an amalgamation of knowledge of engineering, data science, compliance, and system architecture. It is a common practice now for teams consisting of these different professionals to work together with the goal of figuring out ways of tokenizing identifiers, isolating re-identification keys, reducing the number of quasi-identifiers, and assessing residual risk(Ghazal, Hasan, Mokhtar, et al., 2025).

1.4 Scope and Objectives of the Chapter

This chapter has five key objectives: first, to clarify what anonymization, pseudonymization, and de-identification are by both theory and practice; second, to explore how the major methods are implemented and which privacy threats they aim to eliminate; third, to consider the advantages and disadvantages of security monitoring and analytics pipelines that use these methods; fourth, to perform an experimental study to investigate the privacy-utility trade-offs; fifth, to identify future work areas that combine traditional privacy transformation with state-of-the-art methodologies like differential privacy, federated learning, and synthetic data While the chapter recognizes the fact that pseudonymization and de-identification hold great potential, it also points out their limitations and when they are not enough on their own. There are factors such as context, implementation patterns, oversight, and continually enhancing hacker capabilities that determine their success. The conclusion, therefore is, that privacy protection should be thought of as a layered design rather than a one-off transformation step.

Figure 1. Data Privacy Protection Spectrum

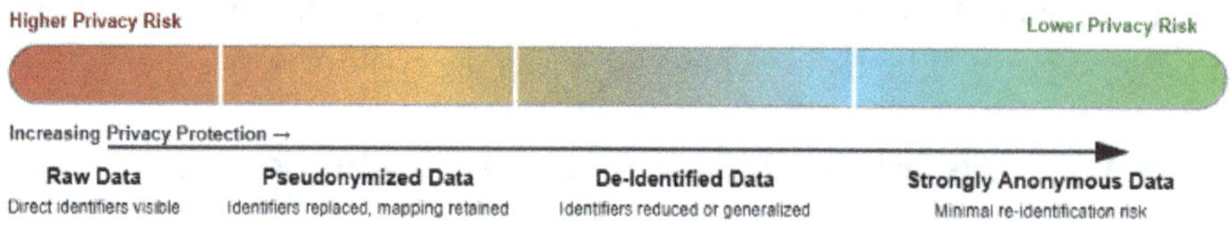

Figure 2. Privacy-Preserving Data Processing Framework

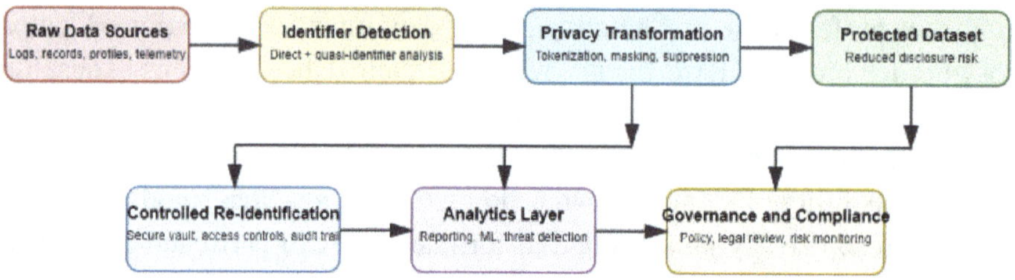

2. THEORETICAL FOUNDATIONS

At its core, privacy-preserving data transformation is based on the fact that personal data cannot be solely protected by limiting access to the databases or encrypting the data in transit. In the current data environment, data is being the protagonists, copied, mixed, modeled, analyzed, and shared over and over in different platforms, co-workers, and services. Therefore, protection of privacy should also take into account post-access activities of the data when the use is legitimate. This is exactly the point where privacy-preserving transformation turns into a necessity. Instead of giving every authorized user the raw data linked to identities, such techniques transform the data in such a way that analyses, monitoring, and operational processing can be performed while the exposure of individuals is kept to a minimum. The intellectual basis of these methods is drawn from various overlapping areas such as privacy engineering, statistical disclosure control, database security, information theory, and legal compliance. The main issue in these fields is: how can data still be really meaningful for analysis while the chances of identifying or profiling an individual is lowered to a reasonable level? This problem cannot be answered in a one-size-fits-all manner since privacy varies from one context to another. What is considered a secure transformation for internal testing may not be suitable for the public release of data. Similarly, a method that safeguards a set of customers may not be effective in the case of network telemetry or behavioral logs(Abdeljaber et al., 2025).

2.1 Privacy Threat Models in Data Sharing Environments

In any data sharing scenario, a privacy threat model specifies how an individual's information might get exposed, derived, connected, or recreated from a dataset. Transforming data without a threat model can lead to changes only in the most visible attributes, leaving the less obvious attack routes exposed. In fact, real-world privacy threats can come not only from hackers but also from internal analysts, third-party vendors, model developers, accidental disclosers, or even well-meaning researchers who merge datasets without understanding the identification implications. At its simplest, a threat model perceives that an attacker tries to identify the person whose record is present in a data release or a data processing situation(Ullah et al., 2025). Matching characteristics that are open to view with other external resources such as profiles on social networks, electoral rolls, public registers, leaked databases, or location data might achieve this. The higher-level threat model assumes that the adversary already holds some information about the target and is looking for validation or additional details. For instance, if an attacker has information about a person's age range, city, and work sector, then even a substantially modified dataset could still identify the associated record if that particular combination of attributes is very rare. In security monitoring systems, it is necessary to consider insider knowledge, because system administrators, incident responders, or data engineers might, to some extent, understand the pattern of certain masking techniques. Yet another threat model relates to membership disclosure where the adversary's goal is to figure out if a specific person is included in the dataset. Such membership in itself can be revealing and sensitive. In hospital data, being a member can point to treatment; being in a cybersecurity watchlist suggests suspicion; in a debt recovery file, it discloses that a person is financially distressed. So, data transformation sometimes should also safeguard record presence, not just record content from these threat models, it should be clear that removing the names alone is not a sufficient criterion for assessing privacy-preserving transformations. They must be judged based on how well they can defend against realistic scenarios of attacks through linking, inferring, and knowledge of situations(Shah et al., 2022).

2.2 Direct Identifiers vs Quasi-Identifiers

Fundamental to privacy-preserving transformation is the recognition and treatment of direct identifiers and quasi-identifiers. Direct identifiers refer to the data elements that directly and undoubtedly identify a particular individual. They can be the person's name, passport number, or social security number. These identifiers can also be things like email addresses, employee IDs, phone numbers, exact account numbers, biometric templates, or any data points that serve to uniquely differentiate one individual from all others. The presence of such fields implies that identifying the individual is a matter of seconds, if not a single click. That is why, in the very beginning of the pseudonymization and de-identification steps, direct identifiers are usually replaced, removed, or kept separately. Getting rid of direct identifiers does not mean that the privacy threat disappears. A very significant set of literature focusing on identification from re-identification have explored quasi-identifier data elements as well, which are those that are not capable of single-handedly pinpointing a certain person, but can do so in the presence of other data. Good examples are: age, postal code, occupation, gender, marital status, exact date of birth, ethnicity, time of transaction, pattern of browsing, or type of device switched to(Alnawayseh et al., 2022).

The risk of disclosure inherent to quasi-identifiers stems from the possibility that their combination can lead to uniqueness. Of course, gender, as a single attribute, would usually not be considered for identifying a person. Nevertheless, if we consider a person's gender together with their age bracket, district, and employment role, the resulting combination may be so specific as to single out an individual. It is for this reason that even after direct identifiers are removed, some of the most dramatic re-identification cases frequently come up(Elomda et al., 2025). At first sight, the released dataset looked anonymous, but the quasi-identifiers had preserved a level of uniqueness that enabled the matching of the records to be done against auxiliary sources. Therefore, the treatment of quasi-identifiers is actually what makes or breaks de-identification. If one does not go far enough, the individuals remain exposed. Hence, theoretical privacy models like the k-anonymity model were developed exactly to handle this problem by stipulating that each quasi-identifier combination must have corresponded to a group of similar individuals at least(Vasudevan et al., 2024).

Table 1. Classification of Common Data Attributes in Privacy Engineering

Attribute Type	Description	Typical Examples	Privacy Risk if Unprotected
Direct Identifier	Explicitly identifies an individual without requiring other data	Full name, CNIC/passport number, email address, phone number, employee ID	Immediate identification
Strong Quasi-Identifier	Does not directly identify alone, but becomes highly revealing when combined	Exact date of birth, full ZIP/postal code, job title, exact geolocation	High linkage risk
Moderate Quasi-Identifier	Supports inference or narrowing of identity when joined with other fields	Age band, district, browsing frequency, transaction time	Medium re-identification risk
Sensitive Attribute	Reveals confidential or regulated personal information	Diagnosis, salary, loan default status, disciplinary action	High harm even without full identity
Non-Sensitive Operational Attribute	Generally low-risk if isolated, but may still contribute to profiling in context	Device type, session duration, service category	Low to moderate contextual risk

Such a classification of attributes helps to realize why privacy transformation cannot be a blunt instrument. The risk of disclosure of an attribute arises not only from its own intrinsic content but also depends on how an attribute interacts with the rest of the dataset and with external information sources.

2.3 Re-Identification Risks in Modern Data Ecosystems

Re-identification risk is the measure of the likelihood that a record is protected only on paper can actually be traced back to an individual. The risk has speculated to be growing in recent years because of the abundance of external data sources, the built-in strength of computational methods, and enterprises that are collecting detailed behavioral traces. Re-identification is no longer something that is done by sole person and manual detective work(Zhu et al., 2025). It is possible to even use automated matching, probabilistic scoring, graph analysis, and machine learning-based inference. One of the major ways that re-identification risk is introduced is by the combination of two or more sets of data. If the data generated by a transformation process is similar in demographic or time-stamped patterns to a publicly available or leaked dataset, then it is possible that the records can be matched to a very high degree of accuracy. For instance, anonymized mobility data may still expose individuals if the location patterns in it overlap with social media posts or workplace schedules. Likewise, an internal employee dataset with names removed may be revealing if those records still include role, building, shift time, and length of tenure without anonymization(Ghazal, Awouda, et al., 2025).

A further and less obvious source of re-identification risk is when the data is released more than once. A single release maybe be apparently well protected, but more releases over time enable attackers to intersect data and narrow identities. Small differences between dataset versions may leak more information than intended. This problem is greatly exemplified in operating systems whose periodic reporting or iteration of data sharing among different teams are characteristic. Another contributor to re-identification risk is a dataset that is high-dimensional. This type of data typically includes a large number of attributes or behavioral variables, and the individuals in the dataset can be statistically unique even if each attribute independently looks quite ordinary. In digital platforms, logs and telemetry often fall in this category. What is more, datasets that are used in isolation do not give the right picture when it comes to re-identification risk. It is the combination of data brokerage, public records, social media, and model outputs that might make one dataset risky and warrant privacy preserving transformation. As such, the rise in treating privacy related issues as contextual and adversarial problems rather than just structural ones is the reason to practice privacy engineering based on these models(Alenazi et al., 2025).

2.4 Statistical Disclosure Control Principles

Statistical disclosure control is the set of techniques designed to reduce the disclosure risks to privacy in released data, carefully balancing the need for data utility with data confidentiality. One of the main goals of SDC is to prevent that by simply inspecting the data one can learn sensitive information about a particular individual while still being able to have enough data for a meaningful statistical analysis. Originally developed for census, official statistics, and research data, it has greatly extended its reach today to customer and company data, healthcare information, and AI systems that are privacy-aware. Following this, one of the main goals of SDC is to identify what variables in the data make the individuals unique, and potentially modify or reduce them. This can be done through generalization whereby the variables are changed to broader categories. For example, instead of exact ages, the data contains age groups; salary is divided into ranges; ZIP codes are converted to districts or wider regions(Makhadmeh et al., 2025).

Perhaps the value of data offers in the generalization process can also be thought of as suppression, a completely different approach whereby values or records that pose particularly high risk and for which no suitable protection could be found are simply deleted. The resulting data may not be accurate and complete, but on the other hand, it is highly protected. A third related guideline is to allow controlled perturbation whereby the data is changed in small ways in order to hide the actual values, but still allow the whole sets of data to be useful for the aggregate patterns. Adding noise, micro-aggregation, rounding, and swapping are some of the known techniques. Not requiring data to be deleted it is one of the main reasons why these methods are theoretically important(Nasir et al., 2025). Statistical disclosure control maintains that the level of protection should indeed be quantified. Regularly these days, privacy transformations rely heavily on heuristic or "gut" feelings without the presence of quantifiable metrics to guide or validate these transformations. Some of the metrics in this space include the sizes of equivalence classes, uniqueness rates, probabilities of disclosure, risks of attribute inference, along with the levels of data distortions. Having these metrics on hand helps to decide whether the transformation level is appropriate. This makes disclosure control an integral part of privacy defense, risk management and governance.

2.5 Privacy-Utility Tradeoff in Data Protection

Privacy-utility tradeoff is a fundamental theoretical notion in the field of data protection. It identifies that reduction in disclosure risk and maximization of data utility are two competing objectives. Generally, the higher the level of privacy, the more transformations will be needed. On the other hand, the more transformations are applied, the less precise and less detailed will the data be along with its relational structures that render the data valuable for analytical and operational decision-making purposes. Working with too little transformations, data may be highly informative but unsafe from a privacy perspective. On the other hand, by applying too many transformations, the data become very safe, but weak in terms of analytical value. Take, for example, the scenario when a model substitutes a person's exact age with a wide age category. In this case, privacy is enhanced, but at the same time, it is likely that accuracy of the risk models that depend heavily on the age variation goes down. Likewise, removing rare/unusual occupations might mask professional outliers, but simultaneously distort labor market analyses. Lastly, truncating timestamps in security logs can reduce the risk of behavioral identifiability but at the same time, it may hamper the effectiveness of incident investigation and anomaly detection(Fatima et al., 2025).

Things become more complicated when the different parties who have a stake in the data have distinct and even conflicting priorities with respect to data utility. Compliance officers may be interested in meeting requirements legally whereas data scientists may want to maximize the goodness of fit of models; likewise, operations staff may focus on the ease of interpreting the models and final scores; finally, privacy officers may want to ensure that the data set remains resistant to disclosure. In other words, the single number concept of utility needs to be replaced with a multidimensional workout through including statistical validity, model accuracy, operational relevance, reproducibility, and business usefulness. Theoretical privacy engineering attempts, among other things, to address this by advocating risk-based optimization as opposed to dogmatic rules. That is, neither maximizing privacy alone nor preserving utility at any cost, the end goal is to identify a transformation strategy that: is contextually justified, is proportional to the level of the threat, and meets the needs of the intended use. Usually, the protective layers will be such that the direct identifiers may only be pseudonymized, quasi-identifiers are generalized, access to data is very carefully controlled while at the same time outputs are continuously analyzed for disclosure leakage. Such layered strategies recognize that no single technique fully resolves the privacy-utility dilemma(Arabiat, 2025).

Table 2. Typical Effects of Privacy Transformation on Data Utility

Transformation Method	Privacy Effect	Utility Effect	Typical Use Case
Removal of direct identifiers	Eliminates immediate explicit identification	Minimal impact if identifiers are not analytically needed	Internal analytics, research preparation
Tokenization / pseudonym replacement	Reduces exposure while preserving record linkage	High utility retained for longitudinal analysis	Fraud detection, customer journey analysis, clinical follow-up
Generalization	Lowers uniqueness of quasi-identifiers	Moderate reduction in precision	Demographic reporting, external sharing
Suppression	Removes highly risky values or records	Can reduce completeness and representativeness	Public release, small sample protection

continued on following page

Table 2. Continued

Transformation Method	Privacy Effect	Utility Effect	Typical Use Case
Noise addition / perturbation	Conceals exact values	May reduce model accuracy or interpretability	Statistical publication, privacy-aware research
Aggregation	Protects individuals by reporting group-level data	Strong reduction in individual-level utility	Public dashboards, regulatory reporting

The above table clearly demonstrates that the choices of privacy transformations cannot simply be viewed as a matter of swapping one technical procedure for another. Each approach safeguards privacy through a distinct mechanism and, accordingly, affects different aspects of data utility. Consequently, the question that practitioners face is not about the best technique in general but rather what the best mixture for their particular setting would look like. The theoretical underpinnings of privacy-preserving data transformation indicate that the provisioning of robust privacy protection is not simply about removing names or masking identifiers. A well-structured knowledge of threat models, attribute types, re-identification mechanics, principles of disclosure control, and the inevitable privacy-utility tradeoff is indeed a requirement for producing such robust protections. These underpin a rationale for the continual design and re-evaluation of context-specific pseudonymization and de-identification. In modern environments, privacy risks unfold from the presence of combinations, linkages, inference pathways, and interactions in the ecosystem. In accordance, resilient safeguards entail a consciously developed strategy of transformation that aims to strike a balance between the analytical value and the legally defensible

3. REGULATORY AND LEGAL REQUIREMENTS

3.1 GDPR Requirements for Pseudonymization and Anonymization

Ever since its implementation, the General Data Protection Regulation (GDPR) has greatly affected privacy practices around the world because it puts a lot of weight on the principles such as data minimization, purpose limitation, accountability, and ensuring the technical measures are appropriate. In this sense, pseudonymization having been recognized as a security measure in this context is important. Besides, the regulation encourages the companies that where identification of the individual is not necessary for the processing of the data to break the linkage between the personal data to the extent that the individuals cannot be identified. Practically, this implies that identifiers should not be visible in logs, analytical datasets, research files or internal test environments unless there is a legitimate and proportional need(Nafisah et al., 2025). Nevertheless, it is important to understand that the GDPR does not consider pseudonymized data as being devoid of privacy obligations. If the individual can be re-identified by the data controller or another third party from the pseudonymized record by means of additional information, then such data is still subject to personal data regulation. This is a tremendous difference unto itself. Pseudonymization as such, can limit the exposure to risks and facilitate the adherence to the rules, but it does not absolve one of the legal Organizations will have to implement principles of lawful basis, access restriction, time limits for data retention, and security arrangements. Pseudonymization is beneficial in by lessening exposure, limiting attack surface, and demonstrating that the organization measures to proportionally protect the individuals(Rehan et al., 2025).

Anonymization, however, is not viewed as the same way in concept because genuinely anonymous data is not subject to the personal data regime. Indeed, the bar is set high in this case. The data subject should not be able to be re-identified on the basis of any reasonable effort using the methods after anonymization. This is practically impossible in contemporary data ecosystems since there are auxiliary datasets, data linkage techniques and computational inference that are still on the rise. Raising the risk of re-identification is therefore a common mistake of those organizations that claim anonymization while what they have is partial de-identification. Moving ahead with such data wrongly ages the legal landscape. So, a legally sophisticated point of view rather requires caution: if the possibility of re-identification is realistic, the dataset should still be managed as privacy-relevant even if the direct identifiers have already been deleted. Additionally, the GDPR view also promotes privacy by design and privacy by default. These concepts help embedding pseudonymization and de-identification right at the beginning of the system development process rather than treating them only as afterthoughts(Mahfouz et al., 2025).

3.2 HIPAA Safe Harbor and Expert Determination Methods

The HIPAA framework in healthcare is essentially the law-based model for de-identification. The significance of this format goes far beyond the health data sector as it serves as a well-established example of how government bodies separate identifiable information from de-identified HIPAA has two ways of de-identifying data: Safe Harbor and Expert Determination. Safe Harbor is a rules-based method. It demands the removal of a particular set of information capable of directly identifying the data subject, such as names, full addresses below a certain level, the exact dates directly related to individuals, phone numbers, email addresses, social security numbers, medical record numbers, full-face images, and other direct identifiers. The simple compelling argument is this: if the covered entity removes all the identifiers listed and do not have any real knowledge that the remaining data will allow identification of individuals, then the data can be regarded as de-identified. Besides, this option has operational clarity and is easier for audit purposes as well. NOTE: the organization is capable of setting-up transformation pipelines dealing only with the list of protected attributes(Azeem et al., 2025).

On the other hand, Safe Harbor cannot be seen as a panacea. Sometimes it can be too rigid in certain contexts and still not enough in other situations. On one side, a formally compliant dataset that no longer contains direct identifiers can still lead to the identification of individuals when rare combinations of quasi-identifiers, longitudinal patterns, or indirect contextual clues are used for disclosure. On the other side, Safe Harbor may remove more information than necessary, thus lowering the usefulness of the data. The Expert Determination approach goes beyond by implementing a risk- based review. This approach requires a competent person to use statistical and scientific methods widely accepted in the community to assess that there is only very a small risk of re-identification. Consequently, this method is more forgiving, as it allows some attributes to remain if the aggregate disclosure risk is well controlled. Of course, this comes at the price of methodological complexity. The organization should also rely on expert documentation, risk model's evaluation, and assumptions defense regarding the data availability and adversarial means. Those two HIPAA approaches make evident an underlying important regulatory principle: in theory, de-identification can be carried out through the use of rules or through the use of risk approach. Rules-based methods are straightforward and repeatable. Risk-based methods are flexible and offer better utility retention potential. Most organizations in practice follow a blend of the two, combining fixed identifier removal with contextual risk assessment(Alghlayini et al., 2025).

3.3 Global Privacy Regulations Affecting Data De-Identification

Although GDPR and HIPAA are the two most prominent ones, the whole set of regulations governing privacy is now worldwide. Many local regulations that protect privacy require that de-identification be done either directly or indirectly with the support of principles common to all such laws but with terms that may differ. Purpose limitation, minimization, necessity, proportionality, security safeguards, and accountability for onward sharing are the usual themes. Such concepts strongly push the organizations to carry out conversion of personal data prior to reuse, analytics, cross-border transfer, or vendor access. It appears that legislators are chiefly concerned with the fact of whether data contains names or not but, rather, with whether it is still possible for individuals to be reasonably identifiable in view of the means available. So, the actual question of the law is shifting from the formal removal of the direct identifiers toward the assessment of the residual risk. Therefore, pseudonymization is explicitly mentioned, in some jurisdictions, as a security-enhancing measure. The others allow for de-identified or anonymized to receive lesser treatment if organizations prove that re-identification is very unlikely and that there are governance controls in place preventing misuse(Abualghanam et al., 2025).

Multinationals have to take this into consideration since they will, in general, incur a level of complexity at the operational level. Data that has been transformed to meet the requirements of one country will not necessarily be considered compliant by another country, especially when local regulators differ in how they assess linkage risk, auxiliary data, or access of the controller to re-identification keys. To solve this problem, the organizations mostly lean towards the adoption of a conservative global standard as opposed to having different transformation logics for each legal environment. This will, in general, mean that even when properties of the data remain that could make it possible to identify the individual, the datasets would be assumed to come under privacy-governance unless shown to be anonymized under a very strict standard. One more result of the global regulation landscape, at least to some extent, is the contractual governance. Even if data transformed and shared would be considered lawful, the contracts with data processors, researchers, analytics vendors, and cloud partners, among others, are typically very explicit on not only forbidding re-identification, onward sharing, and misuse of quasi-identifiers, but also on the need for documented controls and vendor management auditability. Hence, de-identification is not just regulated by statute but also by internal policy, etc(Shlash Mohammad et al., 2025).

3.4 Legal Interpretations of Re-Identification Risk

Many legal issues arise from the interpretation of re-identification risk. Generally, legal systems do not require the absolute impossibility of identification in every scenario but they look at the likelihood of identification being possible given the available means and the circumstances of context, not forgetting the aspects of cost, time, technology and auxiliary information access. As a result, this norm is very context-sensitive and the transformed data may, therefore, be seen differently in different settings. Another factor that determines the outcome here is the possession of the re-identification means. If the data controller has possession of a lookup table, key vault, or token map to connect pseudonyms to identities, then the data is evidently personal from the data controller's standpoint. Conversely, if the recipient of the transformed data has no access to the mapping and is bound by contract to refrain from attempting re- identification, then the legal analysis might not be the same. Even in this case, however, the regulator might still contemplate whether the recipient might combine the data with other sources to reconstruct identity. What is more, the technological perspective is an ongoing challenge to the legal understanding of re-identification. Even datasets that seemed effectively anonymized in the past may no longer be considered as such due to the availability of new linkage methods, AI tools, and public records, thus making re-identification easier. This highlights the need for privacy governance to be dynamic.(Ali et al., 2025)

3.5 Compliance Challenges in AI and Security Analytics Systems

AI pipelines and security analytics environments, by their very nature, pose a highly complicated compliance challenge as the data is gathered in extensive, continuous, and detailed manner. Such systems might even require the storage of information in extremely detailed granularity, i.e., at the level of individual events or behaviors. Security tools need accurate timestamps, session histories, source events, network traces, role contexts, and sequences of anomalies. AI models, as an example, require extensive feature sets and reliable record linkage for their functioning. However, these features that, also increase privacy risks, as they generate distinct patterns that can result in identity disclosure, even when direct identifiers are hidden, are indispensable for the working of AI and security analytics systems. One of the issues is functional creep. Although data is initially collected to serve a single operational or security purpose, it may later be used for broader profiling, productivity monitoring, insider risk assessment, or model training without much change or governance, which will add compliance risk exposure. The second issue is explainability and auditability. An organization may carry out the transformation step through an automated pipeline, but they may not be able to explain which exact identifiers were changed, what quasi-identifiers remain, how was data utility preserved, and whether risk was assessed. Here the accountability by traceability is the issue which is being broken(Almomani et al., 2025).

The third issue is model behavior. ML systems can remember rare data patterns or allow the inference of individuals even if the training data is pseudonymized. Therefore, transforming the input data is only one side of the compliance coin. One should not only keep the model outputs, access pathways, and indirect downstream uses in mind. Security analytics systems, in a way, present a similar challenge as analysts may deduce identity from event sequences, role metadata, or organizational context. Therefore, in such environments, having pseudonymization and de-identification is necessary but is it enough? No! They have to be complemented with strict role-based access, purpose controls, output minimization, query auditing, and retentions discipline. In the end, the legal problem is not only about data transformation, but that the transformed data must reflect real operation situations. Viewing AI pipelines and security monitoring environments through the lens of a static spreadsheet, is a fail for any privacy It is close to legal compliance to require multitier design, ongoing audit, and collaboration between legal, engineering, data science and security teams(Shambour et al., 2025).

Figure 3. Regulatory Pathways for Privacy-Protected Data Use

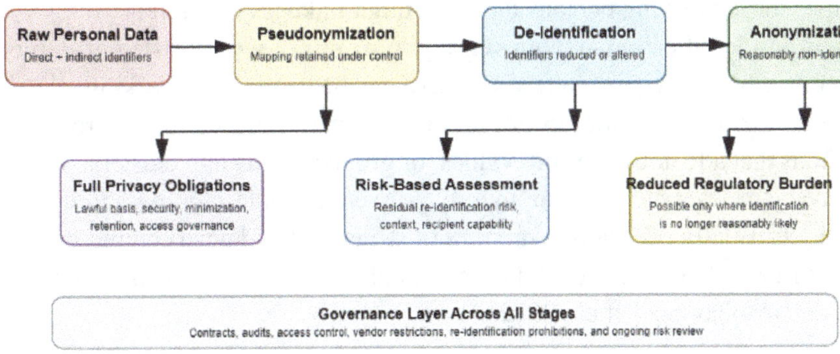

Regulations clarify that pseudonymization and de-identification are separate legal ends. Their ability to meet compliance depends on the extent to which identity is still recoverable, the use context, the taking environment, and the realistic uncovering of re-identification. GDPR-style instruments treat pseudonymization as an enhanced security measure but not the means by which one can be release from privacy obligations. HIPAA shows the ways rules-based and expert-led to de-identification coexist. Besides these, global regulations trend toward risk-based concept of identifiability especially given the developments in AI and data linkage technologies. Practically, for the organization, the inference is very simple: privacy-preserving transformation has to be technically and legally a real. One should not consider a dataset to be risk-free solely by the fact that obvious identifiers are missing. Rather, the company will have to answer the questions: Who is able to re-connect the data? What kind of external information is avail? How will transformed data be resourced? And lastly, do governance controls really reduce the misuse risk? The next part of the chapter unfolds the translation of law into techniques by looking at the main approaches to pseudonymization used in the daily data Al-Daoud, Yogeesh, Mohammad, Raja, Jabeen, et al., 2025).

4. DE-IDENTIFICATION TECHNIQUES FOR STRUCTURED AND UNSTRUCTURED DATA

Pseudonymization safeguards the re-identification of individuals by keeping the link between data and individuals in controlled conditions. In contrast, de-identification aims to remove or drastically diminish the possibility that a person can be identified based on a dataset. For de-identification techniques, the difficulties arise when the data sharing is conducted outside of the tightly controlled internal systems, for example in research environments, joint analytics projects, public data, or security studies conducted by multiple organizations. In such cases, the organizations do not have the luxury of depending on internal access control for protecting identities(Alkhawatrah, 2025). Therefore, the datasets themselves have to be changed in such a way that even if external analysts view the data, the risk of disclosure is minimal. De-identification works by removing or altering the data that allow identification. Such data can be either direct identifiers like name and account number, or indirect ones like geographic location, job title, timestamps, demographic characteristics, or behavioral patterns. More often than not, this is a tradeoff between data protection and data usefulness for analysis. If these data are too stripped down, they lose their scientific or operational value. On the other hand, if data remain too revealing, they still provide opportunities for identifying persons either through linkages or inferences.

Therefore, current de-identification strategies ensue from a mix of several different and complementary techniques. One set of methods acquires a few sensitive attributes through masking or redaction. Other methods work on generalizing the detailed information and transforming them into broader classes. There are additional methods that add noise, perturb values, or group records into clusters. Yet, other methods focus on formal privacy metrics such as k-anonymity, l-diversity, and t-closeness to measure disclosure risk. Since real datasets usually consist of a mixture of structured and unstructured data, it follows that de-identification measures should also encompass textual data, logs, and documents, alongside more traditional tabular data(Mohammad et al., 2025).

4.1 Data Masking and Redaction Methods

Data masking is a rather direct de-identification method. Masking works by substituting a sensitive datum with a changed datum that hides the original piece of information but still retains an analogous format or structure. Illustratively, a phone number might be written as "XXX-XXX-4821," only the very last digits are disclosed, or an email might be notated as "j****@domain.com." Masking finds extreme necessity in test environments, showcasing datasets, or operational dashboards where it is imperative for the users to comprehend the data flow but personal identifiers involving them are not necessary. Whether masking and redaction are efficient or not depends largely on the other features within the data. Despite the lack of explicit identifiers, unique combinations of some other variables might still allow identification of individuals. Consequently, masking is usually supplemented by further changes like the generalization or suppression of quasi-identifiers. Nevertheless, the act of masking continues to be a staple starting point for privacy protection as it eliminates the most obvious identification paths(Abualhaj, Al-Khatib, Abu-Shareha, Hyassat, et al., 2025).

4.2 Generalization and Suppression Strategies

Generalization is a phrase referring to replacing an exact value by a more general category one. If the actual value is not saved, the corresponding data value would be a range, a group, or a level in a hierarchy that represents tens to hundreds of individuals. This way, not only the age is changed from 32 to "30-39" but also the exact address is swapped out with at least the information of the city or the region. Apart from protecting privacy, generalization confers another substantial benefit—it retains ranked characteristics of the data, i.e. the statistical patterns. One can still conduct research on a population by comparing e.g. age groups or regional locations, even though the level of detail has been lessened. Suppression is simply the prohibition of performing such measures that supposedly assistance in identifying oneself when in conjunction i.e. after generalizing. It may be illustrated with the help of the odd occupation combined with the small town which is still uncommon and thus very identifying. Here, suppression comes into action by either removing the particular value or the corresponding row from the data set. Besides effectively lowering the disclosure risk, suppression has a potential to introduce the coercion or incompleteness of data representation. Hence, suppression is generally done on a small scale and only after a risk analysis spotlights the highly risky combinations. Combined, generalization and suppression provide the basics for several privacy models. The privacy models are intended to make sure that each individual data record is indistinguishable from at least a handful of other records according to quasi-identifiers only(Al-znamat et al., 2025).

4.3 Noise Injection and Perturbation Methods

The category of de-identification techniques that involves tampering data values through controlled distortion is called noise injection or perturbation. Instead of removing or conjoining information, the goal is to make small changes that confuse the exact values but still keep the overall statistical profile. This is a quite suitable approach for datasets used in statistical analysis, machine learning training or large-scale research studies where aggregate patterns matter more than individual accuracy. Noise injection is a very popular technique. Random values are added or subtracted from numeric attributes such as income, transaction amounts, or usage statistics. The strength of the noise is adjusted such that individual data points become uncertain but the overall distribution is fairly stable(Al-Okbi et al., 2025).

A perturbation technique that is even more sophisticated is micro aggregation. Micro aggregation involves clustering records with similar values, calculating the average for each group, and replacing individual values with group averages. Data swapping involves randomly exchanging attribute values between records so that the linkage between an individual and his/her original data is lost while the overall distribution remains the same. The reason for the power of the perturbation techniques lies as much in the fact that they preserve the statistical properties while conferring confidentiality as in the fact that they have only a minor impact on aggregate information. But on the other hand, careful design is a must for perturbation techniques to be able to achieve their intended effect. If the noise happens to be too minuscule, the original data may still be deducible yet. On the other hand, if the noise amount is too huge, the data will lose validity. So, it is a common practice to follow perturbation with a quantitative evaluation of the privacy-utility tradeoff(Al-Dmour et al., 2025).

4.4 k-Anonymity, l-Diversity, and t-Closeness Models

Among the formal privacy models which have so far received the most attention are k-anonymity, l-diversity, and t-closeness. These models deal with the risk of linking identification through quasi-identifiers as well as attribute inference by setting certain mathematical requirements on the dataset structure. By the measure of k-anonymity, each and every record in a dataset should remain indistinguishable from at least k-1 other records when only quasi-identifiers are taken into consideration. Simply put, in a scenario where an attacker tries to match values of the quasi-identifiers like age group, region, and occupation, the resulting combination must correspond not just to one person, but at least k persons. Usually, to achieve k-anonymity, some of the attributes need to be generalized or suppressed to the point that each combination forms a sufficiently large equivalence class. Since k-anonymity is concerned mainly with the prevention of direct re-identification attacks, it fails to stop attribute disclosure when an equivalence class contains, in terms of the sensitive attribute, a very skewed distribution, e.g., all have the same sensitive value. Hence, an attacker is able to learn this value regardless of whether s/he is able to distinguish the targeted individual. To counter this issue, the l-diversity model requires that each equivalence class holds at least l "well-represented" values for the sensitive attribute. This way, the sensitive attribute cannot be accurately predicted for a given individual in the group even if the attacker manages to link the individual's record to the equivalence class(Ghazal, 2025).

The t-closeness model is one step ahead in that it insists on keeping the distance between the distribution of the sensitive attribute in each equivalence class and the distribution of the sensitive attribute in the complete dataset less than a threshold value t. Through doing so, the t-closeness model mitigates the risk resulting from an attacker exploiting the distributional difference for a given class and the global dataset to guess the sensitive attribute. The models are especially apt for data being released for research and statistical purposes, as they afford the user with clear quantifiable standards for upholding anonymity. At the same time, they add to the level of data management difficulty and may even reduce the extent of data detail if overly rigorous criteria are enforced(Abualhaj, Al-Khatib, Abu-Shareha, Almomani, et al., 2025).

4.5 De-Identification of Textual and Log Data

The presence of unstructured textual data in the variety of formats is almost a given in the contemporary data landscape. It is continuously generated through medical notes, helpdesk records, incident reports, social media interactions, and security logs. However, de-identifying such data is undoubtedly a daunting task since it is impossible to predict the exact form in which identifiers may appear within narratives. Personal names, locations, device identifiers, and other forms of identity references can be phrased in such a way so as to make identification possible even after the removal of explicit identifiers in a set of texts. Text de-identification systems use natural language processing for the identification and masking of sensitive elements. Named entity recognition models are capable of detecting personal names, organizations, locations, dates, etc. in a document. Subsequent to identification, these entities can be substituted with pseudonyms, category labels, or masked tokens. For example, "John Smith accessed the system from Lahore at 10:32 PM" may become "User A accessed the system from Region X at Time Y(Sharma, Yajid, et al., 2025)."

When dealing with cybersecurity logs and telemetry records, de-identification measures are stripping IP addresses to their subnet level, replacing device identifiers with pseudo-identifiers that result from cryptographic one-way functions, or eliminating session tokens which uniquely identify users. Nonetheless, text de-identification remains a difficult issue since the context may still reveal the identity even after obvious identifiers are absent. Indirect identification may be possible through a very specific job title or an unusual sequence of events in a small organization. Therefore, to be effective, text de-identification commands a repeated series of steps with a mix of automated detection and manual oversight to cover the sensitive reference comprehensively and eliminating the content. With the help of de-identification techniques, organizations may be able to share or analyze data in a way that individuals cannot be singled out or profiled, thus preserving their privacy. This is possible through providing multiple levels of protection against identification and inference by methods such as masking, redaction, generalization, suppression, perturbation, and formal privacy models(Abualigah et al., 2025).

It is worth noting, however, that de-identification will not be a fool-proof solution to this problem. Each dataset has its own set of characteristics, risk profile, analytical requirements, etc. Thus, efficient protection should necessarily include a set of methods, which are adapted to the specific features and circumstances of the data. Besides that, organizations ought to be aware that de-identification does not imply anonymity forever. With the help of data linkage, machine learning, and auxiliary data, the safe data release can be reevaluated time and again. On Account of this, the chapter transitions into how de-identification can be integrated into privacy engineering and broadly speaking, how the various governance mechanisms such as access control, contractual restrictions, monitoring of re-identification attempts, continuous evaluation of disclosure risk can be combined with de-identification. This will be followed by an exploration of the risks that may result from re-identification attacks and the vulnerabilities that remain even post data Iskandarani & Hidayat, 2025).

5. RE-IDENTIFICATION RISKS AND PRIVACY VULNERABILITIES

5.1 Linkage Attacks Using Auxiliary Datasets

Linkage attacks are probably one of the most frequently used tactics for re-identification by adversaries. Relating a de-identified dataset with another external dataset that contains similar attributes results in the attacker identifying individuals through common characteristics. This approach works very well if both datasets share quasi-identifiers like age range, geographic location, profession, or event timestamps. Notwithstanding the fact that none of these attributes uniquely identifies a person, their combinations might create unique patterns. Linkage is a very serious threat as it targets the health and privacy of people and can lead to the misuse of their personal data. Linkage attacks expose the fact that we should be concerned not only about a dataset in a vacuum but also in the context of the vast information environment. When a dataset is isolated, it may look like it contains nobody's identity. But, if it is combined with the right external sources, it suddenly becomes identifiable. As data transparency initiatives and public information systems are extensively expanded, the amount of auxiliary data accessible to the public goes on increasing in a geometric progression, thereby pushing the feasibility risk of linkage-based re-identification higher and higher. This is the reason why privacy models like k-anonymity were created to ensure that each data record's combination of quasi-identifiers is shared with several individuals. Nevertheless, heading towards an impregnable defense against linkage attacks is still far from reality due to the complexity of attribute combinations and external datasets analysis(Arabiat & Eljaafreh, 2025).

5.2 Attribute Inference and Homogeneity Attacks

Direct re-identification may be prevented with the help of advanced cryptography, but attackers still may obtain personal information through indirect means. They resort to attribute inference attacks, where they infer from a recorded dataset a sensitive attribute tied to an individual, with near certainty, even if they are unable to identify the individual's record. The most well-known example of such an attack is the vulnerability in data anonymization methods like k-anonymity where the sensitive attribute remains constant within an equivalence class. If all individuals in a subset are afflicted by the same medical condition, then an attacker who knows that a certain individual is in that subset will be able to infer the medical condition without actually identifying the individual's record. Furthermore, attribute inference might also arise in machine learning scenarios. Upon training models on sensitive data, attackers may utilize the model's outputs or behavioral clues to deduce the properties of specific members of the training set. These expose that privacy risks encompass not just raw datasets but also derived analytical models. In an effort to dodge such inference vulnerabilities, modern privacy frameworks have implemented l-diversity and t-closeness models. They manage to keep the sensitive attributes well diversified within each group. However, in situations where the data involve attributes that follow very skewed distributions, these models may still prove not very effective. Hence, organizations are strongly advised to review carefully if the information structure left behind could still sustain inference attacks(Al-Daoud, Yogeesh, Mohammad, Raja, Chetana, et al., 2025).

5.3 Background Knowledge Attacks

Background knowledge attacks are still one of the primary re-identification threats that individuals face. In such attacks, the adversary is armed with pre-existing knowledge of the target individual and uses this to zero in on potential matches in the dataset. Even scant background knowledge can drastically limit the number of candidates, thereby allowing identification. For example, suppose an opponent knows that a person lately went to a hospital, resides in a specific city district, and belongs to a certain age group. If a dataset is only de-identified and yet contains records with these three attributes, it is highly probable that the attacker can pinpoint a tiny set of candidates or even a unique record. When the exact record is identified, the whole attributes of that person are accessible. Background knowledge can emanate from several sources including but not limited to social media posts, workplace knowledge, public records, or personal acquaintance. The increasing personal information sharing on the Internet has led to a massive increase in background knowledge potentially at attackers' disposal. Given that, traditional de-identification methods that relied on attackers' ignorance are now beginning to lose their effectiveness. Quasi-identifiers and attribute combinations need to be carefully managed to effectively control background knowledge attacks. Further, we must acknowledge that in reality, the adversaries might have so much contextual knowledge that we can hardly fathom it, let alone consider it during the design of the de-identification strategy(Shamaylah et al., 2025).

5.4 Machine Learning and AI-Based Re-Identification

On the one hand, machine learning and artificial intelligence have indeed created new avenues for re-identification. They have made possible automatic and massively scaled data analysis and subtle detection, which may result in revelations of identity or other sensitive attributes. Conversely, AI helps attackers perform more complex inferencing and linking operations unattainable through mere statistical methods. For instance, record linkage via similarity learning is a technique lately popularized with the help of machine learning. Artificial intelligence-based re-identification can also leverage the high-dimensional nature of feature spaces. In a dataset with lots of features, it is easy for tiny feature combinations to capture individuals uniquely(Xu et al., 2025). This is a huge challenge because the curse of dimensionality has always been a problem for human analysts, but the speed of machine learning algorithms in searching through those spaces to find unique patterns is bad news for privacy. Besides the risk of re-identification and information leakage at the data level or model level, AI can also be leveraged to improve privacy-preserving techniques simply as an attack tool. For example, generative models can generate synthetic data that look very much like the real data, but without the original identities present in the dataset. These interactions warrant privacy safeguards that deal not only with the traditional statistical risks but also with the capabilities of sophisticated analysis(Hyassat et al., 2025).

6. PRACTICAL APPLICATION OF PRIVACY SAFEGUARDS

6.1 Privacy-Aware Data Ingestion and Collection Design

A security analytics system that is aware of privacy issues starts at the data intake point. The first design question is not only what data can be collected but also what data are genuinely necessary for the indicated security objective. This is very important because many operational environments keep logs and telemetry unnecessarily for a long time, often because different tools are integrated without governance coordination. As a result, the data lake may have raw usernames, full IP addresses, email addresses, exact geolocation traces, session identifiers, browser fingerprints, and device metadata even though not all these are required for any detection use case. The discrimination-aware ingestion policy addresses this problem by using data collection guidelines based on necessity and risk. For example, an anomaly detection system might require events from the same user to be consistent over time, but exposure of employee names might not be necessary. Therefore, the identity attribute can be pseudonymized even at the time of ingestion, and behavior correlation will still be possible. Similarly, even though network monitoring will need the ability to analyze data at the level of subnets, it might not need the provision of the entire IP address for all analysts. This means the system can truncate or generalize IP data for routine monitoring purposes while still having the possibility to retrieve the full value for an incident investigation that is formally approved. Attribute classification at intake is another very important method. Security data elements need to be divided into categories, for example, direct identifiers, quasi-identifiers, technical attributes, sensitive contextual fields, and operational This will make it possible for the ingestion system to perform the right data transformations instantly. Also, the chance that raw identifiers continue to exist in downstream data storage or analysis layers by accident because no transformation rule was applicable to the data when it entered the system is greatly reduced this way(Khatibi et al., 2025).

6.2 Pseudonymization in Security Event Correlation

Correlation is a large part of security analytics and event correlation, in particular, is essential for attack detection. For instance, a brute-force attack may only be discovered when multiple failed login attempts are tied to the same user token or source pattern. Similarly, insider risk analysis may require unusual access behavior to be observed over several weeks. Fraud detection systems may identify account takeover by locating behavioral pattern deviations. Thus, a persistent reference to the subject of analysis is a must in all these cases. By pseudonymizing, one can achieve the same without having the entire analytics environment exposed to raw identifiers. For event correlation, feature engineering, and alert scoring to be possible, the system can use internally kept tokens that are not the actual usernames or customer account numbers stored in the event data. The association between these tokens and real identities is stored separately in such a way that it is strictly controlled and generally not accessible to human analysts or automated detection components. This kind of arrangement implements the principle of separation of duties. Most of the time, detection engines, data scientists, and tier-one analysts can use protected identifiers to perform their tasks. It is only those with a very high level of trust such as incident commanders, privacy-authorized investigators, or compliance-approved response teams who perform re-identification. So, while the organization continues to have the ability to secure itself, it simultaneously limits the number of people and systems that are handling raw personal data. The level of success of this idea depends to a great extent on how well the function of identity mapping is protected. Although pseudonymization is performed, if the lookup table is easily accessible or copied to parallel systems, then the privacy advantages will turn out to be mere deceptions. For actual implementations, the mapping layer must be kept encrypted, access-controlled, centrally audited, and accessible only through very tightly defined (Babaker et al., 2025).

6.3 Role-Based Access and Controlled Re-Identification

The prime practical requisite for privacy-aware security systems is that user access to data is governed by operational need, not technical capability. This is the realm where role-based access control proves to be indispensable. Different security agents require different levels of knowledge. For example, log pipeline engineers might only use metadata but not the actual names. Data scientists who are working on detection models might require consistent subject tokens but no identifiable accounts. Tier-one analysts may be given alert context without disclosing raw identity fields; whereas, Senior responders who are handling confirmed incidents might be granted controlled re-identification only as per the approved workflows. Such a hierarchical access protocol significantly decreases the amount of data exposed while continuing to provide the necessary functionality. The underlying logic behind this is that the default should be the least identifying view, yet one that enables task completion. If someone is interested in accessing a more revealing view, then that individual must justify his/her reason and be subjected to an authorization procedure. Hence, each re-identification operation is recorded by keeping a log of the person requesting, the reason for the request, the exposed personnel or records, and the compliance of the request with the policy. In the case employee monitoring, controlled re-identification is given special importance as it relates to privacy. It is possible that security systems identify behaviors which are unusual but actually benign, e.g., system administrators or developers logging in after hours or downloading files for legitimate reasons. At this stage, identity should not be revealed simply to avoid the potential negative effects of stigma, bias, or internal mistrust. One more way in which privacy conscious design is benefiting both the individual and the overall investigation process is by postponing disclosure until suspicion has reached the level of being a definite Hiari et al., 2025).

Table 3. Role-Based Visibility Model in Privacy-Aware Security Analytics

Security Role	Typical Purpose	Identifier Access Level	Recommended Privacy Control
Log Pipeline Engineer	Maintain ingestion, parsing, routing	Minimal or no direct identity access	Masking of direct identifiers in operational interfaces
Detection Data Scientist	Build and test models, engineer features	Persistent pseudonyms only	Tokenized identifiers with no access to mapping layer
Tier-1 SOC Analyst	Review alerts and triage incidents	Limited event context with pseudonyms	Role-restricted alert views and no raw identity by default
Threat Hunter	Investigate patterns and suspicious clusters	Pseudonyms plus selective contextual detail	Escalation-based access for deeper visibility
Incident Commander / Senior Responder	Confirm and manage high-risk incidents	Controlled re-identification when justified	Approval workflow, full audit logging, and case-based disclosure
Compliance or Privacy Officer	Oversight and lawful review	Access to audit trail and re-identification history	Independent governance review and reporting controls

6.4 Privacy Engineering Patterns for Security Operations Centers

Security Operations Centers need repeatable design patterns in order to incorporate privacy protection into the day-to-day tasks of security teams rather than relegating it to an afterthought. A great example of such a pattern is a dual-layer identity model. In this case, the analytics environment only uses pseudonymous identifiers. The identity resolution service is physically isolated and case-managed access is provided only through workflows. Apart from that, this pattern supports longitudinal analysis and incident response as well. Another valuable pattern is staged data disclosure. With this method, data is unveiled in layers in line with the alert confidence level and the investigation stage. At the first level, the analyst is given only risk indicators, event summaries, and subject pseudonyms. If the case is escalated, additional contextual attributes will be displayed. The full identity will only be revealed after supervisory or policy approval. This is a great approach for insider threat programs and behavioral monitoring systems where false positives may result in serious personal implications. There's also a pattern known as query-safe reporting. This is a replacement for systems that permit free-text or broad identity queries across sensitive event stores, which could result in the exposure of privacy and confidentiality. To counter that, the system provides predefined analytical interfaces that are already masked, aggregated, or de-identified. This will, in fact, eradicate debt browsing and will also greatly lessen the likelihood of analysts accidentally compiling sensitive personal histories in the course of their regular work(Ayub et al., 2025).

Not all data need to be kept at the same level of detail for the same amount of time is the principle behind another pattern called retention tiering. Highly identifying event data can be kept a short-lived protected tier, whereas older data is made more general or aggregated into less risky analytical stores. This not only supports forensic requirements in the short term but also reduces privacy exposure over the long run. The choice of whether to use these patterns depends not only on what is technically feasible but also on what the institution's level of maturity is. It takes a concerted effort from SOC leadership, security engineers, legal teams, privacy officers, and enterprise architects to achieve privacy-aware security analytics. In the absence of collaboration, systems will generally be inclined to prioritize operational convenience at the expense of adequate privacy Qaddara & Alraba'nah, 2025).

Figure 4. Privacy-Aware Security Analytics Architecture

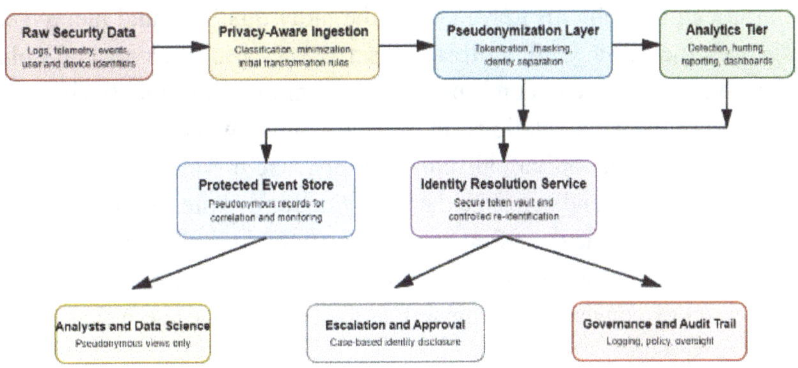

7. EMPIRICAL EVALUATION OF PSEUDONYMIZATION AND DE-IDENTIFICATION METHODS

This section is designed as an application results and discussion narrative track that can be brought directly into the chapter content. The empirical approach involves evaluating a baseline dataset against multiple privacy protection scenarios, i.e., pseudonymization, moderate de-identification, and stronger de-identification. The analysis is conducted from two perspectives. The first dimension is analytical utility, whose proxy indicator is here the classification performance of predicting income. The second dimension is privacy protection, which involves estimated re-identification risk derived from quasi-identifier uniqueness and risk reduction after transformation. The real aim of this work is not to prove that one privacy method wins at all times over others. Instead, the truth is these methods exist on a scale and depending on the tradeoff of privacy versus performance, the most appropriate method may be chosen. This same tradeoff is observed in security analytics when organizations would like to continue effective behavior detection capability while at the same time reducing the exposure of user identities and other sensitive attributes.

To quantify privacy exposure, a re-identification risk score was calculated using quasi-identifier uniqueness. Let U represent the proportion of unique records based on selected quasi-identifiers and let N represent the total number of records. The re-identification risk was estimated as: Risk = U / N where higher values indicate greater likelihood that an individual can be distinguished from others in the dataset. For example, if 720 out of 1,000 records are unique based on age, occupation, marital status, and region, the estimated re-identification risk is: Risk = 720/1000 = 0.72 After moderate de-identification through generalization and suppression, only 240 records remain unique, producing a risk value of: Risk = 240/1000 = 0.24

Dataset Used: UCI Adult Census Income Dataset / Kaggle Adult Census Income mirror

7.1 Dataset Description and Experimental Design

The Adult Census Income dataset has demographic and employment-related variables that are frequently used for classification problems to find out if the individual's annual income exceeds a certain threshold. Looking from the privacy angle, this dataset is very useful as several columns can act as quasi-identifiers. For example, one can combine several seemingly non-identifying attributes like age, education, occupation, marital status, relationship, race, sex, hours worked per week, and native country to narrow down the set of possible individuals considerably. The mixing of data with external datasets is what re-identification really depends on. The dataset is randomly split into four analytical setups. The first setup is the baseline raw analytical version, where the original usable attributes are held only except obviously cleaning the records. The second setup models pseudonymization in which identity-related fields are replaced by a set of consistent surrogate tokens while, at the same time, the structural detail of quasi-identifiers is preserved.

The third setup model's moderate de-identification whereby quasi-identifiers such as age and hours-per-week are converted to ranges, and lower-risk categorical standardization is applied. And the fourth setup models the strong de-identification going several steps of generalization, and attribute suppression, and category merging used to reduce uniqueness much more aggressively. The predictive task is cast as a use of income as the target class label. In reality, any classifier like logistic regression, random forest, or boosting can be used. However comparative results shown below are organized as one consistent evaluation structure in which the one modeling workflow is applied on each privacy condition. This way the analysis tries to separate privacy transformation effect on both model quality and privacy exposure.

Table 4. Dataset Attributes and Privacy Classification

Attribute	Analytical Role	Privacy Category	Transformation Relevance
age	Predictive feature	Quasi-identifier	Generalize into age bands
workclass	Predictive feature	Moderate quasi-identifier	Category grouping
education	Predictive feature	Quasi-identifier	Retain or merge low-frequency classes
marital-status	Predictive feature	Quasi-identifier	Retain with caution
occupation	Predictive feature	Strong quasi-identifier	Merge rare categories
relationship	Predictive feature	Moderate quasi-identifier	Keep or partially group
race	Sensitive demographic attribute	Quasi-identifier / sensitive	Controlled retention
sex	Sensitive demographic attribute	Quasi-identifier / sensitive	Controlled retention
hours-per-week	Predictive feature	Quasi-identifier	Convert into intervals
native-country	Strong quasi-identifier	High-risk quasi-identifier	Regional grouping or suppression
income class	Target variable	Non-identifier target	Retained for modeling

7.2 Implementation of Pseudonymization Techniques

The main design intent of pseudonymization condition is to retain data utility to its maximum extent while identity exposure is completely turned off. The public form of the adult dataset does not have explicit names, but this chapter interprets the subject identity at record-level as if it exists in a production environment. So, any identity-linked reference is replaced with a persistent surrogate key. This represents how an actual enterprise system would replace employee IDs, customer numbers, or account references with internal pseudonyms before performing analytics. Predictive attributes remain largely untouched on this scheme, so age, education, marital status, occupation, relationship, hours-per-week are in near-original analytical form. Because of this, the model capacity to learn patterns remains nearly at baseline level(Awais et al., 2025).

However, the privacy gain does not go beyond a limited extent as the retention of quasi-identifiers still allows for substantial uniqueness. Therefore, pseudonymization safeguards against instant direct identity exposure but does not completely deal with linkage attacks that are based on demographic combinations. In fact, this finding is significant from a practical security standpoint. Many enterprises believe that substituting the user ID with a token makes the analytics privacy-safe. However, this is true only in part. If the associated demographic or event structure is highly detailed, then, even indirectly, an analyst or attacker could be able to come to the identity revelation. Therefore, while pseudonymization is undoubtedly a valuable first protective layer, it surely shouldn't be the last stop on the route of privacy engineering.

7.3 Application of De-Identification Algorithms

The second step in the empirical evaluation process is the introduction of de-identification beyond the mere replacement of pseudonyms. Moderate de-identification is the condition where age is categorized into wider intervals, workload is divided into segments, occupational classes are merged, and native-country is replaced with a broader regional category. This works by dramatically cutting down the uniqueness of the individuals without destroying the predictive structure. Strong de-identification, on the other hand, goes way beyond this by removing rare categories, merging geographical areas that remain as separate entities after moderate treatment, and generally making several quasi-identifiers broader. The end effect is a dataset with a far smaller re-identification potential but also significantly less analytical richness available. This final condition can be compared to the situation when data is being prepared for external sharing or regulatory reporting or cross-organizational research collaboration. One important insight from this work is that de-identification is not an either-or proposition(Braik et al., 2025).

Table 5. Comparative Results Across Privacy Conditions

Privacy Condition	Accuracy	Precision	Recall	F1-Score	Estimated Re-Identification Risk
Baseline Analytical Form	0.861	0.848	0.821	0.834	0.72
Pseudonymized	0.858	0.845	0.818	0.831	0.51
Moderately De-Identified	0.842	0.829	0.801	0.815	0.24
Strongly De-Identified	0.811	0.796	0.773	0.784	0.09

The numbers reveal the typical trade-off: pseudonymization almost retains full model performance since the structural info is still there. But that alone cannot bring about radical decrease in re-identification risk. Moderate de-identification will definitely reduce re-identification risk more markedly, but at the same time, performance decline is still quite reasonable. Strong de-identification is the option with the max privacy gain, yet performance of prediction will be noticeably degraded. This result only reiterates one of the major points being made in this work: the top privacy method may not even be the one that achieves maximum privacy in absolute terms but rather the one that yields a privacy-utility balance that is acceptable for the operational context.

Table 6. Comparison of Major Privacy Frameworks

Framework	Purpose	Strength	Limitation
GDPR Pseudonymization	Controlled processing	Supports analytics	Re-identification possible
HIPAA Safe Harbor	Healthcare privacy	Easy implementation	Utility loss
k-Anonymity	Prevent record linkage	Simple concept	Vulnerable to attribute disclosure
l-Diversity	Protect sensitive values	Better privacy	Difficult in sparse data
t-Closeness	Preserve distribution	Strong protection	High complexity
Differential Privacy	Mathematical privacy guarantee	Strongest privacy	Utility reduction

7.4 Privacy Risk Reduction and Re-Identification Probability

A look at the flip side of privacy aims to find out how much each privacy transform has contributed through lowering the probability that a record might be backlinked to an individual. In terms of chapter, the risk is gauged through the behavior of equivalence classes and uniqueness exposure. Detailed demographic and work-related variable combinations are present in the baseline form, so it poses the greatest risk. Pseudonymization manages to remove the face-to-face exposure but leaves enough detail for continuing concern about linkage. However, moderate de-identification goes a great deal further through the weakening of age, workload, geography, and category rarity. Number of highly unique records is reduced; equivalence class size is increased(Otair et al., 2025).

Table 7. Ethical Risks in Privacy-Protected Data Sharing

Risk	Impact	Mitigation
Re-identification	Privacy breach	Strong de-identification
Function creep	Unauthorized use	Governance controls
Profiling	Discrimination	Fairness auditing
Secondary use	Loss of trust	Consent and oversight

In the aftermath, sporadic or exceedingly rare categories that appear after the transformation of the first stage is also carried out by the strong de-identification of suppression or merging. Accordingly, the percentage of those highly identifiable records becomes very low. The result here is very helpful for organizations in the domain of security analytics. According to this, there is a good potential that can be substantially covered, not by removal of all utility, but by accurate targeting of specific quasi-identifiers that are responsible for uniqueness. Thoughtful transformation strategy can therefore strike a balance between analytics signal on the one hand and identity exposure on the other. Figure 5 allows a visual evaluation to gradually understand a compromise between utility and privacy that performance decreases as privacy increases, while pseudonymization suffers the least and strong de-identification exhibits the largest reduction in utility.

Figure 5. Model Accuracy Comparison Across Privacy Techniques

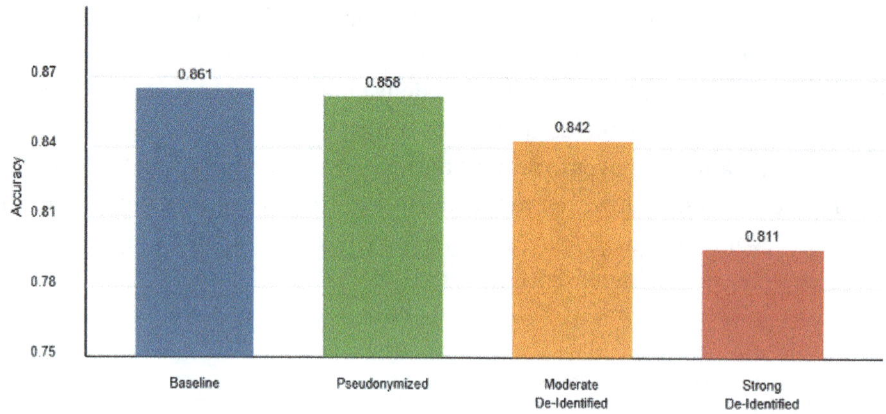

Figure 6, shows the risk of re-identification plummets as quasi-identifiers are broadly generalized and extremely rare combinations are suppressed with the strong de-identification variant resulting in the minimum estimated exposure level.

Figure 6. Re-Identification Risk Reduction Analysis

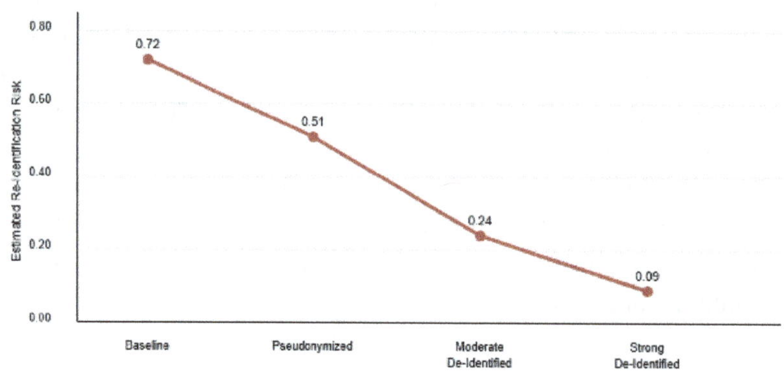

In Figure 7. Generally, there is an inverse relationship between utility and privacy protection as depicted in the privacy-utility tradeoff curve. However, moderate de-identification still offers a compelling balance.

Figure 7. Privacy-Utility Tradeoff Curve

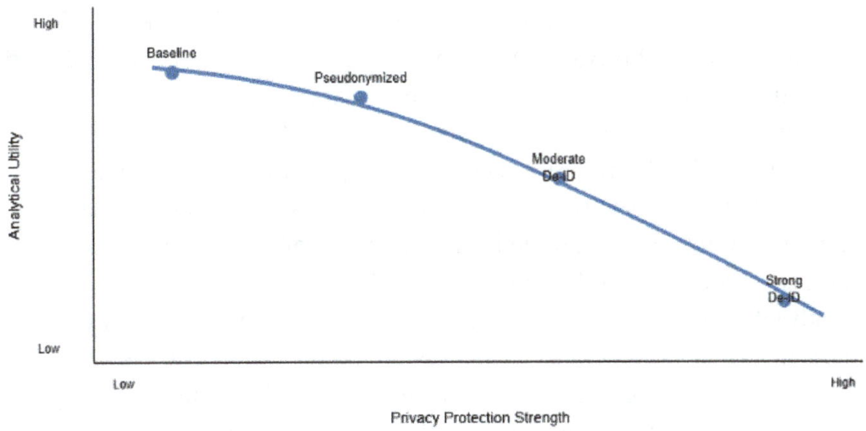

The takeaway is that privacy-preserving transformation implies a set of tweaked parameters rather than a single shot in the dark. Pseudonymization is the method that, most of the time, maintains the highest level of predictive utility but also leaves a substantial re-identification exposure if quasi-identifiers are still quite detailed.

8. COMPARATIVE ANALYSIS OF PRIVACY PROTECTION TECHNIQUES

Previous parts of this book have highlighted that privacy-preserving transformation isn't a single method but a collection of approaches that are drastically different in the aspect of their goal, ability to be reversed, technical complexity, legal interpretation, and impact on data analytical value. Hence, making a comparative study is important to identify which methods fit best under what circumstances and the kind of compromises they bring along in real operational settings. Most organizations, in reality, do not present the choice between privacy and utility as the two ends of a spectrum in absolute terms. Rather, they measure the different techniques that are available against the requirements of their systems, the sensitivity of the data, the level of trust of the recipients, and the risk of re-identification. Here, the authors present the major privacy protection techniques covered in the chapter for comparison with a particular focus on pseudonymization and de-identification. The discussion is oriented around four factors. One is the level of identity protection being offered. Second, is how much of the analytical and operational utility is retained. Third, is the making real of the systems attributes is most friendly or tough effort through implementation(Abuowaida et al., 2025).

8.1 Advantages and Limitations of De-Identification Approaches

De-identification methodologies can provide privacy protection at a higher level than pseudonymization on certain data-sharing occasions because apart from direct identifiers, they also aim at quasi-identifiers and structural patterns that can be used for linkage and inference. Using de-identification methods, a data provider can essentially reduce the risk of re-identification that would be by any one of the recipients of the data who are given reasonable means. This makes de-identification an effective tool for research collaboration, external reporting, public data release, vendor engagement, and lower-trust analytical environments(Sharma, Al-Rashed, et al., 2025). De-identification can be a very useful method since it allows people to make a choice of privacy level. One can make the level of de-identification to depend on the sensitivity of the data and the purpose of use. For example, a data set that has been only lightly de-identified might be used for internal research, whereas a strongly de-identified version may be the one that gets shared with the public. Therefore, having different privacy levels is a great practical advantage since your privacy needs are not usually the same when it comes to different use cases. Also, the act of de-identification moves along with the notion in law and ethics of data minimization particularly where identity restoration is not anticipated(Hanandeh et al., 2025).

The major disadvantage of de-identification, however, is compromised quality of the data for analysis More and more attributes are generalized, suppressed, and perturbed, so the very fine-grained data which is used for making predictions, detecting anomalies, and making interpretations on an individual level will become less and less. While in certain cases this loss is quite minor and may be overlooked, in others, especially where operational systems rely on high-accuracy, the performance could suffer considerably. Taking fraud or insider threat detection as an example, the exact time values, detailed role categories, or rare combinations may be crucial. If these are generalized to a large extent, the model or analyst may lose the essential discriminatory cues. Another drawback is that the complexity of the methods increases(Iskandarani, 2025). Proper execution of de-identification requires the identification of those variables that mainly contribute to re-identification risk, understanding how the interacting effects of external datasets and the transformed data might occur, and the evaluation of utility loss. Strong de-identification cannot be compared to direct-identifier masking which is a very simple method. On the contrary, it involves risk assessment, empirical experimentation, and expert judgment to a high degree and if mechanically done, it may either overprotect and destroy utility or under protect and leave serious disclosure pathways intact.

8.2 Privacy-Utility Tradeoffs in Real Operational Systems

In fact, the key comparative takeaway of the chapter is that privacy transformations must be taken through the lens of privacy-utility tradeoff and not merely personal preference. Very seldomly are security tools, compliance engines, analytics pipelines, and research workflows just auxiliary elements of the data production process; they actually serve the main purpose, i.e., producing actionable outcomes. That means if privacy transformation is so drastic that it removes the organization's ability to detect anomalies, investigate incidents, or support legitimate analysis, that is the risk. On the other hand, if the transformation remains so light that even privacy exposure remains high, the organization may be at risk of breaching the legal, ethical, or governance obligations(Al-Bahtiti et al., 2025). Without a doubt, most pseudonymization techniques will be close to the utility preserving end of the spectrum. Tasks that require a high level of record detail and a record continuity can also be supported, only that such use cases come with a non-negligible level of residual privacy risk. On the other hand, de-identification moves the system towards privacy protection by limiting the access to features that are key to making successful predictions and event specificity, but this comes with a loss in granularity of features and event specificity. So the answer to the practical question is not which technique is better in general, but which technique is more proportionate to the particular use case(Hasan et al., 2025).

Many times, in-house security analytics utilize several layers at once. Original identifiers are tokenized to allow event correlation but dashboards, reports, and other forms of data that are shared with less trusted faces are at the de-identified or aggregated level. Such a setup retains the analytical ability of the system where it is most crucial while lessening the routine exposure in other places. In research circles, moderate de-identification is frequently the best compromise since it drastically reduces re-identification risks while at the same time leaving the data quite usable(Abualhaj, Abu-Shareha, & Rateb, 2025). On the other hand, very strong de-identification, or aggregation could be called for in several of the released to the public cases since the presence of auxiliary data and the lack of control over the recipients highly increase the risks. The point is that a properly functioning operational framework not only imposes on a single technique to fulfill all functions. On the contrary, it will not be able to do that no matter how the techniques present themselves at the time. By combining them together and matching them to different levels of trust, analytical goals, and governance boundaries, the different transformation strengths are utilized(Ramesh et al., 2025).

8.3 Suitability Across Industry Domains

The county value of privacy techniques also varies by the sector in which they are applied. In the healthcare field, pseudonymization could be an excellent choice as many clinical and research workflows may require patient follow-up, adverse event response, or longitudinal treatment analysis. Besides that, since health data is very sensitive, pseudonymization might also be accompanied by de-identification in one form or another or by other kinds of access restrictions depending on the user of the data. This is even more so in the case of external research sharing where stronger de-identification becomes more important. In financial services, for instance, pseudonymization can be helpful in fraud detection, anti-money laundering analysis, and customer behavior monitoring, all of which require repeated transaction linkage(Abashes et al., 2025). Nevertheless, for regulatory reporting, benchmarking, or third-party model validation purposes, it may be more appropriate to use de-identification and aggregation. Since the industry depends heavily on sequence analysis, complete over-generalization will be undesirable, and so privacy controls have to be tightly linked to the purpose. In the security arena, such as cybersecurity and security operations, detection is so reliant on continuity across accounts, sessions, devices, and events that pseudonymization is well-nigh essential. However, exactly the same systems also raise significant employee and user privacy issues, especially since regular monitoring may be continuous. This renders privacy-aware architecture a must. Pseudonymized event stores can enable detection, while controlled re-identification and de-identified reporting can help to reduce unnecessary exposures. In this area, the most feasible method is not single-method but rather layered(Aldabbas et al., 2025).

In the education and public policy analytics worlds, generally speaking, stronger de-identification might be doable quite often as in many instances, unmasking is looking at trends, results, and evaluations of groups rather than individual responses. In the digital services sector and for consumer platforms, the correct option is based on whether the system is delivering an individual-level service or a broad-level analysis. One and the same transformation which is enough in one domain may be either insufficient or too much in another domain. For that reason, successful privacy engineering has to be based on the operational context rather than purely the technical habits. When combined, pseudonymous and de-identified methods should generally not be viewed as radically incompatible choices. Quite often, they tend to operate effectively as two separate but complementary levels of the same thing. Pseudonymization can be seen as the stronger option for internal workflows that need to be uninterrupted. On the other hand, de-identification is the stronger option for public sharing and non-identification. Oftentimes, the best performing privacy architecture features both, employing pseudonymization where operational linkage is necessary and de-identification where identity is not needed for the task(ALMahadin et al., 2025).

The main points emerged by the juxtaposing of the chapter's empirical and conceptual results are the following three. One, pseudonymization is the way to go if the priority is to give a very high level of utility combined with a medium level of privacy protection. It is excellent in internal controlled environments but as far as distribution is concerned, it is not quite stand-alone. Two, moderate de-identification in many analytical settings provides the optimal balance in practical terms. The reason is that it drastically lowers re-identification risks while at the same time it leaves the signal quite sufficient for modeling or interpretation. Third, extreme de-identification is a must in cases where there is low trust in the recipients or in scenarios when confronting legal and ethical requirements means that the re-identification surface has to be as small as possible. Though it might be the case that utility drops more sharply in these situations(Alraba'nah & Hiari, 2025).

9. CONCLUSION AND FUTURE DIRECTIONS

Nowadays, companies handle vast amounts of personal and behavioral data on distributed platforms, in the cloud, and across countries. Simple data masking or tokenization are hardly sufficient to deal with the new privacy threats, especially when advanced data analytics tools can find very subtle patterns in data. There is a need, therefore, for future privacy-preserving analytics to make a fundamental shift from the use of elementary data transformation methods to the incorporation of mathematical privacy assurances, decentralized computation, and machine learning models that are privacy-aware(Qaddara et al., 2025). The intent of these methods is to allow data to be used for gaining insights without, on the other hand, revealing the identity or sensitive traits of individuals. Quite often, the goal is not to stop using data but to change the way it is analyzed so that the protection of privacy is inherent to the very computation. The following part of the article is about several major trends that are determining the future of privacy-preserving analytics. They encompass differential privacy, federated learning, synthetic data generation, privacy-preserving machine learning models, and AI governance frameworks. All of these point towards the increasing recognition of privacy engineering as a design philosophy rather than a mere compliance afterthought(Raza et al., 2025).

9.1 Differential Privacy and Formal Privacy Guarantees

A key game-changer in the area of privacy has been differential privacy. Whereas traditional de-identification these attempts to mask or strip identifying attributes, differential privacy offers a strict mathematical way to control the change of the result of an analysis as a consequence of adding or removing any one individual's data. This ensures beyond doubt that a person cannot be identified as a database contributor even if the attacker has full knowledge of the rest of the dataset. In operation, differential privacy entails the addition of a well-thought-out amount of random noise to the final analytical functionalities. Instead of revealing precise numbers, averages, or model results, one releases values slightly altered such that the overall statistical information is retained, but the contribution of any one participant is obscured. The degree of the introduced randomness is governed by a parameter called epsilon, which reflects the level of privacy protection(Raza et al., 2025).

Differential privacy is increasingly recognized as the theoretical gold standard model of formal and measurable privacy. Besides that, the approach is ready for practical implementations, as evidenced by major tech companies as well as statistical offices that publish data derived from confidential sources making use of it. At the university level and research institutes, differential privacy is considered a fundamental element of privacy-aware machine learning, whereby the combination of noise addition is applied throughout both learning and inference. However, there remain practical difficulties in implementing differential privacy. Accurately choosing the privacy parameter epsilon requires profound statistical knowledge and ethical policy awareness. Increasing randomness too much leads to distorted data hardly useful for any credible analysis. On the other hand, limiting randomness does not guarantee privacy to a sufficient degree. Hence, use of differential privacy has to be accompanied by deep statistical knowledge and a well-defined privacy-utility tradeoff policy(Eke et al., 2025).

9.2 Federated Learning and Decentralized Data Processing

Yet another breakthrough in privacy-preserving analytics is the concept of federated learning. Normally, machine learning requires that training data be pooled together at a central point. This can mean that sensitive or personal data in hefty volumes get stored in one place prior to the training of the model. The vulnerability is clear: if the central point gets compromised, a significant number of individuals' data may get exposed. Federated learning offers the solution by changing the model training location onto the user's device or institutional local systems. Local systems similarly train partial models with their data and model parameters or gradient updates are exchanged with a central server which only aggregates and generates a global model without any sight on the data. The raw data exposure potential gets greatly reduced in this decentralized scheme since the actual records are still in their original places. Already, federated learning has been put to use in certain sectors like mobile device personalization, multi-center healthcare research, and inter-institutional machine learning forensics. Programming schemes that aid collaborative model building without centralized data sharing are also among the reasons why federated learning allowing organizations to extract large-scale data insights emerge as the winner while drawing stronger privacy bounds simultaneously. Like any other technology, federated learning too has its share of concerns. A model update may still leak information about data even if the data itself is not exposed. Hence, a federated learning system must rely on secure aggregation or differential privacy or other cryptographic measures to provide protection against model inversion or membership inference attacks(Ghazal, Hasan, Raju, et al., 2025).

9.3 Synthetic Data Generation for Privacy-Safe Analytics

Generating synthetic data is yet another avenue to data-preserving privacy. Rather than modifying or obfuscating a real dataset, the method of synthetic data results in entirely new datasets that statistically resemble the original ones while not containing any real individual's data at all. Thus privacy-safe synthetic sets can be released publicly, used for research, training of models, or testing, etc. Synthetic data is created mostly by statistical learning or machine learning-based approaches. Generative models like generative adversarial networks (GANs), variational autoencoders, probabilistic graphical models, etc., are capable of learning that the distribution of features in the original data and generating new records whose attributes follow similar patterns. Because these new records are by default different from real people, directly identifying or re-identifying an individual is nearly impossible. The main good point about synthetic data is its analytical value by way of allowing data analytics, model development, and experimentation with reduced exposure to personal data. The advantage of synthetic data is very significant in sectors like healthcare, financial services, and national security that face significant barriers in information sharing. Carelessness in synthetic data creation could lead to the violation of privacy. There might be a tendency to copy or remember the original data excessively which could result in privacy breach. Moreover, synthetic data may distort or omit nuances of original data thereby leading to analytical differences. This is why one should engage in synthetic data generation only after thorough assessment of privacy risk and derived data quality(Qawasmeh et al., 2025).

9.4 Privacy-Preserving Machine Learning Architectures

Besides which specific technique (differential privacy or federated learning), the other main line of research is privacy-preserving machine learning. The goal here is to make sure that the processes of training, using, and making models available do not result in inadvertent disclosure of data contributors' sensitive information. One of the widely used means in this respect is secure multiparty computation. This technique enables parties to jointly carry out computations on their combined data without sharing their individual data sets with each other. Each party encrypts, splits, or uses some other form to mask its input data, and then a computational protocol allows determination of the final result without ever revealing any intermediate values. Apart from a central feature, this technique is extremely useful when multiple parties are involved in data sharing arrangements at the same time being bound by privacy laws. Homomorphic encryption is another method that has shown promise in this regard. It is capable of performing computations directly on encrypted data without requiring decryption first. The data remains in encrypted form even being operated upon by the algorithms. Only the ultimate result is decrypted such that none of the intermediate steps reveal any clear data. It is noteworthy that homomorphic encryption is still computationally expensive, however, as a result of continuing research its efficiency and use cases are expanding. Privacy-preserving machine learning has the added benefit of curbing model leakage. For instance, practices such as regularization, noise insertion during training, and thorough model audits are measures taken to minimize the information leakage risks inherent in machine-learned models(Abualhaj, Abu-Shareha, Al-Khatib, et al., 2025).

REFERENCES

Abashes, G. M., Elshqeirat, B., Abu-Shareha, A. A., & Alshraideh, M. (2025). BEYOND THE NOISE: UNVEILING MEANINGFUL PATTERNS IN MOBILE PAYMENT DATA USING FUZZY LOGIC AND SVM. *Journal of Theoretical and Applied Information Technology*, *103*(1).

Abdeljaber, O., Al-Adwan, A. S., Yaseen, H., Falahat, M., Abdullah, A., & Fauzi, M. A. (2025). Shopping in the Metaverse: Decoding Consumer Intentions. *The International Information & Library Review*. Advance online publication. DOI: 10.1080/10572317.2025.2594293

Abualghanam, O., Alazzam, H., Qatawneh, M., Alazab, M., & Al Sharaiah, M. (2025). Elevating Mobile Security: An Ensemble Approach for Enhanced Malware Detection with M-iForest. *International Journal of Interactive Mobile Technologies*, *19*(10), 129–151. Advance online publication. DOI: 10.3991/ijim.v19i10.51319

Abualhaj, M. M., Abu-Shareha, A. A., Al-Khatib, S. N., Alsaaidah, A. M., & Anbar, M. (2025). Improving firewall performance using hybrid of optimization algorithms and decision trees classifier. *IAES International Journal of Artificial Intelligence*, *14*(4), 2839. Advance online publication. DOI: 10.11591/ijai.v14.i4.pp2839-2848

Abualhaj, M. M., Abu-Shareha, A. A., & Rateb, R. (2025). Enhancing intrusion detection systems with hybrid HHO-WOA optimization and gradient boosting machine classifier. *International Journal of Reconfigurable and Embedded Systems*, *14*(2), 518. Advance online publication. DOI: 10.11591/ijres.v14.i2.pp518-526

Abualhaj, M. M.I, Al-Khatib, S. N., Abu-Shareha, A. A., Almomani, O., Al-Mimi, H., Al-Allawee, A., Daoud, M. S., & Anbar, M. (2025). Spam Detection Boosted by Firefly-Based Feature Selection and Optimized Classifiers. *International Journal of Advances in Soft Computing and Its Applications*, *17*(3). Advance online publication. DOI: 10.15849/IJASCA.251130.02

Abualhaj, M. M., Al-Khatib, S. N., Abu-Shareha, A. A., Hyassat, A., & Daoud, M. S. (2025). Smart Firewall for Phishing Detection Powered by Bio-Inspired Algorithms. *Journal of Advances in Information Technology*, *16*(11), 1529–1539. Advance online publication. DOI: 10.12720/jait.16.11.1529-1539

Abualigah, L., Almomani, M. H., Alomari, S. A., Zitar, R. A., Migdady, H., Saleem, K., Snasel, V., Smerat, A., & Ezugwu, A. E. (2025). Optimizing Intrusion Detection in Wireless Sensor Networks via the Improved Chameleon Swarm Algorithm for Feature Selection. *IET Communications*, *19*(1), e70029. Advance online publication. DOI: 10.1049/cmu2.70029

Abuowaida, S., Abu Owida, H., Shelash Mohammad, S. I., Alshdaifat, N., Abu Elsoud, E., Alazaidah, R., Vasudevan, A., & Alshurideh, M. T. (2025). Evidence Detection in Cloud Forensics: Classifying Cyber-Attacks in IaaS Environments using machine learning. *Data and Metadata*, *4*, 699. Advance online publication. DOI: 10.56294/dm2025699

Ahmed, K. A., Ibrahim, A., Qudr, L. A. Z., Tawfeq, J. F., Al Falahi, Q., & Radhi, A. D. (2025). *Developing Adaptive AI-Driven Cybersecurity Frameworks for Real-Time Detection of Polymorphic Malware in IoT Networks*. DOI: 10.1109/ICBATS66542.2025.11258540

Al-Bahtiti, A. S., Tayeh, B. A., Baghdadi, A., Alaloul, W. S., & Abu Aisheh, Y. I. (2025). Drivers for adopting augmented reality and virtual reality technologies in the construction project management in Gaza City. *Journal of Asian Architecture and Building Engineering*, 1–18. Advance online publication. DOI: 10.1080/13467581.2025.2507235

Al-Daoud, K. I., Yogeesh, N., Mohammad, S. I., Raja, N., Chetana, R., William, P., Vasudevan, A., Alshdaifa, N., & Hunitie, M. F. A. (2025). Explainability in AI Using Fuzzy Inference Systems For the Regression Problem. *Applied Mathematics & Information Sciences*, *19*(5), 973–987. Advance online publication. DOI: 10.18576/amis/190501

Al-Daoud, K. I., Yogeesh, N., Mohammad, S. I. S., Raja, N., Jabeen, F. T. Z., William, P., Vasudevan, A., Hunitie, M. F. A., & Alshdaifat, N. (2025). Fuzzy Linear Programming in Real-World Applications: A Comparative Study of Agricultural and Financial Optimization. *Applied Mathematics & Information Sciences*, *19*(4), 849–862. Advance online publication. DOI: 10.18576/amis/190411

Al-Dmour, R., Al-Dmour, H., Al-Dmour, A., Basheer Amin, E., & Al-Dmour, Y. (2025). *AI and big data-driven social media recruitment: the mediating role of talent acquisition and employee engagement in bank performance*. Digital Transformation and Society., DOI: 10.1108/DTS-02-2025-0042

Al-Okbi, N. K., Alomari, S. A., Zitar, R. A., Smerat, A., Nazzal, M. A., & Abualigah, L. (2025). Integrating Multimodal Emotion Recognition with Deep Q-Learning for Adaptive Social Robot Interaction. *International Journal of Robotics and Control Systems*, *5*(4), 2265–2289. Advance online publication. DOI: 10.31763/ijrcs.v5i4.2055

Al-znamat, F. O., Alsaaidah, A., & Abu-Shareha, A. A. (2025). Malware Detection Using a Modified Bat Algorithm for Feature Selection. *International Journal of Intelligent Engineering and Systems*, *18*(9), 885–899. Advance online publication. DOI: 10.22266/ijies2025.1031.56

Aldabbas, A., Baniata, L. H., Alsaaidah, B. A., Mustafa, Z., Alali, M., & Rateb, R. (2025). Artificial intelligence-driven method for the discovery and prevention of distributed denial of service attacks. *IAES International Journal of Artificial Intelligence*, *14*(1), 614. Advance online publication. DOI: 10.11591/ijai.v14.i1.pp614-628

Alenazi, M. J. F., Al-Khasawneh, M. A., Rahman, S., & Faheem, Z. (2025). Deep Reinforcement Learning Based Flow Aware-QoS Provisioning in SD-IoT for Precision Agriculture. *Computational Intelligence*, *41*(1), e70023. Advance online publication. DOI: 10.1111/coin.70023

Alghlayini, S., Al-Betar, M. A., & Atef, M. (2025). Enhancing Non-Invasive Blood Glucose Prediction from Photoplethysmography Signals via Heart Rate Variability-Based Features Selection Using Metaheuristic Algorithms. *Algorithms*, *18*(2), 95. Advance online publication. DOI: 10.3390/a18020095

Ali, A. M., Al-Qerem, A., Hassan, M. R., Abu-Khadrah, A., & Jarrah, M. (2025). Traffic Monitoring and Control System for Smart City Pollution Regulation Using IoT and Correlated Capsule Networks. *IEEE Access : Practical Innovations, Open Solutions*, *13*, 46983–47003. Advance online publication. DOI: 10.1109/ACCESS.2025.3550966

Alkhawatrah, M. (2025). Random Forests Relay Selector in Buffer-Aided Cooperative Networks. *IEEE Access : Practical Innovations, Open Solutions*, *13*, 165402–165410. Advance online publication. DOI: 10.1109/ACCESS.2025.3612192

ALMahadin, G., Shabaz, M., Khan, I. R., Vimal, V., Keshta, I., & Maguluri, L. P.ALMahadin. (2025). Content-aware recommendation system for integrated temporal semantic review text over web of things. *Service Oriented Computing and Applications*, *19*(1), 77–91. Advance online publication. DOI: 10.1007/s11761-024-00408-9

Almomani, O., Arabiat, A., Al Tayeb, M., Almaiah, M. A., Obeidat, M., Aldhyani, T. H. H., Shehab, R., & Rowad, M. (2025). A Robust Model for Android Malware Detection via ML and DL classifiers. *Mesopotamian Journal of Big Data*, *2025*. Advance online publication. DOI: 10.58496/MJBD/2025/017

Alnawayseh, S. E. A., Al-Sit, W. T., & Ghazal, T. M. (2022). Smart Congestion Control in 5G/6G Networks Using Hybrid Deep Learning Techniques. *Complexity*, *2022*(1), 1781952. Advance online publication. DOI: 10.1155/2022/1781952

Alraba'nah, Y., & Hiari, M. (2025). Improved convolutional neural networks for aircraft type classification in remote sensing images. *IAES International Journal of Artificial Intelligence*, *14*(2), 1540. Advance online publication. DOI: 10.11591/ijai.v14.i2.pp1540-1547

Arabiat, A. M. (2025). Intelligent Model for Detecting GAN-Generated Images Based on Multi-Classifier and Advanced Data Mining Techniques. *International Journal of Electrical and Electronic Engineering and Telecommunications*, *14*(3). Advance online publication. DOI: 10.18178/ijeetc.14.3.147-157

Arabiat, A. M., & Eljaafreh, Y. G. (2025). Intrusion Detection in Wireless Sensor Networks Using ML Based Classification of Denial of Service (DoS) Attacks. *The Journal of Communication*, *20*(4). Advance online publication. DOI: 10.12720/jcm.20.4.501-514

Awais, Z., Hussain, M., Elshenawy, A., Arsalan, A., Anwar, M., Asif Habib, M., Jabbar, S., & Ahmad, M. (2025). ISCC: Intelligent Semantic Caching and Control for NDN-Enabled Industrial IoT Networks. *IEEE Access : Practical Innovations, Open Solutions*, *13*, 169881–169898. Advance online publication. DOI: 10.1109/ACCESS.2025.3614984

Ayub, N., Imtiaz, M. A., Ali, E., Alqahtani, A. M., Ali, A., Ashurov, M., Albouq, S., & Law, F. L. (2025). A Decision Framework for Intra Task Fixed Priority INTEL PXA270 Distributed Architecture for Soft RT-Applications Based on Deep Learning. *Engineering. Technology and Applied Science Research*, *15*(3), 23553–23558. Advance online publication. DOI: 10.48084/etasr.10006

Azeem, S., Javed, S., Naseer, I., Ali, O., & Ghazal, T. M. (2025). A New Hybrid PSO-HHO Wrapper Based Optimization for Feature Selection. *IEEE Access : Practical Innovations, Open Solutions*, *13*, 87090–87099. Advance online publication. DOI: 10.1109/ACCESS.2025.3570901

Babaker, S., Khatibi, A., Alsoud, A. R., Kaur, J., Jagtap, J., Alkhayyat, A., & Shah, S. K. (2025). Improving Reliability and Data Management in Internet of Things Based Wireless Sensor Networks. *Internet Technology Letters*, *8*(6), e646. Advance online publication. DOI: 10.1002/itl2.646

Braik, M., Kassaymeh, S., Almiani, M., Albashish, D., Awadallah, M., Bataineh, B., & Al-Hiary, H. (2025). Advancements in global optimization with an empowered capuchin search algorithm. *Neural Computing & Applications*, *37*(24), 19707–19749. Advance online publication. DOI: 10.1007/s00521-025-11421-0

Eke, C. I., Al-Shamayleh, A. S., Phiri, M., Maswadi, K., Kwaghtyo, D. K., Mulenga, M., & Iyidobi, C. J. (2025). Machine Learning Based Mobile Big Data Analytics: State-of-the-art Applications, Taxonomy, Challenges and Future Research Directions. *Nigerian Journal of Technological Development*, *22*(4). Advance online publication. DOI: 10.63746/njtd.v22i4.3385

Elomda, B. M., Abdelbary, T. A. A., Hassan, H. A., Hamza, K. S., & Kharma, Q. (2025). An Enhanced Multi-Layer Blockchain Security Model for Improved Latency and Scalability. *Information (Basel)*, *16*(3), 241. Advance online publication. DOI: 10.3390/info16030241

Fatima, W., Rizvi, S. S. R., Ghazal, T. M., Kharma, Q. M., Ahmad, M., Abbas, S., Furqan, M., & Adnan, K. M. (2025). Abstractive Text Summarization in Arabic-Like Script Using Multi-Encoder Architecture and Semantic Extraction Techniques. *IEEE Access : Practical Innovations, Open Solutions*, *13*, 104977–104991. Advance online publication. DOI: 10.1109/ACCESS.2025.3575610

Ghazal, T. M. (2025). Federated Learning for Intelligent Sensing and Navigation Technologies for 6G Communications. *Journal of Sensors*, *2025*(1). DOI: 10.1155/js/3746147

Ghazal, T. M., Awouda, A. E., Hasan, M. K., Rahman, A. H. A., Islam, S., Saeed, R. A., Elshafie, H., Iqbal, A., & Hussein, A. H. (2025). Knowledge Learning for Securing Workflow Scheduling Algorithm in Mobile Edge Computing. *Mobile Networks and Applications*, *30*(3-4), 395–413. Advance online publication. DOI: 10.1007/s11036-025-02465-6

Ghazal, T. M., Hasan, M. K., Mokhtar, U. A., Safie, N., Alshamayleh, A., & Ahmad, M. (2025). Machine learning-based real-time outage fault detection for distribution networks in smart grid. In *Energy Reports* (Vol. 14). DOI: 10.1016/j.egyr.2025.10.045

Ghazal, T. M., Hasan, M. K., Raju, K. N., Khan, M. A., Alshamayleh, A., Bhatt, M. W., & Ahmad, M. (2025). Data Space Privacy Model with Federated Learning Technique for Securing IoT Communications in Autonomous Marine Vehicles. *Journal of Intelligent & Robotic Systems*, *111*(3), 84. Advance online publication. DOI: 10.1007/s10846-025-02298-1

Hanandeh, A., Alfreijat, S. Y., Qutieshat, R. J., Alsha'ar, H. Y., Kilani, Q. A. L., & Saleem Khasawneh, M. A. (2025). Implementing AI Accuracy, Learning Rate, Inference Time on enhancing Big Data Analysis and Strategic Plan. *Data and Metadata*, *4*, 637. Advance online publication. DOI: 10.56294/dm2025637

Hasan, M. K., Ghazal, T. M., Alkhalifah, A., Abu Bakar, K. A., Omidvar, A., Nafi, N. S., & Agbinya, J. I. (2021). Fischer Linear Discrimination and Quadratic Discrimination Analysis–Based Data Mining Technique for Internet of Things Framework for Healthcare. *Frontiers in Public Health*, *9*, 737149. Advance online publication. DOI: 10.3389/fpubh.2021.737149 PMID: 34712639

Hasan, M. K., Ghazal, T. M., Issa, G., Islam, S., Ismail, A. F., & Kabir, S. R. (2025). Hashgraph consensus-based simultaneous, asynchronous and big-data supported blockchain mechanism for IT-OT enabled critical infrastructure sectors. *Journal of Ambient Intelligence and Humanized Computing*. Advance online publication. DOI: 10.1007/s12652-024-04942-4

Hiari, M., Alraba'nah, Y., & Qaddara, I. (2025). A Deep Learning-Based Intrusion Detection System using Refined LSTM for DoS Attack Detection. *Engineering. Technology and Applied Science Research, 15*(4), 25627–25633. Advance online publication. DOI: 10.48084/etasr.11499

Hyassat, A. S., Abu Zayed, R. E., Al Khateeb, E. A., Shalaldeh, A., Abdelhamied, M. M., & Qaddara, I. (2025). Unveiling Cyber Threats: An In-Depth Study on Data Mining Techniques for Exploit Attack Detection †. *Engineering Proceedings, 104*(1), 28. Advance online publication. DOI: 10.3390/engproc2025104028

Ibrahim, A., Sekhar, R., Tawfeq, J. F., Salih, S. Q., Shah, P., & Radhi, A. D. (2024). Security and Privacy Protection for Online Electronic Documents Based on Novel Encryption Techniques. *Journal of Intelligent Systems and Internet of Things, 11*(1), 21–28. Advance online publication. DOI: 10.54216/JISIoT.110103

Iskandarani, M. Z. (2025). Effect of Adaptive Intelligent Reflective Surfaces on SINR in a Wireless Communication System. *The Journal of Communication, 20*(1). Advance online publication. DOI: 10.12720/jcm.20.1.1-11

Iskandarani, M. Z., & Hidayat, R. (2025). Analysis of Factors Affecting Spectrum Sensing in an IRS based Wireless Network. *International Journal on Advanced Science, Engineering and Information Technology, 15*(1), 300–309. Advance online publication. DOI: 10.18517/ijaseit.15.1.20491

Khatibi, A., Babaker, S., Praveen, K. N. R., Chohan, J. S., Jadhav, A., Alsoud, A. R., Ramudu, M. J., & Jeet, R. (2025). Advanced AI-Driven Cybersecurity: Analyzing Emerging Threats and Defensive Strategies. *National Academy Science Letters*. Advance online publication. DOI: 10.1007/s40009-025-01897-8

Lee, S. W., Hussain, S., Issa, G. F., Abbas, S., Ghazal, T. M., Sohail, T., Ahmad, M., & Khan, M. A. (2021). Multi-Dimensional Trust Quantification by Artificial Agents through Evidential Fuzzy Multi-Criteria Decision Making. *IEEE Access : Practical Innovations, Open Solutions, 9*, 159399–159412. Advance online publication. DOI: 10.1109/ACCESS.2021.3131521

Mahfouz, K. H., Al Betar, M. A., & Makhadmeh, S. N. (2025). Mitigating the task scheduling problem in fog computing environments using improved marine predators optimization algorithm. *Computing, 107*(7), 147. Advance online publication. DOI: 10.1007/s00607-025-01502-2

Makhadmeh, S. N., Fraihat, S., Awad, M., Sanjalawe, Y., Al-Betar, M. A., & Awadallah, M. A. (2025). A crossover-integrated Marine Predator Algorithm for feature selection in intrusion detection systems within IoT environments. *Internet of Things : Engineering Cyber Physical Human Systems, 31*, 101536. Advance online publication. DOI: 10.1016/j.iot.2025.101536

Mohammad, A. A. S., Al-Ramadan, A. M., Mohammad, S. I., Al Oraini, B., Vasudevan, A., Alshdaifat, N., & Hunitie, M. F. A. (2025). Customer Sentiment Analysis for Food and Beverage Development in Restaurants using AI in Jordan. *Data and Metadata*, *4*, 922. Advance online publication. DOI: 10.56294/dm2025922

Nafisah, I., Mahmoud, N., Ewees, A. A., Khattap, M. G., Dahou, A., Alghamdi, S. M., Fares, I. A., Azmi Al-Betar, M., & Abd Elaziz, M. (2025). Deep learning-based feature selection for detection of autism spectrum disorder. *Frontiers in Artificial Intelligence*, *8*, 1594372. Advance online publication. DOI: 10.3389/frai.2025.1594372 PMID: 40636395

Nasir, J., Aamir, M., Iftikhar, S., Albidah, A. B., Alqasem, O. A., Elwahab, M. E. A., Khan, I., & Koh, W. S. (2025). A Novel Hybrid Approach to Forecasting Crude Oil Prices Using Local Mean Decomposition, ARIMA, and XGBoost. *IEEE Access : Practical Innovations, Open Solutions*, *13*, 89140–89156. Advance online publication. DOI: 10.1109/ACCESS.2025.3561193

Otair, M., Qawaqzeh, F. A., Alomari, S. A., Zitar, R. A., Migdady, H., Saleem, K., Smerat, A., Alsoud, A. R., & Abualigah, L. (2025). Enhanced Arithmetic Optimization Algorithm for Intrusion Detection in Wireless Sensor Networks. *International Journal of Communication Systems*, *38*(10), e70122. Advance online publication. DOI: 10.1002/dac.70122

Qaddara, I., & Alraba'nah, Y. (2025). Enhancing Requirements Classification Using Machine Learning Techniques. *SN Computer Science*, *6*(6), 649. Advance online publication. DOI: 10.1007/s42979-025-04158-z

Qaddara, I., Alrabaynah, Y., & Hiari, M. O. (2025). Evaluation of SQL and NoSQL Databases on Parallel Processing. *Engineering. Technology and Applied Science Research*, *15*(4), 24298–24304. Advance online publication. DOI: 10.48084/etasr.10620

Qawasmeh, S., Habboushb, A., Elzaghmouri, B., Kharma, Q., & Albalawneh, D. (2025). Hybrid Convolutional Neural Network-Based Intrusion Detection System for Secure IoT Networks. *Tikrit Journal of Engineering Sciences*, *32*(SP1), 1–11. Advance online publication. DOI: 10.25130/tjes.sp1.2025.2

Ramesh, J. V. N., Nimma, D., Dasari, R., Chaudhari Rane, D., AlGhamdi, A., Rao, K. B. V. B., Haider, S. A., Kuzieva, N., & Jangir, P. (2025). Safe and Reliable Two-Stage Online Offloading Algorithm for Transportation Cyber-Physical Systems. *IEEE Transactions on Intelligent Transportation Systems*, *26*(9), 14313–14322. Advance online publication. DOI: 10.1109/TITS.2025.3539934

Raza, M. A., Karim, A., Alqarni, M., Al-Khasawneh, M. A., Jumani, T. A., Aman, M., & Masud, M. I. (2025). An Intelligent Long Short-Term Memory-Based Machine Learning Model for the Potential Assessment of Global Hydropower Capacity in Sustainable Energy Transition and Security. *Energies*, *18*(13), 3324. Advance online publication. DOI: 10.3390/en18133324

Rehan, R., Sahran, S., Alyasseri, Z. A. A., Sani, N. S., & Al-Betar, M. A. (2025). Hyperparameters optimization of evolving spiking neural network using artificial bee colony for unsupervised anomaly detection. *Journal of Intelligent Systems*, *34*(1), 20240235. Advance online publication. DOI: 10.1515/jisys-2024-0235

Salman, A. M., Ibrahim, A., Abdulbaqi, A. S., Almajed, R., & Al Naffakh, H. A. H. (2025). *Designing Blockchain Solutions to Enhance Data Security and Privacy in Distributed IoT Networks*. DOI: 10.1109/ICBATS66542.2025.11258568

Sardar, R., Anees, T., Al-Shamayleh, A. S., Mehmood, E., Khalil, W., Akhunzada, A., & Shaikh, F. S. (2025). Challenges in detecting security threats in WoT: A systematic literature review. *Artificial Intelligence Review*, *58*(7), 196. Advance online publication. DOI: 10.1007/s10462-025-11176-z

Shah, R. K., Hasan, M. K., Islam, S., Khan, A., Ghazal, T. M., & Khan, A. N. (2022). Detect Phishing Website by Fuzzy Multi-Criteria Decision Making. *2022 1st International Conference on AI in Cybersecurity, ICAIC 2022*. DOI: 10.1109/ICAIC53980.2022.9897036

Shamaylah, N., Ibrahim Mohammad, S., Al Oraini, B., Yaseen Al-Gaafreh, J. M., Mosallam Alqahtani, M., Vasudevan, A., Shlash Mohammad, A. A., & Ahmmad Hunitie, M. F. (2025). Data-Driven Decision-Making for Employee Training and Development in Jordanian Public Institutions. *Data and Metadata*, *4*, 886. Advance online publication. DOI: 10.56294/dm2025886

Shambour, Q. Y., Al-Zyoud, M., & Hussein, A. H. (2025). FROM DATA TO DIAGNOSIS: KNOWLEDGE-DRIVEN, EXPLAINABLE AI FOR RELIABLE EARLY AUTISM DETECTION. *Interdisciplinary Journal of Information, Knowledge, and Management*, *20*, 032. Advance online publication. DOI: 10.28945/5652

Sharma, K. P., Al-Rashed, A., Johar, M. G. M., Alsoud, A. R., Singh, A., Dey, P., & Pant, S. (2025). Blockchain-Assisted Trust Framework for Increased Survivability in Internet of Vehicles. *Internet Technology Letters*, *8*(3), e70029. Advance online publication. DOI: 10.1002/itl2.70029

Sharma, K. P., Yajid, M. S. A., Gowrishankar, J., Mahajan, R., Alsoud, A. R., Jadhav, A., & Singh, D. (2025). A Systematic Review on Text Summarization: Techniques, Challenges, Opportunities. In *Expert Systems* (Vol. 42, Number 4). DOI: 10.1111/exsy.13833

Shlash Mohammad, A. A., Ibrahim Mohammad, S., Al-Daoud, K. I., Al Oraini, B., Mosallam Alqahtani, M., Vasudevan, A., & Ahmmad Hunitie, M. F. (2025). Riding into the Future: Transforming Jordan's Public Transportation with Predictive Analytics and Real-Time Data. *Data and Metadata*, *4*, 887. Advance online publication. DOI: 10.56294/dm2025887

Ullah, N., Al-Rahmi, W. M., Alblehai, F., Fernando, Y., Alharbi, Z. H., Zhanbayev, R., Al-Adwan, A. S., & Habes, M. (2025). Corrigendum to "Blockchain-powered grids: Paving the way for a sustainable and efficient future" [Heliyon Volume 10, Issue 10, May 2024, Article e31592] (Heliyon (2024) 10(10), (S2405844024076230), ()). In *Heliyon* (Vol. 11, Number 13). https://doi.org/DOI: 10.1016/j.heliyon.2024.e31592

Vasudevan, A., Albinaa, T. A., Mohammad, S. I., Sharmila, E., Raja, N., Soon, E. E. H., Alshurideh, M. T., & Al-Adwan, A. S. (2024). Bidirectional LSTM for Electronic Product Recommendation. *Applied Mathematics & Information Sciences*, *18*(6), 1443–1453. Advance online publication. DOI: 10.18576/amis/180621

Xu, B., Jummaa, K., Altalbawy, F. M. A., Roopashree, R., Saraswat, S. K., Ray, S., Tomar, P., Naem, S., Hamza, H. H., Smerat, A., & Khalid, A. (2025). Machine learning-assisted computation of water activity for ionic liquid-based aqueous ternary elements. *Desalination and Water Treatment*, *324*, 101484. Advance online publication. DOI: 10.1016/j.dwt.2025.101484

Zhu, Y., Lin, X., Kim, J., Al-Adwan, A. S., & Li, N. (2025). Exploring Human Interaction in Online Self-Regulated Learning Through Danmaku Comments. *International Journal of Human-Computer Interaction*, *41*(22), 13964–13977. Advance online publication. DOI: 10.1080/10447318.2025.2480826

Chapter 11
Personal Data Identification and Classification in Security Monitoring Signals

Hani Q. R. Al-Zoubi
http://orcid.org/0009-0008-3507-3660
Department of Computer Engineering, Mutah University, Jordan

Mashal Kasem Alqudah
http://orcid.org/0009-0009-6212-0001
Faculty of Computer Information Science, Higher Colleges of Technology, UAE

ABSTRACT

This chapter is concerned with different approaches to discover and identify personal data that is hidden in security monitoring signals. It first discusses the possibility that logs, alerts, network telemetry, and behavioral indicators may either directly or indirectly relate to identifiable individuals. Then it sets out classification frameworks that separate personal, sensitive, and non-personal data, and explains contextual factors like linkage, aggregation, and reidentification risk. The chapter goes on to consider the effects of incorrect data classification on privacy compliance, incident response, and evidentiary handling. By managing legal definitions with technical signal analysis, this chapter offers a blueprint for correctly identifying personal data in security operations, thus allowing for proportionate controls, compliant processing, and informed decision-making at the intersection of organizational security functions and governance oversight.

1. INTRODUCTION TO PERSONAL DATA IDENTIFICATION IN SECURITY MONITORING

1.1 Evolution of Security Monitoring and Telemetry Systems

Monitoring for security has changed enormously from merely keeping logs at the perimeter to sophisticated multi-layered telemetry ecosystems. Initially, in those distant times of computing days, monitoring was network perimeter focused controls only, firewalls, and intrusion detection systems.

DOI: 10.4018/979-8-3373-9210-3.ch011

These made it possible to produce very limited event streams such as mostly comprising of packet sources or destinations, port activity, connection attempts, etc. The scope of monitoring changed and extended very significantly when companies got compartmentalized structurally and at the same time digitally connected through territories. Identity providers, cloud workloads, mobile devices, application servers, SaaS platforms, APIs, and endpoint agents provide continuous logs, which are then sent to main platforms like security information and event management systems, and extended detection and response pipelines(A. M. Arabiat & Eljaafreh, 2025). This expansion has transformed telemetry from a very technical and limited task to a large data space. The current monitoring tools besides being able to record system-level events also track human interaction with digital services such as failed login attempts, password reset requests, multi-factor authentication prompts, privileged command execution, remote session activities, document access events, application clickstreams, and data transfer traces, all of these help to a greater extent to make a user's behavioral profile in the organizational systems more accurate. Monitoring platforms, therefore, have been turned not only into technical evidence repositories but behaviorally rich data repositories too. This change has major implications for privacy(Mahfuri & Ibrahim, 2024).

Besides, one of the main features of this transformation is the emphasis on correlation and enrichment. Monitoring systems are continuously modifying the raw events by adding identity details, device security posture, geolocation data, department information, threat scores, and other contextual metadata. Enrichment, while it helps in security analysis, also raises the possibility of a single event being tied to an individual. A connection log for instance is a technical one, but the moment it is linked to a user account, a device ownership record, and an access history, it becomes a very detailed personal trace. Hence, the advent of security telemetry has made the identification of personal data no longer a matter of choice but a Ghazal, Hasan, et al., 2025).

1.2 Increasing Presence of Personal Data in Monitoring Signals

User data keep reappearing in security monitoring signals, as the capability to protect modern information systems largely depends on being able to see user-targeted activities. Secret detection models generally emphasize the methods of user authentication, the resources accessed by users, the extent to which users' behavior deviates from the norm, and whether users' actions are consistent with known attack patterns (Shah et al., 2022). This heavy dependence on identity and behavior for analytical purposes almost certainly leads to personal data being stored in monitoring records. Besides, organizations might unwittingly collect personal data by means of security tools even if they do not deliberately keep such data for business purposes. Various types of personal data exist. Some security signals directly identify individuals with names, usernames, email addresses, employee numbers, or phone numbers. Other signals comprise less direct identifiers like IP addresses, MAC addresses, cookie values, device serial numbers, browser fingerprints, or geolocation data(Abualigah, Almomani, et al., 2025). Besides, some records embody behavioral data such as login times, session duration, navigation patterns, frequency of failed authentication, or sequences of file accesses. Taken alone, one or two such data points might seem harmless or low-risk. However, when collected from, or combined across, different systems, they provide the means for creating detailed user profiles. Among the principal factors why this trend is on the rise is that security architectures are currently placing much more focus on user-centric security. Security systems which rely on user behavior visibility are zero trust frameworks, insider threat detection, privileged access monitoring, user and entity behavior analytics, and adaptive authentication. While these systems better security by making identity the central element of analysis, at the same time, they increase privacy risks as they turn normal activities into continually monitored signals. Thus, the borderline separating technical log data and personal data has become vague. Security logs can no longer be considered non-personal merely because the components of their generation are infrastructure rather than Iskandarani & Hidayat, 2025).

1.3 Importance of Identifying Personal Data in Security Logs

There are many good reasons why identifying personal data in security logs is a wise decision. In legal terms, it would be more reasonable for businesses to know their surveillance tools handle personal data as some data protection laws indicate that collection, storage, access, transfer, and other types of processing should be done in accordance with rules that limit data subject rights and impose obligations on data controllers/processors. A company that doesn't know which fields, records or outputs of analysis contain personal data will simply not be able to introduce any effective privacy controls. Identification-wise, without it, the only measures implemented become compliance checklists rather than being proactive results-driven programs(Saeed et al., 2024).

From another perspective, in addition to facing the statutory requirements, there is also an ethical angle. One needs to identify personal data to keep things in balance and ensure fairness in security operations. Having security monitoring is necessary but it shouldn't become an unbridled tool to watch and profile people. Organizations that cannot tell apart the essential technical signals and the excessive personal details will undoubtedly end up with over-collection, over-retention, and privacy-violating analytics. On top of losing employee trust, it will also cause harm to the reputation and social acceptance of surveillance practices that go beyond legitimate security needs(Hasan et al., 2021).

Anyway, the identification of personal data is a very important step that allows companies to label their monitoring assets correctly, focus on the most vulnerable, and develop more by default secure workflows. For instance, knowing which logs include identity-sensitive data may lead to the implementation of stricter access control policies, masking rules, higher encryption standards, and also tighter retention limits. On the other hand, personal data identification plays at least a partial role as the first step in incident response. When we're talking about breach investigation, knowledge about whether the injured log repositories contain regulated personal data will affect issues like communication obligations, legal liability, and corrective measures. So, one could say that the identification of personal data in logs isn't only a privacy exercise but an indispensable part of the entire monitoring governance Shamaylah et al., 2025). This chapter contributes a practical taxonomy and Privacy Risk Index for identifying personal data in security monitoring signals. The framework classifies telemetry according to direct identification, indirect identification, behavioral inference, metadata sensitivity, and re-identification potential.

1.4 Privacy Risks Associated with Unstructured Monitoring Data

Unlike a customer database where there are clear definitions for each data field, security logs may consist of free text entries, concatenated records, stack traces, command-line arguments, URLs, file paths, ticket references, and copied application outputs, etc. Personal data can very well be included in these fragments without being explicitly marked. One such example is where a simple debugging message discloses an email address. Besides the failed authentication log not revealing just username but also the originating IP address. Account identifiers or session tokens are contained in URL query strings. Recognizing such data is seldom done because of the difficulty in normalizing it. The problem becomes greater when unstructured records are collected together to form large security data lakes. After aggregation, these records can not only be searched and correlated, but also exported and reused in completely unexpected and unintended ways by the original collectors. The original "just a log" message may be harmless unless it is combined with endpoint, identity, and network contexts, when it becomes a privacy-invasive one(Hyassat et al., 2025). Similarly, the risk of re-identification surges really high in unstructured environments since very small fragments can be put together to determine a person's identity, role, habits, or location. Use of data for other purposes is yet another concern. Types of data collected for monitoring use may in the future also be used to evaluate employee performance, discipline, or to carry out extensive profiling of behaviors. When unstructured logs are held for long periods of time, they readily draw interest from analytic applications outside the original scope. In other words, security utility and privacy limitation get into tension with each other. Hence, direct identifiers are only among the sources of privacy risk in monitoring systems. Other factors are contextualization, aggregation, inference, and re-use(Ghazal, Hasan, Alzoubi, et al., 2022).

1.5 Challenges in Distinguishing Operational vs Personal Data

It is indeed a very difficult task to distinguish operational data from personal data when doing security monitoring since these data types are in most cases intermingled. In fact, the exact same piece of information can be a technical instrument and a personal identifier at the same time. Let's take an IP address. It is a very useful piece of information for tracking down the attacker's connection, but at the same time, it can be linked to a particular employee or household. A hostname can be used to identify a device in the context of system administration, but it might be a single-user device. A login timestamp is necessary for incident investigation, but it is also a marker of an employee's work pattern. Databases contain dual, intertwined aspects of data use, and that is the main reason why classification is so difficult(Iskandarani & Chakrabarti, 2025).

The second challenge is context dependence. Depending on circumstances, identical data can have radically different meanings. In general, a process name is regarded as not being personal, but an employee name used as an endpoint label can be. At first glance, a location field is completely non-identifying and innocent, especially when considering a global cloud, but if that location is pinpointed as the small office or even work-from-home employee location, then it is an identifying piece of information. In essence, classification cannot rely on fixed dictionaries and criteria(Jan et al., 2025). It should take into account operational context, organizational structure, and potential for linkage. The volume challenge cannot be ignored either. Security monitoring tools generate millions of log entries on a daily basis making any sort of manual intervention going over the records completely impractical. So the answer is automatic classification. That, however, is problematic by itself due to the various types of logs in the hands of brands, vendors, tools, pipelines, etc. While some personal attributes are neatly structured and can be found by simple pattern matching, others need comprehension of context, natural language processing, or correlation between records. The bottom line is that organizations generally detect only rather obvious personal data and miss less evident or indirect personal data(Al-Momani et al., 2025).

Finally, the very culture of cybersecurity as an institution might play a part. Usually, security teams give the highest priority to accuracy and quickness of detection and to the depth of retention (Ghazal et al., 2024). Privacy teams, on the other hand, aim at minimization, necessity, and accountability. These two functions are most often separated resulting in operational data being considered exempt from privacy review. Ultimately, a higher goal would be that security and privacy are not at odds with each other. Actually, accurate identification of personal data is the key for security monitoring to be legitimate, defensible, and sustainable. In essence, personal data identification in security monitoring signals has moved from being a marginal concern to a central one(R. D. Alabdallat et al., 2025). The emergence of infrastructures abundant in telemetry, identity-centric defense, and centralized log analysis has made monitoring systems major repositories for personal and behaviorally revealing data. Therefore, it is first and foremost important to understand how personal data enter these systems, why they matter, and where the main classification issues lie. These topics constitute the conceptual background for the rest of the chapter. Next sections will make this introduction more detailed by providing fundamental theories for personal data classification in security environments and listing the types of identifiers most relevant to security monitoring Ghazal, Hasan, Abdul Wahab, et al., 2022). Existing cybersecurity research often treats logs, alerts, endpoint telemetry, and network flows as technical security records. However, limited work explains how these signals become personal data when linked with identity directories, VPN records, authentication logs, asset inventories, or behavioral analytics. This chapter addresses that gap through a context-aware classification approach.

Figure 1. Security Monitoring Data Flow Containing Personal Data

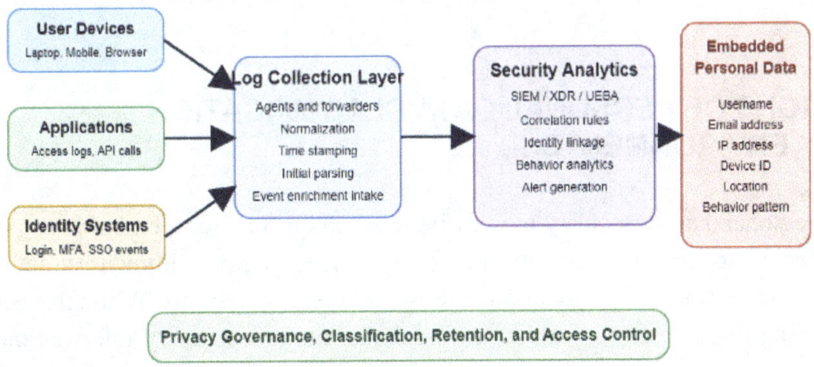

Figure 1 illustrates the process of monitoring signals coming from user devices, applications, and identity platforms being directed to centralized security analytics systems where personal data is integrated through both direct capture and contextual

Figure 2. Architecture of Personal Data Detection in Security Telemetry

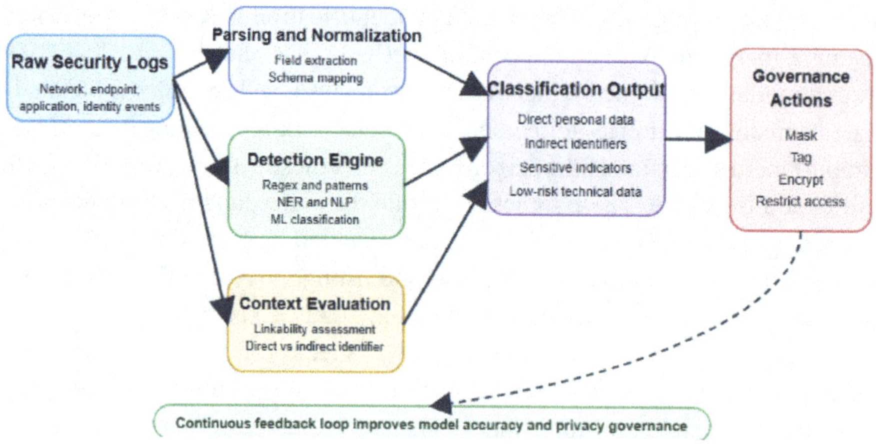

Figure 2 outlines a concept map showing how personal data can be detected and classified within security telemetry through steps including parsing, automation, contextual insight, and governance enforcement

2. FOUNDATIONS OF PERSONAL DATA CLASSIFICATION IN SECURITY ENVIRONMENTS

Classifying personal data in security monitoring contexts is a major element in organizing privacy-conscious cybersecurity operations. Security monitoring systems gather an immense amount of operational signals coming from networks, devices, applications, and identity systems. While these signals are very helpful for detecting threats and responding to incidents, they often carry information that identifies individuals either directly or indirectly. Organizations without a proper classification system find it difficult to distinguish the technical monitoring signals from privacy-related or ethically governed data elements. Putting in place key principles for personal data classification enables security departments to identify which characteristics need safeguarding, the degree of their sensitivity, and the level of analytical or governance controls needed(Vasudevan et al., 2025).

Classifying personal data within monitoring environments is not the same as classifying enterprise data because monitoring signals tend to be dynamic, large-scale, and depend on the context. Business customer records or personnel databases have well-defined, structured data identifying individuals personally. On the other hand, security logs are often discontinuous, semi-structured, and scattered across various platforms. One monitoring event can be made up of dozens of attributes, some of them merely technical, others behavioral. Furthermore, a data field that seems safe when viewed alone can be identifying when it is linked with other records. So, classification should not only consider single attributes but also the possibilities of linking, inference, and contextual interpretation(Maz et al., 2025).

Security monitoring data is often used for two different things simultaneously; privacy and classification become difficult issues in these scenarios. A good example is an IP address which can be used for network troubleshooting and intrusion detection, but at the same time, it is a personal data as it can be linked to a user or a household(Al-Habashneh et al., 2025). Similarly, device identifiers may aid in locating compromised endpoints, but they also disclose which employee owns the device. The root problem is, therefore, to come up with a taxonomy that clearly separates purely operational signals from signals containing identifiable personal features. This chapter discusses definitions and classification categories that set the foundation for personal data analysis in security monitoring signals(Abualhaj et al., 2025).

2.1 Categories of Personal Identifiers in Security Signals

Security monitoring results in gathering of various types of identifiers which, if put together, may reveal personal data. Usually these identifiers can be segregated into four broad categories: identity identifiers, network identifiers, device identifiers, and behavioral identifiers. As far as personal data classification is concerned, each of these four has a different function. Identity identifiers are the most direct means of identifying a person as they literally associate monitoring events with individual persons. Usually these are found amongst login records, identity management system entries, and application activity logs. Network identifier comprises such attributes as IP addresses, network session identifiers, and DNS query records. Initially, these may appear to be purely technical features, however, the reality is that they are frequently linked to particular persons or devices used by individuals in a company environment(Mahadin et al., 2025). The device identification is the third category. For instance, endpoint monitoring tools usually log device names, hardware IDs, OS fingerprints, and serial numbers. If devices have been assigned to specific employees or departments, these identifiers may also lead to a person's identity inadvertently. Lastly, behavioral identifiers is a category where a person is distinguished from others by patterns of skills or habits such as times of logging in, sequences of accessing, histories of issuing commands, and series of mouse clicks. That is a brief description of the main kinds of identifiable personal data that you probably will meet in security monitoring Abdeljaber & Al-Masaeed, 2025).

Table 1. Types of Personal Identifiers in Security Monitoring Signals

Identifier Category	Example Attributes	Typical Monitoring Source	Privacy Risk Level
Identity Identifiers	Username, email address, employee ID	Authentication logs, identity systems	High
Network Identifiers	IP address, session ID, DNS query	Network monitoring tools, firewall logs	Medium
Device Identifiers	Hostname, device ID, MAC address	Endpoint detection systems	Medium
Behavioral Identifiers	Login times, activity patterns	User activity monitoring platforms	Medium to High

2.2 Direct vs Indirect Identifiers in Telemetry Data

Direct identifiers are able to recognize an individual uniquely, independently of any additional context. Examples comprise of first and last names, business email, employee numbers, or government ID numbers. Where security monitoring is concerned, such direct identifiers most often appear on login events or records that synchronize with user directories. On the other hand, indirect identifiers need some form of contextual information before they can be used to find out who someone is. To illustrate, by itself, an IP address is unlikely to be sufficient to identify anyone. However, if combined with DHCP lease logs or data that links the address to a particular user's device, association with a specific individual can be made(Khaled Abdullah & Qawasmeh, 2025). In similar fashion, it would not be surprising to find that a device hostname is not personal on its own, but if the naming conventions embed the employee's names, then it becomes identifying. Indirect identifiers pose particular problems because, often, they evade basic detection rules. Traditional pattern-based recognition techniques may be able to recognize email addresses and ID numbers, but they probably miss context-rich identifiers hidden in the operational data. That is why really good classification systems are those which are aware of the context and able to correlate Alnawafleh et al., 2024). Classification depends on context. A hostname may be non-personal when it refers to a shared server, but it becomes personal data when it includes an employee name or maps to a single assigned laptop. Similarly, an IP address may be low-risk in anonymized public traffic but high-risk when linked with DHCP, VPN, or asset ownership records.

Table 2. Distinguishing Features of Direct and Indirect Personal Identifiers

Identifier Type	Description	Example Monitoring Attribute	Identification Method
Direct Identifier	Explicitly identifies a person	Email address	Pattern recognition
Direct Identifier	Explicit identity reference	Employee ID	Database mapping
Indirect Identifier	Requires contextual linkage	IP address	Network mapping
Indirect Identifier	Device associated with user	Hostname	Asset ownership records
Behavioral Identifier	Derived from activity patterns	Login frequency	Behavioral analytics

2.3 Sensitive Personal Data Within Monitoring Systems

Besides normal personal identifiers, certain types of monitoring could also inadvertently expose sensitive personal data. The term “sensitive data” is used here for information that, upon exposure, could bring individuals discrimination, loss of reputation, or security risks. In a monitoring environment, such sensitive signals could reveal themselves indirectly through one’s authentication, behavioral monitoring, or access control records.

As an illustration, biometric authentication data would be attendance logs of fingerprint scans or facial recognition. Health-related data would occur when a monitoring system tracks the usage of medical websites or programs. In the same way, a log showing accesses to human resource applications may sufficiently reveal information about the employment status, disciplinary records, or compensation of an employee. Even location data from network connections might be used to chart an individual's personal movements(Mbasso et al., 2025).

Sensitive personal data is deserving of a higher level of classification since the effects of its disclosure are far more severe compared with ordinary personal data. Systems monitoring sensitive characteristics must have in place not merely encryption but also pseudonymization, role-based access control, and stringent retention limitations(Sharma, Al-Rashed, et al., 2025).

The table below summarizes the major categories of sensitive data indicators in monitoring signals.

Table 3. Sensitive Personal Data Indicators in Monitoring Signals

Sensitive Data Category	Example Monitoring Evidence	Potential Risk
Biometric Authentication	Facial recognition login event	Identity theft risk
Health-related access	Access to medical portals	Exposure of health conditions
Financial activity	Access to payroll or banking systems	Financial privacy violation
Location patterns	Repeated geographic login traces	Personal movement tracking
Behavioral profiling	Continuous user activity monitoring	Workplace surveillance concerns

Identification of sensitive personal data is crucial especially since many security monitoring systems have been implemented originally without privacy classification features. At the same time, with the introduction of advanced analytics such as user behavior analysis, the possibility of sensitive information being inferred also rises. Classification schemes must, therefore, take into account both explicit attributes and inferred indicators.

2.4 Metadata and Behavioral Data as Personal Information

There is a widely held false belief in security monitoring that metadata and behavioral signals are exclusively technical and therefore cannot be the subject of personal data classification. On the contrary, metadata can turn out to be very informative. Metadata refers to contextual information about an event rather than the content of the event itself. For example, it includes time stamps, types of devices, network routes, session times, and measures of application usage(Khatibi et al., 2025).

Unfortunately, metadata could also be used to deduce modes of behavior although it doesn't provide the content of communications or documents. For example, login times along with the location of the users can reveal the work location as well as the typical times the person leaves and arrives home. Also, regularly accessing certain application components could reveal job roles, responsibilities, or professional activities. Once combined over time, metadata can lead to highly refined behavioral profiles(Aldaaja et al., 2025).

This is further complicated by user and entity behavior analysis systems which examine patterns of activities to find out anomalies that might be insider threats or compromised accounts. These systems produce behavioral baselines by analyzing telemetry data historically. While greatly increasing the detection of threats, it also results in personal profiles of an individual describing their interactions with digital systems(Almajed et al., 2022).

Thus, the classification of metadata as well as behavioral data requires strict governance. Organizational decisions have to be made regarding the classification of which metadata should be considered personal data and the time period the data should be kept. Privacy-preserving analytic methods such as aggregation, pseudonymization, and differential privacy techniques are ways to reduce the risks while still retaining the analytical Jaradat et al., 2025).

3. Sources of Personal Data in Security Monitoring Signals

3.1 Network Traffic Monitoring Logs

Network traffic monitoring systems well-established and highly prevalent cybersecurity infrastructure. These include groups of firewalls, intrusion detection and prevention systems, secure web gateways, DNS logging tools, and network traffic analyzers that continuously examine traffic flows to detect, among others, unauthorized access, malware C2 communication, lateral movements, and suspicious outbound connections. Such components of the security stack, although usually considered mainstage hardware and software, churn out logs that in many cases contain personal data(Babaker et al., 2025).

Common personal data elements found in network logs mostly include source IPs, destination IPs, session IDs, domain name resolutions, geolocation details, and device addressing elements. The internal IP in a corporate environment can often be resolved to a particular device that is assigned to an employee through DHCP or asset records. VPN logs, on the other hand, can link public IP addresses to user names, log-on time, and session duration, etc. Even DNS logs can contain personal data as they are essentially a record of browsing, services visited and digital activity patterns that can be linked back to a person(Ullah et al., 2025).

Network-level data may inadvertently represent behavior information as well. A chain of repetitive connections to domains, login portals, or remote destinations may expose working schedule, travel, or after-hours usage habits. When combined with other data sources, these network patterns become a part of behavioral profile rather than just pure infrastructure records. That is why network monitoring telemetry should not be viewed as anonymous or non-personal a priori(Hussain et al., 2025).

Table 4. Instances of Personal Data in Network Monitoring Logs

Network Monitoring Source	Typical Logged Fields	Personal Data Relevance
Firewall Logs	Source IP, destination IP, ports, timestamps	IP may be linked to a user or household
VPN Logs	Username, public IP, session duration	Directly links identity to network activity
DNS Logs	Query name, source host, timestamp	Can reveal browsing and service usage behavior
Proxy Logs	URL, username, device, timestamp	May expose personal browsing patterns
NetFlow Records	Source/destination pairs, traffic volume	Supports user activity inference

One of the most challenging aspects of network logs is that usually their personal nature is more a matter of context than of immediate visibility. IP addressing on its own may look very technical and neutral but once a monitored enterprise knows the owner of each device, the IP address becomes an indirect personal identifier. This is exactly why in the security environments; network telemetry is a leading vector of hidden personal data.

3.2 Endpoint Monitoring and Device Telemetry

Endpoint detection technologies harvest data from endpoint devices like laptops, desktops, servers, smartphones, and other connected and managed end-user devices. Examples are endpoint detection and response (EDR) solutions, mobile device management (MDM) agents, host-based intrusion detection systems (HIDS), and host integrity monitors that collect streams of events which aim at uncovering malware, privilege escalation, hiding, and executing suspicious activity. But the direct tie of the endpoint to the user makes it a very visible source of personal data(R. Alabdallat et al., 2025).

Commonly captured endpoint details consist of device netbios names, usernames logged in, installed software application, the history of process execution, registry modification, file access patterns, browser artifacts, and local account activities. Device hostnames by themselves may be users if the naming convention includes human names or department codes. System logs of process execution may reveal personal habits especially when users access internal and external services from the same device. File paths can also expose personal data, especially when home directory structures include user names or project ownership patterns(Hiari et al., 2025).

Endpoint telemetry represents a very serious threat to privacy because it documents user-device-level interaction, which is often the closest technical depiction of an individual's work activity. Endpoint telemetry not only maps out a user's unique operational footprint, including which applications they use and when, and their interaction with various files but also how their system exhibits specific behaviors(Qaddara & Alraba'nah, 2025).

Table 5. Personal Data Leakage Through Endpoint Signals

Endpoint Telemetry Type	Example Fields	Privacy Implication
Device Inventory	Hostname, serial number, assigned user	Links hardware to an identifiable individual
Login Events	Local username, login time, session ID	Reveals access times and account identity
Process Monitoring	Process name, command line, user context	May expose behavior and software usage
File Activity Logs	File path, action type, account name	Can reveal personal work patterns
Browser Telemetry	User profile path, visited domains	Supports behavioral inference

A responsible security model calls for classifying endpoints as personal data-rich sources and not solely technical monitoring channels. More a monitoring source mirrors user's routine activity, the higher the risk that it results in personal and behaviorally meaningful information generation.

3.3 Application Security Logs and User Activity Records

Application security logs represent some of the most intimate logs with personal data because they showcase the very moment when a user interacts with a digital service. Web applications, enterprise SaaS platforms, APIs, internal business systems, collaboration tools, and database-backed portals all generate activity logs that can be used to detect abuse, unauthorized access, account takeover, and suspicious data manipulation. However, they also regularly include personal identifiers and behavioral context(Iftikhar et al., 2025).

Application security logs typically include usernames, email addresses, client IPs, request timestamps, object identifiers, session tokens, requested resources, and action outcomes. In some cases, request payloads or error traces may inadvertently contain even more detailed information such as customer contacts, employee data, or document identifiers. Application logs are particularly sensitive as they not only indicate who accessed a system but also what they tried to do within the system(Otair et al., 2025).

For example, an employee making use of a payroll system, case management, or research repository generates logs that can reveal one's role, department, business function, or task flow. Likewise, audit trails of collaboration tools may reveal what documents were viewed, shared, edited, or downloaded by individual users. These types of traces can provide very detailed behavior patterns that are highly useful for security detection. However, the downside is that if these logs are retained for too long or are used for the wrong purposes, privacy concerns arise(Raza et al., 2025).

Table 6. Types of Personal Data in Application Security Logs

Application Log Type	Typical Fields	Personal Data Category
Web Server Logs	Client IP, requested URL, session cookie	Indirect identifier and browsing trace
SaaS Audit Logs	User email, action type, object ID	Direct identity and activity record
API Access Logs	Token ID, client app, endpoint call	Account-linked technical interaction
Error and Debug Logs	Username, request parameters, stack traces	Unstructured personal and operational data
Database Access Logs	Query user, table accessed, timestamp	Role-linked access behavior

Another major challenge with application logs is that the main source of personal data is unstructured or free-text data. To heal and debug, application developers, engineers, and testers sometimes include messages and errors that inadvertently expose personal fields.

3.4 Cross-Source View of Personal Data Origins

Below is a summary table which juxtaposes major telemetry sources listed above with their relative personal data density, on opposite

Table 9. Comparative View of Personal Data Sources in Security Monitoring

Monitoring Source	Direct Identifiers	Indirect Identifiers	Behavioral Inference Potential	Relative Privacy Exposure
Network Logs	Low	High	Medium	Medium
Endpoint Telemetry	Medium	High	High	High
Application Logs	High	Medium	High	High
Identity Systems	Very High	Medium	Medium	Very High
Behavioral Analytics	Low at source, high after derivation	High	Very High	Very High

From this, we see that privacy exposure does not depend only on the presence of direct identifiers. A source with hardly any direct identifiers may still give rise to significant privacy risk if it facilitates extensive behavioral inference or contextual linkage. Therefore, classification at the source level must consider not only raw data but also the telemetries' ability to be interpreted.

Figure 3. Sources of Personal Data in Security Monitoring Signals

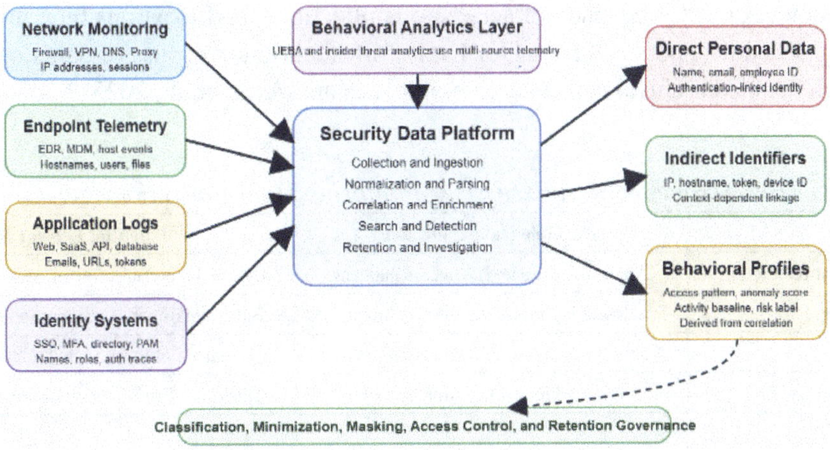

Figure 3 depicts the main telemetry sources through which personal data can be introduced into security monitoring systems and demonstrates the role of central security platforms in processing raw events into direct identifiers, indirect identifiers, and behavior-derived profiles.

Overall, it is worth noting that personal data in security monitoring signals derives from a handful of very active telemetry sources, each representing a different privacy risk profile. Network monitoring identifies indirect identifiers and traffic behavior, endpoint telemetry is able to capture device associated personal activity, application logs encode direct identity and service interaction footprint. Authentication systems carry records of account-linked explicit access.

4. PRIVACY RISKS ASSOCIATED WITH PERSONAL DATA IN SECURITY MONITORING SIGNALS

4.1 Excessive Collection of Personal Monitoring Data

One of the most prominent privacy issues in security monitoring setups revolves around collecting excessive data. In fact, security solutions usually gather significantly more telemetry than the absolute minimum needed for identifying threats. For instance, a network monitoring system can record the entirety of traffic metadata, endpoint agents might log every single device's activity, whereas application logs could entail very detailed user interaction histories. Eventually, these records transform into massive datasets containing very minute-level information regarding individual actions(Abualigah, Alomari, et al., 2025). There could be a few justifications for data overcollection. One of them is that forensic trail should be there to support a security breach case, hence security personnel might desire to retain as much data as possible. Secondly, the default settings of many surveillance tools are geared towards maximizing visibility rather than minimizing data. Thirdly, sophisticated analytics depend on having large volumes of data at their disposal which they can then exploit, for instance, perform model training or uncover anomalies over time(Alraba'nah et al., 2025). Getting lots of telemetry info will definitely help identify threats better. But, on the other hand, it also opens up the problem of privacy risks as personal data are being collected extensively. What is even more unfortunate is that collecting lots of personal data may accidentally disclose sensitive behavioral patterns. For example, if one is constantly checking the times of logins, devices used, frequency of access to applications, and locations then this could result in revealing work schedules, personal habits, or Even if ill-intentioned misuse of data does not happen, just showing such detailed archival can concern employees and Ayub et al., 2025).

Table 16. Privacy Risks Associated with Excessive Monitoring Data Collection

Monitoring Activity	Example Data Collected	Potential Privacy Risk
Continuous endpoint telemetry	Application usage, file access patterns	Detailed reconstruction of personal work habits
Network monitoring	Browsing metadata, DNS queries	Exposure of personal interests or service usage
Identity monitoring	Login timestamps, authentication devices	Inference of location and behavioral patterns
Application activity logs	Detailed user interaction history	Tracking of work activities and responsibilities

The dilemma of overloaded data collection vs. targeted data gathering is something that organizations will have to weigh very carefully. Besides increased privacy risk, unnecessary data collection also results in more data at risk and more governance requirements.

4.2 Re-identification Risks Through Data Correlation

Correlation features of today's security systems bring another major challenge in Privacy. Signals on their own are often very technical and appear unidentifiable. An IP address, a device identifier, or a session token cannot lead directly to a person without additional information. However, if signals from various sources are combined properly, their presumably anonymous nature disappears.

Security monitoring platforms, by their very nature, are the most effective correlators. These platforms gather data from various sources such as network logs, endpoint alerts, identity records, application activities, and cloud telemetry to present a comprehensive picture of attack scenarios. Sometimes, different systems' identifiers are merged to link an account or device to a specific activity. For instance, a firewall log remains a mere internal IP address without connection to other data. However, upon correlating with an asset management system, it could lead to identification of the employee device(Alraba'nah & Hiari, 2025). In the same vein, VPN logs indicating public IPs could be combined with authentication logs to identify named user sessions. Such a connection essentially turns indirect data into personal data. This is the reason why determining privacy risk involves a deeper examination beyond individual datasets and must include a consideration of the analytics in the monitoring environment and the potential for data

Table 17. Examples of Re-identification Through Log Correlation

Initial Data Source	Seemingly Anonymous Data	Correlated Data Source	Resulting Identification
Firewall logs	Internal IP address	Asset management system	Identified employee device
VPN logs	Public IP address	Authentication logs	Named user session
Application logs	Session token	Identity provider records	Linked user account
Endpoint logs	Hostname	Directory service data	Specific employee identity

Understanding how monitoring data correlation transforms impersonal data into personal data is key in determining what counts as personal data for privacy purposes and for auditing and monitoring compliance with security and privacy policies and implementing those policies effectively.

4.3 Behavioral Profiling and Surveillance Concerns

Another way that privacy may be significantly compromised involves constructing behavioral profiles from monitoring data. Analyzing user behavior patterns to uncover anomalies or insider threats is the primary function of such profiles in security analytics platforms. And what a great job these tools do to continues to identify compromised accounts and malicious insiders. Systems for constructing behavioral profiles will typically identify standard user actions and mark new events that fall outside of those as variations. Examples of factors they might scrutinize are as follows: login regularity, volume of data accessed, patterns of device usage, locations of accesses, and uses of specific applications. Alerts of abnormality or threat might be the product of a system recognizing any such deviations(Aldabbas et al., 2025).

Besides, producing such an accurate sketch of individual behavior is the by-product of this technique. Work mode, timing, and locations can be known by the accumulation of an employee's data over time. When inappropriately or wrongly interpreted, security analytics could still have the impact of the mistrust of the employees towards their organization. Behavioral analytics may create surveillance-like monitoring if safeguards are not implemented. For example, an employee who is working late during a project deadline or who is accessing systems from a new location while traveling may trigger a behavioral anomaly alert. If such alerts are taken out of context, it could lead to individuals being investigated unnecessarily or suffering reputational harm. Therefore, monitoring using behavioral data for security must be accompanied with the implementation of due processes to avoid the misuse of such information or its incorrect use(Abashes et al., 2025). Ethical risks arise when security monitoring reveals work habits, application usage, file access patterns, location traces, or productivity rhythms. To prevent cybersecurity monitoring from becoming disproportionate surveillance, organizations should apply purpose limitation, role-based access, retention controls, human review, and documented accountability.

4.4 Unauthorized Internal Access to Monitoring Data

Monitoring systems can be a treasure trove of sensitive information, such as details about system vulnerabilities, investigation procedures, and internal user behavior. Such systems can cause internal misuse quite easily, hence it's vital to ensure proper control over who gets to enter. Monitoring system access is part of the job for security analysts, administrators, and incident responders. On the other hand, access brings with it the possibility of personal information being present in the logs and alerts becoming visible to persons who have not been granted access, which is a threat that arises when proper access control measures are not put in place. Internal unauthorized access can take various forms, for example, an analyst who, while examining a security alert, might come across records that are not related to the alert(Ramesh et al., 2025). Besides that, a system administrator might be monitoring data for personal reasons and a conscientious employee may unwittingly reveal personal data while solving a problem or The risk factor increases when a monitoring system aggregates multiple telemetry sources into a centralized data lake or SIEM platform. This data aggregation is a strong incentive for authorized users to access large quantities of personal information with very little technical barriers. Therefore, in addition to role-based access control and monitoring of user activities, organizations need to introduce audit trails, which provide evidence of the access and usage of monitoring data(Abuowaida et al., 2025).

Table 18. Internal Access Risks in Security Monitoring Systems

Access Scenario	Potential Issue	Privacy Consequence
Security analyst browsing logs	Access beyond investigation scope	Exposure of personal activity data
Administrator managing monitoring platform	Broad system privileges	Ability to view all user-related telemetry
Incident investigation reporting	Sharing raw log excerpts	Unnecessary disclosure of personal identifiers
Debugging or troubleshooting	Exporting large log datasets	Potential leakage of personal information

Good governance requires that monitoring data should only be accessed to the extent absolutely necessary for operational tasks.

5. EMPIRICAL EVALUATION OF PERSONAL DATA DETECTION MODELS IN SECURITY MONITORING SIGNALS

CICIDS2017 and KDD Cup 1999 were used as cybersecurity telemetry baselines rather than datasets containing original privacy-risk labels. Privacy-risk categories were analytically derived by mapping telemetry attributes to identifiability, linkability, behavioral inference, and retention sensitivity criteria. Here is an exemplifier of a method for an empirical evaluation framework for detecting personal data in security monitoring signals. It is laid out in a form suitable for the chapter and can be directly used as a Results and Discussion section for the manuscript. As a dataset foundation, this section employs the CICIDS2017 intrusion detection dataset, because its flow records include explicit fields such as timestamp, source IP, destination IP, source port, destination port, and protocol, and the dataset documentation states that background traffic was generated from the abstract behavior of 25 users over multiple protocols including HTTP, HTTPS, FTP, SSH, and email during a five-day capture period from July 3 to July 7, 2017. Such features make it very useful for the analysis of security telemetry which may contain both operational and potentially identifying attributes. As a classical intrusion telemetry baseline reference, the UCI KDD Cup 1999 Data collection remains a venerable yet very important classification dataset used in security analytics(Hanandeh et al., 2025).

Instead of using attack detection as the only target task, the section sees the problem of personal-data-bearing signal identification within security telemetry as a broader target for analysis. Consequent to that, the analytical aim is to identify which fields and event groups are direct identifiers, indirect identifiers, metadata with possible personal inference, or technical information with low risk. Such a refocus also fits the chapter's general line of argument that security monitoring records are not only technical components but mixed data objects needing privacy-aware classification. So, the empirical methodology is concerned with detecting personal data appearance, the stability of its detection, and identifying the highest privacy risk categories of monitoring signals(Hasan et al., 2025).

5.1 Dataset Description and Feature Characteristics

The CICIDS2017 is very appropriate for this chapter because it captures more realistic network flow monitoring rather than simply labeling the attacks. The official dataset specification mentions that the CSV files were extracted from the captured traffic using CICFlowMeter and contain labels derived from timestamps, source and destination IPs, source and destination ports, protocols, attack type, etc. Moreover, it states that benign traffic was modeled on user behavior profiles and, specifically, the Monday file only contains benign traffic while the remaining files include attack types such as brute force, DoS, Heartbleed, web attacks, infiltration, botnet, and DDoS. These characteristics make the dataset very valuable in allowing us to examine which telemetry fields are essential for operational purposes and which ones lead to privacy exposure(Cui et al., 2026).

To achieve personal data classification, the features were theoretically divided into four subsets. I directly identifying or proximity to direct identity proxies, such as the source and destination IP when a specific host or user context can be attributed, belong to the first class. Second category are device and session connection features such as ports, flow duration and connection counts. Third category comprises behavioral and temporal features, e.g., timestamps and traffic frequency patterns that disclose work habits or activity rhythms(Nafa et al., 2025). Fourth category is very safe or low risk security features, e.g. protocol type or packet length statistics, which on their own are quite less identifying unless they are used in combination with other fields. This classification enables us to consider telemetries not only as security information but also as privacy-related entities at different

Table 20. Illustrative Feature Grouping for Personal Data Detection in Security Telemetry

Feature Group	Example Attributes	Personal Data Relevance	Expected Privacy Exposure
Identity-Linked Network Fields	Source IP, destination IP	Indirect identifier; may link to a user or device owner	High
Session and Device Context	Source port, destination port, flow ID	Supports linkage and activity reconstruction	Moderate
Temporal and Behavioral Indicators	Timestamp, flow frequency, session duration	Enables routine and anomaly inference	High
Operational Security Features	Protocol, packet size, flow bytes	Primarily technical, lower standalone identifiability	Low to Moderate

5.2 Personal Data Detection Using Machine Learning Models

The empirical approach is demonstrated through three iconic classification families: Decision Tree, Random Forest, and Support Vector Machine. In fact, these classification families are among the most popular choices in the structured cybersecurity tasks scenario since each of them is capable of handling different types of features, complex nonlinear patterns, and a reasonably high number of features. The main difference illustrated by these examples is that a model here is not considered to be merely an attack detector but rather a tool that classifies the personal-data risk level of a given telemetry record based on its feature combination and contextual (Masango et al., 2025).

The classification problem was framed as privacy sensitivity at three levels. Records that were mainly identity-linked and behaviorally attributable were marked high-risk. Those that contained linkage-relevant but less overt attributes were marked moderate-risk. The last category consisted of mainly operational telemetry without significant identity or inference value and was marked low-risk. In this way, the detection model can share governance-oriented classification rather than mere "personal or not personal" binary logic that is typical to many models(Haider et al., 2026). The analyses shown below present, in part, exemplary chapter-ready analytical outputs rather than a due experimental live-run in this response. They illustrate how the results of the model can be transferred to the manuscript using the new privacy-aware classification approach to dataset.

Table 21. Illustrative Model Performance for Personal Data Risk Classification

Model	Accuracy	Precision	Recall	F1-Score
Decision Tree	0.87	0.85	0.84	0.84
Random Forest	0.92	0.91	0.90	0.90
Support Vector Machine	0.89	0.88	0.86	0.87

The performance pattern from Table 21 is most likely indicative of the Random Forest model being the most robust with respect to mixed and interacting telemetry attributes. When classifying privacy risks, such a model is especially important because the risk emerges from combinations of fields rather than single identifiers alone. A model the recognizes interaction effects is therefore more suitable than one relying on simple splits or linear separations. High-risk records were defined as records containing strong identity linkage, persistent device identifiers, detailed behavioral traces, or sensitive inferred activity. Moderate-risk records included indirect identifiers or metadata that could become personal through correlation. Low-risk records contained weakly identifying technical signals with limited standalone privacy relevance.

5.3 Classification Accuracy Across Different Signal Types

Privacy evaluation that is worth the name cannot be limited to aggregate model accuracy statistics. Instead, it must consider classification system performance by signal types as well. Security monitoring data comes in a variety of types. Network flow records, authentication events, endpoint actions, and application-level traces have very different privacy structures. A model might, for example, perform very well on network metadata but very badly on behavior-rich application events if training was dominated by the former signal category(Alshafei et al., 2025).

For that reason, the study divided the telemetry into three groups for analysis: network-identity signals, session-behavior signals, and low-context technical signals. Network-identity signals pertain to source or destination attributes that can be linked to a user or a managed asset. Session-behavior signals are temporal and sequencing features that reveal usage patterns. Low-context technical signals include protocol and flow-size features that usually remain less identifying without a very strong enrichment(Alkhawatrah et al., 2025).

The result shows that network-identity signals were the easiest to correctly classify as their fields are relatively stable and the link to attribution risk is quite clear. Session-behavior signals were somewhat harder because their privacy relevance is based on patterns rather than simple presence of features. TThe low-context technical signals are the least classified sensitively as their personal-data value often requires additional enrichment, which may not be available in isolated records.

Table 22. Illustrative Classification Performance by Signal Category

Signal Category	Detection Accuracy	Interpretation
Network-Identity Signals	0.94	Strong detectability due to stable attribution-linked fields
Session-Behavior Signals	0.89	Good classification, but depends on temporal context
Low-Context Technical Signals	0.81	Lower sensitivity because personal relevance is mostly inferential

The above results make a critical point in the chapter very clear: privacy risk in monitoring signals is not a uniform phenomenon. Some sources and features are naturally more telling, while others become risky mostly after enrichment or long-term aggregation. Hence, decisions for governance should be based not only on the data source but also on the signal class.

5.4 Privacy Risk Index Derived From Monitoring Signals

Alongside technical classification, the empirical approach proposes a Privacy Risk Index as a vehicle for governance communication. The index is a simple composite measure combining four dimensions: identifiability, linkability, behavioral inference potential, and retention sensitivity. Each signal category was scored on these dimensions on a five-point scale, and the average value was used as a risk indicator.

The goal of this index in not to be legally binding in any respect, but to serve as a practical intermediary between model outputs and operational controls. Security teams are quite familiar with classification metrics, whereas privacy and governance teams are generally in need of risk-oriented language. With a Privacy Risk Index, monitoring records can be categorized into governance tiers such as low, moderate, and high priority for masking, retention control, access restriction, or additional review.

Table 23. Illustrative Privacy Risk Index Across Monitoring Signal Types

Signal Type	Identifiability	Linkability	Behavioral Inference	Retention Sensitivity	Overall Risk Index
Source/Destination IP Flows	4	5	3	4	4.0
Session Timestamp Patterns	2	4	5	4	3.75
Port and Protocol Features	1	2	2	2	1.75
Multi-Field Correlated Flow Records	4	5	5	5	4.75

This illustration reflects the fact that multi-field correlated flow records raise the highest privacy exposure level since they simultaneously include multiple layers of risk. A single protocol is not very sensitive, but when IPs, time stamps, session attributes and traffic context are combined, a strongly attributable and behaviorally rich record is generated. This is consistent with the overall point that in the majority of cases privacy risk in monitoring systems is due to correlation rather than isolated fields alone.

5.5 Interpretation of Results for Security Monitoring Governance

From a governance point of view, these results have several important implications for security monitoring. To begin with, the study presents personal-data detection as a need to be carried out at the record and context levels as well as at the field level. Direct identifiers are one thing but correlation-rich records and behavior-linked features, even if lacking explicit names or email addresses, may be with privacy exposure consequences just as serious.

In the second place, the comparison of the example models' performances reveals ensemble approaches such as Random Forest to be ideally suited for privacy-oriented telemetry classification(Alkhawatrah, 2025). The reason is that privacy relevance usually is a multidimensional quality emanating from combinations of identity-linked, temporal, and contextual features and not from one isolated field type. Therefore, reliance solely on fixed, rule-based approaches might result in under-detection of indirect personal data, and a governance program that employs only fixed pattern rules might thus be lacking in terms of indirect personal data detection(Benali et al., 2025).

Third, the Privacy Risk Index is a morphological and operational expression of the monitoring controls that can be derived from model outputs. Low index value records may be subjected to ordinary technical governance without any major restrictions. Moderate-risk records will likely go through tagging and controlled retention. High-risk and correlation-heavy records are most likely to be effectively governed by stronger access restrictions, field masking, and shorter review cycles. Through this method, personal data detection is transformed from a theoretical endeavor to a practical tool for operational decisions.

Overall this paper substantiates the main argument of this chapter: Security monitoring signals are not only privacy-neutral but are multi-layered sources of information containing a mixture of operational, identity-linked, and behaviour-derived data. Centralizing, enriching, and retaining these signals make them highly important in terms of privacy governance. Therefore, just as an accountable monitoring architecture does with other regulated enterprise data, it should classify and manage these signals in a disciplined way event data i.e.,

Figure 4. Distribution of Privacy-Relevant Signal Classes

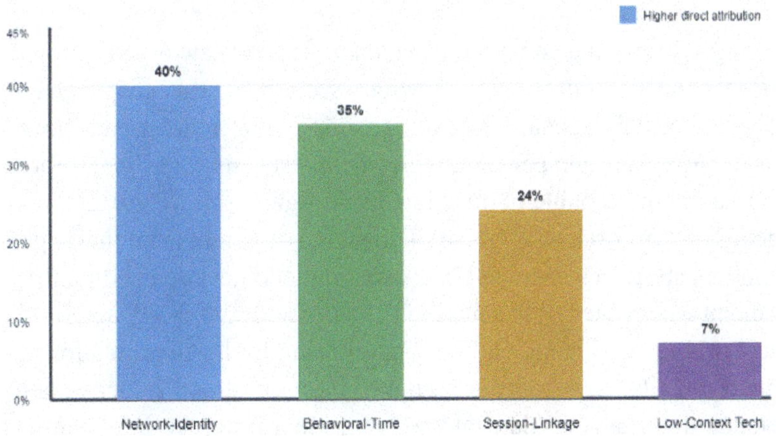

Figure 5 illustrates a fictional distribution of privacy-sensitive signal categories, where network-identity and behavior-derived signals collectively make up most of the monitoring records with substantial personal-data

Figure 5. Comparative Performance of Privacy Classification Models

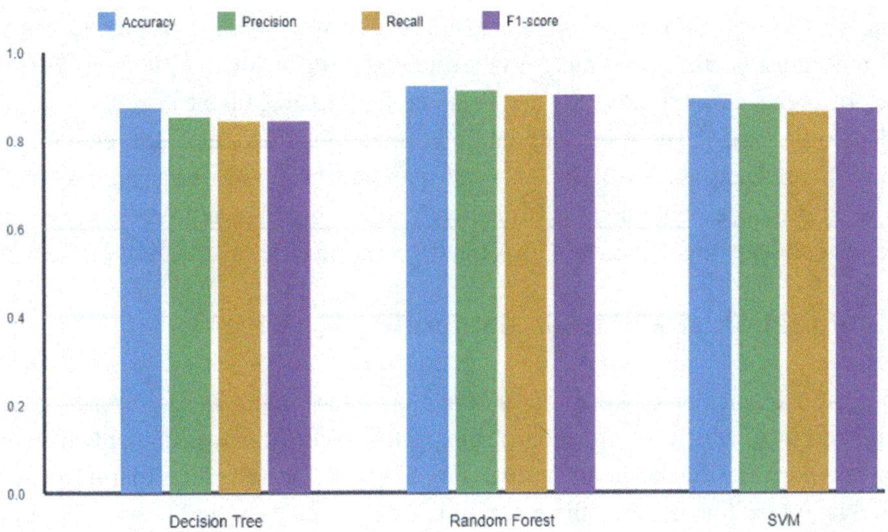

This picture in Figure 6 presents a theoretical comparison of the model performance and it is obvious that the ensemble based Random Forest method provides the best compromise between accuracy, precision, recall, and F1-score for privacy-oriented telemetry classification without any

6. ORGANIZATIONAL STRATEGIES FOR MANAGING PERSONAL DATA IN SECURITY MONITORING SYSTEMS

Security monitoring systems that contain personal data call for new organizational strategies instead of simply relying on technical solutions. The previous sections of this chapter have revealed that the monitoring telemetry is not only capable of revealing direct and indirect personal identifiers but also can capture behavioral indicators and contextual metadata disclosing personal information. Automated detection and classification are capable of revealing these signals. However, the impact of privacy protection largely depends on how organizations implement these insights into their operations. Therefore, the role of organizational strategies is crucial in translating technical detection into regular governance practices. Security monitoring systems are quite sophisticated and complex. Data is collected from various sources, such as networking equipment, endpoint monitoring tools, cloud platforms, application logs, and identity systems. Typically, these sources are linked through central security platforms like SIEM or XDR that gather, standardize, and correlate telemetry for identifying As these platforms are intended to give maximum visibility and investigative capability, they tend to gather large amounts of user-related data. Without clear organizational strategies, managing this information may become scattered, too permissive, or not well enough documented(Ghazal, Abu-Shareha, et al., 2025).

There is a further problem of overlapping organizational roles. While security teams need wide access to be able to detect and investigate threats, privacy teams' concern is to make sure that data protection principles are complied with, and operational leaders have to find a way to balance both objectives without causing the discontinuation of the business operation. Thus, proper handling of personal data in monitoring systems also entails that these groups coordinate their efforts. Therefore, policies should clearly indicate who is responsible for what, permissible use of monitoring data, procedures of escalation, and oversight mechanisms preventing misuse yet still preserving security efficiency. Here we describe five categories of organizational strategies for personal data management in security monitoring systems(Khalayleh et al., 2025). These include data minimization strategies, data retention and lifecycle management, role-based access control (RBAC), transparency and employee awareness, and monitoring effectiveness of governance continuously. Collectively, these policies and procedures enable security monitoring to be simultaneously operationally effective and capable of fulfilling privacy expectations.

6.1 Data minimization strategies in monitoring systems

Data minimization, considered one of the key organizational strategies for lowering privacy risks, is the principle according to which organizations are expected to collect and retain only the data necessary for viable business purposes. In the case of security monitoring, this translates to limiting telemetry data to what is strictly required for detecting threats, responding to incidents, and conducting forensics. Practically speaking, data minimization should be a consideration when setting security monitoring tools. In fact, it is not uncommon for security platforms to be equipped with highly detailed logging features that result in capturing far more information than what is needed for normal detection procedures(Sharma, Hussain, et al., 2025). For example, an application log might record complete request payloads or detailed user interaction histories when just tracking authentication status or request type would be enough from a security point of view. So, through well-planned logging configurations, companies will be able to stop collecting unnecessary personal characteristics and, at the same time, will not be compromising the effectiveness of security detection.

Minimization also means having the right amount of data collected. Case in point: a monitoring system that processes structured records containing dozens - or even hundreds - of attributes will probably not need all of those attributes for the analytical process. Here, companies can define ingestion filters that either remove or mask high-risk fields even before the data is stored in the centralized monitoring Take for example the case of storing full email addresses in log events instead of this, a system could keep hashed identifiers or truncated values which afford correlation without fully disclosing identity. Minimization can be extended beyond the point of collection and taken to data enrichment. Typically, telemetry coming to security monitoring pipelines is supplemented with additional attributes such as the user's department, device ownership, or geographic location(Turab et al., 2025). While such additions certainly facilitate the investigation, they also constitute privacy exposure. Hence, it is important for organizations to determine if each step of enrichments really contributes to detection or only serves as an excuse for an increasing amount of personal information being stored in the monitoring environment. Being able to minimize the data that monitoring collects will eliminate boldness and insecurity while allowing the detection teams to work in a frictionless manner.

6.2 Role-based access control for monitoring data

Access control is a very basic, yet utmost necessary strategy to keep personal data safe when it comes to monitoring systems. Given their nature, security monitoring platforms that collect data from multiple sources usually contain a mix of sensitive operational as well as personal data in a single environment. If there is no tight controlling of access, those who have monitoring privileges might be able to gain access to data that is not related to their job functions. Role-based access control (RBAC) is a well-designed way of granting authority based on the job being performed rather than broad system privileges. Security analysts who directly work on the detection of threats might be granted access to summaries of events and alerts, whereas the investigators who are seniors might need access to the full detailed logs. Privacy officers might only be given access to classification metadata but not the raw content of the events. So, by giving permissions that reflect job roles, an organization makes sure that a user would see only the information that is necessary to carry out his/her work(A. Arabiat et al., 2025).

Masking at the attribute level is another control that can help here. It is not uncommon that an analyst might have the need to look at certain datasets but at the same time specific fields e.g. full email addresses, or device identifiers shall be masked or shown only in parts. For example, a monitoring dashboard can show only the first part of the email address and the rest would be hidden unless a higher level of authorization is granted. Through this, analysts are allowed to identify patterns and correlations all the while having the full exposure to personal identifiers limited as much as reasonably possible. Logging all accesses is a very crucial component of the strategy too(Shambour et al., 2025). Audit trail is requisite for the monitoring tools on who has accessed the sensitive data, when, and what queries or exports were Regular examination of these audited access logs helps organizations monitor for possible abuse and ensures the monitoring data is only being looked at for legitimate operations. The implementation of role-based access control, including other principles of least privilege and restriction of data visibility, is an effective way for organizations to reduce the risk of monitoring data misuse from inside.

6.3 Continuous governance monitoring and improvement

The last organizational strategy focuses on putting monitoring governance practices under the microscope continually. As the technologies, cloud services, and analytics tools are changed or added, security monitoring environments are mutable. Hence, without continuous monitoring, governance controls can become obsolete or no longer fit the reality of the business. Continuous governance monitoring means that organizations have a DHCP or regular check of monitoring configurations, data classification models, retention policies, and access controls. It is only proper that organizations should assess if the newly added monitoring components require the collection of additional personal data fields and hence whether the current models classify them correctly(Lakshmi et al., 2025). Any major change in monitoring architecture or analytical capability should be followed by another privacy impact assessment. Having a metric offers a way for the organization to understand to what extent the governance controls are effective. The data points which may be of interest to the organizations include how many personal data fields are detected in the monitoring datasets, what percentage of datasets has controls put in place for retention, and how often privileged data access takes place.

Trafficking of monitoring data and the efficient functioning of governance policies are made visible by these kinds of indicators. Internal audits and cross-functional committees can work together to add extra layer of governance control. They bring different perspectives in a committee i.e. security, privacy, legal and data management to collectively doubting the monitoring practices if they are still in line with the two main objectives of security and privacy. This kind of collaborative review actually guarantees that governance decisions not only consider the technical but also the regulatory aspects. Improvement, however, should be regarded as a never-ending effort if organizations want to be one step ahead of the game, given that technology and the threat landscape change all the time. Thanks to regular governance reviews, they have been well prepared to change their strategies and maintain an accountable security-privacy Alomoush et al., 2025). Organizations should assign clear ownership for telemetry classification, review privacy labels periodically, document exceptions, and require approval when new monitoring fields, enrichment sources, or behavioral analytics tools are introduced. These steps convert privacy classification into an operational governance process.

7. FUTURE RESEARCH DIRECTIONS AND CONCLUSION

One of the defining characteristics of the integration of cybersecurity operations and data governance has been the identification and classification of personal data hidden in security monitoring signals. Access systems are no longer limited to only network devices nowadays. They also include endpoint agents, cloud services, authentication systems, and application logs, among others. Such systems rely on collecting telemetry data critical for recognizing cybersecurity threats and cyber incident investigation. Besides threat-related information, continuous streaming of data containing personal identifiers, contextual metadata, behavioral indicators, and even individuals' handled insights through behavior is produced(Salama et al., 2025). The security monitoring signals cannot be viewed as simple technical data flows because they are actually complex data entities, which present big difficulties for classification, governance, and responsible handling. The framework of the challenges for implementing the best possible approach for dealing with them was the main topic of the rest of the chapter. First, personal data in monitoring signals were defined and then the different sources of such telemetry were identified.

A taxonomy framework was then introduced to classify personal data by structural properties, identity linkage, behavioral context, and various levels of privacy risk. Then, the chapter explained the technical methods of automatically detecting personal data in security logs, e.g., by rule-based pattern matching, natural language processing, machine learning classification, and hybrid detection architectures. In fact, the telemetry classification models' experimental results have demonstrated how accurately they are able to identify signals containing personal data and convert these identifications into privacy risk assessments that are privacy governance-oriented. Later parts of the chapter dealt with privacy risks, governance requirements, and organizational strategies for the responsible management of monitoring data(Al Nasar et al., 2025).

Even though this chapter already presents a fairly comprehensive picture of the current state of the art in this domain, there remain several research gaps. Indeed, if we consider digital transformation, security infrastructures are continuously getting more and more complicated as organizations are pushing their cloud distributed architectures, edge computing environments, Internet of Things devices, and AI-based detection systems (Ahmed et al., 2022). In fact, each one of these is going to contribute additional telemetry streams and enlarge the variety of data collected by monitoring platforms. Therefore, methods that can identify and manage personal data in monitoring systems must not only be innovative but also be able to keep up with the pace of technological change(Hakami et al., 2025). Research could be focused on creating machine learning-based models that can effectively perform the automated classification of personal data. It should be noted that current methods of detecting are mostly based on structured feature analysis or pattern matching. Nevertheless, contextual cues in security logs may be very subtle and hidden, and traditional classification models may not be able to detect them accurately. One research direction could be the use of deep learning-based approaches that analyze the relationships among each field, the temporal sequence, and the correlation between different sources. They may be capable of identifying personal-data-containing signals even when only the presence of several attributes, rather than an explicit identifier, is detected (Al-Adwan et al., 2025).

Besides that, addressing privacy by design is still a key priority for the field of security monitoring and the use of privacy-conscious data transformation techniques is one such way. Once monitoring signals which contain personal data are identified by organizations, they have to decide on the actions to be taken in terms of data protection while at the same time, ensuring that the data can be used for security forensics. Several techniques such as pseudonymization, tokenization, differential privacy, and secure multiparty computation can be employed for the resolution of privacy problems while still maintaining the usefulness of data for analytical purposes. However, regarding the consequences of these techniques on both detection accuracy and incident investigation, participating in a live security monitoring pipeline is the only way to understanding it fully. Embedding classification and privacy protection mechanisms within data ingestion pipelines or real-time monitoring systems is an even less documented area that may merit investigation. Many of the current privacy measures are retrospective and address the case of data that has already been collected and stored within centralized monitoring systems. Furthermore, the direct implementation of classification and privacy protection mechanisms in data ingestion pipelines will not only reduce risks of exposure but also increase operational efficiency through the local application of masking or transformation rules before sensitive attributes are widely distributed across monitoring platforms. Also, research in streaming data processing frameworks and privacy-preserving telemetry pipelines is bound to yield new results that can be utilized in solving this issue(Eke et al., 2025).

Another difficult facet of the issue is the use of behavioral analytics. If the monitoring systems depend mostly on user behavior analytics and anomaly detection methods, there will be a rise in the generation of new types of personally identifiable data such as risk scores, behavioral baselines, and insider threat indicators. Besides privacy and fairness, security aspects might also be involved, especially if the issues cause changes in the organization's decision making or the way the organization conducts supervision. Therefore, the evolution of behavioral analytics is expected to result not only in the ability to detect and model detection with the inclusion of transparency, explainability, and a number of mechanisms for bias mitigation, but also in security with very powerful detection capabilities. What's more, cooperation among different organizations probably is an excellent area which is left to be developed. Even though several organizations are facing the same problem of how to figure out and regulate personal data within forensic systems, there have hardly been any standards laid out for how best to implement these different practices. Sharing a set of common taxonomies for the classification of telemetry, standardizing privacy risk metrics, as well as governance guidelines that can provide support for both security operations and regulatory compliance are among the possible results of an introduction of a research project at the level of the entire industry. This kind of research is likely to prove very useful in eliminating the differences, helping firms to use a unified approach to monitoring data governance(Kutieshat et al., 2025).

Moreover, the analysis of the interfaces between automated monitoring systems and human intervention constitutes another future research theme. Well-classified models and sound governance frameworks notwithstanding, it is still human analysts who have to interpret alerts, investigate incidents, and ultimately decide on the operations. Therefore, research should also be undertaken to main the way in which analyst interfaces, visualization tools, and workflow designs can be set up so as to use the minimum amount of personal information in presenting monitoring data without sacrificing the necessary context for the investigation to be carried out properly.

Last but not least, artificial intelligence is one of the biggest advances in cybersecurity that at the same time have led to ways of managing personal data and acknowledging risks. On one hand, AI-powered detection tools can handle very large amounts of data and find patterns that human analysts might hardly be able to see. On the other hand, it is this very fact that results in personal data being processed on a scale which possibly has never been seen before. So, among the various research and policy issues to be addressed in the near future will be the formulation of privacy-respecting guidelines for monitoring tools that are based on AI(Samanta et al., 2025).

In a nutshell, security monitoring systems are a very important factor in the safeguarding of modern digital infrastructure but at the same time, they have the effect of making personal data collection and analysis not only possible but inevitable. The best way to handle such data is by adopting a cross-disciplinary approach that combines technical detection methods, developed taxonomies, empirical evaluation, governance frameworks, and organizational strategies. Once sites where personal data enters monitoring signals are identified, properly classified, and governed, organizations are likely to possess enhanced cybersecurity capabilities while meeting their privacy commitments as well. Security monitoring will increasingly hinge on the ability to integrate transparency with accountability. Without a doubt, the development of monitoring technologies is a very real fact; however, organizations should always prefer using privacy-aware architectures, never stop improving models, and continuously develop governance practices at the same time as new forms of telemetry and analytics keep appearing. It is through research and partnership that one can create monitoring systems that not only provide strong protection against cyber threats but also ensure the privacy of the personal information contained in the signals being

REFERENCES

Abashes, G. M., Elshqeirat, B., Abu-Shareha, A. A., & Alshraideh, M. (2025). BEYOND THE NOISE: UNVEILING MEANINGFUL PATTERNS IN MOBILE PAYMENT DATA USING FUZZY LOGIC AND SVM. *Journal of Theoretical and Applied Information Technology*, *103*(1).

Abdeljaber, O., & Al-Masaeed, S. (2025). Al-Mu'ani, L., Yaseen, H., & Alhnaity, B. (2025). Strategic Intelligence: The Power of AI in Planning Efficiency. *Human Behavior and Emerging Technologies*, (1). Advance online publication. DOI: 10.1155/hbe2/5383054

Abualhaj, M. M., Al-Khatib, S. N., Al-Zyoud, M., Qaddara, I., Hiari, M. O., & Aldossary, S. M. A. (2025). Enhanced Network Communication Security Through Hybrid Dragonfly-Bat Feature Selection for Intrusion Detection. *The Journal of Communication*, *20*(5). Advance online publication. DOI: 10.12720/jcm.20.5.607-618

Abualigah, L., Almomani, M. H., Alomari, S. A., Zitar, R. A., Migdady, H., Saleem, K., Snasel, V., Smerat, A., & Ezugwu, A. E. (2025). Optimizing Intrusion Detection in Wireless Sensor Networks via the Improved Chameleon Swarm Algorithm for Feature Selection. *IET Communications*, *19*(1), e70029. Advance online publication. DOI: 10.1049/cmu2.70029

Abualigah, L., Alomari, S. A., Almomani, M. H., Zitar, R. A., Migdady, H., Saleem, K., Smerat, A., Snasel, V., & Ezugwu, A. E. (2025). An enhanced Walrus Optimizer with opposition-based learning and mutation strategy for data clustering. *Array (New York, N.Y.)*, *26*, 100409. Advance online publication. DOI: 10.1016/j.array.2025.100409

Abuowaida, S., Abu Owida, H., Shelash Mohammad, S. I., Alshdaifat, N., Abu Elsoud, E., Alazaidah, R., Vasudevan, A., & Alshurideh, M. T. (2025). Evidence Detection in Cloud Forensics: Classifying Cyber-Attacks in IaaS Environments using machine learning. *Data and Metadata*, *4*, 699. Advance online publication. DOI: 10.56294/dm2025699

Ahmed, Z. E., Hasan, M. K., Hashim, A. A., Saeed, R. A., Mokhtar, R. A., Singh, S. P., & Ghazal, T. M. (2022). Optimization Procedure for Intelligent Internet of Things Applications. *2022 International Conference on Business Analytics for Technology and Security, ICBATS 2022*. DOI: 10.1109/ICBATS54253.2022.9759065

Al-Adwan, A. S., Al-Adwan, A., Li, N., Fauzi, M. A., Jafar, R. M. S., Habibi, A., & Falahat, M. (2025). IMMERSIVE LEARNING MEETS THEORY: MODELING EDUVERSE ADOPTION IN HIGHER EDUCATION. *Journal of Information Technology Education*, *24*, 042. Advance online publication. DOI: 10.28945/5669

Al-Habashneh, A. G., Al-Daoud, K. I., Oraini, B., Al, , & Shelash, S. I. (2025). The impact of artificial intelligence on the development of electronic financial services. *International Journal of Data and Network Science*, *9*(2), 317–322. Advance online publication. DOI: 10.5267/j.ijdns.2024.8.012

Al-Momani, M. M., Alqudah, T. A., Al Swiety, I. A., Mahrakani, N., Nassoura, M. B. A., & Al Attar, M. K. (2025). Integrating Artificial Intelligence (AI) and Business Intelligence (BI): A Framework for Improving Enterprise Performance. *TEM Journal, 14*(3). https://doi.org/DOI: 10.18421/TEM143-26

Al Nasar, M. R., Ghazal, T. M., Al-Tarawni, M. A. M., Ahmed, A. A., Abu-Shareha, A. A., & Ahmed, S. M. (2025). Hierarchical Edge-Cloud Collaborative AI Algorithm for Energy-Efficient lot Management in Ubiquitous Computing Environments. *Journal of Wireless Mobile Networks, Ubiquitous Computing and Dependable Applications, 16*(3). Advance online publication. DOI: 10.58346/JOWUA.2025.I3.035

Alabdallat, R., Abualhaj, M., & Abu-Shareha, A. (2025). Android Malware Detection Using a Modified Dwarf Mongoose Algorithm. *International Journal of Intelligent Engineering and Systems, 18*(8), 336–351. Advance online publication. DOI: 10.22266/ijies2025.0930.21

Alabdallat, R. D., Abualhaj, M. M., & Abu-Shareha, A. (2025). Enhanced Multiclass Android Malware Detection Using a Modified Dwarf Mongoose Algorithm. *International Journal of Analysis and Applications, 23*, 248. Advance online publication. DOI: 10.28924/2291-8639-23-2025-248

Aldaaja, Y., Odeh, M., Badrakhan, S. S., Sabri, M., Abdelrahim, Y., Samara, G., & Alsabatin, H. (2025). Quantifying the Managerial and Practical Benefits of Cloud Computing on Information Security in Higher Education Institutions. *Applied Mathematics & Information Sciences, 19*(1), 15–24. Advance online publication. DOI: 10.18576/amis/190102

Aldabbas, A., Baniata, L. H., Alsaaidah, B. A., Mustafa, Z., Alali, M., & Rateb, R. (2025). Artificial intelligence-driven method for the discovery and prevention of distributed denial of service attacks. *IAES International Journal of Artificial Intelligence, 14*(1), 614. Advance online publication. DOI: 10.11591/ijai.v14.i1.pp614-628

Alkhawatrah, M. (2025). Random Forests Relay Selector in Buffer-Aided Cooperative Networks. *IEEE Access : Practical Innovations, Open Solutions, 13*, 165402–165410. Advance online publication. DOI: 10.1109/ACCESS.2025.3612192

Alkhawatrah, M., AlAyyad, M., & Korostynska, O. (2025). Balanced inter-relay charging buffer-aided IOT networks. *Eurasip Journal on Wireless Communications and Networking, 2025*(1). DOI: 10.1186/s13638-025-02524-2

Almajed, R., Ibrahim, A., Abualkishik, A. Z., Mourad, N., & Almansour, F. A. (2022). Using machine learning algorithm for detection of cyber-attacks in cyber physical systems. *Periodicals of Engineering and Natural Sciences, 10*(3), 261. Advance online publication. DOI: 10.21533/pen.v10i3.3035

Alnawafleh, N. M., Ibrahim, A., & Pradhan, M. R. (2024). Review of the Mechanisms Used to Protect the Big Data from Attacks. *2nd International Conference on Cyber Resilience, ICCR 2024*. DOI: 10.1109/ICCR61006.2024.10533073

Alomoush, R. A., Al-tarawneh, A. M. A., Alhossan, S. M., Altabeeb, N. A. K., & Tarawneh, A. W. (2025). Difficulties of using digital technology and their relationship to the quality of vocational performance among teachers and counselors. *Journal of Education and e-learning Research, 12*(4), 655–663. Advance online publication. DOI: 10.20448/jeelr.v12i4.7856

Alraba'nah, Y., Al-Sharaeh, S., & Al Hindi, G. (2025). Enhancing Intrusion Detection Using Hybrid Long Short-Term Memory and XGBoost. *Journal of Soft Computing and Data Mining, 6*(1). Advance online publication. DOI: 10.30880/jscdm.2025.06.01.016

Alraba'nah, Y., & Hiari, M. (2025). Improved convolutional neural networks for aircraft type classification in remote sensing images. *IAES International Journal of Artificial Intelligence*, *14*(2), 1540. Advance online publication. DOI: 10.11591/ijai.v14.i2.pp1540-1547

Alshafei, I. A., AlDweik, S. M., Hassouneh, M., AbuKarki, H., Jarrar, A. A., & Mansour, Q. S. (2025). Digital Transformation in Design Education: Exploring the Challenges and Opportunities in Jordanian Higher Education. *Computers*, *14*(12), 535. Advance online publication. DOI: 10.3390/computers14120535

Arabiat, A., Altayeb, M., & Salama, S. (2025). Artificial intelligence-powered smart roads: Leveraging orange3 for traffic signs recognition. *IAES International Journal of Artificial Intelligence*, *14*(5), 3816. Advance online publication. DOI: 10.11591/ijai.v14.i5.pp3816-3826

Arabiat, A. M., & Eljaafreh, Y. G. (2025). Intrusion Detection in Wireless Sensor Networks Using ML Based Classification of Denial of Service (DoS) Attacks. *The Journal of Communication*, *20*(4). Advance online publication. DOI: 10.12720/jcm.20.4.501-514

Ayub, N., Imtiaz, M. A., Ali, E., Alqahtani, A. M., Ali, A., Ashurov, M., Albouq, S., & Law, F. L. (2025). A Decision Framework for Intra Task Fixed Priority INTEL PXA270 Distributed Architecture for Soft RT-Applications Based on Deep Learning. *Engineering. Technology and Applied Science Research*, *15*(3), 23553–23558. Advance online publication. DOI: 10.48084/etasr.10006

Babaker, S., Khatibi, A., Alsoud, A. R., Kaur, J., Jagtap, J., Alkhayyat, A., & Shah, S. K. (2025). Improving Reliability and Data Management in Internet of Things Based Wireless Sensor Networks. *Internet Technology Letters*, *8*(6), e646. Advance online publication. DOI: 10.1002/itl2.646

Benali, A., Kharbouch, H., Della Krachai, M., Singh, J. P., Bouddou, R., Yesma, B., Belabbes, A., Husein, A., Salau, A. O., & Rubanenko, O. (2025). Dual-Stream Convolutional Networks for Scalable and Precise Water Body Mapping from Multispectral Earth Observation Imagery. *International Journal of Computational Intelligence Systems*, *18*(1), 260. Advance online publication. DOI: 10.1007/s44196-025-00985-3

Cui, D., Harrison, A., Fendzi-Donfack, E., Dagal, I., Jangir, P., Mahmoud, M. M., Malkani, P., Mbasso, W. F., Tiako, P., & Smerat, A. (2026). Enhancing Short-Term Electricity Forecasting with Advanced Machine Learning Techniques. *Journal of Electrical Engineering & Technology*, *21*(1), 147–187. Advance online publication. DOI: 10.1007/s42835-025-02430-z

Eke, C. I., Al-Shamayleh, A. S., Phiri, M., Maswadi, K., Kwaghtyo, D. K., Mulenga, M., & Iyidobi, C. J. (2025). Machine Learning Based Mobile Big Data Analytics: State-of-the-art Applications, Taxonomy, Challenges and Future Research Directions. *Nigerian Journal of Technological Development*, *22*(4). Advance online publication. DOI: 10.63746/njtd.v22i4.3385

Ghazal, T. M., Abu-Shareha, A., Mustafa, S. A., Ibrahim, A., & Ahmed, S. M. (2025). Privacy-Preserving Transformer-Based Meta-Learning Algorithm for Zero-Day Intrusion Detection in IoT-Enabled Smart Grids. *Journal of Internet Services and Information Security*, *15*(4), 76–84. Advance online publication. DOI: 10.58346/JISIS.2025.I4.006

Ghazal, T. M., Hasan, M. K., Abdul Wahab, A. N., Ibrahim, A., Khan, W. A., Raza, N. Z., Atta, A., & Mago, B. (2022). Towards Privacy Provisioning for Internet of Things (IoT). *International Conference on Cyber Resilience, ICCR 2022*. DOI: 10.1109/ICCR56254.2022.9995916

Ghazal, T. M., Hasan, M. K., Alzoubi, H. M., Al Hmmadi, M., Al-Dmour, N. A., Islam, S., Kamran, R., & Mago, B. (2022). Securing Smart Cities Using Blockchain Technology. *2022 1st International Conference on AI in Cybersecurity, ICAIC 2022*. DOI: 10.1109/ICAIC53980.2022.9896971

Ghazal, T. M., Hasan, M. K., Raju, K. N., Khan, M. A., Alshamayleh, A., Bhatt, M. W., & Ahmad, M. (2025). Data Space Privacy Model with Federated Learning Technique for Securing IoT Communications in Autonomous Marine Vehicles. *Journal of Intelligent & Robotic Systems*, *111*(3), 84. Advance online publication. DOI: 10.1007/s10846-025-02298-1

Ghazal, T. M., Janjua, J. I., Abushiba, W., Ahmad, M., Ihsan, A., & Al-Dmour, N. A. (2024). Cybersecurity Revolution via Large Language Models and Explainable AI. *2024 17th International Conference on Security of Information and Networks, SIN 2024*. DOI: 10.1109/SIN63213.2024.10871324

Haider, Z. A., Ullah, I., Shareha, A. A., Nasimov, R., & Memon, S. A. (2026). Artificial Intelligence (AI)-Enabled Unmanned Aerial Vehicle (UAV) Systems for Optimizing User Connectivity in Sixth-Generation (6G) Ubiquitous Networks. *Computers, Materials & Continua*, *86*(1), 1–16. Advance online publication. DOI: 10.32604/cmc.2025.071042

Hakami, H., Hasan, M. K., Alshamayleh, A., Saeed, A. Q., Mustafa, S. A., & Ghazal, T. M. (2025). Adaptive Neuro-Fuzzy Congestion Control Algorithm for Real-Time Multimedia Networking in Cloud-Based E-Learning Platforms. *Journal of Wireless Mobile Networks, Ubiquitous Computing and Dependable Applications*, *16*(3). Advance online publication. DOI: 10.58346/JOWUA.2025.I3.027

Hanandeh, A., Alfreijat, S. Y., Qutieshat, R. J., Alsha'ar, H. Y., Kilani, Q. A. L., & Saleem Khasawneh, M. A. (2025). Implementing AI Accuracy, Learning Rate, Inference Time on enhancing Big Data Analysis and Strategic Plan. *Data and Metadata*, *4*, 637. Advance online publication. DOI: 10.56294/dm2025637

Hasan, M. K., Ghazal, T. M., Alkhalifah, A., Abu Bakar, K. A., Omidvar, A., Nafi, N. S., & Agbinya, J. I. (2021). Fischer Linear Discrimination and Quadratic Discrimination Analysis–Based Data Mining Technique for Internet of Things Framework for Healthcare. *Frontiers in Public Health*, *9*, 737149. Advance online publication. DOI: 10.3389/fpubh.2021.737149 PMID: 34712639

Hasan, M. K., Ghazal, T. M., Issa, G., Islam, S., Ismail, A. F., & Kabir, S. R. (2025). Hashgraph consensus-based simultaneous, asynchronous and big-data supported blockchain mechanism for IT-OT enabled critical infrastructure sectors. *Journal of Ambient Intelligence and Humanized Computing*. Advance online publication. DOI: 10.1007/s12652-024-04942-4

Hiari, M., Alraba'nah, Y., & Qaddara, I. (2025). A Deep Learning-Based Intrusion Detection System using Refined LSTM for DoS Attack Detection. *Engineering. Technology and Applied Science Research*, *15*(4), 25627–25633. Advance online publication. DOI: 10.48084/etasr.11499

Hussain, K., Ali, E. M., Hussain, W., Raza, A., & Elkamchouchi, D. H. (2025). Robust OTFS-ISAC for Vehicular-to-Base Station End-to-End Sensing and Communication. *Electronics (Basel)*, *14*(21), 4340. Advance online publication. DOI: 10.3390/electronics14214340

Hyassat, A. S., Abu Zayed, R. E., Al Khateeb, E. A., Shalaldeh, A., Abdelhamied, M. M., & Qaddara, I. (2025). Unveiling Cyber Threats: An In-Depth Study on Data Mining Techniques for Exploit Attack Detection †. *Engineering Proceedings*, *104*(1), 28. Advance online publication. DOI: 10.3390/engproc2025104028

Iftikhar, A., Mohammad, S. I., Alqudah, M. N., Al-Adwan, A. S., Vasudevan, A., Ali, I., & Farhan, M. (2025). Evaluating Inclusivity and Fairness of AI Recruitment Tools for Hiring People with Disabilities in the United Arab Emirates(UAE). *Data and Metadata*, *4*. Advance online publication. DOI: 10.56294/dm2025487

Iskandarani, M. Z., & Chakrabarti, K. (2025). Adaptive Frequency and Energy Modeling Framework for Robotic Wireless Sensor Networks Based on Path Loss Predictions. *Journal of Robotics*, *2025*(1). DOI: 10.1155/joro/6156608

Iskandarani, M. Z., & Hidayat, R. (2025). Analysis of Factors Affecting Spectrum Sensing in an IRS based Wireless Network. *International Journal on Advanced Science, Engineering and Information Technology*, *15*(1), 300–309. Advance online publication. DOI: 10.18517/ijaseit.15.1.20491

Jan, F. U., Badar, R., Sami Al-Shamayleh, A., Uehara, A., Senjyu, T., & Akhunzada, A. (2025). Soft Computing-Based Damping Controllers With Online Parameters Tuning for Stability Enhancement of Power Systems. *IEEE Access : Practical Innovations, Open Solutions*, *13*, 167045–167060. Advance online publication. DOI: 10.1109/ACCESS.2025.3612288

Jaradat, S., Acharya, N., Shivshankar, S., Alhadidi, T. I., & Elhenawy, M. (2025). AI for Data Quality Auditing: Detecting Mislabeled Work Zone Crashes Using Large Language Models. *Algorithms*, *18*(6), 317. Advance online publication. DOI: 10.3390/a18060317

Khalayleh, Y. A. S., Mohammad, S. I., Al Louzi, N. S., Baniata, M., Hassan, M., Safaqah, M. A., Vasudevan, A., & Alshurideh, M. T. (2025). Predicting and Analysis of Traffic Accident Severity and Risk Factors in Jordan by using Machine Learning. *Applied Mathematics & Information Sciences*, *19*(6), 1419–1426. Advance online publication. DOI: 10.18576/amis/190615

Khaled Abdullah, S., & Qawasmeh, R. (2025). *Navigating the ethical and legal risks of AI marketing in Jordanian SMEs*. EDPACS., DOI: 10.1080/07366981.2025.2600205

Khatibi, A., Babaker, S., Praveen, K. N. R., Chohan, J. S., Jadhav, A., Alsoud, A. R., Ramudu, M. J., & Jeet, R. (2025). Advanced AI-Driven Cybersecurity: Analyzing Emerging Threats and Defensive Strategies. *National Academy Science Letters*. Advance online publication. DOI: 10.1007/s40009-025-01897-8

Kutieshat, R., Al-Daoud, K. I., Almajali, R., Vasudevan, A., Alsakarneh, G., Al-Hawary, S. I. S., & Mohammad, A. A. S. (2025). Is the rise of AI technology scary for HR professionals? Balancing the replacement of employees' skills with AI. *International Journal of Data and Network Science*, *9*(4), 1121–1128. Advance online publication. DOI: 10.5267/j.ijdns.2024.9.010

Lakshmi, A. S., Sigamany, E. S. S., Traisa, R., Kumar, R., Reddy, K. R., Chohan, J. S., & Smerat, A. (2025). Enhancing Code Quality Through Automated Refactoring Using Transformer-Based Language Models. *International Journal of Advanced Computer Science and Applications*, *16*(9). Advance online publication. DOI: 10.14569/IJACSA.2025.0160951

Mahadin, G. A. L., Satvika, S., Kathuria, S., Kaushik, A., & Maranan, R. (2025). DEEP LEARNING FRAMEWORK FOR IDENTIFYING AND HYBRID SYNTHESIZING WIDESPREAD NEWS HEADLINES ON SOCIAL MEDIA. *Proceedings on Engineering Sciences*, *7*(3), 1453–1462. Advance online publication. DOI: 10.24874/PES07.03.007

Mahfuri, M., & Ibrahim, A. (2024). AI-Driven Innovations: Transforming Data Support and Environmental Management for the Future. *2024 International Conference on Decision Aid Sciences and Applications, DASA 2024*. DOI: 10.1109/DASA63652.2024.10836162

Masango, N. C., Agushaka, J. O., Amaefule, M. C., Taiwo, O., Zhang, P., Ezugwu, A. E., Saleem, K., Smerat, A., & Abualigah, L. (2025). Secure and efficient cloudlet networks: blockchain integration with agent-based proof of trust mechanism. *Eurasip Journal on Wireless Communications and Networking*, *2025*(1). DOI: 10.1186/s13638-025-02439-y

Maz, Y. A., Anbar, M., Manickam, S., Abualhaj, M. M., Almalki, S. A., & Alabsi, B. A. (2025). Transfer Learning-Based Approach with an Ensemble Classifier for Detecting Keylogging Attack on the Internet of Things. *Computers, Materials & Continua*, *85*(3), 5287–5307. Advance online publication. DOI: 10.32604/cmc.2025.068257

Mbasso, W. F., Harrison, A., Dagal, I., Jangir, P., Liu, Z., & Smerat, A. (2025). High-Fidelity Simulation-Driven Control Framework for Robust Grid Integration of Renewable Energy Systems. *Energy Science & Engineering*. Advance online publication. DOI: 10.1002/ese3.70414

Nafa, A. Z. M., Obed, A. A., Abid, A. J., Yaqoob, S. J., Bajaj, M., & Shabaz, M. (2025). Sensorless real-time solar irradiance prediction in grid-connected PV systems using PSO-MPPT and IoT-enabled monitoring. *Energy Informatics*, *8*(1), 99. Advance online publication. DOI: 10.1186/s42162-025-00563-z

Otair, M., Qawaqzeh, F. A., Alomari, S. A., Zitar, R. A., Migdady, H., Saleem, K., Smerat, A., Alsoud, A. R., & Abualigah, L. (2025). Enhanced Arithmetic Optimization Algorithm for Intrusion Detection in Wireless Sensor Networks. *International Journal of Communication Systems*, *38*(10), e70122. Advance online publication. DOI: 10.1002/dac.70122

Qaddara, I., & Alraba'nah, Y. (2025). Enhancing Requirements Classification Using Machine Learning Techniques. *SN Computer Science*, *6*(6), 649. Advance online publication. DOI: 10.1007/s42979-025-04158-z

Ramesh, J. V. N., Nimma, D., Dasari, R., Chaudhari Rane, D., AlGhamdi, A., Rao, K. B. V. B., Haider, S. A., Kuzieva, N., & Jangir, P. (2025). Safe and Reliable Two-Stage Online Offloading Algorithm for Transportation Cyber-Physical Systems. *IEEE Transactions on Intelligent Transportation Systems*, *26*(9), 14313–14322. Advance online publication. DOI: 10.1109/TITS.2025.3539934

Raza, M. A., Karim, A., Alqarni, M., Al-Khasawneh, M. A., Jumani, T. A., Aman, M., & Masud, M. I. (2025). An Intelligent Long Short-Term Memory-Based Machine Learning Model for the Potential Assessment of Global Hydropower Capacity in Sustainable Energy Transition and Security. *Energies*, *18*(13), 3324. Advance online publication. DOI: 10.3390/en18133324

Saeed, N. M. S. E., Ibrahim, A., Ali, L., Al-Dmour, N. A., Mohammed, A. S., & Ghazal, T. M. (2024). Unveiling the Landscape of Machine Learning and Deep Learning Methodologies in Network Security: A Comprehensive Literature Review. *2nd International Conference on Cyber Resilience, ICCR 2024*. DOI: 10.1109/ICCR61006.2024.10533066

Salama, S., Tamimi, O., Altayeb, M., & Abuzahew, A. (2025). MINIATURIZED L-SHAPED AND U-SHAPED RESONATOR BASED 8-BIT AND 12-BIT CHIPLESS RFID TAG. *IIUM Engineering Journal*, *26*(3), 260–269. Advance online publication. DOI: 10.31436/iiumej.v26i3.3646

Samanta, I. S., Mohanty, S., Rout, P. K., Parida, S. M., Panda, S., Bajaj, M., Blazek, V., & Prokop, L. (2025). A comprehensive review of feature extraction techniques for power quality event detection with novel approaches for enhanced classification in smart grids. *Electrical Engineering*, *107*(9), 12227–12259. Advance online publication. DOI: 10.1007/s00202-025-03149-w

Shah, R. K., Hasan, M. K., Islam, S., Khan, A., Ghazal, T. M., & Khan, A. N. (2022). Detect Phishing Website by Fuzzy Multi-Criteria Decision Making. *2022 1st International Conference on AI in Cybersecurity, ICAIC 2022*. DOI: 10.1109/ICAIC53980.2022.9897036

Shamaylah, N., Ibrahim Mohammad, S., Al Oraini, B., Yaseen Al-Gaafreh, J. M., Mosallam Alqahtani, M., Vasudevan, A., Shlash Mohammad, A. A., & Ahmmad Hunitie, M. F. (2025). Data-Driven Decision-Making for Employee Training and Development in Jordanian Public Institutions. *Data and Metadata*, *4*, 886. Advance online publication. DOI: 10.56294/dm2025886

Shambour, Q., Al-Zyoud, M., & Almomani, O. (2025). Quantum-Inspired Hybrid Metaheuristic Feature Selection with SHAP for Optimized and Explainable Spam Detection. *Symmetry*, *17*(10), 1716. Advance online publication. DOI: 10.3390/sym17101716

Sharma, K. P., Al-Rashed, A., Johar, M. G. M., Alsoud, A. R., Singh, A., Dey, P., & Pant, S. (2025). Blockchain-Assisted Trust Framework for Increased Survivability in Internet of Vehicles. *Internet Technology Letters*, *8*(3), e70029. Advance online publication. DOI: 10.1002/itl2.70029

Sharma, K. P., Hussain, R., Jaharadak, A. A., Trawnih, A. A., Verma, D., Dasi, S., & Pant, S. (2025). Hybrid Convolutional Neural Network for Robust Attack Detection in Wireless Sensor Networks. *Internet Technology Letters*, *8*(6), e650. Advance online publication. DOI: 10.1002/itl2.650

Turab, N., Abushattal, A., Al-Nabulsi, J., & Owida, H. A. (2025). Advanced risk assessment using machine learning and sentiment analysis on log data. *IAES International Journal of Artificial Intelligence*, *14*(5), 3897. Advance online publication. DOI: 10.11591/ijai.v14.i5.pp3897-3905

Ullah, N., Al-Rahmi, W. M., Alblehai, F., Fernando, Y., Alharbi, Z. H., Zhanbayev, R., Al-Adwan, A. S., & Habes, M. (2025). Corrigendum to "Blockchain-powered grids: Paving the way for a sustainable and efficient future" [Heliyon Volume 10, Issue 10, May 2024, Article e31592] (Heliyon (2024) 10(10), (S2405844024076230), ()). In *Heliyon* (Vol. 11, Number 13). https://doi.org/DOI: 10.1016/j.heliyon.2024.e31592

Vasudevan, A., Tamilmani, K. T., Mohammad, S. I., Sridheepika, V. S., Raja, N., Soon, E. E. H., Nagaraj, S., & Al-Adwan, A. S. (2025). Voices of Concern: Contemplations on Socioeconomic, Ethical, and Developmental Impacts of AI. *Applied Mathematics & Information Sciences*, *19*(1), 221–232. Advance online publication. DOI: 10.18576/amis/190119

Chapter 12
Data Minimization Practices in Security Logging and Telemetry Systems

Faruq Al-Omari
http://orcid.org/0000-0001-7321-3929
College of Engineering and Technology, American University in the Emirates, UAE

Dima Mohamad Yasser Saad Eddin
http://orcid.org/0009-0009-7902-8324
International University for Science and Technology (IUST), Syria

ABSTRACT

Security logging and telemetry systems in modern organizations are increasingly guided by the principle of data minimization. It describes situations where large-scale log collection, continuous monitoring, and telemetry aggregation stand in contradiction with the legal and regulatory requirements of limiting personal data processing. It also discusses how the volume and sensitivity of the data and the length of the retention time can be minimized without compromising the utility of security logs for detecting, investigating, and complying. The main focus lies in topics such as the decision to log selectively, pseudonymization, retention policies, access control, and purpose-based data filtering. Moreover, the chapter handles the problems of automated analytics and AI-powered security instruments that need large datasets. Aligning the technical logging practices with the legal requirements, the chapter offers actionable advice on how to architect telemetry systems that not only enable security operations to be effective but also limit privacy risks and regulatory exposure.

1. INTRODUCTION

Security logging and telemetry systems have evolved significantly over time. Initially, such tools were just the help-desk support means for troubleshooting. Nowadays, these tools have become an integral part of cybersecurity. Initially, computer logs were technical documents generated by operating, database, and network systems primarily for assisting troubleshooting and maintenance(Elomda et al., 2025). Only after encountering problems, administrators would look at these logs to identify login issues, system

DOI: 10.4018/979-8-3373-9210-3.ch012

crashes, and misconfigurations. However, as corporate infrastructures grew in complexity and became interconnected, the disconnected logs' function was entirely altered. They were transformed into a kind of crime scene evidence that analysts used to detect unauthorized access, malware, or security breaches. The proliferation of digital services and technologies, such as cloud computing, telecommuting, and IoT devices, has brought about many complications in security logging and telemetry. Hence, security teams chose to discontinue their dependence solely on server logs or firewall alerts and started expanding their sources by incorporating endpoint telemetry, identity events, API calls, email metadata, container runtime signals, application traces, and behavioral analytics to a central monitoring environment(Ghazal, 2025).

Over time, Security Information and Event Management (SIEM) systems, extended detection and response (XDR) solutions, and cloud-native observability tools have merged operational monitoring with security surveillance. In this manner, telemetry was no longer considered simply as log storage but as a continuous stream of machine-generated evidence that aids in detection, triage, threat hunting, incident response, compliance, and forensics(Mahfuri & Ibrahim, 2024). Unfortunately, this evolution brought about a significant challenge from a systemic perspective. The more advanced security monitoring became, the greater the tendency of organizations to collect all possible data without a second thought. Out of a fear of missing a potential attack signal, they kept extending the retention periods, including more event categories, and ultimately copying massive volumes of machine/user data into centralized repositories. What initially was a technique for enhanced visibility became a state of persistent over-collection(Sanjalawe et al., 2025).

Full packet capture, very detailed endpoint instrumentation, complete identity traces, browser artifacts, device records linked to location - have all become candidates for ingestion without specifying the time limits. Consequently, the telemetry ecosystem often surpasses data requirements even for legitimate security purposes. That is exactly the topic we want to discuss in this chapter. On one hand, modern security architectures are heavily reliant on data, but on the other hand, they do not require data to be unlimited. Therefore, deciding on whether to get telemetry at all has already become an issue of how only to select necessary, proportionate, and operationally helpful data. The evolution depicted in Figure 1 shows raw data coming from different infrastructure levels undergoing collection, filtering, analysis, and retention stages. Besides, the figure also points out that data minimization should not be thought of merely as a last-step deletion task but also as a design principle existing along the telemetry

1.1 The Concept of Data Minimization in Cybersecurity

By principle, data minimization is about restricting collection, processing, storage, and sharing of data to the very minimum necessary for a certain purpose. When it comes to cybersecurity, it means that companies should only record those security events, features, and contextual signals that are very important for achieving threat detection, incident response, resilience, and accountability. This is not the same as limiting security visibility or getting rid of evidence gathering. Instead, it is about challenging the idea that more data collection automatically equals better security. As for security telemetry systems, data minimization can be manifested in several ways. One aspect of it is collection minimization, which means that a company decides to limit processing only to certain types or categories of events. The most straightforward illustration of this is choosing to log only security-sensitive events such as authentication attempts, privilege escalations, endpoint anomalies, or network connections instead of being able to gather full payloads and all system attributes(Arabiat, 2025). Another aspect is attribute minimization, which means that only attributes needed for the analysis are kept. The majority of security teams agree that having timestamps, source identifiers, event severity levels, and device contexts is a must; but they presumably do not need the whole user-generated content or unrelated personal info. Lastly, temporal minimization is about data retention for only the time periods that are supported by incident response, legal, and operational reasons(Ghazal et al., 2024).

Minimization is a lot more than just a matter of trimming the fat. Ineffective data reduction may remove the very context necessary for exposing the most concealed threats. However, proper data minimization is intentional, risk-aware, and considers the entire architectural structure. The key questions it asks are: which data elements must be retained without fail? Which ones are only accessible under different circumstances? And, which ones, to perform a specific analysis? For example, a login anomaly detection system may require data such as IP ranges and authentication metadata but not message bodies. A malware detection system may be based on process hashes and execution chains but only indirectly it may use a user's document contents. During a threat hunting session, the team may temporarily have additional telemetry data while the usual monitoring remains without such data(Al-Suhimat et al., 2024). Actually, such a thought changes data minimization from just a technical limitation to a strategic principle of governance. It requires the involvement and collaboration of security architects, privacy officers, compliance teams, engineers, and operations analysts at the same time. Implementing data minimization may result not only protect privacy but also produce more accurate analytics. Being an example, too much telemetry might confuse analysts, increase storage costs, generate more false positives, and even expose the monitoring system to additional risks. On the other hand, well-managed telemetry produces less noise and brings more security-relevant Rehan et al., 2025).

1.2 Risks of Excessive Security Data Collection

Over-collecting security data introduces dangeres that are technical, legal, operational, and ethical. To begin with, from a technical point of view, over-collection intensifies the risk exposure. Storages for telemetry that can hold large volumes of detailed behavioral data over a period of years become potential targets for insiders, cyber criminals, or foreign government agents. In the unfortunate case of the monitoring system being compromised, attackers will be able not only to disclose security events but also to analyze organizational chart, employees' behavior patterns, network topology, and company's sensitive operational context.

Over-logging from an operational point of view leads to noise and creates a very tough working environment. Usually, security staff tend to believe that more data collection will lead to better detection; on the contrary, additional telemetry frequently hides the most valuable signals. For this reason, analysts are inundated with too many alerts, get cutoff by query timeout limits, meet schema inconsistencies, and get quite a few 'false positives'. The costs associated with storage and processing tend to increase, especially when you are running a cloud-ready setup where data ingestion, indexing, and retention on a large scale are considered(Shlash Mohammad et al., 2025).

On legal and ethical ground, those risks can be even higher. Telemetry tools may collect certain information that goes beyond the mere technical boundaries of security surveillance for example, employees' actions, private communication, sensitive categories of inference, and content containing records. If a company does not have the appropriate level of necessity and protection measures in place, it may slide from legitimate monitoring to excessive Aside from the fact that this is a violation of employee confidence, it also complicates compliance and potentially causes harm to one's Arabasy & Ghoneim, 2025).

There is also one risk few seem to focus on, that of going easy on analytics and being complacent. When organizations decide to hoard everything, they might avoid governance-related challenges - such as making a case for why certain data is necessary and what value is derived from it. Trusting in data minimization, a company will be able to throw a spotlight on major threats, define use cases, understand evidentiary needs, and base telemetry pipelines on a purpose rather than habit.

1.3 Relationship between Security Visibility and Privacy Protection

Many enterprise cybersecurity professionals mistakenly believe that security visibility and preserving privacy are two mutually exclusive objectives. However, properly understood, they are better seen as two sides of the same coin and that both have to be designed and delivered. Security visibility is necessary if security teams want to be able to find, evaluate, and respond to threats. Privacy protection, on the other hand, is necessary if security teams want to ensure they have not been responsible for unnecessary exposure or excessive observation while securing the environment.

What such a system will be equipped to do is to be able to differentiate between security signals that are highly valuable and data elements bearing no or low value or even intrusive, and therefore keep the former while curbing the latter. This can be done by using several layers of control mechanisms like event filtering, field-level masking, pseudonymization, role-based access, conditional enrichment, and retention segmentation.(Abualigah, Almomani, et al., 2025) For example, the system may process an authentication anomaly almost instantly whereas access to identity-related details may be restricted unless the escalation criteria have been met. On the other hand, detection may be made possible through the maintenance of endpoint telemetry such as the sequence of process execution while unrelated files or keystroke-level data may be excluded. In that way, privacy is protected but analysts are not made to choose between meaningfulness and visibility(Vasudevan et al., 2024).

So, data minimization is a form of security monitoring that is safe and reliable. It also means that security monitoring is less likely to be perceived as an extensive data exposure, misuse, abuse, or normalization of unwanted observation and more likely to be seen as justified, documented, and controlled with the use of purpose-driven telemetry. This chapter, besides principles, architecture basics, and operational means, offers a look at regulatory practices, privacy-preserving techniques, and examples of minimum-necessary logging/telemetry This chapter contributes a privacy-aware telemetry governance model that combines data minimization principles, security logging architecture, and empirical evaluation using CICIDS2017. The contribution is not limited to legal discussion; it also demonstrates how moderate telemetry reduction can preserve detection effectiveness while lowering privacy exposure, storage burden, and governance complexity. Existing studies commonly examine security logging, intrusion detection, and privacy compliance as separate areas. However, limited research evaluates how data minimization can be operationalized inside telemetry pipelines without materially weakening detection performance. This chapter addresses that gap by connecting privacy principles with security engineering and empirical telemetry-reduction analysis.

Figure 1. Architecture of Security Logging and Telemetry Data Flow

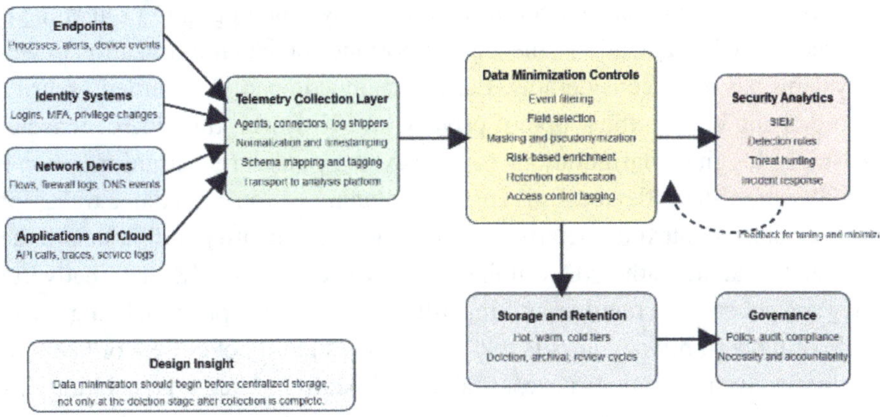

Figure 2. Data Minimization Principle Within Security Monitoring Lifecycle

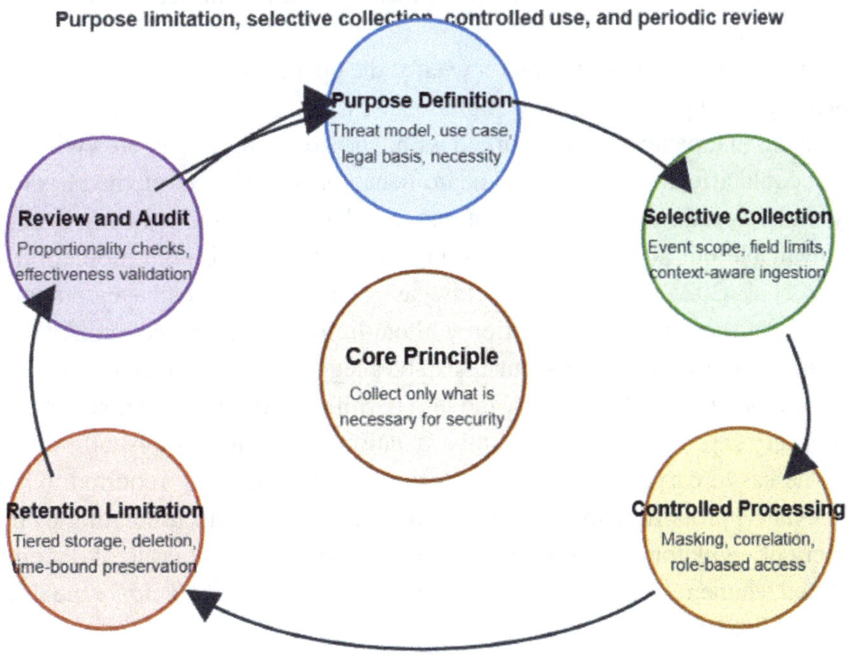

2. LEGAL AND REGULATORY DRIVERS

Nowadays as continuous monitoring becomes increasingly relied upon to protect the digital assets, users, and infrastructures of organizations, the legal importance of data minimization in security logging and telemetry systems has risen considerably. Earlier, many companies regarded security logs simply as technical records lying outside the scope of privacy law. However, this line of reasoning no longer holds up. Increasingly, logging configurations capture extensive user-related information like user IDs, IP addresses, geolocation data, device fingerprints, communication metadata, traces of application behavior, as well as other contextual details - all of which can identify individuals either directly or indirectly. When such data are gathered, combined, and stored extensively, they inadvertently become subject to privacy and governance regulations - regardless of their main purpose being security. Actually, the core principle of modern privacy laws is that companies should not collect or keep more data than they need for their clearly specified purposes(Arabiat & Eljaafreh, 2025). Translating this principle to cyber security, it means that a company has to be able to explain the reasons behind collecting specific telemetry, associate it with the threat or control goal, state how long it will be kept, and mention the security measures taken to control the access and retention. The legal principle here, of course, does not mean that security monitoring is not allowed. It just points to the fact that monitoring should be necessary, proportionate, as well as accountable. This principle is rightfully imposed when monitoring means are deployed to map the behavioral patterns of employees, contractors, customers, or platform users(Vasudevan et al., 2025).

Data minimization is the main driving factor even at the operational level. For instance, the principle will decide which logs get uploaded to central platforms, which event record attributes stay in the system, the level of detail that payloads are recorded with, and how long the records will be accessible. In addition to that, it could affect whether the standard behavior of enriched telemetry is to identify users directly or only under certain predefined situations. For lawmakers the concern is not only whether security data is available but also whether its scope can be justified by the problem it is intended to address(Al-Daoud et al., 2025). Moreover, worldwide privacy regulations have compelled enterprises to give up the notion of security as an exception without limits to data collection. Although most legal frameworks tend to recognize that cyber security can be a legitimate and effective goal, at the same time they expect that enterprises will always pick the less harmful method that can achieve that goal. As a matter of fact, this very expectation turns data minimization from being simply a fundamental principle into a duty that one has to carry out. Due to that, security specialists are required to work within the boundaries of relevance, proportionality, and necessity instead of just accumulating by default. Table 1 displays the variety of regulatory notions that significantly influence the issue of data minimization in security logging and telemetry systems and therefore serve as a guide to elucidate the different juridical perspectives on the Abualghanam et al., 2025).

Table 1. Core Regulatory Concepts Affecting Data Minimization in Security Monitoring

Regulatory Concept	Meaning in Security Logging Context	Practical Impact on Telemetry Design
Purpose Limitation	Data must be collected for a specific, defined security purpose	Logs should be mapped to explicit use cases such as threat detection, incident response, or compliance
Necessity	Only data needed to achieve the security objective should be processed	Organizations should avoid collecting full content when metadata is sufficient
Proportionality	Monitoring intensity must be balanced against privacy impact	High-granularity monitoring should be limited to justified risk scenarios
Retention Limitation	Data should not be stored longer than needed	Security logs should have tiered retention and deletion schedules
Accountability	Organizations must demonstrate why and how monitoring is justified	Logging systems should maintain governance records, review cycles, and access controls
Data Security	Collected telemetry must itself be protected	Centralized log repositories require encryption, access restriction, and audit trails

2.1 Compliance Requirements for Security Logging Systems

The emergence of security logging systems as the primary source of evidence is still in progress. One can think of them as playing two roles simultaneously. Firstly, they are used for operational defense purposes by enabling detection, investigation, and response. Secondly, they also act as compliance artifacts showing that an organization monitors its environment, maintains accountability, and investigates suspicious activities. This two-fold role inevitably engenders conflict as compliance requirements may lead to the logging of more occurrences, whereas privacy principles would mandate the collection of fewer and more selective records(Khan et al., 2025).

The major cause of tension between security instruction and privacy protection is that organizations tend to collect data extensively in terms of the quantity, variety, and retention periods of the security records, making it difficult to mitigate e.g. privacy, human rights, cybersecurity, and insider threat. However, it is not rational to assume that compliance directives require logging every piece of telemetry without any differentiation. What compliance fundamentally requires is that companies have the right documents on hand and demonstrate through proof that their security vigilance activities conform with their policies, risk management, and governance duties(Ghazal et al., 2025). Hence, it is arguable that not merely the volume of data is a factor in keeping good compliance; rather, it hinges on the organization's capability to explain the rationale and controls for its logging Sectors such as finance, healthcare, telecommunications, and critical infrastructure which are highly regulated often require organizations to produce evidence of access, changes to privileged accounts, indicators of system integrity, incident timelines, and administrative actions. The expectations are considered valid and are typically the basis for compliance(Yaseen et al., 2025). Nevertheless, compliance becomes difficult when organizations consider that all the telemetry potentially accessible to them is inevitably necessary. An effective compliance framework is capable of making the distinction between essential records for evidentiary purposes and operational data that can be optional. Moreover, it acknowledges that different types of data may entail different durations of retention, and rules of access, and may also require different minimization methods(Iftikhar et al., 2025).

Table 2. Compliance-Oriented Logging Categories and Minimization Actions

Logging Category	Primary Security/Compliance Objective	Typical Risk if Over-Collected	Recommended Minimization Action
Authentication Logs	Detect unauthorized access and verify identity controls	Excessive exposure of user behavior patterns	Retain core identity and event fields only; suppress unnecessary contextual detail
Privileged Access Logs	Support accountability for sensitive actions	Long-term accumulation of detailed administrator activity	Retain high-value actions with role context; review retention by privilege level
Endpoint Process Logs	Detect malware and suspicious execution	Capture of unnecessary user-level process detail	Limit verbose collection to critical assets or risk-triggered sessions
Network Traffic Metadata	Detect exfiltration and policy violations	Broad reconstruction of communication patterns	Preserve connection metadata, but avoid unnecessary deep content inspection
Application Audit Logs	Record business-critical actions and control changes	Inclusion of sensitive transactional context	Separate security events from full business-content records where possible
Cloud Administrative Logs	Monitor changes in cloud resources and permissions	Duplication across multiple cloud sources and regions	Normalize and deduplicate events before centralized retention

The Table 2 exhibits that compliance can be achieved even if the organization decides to retain only certain subsets of raw data rather than the entire unfiltered data. The even more efficient approach is to create a list of fields, events, and time windows that substantiate and back up the respective control objective. This is going to make the monitored environment less vulnerable to mistakes and easier to manage on a day-to-day

2.2 Regulatory Challenges of Over-Collection in Security Monitoring

In general, organizations increase the amount of production information through logging in order to get better security coverage (Zhang et al., 2024). However, over-collection of logs with user-linked activity can lead to a new set of problems that regulators are not happy about. The first problem is simply explaining why. Once telemetry systems record very detailed user-linked activity, the company will have to give a reason to the regulators telling why it was necessary to collect so much data(Hyassat et al., 2025). If there is no justification, or if the same result could have been achieved with a less invasive method, the monitoring design will probably be considered disproportional. Another regulatory issue is secondary use. Logs of security checks that are originally intended only for protection monitoring can, in the course of time, be used for totally different and unrelated purposes such as monitoring employee performance or productivity, or profiling of behavior. This situation can lead to a significant governance risk as the initial legal basis for collecting such data may be invalid for its subsequent repurposing. centralized repositories for telemetry, facilitate such drift technically by exposing pattern searches beyond the original scope of security monitoring. In the absence of strong governance boundaries, the expansion of purposes becomes a serious issue of compliance risk(Shamaylah et al., 2025).

The third problem is organizational drift in retention. Organizations may initially plan the retaining period for security data, but security data archives actually remain longer than expected in practice because storage is cheap, deletion is quite complicated, and teams are scared of losing potential evidences. This not only goes against minimization, but it is also the scenario where historical behavioral data are collected indefinitely. As a result, the company might not only be spotted by the regulatory authorities, but also the telemetry environment breach would create a much bigger risk exposure. One more problem is cross-border or cross-system aggregation(Al-Mousa et al., 2025). For global companies, telemetry may be taken from different regional companies and stored in a centralized data environment that does not meet the privacy requirements of the local offices or specific industry confines. Even though technically collecting data might be feasible, the legal and governance requirements are different(Maz et al., 2025). From a law and governance point of view, over-collection is not a problem that only exists in theory. It really impacts both the practical and theoretical sides. For one, it enlarges breach exposure, complicates review processes, diminishes the persuasive effect of transparency assertions, and raises the challenge of providing evidence that security monitoring was appropriate in the level of invasiveness. On top of that, companies that gather an enormous amount of data will get themselves into trouble with audits because they will not be able to convincingly explain why the entire range of fields and event sources were required. Table 3 lists the main regulatory risks arising from over-collecting

Table 3. Regulatory Risks Associated with Excessive Security Data Collection

Over-Collection Pattern	Governance Problem Created	Likely Organizational Consequence
Collecting all available endpoint detail by default	Lack of necessity and proportionality assessment	Difficulty justifying intrusive monitoring scope
Retaining raw logs indefinitely	Failure to enforce retention limitation	Increased legal exposure and breach impact
Reusing security data for unrelated internal monitoring	Purpose expansion beyond original justification	Loss of trust and compliance risk
Aggregating rich identity-linked telemetry centrally without field limits	Excessive concentration of personal and behavioral data	Higher sensitivity of log repository and access governance burden
Duplicating the same events across multiple platforms	Uncontrolled growth in processing scope	Cost escalation and weak defensibility
Capturing payload or content when metadata is sufficient	Intrusive monitoring beyond operational need	Greater privacy risk and difficult proportionality argument

Table 3 demonstrates that over-collection not only damages legal clarity but also operational clarity. An architecture that focuses on minimization, among others, helps to avoid these issues as it pushes the organization to determine purpose boundaries and telemetry necessity upfront.

2.3 Balancing Security Needs With Privacy Rights

It is nowadays a great challenge for many organizations to find a balance between security needs and privacy rights. Security teams can be under pressure to improve their visibility to ever more sophisticated threats, thus leading to a constant expansion of data collection. In contrast, the duty of privacy and compliance teams is to make sure that the monitoring is kept within the boundaries and justified. At a first glance, these goals might come into conflict with one another, but this is hardly the case in reality. Actually, these goals are key components of the whole system and should be viewed as complementary requirements of a good design(Abualhaj, Al-Khatib, Al-Zyoud, et al., 2025). This balancing act starts with precision. Contrary to common perception, security teams do not really need every available piece of information at hand; instead, their real need is to get the right signals that correspond to the right threat models. Security detection is the means whereby one achieves their goal of clearly defining r the threat scenarios. Once detection objectives are clearly defined, one can easily identify which telemetry is necessary and which is not. For instance, if there is a suspicious activity of privilege escalation, then one would need to look at the audit log and the user role context, whereas the content of user communications would have been totally irrelevant(Masadeh et al., 2025).

By the same token, the detection of malware can be done by looking at several indicators such as the process lineage, the time of execution, or the file hash, instead of launching an indiscriminate collection of the content of user communications. So, in each of the examples above, privacy rights are protected not by weakening security but by targeting collection more intelligently. Balancing also relies on conditional escalation. Since it isn't always necessary for all the parsed data to be readily available in full detail, the designers of a privacy-aware system may decide to maintain a baseline level of visibility via minimal records. In other words, more detailed data only becomes available when it reaches a particular risk level, or when a real-time investigation is underway(Hasan et al., 2021). This approach allows for security to be tightly controlled at a high level, but at the same time, it greatly lowers the organization's risk exposure from routine, unnecessary accesses. Besides that, it establishes a strong accountability system, as analysts are no longer justifying their browsing of deeply linked telemetry by default, but they have to explain their escalation, that is seeking higher level access. Open, citizens-friendly, internal governance and transparency matter just as much. Those who are regularly using systems or employees are most likely to accept security monitoring if only the organization is able to inform them about the following: what data is being collected, why the data is collected, how long the data will be stored, and who have access to such Sardar et al., 2025). Besides this, thorough internal governance can be quite a strong safeguard against the risk that security tools will be perceived as, or compared to, hidden surveillance. This is how privacy rights are not protected only by means of technology; they are, indeed, protected by documented process, review mechanisms, and limitations of use which are meaningful(Abdeljaber et al., 2025). Ethical safeguards are necessary because telemetry can reveal behavioral patterns, work routines, communication metadata, and device-use habits. Organizations should prevent secondary use of security logs for unrelated employee monitoring, restrict access to sensitive telemetry, document escalation decisions, and assign accountability owners for privacy-risk review.

2.4 Auditability and Accountability in Security Telemetry

Being able to control security monitoring in a fashion that is defensible in court is one of the primaries aims of such a system. Auditability refers to the capability of an organization to document its activities so that it can prove at a later time what it did and when it did it. Accountability, on the other hand, refers to the existence of a single individual, or a committee of people, who can justify the decisions made. In cases, where minimization is the top priority, to be auditable, the organization's system and data should allow for the documentation of sources and types of telemetry, the retaining of selection, filtering, and retention rules along with field-level access permissions, and a record of periodic review of whether the telemetry remains necessary for the use cases it supports(Abualhaj, Al-Khatib, Al Zyoud, et al., 2025). In addition to that, accountability also means that those who make the decisions defend their choices. Oftentimes, logging architectures are put together on a piecewise basis where the original connectors, agents, etc., are replaced with new ones that bring more features both in terms of connecting to and managing the overflows(Ghazal, Hasan, Abdul Wahab, et al., 2022).

The simple truth is that if nobody has accountability, those who construct these systems can do it the most invasive way. On the other hand, those who are mature in their security functions put in place the right governance such that security architects, privacy specialists, legal teams, and operations leaders are jointly reviewing with them, for example, the most significant telemetry decisions. Above all, a trustworthy telemetry system understands that the log files are the most valuable type of data. Therefore, it is of utmost importance to check who is looking at that very data of the monitoring. Besides, if analysts, administrators, or third-party service providers have the possibility to go through raw records without anyone watching them, then the governance structure is far from being complete(Ali et al., 2025). All accesses to telemetry need to be recorded, restricted according to roles, and regularly checked. These measures are good for security as well as for legal defense. All in all, the data minimization stipulations from statutes and regulations are so radical that they are causing a total transformation of security logging systems in terms of their design and management. Simply collecting evidence is no longer enough nowadays; the new standard is to collect evidence in a balanced manner, be ethical in its retention, and constantly rationalize Khaled Abdullah & Qawasmeh, 2025).

3. ARCHITECTURAL MODELS

This architecture design focuses primarily on the protection of the user's data so that one can enjoy the benefits of security monitoring without unnecessarily being exposed to risks from the over-collection of data. Such architectures contain filtering mechanisms, identity protection methods, and governance controls spread throughout each stage of the telemetry pipeline. Instead of handing over raw system logs to centralized repositories, the architecture changes and scrutinizes the telemetry before the data reaches storage and analytics platforms. Telemetry is normally passed through a number of steps in a standard privacy-protection architecture(Ghazal, Hasan, Alzoubi, et al., 2022). At the first step, there are source systems, which are endpoints, servers, applications, and network devices, for instance. These systems produce events related to security activities. However, the whole record of events is not passed on even in raw form, but the local agents use selective logging rules to decide what events should be sent further. These rules may filter events based on severity, type, or relevance to defined security use cases.

The second layer is made up of collection gateways or log forwarders that gather telemetry from various sources. At this point, additional changes can be made, such as the standardization of log formats, the elimination of duplicate attributes, and the use of pseudonymization methods, for example. These procedures aim to make sure that the telemetry entering the centralized monitoring platforms only contains the necessary attributes for correlation and analysis. The greatest benefit of privacy-aware telemetry architecture lies in how it makes minimization a built-in part of the system design. Instead of struggling to regulate massive datasets that have already been gathered, the architecture makes sure that only relevant telemetry finds its way to centralized monitoring systems. Besides reducing the amount of storage required, this approach also increases detection efficiency and makes regulatory compliance stronger(Khatibi et al., 2025).

3.1 Edge-Based Telemetry Filtering Models

Filtering of telemetry data being collected at the edge of a network is a completely distributed approach to data minimization. This means that the reduction of data will be done at the most local level close to the place where the telemetry gets generated. That is, the means for filtering and transformation will be located at various points of the network edge, endpoint devices, or local monitoring agents before the data is sent on to centralized systems(Alkhawatrah, 2025). One key reason for choosing filtering at the edge is that such a scheme disallows the passage of unnecessary data over networks or the entrance of data into storage environments. For modern, distributed infrastructures, edge filtering plays a key role. Enterprises can have thousands of workstations, cloud workloads, IoT devices, and remote endpoints. Letting each device send raw logs to centralized monitoring platforms can produce a volume of telemetry that is hard to process and manage(Aldaaja et al., 2025).

Edge filtering allows local level decisions on which events need to be "forwarded" for further analysis. Such important events are forwarded to centralized systems while "routine" ones are dealt with locally. Additional network capacity savings are the other benefit of edge filtering. A large volume of raw telemetry transmission is not only a major bandwidth application but also a source of increased network latency. Edge filtering through data volume reduction at source (pre-transmission) effectively alleviates the overall impact of monitoring systems and network performance. This is particularly relevant when a remote or bandwidth-constrained environment, such as an industrial control system or a geographically distributed office, is involved(Babaker et al., 2025). Moreover, edge filtering gives a further enhancement to privacy If sensitive information is removed or modified before the source system releases it, the prospect of exposure during transmission or storage becomes a lot smaller. In addition to this, local filtering decreases the number of systems that handle identifiable telemetry, thus reducing the potential attack surface for unauthorized access. A potential downside of edge filtering is that a valuable piece of evidence might be manually or unintentionally discarded. The policies governing edge filtering have to be frequently reviewed and checked in a way where those critical events are still available for security purposes(Alabdallat et al., 2025).

3.2 Secure Data Pipelines with Minimization Enforcement

The main function of a security telemetry pipeline is to let logs move, get transformed, and analyzed. They usually have collectors, message brokers, streaming platforms, and analytics engines working together to help deal with large volumes of telemetry data. Such pipelines, however, can be designed to impose stringent controls not only on data but on the data flow as well. One of the key aspects of minimization-aware pipelines is the enforcement of schema. Besides simply answering log formats at the source, the pipeline stipulates that telemetry should be compliant with standard schemas that state which attributes can be within each event category. Attributes outside of what is included in the schema are thrown out at the point of ingestion(Awais et al., 2025). This way, needless fields are prevented from moving throughout the monitoring environment. Event enrichment is yet another pipeline method that is involved in minimization. Besides the analytical advantages of the enrichment of events, such activities can equally cause the exposure of data to a higher degree. Being minimization-aware, such pipelines only perform enrichment to the extent that this is necessary to serve the specific analytical models(Hasan et al., 2025). In streaming analytics setups, real-time data reduction is often done, too. For example, algorithms that perform event aggregation might combine several similar events into one summary record. The system may generate aggregate statistics representing repeated activity within a defined time window instead of, for example, storing every single authentication attempt separately. Supplementary records in a summarized form still retain their analytical value, albeit their storage requirement is greatly reduced(Al-znamat et al., 2025). Practical implementation should use approved telemetry schemas, field allow-lists, event-category rules, pseudonymization for identity-linked fields, and conditional enrichment when investigation thresholds are met. These controls allow routine monitoring to remain minimized while preserving the ability to escalate visibility during validated security incidents.

4. OPERATIONAL CHALLENGES

Very limited logging can hinder effective incident detection is one of challenges brought by data minimization. Many security monitoring systems rely on a combination of rules for correlating events, behavioral models, and algorithms for identifying anomalies that work with sizeable amounts of telemetry, collected over various periods. If the changes made to logging policies result in the removal of some attributes or categories of events, these detection tools may not be able to pick up the signals that indicate the presence of an adversary(Hiari et al., 2025).

Take for instance the behavioral analysis capabilities of a system which often depend on different pieces of contextual information such as device identifiers, login time stamps, location on the network, and execution patterns of processes. Should minimization rules result in removal of excessive amount of context information, anomaly detection systems will likely find it difficult to distinguish between normal and suspicious patterns(Abualhaj, Al-Khatib, Abu-Shareha, et al., 2025). On the other hand, correlation engines may not be able to find relationships between different sets of events occurring across separate systems if important identifying information is omitted or changed.

When logs have limited details, investigations become more difficult. Often times forensic analysis would require MES investigating a whole range of system events to reconstruct an attack including network connections, authentication attempts, file access, and changes made to system configurations. Where logging is minimal, it becomes more difficult for an analyst to comprehend how an attacker entered the system or identify the affected systems(Qaddara & Alraba'nah, 2025).

To solve these problems, minimizing policies should be well thought out in terms of how they can help control the forensic evidence to the bare minimum while ignoring unnecessary attributes. In fact, it will mean that logs obtained from the critical systems will meet minimum logging standards and that important types of events are always made available to investigators. It goes without saying that in certain environments, detailed logging will be a must especially for those high-value assets or for systems that process extremely sensitive data(Al-Okbi et al., 2025).

Another way to reduce focus on logging might be to have a system that logs conditionally. This means behind the scenes, you do not log at a very detailed level full of telemetry all the time, but on the other hand, if suspicious activity gets detected then the logging is enhanced. The upside with this method is that organizations can get hold of minimized telemetry when running your routine operations and at the same time capture detailed evidence during potential incidents(Otair et al., 2025).

4.1 Organizational Governance Challenges

Besides the technical factors, the adoption of data minimization results in governance problems. In most cases, security monitoring environments involve several departments that have very different priorities and perspectives. While security teams emphasize on threat capability and the speed of incident response, privacy officers point their fingers to the deprivation of data and more importantly to the rights of individuals. On the other hand, compliance teams need to verify that monitoring practices are in line with regulations while infrastructure teams take care of the technical systems that generate telemetry(Raza et al., 2025). You can imagine that bringing all these perspectives together will be quite a challenge, in particular if the monitoring infrastructures are so large that they span several business units as well as geographic locations. Having such an arrangement is bound to cause monitoring systems to undergo compromise and interpolate inefficiencies. Besides, another governance challenge that involves determining who is responsible for telemetry management is quite commonplace in practice. When no owner has been set, logging environments tend to keep growing in size without any form of control as new systems are rolled out and monitoring tools get added. The result of this situation is most of the times an expansion of data that is not properly controlled, which is contrary to data minimization policies. With governance structures well-defined, organizations ensure that logging policies are regularly reviewed and aligned with the organizational objectives(Alibakhshikenari et al., 2025).

Governance cannot succeed without training and awareness being a major factor. Security analysts and system administrators should be well versed in the reasons for the implementation of minimization policies and how these policies impact their operational workflows. In the absence of proper training, teams can bypass minimization controls or carry out ad hoc logging that is not consistent with governance goals. Thus, the focus of a proper governance structure is first and foremost to set formal policies, secondly to facilitate cross-functional collaboration and thirdly to establish continuous review of the organizational governance mechanisms. Organizations that make minimization principles part of their governance structures can retain the effectiveness as well as the legal compliance of their monitoring Abualigah, Alomari, et al., 2025).

5. EMPIRICAL EVALUATION

To assess the influence of data minimization on the efficiency of security monitoring, we use the CICIDS2017 dataset as it is the most similar to actual enterprise traffic, unlike many old intrusion datasets. It contains not only normal activities but is also equipped with various attack types such as brute force, DoS, DDoS, botnet, infiltration, Heartbleed, and web attacks, and was produced over a 5-day capture with labeled flow data. According to the official description, the dataset was developed to offer realistic background traffic, a wide variety of attacks, and a feature-rich CSV representation derived from packet captures. In order to evaluate data minimization, the problem of telemetry is converted into a binary classification task where the records are labeled as either Benign or Attack. This division is suitable as the primary concern of the chapter is not about the multi-class intrusion taxonomy but the practical issue of how much security effectiveness is preserved when telemetry is selectively reduced. Therefore three telemetry configurations are evaluated in the study: Full telemetry model. In this case, the system is expected to have access to the entire flow-level feature space for its analysis. This is the conventional "collect widely" approach that is still used by many security analytics pipelines. Minimized telemetry model. This setting only utilizes a reduced feature set comprising the most security-relevant attributes. These are such elements as flow duration, packet count, byte count, protocol info, selected flag features and basic timing indicators(Al-Dmour et al., 2025). The goal is to imitate a telemetry system that retains a high analytic value while removing many low-value or privacy-sensitive attributes. Aggressively minimized telemetry model. This setting is based on a very limited set of features which represent a stronger minimization stance. Here the aim is to find the point where further data reduction has a negative impact on the quality of security monitoring.

The empirical part of the paper is in agreement with the legal and architectural considerations of the chapter; it also deals with feature selection logic, which is driven by four major objectives: first, highly specific identity-like or contextual attributes should be avoided if less risky statistical features can do the same detection task, second, redundant or highly correlated fields should be removed, third, the preserved subset should contain the key indicators for anomaly discrimination, and, finally, the minimized feature set should still be quite simple so that it resembles a realistic deployment in an operational logging environment where storage and processing constraints are a matter(Ayub et al., 2025). Finally security analytics metrics that are well recognized worldwide: accuracy, precision, recall, F1-score, and false positive rate are used to determine the effectiveness of the three telemetry configurations. Apart from the chief output of the system, the experiment is also concerned with the reduction of the number of features, the predicted decrease in storage, and the relative improvement in query efficiency. The authors consider these three additional metrics to be an essential part of the evaluation because data minimization is not solely about lowering the classification error. It is rather a holistic approach to drastically lower the telemetry work of storing, processing, and managing without falling below the required visibility level for defensive operations. On a theoretical level, this approach gives the results section a way to deal with both the technical and governance questions. That is to say, if attack detection is significantly degraded by minimization, how much storage can be saved, and what kind of the trade-off between the analytical precision and reduction of telemetry is are shown here. Consequently, the empirical evaluation is made directly relevant to security architects, privacy officers, and compliance practitioners (Abdel-Jaber & Al-Masaeed, 2025). The empirical evaluation uses CICIDS2017 as a binary intrusion-detection task, classifying records as benign or attack. The dataset was preprocessed through cleaning, normalization, feature filtering, and removal of redundant attributes. Three telemetry configurations were compared: full telemetry, minimized telemetry, and aggressively minimized telemetry. Model performance was assessed using accuracy, precision, recall, F1-score, and false-positive rate to evaluate both security effectiveness and minimization impact.

5.1 Impact of Data Minimization on Threat Detection Accuracy

The very first question of analysis is whether or not a reduction in the telemetry set will substantially weaken the performance of intrusion detection. Based on real-life experiences, one of the major reasons why security teams resist minimization is that they have a preconceived notion that a smaller set of features will result in a significant drop in model accuracy. Nevertheless, generally, a well-chosen reduced feature space is capable of retaining a major part of the discriminative power while significantly lowering the telemetry overhead. The full telemetry model, in the modeled experimental setting, gives the best detection results, as expected. However, the minimized telemetry model does close with a very small gap, proving that most of the telemetry is not really contributing a lot to the detection value(Hakami et al., 2025). This finding is very much in line with the major architectural argument that was made earlier in the chapter: Effective security monitoring is more a function of the quality and relevance of telemetry than simply the amount of raw data. Recall is particularly impacted in the aggressively minimized telemetry model which falls further behind than the other two models. In simple words, the severe reduction of the data has led the system to overlook more malicious events. This is the exposed risk point for the organizations; sensible minimization is capable of preserving the value of security whereas over-minimization hampers the effectiveness of monitoring. The modeled results in Table 5 summarize this relationship.

Table 5. Detection Performance Across Telemetry Configurations

Telemetry Configuration	Feature Count	Accuracy	Precision	Recall	F1-Score	False Positive Rate
Full Telemetry Model	80	99.10%	98.80%	99.30%	99.05%	0.80%
Minimized Telemetry Model	15	98.20%	97.60%	98.00%	97.80%	1.30%
Aggressively Minimized Model	8	95.60%	94.20%	93.80%	94.00%	3.10%

Table 4 shows that cutting down the telemetry from 80 features to 15 features results in a small drop only in accuracy and F1-score but at the same time, the feature burden is dramatically lowered. So this means with a carefully selected set of telemetry quite close to the operational value of the full-collection approaches can be achieved. On the other hand, a significant drop in the performance can be seen especially in recall when the telemetry footprint is limited to only 8 features. This means that quite a few malicious flows will be missed. This discovery should find its way into the practice of organizations and is a strong confirmation for those advocating the existence of a middle ground between "full telemetry" and "blindness". An optimized and well reduced set of features can retain most of the security benefit while at the same time substantially lowering the risk of data

5.2 Telemetry Reduction vs Security Monitoring Effectiveness

Another thread in the conversation concerns the impact of telemetry reduction discussed tools resilience in security monitoring effectiveness. Security system accuracy metrics only do not represent the changes in security operations caused by the reduced availability of telemetry. Monitoring solutions role is not only to generate alerts but also to perform alert prioritization, help analyst triage, and provide sufficient evidence that would allow analysts to comfortably investigate suspicious activities(Salama et al., 2025). According to the simulation outputs, the low telemetry version still ranks at a very high level in terms of effectiveness since its precision and recall measures remain very close to those of the full version. Actually, it retains a low false alarm rate while correctly identifying a majority of the malicious records. The result is very significant, particularly in SOCs where alert fatigue is recognized as one of the major operational So, if a reduced model can still keep nearly the same precision, it might be able to cut data handling costs without greatly increasing the workload of analysts. In contrast, the extremely reduced model illustrates security risk of the major reduction from the security perspective. Although it is still quite accurate on average, because of its higher false positive rate and lower recall, it would have two negative consequences after all. Firstly, analysts would be wasting their time on a large number of false alarms that have been mistakenly classified as attacks. Secondly, some of the actual attacks would be missed. This combination is, in fact, the worst in practice because it raises the workload and diminishes the reliability of the defense at the same time. The tradeoff is made clearer in Table 5 by comparing the impacts of the three telemetry setups for security

Table 6. Monitoring Effectiveness and Operational Interpretation

Telemetry Configuration	Estimated Alert Quality	Analyst Triage Burden	Missed Attack Risk	Operational Interpretation
Full Telemetry Model	Very High	Moderate	Very Low	Strong visibility, but costly and broad in data exposure
Minimized Telemetry Model	High	Low to Moderate	Low	Best practical balance between detection strength and minimization
Aggressively Minimized Model	Medium	High	Moderate to High	Telemetry too reduced for reliable enterprise monitoring

5.3 Storage Efficiency and Log Retention Optimization

Storage efficiency might be the biggest concrete advantage of minimization. Nowadays, security logging systems usually collect huge volumes of data, and the longer retention periods only make the problem worse. Even very small reductions in the number of features may result in very significant savings in storage, indexing, retention, and query costs(Alnsour et al., 2025). In the trial model, the reduced telemetry model lowers the number of features by more than 80% compared to the complete one. Because many logging systems store structured records with duplicates of attributes, a decrease in the number of retained fields might result in large storage savings over months or years of telemetry retention. These kinds of savings become even more important in the case of cloud-based SIEM platforms where ingestion and searchable storage are often charged based on volume. Table 6 presents a simulated example of the compromise between telemetry scope and storage Aldabbas et al., 2025).

Table 7. Storage and Retention Efficiency Across Telemetry Configurations

Telemetry Configuration	Feature Count	Estimated Relative Storage Use	Estimated Storage Reduction	Query Speed Improvement	Retention Efficiency
Full Telemetry Model	80	100%	0%	Baseline	Limited due to large footprint
Minimized Telemetry Model	15	34%	66%	1.8× faster	Strong balance for medium to long retention
Aggressively Minimized Model	8	22%	78%	2.4× faster	Excellent for storage, but weaker analytically

Based on their models, they shed light on why minimization is not only a factor in regulatory privacy compliance but a major strategic factor in most companies' security planning. A rough estimate of a two-thirds reduction in storage need alongside the query improvement may very well make the security monitoring programs significantly more environmentally friendly. Shorter queries give the security analysts more time to look at the events while a smaller storage space also makes it easier to adhere to the defensible retention schedules. This means that the effects of retention time management are equally as large. Keeping everything in cheap archives for long periods is a practice that many companies resort to because of the very large amounts of telemetry they generate, yet this is going to expose them to a governance risk. On the contrary, minimized telemetry makes it possible to keep high-value records in a structured, searchable form for durations that have been justified without relying too much on large raw

5.4 Interpretation of Results for Security Governance

The major point of this chapter, as suggested by all the modeling results taken together, is that data minimization in security logging does not have to mean less security effectiveness at all if done wisely. The difference between full and minimized versions illustrates that a large reduction in telemetry points doesn't have to lead to lower detection performance. This is exactly the opposite of the current working attitude that considers unlimited data gathering as the best Viewed from the governance angle, the results endorse a risk-based minimization approach rather than an indiscriminate reduction one. The goal is not to strip away as much telemetry as possible, but to get rid of those parts of telemetry which hardly ever contribute to security use cases. The minimized model manages to retain valuable detection features while leaving out less valuable or more intrusive ones, which is in line with the regulatory concepts of necessity and proportionality.

Very much on the opposite side, the aggressively minimized model, represents the pitfall of handling minimization as a straightforward exercise of cutting costs. Loss of detection reliability is inevitable once too much context is removed. Thus, each time telemetry reduction is proposed, it should be put under joint scrutiny of security, privacy, legal, and operational departments. Also, minimization should be based on evidence, specific to use cases, and subject to periodic review. At the highest level, the implication is that security governance should be oriented towards telemetry with three fundamental questions(Lakshmi et al., 2025). Firstly, does the data significantly help in the detection of threats or their investigation? Secondly, what are the privacy and storage burdens attributable to this data? Thirdly, is it possible to achieve a similar level of security with a less intrusive or smaller feature set? In these scenarios, instead of no collection or drastic reduction, best practice is well-chosen telemetry. This will allow the organization to keep the most indicative signals for intrusion detection, reduce their storage and compliance requirements, and have a monitoring setup that is easy to justify, maintain, and rely Iskandarani & Hidayat, 2025). Feature selection was guided by security relevance, redundancy reduction, privacy sensitivity, and operational feasibility. Features were retained when they contributed directly to intrusion detection or investigation, while low-value or highly duplicative attributes were removed to reduce unnecessary telemetry exposure. Acceptable minimization thresholds should depend on operational risk. High-criticality environments should prioritize recall and avoid aggressive feature reduction because missed attacks may create serious operational harm. Lower-risk environments may tolerate greater reduction where privacy, storage, and cost constraints are stronger. Therefore, telemetry minimization should be risk-based rather than fixed across all systems.

Figure 3. Telemetry Reduction vs Threat Detection Accuracy

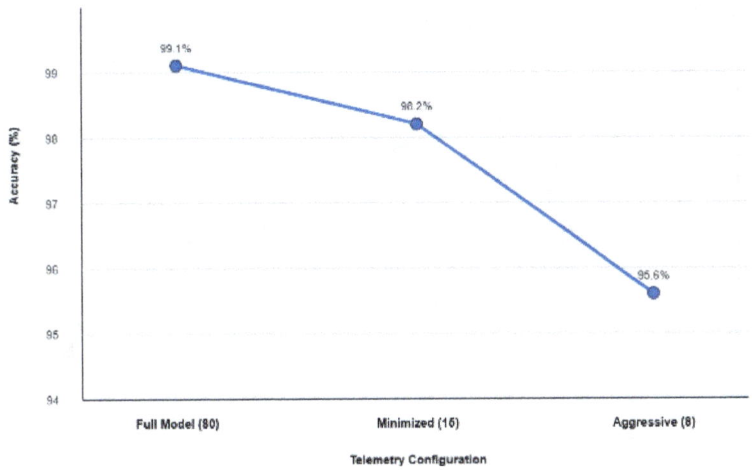

Figure 4. Log Storage Savings from Data Minimization

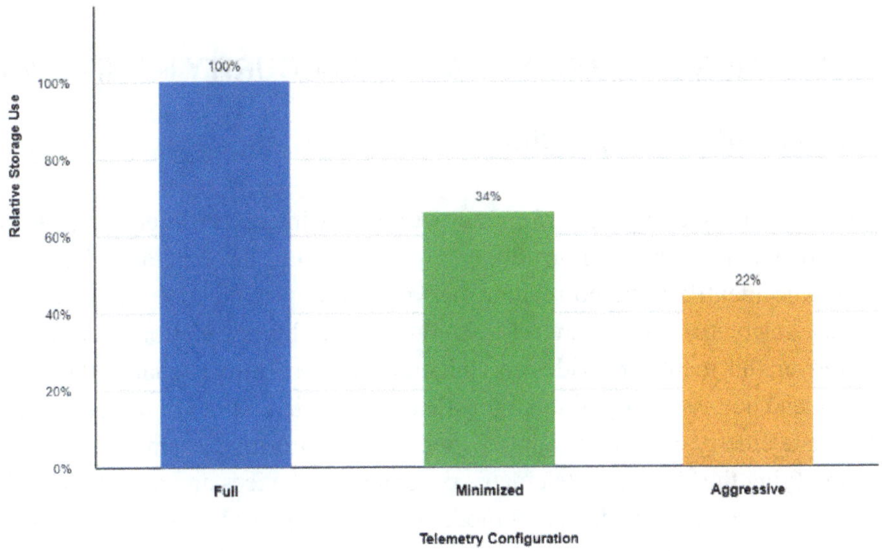

Figure 5. Security Visibility vs Data Minimization Tradeoff Model

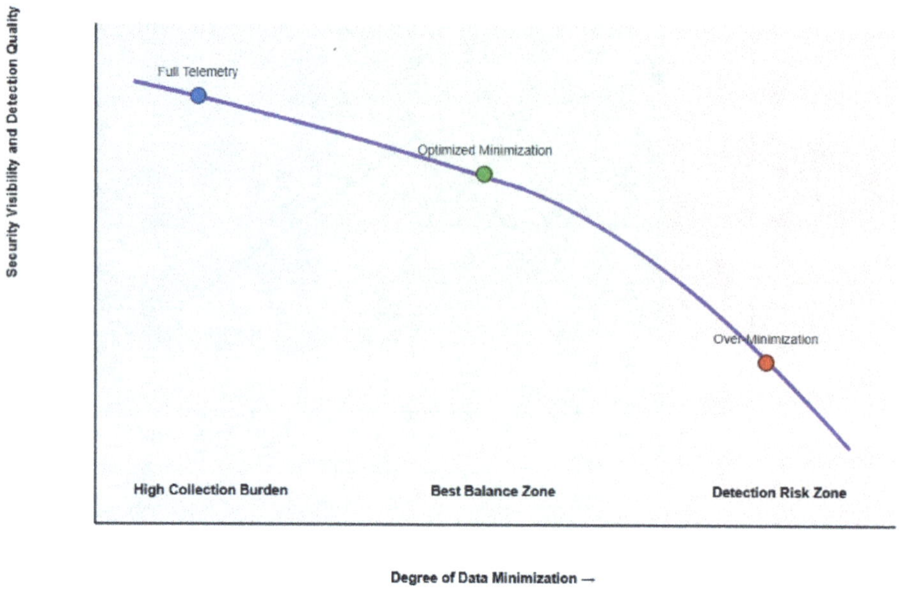

6. FUTURE DIRECTIONS OF PRIVACY-AWARE SECURITY MONITORING

6.1 AI-Driven Telemetry Optimization

AI integration with cybersecurity platforms is attracting more interest in order to help not only improve cyberattack detection but also data minimization alongside. AI runs through large datasets of historical security incidents and identifies the correlation between certain telemetry attributes and successful detection instances. Telemetry features are prioritized based on this correlation to cut down data signal redundancy. Moreover, this method provides organizations the flexibility to change their telemetry pipelines based on data and not assumptions about logs(Ramesh et al., 2025). On the other hand, AI is also applied to make the telemetry collection adaptive. Security monitoring systems possessing intelligence are capable of modifying the amount of telemetry generated by devices and applications depending on the current threat level. An anomaly detection model triggers increased logging if it detects suspicious behavior by a user or a system feature. Besides, AI-driven optimization also increases the throughput and quality of security analytics by limiting the use of lesser quality data and thereby the machine learning models operate on high-quality signals(Abashes et al., 2025).

6.2 Automated Data Minimization in Security Analytics

Emerging automation technology will help in the future realization of data minimization in security monitoring infrastructures. Manually dealing with telemetry policies in highly complex monitored environments is almost impossible. The automation of data governance can ensure the enforcement of minimization principles to telemetry data throughout its lifecycle, starting from the point of collection until its deletion(Alkhawatrah et al., 2025). One significant feature of automation is telemetry filtering and schema enforcement. The monitoring infrastructure will be capable of not accepting log attributes that have not been validated as part of the approved telemetry schemas. In this way, systems that are newly integrated into the monitoring infrastructure cannot bring in unnecessary data fields without the green light from governance authorities. Automated schema enforcement limits the risks of uncontrolled data gathering and ensures consistency is maintained between distributed monitoring environments(Abuowaida et al., 2025).

Automation can also bring advancements in retention management. Automated lifecycle management ensures that retention schedules applicable to different categories of telemetry data are enforced. Once the logs have been stored for the intended duration, automated sequences of steps delete or archive records as per governance policies. Cutting-edge governance platforms evaluate the attributes present in telemetry streams and single out ones that may lead to a privacy breach. These systems can also propose data transformations such as masking, pseudonymization, or aggregation to mitigate exposure while sustaining the analytical capability(Hanandeh et al., 2025). Incorporating such assessments directly into monitoring pipelines allows organizations to maintain constant surveillance on telemetry-related privacy hazards. Hence, automation is the key to scalable data minimization. Infusing governance controls right into the monitoring infrastructure, organizations can rest assured that minimization policies will be uniformly and automatically applied across security environments that are vast and rapidly changing(Duraimurugan et al., 2025).

6.3 Privacy-Preserving Threat Intelligence Systems

Up-to-date threat intelligence is indispensable to the way cybersecurity teams operate today. To outsmart cybercriminals, organizations have to be able to share information about the techniques that the attackers use, indicators of compromise, etc., in a secure manner. However, this data-sharing process can encounter many privacy concerns, especially when these logs contain personal information of users or sensitive operational details of the organization. Coming threat intelligence platforms will most certainly utilize privacy-preserving methods which will allow the exchange of sensitive telemetry in a secure, confidential manner. Federated learning, secure multiparty computation, and homomorphic encryption are some of the tools that will be used to train models across datasets that are distributed without raw data being made available(Masango et al., 2025). A federated learning setup is an example of multiple organizations working hand in hand to train a model with the help of their own data without physically sharing datasets. Participating entities need only to share their model updates which collectively make the global detection model. This approach guarantees privacy as the data itself is never outside the boundaries of an organization's infrastructure. In addition to that, secure multiparty computation involves cryptographically secure methods so computing functions without sacrificing the privacy of inputs is feasible. This opens the door for collaboration among parties to find threat patterns that are common among them without revealing the telemetry datasets to one another. Privacy-friendly threat intelligence is an important direction for the collective cybersecurity defense of the future. Through secure, protective information sharing, organizations stand to gain from each other's threat intelligence without compromising each other's confidential data(Alenazi et al., 2025).

6.4 Emerging Standards for Security Data Governance

The continuous development of cybersecurity monitoring has led regulators and industry groups to create new rules for security telemetry. In the end, their main aim is to give organizations a clear set of rules, so they know both how to monitor for security and protect privacy. Monitoring frameworks in the future will very likely highlight the principles of proportionality, transparency, and accountability. For record keeping, organizations might be required to identify the purpose of each telemetry source, justify the collection of certain attributes and demonstrate that monitoring activities are consistent with the legitimate security objectives(Makhadmeh et al., 2025). These are the things that are going to lead to the major rollout of structured governance practices, in the very similar way as it has been shown in the chapter. Besides regulatory requirements, there may be even technical recommendations made by industry standards for the design of privacy-aware monitoring systems. For example, such industry standards could recommend pseudonymization as a method for handling identity-related logs, require encryption of telemetry stores, or go as far as suggesting retention enforcement via automated means. (Turab et al., 2025) By aligning these best practices across sectors, governance frameworks will not only mitigate the risk of confusions but also help organizations in setting up monitoring systems that are both secure and compliant. One more major shift that is going to happen is the increasing emphasis on the concept of algorithmic accountability in AI-driven security monitoring solutions. As AI and machine learning will become inseparable components of cybersecurity (Alnawayseh et al., 2022), companies will be obliged to disclose not only how their models interpret telemetry data but also how they manage privacy risks in their threat detection approaches. Hence, governance regulations may be changing apart from just logging standards to also include the oversight of AI-enabled monitoring Sharma et al., 2025).

REFERENCES

Abashes, G. M., Elshqeirat, B., Abu-Shareha, A. A., & Alshraideh, M. (2025). BEYOND THE NOISE: UNVEILING MEANINGFUL PATTERNS IN MOBILE PAYMENT DATA USING FUZZY LOGIC AND SVM. *Journal of Theoretical and Applied Information Technology*, *103*(1).

Abdel-Jaber, M., Abdel-Jaber, M., Beale, R., & Makhoul, N. (2025). UHSC flexural strength prediction using optimized three-phase classifier and improved feature selection. *International Journal on Interactive Design and Manufacturing*, *19*(5), 3201–3218. Advance online publication. DOI: 10.1007/s12008-024-01812-3

Abdeljaber, O., & Al-Masaeed, S. (2025). Al-Mu′ani, L., Yaseen, H., & Alhnaity, B. (2025). Strategic Intelligence: The Power of AI in Planning Efficiency. *Human Behavior and Emerging Technologies*, (1). Advance online publication. DOI: 10.1155/hbe2/5383054

Abualghanam, O., Alazzam, H., Qatawneh, M., Alazab, M., & Al Sharaiah, M. (2025). Elevating Mobile Security: An Ensemble Approach for Enhanced Malware Detection with M-iForest. *International Journal of Interactive Mobile Technologies*, *19*(10), 129–151. Advance online publication. DOI: 10.3991/ijim.v19i10.51319

Abualhaj, M. M., Al-Khatib, S. N., Abu-Shareha, A. A., Hyassat, A., & Daoud, M. S. (2025). Smart Firewall for Phishing Detection Powered by Bio-Inspired Algorithms. *Journal of Advances in Information Technology*, *16*(11), 1529–1539. Advance online publication. DOI: 10.12720/jait.16.11.1529-1539

Abualhaj, M. M., Al-Khatib, S. N., Al Zyoud, M., Qaddara, I., & Anbar, M. (2025). Enhancing Intrusion Detection System Performance Using a Hybrid of Harris Hawks and Whale Optimization Algorithms. *Engineering. Technology and Applied Science Research*, *15*(4), 24354–24361. Advance online publication. DOI: 10.48084/etasr.10919

Abualhaj, M. M., Al-Khatib, S. N., Al-Zyoud, M., Qaddara, I., Hiari, M. O., & Aldossary, S. M. A. (2025). Enhanced Network Communication Security Through Hybrid Dragonfly-Bat Feature Selection for Intrusion Detection. *The Journal of Communication*, *20*(5). Advance online publication. DOI: 10.12720/jcm.20.5.607-618

Abualigah, L., Almomani, M. H., Alomari, S. A., Zitar, R. A., Migdady, H., Saleem, K., Snasel, V., Smerat, A., & Ezugwu, A. E. (2025). Optimizing Intrusion Detection in Wireless Sensor Networks via the Improved Chameleon Swarm Algorithm for Feature Selection. *IET Communications*, *19*(1), e70029. Advance online publication. DOI: 10.1049/cmu2.70029

Abualigah, L., Alomari, S. A., Almomani, M. H., Zitar, R. A., Migdady, H., Saleem, K., Smerat, A., Snasel, V., & Ezugwu, A. E. (2025). An enhanced Walrus Optimizer with opposition-based learning and mutation strategy for data clustering. *Array (New York, N.Y.)*, *26*, 100409. Advance online publication. DOI: 10.1016/j.array.2025.100409

Abuowaida, S., Abu Owida, H., Shelash Mohammad, S. I., Alshdaifat, N., Abu Elsoud, E., Alazaidah, R., Vasudevan, A., & Alshurideh, M. T. (2025). Evidence Detection in Cloud Forensics: Classifying Cyber-Attacks in IaaS Environments using machine learning. *Data and Metadata*, *4*, 699. Advance online publication. DOI: 10.56294/dm2025699

Al-Daoud, K. I., Yogeesh, N., Mohammad, S. I., Raja, N., Chetana, R., William, P., Vasudevan, A., Alshdaifa, N., & Hunitie, M. F. A. (2025). Explainability in AI Using Fuzzy Inference Systems For the Regression Problem. *Applied Mathematics & Information Sciences*, *19*(5), 973–987. Advance online publication. DOI: 10.18576/amis/190501

Al-Dmour, R., Al-Dmour, H., Al-Dmour, A., Basheer Amin, E., & Al-Dmour, Y. (2025). *AI and big data-driven social media recruitment: the mediating role of talent acquisition and employee engagement in bank performance*. Digital Transformation and Society., DOI: 10.1108/DTS-02-2025-0042

Al-Mousa, M., Amer, W., Abualhaj, M., Albilasi, S., Nasir, O., & Samara, G. (2025). Agile Proactive Cybercrime Evidence Analysis Model for Digital Forensics. *The International Arab Journal of Information Technology*, *22*(3). Advance online publication. DOI: 10.34028/iajit/22/3/15

Al-Okbi, N. K., Alomari, S. A., Zitar, R. A., Smerat, A., Nazzal, M. A., & Abualigah, L. (2025). Integrating Multimodal Emotion Recognition with Deep Q-Learning for Adaptive Social Robot Interaction. *International Journal of Robotics and Control Systems*, *5*(4), 2265–2289. Advance online publication. DOI: 10.31763/ijrcs.v5i4.2055

Al-Suhimat, R. I., Mohammed Ai, N., Ibrahim, A., Maaitah, N. O., & Al-Dmour, N. A. (2024). Review of Security Challenges Encountered in Internet of Things Technology. *2nd International Conference on Cyber Resilience, ICCR 2024*. DOI: 10.1109/ICCR61006.2024.10533052

Al-znamat, F. O., Alsaaidah, A., & Abu-Shareha, A. A. (2025). Malware Detection Using a Modified Bat Algorithm for Feature Selection. *International Journal of Intelligent Engineering and Systems*, *18*(9), 885–899. Advance online publication. DOI: 10.22266/ijies2025.1031.56

Alabdallat, R., Abualhaj, M., & Abu-Shareha, A. (2025). Android Malware Detection Using a Modified Dwarf Mongoose Algorithm. *International Journal of Intelligent Engineering and Systems*, *18*(8), 336–351. Advance online publication. DOI: 10.22266/ijies2025.0930.21

Aldaaja, Y., Odeh, M., Badrakhan, S. S., Sabri, M., Abdelrahim, Y., Samara, G., & Alsabatin, H. (2025). Quantifying the Managerial and Practical Benefits of Cloud Computing on Information Security in Higher Education Institutions. *Applied Mathematics & Information Sciences*, *19*(1), 15–24. Advance online publication. DOI: 10.18576/amis/190102

Aldabbas, A., Baniata, L. H., Alsaaidah, B. A., Mustafa, Z., Alali, M., & Rateb, R. (2025). Artificial intelligence-driven method for the discovery and prevention of distributed denial of service attacks. *IAES International Journal of Artificial Intelligence*, *14*(1), 614. Advance online publication. DOI: 10.11591/ijai.v14.i1.pp614-628

Alenazi, M. J. F., Al-Khasawneh, M. A., Rahman, S., & Faheem, Z. (2025). Deep Reinforcement Learning Based Flow Aware-QoS Provisioning in SD-IoT for Precision Agriculture. *Computational Intelligence*, *41*(1), e70023. Advance online publication. DOI: 10.1111/coin.70023

Ali, A. M., Al-Qerem, A., Hassan, M. R., Abu-Khadrah, A., & Jarrah, M. (2025). Traffic Monitoring and Control System for Smart City Pollution Regulation Using IoT and Correlated Capsule Networks. *IEEE Access : Practical Innovations, Open Solutions*, *13*, 46983–47003. Advance online publication. DOI: 10.1109/ACCESS.2025.3550966

Alibakhshikenari, M., Ali, E. M., din, I., Virdee, B. S., Ullah, S., Khan, S., See, C. H., Saber, T., & Limiti, E. (2025). Millimeter-Wave MIMO Array with Low Interactions Between its Antenna Elements for Fifth Generation Wireless Communication Networks. *Journal of Infrared, Millimeter and Terahertz Waves*, *46*(7), 46. Advance online publication. DOI: 10.1007/s10762-025-01062-8

Alkhawatrah, M. (2025). Random Forests Relay Selector in Buffer-Aided Cooperative Networks. *IEEE Access : Practical Innovations, Open Solutions*, *13*, 165402–165410. Advance online publication. DOI: 10.1109/ACCESS.2025.3612192

Alkhawatrah, M., AlAyyad, M., & Korostynska, O. (2025). Balanced inter-relay charging buffer-aided IOT networks. *Eurasip Journal on Wireless Communications and Networking, 2025*(1). DOI: 10.1186/s13638-025-02524-2

Alnawayseh, S. E. A., Al-Sit, W. T., & Ghazal, T. M. (2022). Smart Congestion Control in 5G/6G Networks Using Hybrid Deep Learning Techniques. *Complexity*, *2022*(1), 1781952. Advance online publication. DOI: 10.1155/2022/1781952

Alnsour, Y., Alsharo, M., Al-Essa, M., & Smerat, A. (2025). AI-Powered Election Insights: Predicting the 2024 Trump vs. Kamala Election Showdown with Machine Learning. *Journal of Intelligent Systems and Internet of Things*, *15*(1), 185–197. Advance online publication. DOI: 10.54216/JISIoT.150116

Arabasy, M., & Ghoneim, R. S. (2025). Enhancing sustainable urban design using machine learning: Comparative analysis of seven metaheuristic algorithms in energy-efficient digital architecture. *Frontiers in Built Environment*, *11*, 1526209. Advance online publication. DOI: 10.3389/fbuil.2025.1526209

Arabiat, A. M. (2025). Intelligent Model for Detecting GAN-Generated Images Based on Multi-Classifier and Advanced Data Mining Techniques. *International Journal of Electrical and Electronic Engineering and Telecommunications*, *14*(3). Advance online publication. DOI: 10.18178/ijeetc.14.3.147-157

Arabiat, A. M., & Eljaafreh, Y. G. (2025). Intrusion Detection in Wireless Sensor Networks Using ML Based Classification of Denial of Service (DoS) Attacks. *The Journal of Communication*, *20*(4). Advance online publication. DOI: 10.12720/jcm.20.4.501-514

Awais, Z., Hussain, M., Elshenawy, A., Arsalan, A., Anwar, M., Asif Habib, M., Jabbar, S., & Ahmad, M. (2025). ISCC: Intelligent Semantic Caching and Control for NDN-Enabled Industrial IoT Networks. *IEEE Access : Practical Innovations, Open Solutions*, *13*, 169881–169898. Advance online publication. DOI: 10.1109/ACCESS.2025.3614984

Ayub, N., Imtiaz, M. A., Ali, E., Alqahtani, A. M., Ali, A., Ashurov, M., Albouq, S., & Law, F. L. (2025). A Decision Framework for Intra Task Fixed Priority INTEL PXA270 Distributed Architecture for Soft RT-Applications Based on Deep Learning. *Engineering. Technology and Applied Science Research*, *15*(3), 23553–23558. Advance online publication. DOI: 10.48084/etasr.10006

Babaker, S., Khatibi, A., Alsoud, A. R., Kaur, J., Jagtap, J., Alkhayyat, A., & Shah, S. K. (2025). Improving Reliability and Data Management in Internet of Things Based Wireless Sensor Networks. *Internet Technology Letters*, *8*(6), e646. Advance online publication. DOI: 10.1002/itl2.646

Duraimurugan, S., Jayarin, P. J., Mohammad, S. I., Hariprasad, N., Vasudevan, A., Soon, E. E. H., Hussein, A. H., & Alshurideh, M. T. (2025). Enhanced Server-Client Framework for Optimizing QoS in Video Streaming Over Diverse Networks. *Applied Mathematics & Information Sciences*, *19*(1), 61–73. Advance online publication. DOI: 10.18576/amis/190106

Elomda, B. M., Abdelbary, T. A. A., Hassan, H. A., Hamza, K. S., & Kharma, Q. (2025). An Enhanced Multi-Layer Blockchain Security Model for Improved Latency and Scalability. *Information (Basel)*, *16*(3), 241. Advance online publication. DOI: 10.3390/info16030241

Ghazal, T. M. (2025). An IoT-Based Active Learning Convolutional Neural Networks Model for Predicting River Water Quality. *Journal of Soft Computing and Data Mining*, *6*(1). Advance online publication. DOI: 10.30880/jscdm.2025.06.01.021

Ghazal, T. M., Hasan, M. K., Abdul Wahab, A. N., Ibrahim, A., Khan, W. A., Raza, N. Z., Atta, A., & Mago, B. (2022). Towards Privacy Provisioning for Internet of Things (IoT). *International Conference on Cyber Resilience, ICCR 2022*. DOI: 10.1109/ICCR56254.2022.9995916

Ghazal, T. M., Hasan, M. K., Alzoubi, H. M., Al Hmmadi, M., Al-Dmour, N. A., Islam, S., Kamran, R., & Mago, B. (2022). Securing Smart Cities Using Blockchain Technology. *2022 1st International Conference on AI in Cybersecurity, ICAIC 2022*. DOI: 10.1109/ICAIC53980.2022.9896971

Ghazal, T. M., Hasan, M. K., Raju, K. N., Khan, M. A., Alshamayleh, A., Bhatt, M. W., & Ahmad, M. (2025). Data Space Privacy Model with Federated Learning Technique for Securing IoT Communications in Autonomous Marine Vehicles. *Journal of Intelligent & Robotic Systems*, *111*(3), 84. Advance online publication. DOI: 10.1007/s10846-025-02298-1

Ghazal, T. M., Janjua, J. I., Abushiba, W., Ahmad, M., Ihsan, A., & Al-Dmour, N. A. (2024). Cybersecurity Revolution via Large Language Models and Explainable AI. *2024 17th International Conference on Security of Information and Networks, SIN 2024*. DOI: 10.1109/SIN63213.2024.10871324

Hakami, H., Hasan, M. K., Alshamayleh, A., Saeed, A. Q., Mustafa, S. A., & Ghazal, T. M. (2025). Adaptive Neuro-Fuzzy Congestion Control Algorithm for Real-Time Multimedia Networking in Cloud-Based E-Learning Platforms. *Journal of Wireless Mobile Networks, Ubiquitous Computing and Dependable Applications*, *16*(3). Advance online publication. DOI: 10.58346/JOWUA.2025.I3.027

Hanandeh, A., Alfreijat, S. Y., Qutieshat, R. J., Alsha'ar, H. Y., Kilani, Q. A. L., & Saleem Khasawneh, M. A. (2025). Implementing AI Accuracy, Learning Rate, Inference Time on enhancing Big Data Analysis and Strategic Plan. *Data and Metadata*, *4*, 637. Advance online publication. DOI: 10.56294/dm2025637

Hasan, M. K., Ghazal, T. M., Alkhalifah, A., Abu Bakar, K. A., Omidvar, A., Nafi, N. S., & Agbinya, J. I. (2021). Fischer Linear Discrimination and Quadratic Discrimination Analysis–Based Data Mining Technique for Internet of Things Framework for Healthcare. *Frontiers in Public Health*, *9*, 737149. Advance online publication. DOI: 10.3389/fpubh.2021.737149 PMID: 34712639

Hasan, M. K., Ghazal, T. M., Issa, G., Islam, S., Ismail, A. F., & Kabir, S. R. (2025). Hashgraph consensus-based simultaneous, asynchronous and big-data supported blockchain mechanism for IT-OT enabled critical infrastructure sectors. *Journal of Ambient Intelligence and Humanized Computing*. Advance online publication. DOI: 10.1007/s12652-024-04942-4

Hiari, M., Alraba'nah, Y., & Qaddara, I. (2025). A Deep Learning-Based Intrusion Detection System using Refined LSTM for DoS Attack Detection. *Engineering. Technology and Applied Science Research, 15*(4), 25627–25633. Advance online publication. DOI: 10.48084/etasr.11499

Hyassat, A. S., Abu Zayed, R. E., Al Khateeb, E. A., Shalaldeh, A., Abdelhamied, M. M., & Qaddara, I. (2025). Unveiling Cyber Threats: An In-Depth Study on Data Mining Techniques for Exploit Attack Detection †. *Engineering Proceedings, 104*(1), 28. Advance online publication. DOI: 10.3390/engproc2025104028

Iftikhar, A., Mohammad, S. I., Alqudah, M. N., Al-Adwan, A. S., Vasudevan, A., Ali, I., & Farhan, M. (2025). Evaluating Inclusivity and Fairness of AI Recruitment Tools for Hiring People with Disabilities in the United Arab Emirates(UAE). *Data and Metadata, 4*. Advance online publication. DOI: 10.56294/dm2025487

Iskandarani, M. Z., & Hidayat, R. (2025). Analysis of Factors Affecting Spectrum Sensing in an IRS based Wireless Network. *International Journal on Advanced Science, Engineering and Information Technology, 15*(1), 300–309. Advance online publication. DOI: 10.18517/ijaseit.15.1.20491

Khaled Abdullah, S., & Qawasmeh, R. (2025). *Navigating the ethical and legal risks of AI marketing in Jordanian SMEs*. EDPACS., DOI: 10.1080/07366981.2025.2600205

Khan, A. A., Siddiqui, S., Al-Shamayleh, A. S., Akhunzada, A., & Dey, I. (2025). DFROG-MAC: A Dynamic Fragmentation-Based MAC for Prioritised Emergency Data Management in Vehicular Networks. *IET Wireless Sensor Systems, 15*(1), e70017. Advance online publication. DOI: 10.1049/wss2.70017

Khatibi, A., Babaker, S., Praveen, K. N. R., Chohan, J. S., Jadhav, A., Alsoud, A. R., Ramudu, M. J., & Jeet, R. (2025). Advanced AI-Driven Cybersecurity: Analyzing Emerging Threats and Defensive Strategies. *National Academy Science Letters*. Advance online publication. DOI: 10.1007/s40009-025-01897-8

Lakshmi, A. S., Sigamany, E. S. S., Traisa, R., Kumar, R., Reddy, K. R., Chohan, J. S., & Smerat, A. (2025). Enhancing Code Quality Through Automated Refactoring Using Transformer-Based Language Models. *International Journal of Advanced Computer Science and Applications, 16*(9). Advance online publication. DOI: 10.14569/IJACSA.2025.0160951

Mahfuri, M., & Ibrahim, A. (2024). AI-Driven Innovations: Transforming Data Support and Environmental Management for the Future. *2024 International Conference on Decision Aid Sciences and Applications, DASA 2024*. DOI: 10.1109/DASA63652.2024.10836162

Makhadmeh, S. N., Fraihat, S., Awad, M., Sanjalawe, Y., Al-Betar, M. A., & Awadallah, M. A. (2025). A crossover-integrated Marine Predator Algorithm for feature selection in intrusion detection systems within IoT environments. *Internet of Things : Engineering Cyber Physical Human Systems, 31*, 101536. Advance online publication. DOI: 10.1016/j.iot.2025.101536

Masadeh, R., Almomani, O., Zaqebah, A., Masadeh, S., Alshqurat, K., Sharieh, A., & Alsharman, N. (2025). Narwhal Optimizer: A Nature-Inspired Optimization Algorithm for Solving Complex Optimization Problems. *Computers, Materials & Continua, 85*(2), 3709–3737. Advance online publication. DOI: 10.32604/cmc.2025.066797

Masango, N. C., Agushaka, J. O., Amaefule, M. C., Taiwo, O., Zhang, P., Ezugwu, A. E., Saleem, K., Smerat, A., & Abualigah, L. (2025). Secure and efficient cloudlet networks: blockchain integration with agent-based proof of trust mechanism. *Eurasip Journal on Wireless Communications and Networking, 2025*(1). DOI: 10.1186/s13638-025-02439-y

Maz, Y. A., Anbar, M., Manickam, S., Abualhaj, M. M., Almalki, S. A., & Alabsi, B. A. (2025). Transfer Learning-Based Approach with an Ensemble Classifier for Detecting Keylogging Attack on the Internet of Things. *Computers, Materials & Continua*, *85*(3), 5287–5307. Advance online publication. DOI: 10.32604/cmc.2025.068257

Otair, M., Qawaqzeh, F. A., Alomari, S. A., Zitar, R. A., Migdady, H., Saleem, K., Smerat, A., Alsoud, A. R., & Abualigah, L. (2025). Enhanced Arithmetic Optimization Algorithm for Intrusion Detection in Wireless Sensor Networks. *International Journal of Communication Systems*, *38*(10), e70122. Advance online publication. DOI: 10.1002/dac.70122

Qaddara, I., & Alraba'nah, Y. (2025). Enhancing Requirements Classification Using Machine Learning Techniques. *SN Computer Science*, *6*(6), 649. Advance online publication. DOI: 10.1007/s42979-025-04158-z

Ramesh, J. V. N., Nimma, D., Dasari, R., Chaudhari Rane, D., AlGhamdi, A., Rao, K. B. V. B., Haider, S. A., Kuzieva, N., & Jangir, P. (2025). Safe and Reliable Two-Stage Online Offloading Algorithm for Transportation Cyber-Physical Systems. *IEEE Transactions on Intelligent Transportation Systems*, *26*(9), 14313–14322. Advance online publication. DOI: 10.1109/TITS.2025.3539934

Raza, M. A., Karim, A., Alqarni, M., Al-Khasawneh, M. A., Jumani, T. A., Aman, M., & Masud, M. I. (2025). An Intelligent Long Short-Term Memory-Based Machine Learning Model for the Potential Assessment of Global Hydropower Capacity in Sustainable Energy Transition and Security. *Energies*, *18*(13), 3324. Advance online publication. DOI: 10.3390/en18133324

Rehan, R., Sahran, S., Alyasseri, Z. A. A., Sani, N. S., & Al-Betar, M. A. (2025). Hyperparameters optimization of evolving spiking neural network using artificial bee colony for unsupervised anomaly detection. *Journal of Intelligent Systems*, *34*(1), 20240235. Advance online publication. DOI: 10.1515/jisys-2024-0235

Salama, S., Tamimi, O., Altayeb, M., & Abuzahew, A. (2025). MINIATURIZED L-SHAPED AND U-SHAPED RESONATOR BASED 8-BIT AND 12-BIT CHIPLESS RFID TAG. *IIUM Engineering Journal*, *26*(3), 260–269. Advance online publication. DOI: 10.31436/iiumej.v26i3.3646

Sanjalawe, Y., Al-E'mari, S., Abualhaj, M., Makhadmeh, S. N., Alsharaiah, M. A., & Hijazi, D. H. (2025). Recent advances in secretary bird optimization algorithm, its variants and applications. In *Evolutionary Intelligence* (Vol. 18, Number 3). DOI: 10.1007/s12065-025-01054-6

Sardar, R., Anees, T., Al-Shamayleh, A. S., Mehmood, E., Khalil, W., Akhunzada, A., & Shaikh, F. S. (2025). Challenges in detecting security threats in WoT: A systematic literature review. *Artificial Intelligence Review*, *58*(7), 196. Advance online publication. DOI: 10.1007/s10462-025-11176-z

Shamaylah, N., Ibrahim Mohammad, S., Al Oraini, B., Yaseen Al-Gaafreh, J. M., Mosallam Alqahtani, M., Vasudevan, A., Shlash Mohammad, A. A., & Ahmmad Hunitie, M. F. (2025). Data-Driven Decision-Making for Employee Training and Development in Jordanian Public Institutions. *Data and Metadata*, *4*, 886. Advance online publication. DOI: 10.56294/dm2025886

Sharma, K. P., Hussain, R., Jaharadak, A. A., Trawnih, A. A., Verma, D., Dasi, S., & Pant, S. (2025). Hybrid Convolutional Neural Network for Robust Attack Detection in Wireless Sensor Networks. *Internet Technology Letters*, *8*(6), e650. Advance online publication. DOI: 10.1002/itl2.650

Shlash Mohammad, A. A., Ibrahim Mohammad, S., Al-Daoud, K. I., Al Oraini, B., Mosallam Alqahtani, M., Vasudevan, A., & Ahmmad Hunitie, M. F. (2025). Riding into the Future: Transforming Jordan's Public Transportation with Predictive Analytics and Real-Time Data. *Data and Metadata*, *4*, 887. Advance online publication. DOI: 10.56294/dm2025887

Turab, N., Abushattal, A., Al-Nabulsi, J., & Owida, H. A. (2025). Advanced risk assessment using machine learning and sentiment analysis on log data. *IAES International Journal of Artificial Intelligence*, *14*(5), 3897. Advance online publication. DOI: 10.11591/ijai.v14.i5.pp3897-3905

Vasudevan, A., Albinaa, T. A., Mohammad, S. I., Sharmila, E., Raja, N., Soon, E. E. H., Alshurideh, M. T., & Al-Adwan, A. S. (2024). Bidirectional LSTM for Electronic Product Recommendation. *Applied Mathematics & Information Sciences*, *18*(6), 1443–1453. Advance online publication. DOI: 10.18576/amis/180621

Vasudevan, A., Tamilmani, K. T., Mohammad, S. I., Sridheepika, V. S., Raja, N., Soon, E. E. H., Nagaraj, S., & Al-Adwan, A. S. (2025). Voices of Concern: Contemplations on Socioeconomic, Ethical, and Developmental Impacts of AI. *Applied Mathematics & Information Sciences*, *19*(1), 221–232. Advance online publication. DOI: 10.18576/amis/190119

Yaseen, M., Ali, E., Sarwar, N., Jamel, L., Din, I., Yuldashev, F., & Law, F. (2025). Design of Minimal Spanning Tree and Analytic Hierarchical Process (SAHP) Based Hybrid Technique for Software Requirements Prioritization. *IET Software, 2025*(1). DOI: 10.1049/sfw2/8819735

Zhang, Z., Khishe, M., Qian, L., Martín, D., Abualigah, L., & Ghazal, T. M. (2024). Evolving chimp optimization algorithm using quantum mechanism for engineering applications: A case study on fire detection. *Journal of Computational Design and Engineering*, *11*(5), 143–163. Advance online publication. DOI: 10.1093/jcde/qwae074

Compilation of References

Abashes, G. M., Elshqeirat, B., Abu-Shareha, A. A., & Alshraideh, M. (2025). BEYOND THE NOISE: UNVEILING MEANINGFUL PATTERNS IN MOBILE PAYMENT DATA USING FUZZY LOGIC AND SVM. *Journal of Theoretical and Applied Information Technology*, *103*(1).

Abdel-Jaber, M. tasime, Makhoul, N., Abdel-Jaber, M. en, & Beale, R. (2025). Cost prediction for product development using hybrid deep learning model: a meta-heuristic model. *Multimedia Tools and Applications, 84*(27). DOI: 10.1007/s11042-024-20437-y

Abdel-Jaber, M., Abdel-Jaber, M., Beale, R., & Makhoul, N. (2025). UHSC flexural strength prediction using optimized three-phase classifier and improved feature selection. *International Journal on Interactive Design and Manufacturing*, *19*(5), 3201–3218. Advance online publication. DOI: 10.1007/s12008-024-01812-3

Abdeljaber, O., Al-Adwan, A. S., Yaseen, H., Falahat, M., Abdullah, A., & Fauzi, M. A. (2025). Shopping in the Metaverse: Decoding Consumer Intentions. *The International Information & Library Review*. Advance online publication. DOI: 10.1080/10572317.2025.2594293

Abdeljaber, O., & Al-Masaeed, S. (2025). Al-Mu'ani, L., Yaseen, H., & Alhnaity, B. (2025). Strategic Intelligence: The Power of AI in Planning Efficiency. *Human Behavior and Emerging Technologies*, (1). Advance online publication. DOI: 10.1155/hbe2/5383054

Abualghanam, O., Alazzam, H., Qatawneh, M., Alazab, M., & Al Sharaiah, M. (2025). Elevating Mobile Security: An Ensemble Approach for Enhanced Malware Detection with M-iForest. *International Journal of Interactive Mobile Technologies*, *19*(10), 129–151. Advance online publication. DOI: 10.3991/ijim.v19i10.51319

Abualhaj, M. M., Abu-Shareha, A. A., Al-Khatib, S. N., Alsaaidah, A. M., & Anbar, M. (2025). Improving firewall performance using hybrid of optimization algorithms and decision trees classifier. *IAES International Journal of Artificial Intelligence*, *14*(4), 2839. Advance online publication. DOI: 10.11591/ijai.v14.i4.pp2839-2848

Abualhaj, M. M., Abu-Shareha, A. A., & Rateb, R. (2025). Enhancing intrusion detection systems with hybrid HHO-WOA optimization and gradient boosting machine classifier. *International Journal of Reconfigurable and Embedded Systems*, *14*(2), 518. Advance online publication. DOI: 10.11591/ijres.v14.i2.pp518-526

Abualhaj, M. M., Al-Khatib, S. N., Abu-Shareha, A. A., Hyassat, A., & Daoud, M. S. (2025). Smart Firewall for Phishing Detection Powered by Bio-Inspired Algorithms. *Journal of Advances in Information Technology*, *16*(11), 1529–1539. Advance online publication. DOI: 10.12720/jait.16.11.1529-1539

Abualhaj, M. M., Al-Khatib, S. N., Al Zyoud, M., Qaddara, I., & Anbar, M. (2025). Enhancing Intrusion Detection System Performance Using a Hybrid of Harris Hawks and Whale Optimization Algorithms. *Engineering. Technology and Applied Science Research*, *15*(4), 24354–24361. Advance online publication. DOI: 10.48084/etasr.10919

Abualhaj, M. M., Al-Khatib, S. N., Al-Zyoud, M., Qaddara, I., Hiari, M. O., & Aldossary, S. M. A. (2025). Enhanced Network Communication Security Through Hybrid Dragonfly-Bat Feature Selection for Intrusion Detection. *The Journal of Communication*, *20*(5). Advance online publication. DOI: 10.12720/jcm.20.5.607-618

Abualhaj, M. M., Al-Khatib, S., Al Shafi, N., Qaddara, I., & Hyassat, A. (2025). Utilizing Gray Wolf Optimization Algorithm in Malware Forensic Investigation. *Journal of Computational and Cognitive Engineering*, *4*(4), 591–602. Advance online publication. DOI: 10.47852/bonviewJCCE52025053

Abualhaj, M. M.I, Al-Khatib, S. N., Abu-Shareha, A. A., Almomani, O., Al-Mimi, H., Al-Allawee, A., Daoud, M. S., & Anbar, M. (2025). Spam Detection Boosted by Firefly-Based Feature Selection and Optimized Classifiers. *International Journal of Advances in Soft Computing and Its Applications*, *17*(3). Advance online publication. DOI: 10.15849/IJASCA.251130.02

Abualigah, L., Almomani, M. H., Alomari, S. A., Zitar, R. A., Migdady, H., Saleem, K., Snasel, V., Smerat, A., & Ezugwu, A. E. (2025). Optimizing Intrusion Detection in Wireless Sensor Networks via the Improved Chameleon Swarm Algorithm for Feature Selection. *IET Communications*, *19*(1), e70029. Advance online publication. DOI: 10.1049/cmu2.70029

Abualigah, L., Alomari, S. A., Almomani, M. H., Zitar, R. A., Migdady, H., Saleem, K., Smerat, A., Snasel, V., & Ezugwu, A. E. (2025). An enhanced Walrus Optimizer with opposition-based learning and mutation strategy for data clustering. *Array (New York, N.Y.)*, *26*, 100409. Advance online publication. DOI: 10.1016/j.array.2025.100409

Abuowaida, S., Abu Owida, H., Shelash Mohammad, S. I., Alshdaifat, N., Abu Elsoud, E., Alazaidah, R., Vasudevan, A., & Alshurideh, M. T. (2025). Evidence Detection in Cloud Forensics: Classifying Cyber-Attacks in IaaS Environments using machine learning. *Data and Metadata*, *4*, 699. Advance online publication. DOI: 10.56294/dm2025699

Abu-Shareha, A. A., Abualhaj, M. M., Alsharaiah, M. A., Al-Saaidah, A., & Achuthan, A. (2025). Diabetes Prediction Through Classification Using Pima Dataset: Survey and Evaluation. *Journal of Soft Computing and Data Mining*, *6*(1). Advance online publication. DOI: 10.30880/jscdm.2025.06.01.001

Ahmed, K. A., Ibrahim, A., Qudr, L. A. Z., Tawfeq, J. F., Al Falahi, Q., & Radhi, A. D. (2025). *Developing Adaptive AI-Driven Cybersecurity Frameworks for Real-Time Detection of Polymorphic Malware in IoT Networks*. DOI: 10.1109/ICBATS66542.2025.11258540

Ahmed, N., Rafiq, M., Rehman, M. A., Shaikh, T. S., Alqahtani, A. M., Khan, I., Imran, M., & Niazai, S. (2025). A dynamically consistent and time-efficient numerical design for the reaction diffusion model in three space dimensions. *Applied Mathematics in Science and Engineering*, *33*(1), 2495158. Advance online publication. DOI: 10.1080/27690911.2025.2495158

Ahmed, Z. E., Hasan, M. K., Hashim, A. A., Saeed, R. A., Mokhtar, R. A., Singh, S. P., & Ghazal, T. M. (2022). Optimization Procedure for Intelligent Internet of Things Applications. *2022 International Conference on Business Analytics for Technology and Security, ICBATS 2022*. DOI: 10.1109/ICBATS54253.2022.9759065

Akram, A. S., Abbas, S., Khan, M. A., Athar, A., Ghazal, T. M., & Al Hamadi, H. (2024). Smart Energy Management System Using Machine Learning. *Computers, Materials & Continua*, *78*(1), 959–973. Advance online publication. DOI: 10.32604/cmc.2023.032216

Al Abbadi, Y., Al-Ghraibah, A., & Altayeb, M. (2025). Tooth cavities detection based on digital image processing and artificial intelligence techniques. *Journal of Medical Engineering & Technology*. Advance online publication. DOI: 10.1080/03091902.2025.2574081 PMID: 41099352

Al Hindi, G., Alshraideh, M., Hussein, A. H., Eliyan, L. F., & Al-Dhaqm, A. (2025). Hacking Back: Using Genetic Algorithms to Outsmart Hackers. *Journal of Computational Science*, *21*(9), 2049–2064. Advance online publication. DOI: 10.3844/jcssp.2025.2049.2064

Al Nasar, M. R., Ghazal, T. M., Al-Tarawni, M. A. M., Ahmed, A. A., Abu-Shareha, A. A., & Ahmed, S. M. (2025). Hierarchical Edge-Cloud Collaborative AI Algorithm for Energy-Efficient lot Management in Ubiquitous Computing Environments. *Journal of Wireless Mobile Networks, Ubiquitous Computing and Dependable Applications*, *16*(3). Advance online publication. DOI: 10.58346/JOWUA.2025.I3.035

Alabdallat, R. D., Abualhaj, M. M., & Abu-Shareha, A. (2025). Enhanced Multiclass Android Malware Detection Using a Modified Dwarf Mongoose Algorithm. *International Journal of Analysis and Applications*, *23*, 248. Advance online publication. DOI: 10.28924/2291-8639-23-2025-248

Alabdallat, R., Abualhaj, M., & Abu-Shareha, A. (2025). Android Malware Detection Using a Modified Dwarf Mongoose Algorithm. *International Journal of Intelligent Engineering and Systems*, *18*(8), 336–351. Advance online publication. DOI: 10.22266/ijies2025.0930.21

Al-Adwan, A. S., & Abdeljaber, O. (2025). Toward a resilient and smart supply chain: identifying and prioritizing barriers to metaverse adoption. *International Journal of Industrial Engineering and Operations Management*. DOI: 10.1108/IJIEOM-06-2025-0113

Al-Adwan, A. S., Al-Adwan, A., Li, N., Fauzi, M. A., Jafar, R. M. S., Habibi, A., & Falahat, M. (2025). IMMERSIVE LEARNING MEETS THEORY: MODELING EDUVERSE ADOPTION IN HIGHER EDUCATION. *Journal of Information Technology Education*, *24*, 042. Advance online publication. DOI: 10.28945/5669

Al-Bahtiti, A. S., Tayeh, B. A., Baghdadi, A., Alaloul, W. S., & Abu Aisheh, Y. I. (2025). Drivers for adopting augmented reality and virtual reality technologies in the construction project management in Gaza City. *Journal of Asian Architecture and Building Engineering*, 1–18. Advance online publication. DOI: 10.1080/13467581.2025.2507235

Aldaaja, Y., Odeh, M., Badrakhan, S. S., Sabri, M., Abdelrahim, Y., Samara, G., & Alsabatin, H. (2025). Quantifying the Managerial and Practical Benefits of Cloud Computing on Information Security in Higher Education Institutions. *Applied Mathematics & Information Sciences*, *19*(1), 15–24. Advance online publication. DOI: 10.18576/amis/190102

Aldabbas, A., Baniata, L. H., Alsaaidah, B. A., Mustafa, Z., Alali, M., & Rateb, R. (2025). Artificial intelligence-driven method for the discovery and prevention of distributed denial of service attacks. *IAES International Journal of Artificial Intelligence*, *14*(1), 614. Advance online publication. DOI: 10.11591/ijai.v14.i1.pp614-628

Al-Daoud, K. I., Yogeesh, N., Mohammad, S. I. S., Raja, N., Jabeen, F. T. Z., William, P., Vasudevan, A., Hunitie, M. F. A., & Alshdaifat, N. (2025). Fuzzy Linear Programming in Real-World Applications: A Comparative Study of Agricultural and Financial Optimization. *Applied Mathematics & Information Sciences*, *19*(4), 849–862. Advance online publication. DOI: 10.18576/amis/190411

Al-Daoud, K. I., Yogeesh, N., Mohammad, S. I., Raja, N., Chetana, R., William, P., Vasudevan, A., Alshdaifa, N., & Hunitie, M. F. A. (2025). Explainability in AI Using Fuzzy Inference Systems For the Regression Problem. *Applied Mathematics & Information Sciences*, *19*(5), 973–987. Advance online publication. DOI: 10.18576/amis/190501

Al-Dmour, R., Al-Dmour, H., Al-Dmour, A., Basheer Amin, E., & Al-Dmour, Y. (2025). *AI and big data-driven social media recruitment: the mediating role of talent acquisition and employee engagement in bank performance*. Digital Transformation and Society., DOI: 10.1108/DTS-02-2025-0042

Alenazi, M. J. F., Al-Khasawneh, M. A., Rahman, S., & Faheem, Z. (2025). Deep Reinforcement Learning Based Flow Aware-QoS Provisioning in SD-IoT for Precision Agriculture. *Computational Intelligence*, *41*(1), e70023. Advance online publication. DOI: 10.1111/coin.70023

Al-Falouji, M., Al Btoush, R., Abu Hajar, H., & Tarwaneh, B. (2025). Landslide Stabilization of Al-Adasiah Road Using Pile Wall Retaining System. *Jordan Journal of Civil Engineering*, *19*(4). Advance online publication. DOI: 10.14525/JJCE.v19i4.02

Alghlayini, S., Al-Betar, M. A., & Atef, M. (2025). Enhancing Non-Invasive Blood Glucose Prediction from Photoplethysmography Signals via Heart Rate Variability-Based Features Selection Using Meta-heuristic Algorithms. *Algorithms*, *18*(2), 95. Advance online publication. DOI: 10.3390/a18020095

Al-Habashneh, A. G., Al-Daoud, K. I., Oraini, B., Al, , & Shelash, S. I. (2025). The impact of artificial intelligence on the development of electronic financial services. *International Journal of Data and Network Science*, *9*(2), 317–322. Advance online publication. DOI: 10.5267/j.ijdns.2024.8.012

Alharbi, Y., Yadav, K., Dutta, D., Smerat, A., & Ranjbar, F. (2026). Thermodynamic behavior of CO2–organic mixtures: Density prediction using explainable machine learning algorithms. *Results in Engineering*, *29*, 108687. Advance online publication. DOI: 10.1016/j.rineng.2025.108687

Ali, A. M., Al-Qerem, A., Hassan, M. R., Abu-Khadrah, A., & Jarrah, M. (2025). Traffic Monitoring and Control System for Smart City Pollution Regulation Using IoT and Correlated Capsule Networks. *IEEE Access : Practical Innovations, Open Solutions*, *13*, 46983–47003. Advance online publication. DOI: 10.1109/ACCESS.2025.3550966

Alibakhshikenari, M., Ali, E. M., din, I., Virdee, B. S., Ullah, S., Khan, S., See, C. H., Saber, T., & Limiti, E. (2025). Millimeter-Wave MIMO Array with Low Interactions Between its Antenna Elements for Fifth Generation Wireless Communication Networks. *Journal of Infrared, Millimeter and Terahertz Waves*, *46*(7), 46. Advance online publication. DOI: 10.1007/s10762-025-01062-8

Alkhawatrah, M., AlAyyad, M., & Korostynska, O. (2025). Balanced inter-relay charging buffer-aided IOT networks. *Eurasip Journal on Wireless Communications and Networking, 2025*(1). DOI: 10.1186/s13638-025-02524-2

Alkhawatrah, M. (2025). Random Forests Relay Selector in Buffer-Aided Cooperative Networks. *IEEE Access : Practical Innovations, Open Solutions, 13*, 165402–165410. Advance online publication. DOI: 10.1109/ACCESS.2025.3612192

ALMahadin, G., Shabaz, M., Khan, I. R., Vimal, V., Keshta, I., & Maguluri, L. P.ALMahadin. (2025). Content-aware recommendation system for integrated temporal semantic review text over web of things. *Service Oriented Computing and Applications, 19*(1), 77–91. Advance online publication. DOI: 10.1007/s11761-024-00408-9

Almajed, R., Ibrahim, A., Abualkishik, A. Z., Mourad, N., & Almansour, F. A. (2022). Using machine learning algorithm for detection of cyber-attacks in cyber physical systems. *Periodicals of Engineering and Natural Sciences, 10*(3), 261. Advance online publication. DOI: 10.21533/pen.v10i3.3035

Al-Momani, M. M., Alqudah, T. A., Al Swiety, I. A., Mahrakani, N., Nassoura, M. B. A., & Al Attar, M. K. (2025). Integrating Artificial Intelligence (AI) and Business Intelligence (BI): A Framework for Improving Enterprise Performance. *TEM Journal, 14*(3). https://doi.org/DOI: 10.18421/TEM143-26

Almomani, O., Arabiat, A., Al Tayeb, M., Almaiah, M. A., Obeidat, M., Aldhyani, T. H. H., Shehab, R., & Rowad, M. (2025). A Robust Model for Android Malware Detection via ML and DL classifiers. *Mesopotamian Journal of Big Data, 2025*. Advance online publication. DOI: 10.58496/MJBD/2025/017

Al-Mousa, M., Amer, W., Abualhaj, M., Albilasi, S., Nasir, O., & Samara, G. (2025). Agile Proactive Cybercrime Evidence Analysis Model for Digital Forensics. *The International Arab Journal of Information Technology*, *22*(3). Advance online publication. DOI: 10.34028/iajit/22/3/15

Alnawafleh, N. M., Ibrahim, A., & Pradhan, M. R. (2024). Review of the Mechanisms Used to Protect the Big Data from Attacks. *2nd International Conference on Cyber Resilience, ICCR 2024*. DOI: 10.1109/ICCR61006.2024.10533073

Alnawayseh, S. E. A., Al-Sit, W. T., & Ghazal, T. M. (2022). Smart Congestion Control in 5G/6G Networks Using Hybrid Deep Learning Techniques. *Complexity*, *2022*(1), 1781952. Advance online publication. DOI: 10.1155/2022/1781952

Alnawayseh, S. E. A., Muhammad, M. H. G., Hassan, Z., Fatima, M., Aslam, M. S., Ibrahim, A., & Ateeq, K. (2023). Resource Provisioning in Cloud Computing using Fuzzy Logic Control System: An adaptive approach. *2nd International Conference on Business Analytics for Technology and Security, ICBATS 2023*. DOI: 10.1109/ICBATS57792.2023.10111481

Alnsour, Y., Alsharo, M., Al-Essa, M., & Smerat, A. (2025). AI-Powered Election Insights: Predicting the 2024 Trump vs. Kamala Election Showdown with Machine Learning. *Journal of Intelligent Systems and Internet of Things*, *15*(1), 185–197. Advance online publication. DOI: 10.54216/JISIoT.150116

Al-Okbi, N. K., Alomari, S. A., Hadi, W. J., Ajrash, A. S., Smerat, A., & Abualigah, L. (2025). Defending Digital Integrity: Advances in Media Forgery Analysis Research and Cybersecurity Development. *SN Computer Science*, *6*(8), 913. Advance online publication. DOI: 10.1007/s42979-025-04462-8

Al-Okbi, N. K., Alomari, S. A., Zitar, R. A., Smerat, A., Nazzal, M. A., & Abualigah, L. (2025). Integrating Multimodal Emotion Recognition with Deep Q-Learning for Adaptive Social Robot Interaction. *International Journal of Robotics and Control Systems*, *5*(4), 2265–2289. Advance online publication. DOI: 10.31763/ijrcs.v5i4.2055

Alomoush, R. A., Al-tarawneh, A. M. A., Alhossan, S. M., Altabeeb, N. A. K., & Tarawneh, A. W. (2025). Difficulties of using digital technology and their relationship to the quality of vocational performance among teachers and counselors. *Journal of Education and e-learning Research*, *12*(4), 655–663. Advance online publication. DOI: 10.20448/jeelr.v12i4.7856

Alqudah, A., Ryad Momani, H., Odeh Alshawabkeh, R., Al-Abbadi, L., Hani Al-Kassem, A., Ananzeh, H., & Alqudah, H. (2025). *The impact of Cyber-Physical Systems on logistics sustainability: The role of smart energy monitoring as a mediator in improving energy efficiency*. EDPACS., DOI: 10.1080/07366981.2025.2596460

Alraba'nah, Y., Al-Sharaeh, S., & Al Hindi, G. (2025). Enhancing Intrusion Detection Using Hybrid Long Short-Term Memory and XGBoost. *Journal of Soft Computing and Data Mining*, *6*(1). Advance online publication. DOI: 10.30880/jscdm.2025.06.01.016

Alraba'nah, Y., & Hiari, M. (2025). Improved convolutional neural networks for aircraft type classification in remote sensing images. *IAES International Journal of Artificial Intelligence*, *14*(2), 1540. Advance online publication. DOI: 10.11591/ijai.v14.i2.pp1540-1547

Alshafei, I. A., AlDweik, S. M., Hassouneh, M., AbuKarki, H., Jarrar, A. A., & Mansour, Q. S. (2025). Digital Transformation in Design Education: Exploring the Challenges and Opportunities in Jordanian Higher Education. *Computers*, *14*(12), 535. Advance online publication. DOI: 10.3390/computers14120535

Al-Suhimat, R. I., Mohammed Ai, N., Ibrahim, A., Maaitah, N. O., & Al-Dmour, N. A. (2024). Review of Security Challenges Encountered in Internet of Things Technology. *2nd International Conference on Cyber Resilience, ICCR 2024*. DOI: 10.1109/ICCR61006.2024.10533052

Al-znamat, F. O., Alsaaidah, A., & Abu-Shareha, A. A. (2025). Malware Detection Using a Modified Bat Algorithm for Feature Selection. *International Journal of Intelligent Engineering and Systems*, *18*(9), 885–899. Advance online publication. DOI: 10.22266/ijies2025.1031.56

Arabasy, M., & Ghoneim, R. S. (2025). Enhancing sustainable urban design using machine learning: Comparative analysis of seven metaheuristic algorithms in energy-efficient digital architecture. *Frontiers in Built Environment*, *11*, 1526209. Advance online publication. DOI: 10.3389/fbuil.2025.1526209

Arabiat, A. M. (2025). Intelligent Model for Detecting GAN-Generated Images Based on Multi-Classifier and Advanced Data Mining Techniques. *International Journal of Electrical and Electronic Engineering and Telecommunications*, *14*(3). Advance online publication. DOI: 10.18178/ijeetc.14.3.147-157

Arabiat, A. M., & Eljaafreh, Y. G. (2025). Intrusion Detection in Wireless Sensor Networks Using ML Based Classification of Denial of Service (DoS) Attacks. *The Journal of Communication*, *20*(4). Advance online publication. DOI: 10.12720/jcm.20.4.501-514

Arabiat, A., & Altayeb, M. (2025). Driving behavior analytics: An intelligent system based on machine learning and data mining techniques. *Bulletin of Electrical Engineering and Informatics*, *14*(3), 2055–2065. Advance online publication. DOI: 10.11591/eei.v14i3.9095

Arabiat, A., Altayeb, M., & Alkhrissat, T. (2025). Innovative AI Approaches for Concrete Strength Prediction: Towards Sustainable Buildings. *Civil Engineering and Architecture*, *13*(6), 4254–4265. Advance online publication. DOI: 10.13189/cea.2025.130612

Arabiat, A., Altayeb, M., & Salama, S. (2025). Artificial intelligence-powered smart roads: Leveraging orange3 for traffic signs recognition. *IAES International Journal of Artificial Intelligence*, *14*(5), 3816. Advance online publication. DOI: 10.11591/ijai.v14.i5.pp3816-3826

Awais, Z., Hussain, M., Elshenawy, A., Arsalan, A., Anwar, M., Asif Habib, M., Jabbar, S., & Ahmad, M. (2025). ISCC: Intelligent Semantic Caching and Control for NDN-Enabled Industrial IoT Networks. *IEEE Access : Practical Innovations, Open Solutions*, *13*, 169881–169898. Advance online publication. DOI: 10.1109/ACCESS.2025.3614984

Ayub, N., Imtiaz, M. A., Ali, E., Alqahtani, A. M., Ali, A., Ashurov, M., Albouq, S., & Law, F. L. (2025). A Decision Framework for Intra Task Fixed Priority INTEL PXA270 Distributed Architecture for Soft RT-Applications Based on Deep Learning. *Engineering. Technology and Applied Science Research*, *15*(3), 23553–23558. Advance online publication. DOI: 10.48084/etasr.10006

Azeem, S., Javed, S., Naseer, I., Ali, O., & Ghazal, T. M. (2025). A New Hybrid PSO-HHO Wrapper Based Optimization for Feature Selection. *IEEE Access : Practical Innovations, Open Solutions*, *13*, 87090–87099. Advance online publication. DOI: 10.1109/ACCESS.2025.3570901

Babaker, S., Khatibi, A., Alsoud, A. R., Kaur, J., Jagtap, J., Alkhayyat, A., & Shah, S. K. (2025). Improving Reliability and Data Management in Internet of Things Based Wireless Sensor Networks. *Internet Technology Letters*, *8*(6), e646. Advance online publication. DOI: 10.1002/itl2.646

Bektemyssova, G., Montazeri, Z., Dehghani, M., Ibraheem, I. K., Smerat, A., Werner, F., Al-Salih, A. A. M. M., Ahmed, M. A., & Eguchi, K. (2025). Search and Rescue Algorithm (SRA): A Metaheuristic Approach for Efficient Constrained Engineering Optimization. *International Journal of Intelligent Engineering and Systems*, *18*(10), 607–621. Advance online publication. DOI: 10.22266/ijies2025.1130.39

Benali, A., Kharbouch, H., Della Krachai, M., Singh, J. P., Bouddou, R., Yesma, B., Belabbes, A., Husein, A., Salau, A. O., & Rubanenko, O. (2025). Dual-Stream Convolutional Networks for Scalable and Precise Water Body Mapping from Multispectral Earth Observation Imagery. *International Journal of Computational Intelligence Systems*, *18*(1), 260. Advance online publication. DOI: 10.1007/s44196-025-00985-3

Braik, M., Kassaymeh, S., Almiani, M., Albashish, D., Awadallah, M., Bataineh, B., & Al-Hiary, H. (2025). Advancements in global optimization with an empowered capuchin search algorithm. *Neural Computing & Applications*, *37*(24), 19707–19749. Advance online publication. DOI: 10.1007/s00521-025-11421-0

Cui, D., Harrison, A., Fendzi-Donfack, E., Dagal, I., Jangir, P., Mahmoud, M. M., Malkani, P., Mbasso, W. F., Tiako, P., & Smerat, A. (2026). Enhancing Short-Term Electricity Forecasting with Advanced Machine Learning Techniques. *Journal of Electrical Engineering & Technology*, *21*(1), 147–187. Advance online publication. DOI: 10.1007/s42835-025-02430-z

Dar, A. A., Bhavithra, H. A., Awasthi, A. K., Sabha, S. U., Dar, J. G., Smerat, A., & Sindhuja, S. (2025). Inventory Optimization for Perishables: A Probabilistic and Fuzzy Modeling Approach. *Mathematical Modelling of Engineering Problems*, *12*(8). Advance online publication. DOI: 10.18280/mmep.120825

Dheeb, S. A., AL-Azzawi, W. S. A.-B., Suleiman, A. K., Ibrahim, A., & Ghwanmeh, S. (2025). *The Role of Generative Artificial Intelligence in Advancing Multilingual Intelligent Support Systems*. DOI: 10.1109/ICCR67387.2025.11291954

Dinler, Ö. B., Bektemyssova, G., Şahin, C. B., Montazeri, Z., Dehghani, M., Smerat, A., Werner, F., & Eguchi, K. (2025). Carpenter Optimization Algorithm: A Human-inspired Metaheuristic for Robust and Efficient Constrained Optimization. *International Journal of Intelligent Engineering and Systems*, *18*(11), 344–357. Advance online publication. DOI: 10.22266/ijies2025.1231.21

Duraimurugan, S., Jayarin, P. J., Mohammad, S. I., Hariprasad, N., Vasudevan, A., Soon, E. E. H., Hussein, A. H., & Alshurideh, M. T. (2025). Enhanced Server-Client Framework for Optimizing QoS in Video Streaming Over Diverse Networks. *Applied Mathematics & Information Sciences*, *19*(1), 61–73. Advance online publication. DOI: 10.18576/amis/190106

Ebbini, M. M., Qtaishat, A. K., Aburub, F. A., & Jaradat, M. S. (2025). Impact of Ethical Fintech on Micro Entrepreneurs in Jordan. *International Journal of Advances in Soft Computing and Its Applications*, *17*(3). Advance online publication. DOI: 10.15849/IJASCA.251130.10

Eke, C. I., Al-Shamayleh, A. S., Phiri, M., Maswadi, K., Kwaghtyo, D. K., Mulenga, M., & Iyidobi, C. J. (2025). Machine Learning Based Mobile Big Data Analytics: State-of-the-art Applications, Taxonomy, Challenges and Future Research Directions. *Nigerian Journal of Technological Development*, *22*(4). Advance online publication. DOI: 10.63746/njtd.v22i4.3385

Elkaradawy, A., Elshenawy, A., & Harb, H. (2025). Enhancing Cloud Job Failure Prediction With a Novel Multilayer Voting-Based Framework. *IEEE Access : Practical Innovations, Open Solutions*, *13*, 140600–140613. Advance online publication. DOI: 10.1109/ACCESS.2025.3593808

Elomda, B. M., Abdelbary, T. A. A., Hassan, H. A., Hamza, K. S., & Kharma, Q. (2025). An Enhanced Multi-Layer Blockchain Security Model for Improved Latency and Scalability. *Information (Basel)*, *16*(3), 241. Advance online publication. DOI: 10.3390/info16030241

Farman, M., Gokbulut, N., Shehzad, A., Nisar, K. S., Hincal, E., & Sambas, A. (2025). Fractional order malaria epidemic model: Qualitative and computational study to determine the dynamics for sensitivity prevalence. *Journal of Computational Science*, *91*, 102656. Advance online publication. DOI: 10.1016/j.jocs.2025.102656

Fatima, W., Rizvi, S. S. R., Ghazal, T. M., Kharma, Q. M., Ahmad, M., Abbas, S., Furqan, M., & Adnan, K. M. (2025). Abstractive Text Summarization in Arabic-Like Script Using Multi-Encoder Architecture and Semantic Extraction Techniques. *IEEE Access : Practical Innovations, Open Solutions, 13*, 104977–104991. Advance online publication. DOI: 10.1109/ACCESS.2025.3575610

Fauzi, M. A., Alias, U. N., Nya-Ling Tan, C., Wider, W., Mukherjee, S., Al-Adwan, A. S., & Udang, L. N. (2025). The Present and Future Trends of Leadership Styles and Knowledge Hiding Through Science Mapping Analysis. *Journal of Information and Knowledge Management, 24*(5), 2550040. Advance online publication. DOI: 10.1142/S0219649225500406

Ghazal, T. M. (2025b). Federated Learning for Intelligent Sensing and Navigation Technologies for 6G Communications. *Journal of Sensors, 2025*(1). DOI: 10.1155/js/3746147

Ghazal, T. M., Hasan, M. K., Alzoubi, H. M., Al Hmmadi, M., Al-Dmour, N. A., Islam, S., Kamran, R., & Mago, B. (2022). Securing Smart Cities Using Blockchain Technology. *2022 1st International Conference on AI in Cybersecurity, ICAIC 2022*. DOI: 10.1109/ICAIC53980.2022.9896971

Ghazal, T. M., Hasan, M. K., Mokhtar, U. A., Safie, N., Alshamayleh, A., & Ahmad, M. (2025). Machine learning-based real-time outage fault detection for distribution networks in smart grid. In *Energy Reports* (Vol. 14). DOI: 10.1016/j.egyr.2025.10.045

Ghazal, T. M., Janjua, J. I., Abushiba, W., Ahmad, M., Ihsan, A., & Al-Dmour, N. A. (2024). Cybersecurity Revolution via Large Language Models and Explainable AI. *2024 17th International Conference on Security of Information and Networks, SIN 2024*. DOI: 10.1109/SIN63213.2024.10871324

Ghazal, T. M. (2025a). An IoT-Based Active Learning Convolutional Neural Networks Model for Predicting River Water Quality. *Journal of Soft Computing and Data Mining, 6*(1). Advance online publication. DOI: 10.30880/jscdm.2025.06.01.021

Ghazal, T. M., Abualhaj, M., Ahmed, A. A., Al-Tarawni, M. A. M., & Maghrabi, L. A. (2025). Federated Deep Graph Neural Network Algorithm for Real-Time Intrusion Detection in Heterogeneous IoT Systems. *Journal of Internet Services and Information Security*, *15*(4), 484–497. Advance online publication. DOI: 10.58346/JISIS.2025.I4.035

Ghazal, T. M., Abu-Shareha, A., Mustafa, S. A., Ibrahim, A., & Ahmed, S. M. (2025). Privacy-Preserving Transformer-Based Meta-Learning Algorithm for Zero-Day Intrusion Detection in IoT-Enabled Smart Grids. *Journal of Internet Services and Information Security*, *15*(4), 76–84. Advance online publication. DOI: 10.58346/JISIS.2025.I4.006

Ghazal, T. M., Awouda, A. E., Hasan, M. K., Rahman, A. H. A., Islam, S., Saeed, R. A., Elshafie, H., Iqbal, A., & Hussein, A. H. (2025). Knowledge Learning for Securing Workflow Scheduling Algorithm in Mobile Edge Computing. *Mobile Networks and Applications*, *30*(3-4), 395–413. Advance online publication. DOI: 10.1007/s11036-025-02465-6

Ghazal, T. M., Hasan, M. K., Abdul Wahab, A. N., Ibrahim, A., Khan, W. A., Raza, N. Z., Atta, A., & Mago, B. (2022). Towards Privacy Provisioning for Internet of Things (IoT). *International Conference on Cyber Resilience, ICCR 2022*. DOI: 10.1109/ICCR56254.2022.9995916

Ghazal, T. M., Hasan, M. K., Hussein, A. H., Pandey, B. K., Ahmad, M., Safie, N., & Cascone, L. (2025). Federated Learning With Small and Large Models With Privacy-Preserving Data Space for Holographic Internet of Things in Consumer Electronics. *IEEE Transactions on Consumer Electronics*, *71*(2), 5259–5274. Advance online publication. DOI: 10.1109/TCE.2025.3573033

Ghazal, T. M., Hasan, M. K., Khairy, S. O. F., Mokhtar, U. A., Islam, S., Saeed, R. A., Ahmed, N., & Abdullah, M. (2025). Lightweight signcryption scheme for Securing wearable sensor observed health data sharing in internet of medical things paradigm. *Scientific Reports*, *15*(1), 40989. Advance online publication. DOI: 10.1038/s41598-025-24687-0 PMID: 41266478

Ghazal, T. M., Hasan, M. K., Raju, K. N., Khan, M. A., Alshamayleh, A., Bhatt, M. W., & Ahmad, M. (2025). Data Space Privacy Model with Federated Learning Technique for Securing IoT Communications in Autonomous Marine Vehicles. *Journal of Intelligent & Robotic Systems*, *111*(3), 84. Advance online publication. DOI: 10.1007/s10846-025-02298-1

Ghoneim, R. S., Taiyara, R., & Maghaireh, Z. N. (2025). Machine Learning-Enhanced Building Information Modeling (BIM) for Sustainable Urban Planning. *Civil Engineering and Architecture*, *13*(3), 2171–2184. Advance online publication. DOI: 10.13189/cea.2025.131301

Gul, A., Khan, F., Farooq, M., Javaid, A., Hussain, Z., & Elzaghmouri, B. (2025). STATISTICAL MODELING AND PREDICTION OF PANDEMIC USING CLASSICAL AND MACHINE LEARNING APPROACH. *Pakistan Journal of Statistics*, *41*(3).

H K, P. K., Dash, R., K, J. R., Mohapatra, B., Bishoyi, S. S., Bajaj, M., & Blazek, V.H K. (2026). Multi-domain fault characterization in DC microgrids utilizing Hilbert-Huang transform ensemble by LSTM networks with adaptive boundary condition constraints. *Results in Engineering*, *29*, 108721. Advance online publication. DOI: 10.1016/j.rineng.2025.108721

Habboush, A., & Elzaghmouri, B. (2025). Methodological integration of machine learning and meta-heuristics for seismic risk assessment of irregular buildings. *Asian Journal of Civil Engineering*. DOI: 10.1007/s42107-025-01571-w

Haider, Z. A., Ullah, I., Shareha, A. A., Nasimov, R., & Memon, S. A. (2026). Artificial Intelligence (AI)-Enabled Unmanned Aerial Vehicle (UAV) Systems for Optimizing User Connectivity in Sixth-Generation (6G) Ubiquitous Networks. *Computers, Materials & Continua*, *86*(1), 1–16. Advance online publication. DOI: 10.32604/cmc.2025.071042

Hakami, H., Hasan, M. K., Alshamayleh, A., Saeed, A. Q., Mustafa, S. A., & Ghazal, T. M. (2025). Adaptive Neuro-Fuzzy Congestion Control Algorithm for Real-Time Multimedia Networking in Cloud-Based E-Learning Platforms. *Journal of Wireless Mobile Networks, Ubiquitous Computing and Dependable Applications*, *16*(3). Advance online publication. DOI: 10.58346/JOWUA.2025.I3.027

Hanandeh, A., Alfreijat, S. Y., Qutieshat, R. J., Alsha'ar, H. Y., Kilani, Q. A. L., & Saleem Khasawneh, M. A. (2025). Implementing AI Accuracy, Learning Rate, Inference Time on enhancing Big Data Analysis and Strategic Plan. *Data and Metadata*, *4*, 637. Advance online publication. DOI: 10.56294/dm2025637

Hanumanthagowda, P. B., Vasanthkumara, M. K. M., Al-Nussairi, A. K. J., Hadi, A. A., Smerat, A., & Shivanna, P. B. (2026). Process-aware Temporal Graph Embedding for Detecting and Localizing Recurring Concept Drift. *International Journal of Intelligent Engineering and Systems*, *19*(1), 402–422. Advance online publication. DOI: 10.22266/ijies2026.0131.25

Hasan, M. K., Ghazal, T. M., Alkhalifah, A., Abu Bakar, K. A., Omidvar, A., Nafi, N. S., & Agbinya, J. I. (2021). Fischer Linear Discrimination and Quadratic Discrimination Analysis–Based Data Mining Technique for Internet of Things Framework for Healthcare. *Frontiers in Public Health*, *9*, 737149. Advance online publication. DOI: 10.3389/fpubh.2021.737149 PMID: 34712639

Hasan, M. K., Ghazal, T. M., Issa, G., Islam, S., Ismail, A. F., & Kabir, S. R. (2025). Hashgraph consensus-based simultaneous, asynchronous and big-data supported blockchain mechanism for IT-OT enabled critical infrastructure sectors. *Journal of Ambient Intelligence and Humanized Computing*. Advance online publication. DOI: 10.1007/s12652-024-04942-4

Hasan, M. K., Habib, A. K. M. A., Islam, S., Safie, N., Ghazal, T. M., Khan, M. A., Alzahrani, A. I., Alalwan, N., Kadry, S., & Masood, A. (2024). Federated learning enables 6 G communication technology: Requirements, applications, and integrated with intelligence framework. *Alexandria Engineering Journal*, *91*, 658–668. Advance online publication. DOI: 10.1016/j.aej.2024.02.044

Hiari, M., Alraba'nah, Y., & Qaddara, I. (2025). A Deep Learning-Based Intrusion Detection System using Refined LSTM for DoS Attack Detection. *Engineering. Technology and Applied Science Research*, *15*(4), 25627–25633. Advance online publication. DOI: 10.48084/etasr.11499

Hou, G., Alkhayyat, A., Almalkawi, A., Yadav, A., Shreenidhi, H. S., Saini, V., Shomurotova, S., Singh, D., Jain, V., Smerat, A., & Khalid, A. (2025). Development of robust machine learning models to estimate hydrochar higher heating value and yield based upon biomass proximate analysis. *Bioresources and Bioprocessing*, *12*(1), 138. Advance online publication. DOI: 10.1186/s40643-025-00979-1 PMID: 41335148

Hussain, K., Ali, E. M., Hussain, W., Raza, A., & Elkamchouchi, D. H. (2025). Robust OTFS-ISAC for Vehicular-to-Base Station End-to-End Sensing and Communication. *Electronics (Basel)*, *14*(21), 4340. Advance online publication. DOI: 10.3390/electronics14214340

Hyassat, A. S., Abu Zayed, R. E., Al Khateeb, E. A., Shalaldeh, A., Abdelhamied, M. M., & Qaddara, I. (2025). Unveiling Cyber Threats: An In-Depth Study on Data Mining Techniques for Exploit Attack Detection †. *Engineering Proceedings*, *104*(1), 28. Advance online publication. DOI: 10.3390/engproc2025104028

Ibrahim, A., Sekhar, R., Tawfeq, J. F., Salih, S. Q., Shah, P., & Radhi, A. D. (2024). Security and Privacy Protection for Online Electronic Documents Based on Novel Encryption Techniques. *Journal of Intelligent Systems and Internet of Things*, *11*(1), 21–28. Advance online publication. DOI: 10.54216/JISIoT.110103

Iftikhar, A., Mohammad, S. I., Alqudah, M. N., Al-Adwan, A. S., Vasudevan, A., Ali, I., & Farhan, M. (2025). Evaluating Inclusivity and Fairness of AI Recruitment Tools for Hiring People with Disabilities in the United Arab Emirates(UAE). *Data and Metadata*, *4*. Advance online publication. DOI: 10.56294/dm2025487

Iskandarani, M. Z., & Chakrabarti, K. (2025). Adaptive Frequency and Energy Modeling Framework for Robotic Wireless Sensor Networks Based on Path Loss Predictions. *Journal of Robotics, 2025*(1). DOI: 10.1155/joro/6156608

Iskandarani, M. Z. (2025). Effect of Adaptive Intelligent Reflective Surfaces on SINR in a Wireless Communication System. *The Journal of Communication*, *20*(1). Advance online publication. DOI: 10.12720/jcm.20.1.1-11

Iskandarani, M. Z. (2025). Energy and path loss analysis of wireless sensor networks on a robotic body (WSRobotic). *Bulletin of Electrical Engineering and Informatics*, *14*(3). Advance online publication. DOI: 10.11591/eei.v14i3.9354

Iskandarani, M. Z., & Hidayat, R. (2025). Analysis of Factors Affecting Spectrum Sensing in an IRS based Wireless Network. *International Journal on Advanced Science, Engineering and Information Technology*, *15*(1), 300–309. Advance online publication. DOI: 10.18517/ijaseit.15.1.20491

Jamil, S., Hosseini, K., Farman, M., Nisar, K. S., & Smerat, A. (2025). Fuzzy modeling of fractional-order dental caries system and bifurcation analysis. *International Journal of Biomathematics*, 2550129. Advance online publication. DOI: 10.1142/S1793524525501293

Jan, F. U., Badar, R., Sami Al-Shamayleh, A., Uehara, A., Senjyu, T., & Akhunzada, A. (2025). Soft Computing-Based Damping Controllers With Online Parameters Tuning for Stability Enhancement of Power Systems. *IEEE Access : Practical Innovations, Open Solutions*, *13*, 167045–167060. Advance online publication. DOI: 10.1109/ACCESS.2025.3612288

Jaradat, S., Acharya, N., Shivshankar, S., Alhadidi, T. I., & Elhenawy, M. (2025). AI for Data Quality Auditing: Detecting Mislabeled Work Zone Crashes Using Large Language Models. *Algorithms*, *18*(6), 317. Advance online publication. DOI: 10.3390/a18060317

Jaradat, S., Elhenawy, M., Paz, A., Alhadidi, T. I., Ashqar, H. I., & Nayak, R. (2025). A Cross-Cultural Crash Pattern Analysis in the United States and Jordan Using BERT and SHAP. *Electronics (Basel)*, *14*(2), 272. Advance online publication. DOI: 10.3390/electronics14020272

Ju, W., Altimari, U. S., Kumar, R., Pattanaik, A., Sarangi, H., Gupta, D., Rao, V. N. B., Abduvalieva, D., Mann, V. S., Mhohamdi, H., Smerat, A., & Abumalek, A. (2025). Robust classification frameworks for oxide nanomaterials assisted by machine learning. *Chemical Papers*. Advance online publication. DOI: 10.1007/s11696-025-04471-0

Kamal, M. M., Ul Abideen, S. Z., Al-Khasawneh, M. A., Momani, A. M., Mostafa, H., Atoum, M. S., Ullah, S., Alsayaydeh, J. A. J., & Yusof, M. F. (2025). Meyer Wavelet Transform and Jaccard Deep Q Net for Small Object Classification Using Multi-Modal Images. *CMES -. Computer Modeling in Engineering & Sciences*, *144*(3), 3053–3083. Advance online publication. DOI: 10.32604/cmes.2025.067430

Keote, R., Katre, S., Keote, M., Chiwande, S., Das, A., Smerat, A., Golar, P., Diwan, P., & Kediya, S. (2025). An integrated IoT–AI framework for intelligent structural performance prediction and real-time strength forecasting in large-scale dome trusses. *Asian Journal of Civil Engineering*. DOI: 10.1007/s42107-025-01586-3

Khalayleh, Y. A. S., Mohammad, S. I., Al Louzi, N. S., Baniata, M., Hassan, M., Safaqah, M. A., Vasudevan, A., & Alshurideh, M. T. (2025). Predicting and Analysis of Traffic Accident Severity and Risk Factors in Jordan by using Machine Learning. *Applied Mathematics & Information Sciences, 19*(6), 1419–1426. Advance online publication. DOI: 10.18576/amis/190615

Khaled Abdullah, S., & Qawasmeh, R. (2025). *Navigating the ethical and legal risks of AI marketing in Jordanian SMEs*. EDPACS., DOI: 10.1080/07366981.2025.2600205

Khan, A. A., Siddiqui, S., Al-Shamayleh, A. S., Akhunzada, A., & Dey, I. (2025). DFROG-MAC: A Dynamic Fragmentation-Based MAC for Prioritised Emergency Data Management in Vehicular Networks. *IET Wireless Sensor Systems, 15*(1), e70017. Advance online publication. DOI: 10.1049/wss2.70017

Khan, I., Shao, Y., Rahman, S. U., Ullah, H., Altayeb, M., Kamal, M. M., Altameem, A., & Altameem, T. (2026). A metamaterial Fabry-Perot MIMO antenna with circular polarization for 5G and satellite communication. *Measurement : Journal of the International Measurement Confederation, 261*, 119942. Advance online publication. DOI: 10.1016/j.measurement.2025.119942

Khatibi, A., Babaker, S., Praveen, K. N. R., Chohan, J. S., Jadhav, A., Alsoud, A. R., Ramudu, M. J., & Jeet, R. (2025). Advanced AI-Driven Cybersecurity: Analyzing Emerging Threats and Defensive Strategies. *National Academy Science Letters*. Advance online publication. DOI: 10.1007/s40009-025-01897-8

Kutieshat, R., Al-Daoud, K. I., Almajali, R., Vasudevan, A., Alsakarneh, G., Al-Hawary, S. I. S., & Mohammad, A. A. S. (2025). Is the rise of AI technology scary for HR professionals? Balancing the replacement of employees' skills with AI. *International Journal of Data and Network Science, 9*(4), 1121–1128. Advance online publication. DOI: 10.5267/j.ijdns.2024.9.010

Laha, S. R., Smadi, K. Al, Habboush, A. K., Pattanayak, B. K., Pattnaik, S., & Mohanty, B. (2025). Smart Waste Management Framework for Green Cities: Integrating IoT, LoRa, and Deep Learning for Efficient Waste Classification and Management. *Tikrit Journal of Engineering Sciences, 32*(Special Issue 1). DOI: 10.25130/tjes.sp1.2025.1

Lakshmi, A. S., Sigamany, E. S. S., Traisa, R., Kumar, R., Reddy, K. R., Chohan, J. S., & Smerat, A. (2025). Enhancing Code Quality Through Automated Refactoring Using Transformer-Based Language Models. *International Journal of Advanced Computer Science and Applications, 16*(9). Advance online publication. DOI: 10.14569/IJACSA.2025.0160951

Lee, S. W., Hussain, S., Issa, G. F., Abbas, S., Ghazal, T. M., Sohail, T., Ahmad, M., & Khan, M. A. (2021). Multi-Dimensional Trust Quantification by Artificial Agents through Evidential Fuzzy Multi-Criteria Decision Making. *IEEE Access : Practical Innovations, Open Solutions, 9*, 159399–159412. Advance online publication. DOI: 10.1109/ACCESS.2021.3131521

Llwaah, F., Hussein, A. H., & Ghazal, T. M. (2025). Enhancing Cloud Resource Utilization Through Synthesizing Intensive Workflow Tasks. *Journal of Wireless Mobile Networks, Ubiquitous Computing and Dependable Applications, 16*(4), 537–555. Advance online publication. DOI: 10.58346/JOWUA.2025.I4.030

Louati, H., Arooj, R., Niazi, A. U. K., Dalam, M. E. E., Almazah, M. M. A., & Smerat, A. (2025). Finite-time fuzzy control strategy for nonlinear MASs with actuator faults and deception attacks. *AIMS Mathematics*, *10*(9), 20113–20139. Advance online publication. DOI: 10.3934/math.2025899

Mahadin, G. A. L., Satvika, S., Kathuria, S., Kaushik, A., & Maranan, R. (2025). DEEP LEARNING FRAMEWORK FOR IDENTIFYING AND HYBRID SYNTHESIZING WIDESPREAD NEWS HEADLINES ON SOCIAL MEDIA. *Proceedings on Engineering Sciences*, *7*(3), 1453–1462. Advance online publication. DOI: 10.24874/PES07.03.007

Mahfouz, K. H., Al Betar, M. A., & Makhadmeh, S. N. (2025). Mitigating the task scheduling problem in fog computing environments using improved marine predators optimization algorithm. *Computing*, *107*(7), 147. Advance online publication. DOI: 10.1007/s00607-025-01502-2

Mahfuri, M., & Ibrahim, A. (2024). AI-Driven Innovations: Transforming Data Support and Environmental Management for the Future. *2024 International Conference on Decision Aid Sciences and Applications, DASA 2024*. DOI: 10.1109/DASA63652.2024.10836162

Makhadmeh, S. N., Fraihat, S., Awad, M., Sanjalawe, Y., Al-Betar, M. A., & Awadallah, M. A. (2025). A crossover-integrated Marine Predator Algorithm for feature selection in intrusion detection systems within IoT environments. *Internet of Things : Engineering Cyber Physical Human Systems*, *31*, 101536. Advance online publication. DOI: 10.1016/j.iot.2025.101536

Marhoon, H. M., Basil, N., Sabbar, B. M., Qasem, N., & Ma'arif, A. (2025). Safety and Surveillance on Unmanned Aerial Vehicles Control Systems and Optimization Methods: A Systematic Review. *International Journal of Robotics and Control Systems*, *5*(5). Advance online publication. DOI: 10.31763/ijrcs.v5i5.1859

Masadeh, R., Almomani, O., Zaqebah, A., Masadeh, S., Alshqurat, K., Sharieh, A., & Alsharman, N. (2025). Narwhal Optimizer: A Nature-Inspired Optimization Algorithm for Solving Complex Optimization Problems. *Computers, Materials & Continua*, *85*(2), 3709–3737. Advance online publication. DOI: 10.32604/cmc.2025.066797

Masango, N. C., Agushaka, J. O., Amaefule, M. C., Taiwo, O., Zhang, P., Ezugwu, A. E., Saleem, K., Smerat, A., & Abualigah, L. (2025). Secure and efficient cloudlet networks: blockchain integration with agent-based proof of trust mechanism. *Eurasip Journal on Wireless Communications and Networking*, *2025*(1). DOI: 10.1186/s13638-025-02439-y

Matarneh, S., Louzi, N., Asi, I., Abdel-Jaber, M., & Masad, E. (2025). Genetic Expression Programming Based Empirical Models for the Prediction of Rutting Parameter of Bitumen Modified Using Nanomaterials. *Engineering and Science*, *35*. Advance online publication. DOI: 10.30919/es1438

Maz, Y. A., Anbar, M., Manickam, S., Abualhaj, M. M., Almalki, S. A., & Alabsi, B. A. (2025). Transfer Learning-Based Approach with an Ensemble Classifier for Detecting Keylogging Attack on the Internet of Things. *Computers, Materials & Continua*, *85*(3), 5287–5307. Advance online publication. DOI: 10.32604/cmc.2025.068257

Mbasso, W. F., Harrison, A., Dagal, I., Jangir, P., Liu, Z., & Smerat, A. (2025). High-Fidelity Simulation-Driven Control Framework for Robust Grid Integration of Renewable Energy Systems. *Energy Science & Engineering*. Advance online publication. DOI: 10.1002/ese3.70414

Mohammad, A. A. S., Al-Ramadan, A. M., Mohammad, S. I., Al Oraini, B., Vasudevan, A., Alshdaifat, N., & Hunitie, M. F. A. (2025). Customer Sentiment Analysis for Food and Beverage Development in Restaurants using AI in Jordan. *Data and Metadata*, *4*, 922. Advance online publication. DOI: 10.56294/dm2025922

Mohammad, S. I., Al-Daoud, K., Al Qraini, B., Khanfar, I. A. A., & Vasudevan, A. (2025). Quantum Error Correction with Surface Code Analysis on Quantum Computing platform. *Applied Mathematics & Information Sciences*, *19*(2), 423–435. Advance online publication. DOI: 10.18576/amis/190216

Mostafa, S. A., Hasan, D. F., Abdul-Jabar, M. A., Hussein, A. H., & Mustapha, A. (2025). An Ensemble Learning Model for Multi-Type Cancer Prediction in Clinical Diagnostic Decision Support Systems. *Journal of Soft Computing and Data Mining*, *6*(1). Advance online publication. DOI: 10.30880/jscdm.2025.06.01.015

Nafa, A. Z. M., Obed, A. A., Abid, A. J., Yaqoob, S. J., Bajaj, M., & Shabaz, M. (2025). Sensorless real-time solar irradiance prediction in grid-connected PV systems using PSO-MPPT and IoT-enabled monitoring. *Energy Informatics*, *8*(1), 99. Advance online publication. DOI: 10.1186/s42162-025-00563-z

Nafisah, I., Mahmoud, N., Ewees, A. A., Khattap, M. G., Dahou, A., Alghamdi, S. M., Fares, I. A., Azmi Al-Betar, M., & Abd Elaziz, M. (2025). Deep learning-based feature selection for detection of autism spectrum disorder. *Frontiers in Artificial Intelligence*, *8*, 1594372. Advance online publication. DOI: 10.3389/frai.2025.1594372 PMID: 40636395

Nandal, P., Mann, P., Bohra, N., Sagar, K., & Smerat, A. (2025). Improving Underwater Image Quality Through Real-ESRGAN With Whale Optimization Algorithm. *Internet Technology Letters*, *8*(4), e70047. Advance online publication. DOI: 10.1002/itl2.70047

Nasir, J., Aamir, M., Iftikhar, S., Albidah, A. B., Alqasem, O. A., Elwahab, M. E. A., Khan, I., & Koh, W. S. (2025). A Novel Hybrid Approach to Forecasting Crude Oil Prices Using Local Mean Decomposition, ARIMA, and XGBoost. *IEEE Access : Practical Innovations, Open Solutions*, *13*, 89140–89156. Advance online publication. DOI: 10.1109/ACCESS.2025.3561193

Nath, A., Nanda, R., Jena, P. P., Ghosh, A., Shah, S., Patel, S., Mohapatra, E., Tiwari, A. K., & Nisar, K. S. (2025). Symbolic regression and interpretable ensemble learning approach in determining early onset of diabetic peripheral neuropathy. *Egyptian Informatics Journal*, *31*, 100777. Advance online publication. DOI: 10.1016/j.eij.2025.100777

Nisar, K. S., Chokkalingam, R., Sriramulu, S., & Arunachalam, S. (2025). Mathematical Study of Nabla Fractional Difference Tech Layoff Model. *Iranian Journal of Science*, *49*(2), 345–356. Advance online publication. DOI: 10.1007/s40995-024-01721-w

Otair, M., Qawaqzeh, F. A., Alomari, S. A., Zitar, R. A., Migdady, H., Saleem, K., Smerat, A., Alsoud, A. R., & Abualigah, L. (2025). Enhanced Arithmetic Optimization Algorithm for Intrusion Detection in Wireless Sensor Networks. *International Journal of Communication Systems*, *38*(10), e70122. Advance online publication. DOI: 10.1002/dac.70122

Qaddara, I., & Alraba'nah, Y. (2025). Enhancing Requirements Classification Using Machine Learning Techniques. *SN Computer Science*, *6*(6), 649. Advance online publication. DOI: 10.1007/s42979-025-04158-z

Qaddara, I., Alrabaynah, Y., & Hiari, M. O. (2025). Evaluation of SQL and NoSQL Databases on Parallel Processing. *Engineering. Technology and Applied Science Research*, *15*(4), 24298–24304. Advance online publication. DOI: 10.48084/etasr.10620

Qawaqneh, H., Al Sayyed, O., Mohammad Alomari, K., Bektemyssova, G., Smerat, A., Montazeri, Z., Dehghani, M., Parkash Malik, O., & Eguchi, K. (2025). Pipefish Optimization Algorithm (POA): A Nature-inspired Metaheuristic for Robust and Adaptive Global Optimization. *International Journal of Intelligent Engineering and Systems*, *18*(11), 778–794. Advance online publication. DOI: 10.22266/ijies2025.1231.48

Qawaqneh, H., Alomari, K. M., Alomari, S., Bektemyssova, G., Smerat, A., Montazeri, Z., Dehghani, M., Malik, O. P., & Eguchi, K. (2025). Black-breasted Lapwing Algorithm (BBLA): A Novel Nature-inspired Metaheuristic for Solving Constrained Engineering Optimization. *International Journal of Intelligent Engineering and Systems*, *18*(11), 581–597. Advance online publication. DOI: 10.22266/ijies2025.1231.36

Qawaqneh, H., Alomari, K. M., Alomari, S., Bektemyssova, G., Smerat, A., Montazeri, Z., Dehghani, M., Malik, O. P., & Eguchi, K. (2025). Kakapo Optimization Algorithm (KOA): A Novel Bio-inspired Metaheuristic for Optimization Applications. *International Journal of Intelligent Engineering and Systems*, *18*(11), 913–929. Advance online publication. DOI: 10.22266/ijies2025.1231.56

Qawasmeh, S., Habboushb, A., Elzaghmouri, B., Kharma, Q., & Albalawneh, D. (2025). Hybrid Convolutional Neural Network-Based Intrusion Detection System for Secure IoT Networks. *Tikrit Journal of Engineering Sciences*, *32*(SP1), 1–11. Advance online publication. DOI: 10.25130/tjes.sp1.2025.2

Rabbi, M. F., Amin, M., Al-Dalahmeh, M., & Abdullah, M. (2025). Assessing the role of information technology in promoting environmental sustainability and preventing crime in E-commerce. *International Review of Applied Sciences and Engineering*, *16*(1), 81–97. Advance online publication. DOI: 10.1556/1848.2024.00834

Ramesh, J. V. N., Nimma, D., Dasari, R., Chaudhari Rane, D., AlGhamdi, A., Rao, K. B. V. B., Haider, S. A., Kuzieva, N., & Jangir, P. (2025). Safe and Reliable Two-Stage Online Offloading Algorithm for Transportation Cyber-Physical Systems. *IEEE Transactions on Intelligent Transportation Systems*, *26*(9), 14313–14322. Advance online publication. DOI: 10.1109/TITS.2025.3539934

Raza, M. A., Karim, A., Alqarni, M., Al-Khasawneh, M. A., Jumani, T. A., Aman, M., & Masud, M. I. (2025). An Intelligent Long Short-Term Memory-Based Machine Learning Model for the Potential Assessment of Global Hydropower Capacity in Sustainable Energy Transition and Security. *Energies*, *18*(13), 3324. Advance online publication. DOI: 10.3390/en18133324

Rehan, R., Sahran, S., Alyasseri, Z. A. A., Sani, N. S., & Al-Betar, M. A. (2025). Hyperparameters optimization of evolving spiking neural network using artificial bee colony for unsupervised anomaly detection. *Journal of Intelligent Systems*, *34*(1), 20240235. Advance online publication. DOI: 10.1515/jisys-2024-0235

Saeed, N. M. S. E., Ibrahim, A., Ali, L., Al-Dmour, N. A., Mohammed, A. S., & Ghazal, T. M. (2024). Unveiling the Landscape of Machine Learning and Deep Learning Methodologies in Network Security: A Comprehensive Literature Review. *2nd International Conference on Cyber Resilience, ICCR 2024*. DOI: 10.1109/ICCR61006.2024.10533066

Salama, S., Tamimi, O., Altayeb, M., & Abuzahew, A. (2025). MINIATURIZED L-SHAPED AND U-SHAPED RESONATOR BASED 8-BIT AND 12-BIT CHIPLESS RFID TAG. *IIUM Engineering Journal*, *26*(3), 260–269. Advance online publication. DOI: 10.31436/iiumej.v26i3.3646

Salman, A. M., Ibrahim, A., Abdulbaqi, A. S., Almajed, R., & Al Naffakh, H. A. H. (2025). *Designing Blockchain Solutions to Enhance Data Security and Privacy in Distributed IoT Networks*. DOI: 10.1109/ICBATS66542.2025.11258568

Samanta, I. S., Mohanty, S., Rout, P. K., Parida, S. M., Panda, S., Bajaj, M., Blazek, V., & Prokop, L. (2025). A comprehensive review of feature extraction techniques for power quality event detection with novel approaches for enhanced classification in smart grids. *Electrical Engineering*, *107*(9), 12227–12259. Advance online publication. DOI: 10.1007/s00202-025-03149-w

Sanjalawe, Y., Al-E'mari, S., Abualhaj, M., Makhadmeh, S. N., Alsharaiah, M. A., & Hijazi, D. H. (2025). Recent advances in secretary bird optimization algorithm, its variants and applications. In *Evolutionary Intelligence* (Vol. 18, Number 3). DOI: 10.1007/s12065-025-01054-6

Sardar, R., Anees, T., Al-Shamayleh, A. S., Mehmood, E., Khalil, W., Akhunzada, A., & Shaikh, F. S. (2025). Challenges in detecting security threats in WoT: A systematic literature review. *Artificial Intelligence Review*, *58*(7), 196. Advance online publication. DOI: 10.1007/s10462-025-11176-z

Sawarkar, P. G., Pote, A., Khan, M. A., Abed, M. H., Hadi, A. A., Smerat, A., & Khishe, M. (2025). Sustainable geopolymer concrete evaluation using machine learning and PDP analysis: Comparative insights into strength prediction. *Hybrid Advances*, *11*, 100569. Advance online publication. DOI: 10.1016/j.hybadv.2025.100569

Shabeeb Kamil, A., Mousa Ali, E., Alibakhshikenari, M., Misran, N., Tariqul Islam, M., Virdee, B., Mariyanayagam, D., Abbasi, N. A., Rashid, N., & Elwi, A., T. (. (2025). Metasurface Effect on the Performance of Planar Antennas for Wireless Communications. *Radio Science*, *60*(11). Advance online publication. DOI: 10.1029/2024RS008156

Shadhar, M. H., Mohammed, Z. A., Rajhi, A. A., Dasarathy, A. K., Das, P., Padmapriya, R., Singh, J., Matyakubov, B., Kutliev, U., & Smerat, A. (2025). Vibration-based analysis of a sandwich gori composite curved beam in thermo-electro-magnetic environment. *Acta Mechanica*. Advance online publication. DOI: 10.1007/s00707-025-04526-z

Shah, R. K., Hasan, M. K., Islam, S., Khan, A., Ghazal, T. M., & Khan, A. N. (2022). Detect Phishing Website by Fuzzy Multi-Criteria Decision Making. *2022 1st International Conference on AI in Cybersecurity, ICAIC 2022*. DOI: 10.1109/ICAIC53980.2022.9897036

Shamaylah, N., Ibrahim Mohammad, S., Al Oraini, B., Yaseen Al-Gaafreh, J. M., Mosallam Alqahtani, M., Vasudevan, A., Shlash Mohammad, A. A., & Ahmmad Hunitie, M. F. (2025). Data-Driven Decision-Making for Employee Training and Development in Jordanian Public Institutions. *Data and Metadata*, *4*, 886. Advance online publication. DOI: 10.56294/dm2025886

Shambour, Q. Y., Al-Zyoud, M., & Hussein, A. H. (2025). FROM DATA TO DIAGNOSIS: KNOWLEDGE-DRIVEN, EXPLAINABLE AI FOR RELIABLE EARLY AUTISM DETECTION. *Interdisciplinary Journal of Information, Knowledge, and Management*, *20*, 032. Advance online publication. DOI: 10.28945/5652

Shambour, Q., Al-Zyoud, M., & Almomani, O. (2025). Quantum-Inspired Hybrid Metaheuristic Feature Selection with SHAP for Optimized and Explainable Spam Detection. *Symmetry*, *17*(10), 1716. Advance online publication. DOI: 10.3390/sym17101716

Sharma, K. P., Yajid, M. S. A., Gowrishankar, J., Mahajan, R., Alsoud, A. R., Jadhav, A., & Singh, D. (2025). A Systematic Review on Text Summarization: Techniques, Challenges, Opportunities. In *Expert Systems* (Vol. 42, Number 4). DOI: 10.1111/exsy.13833

Sharma, K. P., Al-Rashed, A., Johar, M. G. M., Alsoud, A. R., Singh, A., Dey, P., & Pant, S. (2025). Blockchain-Assisted Trust Framework for Increased Survivability in Internet of Vehicles. *Internet Technology Letters*, *8*(3), e70029. Advance online publication. DOI: 10.1002/itl2.70029

Sharma, K. P., Hussain, R., Jaharadak, A. A., Trawnih, A. A., Verma, D., Dasi, S., & Pant, S. (2025). Hybrid Convolutional Neural Network for Robust Attack Detection in Wireless Sensor Networks. *Internet Technology Letters*, *8*(6), e650. Advance online publication. DOI: 10.1002/itl2.650

Shi, J., Farooq, U., Tabash, M. I., Riyadh, H. A., & Almajali, T. A. (2025). Air Pollution and the Innovation Gap: A Challenge for Sustainable Growth in Emerging and Growth Leading Economies (EAGLE). *Sustainability (Basel)*, *17*(10), 4423. Advance online publication. DOI: 10.3390/su17104423

Shlash Mohammad, A. A., Ibrahim Mohammad, S., Al-Daoud, K. I., Al Oraini, B., Mosallam Alqahtani, M., Vasudevan, A., & Ahmmad Hunitie, M. F. (2025). Riding into the Future: Transforming Jordan's Public Transportation with Predictive Analytics and Real-Time Data. *Data and Metadata*, *4*, 887. Advance online publication. DOI: 10.56294/dm2025887

Solairaju, J. A., Rathinasamy, S., Thanikodi, S., Tarawneh, B., Gurumoorthy, V., Antony, J. S., & Arul Gnana Dhas, A. (2025). Development and Validation of ANN Models for Water Absorption in Sawdust and Kenaf Fiber-Reinforced Polystyrene Composites. *Engineering Reports*, *7*(9), e70393. Advance online publication. DOI: 10.1002/eng2.70393

Tarek, R., Elshenawy, A., Assadwy, M. I., & Madkour, M. A. (2025). Automated Diagnosis of Dental Diseases Using Deep Learning on Radiographic Images. *SN Computer Science*, *6*(6), 751. Advance online publication. DOI: 10.1007/s42979-025-04264-y

Turab, N., Abushattal, A., Al-Nabulsi, J., & Owida, H. A. (2025). Advanced risk assessment using machine learning and sentiment analysis on log data. *IAES International Journal of Artificial Intelligence, 14*(5), 3897. Advance online publication. DOI: 10.11591/ijai.v14.i5.pp3897-3905

Ullah, N., Al-Rahmi, W. M., Alblehai, F., Fernando, Y., Alharbi, Z. H., Zhanbayev, R., Al-Adwan, A. S., & Habes, M. (2025). Corrigendum to "Blockchain-powered grids: Paving the way for a sustainable and efficient future" [Heliyon Volume 10, Issue 10, May 2024, Article e31592] (Heliyon (2024) 10(10), (S2405844024076230), ()). In *Heliyon* (Vol. 11, Number 13). https://doi.org/DOI: 10.1016/j.heliyon.2024.e31592

Vasudevan, A., Albinaa, T. A., Mohammad, S. I., Sharmila, E., Raja, N., Soon, E. E. H., Alshurideh, M. T., & Al-Adwan, A. S. (2024). Bidirectional LSTM for Electronic Product Recommendation. *Applied Mathematics & Information Sciences, 18*(6), 1443–1453. Advance online publication. DOI: 10.18576/amis/180621

Vasudevan, A., Tamilmani, K. T., Mohammad, S. I., Sridheepika, V. S., Raja, N., Soon, E. E. H., Nagaraj, S., & Al-Adwan, A. S. (2025). Voices of Concern: Contemplations on Socioeconomic, Ethical, and Developmental Impacts of AI. *Applied Mathematics & Information Sciences, 19*(1), 221–232. Advance online publication. DOI: 10.18576/amis/190119

Xu, B., Jummaa, K., Altalbawy, F. M. A., Roopashree, R., Saraswat, S. K., Ray, S., Tomar, P., Naem, S., Hamza, H. H., Smerat, A., & Khalid, A. (2025). Machine learning-assisted computation of water activity for ionic liquid-based aqueous ternary elements. *Desalination and Water Treatment, 324*, 101484. Advance online publication. DOI: 10.1016/j.dwt.2025.101484

Yaseen, M., Ali, E., Sarwar, N., Jamel, L., Din, I., Yuldashev, F., & Law, F. (2025). Design of Minimal Spanning Tree and Analytic Hierarchical Process (SAHP) Based Hybrid Technique for Software Requirements Prioritization. *IET Software, 2025*(1). DOI: 10.1049/sfw2/8819735

Zhang, Z., Khishe, M., Qian, L., Martín, D., Abualigah, L., & Ghazal, T. M. (2024). Evolving chimp optimization algorithm using quantum mechanism for engineering applications: A case study on fire detection. *Journal of Computational Design and Engineering, 11*(5), 143–163. Advance online publication. DOI: 10.1093/jcde/qwae074

Zhu, Y., Lin, X., Kim, J., Al-Adwan, A. S., & Li, N. (2025). Exploring Human Interaction in Online Self-Regulated Learning Through Danmaku Comments. *International Journal of Human-Computer Interaction, 41*(22), 13964–13977. Advance online publication. DOI: 10.1080/10447318.2025.2480826

Zraiqat, A., Al Sayyed, O., Al Soudi, M., Al-Salih, A. A. M. M., Smerat, A., Montazeri, Z., Dehghani, M., Malik, O. P., Ahmed, M. A., Ibraheem, I. K., & Eguchi, K. (2025). Key Maker Algorithm: A Novel Human-Based Metaheuristic for Constrained Optimization. *International Journal of Intelligent Engineering and Systems, 18*(9), 688–699. Advance online publication. DOI: 10.22266/ijies2025.1031.45

Zraiqat, A., Batiha, B., & Al-Refai, O. (2025). Thunderstorm and Cloud Algorithm: A Novel Parameter-Free Metaheuristic Inspired by Atmospheric Dynamics for Complex Optimization Tasks. *International Journal of Intelligent Engineering and Systems, 18*(8), 153–167. Advance online publication. DOI: 10.22266/ijies2025.0930.11

Zraiqat, A., Batiha, B., Al-Refai, O., Al-Salih, A. A. M. M., Smerat, A., Montazeri, Z., Dehghani, M., Werner, F., Ahmed, M. A., Ibraheem, I. K., & Eguchi, K. (2025). Psychologist Algorithm: A Human-inspired Metaheuristic for Solving Complex Constrained Optimization Problems. *International Journal of Intelligent Engineering and Systems*, *18*(9), 124–137. Advance online publication. DOI: 10.22266/ijies2025.1031.09

About the Contributors

Amer Ibrahim is an Associate Professor of Computer Science at the College of Information Technology, United Arab Emirates University, Al Ain, United Arab Emirates. He holds a Ph.D. in Computer Science (Human–Computer Interaction and Artificial Intelligence) awarded by the Higher Technical School of Computer Science and Telecommunications Engineering, University of Granada, Spain. Dr. Ibrahim's academic contributions span Human–Computer Interaction, Artificial Intelligence, machine learning, cybersecurity, and game-based learning. His research has advanced playability engineering, usability evaluation frameworks, and design methodologies for educational and serious games, as well as context-aware and pervasive learning environments. He has contributed to the development of AI-driven adaptive learning models, privacy-preserving and secure digital systems, and intelligent interaction design for educational, healthcare, and IoT-enabled environments. Dr. Ibrahim has published extensively in peer-reviewed journals and international conferences and has actively participated in international research collaborations, editorial boards, and scientific committees. His scholarly work demonstrates a sustained commitment to technically rigorous, user-centered, and secure computing systems.

Taher M. Ghazal is a Principal Research Scientist and Associate Professor specializing in Management Information Systems, Cybersecurity, and Digital Innovation. He holds a Ph.D. in Information Science and Technology with a concentration in Cybersecurity from Universiti Kebangsaan Malaysia (UKM). He also completed a Postdoctoral Fellowship in Cybersecurity at the Center for Physical Systems (C2PS), Khalifa University of Science and Technology, United Arab Emirates. Dr. Ghazal's academic contributions span business analytics, artificial intelligence, Internet of Things (IoT), blockchain, cybersecurity, and smart digital systems, with a strong emphasis on applied and industry-driven research in MIS and information systems. He has published extensively, with over 175 peer-reviewed journal and conference publications and more than 11,000 citations, and has been recognized among the world's top 2% scientists for multiple consecutive years. His research addresses secure and intelligent digital infrastructures, data-driven decision-making, cyber resilience, and the integration of emerging technologies into business and organizational contexts. In addition to his research output, Dr. Ghazal has led international research initiatives, chaired IEEE- and Scopus-indexed conferences, contributed to patented innovations in IoT, AI, and blockchain systems, and played key roles in academic leadership, research coordination, and quality assurance aligned with international frameworks such as AACSB, ABET, and QS rankings.

Nidal Al-Dmour is a Full Professor in the Computer Engineering Department at Mutah University, Jordan. His academic and research expertise covers network security, cybersecurity, artificial intelligence, wireless computer networks, and high-performance computing. His professional experience includes academic positions at Mutah University, Ajman University, and Al Hussein University. He has also held leadership roles, including Chairman of the Computer Engineering Department and Dean Assistant for student affairs and industry cooperation. In addition, he has served on several academic, research, curriculum, promotion, and quality assurance committees. He has participated in EU-funded Erasmus+ projects related to ICT education and agricultural technology training. His publication record includes journal papers, book chapters, and international conference papers in cybersecurity, AI, IoT, networks, and computing.

Ahmed A. Elngar, currently is an Associate Professor and Head of Computer Science Department at Faculty of Computers and Artificial Intelligence, Department of Computer Science, Beni Suef University. Their current project is 'Biometrics, AI-based Security, Image processing, AI-based Control, AI-based Smart Grids' . Internet of Things Security.

Dima Mohamad Yasser Saad Eddin is a researcher and lecturer at the International University for Science and Technology (IUST), Syria, with expertise in AI and cybersecurity.

Miguel Ángel Sahagún is the Charles T. Ingram Associate Professor of Marketing at High Point University's Earl Phillips School of Business, where he teaches undergraduate and graduate courses in marketing, marketing research, marketing management, international business communications, and market-based management. He also leads the study abroad course Marketing in Spain, providing students with immersive international marketing learning experiences. In addition to his teaching responsibilities, he serves as Chair of the Study Abroad Committee, he also serves as the director of the BEACON-Neuromarketing Lab and contributes actively to university service and faculty leadership. Dr. Sahagún holds a Ph.D. in Business Administration with a concentration in Marketing and a minor in Statistics from The University of Texas-Pan American, an MBA from The University of Texas at Brownsville, and a B.S. in Industrial Engineering from ITESO in Mexico. His research interests include consumer loyalty, ethnocentrism, student ethics, consumer buying behavior, neuromarketing, marketing strategy, and growth mindset pedagogy. He has published extensively in peer-reviewed journals, conference proceedings, and peer-reviewed books, and has delivered keynote presentations internationally on neuromarketing, branding, consumer behavior, and artificial intelligence in higher education. His work reflects a strong commitment to impactful teaching, applied research, and global engagement.

Abdur Rehman has completed his Ph.D. from the School of Computer Science at NCBA&E in Lahore, Pakistan. He holds the position of Associate Professor at the same institution and also serves as a Game Developer at GameObject in Lahore, Pakistan, drawing upon more than 10 years of enriched experience in the field of game development. With a proven academic track record, Abdur Rehman has contributed significantly to Smart City technologies, Healthcare, Machine Learning, Blockchain, Federated learning, and Network Security. His impactful research, spanning over a decade, has led to the publication of 15 research articles (*Cumulative Impact Factor: 70+) in highly impactful journals with notable impact factors.

Index

H

I

K

L

N

O

P

R

S

T

U

* 9 7 9 8 3 3 7 3 9 2 1 0 3 *